P9-APP-328

THE SEED

WAS

PLANTED

176737

RCL

THE SEED WAS PLANTED

THE SÃO PAULO ROOTS OF BRAZIL'S RURAL LABOR MOVEMENT, 1924–1964

CLIFF WELCH

THE PENNSYLVANIA STATE UNIVERSITY PRESS
UNIVERSITY PARK, PENNSYLVANIA

Library of Congress Cataloging-in-Publication Data

Welch, Cliff.
    The seed was planted : the São Paulo roots of Brazil's rural labor movement,
1924–1964 / Cliff Welch.
        p.   cm.
    Includes bibliographical references and index.
    ISBN 0-271-01788-0 (cloth : alk. paper)
    ISBN 0-271-01789-9 (pbk. : alk. paper)
    1. Labor movement—Brazil—São Paulo—History—20th century.   2. Labor
movement—Brazil—Political activity—20th century.   3. Trade-unions—Agricultural laborers—History.   4. Trade-unions—Brazil—History—20th century.   5. Brazil—Politics and government—History.   6. Brazil—Social conditions.   I. title.
    HD6613.5.W45   1999
    331.88'0981'61—dc21   97-49347
                                                                        CIP

Copyright © 1999 The Pennsylvania State University
All rights reserved
Printed in the United States of America
Published by The Pennsylvania State University Press
University Park, PA 16802-1003

It is the policy of The Pennsylvania State University Press to use acid-free paper for
the first printing of all clothbound books. Publications on uncoated stock satisfy the
minimum requirements of American National Standard for Information Sciences—
Permanence of Paper for Printed Library Materials, ANSI Z39.48-1992.

For Toni

CONTENTS

176737

MAPS, TABLES, AND FIGURES

Maps

Tables

Figures

ABBREVIATIONS

Organizational Acronyms

AIFLD	American Institute for Free Labor Development
AP	Ação Popular (Popular Action)
BOC	Bloco Operário e Camponês (Worker and Peasant Bloc)
CAIC	Companhia Agrícola de Imigração e Colonização (Agrarian Immigration and Colonization Company)
CGT	Confederação Geral do Trabalho (General Confederation of Labor), circa 1929; Confederação Geral dos Trabalhadores (General Confederation of Laborers), circa 1946; Comando Geral dos Trabalhadores (General Command of Laborers),circa 1962
CLT	Consolidação das Leis do Trabalho (Consolidated Labor Law)
CMT	Comissão Mista de Terras (Mixed Commission of Lands)
CNA	Confederação Nacional de Agricultura (National Confederation of Agriculture)
CNBB	Conferência Nacional dos Bispos Brasileiros (National Conference of Brazilian Bishops)
CNPA	Comissão Nacional de Política Agrária (National Agrarian Policy Commission)
CONSIR	Comissão Nacional de Sindicalização Rural (National Rural Unionization Commission)
CONTAG	Confederação Nacional dos Trabalhadores na Agricultura (National Confederation of Laborers in Agriculture)
CPT	Comissão Pastoral da Terra (Pastoral Land Commission)
CRB	Confederação Rural Brasileira (Brazilian Rural Confederation)
CTNP	Companhia de Terras Norte de Paraná (North Paraná Land Company)
CUT	Central Única dos Trabalhadores (Unified Laborers' Central)
DOPS	Departamento de Ordem Política e Social (Department of Social and Political Order)
ECLA	United Nations Economic Commission for Latin America

ET	Estatuto da Terra (Land Statute)
ETR	Estatuto do Trabalhador Rural (Rural Laborer Statute)
FAESP	Federação Agrícola do Estado de São Paulo (São Paulo State Agrarian Federation)
FALN	Frente Armada de Liberação Nacional (National Liberation Armed Front)
FAO	Food and Agriculture Organization of the United Nations
FAP	Frente Agrária Paulista (Paulista Agrarian Front)
FARESP	Federação das Associaçies Rurais do Estado de São Paulo (São Paulo State Federation of Rural Associations)
FARSUL	Federação dos Agricultores de Rio Grande do Sul (Rio Grande do Sul Federation of Agriculturalists)
FATAESP	Federação de Associaçies de Trabalhadores Agrícolas do Estado de São Paulo (São Paulo State Federation of Agrarian Laborers' Associations)
FECOESP	Federação de Círculos Operários do Estado de São Paulo (São Paulo State Federation of Workers Circles)
FERAESP	Federação de Empregados Rurais Assalariados do Estado de São Paulo (São Paulo State Federation of Rural Employees)
FESTIAESP	Federação dos Sindicatos dos Trabalhadores nas Indústrias de Alimentação do Estado de São Paulo (São Paulo State Federation of Food Industry Laborers' Unions)
FETAESP	Federação de Trabalhadores Agrícolas do Estado de São Paulo (São Paulo State Federation of Agricultural Laborers)
FNT	Frente Nacional de Trabalho (National Labor Front)
FSC	Frente Social Cristão (Christian Social Front)
FTRAESP	São Paulo Federation of Autonomous Rural Laborers
FTRSESP	Federação dos Trabalhadores Rurais e Similares do Estado de São Paulo (São Paulo State Federation of Rural Laborers and Others)
FUNRURAL	Fundo de Assistência ao Trabalhador Rural (Rural Laborer Assistance Fund)
IAA	Instituto de Açúcar e Álcool (Sugar and Alcohol Institute)
IBAD	Instituto Brasileiro de Ação Democrático (Brazilian Democratic Action Institute)

IBRA	Instituto Brasileiro de Reforma Agrária (Brazilian Agrarian Reform Institute)
ICT	Instituto Cultural de Trabalho (Cultural Institute of Labor)
ILO	International Labor Organization
INDA	Instituto Nacional de Desenvolvimento Agrária (National Agrarian Development Institute)
MAF	Movimento de Arregimentação Feminina (Feminine Regimentation Movement)
MASTER	Movimento dos Agricultores Sem Terra (Landless Farmers' Movement)
MST	Movimento dos Trabalhadores Rurais Sem Terra (Landless Laborers' Movement)
PCB	Partido Comunista Brasileiro (Brazilian Communist Party)
PD	Partido Democrático (Democratic Party)
PDC	Partido Democrata Cristão (Christian Democratic Party)
PM	Polícia Militar (Military Police)
PMDB	Partido do Movimento Democrático Brasileiro (Brazilian Democratic Movement Party)
PR	Partido Republicano (Republican Party)
PRP	Partido Republicano Paulista (Paulista Republican Party)
PSD	Partido Social Democrático (Social Democratic Party)
PSP	Partido Social Progressista (Social Progressive Party)
PT	Partido dos Trabalhadores (Workers' Party)
PTB	Partido Trabalhista Brasileiro (Brazilian Labor Party)
PTN	Partido Trabalhista Nacional (National Labor Party)
PTR	Partido Trabalhista Rural (Rural Labor Party)
PUI	Pacto de Unidade Intersindical (Interunion Unity Pact)
SER	Serviço Economia Rural (Rural Economy Service); Sindicato dos Empregados Rurais (Rural Employees Union), from 1988
SNA	Sociedade Nacional de Agricultura (National Agricultural Society)
SORPE	Serviço de Orientação Rural de Pernambuco (Pernambuco Rural Orientation Service)
SPA	Sociedade Paulista de Agricultura (Paulista Agriculture Society)

SRB	Sociedade Rural Brasileira (Brazilian Rural Society)
SSR	Serviço Social Rural (Rural Social Service)
STR	Sindicato dos Trabalhadores Rurais (Rural Laborers' Union)
SUPRA	Superintendência da Política Agrária (Superintendency of Agrarian Policy)
UDN	União Democrática Nacional (National Democratic Union Party)
UDR	União Democrática Ruralista (Rural Democratic Union Party)
UGT	União Geral dos Trabalhadores (Laborers' General Union)
ULTAB	União dos Lavradores e Trabalhadores Agrícolas do Brasil (Farmers' and Agricultural Laborers' Union of Brazil)
UNICAMP	Universidade Estadual de Campinas (São Paulo State University at Campinas)

Bibliographical Abbreviations

AEL/UNICAMP	Arquivo Edgard Leuenroth, Universidade de Campinas
AmConGen	American Consul General
AmConsul	American Consulate
AmEmbassy	American Embassy
ASP	*Agricultura em São Paulo*
B:NM	Arquivo do Projeto, Brasil: Nunca Mais, AEL/UNICAMP
CPDOC/FGV	Centro de Pesquisa e Documentação, Fundação Getúlio Vargas
DF	Decimal File, DS/USNA
DHBB	*Dicionário histórico-biográfico brasileiro*
DM	*Diário da Manhã*
DN	*Diário de Notícias*
DS/USNA	Department of State, United States National Archives
FL	*Folha de Londrina*
HAHR	*Hispanic American Historical Review*
JT/RP	Junta de Conciliação e Julgamento (Junta de Trabalho), Ribeirão Preto
MTIC	Ministério do Trabalho, Indústria e Comércio
NH	*Notícias de Hoje*
NR	*Novos Rumos*

NR-ss	*Novos Rumos,* 8–14 December 1961, special supplement
OESP	*O Estado de São Paulo*
PR	Processo No.
RG	Record Group, DS/USNA
RLT	*Revista Legislação do Trabalho*
RSRB	*Revista da Sociedade Rural Brasileira*
SEPLAN	Secretaria da Economia e Planejamento
SPR/AN	Fundo da Secretária da Presidência da República, Arquivo Nacional do Brasil
TL	*Terra Livre*
TRE/SP	Arquivo da Tribunal Regional Eleitoral do Estado de São Paulo
UH	*Última Hora*
USDS	United States Department of State

ACKNOWLEDGMENTS

This book has been more than a dozen years in the making, and I am grateful to so many people that I hardly know where to begin. As the book is already long, I have tried to keep this section short and snappy, though it has been difficult, given the size of my debts. If your name is missing here, check the endnotes, which include specific acknowledgments to colleagues who generously shared their research materials, time, and ideas with me. If I have left your name out, please forgive me, for twelve years is a long time to keep track of everyone who contributed to this effort.

When I first started to conceptualize this book, virtually nothing had been published on the subject, and it often seemed an impossible task to put the story together. From time to time, I grew profoundly discouraged, but there was one person who believed it could be done—Michael M. Hall of Universidade Estadual de Campinas (UNICAMP)—and to him I owe my greatest thanks. He may have been moved, as I was, by the ongoing struggles of rural workers in the 1980s, for it seemed that each day's *Folha de São Paulo* brought news of their bitter fight. Once the research got under way, no one sustained it more than the subjects themselves. My contact with such unsung heroes as Irineu Luís de Moraes, João Guerreiro Filho, Celso Ibson de Syllos, and Avelino Ganzer, not to mention dozens of other labor militants, eroded my anxieties and filled me with a sense of duty. Their memories are the *carne e osso* (meat and bones) of this book. Once I met them, I stopped wondering if there was a story to tell and began to focus on how I would repay these courageous spirits for trusting me with their life stories. This book is a partial attempt to do so.

I had just begun to see the outlines of the puzzle that became this book when I met Sebastião Geraldo in the lobby of the Ribeirão Preto archdiocese building. Like me, he was a graduate student of working-class origins who was trying to put together a history of labor in the region. Little by little our friendship grew, and so did our collaboration on a number of personal and professional projects. Given his warm-hearted Italo-Brazilian heritage, it was not long before his house (and kitchen!) became a home away from home for my family and me. I can hardly fathom the depths of knowledge I have gained in his company, nor can I adequately thank him. I am also indebted to the hospitality, teachings, and companionship of Sebastião's wife, Maria Amélia de Oliveira Geraldo, and their children,

Roberta and Lucas, not to mention the entire Geraldo and Oliveira clans.

When I returned to the United States from Brazil in 1989, I was far from certain where I would be taken by the nine suitcases of books, photocopies, notes, and tapes I brought back with me. At that point, I received a kind and encouraging letter from John D. French, then an assistant professor of history at Florida International University. For reasons far beyond my comprehension, this absolute stranger believed in me and this book long before I did, and for that I will be eternally grateful. Although his generosity toward me has been boundless, I am particularly thankful that he introduced me to the challenging world of the Latin American labor history conferences, where I always received—from such commentators as Barbara Weinstein and Daniel James—more than I brought. To this day, I find it difficult to explain John's faith in me, but I cannot doubt it, for his keen historical sensibility has informed every page of this book.

My life and work have been enriched by many good teachers. In addition to Michael, John, Barbara, and Danny, professors Victor Perrera, Michael Cowan, Page Smith, Ira Berlin, Winthrop Wright, Richard Price, Charles Bergquist, John TePaske, Janet Ewald, Hobart Spalding, Emilia Viotti da Costa, Maurício Font, and Paulo Sérgio Pinheiro have been especially important to me. From each I have learned new ways of seeing and knowing the world. Each has gone out of their way to support me through acts large and small. Barbara, for example, was the first "Brazilianist" I came to know and the first to provide comments on this work as a book manuscript. By modeling their own deep respect for humanity, each of these people taught me much about extending compassion to others. I hope this book convinces them I was paying attention at least part of the time.

As I learned from these fine teachers, good history is based on good evidence, and finding such material for this book was a particularly challenging task. More than a few "archives" I worked in were merely tables courteously cleared for my convenience in cramped offices. This was especially true of the Junta de Trabalho in Ribeirão Preto, where Vilma Gimenez Welch and I spent an entire week organizing dusty piles of court records before we were able to begin reading them. At the *junta,* first Wagner Moreira da Cunha and later Zildete Ribeiro do Desterro went out of their way to accommodate me. I also want to thank Judge Valentin Carrion for helping me gain access to the labor court system. Elsewhere in Ribeirão Preto, Pedro Márcio Sant'Anna made way for me in the newsroom of the *Diário da Manhã,* and José Pedro de Miranda made it possible for me to enter the archdiocese curate to look at old copies of *Diário de Notícias*. I like to think that the attention Sebastião and I showed these documents alerted officials to their value, for future researchers will find them more carefully housed in the Arquivo Público e Histórico de Ribeirão Preto, an entity that did not yet exist when I began my work. Hopefully, archivist Divo Marino will take as much care of them as he does of his rich memories. Although Benonio Pitta—a printer for the Ribeirão Preto daily *A Cidade* and a Communist Party activist—had no table to offer me, he was always eager to help me locate the historic militants who were this book's largest storehouse of information. I also want to thank Paulo Sérgio Honório and Patrícia da Silva Montanheiro of the Centro de Direitos Humanos e Educação Popular for their help and good works.

In São Paulo, at the Biblioteca "Mario Andrade," Dona Lourdes treated me like a member of her microfilming staff. I am also grateful to the professional care with which I was received at various libraries and study centers at the Universidade de São Paulo (USP), the Pontifical Universidade Católica of São Paulo (PUC-SP), the Sociedade Rural Brasileira (SRB), the Tribunal Regional Eleitoral (TRE), the Instituto Brasileiro de Geografia e Estatística (IBGE), the Movimento dos Trabalhadores Rurais Sem Terra (MST), the Instituto Económico Brasilerio, the Centro de Documentação e Informação Científico (CEDIC), the Centro Brasileiro de Análise e Pesquisa (CEBRAP), and at the Central Único dos Trabalhadores. At the Arquivo do Estado de São Paulo, Aparecido Oliveira da Silva and Walmir Carlos Zerio were especially helpful to me. At UNICAMP, Marco Aurélio Garcia and Ricardo Antunes greatly assisted my work in the Arquivo Edgard Leuenroth, and the staff of UNICAMP's Centro de Memórias also made my work easier. In São Carlos, São Paulo, Terrie Groth, Valter Roberto Silverio, and José Cláudio Barriguelli facilitated my work. I am grateful to each of them.

In Rio de Janeiro, I was received with great enthusiasm and grace by Professor João C. Portinari, director of the Projeto Cândido Portinari, who helped select the cover art for the book. The staffs of the Arquivo Nacional and the Biblioteca Nacional were always courteous and happy to help a confused foreign researcher. The same can be said of those who operate the Centro de Pesquisa e Documentação at the Fundação Getúlio Vargas, especially Angela Castro Gomes and Aspásia Camargo. I also enjoyed special care and attention from the staffs of the Casa Rui Barbosa and the Centro de Estudos Afro-Asiáticos (CEAA).

Many friends and colleagues in Brazil and the United States

helped me in dozens of ways, large and small, with the completion of this book. In Rio de Janeiro, Paulo Venancio Filho was a constant source of support from the first day I arrived in Brazil. I was also aided there by Nancy Naro, Amaury de Souza, Peter Fry, Roquinaldo Amaral, and Lygia Sigaud. In São Paulo, Maria Silvia Portella de Castro; her father, Mario; and their helper, Rosalinda, helped me enormously. The same can be said of Bill Hinchberger, Maruska Rameck, John Monteiro, Maria Helena Machado, Elide Rugai Bastos, Nena Castro, Jarbas Favoretto, Salvador Sandoval, and Sonia de Avelar—all supporters of many years. In Ribeirão Preto, I was fortunate to be befriended by Aurea Moretti Pires and Moacir Paulo Botelho de Lima ("Paulinho"), two inspiring *lutadores*. In the United States, I have Tony Pereira to thank for many ideas and much encouragement. Additional help and inspiration has come from Teresa Meade, Richard Soderlund, Stanley Gacek, Jeff Smith, Abíódún Gòkè-Paríolá, Jo Ellen Miller, Larry Tosh, Dennis Valdéz, Alberto Macias, Medea Benjamin, David Leaman, Al Walczak, Russell Rhoads, Walter Foote, James and Virginia Goode, Lynn Mapes, Tony Travis, Gary Gerson, and Michelle Duram. I have also found inspiration in debate with students in my Brazilian and Latin American history courses at Grand Valley State University (GVSU).

Another ingredient essential to a successful book is money. I have not had much of it and so am especially grateful for what financial help I have received. Most recently, support has come through the good offices of GVSU's associate vice president, John Gracki, and the Research and Development Committee. Over the years at Grand Valley, their support of me and my work has been invaluable. I also received research fellowships from the Tinker Foundation, Shell International, and the Organization of American States. I was able to prolong my stay in Brazil between 1987 and 1989 with the support of Paulo Sérgio Pinheiro, who kept me busy and financially afloat with interesting translating and interpreting assignments.

My mother and stepfather, Jeanette S. and Arthur C. Rosenbrock, also kept me from starving time and time again. Above and beyond their financial support, however, was their constant love and encouragement. One of the best times of my life was in 1988, when they visited me for ten days in Brazil. My mother has long been a fighter for progressive change, and I thank her for passing that spirit along to me. Art, who was so popular that the forward-looking San Francisco ship clerks of the International Longshoremen's and Warehousemen's Union elected him year after year to the post of secretary-treasurer for more than two decades, taught me about solidarity, work, and being tough but kind. I thank them both as parents and human beings.

Without a publisher, there would be no book to write acknowledgments for, and so I thank Penn State Press director Sanford Thatcher and his board of reviewers for agreeing to publish *The Seed Was Planted*. Under the strain of capitalist reform, university presses are finding it harder and harder to support books that may have limited commercial appeal. Given these pressures, I am particularly grateful for the consistent interest and full investment Sandy has given this project, from the thorough expert reader reports of Thomas Holloway and John French to the painstaking copyediting of Thayer Robins and the decision to stretch the budget to use a Portinari print on the cover of the paperback edition. I also thank Kurt Thompson of the Water Resources Institute at Grand Valley State University for his work on the maps.

I dedicate this book to Toni A. Perrine, my partner in life and love. I've learned a lot about the life of the mind from her sharp intelligence and about family life from her tender nurturing of Andrew and Alida Perrine. The three Perrines in my life are a work in progress that brings much delight, drawing me away from history and into the present, where I gain precious perspective. I thank them all.

9 March 1998, Grand Rapids, Michigan

NOTE ON TRANSLATIONS AND SPELLINGS

Unless otherwise noted, translations from Portuguese to English have been made by the author. Brazilian spelling, especially of names, is notoriously inconsistent. To satisfy North American demands for consistency, the spellings of names have been adjusted to modern Brazilian standards as set forth in Domingos Paschoal Cegalla's *Novíssima gramática da língua portuguesa*.

The president was coming. In just under three weeks, he would be in Ribeirão Preto to inaugurate a regional agrarian reform agency and address a rally of farmworkers, many of them recently unionized with the agency's help. It was a big moment for those who had worked hard to build the rural labor movement in this important agricultural region. Over the years, their activities had inspired constant repression, from dismissals to beatings. Now, in late March 1964, many of those seeking improvements in the living and working conditions of rural laborers gathered together to unify their efforts under the direction of a federal agency that enjoyed the clear support of Brazilian President João "Jango" Goulart.

Dozens of people attended the meeting, including newspaper editors, lawyers, urban and rural union officers, Catholic priests and

PROLOGUE

São Paulo Rural Workers and Modern Brazilian History

lay workers, Communist militants, medical and dental students, and more. The medical students were to address the health needs of rural workers; the dental students, their oral hygiene; the liberal arts students, their education; the editors, the promotional needs of the movement. The lawyers offered to give legal advice and file the workers' labor law claims, and the trade unionists supplied strategic and political support. Brazilian Communist Party (PCB, Partido Comunista Brasileiro) member Irineu Luís de Moraes, a labor organizer since 1929, specialized in generating worker interest in rural unions. Celso Ibson de Syllos, a Catholic priest involved with the movement since 1960, trained worker-leaders in union administration. Whatever their individual contributions and reservations about the process, all supported the plan—although it was far removed from traditional practice—to use the state to help unionize workers and integrate them into the political economy. It was an ambitious project, and they were proud to be part of it.

But the president never came. Within a week of the meeting, Moraes, Padre Celso, and other movement participants were in hiding, fearful of arrest, torture, or worse. On March 31, a long-planned military-civilian conspiracy went on the offensive, overthrowing President Goulart and suppressing his supporters and their programs. The conspirators singled out the agrarian reform agency known as SUPRA—Superintendency of Agrarian Policy (Superintendência de Política Agrária)—for immediate assault. The agency's promise of uplifting some of Brazil's least well-off inhabitants—rural workers—of redistributing land, of improving the country's agricultural productivity through social reform, of empowering farmworkers through voter registration, a plan so passionately embraced by so many communities, was soon torn apart. Goulart, fleeing capture by the army, went into exile, and Ribeirão Preto's grand inauguration rally never took place.

The rally that never was symbolized both achievements and failures of the rural labor movement that took root in São Paulo in the aftermath of World War II. By 1964 the movement had acquired an unprecedented political presence, one built on public sympathy and an increasingly influential position in the agrarian structure, where strikes and other collective and individual actions had caused changes in labor relations on plantations (*fazendas*) and modifications of planter (*fazendeiro*) practices. But at the time of the proposed rally, the movement was disorganized and insecure. It was in an awkward growth stage, a seedling that had taken root yet continued to need the help of supporting stakes and guides. This support network came to be provided by a government and a progressive sector of the landlord class interested, yet not quite committed to, the idea of rearranging rural social relations in order to improve agricultural productivity, slow the exodus of rural workers out of the rural labor market and into the crowded cities, and build a new constituency among farmworkers. São Paulo rural workers and their leaders found ways to push these hesitant elite initiatives in unexpected directions. Neither the government nor the *fazendeiros* accepted the growing autonomy of the movement. The state tried to recapture control, and the planters turned hostile, threatened by the deepening relationship between rural workers and both revolutionary and populist parties and politicians. Fearing the erosion of their authority over national policy and their own property, planters acted to suppress the coalition of rural workers and politicians while it was still forming. *The Seed Was Planted* tells this story, recounting the steps that led to the movement's triumphant expectations and painful collapse in 1964.

Although the *golpe* of 1964 was a turning point for the rural labor movement in Brazil, it neither eradicated the old movement nor planted a completely new one. Several significant continuities carried over from the past into the future rural labor movement. These included two institutional advances from 1963: the Rural Laborer Statute (ETR, Estatuto do Trabalhador Rural), which shaped the laws governing rural labor relations and organizations, and the National Confederation of Laborers in Agriculture (CONTAG, Confederação Nacional dos Trabalhadores na Agricultura), which continues to unite state union federations and represent the interests of rural workers at the national level. Various local unions also remained in place, and some of the people who were active before the *golpe* continued their participation afterward, though in altered ways and without the help of an executive branch agency like SUPRA. Another continuity with the past can be found in the memory of participants in the rural labor struggle.

Rural Worker Voices

The Seed Was Planted takes its title from one such source, João Guerreiro Filho. Guerreiro was working for his father on a small farm in Dumont, São Paulo, when in 1945 he joined the PCB and helped establish one of the founding organizations of the movement, the peasant league of Dumont. Years later, in 1989, my colleague Sebastião

Geraldo and I found Guerreiro living in the city of São Paulo with his son. When we revealed our interest in his past, he directed us outside to the carport and began to talk in a hushed tone, explaining, somewhat whimsically, that his son worked as an officer of the military police, a branch of the state security apparatus that had done much to repress popular social movements like the unions. Guerreiro wanted to avoid irritating him and so kept our conversation quiet. Evidently a popular struggle of sorts had unfolded within the family home as Guerreiro voiced the connections he saw between his activism in 1945 and recent challenges to the military regime that had ruled Brazil since 1964. In 1985, just a few years before we spoke, the military finally relinquished power to civilians, pressured in part by a great sweep of popular mobilization in which opposition marchers frequently numbered in the hundreds of thousands. "The seed was planted and it's germinating," Guerreiro told us. The Dumont league of 1945 had been the seed, and its fruit included the return of popular politics in the 1980s.[1]

Guerreiro's statement lent itself not only to a good title but also to an organizing principle for the book. His vision of a historic rural labor movement whose legacy included redemocratization suggests a new theme of continuity for Brazilian history—a theme of rural worker agency in the making of modern Brazil. Partial support for this theme can be found in the story of a peasant league—organized by Francisco Julião Arruda de Paula in the state of Pernambuco—that successfully pressured the state government into expropriating an old sugar estate and distributing its lands to resident workers. The year of this event—1959—corresponded closely to the Cuban revolution and intensification of the Vietnam insurgency, both of which depended in differing measures on the discontent of rural workers. Suddenly, authorities in Brazil were confronted by a previously quiescent rural mass. Scholars reflected this timing in their writings by emphasizing the increasingly influential presence of rural workers as a political force between 1959 and, in the case of Brazil, the 1964 *golpe*.

It is generally assumed, however, that before 1959, rural workers had no impact on society. A typical summary of this view is encap-

1. João Guerreiro Filho, transcript of interview by author and Sebastião Geraldo, São Paulo, 11 July 1989, Arquivo Edgard Leuenroth, Universidade de Campinas (hereafter AEL/ UNICAMP). In another region of Brazil, the Amazon state of Acre, the internationally recognized rubber-tapper leader Chico Mendes expressed a similar sense of historical continuity before he was killed in 1988. See Andrew Revkin, *The Burning Season: The Murder of Chico Mendes and the Fight for the Amazon Rain Forest* (Boston: Houghton Mifflin, 1990).

sulated in a 1995 analysis of agrarian structure and politics in Brazil: "The lack of any rural organization until the late 1950s meant that landlords were left in the position of ultimate authority on their estates and mostly also controlled local politics."[2] This argument is linked to a larger theory positing that in the course of Brazilian history, the bourgeoisie conspired with landlords to exclude rural workers from the benefits of modernization, thereby protecting the landlord's access to low-cost labor while gaining their support for urban and industrial development. According to this theory, the government cooperated with this pact—even orchestrated it—by helping to repress rural labor organizations while encouraging urban unionization with a variety of measures.[3] The pact began to disintegrate in the early 1960s when the government suddenly opened its doors to the rural labor movement.

One consequence of presenting the rural labor movement as an apparition of the early 1960s has been a tendency to exaggerate its importance during this so-called interregnum of the workers' complacency. This tendency has had two main expressions: either the movement is blamed for creating a sense of anarchy that presented the conspirators with a justification for the 1964 coup d'état—the need to restore order—or it is faulted for being loud and demanding but not sufficiently well planted to successfully resist the takeover.[4] The Brazilian Rural Society (SRB, Sociedade Rural Brasileira), a powerful association of coffee growers and beef exporters based in São Paulo, linked rural unionization to anarchy, blamed the Goulart government for establishing conditions propitious for "subversives," and eagerly supported the *golpe*. "As a participant in the team that brought victory in the struggle against the recently deposed *comunopeleguista* government," wrote SRB president Salvio de Almeida Prado, "the SRB occupied an outstanding place in the national political panorama." Rural labor militants have been just as eager to emphasize the significance of their movement at that moment. "I have no doubts," the PCB activist Gregório Bezerra reflected some years later, "that 50 percent of the *golpe* was caused by the pressure of the

2. Evelyne Huber and John D. Stephens, "Conclusion: Agrarian Structure and Political Power in Comparative Perspective," in *Agrarian Structure and Political Power: Landlord and Peasant in the Making of Latin America*, edited by Evelyne Huber and Frank Safford (Pittsburgh: University of Pittsburgh Press, 1995), 197.

3. Fernando Antônio Azevêdo, *As ligas camponesas* (Rio de Janeiro: Paz e Terra, 1982).

4. On restoring order, see General Olympio Mourão Filho, *Memórias: A verdade de um revolucionário,* 4th ed. (Porto Alegre: L + PM, 1978), 25–47, 158, 162–63, 183. For a critique of the movement's authenticity, see Benno Galjart, "Class and 'Following' in Rural Brazil," *América Latina* 7:3 (July/September 1964), 3–23.

rural bourgeoisie against the advancing peasant movement." Historians generally endorse these views, with Thomas Skidmore citing the conspirators' desires to "'root out'" the rural labor movement and Aspásia Camargo calling peasant mobilization "decisive" in motivating planter reaction.[5]

Guerreiro's perspective roots these arguments in the more distant past. For Guerreiro and other participants, a continuous line connects the peasant leagues of the 1940s to the massive *"Diretas Já!* [Direct Elections Now!]" mobilizations of the mid-1980s. Implicit is a progressive view of history in which rural workers played a central part. In contrast to standard versions, Guerreiro's story legitimates and empowers rural workers like himself. In his memory of the past, his efforts and those of all rural militants are neither shameful nor unremarkable but a way of showing that rural workers were in control of the strings of history all along. There may have been a few setbacks along the way, but to the extent rural workers took part in knocking down the military regime in the present, their work was built on prior efforts, including Guerreiro's 1945 peasant league. In this sense, Guerreiro offers a compelling counternarrative, a "uchronic dream," as the Italian historian Alessandro Portelli calls memories that reflect the "possible worlds" of informants. In the context of triumph for the masses, as perceived in the mid-1980s, the former Communist identifies with "the people" and imagines direct linkages between his militancy and that of present-day activists.[6]

The validity of Guerreiro's possible world is not as improbable

5. Bezerra is quoted in Dênis de Moraes, *A esquerda e o golpe de 64* (Rio de Janeiro, 1989); Aspásia de Alcântara Camargo, "A questão agrária: Crise de poder e reformas de base (1930–1964)," in *História geral da civilização brasileira*, Tomo III, *O Brasil republicano*, vol. 3, *Sociedade e política (1930–1964)*, edited by Boris Fausto, 3d ed. (São Paulo: Difel, 1986), 223. Thomas E. Skidmore, *The Politics of Military Rule in Brazil, 1964–85* (New York: Oxford University Press, 1988), 4. For the planters, see "Sindicalismo e anarquia rural," *A Rural* 43:501 (January 1963), 3; and Salvio de Almeida Prado, "Pronunciamentos da SRB durante a revolução redentora do pais," *A Rural* 44:517 (May 1964), 28–30. (*A Rural* was the new title of the SRB's monthly journal.) See also Cliff Welch, "'Rivalry and Unification': Mobilising Rural Workers in São Paulo on the Eve of the Brazilian Golpe of 1964," *Journal of Latin American Studies* 27 (1995), 161–87.

6. Portelli adopted this concept from science fiction after interviewing dozens of Communist militants in Terni, Italy. He found it useful in recovering "not only the material surface of what happened, but also the narrator's attitude toward events, the subjectivity, imagination, and desire that each individual invests in the relationship with history" (143). So many informants recounted "wrong" versions of the past that he began to notice this "motif," as he calls it: "the narrative shape of the dream of a different personal life and a different collective history" (145). *The Seed Was Planted* uses the concept to interpret oral testimonies, an important source of information for this book. Alessandro Portelli, "Uchronic Dreams: Working Class Memory and Possible Worlds," in *The Myths We Live By*, edited by Raphael Samuel and Paul Thompson (New York: Routledge, 1990), 143–60. (Thanks to Daniel James for introducing me to Portelli's work.)

as it might first appear. Guerreiro's belief that organized rural workers were instrumental in challenging the military government's monopoly of power in the late 1970s and early 1980s is corroborated by other sources.[7] While the present cannot be projected into the past, neither can the contemporary movement be summarily detached from its antecedents in the 1960s, 1950s, and 1940s. This is not to say that scholars have been wrong in emphasizing the continuity of landlord authority and its basis in the suppression of rural worker demands. This historical tendency cannot be denied. But acceptance of this position has long led analysts to assume that rural workers quietly acquiesced in their subjugation until the magical 1959 date, when government tolerance, as much as their autonomous action, suddenly endowed rural workers with historical agency. Guerreiro's alternative recollection of a history driven by rural workers, while too extreme in its own right, prompts a reconsideration of traditional assumptions. By taking Guerreiro's narrative seriously, *The Seed Was Planted* presents considerable evidence to show that rural workers, especially those in São Paulo, contributed much to modern Brazilian history, even though their initiatives were rarely welcomed by the ruling class.

Guerreiro has indeed imagined a direct link between Dumont and the restoration of civilian rule in 1985. But he has not imagined the fact that rural workers began to develop an organized social movement in the 1940s. The formation of this movement in São Paulo and its evolving relationship with the ruling state-landlord alliance is the subject of *The Seed Was Planted*. The book examines both the theory and practice of this relationship, centering on an analysis of the subaltern discourse of rural workers and their interlocutors and the ruling-class discourse of landlords and bureaucrats. Most of the literature on this subject stresses the most conservative voices of the elite discourse, focusing on those who demanded the exclusion of rural workers from politics and ignored their role in history. However, even within this discourse, striking diversity can be found, for some officials pushed hard to improve "rural life" and enhance the power of workers. Moreover, a few *fazendeiros* found it useful to support rural worker demands and form political alliances with Communist labor

7. Key strikes of sugarcane cutters in Pernambuco in 1979 and São Paulo in 1984 represented significant challenges to the government's legitimacy as arbiter of wages and prices. See Lygia Sigaud, *Greve nos engenhos* (Rio de Janeiro: Paz e Terra, 1980); and Maria Conceição D'Incao, "O movimento de Guariba: O papel acelerador da crise econômica," *Política e Administração* 1:2 (1985), 201–22. See also Anthony W. Pereira, *The End of the Peasantry: The Rural Labor Movement in Northeast Brazil (1961–1984)* (Pittsburgh: University of Pittsburgh Press, 1996).

militants. Among rural workers, the subaltern discourse is limited and divided in various ways. On the one hand, the voices of the vast majority of rural workers remains silent, their hopes and aspirations forever lost in the void of neglectful documentation. On the other hand, the loudest voices in the surviving record are those of interlocutors like the PCB, Francisco Julião's Peasant Leagues, and populist politicians. Through oral testimony, the voices of some participants and rural worker leaders like Guerreiro can also be heard. Depending on the source, the subaltern voice may stress rural labor's role in the overthrow of capitalism, the need for land reform, rural unionization, or the improvement of living and working conditions for the rural poor.

The difficulty of defining who was a rural worker complicated activism and hence the historical record. Participants in the rural labor movement recognized the need to treat people in different job categories differently, for each group had their own unique interests. Thus, a rural wage earner (*operário rural* or *assalariado rural*) first sought higher wages, a tenant farmer (*arrendatário*) wanted his or her rent lowered and access to markets improved, and insecure sharecroppers (*parceiros*) and day laborers (*diários*) desired land they could call their own, a dream thought to flower in the minds of all rural workers. Until the 1960s, the generic term used to define the rural working classes was *camponeses*. This word is generally translated as "peasants," though in the 1950s and 1960s it applied in political dialog not only to smallholders but to many other categories of the rural poor, including wage earners, tenant farmers, sharecroppers, migrants, and contract workers. In the early 1960s, *trabalhador agrícola* (agricultural laborer) began to displace *camponês* as a catchall term. This lexical transition was captured in the title of CONTAG, the movement's first official national organization, which was charged with representing all categories of rural workers from its inception in 1963. Today, *trabalhador rural* (rural laborer/worker) is a more common universalizing term, though increasingly overarching terminology is avoided in preference for more specific and accurate labels.

São Paulo's Unique Story

The shift in terminology reflects a shift in modern Brazilian agriculture from a sector characterized by varied and informal land-labor relationships (befitting *camponês*) to one characterized by large agricultural establishments where market relations predominate (befitting *trabalhador rural*). Because São Paulo was on the forefront of the transition from traditional estates to modern agro-industry, the history of rural social relations in this state is particularly interesting. Far from being a representative case, São Paulo offers a unique setting in which to examine some aspects of what promised to become more common in other states. Though each region developed in its own way, São Paulo's history forecast the future as both a warning and an example. *The Seed Was Planted* uses the São Paulo story to detail the modernization process in agriculture, especially how it affected and was affected by the people involved. Rural workers wanted greater security and dignity of modernization; landlords wanted greater profits and the preservation of their sovereignty; the federal government wanted more foreign exchange earnings. Each group pressured the land and each other to fulfill their goals. By the early 1960s, they settled on some of the terms of rural worker "incorporation" that would be a part of modern Brazilian history for several decades. In all parts of rural Brazil, incorporation referred to a process of determining how rural workers were to be treated by state institutions, the law, and landlords—how, in other words, they would be formally integrated in the political economy of which they were, by necessity, already an integral part.

In São Paulo, the politics of rural labor incorporation were especially dynamic. Brazil's wealthiest and most powerful state for more than a century, much of São Paulo's growth and development stemmed from the richness of its soil and the energy millions of enslaved Africans and free European laborers expended clearing land and cultivating a variety of crops. Until the 1930s, coffee had no equal among crops grown in São Paulo. Thereafter, its significance declined relative to the ascent of other commercial crops, especially cotton and sugarcane. Nevertheless, coffee remained the state's most lucrative commodity well into the 1960s. The export of coffee also remained Brazil's most important source of foreign currency, a precious resource for a nation seeking to import equipment and technology to build its industrial sector. São Paulo's ruling class owed much of its great political influence to this strategic crop. As coffee prospered, so did the state's industrial base, which eventually included a network of sugar mills and other agro-industries.[8]

8. Essential works on the history of São Paulo include Warren Dean, *The Industrialization of São Paulo, 1880–1945* (Austin: University of Texas Press, 1969); and Mauricio A. Font, *Coffee, Contention, and Change in the Making of Modern Brazil* (New York: Basil Blackwell, 1990).

MAP 1. São Paulo and places of interest in Brazil's history of the rural labor struggle

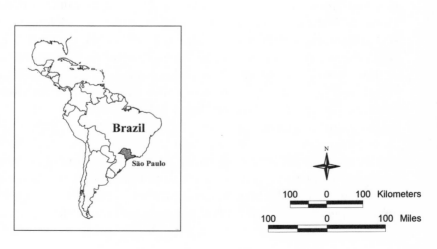

The returns generated by world demand for coffee made São Paulo Brazil's engine and also its engineer. The wealth of São Paulo's planters placed them at the forefront of the national ruling class, thus making them the envy of that class. Their position of dominance eventually generated challengers, and beginning in 1930 the *paulistas* were forced to relinquish some of their political power, although they retained considerable socioeconomic influence over the nation. It could be said that after 1930, a governor had been attached to the São Paulo motor, setting limits on its speed and power.

As key as São Paulo agriculture was to Brazil, it is no wonder that the labor process on São Paulo plantations presented rural workers with considerable leverage over everything from production to politics. The labor process was the first axis of conflict between planter, bureaucrat, worker, and leader, as each pressed their own notion of how plantation life and labor should be organized. The first major initiatives came from the federal government, which challenged the *paulistas* after 1930. The policy and law it generated did not succeed in influencing much change, but it did create a new language that was later grabbed and reshaped by rural workers and their advocates. Although the new policies promised to affect the labor process, they were not implemented. They helped create expectations, however, and as rural workers and their advocates sought to make the ideal real, the axis of conflict shifted to political and institutional realms. Getting the laws implemented required courts, and getting courts established required political pressure. Once courts were established, questions arose about the equitable enforcement of the law and its adequacy, and the rural labor movement grew and acquired enough strength to insist on standards that more closely fit the subaltern discourse than that of bureaucrats and planters. This movement began to shape not only the implementation of the law but the law itself. One partisan source claimed that rural workers in Ribeirão Preto filed 1,530 complaints in 1958 and 1959, winning 1,500 of them. Although an exaggeration, these figures indicate the extraordinary pressures rural workers were beginning to place on a system once owned by the landlords.[9] In reaction, many planters refused to deal with their uppity workers, found new ways to cheat them, expelled them, changed their crops and methods, and finally conspired to overthrow the government. This process took several decades

9. Figures from Nestor Vera, "A sindicalização rural em São Paulo," *Novos Rumos* (hereafter *NR*), 21–27 April 1961, 4. Vera was then an officer of ULTAB, a Communist Party front for organizing rural workers.

before it abruptly culminated in the 1964 *golpe*. Throughout these years, rural workers played an increasingly active role, going from sporadic to more consistent engagement and from plantation to plaza-centered protest.

The Ribeirão Preto rally that never was promised to be an exultant promenade around the city's central plaza, a public display of the movement's youthful vigor. The ground had been cleared and prepared, the seed planted, the soil tended, and a young seedling had grown to bear the fruit of a better life for thousands of rural workers. Mimicking the spread of Brazil's ubiquitous lime tree, seedlings sprouted up in many parts of the country, areas where others like Guerreiro had planted the seeds of rural labor organization in response to local problems. The first fruit developed in the early 1960s, when hundreds of rural labor unions took shape around the country. But the young trees demanded pruning, shaping, and care to produce a full crop. SUPRA, the agrarian reform agency, started to coordinate these activities under the presidency of João Goulart, sending overseers out to tend the trees in all corners of Brazil. The *golpe* of 1964 arrested the process, clearing the orchards of cultivators, letting the fruit rot on the ground, and cutting back the fragile trees. Yet, these plants were not uprooted, and so few died. Some went into hibernation, awaiting better conditions. For a time, the unions turned away from the plaza, from politics, and focused on economic issues and member services. The buds gradually began to appear again, and by the early 1980s, fruit dangled from a thousand branches: the rural labor movement was reborn, changed but stronger than ever before. "The seed was planted and it's germinating," Guerreiro had said. How the ground was cleared, the seeds planted, and the seedlings bore their first fruit only to be cut back at a moment of great promise, their growth suppressed, is the question this book sets out to answer.

Historiography, Sources, and Overview

Larger than the continental United States, Brazil's great size and diversity resist stereotyping and generalization. This is especially true of its social movements, whose complexity complicate summation in the best of circumstances. For the rural labor movement, only one author has attempted a synthesis. Leonilde Sérvolo de Medeiros's *História dos movimentos sociais no campo* is a survey of the movement that begins in 1945 and takes the story up to 1989, when the book was published. Written to serve as a resource for the movement, the book makes many insightful observations and provides an invaluable overview. Lacking adequate monographic sources, its historical chapters are the weakest. Only a series of empirically based studies will reveal the knowledge needed to answer questions about the pre-1964 rural labor movement.[10] More is known about the peasant leagues of the northeast than any other part of the movement. Nevertheless, a few studies have examined the history of rural labor mobilization in the southern and central states of Rio Grande do Sul, Rio de Janeiro, and Goiás, and several studies explore peasant mobilization in Paraná.[11]

This book differs from the work described above by offering an examination of the development of the movement and its leaders in São Paulo—Brazil's most prosperous and influential state—and especially in the state's northwestern agricultural zone, called the Alta Mogiana, of which Ribeirão Preto is the commercial and sociopolitical center. Far from a community study, this book strives to show the relationship between local rural labor mobilization, state and national politics, and international political and economic pressures. Of primary importance is an analysis of the process of political incorporation experienced by rural workers during the period demarcated by the 1930 revolution and the *golpe* of 1964. While some preliminary steps were taken during the years 1930 to 1945, after 1945 rural workers began to push their way into the public sphere, demanding a say in the sociopolitical and economic life of the country. In contrast to the predominant interpretation, this book shows that they could not

10. In addition to Leonilde Sérvolo de Medeiros's *História dos movimentos sociais no campo* (Rio de Janeiro: FASE, 1989), two articles offer surveys of the movement: Clodomir Santos de Moraes, "Peasant Leagues in Brazil," in *Agrarian Problems and Peasant Movements in Latin America,* edited by Rodolfo Stavenhagen (New York: Doubleday, 1970), 453–501; and José de Souza Martins, *Os camponeses e a política no Brasil* (Petrópolis: Vôzes, 1981), 21–102.

11. For the northeast, see, for example, Cynthia Hewitt, "Brazil: The Peasant Movement in Pernambuco, 1961–1964," in *Latin American Peasant Movements,* edited by Henry A. Landsberger (Ithaca: Cornell University Press, 1969), 374–98; Florencia E. Mallon, "Peasants and Rural Laborers in Pernambuco, 1955–1964," *Latin American Perspectives* 5:4 (Fall 1978), 49–70; Azevêdo, *As ligas camponesas;* Elide Rugai Bastos, *As ligas camponesas* (Petrópolis: Vôzes, 1984); and Manuel da Conceição, *Essa terra é nossa: Depoimento sôbre a vida e as lutas de camponeses no estado do Maranhão* (Petrópolis: Vôzes, 1980). For Rio Grande do Sul, see Cordula Eckert, "Movimento dos Agricultores Sem Terra no Rio Grande do Sul, 1960–1964" (master's thesis, Universidade Federal Rural do Rio de Janeiro, 1984). For Rio de Janeiro, consult Mario Grynszpan, "O campesinato fluminense: Mobilização e controle político, 1950–1964," *Revista Rio de Janeiro* 1 (April 1986), 19–27. For Goiás, see Maria Esperança Fernandes Carneiro, *A revolta campnesa de Formoso e Tombas* (Goiánia: Editora da Universidade Federal de Goiás, 1986). For Paraná, see, for example, Iria Zanani Gomes, *1957: A revolta dos posseiros* (Curitiba: Crias Edições, 1986).

MAP 2.   Alta Mogiana region

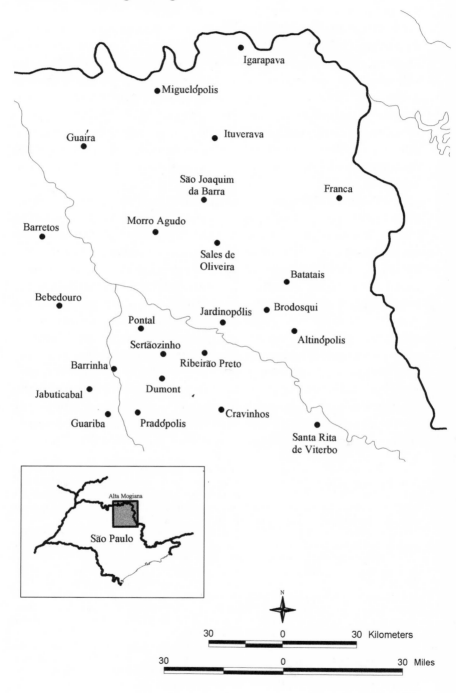

be excluded and that once the elites realized this, they had few choices but to try to control the workers' incorporation.[12]

The Seed Was Planted is not the first book to look at the history of rural workers in São Paulo and treat them as participants rather than victims. The anthropologist Verena Stolcke offered a unique assessment of rural workers in São Paulo in her study *Coffee Planters, Workers, and Wives: Class Conflict and Gender Relations on São Paulo Plantations, 1850–1980*. Like other recent works, *Coffee Planters* sought to explain the appearance of class conscious rural workers in the present. But unlike other authors, Stolcke criticized structural approaches and emphasized human agency as the leading catalyst of change. Economic structures, she argued, arise from social pressures, not the other way around. For the period before 1964, however, her study gave the agency of rural workers only infrequent credit for bringing about change while attributing a determining role to government policymakers, planters, and market forces. For the post-1964 period, rural workers become the central actors in her account. In oral histories Stolcke gathered in the early 1970s, workers revealed how the pre-1964 period was a "time of plenty," a time when "all the poor were singing." Unfortunately, her book fails to fully examine the sources of these beliefs in the 1930s, 1940s, and 1950s and devotes only a few pages to rural labor mobilization during the early 1960s.[13] Despite these shortcomings, her emphasis on class relations and human agency has been an inspiration for the present book.

A wide range of sources was utilized in writing *The Seed Was Planted*. State and federal government documents, particularly those related to the formulation of rural labor law and policy, provided much valuable information. Some rural social history was gleaned

12. For most authors, agency lies in the hands of the government and landlords, who "exclude" rural workers from the "benefits of modernization" and block the incorporation of rural labor. As discussed above, much agency does lie with the ruling class, but rural workers did not check their own agency at the door of life. They pushed for change as well, insisting on incorporation at the very least. The exclusion argument is best articulated in Azevêdo, *As ligas camponesas:* "If the incorporation and the *controlled participation* of the urban masses in the political system constituted the bases of domination of the agro-industrial block, through the populist state, in the countryside, the foundation of this domination based itself in the *social and political exclusion* of peasants and rural laborers" (37; emphasis in original). Such statements, emphasizing the unilateral power of the dominant class in a book whose subject is peasant activism, demonstrate the elitist tendency of the literature on this topic. A sharp change in this tendency came with Medeiros's *História dos movimentos*, which not only argues the historical links between the pre-1964 movement and the present but also puts rural workers and peasants in the driver's seat, detailing how they drove their way into the political life of the country. See especially "Um Balanço," 79–81, for a summary of the 1945 to 1964 period.

13. Verena Stolcke, *Coffee Planters, Workers, and Wives* (New York: St. Martin's Press, 1988), esp. 159–207.

from the numerous sociological studies of agriculture that began to appear in the 1920s and 1930s. A few later studies were sponsored and collected by SUPRA, whose records were clandestinely photocopied by supporters of the Brasil: Nunca Mais project during the course of military tribunals against the agency and its officials. The journals and bulletins of professional landowner associations, such as the SRB and the National Agricultural Society (SNA, Sociedade Nacional de Agricultura), provided clear evidence of the influence elites had over the composition of Brazilian rural labor law. In addition to these specific sources, standard sources such as censuses and newspapers were also researched.

The most challenging task was to document the role of rural workers in making their own history. For the 1930s and 1940s, the principal documentary source was a collection of letters written to head of state Getúlio Vargas by São Paulo farmworkers. As concern for agricultural productivity increased in the 1940s, so did the number of newspaper reports and investigations of rural labor, and these periodicals were also consulted. Increasingly, farm laborers became the objects of surveys and studies in which their voices occasionally appeared. Moreover, they became an important constituency for aspiring politicians and for a resuscitated PCB that, in 1954, began regular publication of a tabloid about rural workers call 1 *Terra Livre*. This journal and other political reports helped to document an important part of the story. During the 1950s and 1960s, workers made greater use of the courts to resolve employment disputes, and so the records of the Ribeirão Preto labor court (Junta de Conciliação e Julgamento da Justiça de Trabalho) proved exceptionally rich.

Finally, this volume profoundly benefits from a number of interviews conducted with Communist and Catholic labor organizers active in the Alta Mogiana from the 1920s to the *golpe* of 1964 and beyond. These interviews, including various sessions with central participants like Irineu Luís de Moraes and Padre Celso Ibson de Syllos, provided invaluable insight into the tactical details of organizing rural workers in pre-*golpe* Ribeirão Preto and a way to compare written accounts with remembered ones. More than any other source, these interviews revealed the seamless web of history that makes it impossible to detach the present from the past. It was clear from my encounters with these men that the 1950s and 1960s were years of exceptional hope during which it was felt that a revolution of justice and plenty would be upon Brazil at any moment.

The richness of these interviews and the SUPRA documents has tended to skew the book in favor of the movement's leaders rather than the workers who composed its membership. Current fashion in the international field of labor history emphasizes working-class history as the study of working people apart from the unions and other organizations that claimed to represent them. I make no argument against this tendency but side in part with comparative labor historian Charles Bergquist, who has noted the difficulty of attaining the requisite evidence to write the history of Latin American working people.[14] Furthermore, working-class history arose in the United States and Western Europe in reaction to existing literature on labor organizations and their leaders. Very little literature of this sort exists in Latin America to react against; to create such a document, as this work attempts to do, must be seen as contributing to the ability to eventually write more penetrating studies. All the same, I am sensitive to the logic of the social history critique of labor studies and have used other sources to question the opinions of leaders from the perspective of those they sought to lead. I hope others will follow these leads and use the profound questions raised by class and gender studies to fully analyze the Brazilian rural labor movement.[15]

This book is organized as an analytical narrative, proceeding chronologically and examining the interpretive and historiographical debates only insofar as they have become a part of the story of revealing or obscuring the history of the rural labor movement. Chapter 1 describes rural life in São Paulo in the years preceding the Constitutionalist Revolt of 1932, giving special attention to the ways free laborers challenged the rural elite and the legacy of authoritarianism that persisted from nineteenth-century master-slave relations. Chapter 2 shows how rural workers reacted to the turmoil created by political and economic changes in the 1930s and early 1940s. Most of all, the chapter examines elite discussions of rural labor and the discourse of corporatism as it related to rural workers. Chapter 3 uses the example of Guerreiro and the Dumont Peasant League to show how rural workers took advantage of the corporatist discourse and

14. Charles Bergquist, "Latin American Labour History in Comparative Perspective: Notes on the Insidiousness of Cultural Imperialism," *Labour/Le Travail* 25 (Spring 1990), 189–98. Florencia Mallon is one scholar who has been particularly successful in overcoming these difficulties. Having uncovered sophisticated tracts written by community intellectuals in Mexico and Peru, she admirably contrasts elite and subaltern nationalist discourses in *Peasant and Nation: The Making of Postcolonial Mexico and Peru* (Berkeley and Los Angeles: University of California, 1995).

15. For further discussion of Bergquist's views and the development of Latin American labor history, see Jeremy Adelman, "Against Essentialism: Latin American Labour History in Comparative Perspective; A Critique of Bergquist," *Labour/Le Travail* 27 (Spring 1991), 175–84; and Daniel James, "Something Old, Something New? The Emerging Parameters of Latin American Labor History," paper presented at Princeton University, 9 April 1993.

the new laws it generated. The mobilization of rural workers was one of the factors leading to the suppression of the PCB in 1947. Pushed underground, militants experimented with armed struggle, a subject examined in Chapter 4. In the 1950s, a new accommodation between workers and planters came to typify rural labor relations in São Paulo, as recounted in Chapters 5 and 6. The new peace bought by corporatist policies did not last long, however, since bureaucratic processes were inadequate to the task of resolving the long-standing grievances of rural workers. Chapter 7 shows how rural workers turned increasingly to collective direct actions to make their needs known. Emboldened by worker militancy, the more sympathetic federal government of Goulart tried to harness the new militancy by regulating the new organizations and awarding benefits to those who joined the new *sindicatos rurais* (corporatist rural unions), a topic analyzed in Chapter 8. This chapter also shows how the growing success and political influence of the rural labor movement generated considerable hostility on the part of planters and other traditional sectors of the ruling class, such as the military hierarchy. The Epilogue takes one last look at the "germination" process Guerreiro envisioned by examining a 1984 strike wave in the Ribeirão Preto region that helped revive the rural labor movement in the context of the restoration of civilian rule. Once again, as at the climax in 1964, a wide array of supporters gathered around the movement, and its prospects became a measure of democracy in the new era.

1

It was 4:00 A.M. and the cook shouted out the wake-up call: "Olha o moca! Olha o moca! [Coffee's ready!]." Another workday had started on the ranch at the Alberto Moreira rail station, located a few miles outside of Barretos in northwestern São Paulo. Four in the morning and some bread and coffee. Five in the morning and a march to the fields to clear trees and brush and plant grass—all to create pasture for beef cattle owned by Armour, the English meatpacking firm. At 8:00 A.M. the men had "lunch." Six hours later, at two in the afternoon, they broke for supper but not the end of the workday. Under a sun red-hot year in and year out, and in fields where shade removal was the task at hand, the work continued thereafter until dusk. The food—beans and rice, pasta, and meat—was plentiful and good, but after 2:00 P.M., no more food was provided.

FRONTIER TERRITORY

> Confronting the Landlords' World

Returning at dusk to their remote palm-thatched barracks, hunger grabbed at the men and drove them to purchase a hunk of cheese, a slice of bread, or some sweets from the ranch stores—adding debits, charged against their salary credits, many times higher than the item's market price. Such was the life of the peon in Brazil's burgeoning beef industry.[1]

For a time, Irineu Luís de Moraes followed the routine. It was 1929 and Moraes, seventeen years old and already six-feet tall, rose at four, ate lunch at eight, dinner at two, and hiked back to the camp in the evening with everyone else. The son of a railroad construction worker, Moraes was a *caboclo,* rural folk of mixed Amerindian and Portuguese ancestry, and so he seemed little different from the other peons. He had some schooling, and his family lived in Barretos, which, though a frontier town, was a town nonetheless. He had worked there at the British meatpacking plant, the Frigorífico Anglo. Life in Barretos was wilder and labor relations at the plant less personalistic than on the ranch. Rowdy farm laborers and cowboys came to town to relax and gamble in its bars and brothels. Factions of the elite competed for access to power, opening fissures in the monolith of landlord domination. Town residents found that they lived in a flexible labor market and polity where loyalty to one's patron was not as essential as in the countryside. These experiences shaped Moraes's expectations about labor relations.

Moraes saw exploitation in the ranch routine and grew resentful of the injustices of the job. The work was too hard for such long days and long waits between rests and meals. The early dinner hour seemed calculated to make the men dependent on the store for food. Credit there quickly wasted away their earnings, setting up a classic scenario for debt bondage. Fifty men worked at the camp, and as Moraes pointed out the unfairness of their situation, resentment slowly grew among them.

Talking quietly among the men, Moraes sought support for a collective work stoppage. The day should start two hours later, he argued, and mealtimes needed to be better distributed throughout the day, with supper scheduled much later. Their overseer, Bonifácio Ferreira, profited from the store markup, so they figured he would oppose their action. This troubled some of the men, for Ferreira was not only their boss but chief of the ranch's *jagunços,* a private gang of

1. The following anecdote is reconstructed from Cliff Welch and Sebastião Geraldo, *Lutas camponesas no interior paulista: Memórias de Irineu Luís de Moraes* (São Paulo: Paz e Terra, 1992), 35–39.

Sebastiana and Irineu Luís de Moraes, photographed in their Ribeirão Preto home in May 1989. Photo: author

ruffians assembled ad hoc to police the ranch and enforce labor discipline violently when other forms of persuasion failed. This factor did not worry Moraes. A brave youth not easily intimidated, Moraes had a unique relationship with Ferreira: he was a family friend who socialized with Moraes's father in Barretos and who personally provided Moraes with his job on the ranch. Despite this relationship, or perhaps because of it, Moraes convinced the others to stage a confrontation. One morning, when the cook made his call, no one got up. "We're not leaving till six," Moraes announced. "This isn't the time anymore."

Though furious, Ferreira let some time pass before responding to the reluctant workers. He taunted the men by asking them when they might like to get up and work. His voice and very presence scared the men, Moraes thought, for soon after he spoke, they abandoned the strike, tripping over one another in their haste to dress and get to the fields. Rumor had it that Ferreira had already killed three or four men and that he was invincible. "Bullets couldn't stop him," people said. Moraes accused his mates of cowardice but soon found himself the strike's lone picket. The moment was lost by the time Ferreira approached him. "Eat and catch the next train home," he said. "Next time I'm in Barretos, I'll speak with your father, right?"

Moraes left the ranch unconcerned about Ferreira's threat. His parents had always supported him; this was not the first time Moraes had demonstrated a strong sense of right and wrong and a passion for challenging authority, and it would not be the last. In fact, he had gone to the ranch to flee persecution after helping to organize a strike at the Barretos meatpacking plant. As it turned out, he was on the verge of discovering his true vocation: labor agitation, especially among rural workers. Brazil, too, was on the verge of great change. Whereas the Brazilian ruling class had long suppressed revolts among laborers, factions among them were gradually becoming more tolerant, even supportive of a change in social relations that promised greater freedom and material wealth for all people. The change was a long time in coming and resulted from the struggles of many people, from peons to presidents.[2]

The work stoppage Moraes staged near Barretos reflected the typical form of quickly organized, sporadic rural labor protest that was to be strengthened over the course of the next several decades by the evolution of an organized rural labor movement. With few exceptions, peons in the cattle industry were not known for their militancy. Rather, the most forceful demands for change grew out of agro-industrial sectors such as the coffee and sugar industries. On the bottom rung of a long commodity development and export process, these rural workers had more leverage than most agricultural workers. In the years leading up to the October revolution of 1930, when a new national government began projects that would result in fundamentally altered rural social relations, the actions of coffee workers in the state of São Paulo helped generate the country's first liberal agricultural labor relations system. By confronting the world the landlords had built on the backs of enslaved African workers, the new free laborers on coffee plantations cleared the frontier for planting the seeds of the post–World War II rural labor movement. This chapter recounts that early history.

2. Font's *Coffee, Contention, and Change* documents the growing debate among São Paulo coffee planters, bureaucrats, merchants, and industrialists over questions of labor rights and political practice during the 1920s.

From Slave to Free Labor

Slaves and free laborers shaped the process of transition from slavery to free labor in Brazil, a process that began in earnest with the suppression of the slave trade in 1850 and ended officially in May 1888 when Princess Isabel issued the emancipating Golden Law. Neither group of working people can be credited with either initiating or determining the outcome of the process, but they each influenced it. One authority asserts that slave upheavals and flights from plantations in São Paulo were the "most significant factor" behind the federal senate's eventual support for emancipation. But if the freedmen had gotten their way, as historian Maria Helena Machado reports, the government would have set them up as farmers rather than let them slide into the margins of society, as eventually happened. As long as the possibility of smallholding was kept from them, many former slaves preferred life in the margins over continued labor on plantations. This was one way the former bondsmen denied their labor power to the planters. So deprived, planters reluctantly turned toward a reliance on immigrants, encouraging families from Europe to come and work on São Paulo's coffee plantations. These new, free laborers (*colonos*) also expected independence from their move to the New World. They saw coffee plantation labor as the last leg of an ambitious journey toward freeholding. But the planters had foreseen this demand, and with an 1850 land law, they made property holding more difficult to achieve for anyone with little capital and few connections. As the *colonos* confronted one barrier after another, they rebelled as vigorously as the enslaved Africans. During these decades of transition, in fact, the two groups worked side by side, the one comparing conditions with the other, neither satisfied with the parameters imposed by the planter oligarchy. Through multiple acts of resistance, innovation, and flight, slavery disappeared, and the *colonato* labor regime replaced it.[3]

The *colonato* evolved through conflicts between *colonos* and planters. While the *colonos* wanted a system that would promote

3. The significance of slave rebellion is examined in Robert Brent Toplin, "Upheaval, Violence, and the Abolition of Slavery in Brazil: The Case of São Paulo," *Hispanic American Historical Review* (hereafter *HAHR*) 49:4 (1969), 639–55. The transition to free labor is analyzed in Emilia Viotta da Costa, "Sharecroppers and Plantation Owners: An Experiment with Free Labor," *The Brazilian Empire* (Chicago: University of Chicago Press, 1985), 94–124; Verena Stolcke and Michael M. Hall, "The Introduction of Free Labour on São Paulo Coffee Plantations," *Journal of Peasant Studies* 10:2/3 (January/April 1983), 184–205, which appears in revised form as chapter 1 of Verena Stolcke, *Cafeicultura: Homens, mulheres e capital (1850–1980)* (São Paulo: Brasiliense, 1986), 17–52; and Maria Helena Machado, *O plano e o pânico: Os movimentos sociais na década da abolição* (Rio de Janeiro: UFRJ, EDUSP, 1994).

quick social mobility, the planters wanted one that would improve on slavery, offering them reliable, diligent, disciplined, and cheap labor. The first immigrant free workers engaged on coffee plantations were like the Swiss schoolteacher Thomas Davatz, who Senator Nicolaú de Campos Vergueiro hired as a sharecropper, working for halves on his Ibicaba plantation in central São Paulo. In 1856, however, the sharecroppers rebelled against Vergueiro, denouncing "the means used to calculate coffee income, commission charges, the unfavorable exchange rates used to convert debts into Brazilian currency, charges for transporting the coffee from the plantation to the port, and the strange division of profits from selling the coffee," as Davatz later recorded in his memoir. The sharecroppers astutely reasoned that planters manipulated the books to keep them in a state of debt and thereby trap them. In the meantime, the Ibicaba revolt was but one of many, and planters grew weary of their rebellious free workers. One planter, encountered by nineteenth-century traveler Avé-Lallemont, "prided himself since childhood on whipping and chastising his slaves and could hardly tolerate free labor." Vergueiro fired Davatz and others, while some resentful sharecroppers abandoned Ibicaba without collecting any pay for many months' work. They also fled without paying off their debts, a problem that greatly concerned planters. For a time, planters lost interest in sharecropping arrangements, and immigrants lost interest in Brazil.[4]

The abolition of slavery was inevitable, however, and as long as planters wished to remain lords of large agricultural domains, a replacement system had to be found. In the 1860s and 1870s, immigrants and planters experimented with a contract wage system known as *locação de serviços*. Instead of working for shares, which could easily be manipulated, *colonos* and planters arranged set cash payments for harvesting a certain quantity of coffee beans. To weed and care for a set number of coffee trees year round, *colonos* were allowed to use an assigned quantity of land for growing subsistence crops. For *colonos,* the contract labor system had the advantage of supplying them with regular cash income as well as foodstuffs they could use to offset their expenses and sell—should a surplus be generated—thus aiding their goals of independence. Planters, however, were less certain of the system's advantages, and only those with adequate cash reserves fully endorsed it. Until the mid 1870s, only about three thousand *colonos* worked on plantations in any given year, revealing the planter's con-

---

4. The Davatz quote appears in Stolcke, *Cafeicultura,* 23. Avé-Lallemont is cited in Costa, *Brazilian Empire,* 112.

tinued dependence on tens of thousands of enslaved Africans and Afro-Brazilians. Even supporters doubted its efficacy, for *colonos* constantly found ways to alter the system to support their ambitions to be independent.[5]

Planters complained that *colonos* tended to shirk contract obligations regarding the trees, finding it more profitable to develop the land allotted them for crops and livestock. This made them much less productive than slaves. They also found ways to avoid paying debts by moving from plantation to plantation in search of better deals. This made them more expensive than slaves. To resolve these difficulties, the planters pursued two strategies. One was to increase the labor supply through an immigration assistance program, which was first legislated in 1871 and 1872. Another strategy was to enhance planter control over free workers. In 1878 the state convened an agricultural congress to probe the issue, charging delegates with the composition of a detailed contract labor law, including measures to fine and prosecute *colonos* who failed to fulfill their contractual obligations. Once contracted, a *colono* would be bound to a plantation until the work was completed and the debts paid off. Prohibitive penalties would be used to enforce the contract. The measure, which was issued in 1879, also outlawed labor strikes. Although the law sought to freeze workers in place, restricting the mechanisms of an ideal free labor market, planters celebrated the legislation as a liberal labor regulations system that would be useful in attracting more European laborers to Brazil. Responding to labor recruiters and the perception of improved conditions, more than 150,000 Italians and Portuguese immigrated to São Paulo between 1879 and 1887.[6]

Creating the *Colonato*

The *colonato* system finally took hold once slavery had been abolished. The planters' reluctance to adopt it, their collective commitment to find less costly and more authoritarian ways to coerce labor from free men and women, is underscored by the fact that the system first appeared in the 1860s but became widespread only in the 1890s. Its very origins reveal the importance of worker initiative in shap-

---

5. Stolcke, *Cafeicultura*, 31–35; and Costa, *Brazilian Empire*, 121–24.
6. On immigration policy, see Thomas H. Holloway, *Immigrants on the Land: Coffee and Society in São Paulo, 1886–1934* (Chapel Hill: University of North Carolina Press, 1980), 35–36. For the 1879 law, see Maria Lúcia Lamounier, *Da escravidão ao trabalho livre* (Campinas: Papírus, 1988); and Stolcke, *Cafeicultura*, 40.

ing the production system that generated enormous wealth for São Paulo, enabling the transformation of state and nation. In the 1860s *colonos* in the Campinas region of São Paulo frequently objected to the low incomes they received working groves of young trees. A coffee tree must be mature to bear fruit, with the first fruit appearing after four years and full productivity reached only after the sixth year. With income tied to the harvest under both sharecropping and contractual arrangements, *colonos* in new coffee fields might well have no income after years of effort clearing new land, planting coffee trees, and hoeing and weeding the ground around their base several times a year. To quell the demands of disgruntled *colonos,* Campinas planters designed a new system: they would pay *colonos* not only for the harvest but also a set annual amount for cultivating each unit of one thousand trees. In addition, the Campinas *colonos* retained traditional rights to free rent and access to land to grow foodstuffs or raise livestock. Payment provided an incentive for *colonos* to work the new trees, whereas both sharecropping and the contract system had provided only disincentives. This mixed piecework and salaried system, cooked in the cauldron of contentious class relations, became known as the *colonato.*[7]

Two circumstances from the 1880s made this system popular throughout the state. One was the final crisis of slavery, a crisis stimulated by abolitionist agitation and slave flight. These factors forced planters to find a new source and system of dependent labor if they wanted to continue to exercise significant control on large plantations. The other was the 1886 foundation of the Immigration Promotion Society (Sociedade Promotora da Imigração), a state agency designed to recruit European workers, transport them to São Paulo, and put them to work on coffee plantations. The agency's funds came from a tax imposed on slave owners, especially those who employed slaves in non-agricultural activities—these owners had to pay twice as much per slave as those who employed slaves to work in agriculture. The state government was, in the words of historian Thomas Holloway, "the instrument of the coffee planters," and they used its resources to supply them with *colonos* at little cost to those who manumitted their Afro-Brazilian slaves. The state transportation and placement subsidies, combined with the *colonato* system and a growing market for coffee in industrializing Europe and the United States, helped generate a free labor market in São Paulo for the first time. By

---

7. On events in Campinas, see J. B. do Amaral, visconde de Indaiatuba, "Introdução do trabalho livre em Campinas," cited in Stolcke, *Cafeicultura,* 36; and on the early spread of the *colonato* system, see Stolcke, *Cafeicultura,* 35–52.

1898, with slavery abolished for ten years, nearly one million immigrants had come, nearly all destined for work on coffee plantations. With the subsidies in place until World War I, and sporadically thereafter, hundreds of thousands of free laborers from Italy, the Iberian Peninsula, and Asia flooded the state, creating a distinct social formation.[8]

Planters had, in a sense, created a landless peasantry. Where once their capital had been tied up in the purchase of slaves, it was now increasingly invested in land. Control of labor was essential to planter dominance of the land: to keep *colonos* dependent on plantation work for their daily bread, they had to be kept from owning land. To establish a dependent peasantry, planters encouraged the immigration of entire families, and to persevere under these conditions, *colono* men, women, and children pooled their labor. In the early stages of the extraordinary expansion of the coffee frontier, *colonos* fanned out into western São Paulo, where they favored employment on new or recently cleared territory. Here they could maximize their efforts and savings by planting food crops in the open paths between the rows of young coffee plants they cultivated. Thus, *colonos* found they could fulfill their obligation to care for the coffee trees while simultaneously nurturing the food crops that sustained them. Since *colonos* fed themselves, planters attained from the *colonato* reliable, dependent labor that cost them little to attract while gaining, after four or five years, the product of thousands of new coffee trees, each of which would continue to produce for at least another twenty years. "This is how," an Italian correspondent reported, "in a relatively brief period, an owner of good lands, in western São Paulo, could become the proprietor of a lovely and productive coffee plantation, with little to no capital outlay."[9]

Although most of the labor service shifted to immigrant *colonos* after abolition, their efforts were supplemented—just as the slaves had been—by the contributions of *camaradas:* mixed-race Brazilians like Moraes, trusted freedmen, and dependents of the planter (*agregados*), who earned wages on a daily, monthly, or annual basis. Translations of the generic name *camarada*—comrade or crony—further reveal their close relationship to planters and supervisors. *Camaradas* lived around the plantation manor and outbuildings, where they ful-

8. See Costa, *Brazilian Empire,* 125–71; Michael M. Hall, "The Origins of Mass Immigration in Brazil, 1871–1914" (Ph.D. diss., Columbia University, 1969); Holloway, *Immigrants on the Land,* esp. 35–69; and Chiara Vangelista, *Os braços da lavoura: Imigrantes e "caipiras" na formação do mercado de trabalho paulista (1850–1930)* (São Paulo: Hucitec, 1991), esp. 34–78.
9. Vangelista, *Os braços,* 221–23, 192.

176737

filled routine tasks like construction work and repairs and, during the harvest, processed and readied the beans for transport to the port of Santos. The two groups—*colonos* and *camaradas*—complemented each other but tended not to mix due to their differing interests. Immigrant fortunes were tied to the productivity of their crops, the abundance of the harvest, and the payments they could wrest from the planters. In contradistinction to *colonos,* the well-being of Brazilian farmhands rested on the favor of superiors with whom they naturally sought to ingratiate themselves through acts of loyalty and displays of exertion.

Much to the planters' chagrin, *colonos* proved far more demanding than *camaradas.* They frequently protested mistreatment, vigorously asserted their rights to secure fair pay and conditions, and occasionally murdered their employers. Since *colono* challenges worried planters, they tightened discipline on the plantations. The planters drafted their toughest *camaradas* to serve as *capangas* to police their estates. These men—some, bullies who enjoyed violence; others, common rural workers coerced into service—formed a planter's ever present band of enforcers. "I alone command on my plantation," Campinas planter Artur Leite boasted in 1908. "The *colonos'* houses are guarded by loyal *capangas* who don't tolerate the slightest liberties; they're on hand to persuade the *colonos* that against force, reason has no value." Around 1910 the French traveler Pierre Denis described the closed world the planters dictated over. "The planter's task is twofold. He works not only to obtain regularity in the labor process, but also to maintain order and peace among the heterogeneous population he governs. To do so, he functions as the police. As a consequence, the regular police have no role in enforcing respect for the law, for persons, or for property." [10]

Despite such conditions, *colonos* confronted the landlord's world, and the law provided some assistance. Starting with an 1879 law regulating contract labor, São Paulo and national authorities approved numerous measures designed to regulate free labor on coffee plantations. These measures included a unionization scheme, legislated in 1903 and signed into law in 1907, intended to unite employers and employees in the same organization, but no such groupings seem ever to have been formed. Of greatest importance for coffee workers were laws that made the wages owed *colonos* a first lien against the planter's income and required employers to keep a written

10. On early plantation conditions, see Warren Dean, *Rio Claro: A Brazilian Plantation System, 1820–1920* (Stanford: Stanford University Press, 1976). Quotes cited in Vangelista, *Os braços,* 228, 229.

record of their employees' debts and credits. First legislated in 1904 and 1906, a 1907 decree (No. 6,437) required planters to apply the proceeds of a harvest toward *colono* salaries before paying off any other debts. A 1913 law required that immigration agencies provide workers a copy of the account booklet, called the *caderneta agrícola*. A 1934 law directed property owners to distribute the *cadernetas* to their workers at no charge after purchasing them from the state department of labor for a nominal fee. Failure to abide by this new law carried substantial penalties in the form of fines, though it is not known how often such fines were assessed. The booklet gave *colonos* greater control over their salary by making it easier for them to account for their income and more difficult for employers to manipulate debts. Eventually, the book contained a formulaic labor contract, including some standard clauses but numerous lacunae that allowed the parties to tailor the contract to specific situations. After the contract came several printed pages of extant rural labor relations law. Important as these measures were, the burden of enforcement was borne by the *colonos,* and their status as immigrants and paucity of independent resources made it difficult for them to make the law real.[11]

Colono Labor Struggles

Colonos brought a consciousness of themselves as free men and women and protested abuses whenever they could. They found, however, that local power structures permitted few opportunities for protest and alliance. In 1901, for example, *colonos* outside Araraquara, in north central São Paulo, attempted to reenact the recent success of slaves by inviting an urban advocate reminiscent of past abolitionists—in this case a sympathetic lawyer—to intervene in the landlord's world. When the lawyer arrived to meet with the *colonos,* however, he was brutally beaten by a planter and his *capangas.* Two policemen at the station stood by and watched, demonstrating the *colonos'* isolation from power. A 1908 Italian document, quoted by

11. On resistance, see Michael Hall and Verena Martinez Alier, "Greves de colonos na Primeira República" (paper presented at the II Seminário de Relações de Trabalho e Movimentos Sociais, Campinas, São Paulo, May 1979, mimeographed); and Stolcke, *Cafeicultura,* 22–25. On early union laws, see Heloísa Menandro and Dora Flaksman, "Confederação Nacional dos Trabalhadores na Agricultura," in *Dicionário histórico-biográfico brasileiro, 1930–1983* (hereafter *DHBB*), edited by Israel Beloch and Alzira Alves de Abreu, 4 vols. (Rio de Janeiro: Forense-Universitária, 1984), 875. The *caderneta* is described from copies in the author's possession.

economic historian Chiara Vangelista, tells another revealing story about limits on the interventionist power of local authorities:

> I don't believe that the judicial reports of São Paulo State record a single case of a planter who, having beaten a *colono,* was himself legally punished. Quite recently, near the town of Ribeirão-zinho, there was a beating case. The adults of the Italian colony didn't even think about filing a complaint with the judge. Instead, they went directly to the chief of police and implored him, not to take action against the planter, but to make known to the brutal planter that he ought to use other methods with his Italian *colonos* if he didn't want to receive the same sort of treatment, since there were some among them who could dish it out in equal measure.

On the one hand, this anecdote underscores the brutality and predominance of planters under the *colonato* system. The unnamed planter had beaten some *colonos,* and they were convinced the law would neither proscribe their boss nor protect them from further abuse. On the other hand, it also demonstrates Italian solidarity and *colono* resilience, their refusal to be intimidated, and a more sophisticated appreciation of the modern order than that displayed by the planter. Unlike the planter, *colonos* preferred to use state intermediaries to resolve disputes and asked the police chief to educate their boss about proper ways of handling conflicts. Both anecdotes also show how difficult it was for planters to completely intimidate *colonos.*[12]

Complaints by Italian *colonos,* who were the largest single nationality represented among immigrants, inevitably filtered back to Italy and affected the immigrant stream. While Italians composed 73 percent of all immigrants between 1887 and 1900, their percentage dropped considerably thereafter, and their share of total immigration fell to 43 percent for the entire 1887 to 1930 period. To address this decline and perhaps reverse it, in 1911 São Paulo authorities created the Patronato Agrícola, a new state agency designed to enforce the fulfillment of contractual terms on both *colonos* and planters. To maximize its impact on the flow of immigrants, the law's preamble described it as a measure in "defense of the rights and interests of agricultural workers." Indeed, before it was disbanded, the agency responded to hundreds of *colono* complaints and counseled both workers and bosses to abide by their contractual obligations. Through

---

12. Anecdotes from Dean, *Rio Claro,* 174; and Vangelista, *Os braços,* 230–31.

the agency, the state tried to become the new patron, or plantation master, and like an ideal patron, it sought to resolve disputes in a familial way through conciliation.[13]

At its peak in the 1920s, the agency's few inspectors could be found riding horseback through the countryside, resolving conflicts by overcoming the distrust and animosity of planters and *colonos* and persuading them to cooperate with one another. During the decade, the agency built a reputation for relative autonomy from the planter class, but in disputes between unequals, it had few tools to force the compliance of planters. In disputes over oral agreements, so common in the close-knit atmosphere of rural life, especially between *camaradas* and planters, the agents had no authority. Even when its efforts were supplemented by the few rural tribunals introduced by state president Washington Luís Pereira de Sousa around 1925, it proved ineffective at ensuring compliance with obligations composed outside those specified in written *colono* contracts. With the depression of 1930, mass European immigration to São Paulo slowed down, and so did a key justification for the Patronato Agrícola. By 1934 the agency had been discontinued and its responsibilities for providing legal services to rural laborers absorbed by the newly formed state department of labor.[14]

Armed with contracts and promises of social mobility, European immigrant workers continued to find means to resist the caprice of planters and the injustices of plantation life. *Colonos* seized the opportunity presented by the harvest season to withhold their services and force planters to negotiate. These practices were widespread enough to merit comment by Augusto Ramos, a contemporary planter and analyst of the coffee industry: "It little surprises us that on the day the harvest was to begin, each *colono* stayed in his house rather than leaving early for the fields, despite the pressure of overseers. For the planter, this was the critical hour in his whole year of labor. . . . The loss of the harvest would spell his ruin. Perfectly conscious of this situation, the *colonos* take advantage of the moment to make their

13. Immigration statistics from Holloway, *Immigrants on the Land*, 42. State law 1299-A of 27 December 1911 created the patronato, while regulation 2214 of 15 March 1912 activated it. Quoted is article 1 of law 1299-A. See Frances Rocha, "Conflito social e dominação: Um estudo sôbre as leis de regulação das relações de trabalho na empresa agrícola, 1897–1930" (master's thesis, Pontifical Universidade Católica, São Paulo, 1982), esp. 285–337 and appendix.

14. Jorge Miguel Mayer and César Benjamim, "Washington Luís," in Beloch and Abreu, eds., *DHBB*, 3:1953. On the closing of the agency, see Decree Law No. 6,405 of 19 April 1934, "Dispõe sôbre o Departamento Estadual do Trabalho, da Secretária do Trabalho, Indústria e Comercio"; and Vasco de Andrade, "O departamento estadual do trabalho e sua influencia na economia rural," *RLT* 7 (October 1943), 373–76.

demands, just or unjust." Ramos portrayed the *colonos* as having the upper hand, abusing the planter's dependence on their labor. But he also represented the discourse of planters progressive enough in their views to recognize the need to respect *colono* interests and power: "A good administrator needs to have a high degree of foresight and good sense of justice in order to avoid a just strike by his *colonos,* because such a strike is fatal and invincible." As Ramos indicates, in exaggerated fashion, the labor process on coffee plantations created leverage for *colonos* to confront the planter oligarchy.[15]

Despite this leverage, plantation-wide strikes were enormously difficult to pull off. In the Alta Mogiana, vast estates employed thousands of *colonos,* who populated the frontier with their growing families. Figures from 1913 show 8,613 *colonos* on the plantations near Ribeirão Preto owned by Francisco Schmidt. The Dumont Company, headquartered in the village where João Guerreiro Filho later planted the seed of rural labor mobilization, then had five thousand *colonos* contracted to work its vast fields. Since *colono* families averaged around five members each, and only those who were old and strong enough to work the coffee trees counted as *colonos,* the total number of people in and around the plantation was actually much higher. Some plantations, like Dumont, eventually spread out around a central settlement that housed a city of services—from stores to chapel, cinema, clinic, and schools. Here, a planter and his managers could keep a close watch on all their workers from the high porch of the plantation manor. Relations were close and protest difficult to galvanize. Other large *fazendas* were built from separate parcels, with the *colonos* employed by a single planter living in various *colônias,* small clusters of houses set miles apart from one another—a setup that made communication among workers rare and difficult. This was the case for Schmidt's laborers, who worked on thirty-three plantations and lived in a dispersed fashion.[16]

The difficulties of *colono* life were such that even these constraints proved incapable of preventing all collective action. At least seventy *colono* families on the Fazenda Iracema, owned by Schmidt, overcame these obstacles in May 1912, organizing a uniquely suc-

15. Augusto Ramos, *O café no Brasil e no estrangeiro* (Rio de Janeiro: Papelaria Santa Helena, 1923), 209–10.
16. R. Lloyd et al., *Impressões do Brasil no século vinte* (London: Lloyd's Greater Britain Publishing, 1913), cited in Maria Angélica Momenso Garcia, "As greves de 1912 e 1913 nas fazendas de café de Ribeirão Preto," *Estudos de História* (Franca) 2:2 (1995), 169. (Thanks to John French and Sebastião Geraldo for making the Garcia article available to me.) Joseph Love claims that Schmidt employed eleven thousand *colonos,* working ten million trees, in 1914. *São Paulo in the Brazilian Federation, 1889–1937* (Stanford: Stanford University Press, 1980), 79.

cessful eight-day strike at the start of the harvest. According to a close observer known only by the revealing pseudonym "A Socialist," the *colonos* facilitated communication and resisted repression by forming cells of four or five families, with no outstanding leader. Representatives of these cells united in a "Secret Directory" and met for the first time at three in the morning on May 4, "resolving to employ all expedient measures consonant with the reason of free-thought, to resist until death should justice fail to be done," as "A Socialist" phrased it. To protect their jobs and fortify the strike, *colonos* worked underground to discourage workers on neighboring plantations from replacing them. This clandestine strategy proved effective, and the strike ended in a partial victory when Schmidt agreed to raise their wages 20 percent, from five to six hundred *reis* per fifty-liter sack of picked coffee cherries. As Ramos commented, the pressure of the harvest certainly gave these *colonos* leverage. It may also have helped that a modest surge in coffee prices was then under way, allowing Schmidt to pass on the added labor costs to buyers.[17]

Foreshadowing later developments, the strike was no doubt aided by the publicity it received. With reporters like "A Socialist" on hand to witness and perhaps even participate in events, publishing their stories in the socialist and anarchist press of Ribeirão Preto and São Paulo, it was more difficult to isolate and suppress the *colono* cause. The proximity of a plantation to urban centers like Ribeirão Preto, which had a population of 18,732 in 1912, contributed to the ability of *colonos* to organize. Eugenio Bonardelli, who reported on an even larger strike a year after the Iracema victory, made this observation, noting that Ribeirão Preto was a place where otherwise isolated *colonos* could mix and talk without fear. Ideas circulated more freely and in this era, including ideas based on anarchist and socialist notions of freedom and class struggle. The Ribeirão Preto scholar Sebastião Geraldo has made a close study of the numerous working-class journals that circulated in the area during this period, giving credence to Bonardelli's contemporary comment.[18]

Structural conditions also affected the *colonos*' propensity to

17. Contemporary quotes from an article by "Um Socialista" first appearing in *La Battaglia,* an anarchist newspaper published in São Paulo, and reprinted in *A classe operária no Brasil, (1889–1930),* Documentos, vol. 1, edited by Paulo Sérgio Pinheiro and Michael M. Hall (São Paulo: Alfa Omega, 1979), 116–17. Garcia, "As greves de 1912 e 1913," 169–71, elaborates on socialist and anarchist involvement in the strikes. Details of the strikes can also be found in Rocha, "Conflito social e dominação," 169–93. Holloway, *Immigrants on the Land,* 10–11, discusses coffee price fluctuations.

18. Sebastião Geraldo, "Comunicação oral: O resgate da memória proletária em Ribeirão Preto" (master's thesis, Universidade de São Paulo, 1990).

protest. One such factor was price fluctuation in the international coffee market, an issue that seems to have influenced the outcome of the 1912 strike. The age of a coffee-growing region also proved influential. By the time of World War I, the Alta Mogiana was one of the older coffee zones in São Paulo, with commercial coffee cultivation dating from the 1870s. The age of the region's plantations meant several things to *colonos*. First, older trees did not produce as many cherries as ones in their prime. Thus, it took more time and energy on older plantations to earn as much money as one could on a plantation with younger trees. Second, the real economic benefits of the *colonato* were to be found in intercropping beans, corn, and other foodstuffs between rows of coffee seedlings before they reached maturity and their large green leaves prevented the sun from reaching the soil. In the Alta Mogiana, the vast majority of trees had matured by their mid-teens, eliminating intercropping, reducing yields, and increasing the *colonos'* dependence on wages. Over time, this trend would cause wage disputes to grow in importance.[19]

All of these structural and ideological conditions converged in April and May 1913. Coffee prices were in decline internationally, and planters responded by cutting wages while maintaining the high price of goods sold to *colonos* on plantations. *Colonos* suffered further deprivation by having their access to intercropping restricted. As coffee prices fell, planters argued that interrow farming hurt the trees' growth and productivity, and they prohibited the practice, forcing the *colonos* to cultivate less desirable land at more distant locations. Frustrated with these conditions, more than ten thousand *colonos* chose the start of the harvest season to withhold their labor, hoping to improve their lot as had the Iracema *colonos*. The Alta Mogiana strikers, most of them Italian immigrants, mobilized against several of the largest Ribeirão Preto plantations, including Fazenda Macaúbas of the Schmidt company, Fazenda Boa Vista of Joaquim Diniz "Quinzinho" da Cunha Junqueira, and the Companhia Agrícola Dumont. This time, however, the planters resolved not to give in.

On the first of May—ironically, international labor day—proprietors and overseers from each of the concerns involved met together on the shaded porches of Schmidt's palatial headquarters at Monte Alegre, now a historical site on the outskirts of Ribeirão Preto.[20] They combined in their resistance to the strike and developed plans

---

19. Holloway, *Immigrants on the Land,* chap. 4; Stolcke, *Cafeicultura,* chap. 2; and Vangelista, *Os braços,* chap. 3.

20. In addition to Schmidt, the local paper *A Cidade* (3 May 1913, p. 3) listed the presence of the following people: "Jorge Lobato, Theodormiro Uchoa, Affonso Geribello, J. P. Veiga

to suppress it by having selected strikers deported and replaced by Japanese immigrants recently arrived in the country. The Japanese would make good strikebreakers, the planters presumed, because it would be difficult for them to communicate with the Italian *colonos.* They also refused the strikers credit in company stores, hoping to starve them into submission, and agreed to blackball participants. Their list of plans, revealed in the local press, also included their intention to set future *colono* wages in collusion with one another. By publicizing their reaction, they hoped planters outside the region would adopt their proposal. The geographical spread of the event and the large number of workers involved made it impossible for the leaders to escape the punishing raids of *capangas* and police. After two weeks, the strike came to an end with the deportation of 137 Italian workers, who were reviled as "agitators" in the established press.[21] In nearby Cravinhos, in June 1913, planter power was reconfirmed when planter Luís Aleixo—dubbed a "slave master" by an anarchist paper—forced striking *colonos* to return to work through a show of force: the dispatch of eighteen *capangas,* "armed with rifles and machetes and ready to perform a St. Bartholomew Massacre."[22]

Regional historian Maria Angélica Momenso Garcia argues that these strikes marked a "new moment in the movements of rural laborers," due to their size and the recognition they received. Unfortunately, these movements do not seem to have led to a new awakening of rural workers or an enduring level of organization among them. To

Miranda, Leovigildo Uchoa, José Henrique Diederichsen, José Penteado, Saturnino Correa de Carvalho, Major Joaquim de Carvalho, and Srs. Manoel Carvalho Filho, Emílio Moreno de Alag, Arthur Pires, e João Fabrício Alcântara." Quoted in Gifun, "Ribeirão Preto, 1880–1914," 192 n. 21.

21. On Ribeirão Preto, see Thomas Walker, "From Coronelismo to Populism: The Evolution of Politics on a Brazilian Municipality, Ribeirão Preto, São Paulo, 1910–1960" (Ph.D. diss., University of New Mexico, 1974), 54, passim; and Geraldo, "Comunicação oral." The principal eyewitness account of the 1913 strike is Eugenio Bondardelli, *Lo stato di S. Paolo del Brasile e l'emigrazione* (1916), reprinted in Portuguese translation in Pinheiro and Hall, eds., *A classe operária,* 118–27. Several contemporary newspaper accounts are reprinted in José Cláudio Barriguelli, ed., *Subsídios à história das lutas no campo em São Paulo (1870–1956),* vol. 2 (São Carlos: Universidade Federal de São Carlos, Arquivo de História Contemporânea, 1981), 92–94. One of these stories amplified on the results of the strike, claiming among other things that "c) the most conscious *colonos* of the region had been expelled; d) the *colonos* fled the *fazendas* in mass; e) 142 *colonos* arrived in [São Paulo] in a deplorable condition, seeking resources to return to Italy; and f) the owners did not pay back wages they owed the *colonos,* saying they would pay them only after the harvest was completed" (*Jornal La Barricata,* 31 May 1913). See also Holloway, *Immigrants on the Land,* 107; and Garcia, "As greves de 1912 e 1913," 171–76. A discussion of the strike and Schmidt's meeting with other planters can also be found in Gifun, "Ribeirão Preto, 1880–1914," 177–80.

22. "Greve de colonos em Cravinhos" and "Greve de colonos," *Jornal A Barricata* (São Paulo), 8 June 1913 and 15 June 1913, in Barriguelli, ed., *Subsídios à história ,* 94–95.

the contrary, the coffee *colono* strikes of 1912 and 1913 proved to be exceptional events, ones without precedent and with few imitators until the 1950s. A team of researchers led by José Claúdio Barriguelli, scanning dozens of mainstream and leftist newspapers, found no reports of strikes from mid-1913 until the late 1940s. We know from records kept by the Patronato Agrícola that *colonos* did strike during this period, but most of these incidents were small, isolated, and quickly resolved. For example, nearly half of the twenty-three strikes reported for 1923 were associated with *colonos* who protested the prolongation of the harvest season—due to rain—because they were anxious to move on to other plantations. In the eighteen strikes recorded for 1925, only 353 workers were involved. Thus, the "new moment" of 1913 was brief but impressive.[23]

The wide attention the 1912 and 1913 strikes received left a rich, discursive legacy. In the mythology of the coffee economy, planters linked the *colonato* system to the workers' freedom and social mobility. During the strikes, however, *colono* spokesmen regularly equated the *colonato* to slavery and emphasized the misery of *colono* life. "The principle motive" of the 1912 strike, wrote "A Socialist", was to make known "the misery . . . of the conditions of virtual slavery" in which the *colonos* lived and worked. The cause of the planters' resistance to the 1913 strike, said Bonardelli, was "the slave economy that had been toppled only thirty years before," leaving a legacy of master-slave relations. Christian notions of justice also featured in the arguments made in support of the strikers. An article in the anarchist Italian-language journal *La Barricata* emphasized the injustice of the strike's suppression by noting how the *colonos'* struggle was marked by "an absolutely Christian passivity and quietude," in contrast to "a stupid, criminal violence on the part of the planters." Bonardelli, who belonged to the Italica Gens, a federation of Italian religious organizations, shared this conclusion. "One of the notable characteristics of the strikes was the calm with which the *colonos* protested. Although they lived in misery, the *colonos* never acted in a violent way. . . . Despite this, the police intervened at the beck and call of certain planters to frighten the *colonos* into stopping the strike." Another motif contrasted the wealth and splendor of planter life with the poverty and deprivation suffered by the *colonos*. Thus, the bulk of their critique was based in moral arguments and seemed

23. Garcia, "As greves de 1912 e 1913," 169; Barriguelli, ed., *Subsídios à história,* vol. 2; and for the Patronato Agrícola statistics, Font, *Coffee, Contention, and Change,* 138.

sincere yet calculated to generate public sympathy for the *colonos'* cause.[24]

While moral issues remained central to *colono* discourse, the planters sought to steer the conflict in legal and economic directions. The *colonos* had signed their contracts earlier in the year; by what right did they now reject the terms? "The *colonos* have violated their contracts," editorialized the conservative *Jornal Comércio do Jahu;* "the strike, in such conditions, is absolutely unjustifiable." To the contrary, wrote Bonardelli, it was the planters who first violated the contracts. But *colono* solidarity could not yet match the unity of the planter class, and as much as the *colonos* succeeded in identifying their class interests and uniting to defend them, the planters easily pulled together in opposition. Planter confidence, paternalism, and an ominous sense of identity with *colonos* was summed up in a quote from Francisco Schmidt: "I too was a *colono*. My *colonos* and I will fulfill the contract."[25]

To escape the charge that slavery persisted under the guise of the *colonato* in São Paulo, the Patronato Agrícola was asked to become more active in the aftermath of the 1913 strike. Staffed in June 1912, it ruled the 1913 strike outside its purview. Nevertheless, the patronato charged the *colonos* with violating their contracts by refusing to work the harvest. Arguing that it could only intervene to enforce contractual terms, it adopted a laissez-faire attitude toward the Alta Mogiana *colonos*. "It is not possible to intervene," wrote patronato director Eugénio Egas, "in order to benefit the *colonos* . . . by altering the substance of contracts so recently entered into."[26]

The 1913 strike so exposed the brutality of the *colonato* that the Italian consul got involved, and the future of Italian immigration was cast in doubt, a repercussion that truly worried planters. The solution was to make the patronato more effective, and this meant that it had to appear to take the side of *colonos* in a significant number of cases. In 1914 the number of complaints brought to the agency began to climb, and by 1923 its staff had been increased from one to eight lawyers. In that year, 500 complaints against planters were filed by *colonos:* 114 for contract violations, 99 for violent or unjustified firings,

---

24. Um Socialista, 117; Bonardelli, *Lo stato,* 121; and Barriguelli, ed., *Subsídios à história,* 93.

25. Quoted in Love, *São Paulo in the Brazilian Federation,* 79.

26. *Relatório apresentado ao Dr. Carlos Augusto Pereira Guimares, vice presidente do estado, em exercício, pelo Dr. Paulo de Moraes Barros, secretaria de estado: Annos de 1912–1913* (São Paulo: Typographia Brasil de Rothschild & Cia, 1914), 203, quoted in Gifun, "Ribeirão Preto," 179.

71 for stealing *colono* property, 63 for unjustifiable fines, 57 for abusive treatment, 37 for miscellaneous accusations, 25 for failure to pay wages, and 16 for failure to provide services. Ten were deemed unsuitable for adjudication, and eight asked the agency to regulate harvest prices. Between 1912 and 1929, the patronato heard 11,962 cases and formally collected and redistributed more than four million *milreis* in damage awards. Energized and staffed, the agency quickly became an effective means of channeling *colono* protest away from consular offices. "The complaints of the foreign *colonos*," wrote the São Paulo secretary of agriculture in 1914, "which logically used to go to the consulates, now are almost all directed to the patronato, thus depriving the consular files of complaints against our country, with evident advantages for our prestige as a state that seeks manpower for the plantations and good people for settling its land." [27] For the time being, the patronato served as a safety valve for *colono* discontent and planter anxiety, as well as a public relations cover for Brazil's international reputation.

The Politics of *Colono* Social Mobility

Two other processes worked to reduce the tendency toward working-class formation and struggle on São Paulo coffee plantations. One was physical mobility in the tight rural labor market, for *colonos* were constantly on the move, searching for better employment conditions. "At the end of each agricultural year, on nearly all plantations, the pace of dislocation accelerates as workers freely make or break contracts without the slightest hindrance." [28] This was one of the sharpest contrasts between the lives of immigrants and those of the slaves they replaced. Another far less significant development, yet one of importance to our focus on rural labor politics, was the ever so gradual process of political incorporation. By 1920 the ethnic Italian community had given birth to Italian language newspapers, civic organizations, and class stratification. (A few wealthy and powerful Italian industrialists and planters like Francisco Matarazzo and Geremia Lunardelli contrasted with the largely poor majority of Italian *colonos* and artisans.) The community formed a new constituency. Mauricio Font, a historical sociologist, has joined these two tendencies to argue that

27. Garcia, "As greves de 1912 e 1913," 171–73; Rocha, "Conflito social e dominação"; Vangelista, *Os braços,* 160–202; and *Boletim da Secretaria da Agricultura* (1914), 171–72, quoted in Holloway, *Immigrants on the Land,* 109.
28. Ramos, *O café,* 209.

socially mobile immigrant *colonos*, their aspiring Brazilian-born off-spring, and an alternative economy that developed out of their activities eventually evolved into one of the principal forces behind the demise of São Paulo's traditional coffee oligarchy.[29] From the perspective of rural labor, the evidence for this argument remains incomplete yet enticing. The immigrants Font emphasized had either gained economic independence from planters by forming their own farms or had moved to urban areas where they pursued non-agricultural vocations. Nevertheless, the political history of the time had a certain relevancy for rural workers, especially coffee *colonos*.

The cornerstone of planter predominance in the Old Republic (1889–1930) was control of local elections, a control based on the manipulation of voters in county (*município*) elections. As long as the chief of the local association of planters and merchants, the colonel (*coronel*), could produce victories for state and national politicians, he could count on state and national authorities to either leave him alone or help him run local affairs as he and his peers saw fit. Success was ensured by registering to vote only those adult males whose loyalty could be counted on, and rural workers selected by planters and managers composed a portion of the faithful. The historian Frederick Gifun documented one such example in his study of Ribeirão Preto. The preeminent political boss at the time of World War I was Colonel "Quinzinho" da Cunha Junqueira, owner of a *fazenda* struck against in 1913. According to local legend, it was not through coercion that Junqueira wielded the votes of his workers but through the power of his "high esteem." Local informant Sebastião Palma told Gifun that *colonos* supported Junqueira "more because of the good that he did than because of the bad that he could do." Into the 1920s, São Paulo's leading *coronel* institution was the Paulista Republican Party (PRP, Partido Republicano Paulista). From the later teens on, however, socioeconomic pressures began to pound the system, creating factionalism, chipping away at the solidarity of PRP bosses, and fracturing the once monolithic planter oligarchy.[30]

---

29. Font, *Coffee, Contention, and Change*. Variations of this argument can be found in Holloway, *Immigrants on the Land;* Walker, "From Coronelismo to Populism"; and Gifun, "Ribeirão Preto." Font is more explicit and detailed in showing how increased economic diversity, much of it driven by immigrants and their Brazilian-born children, inevitably weakened the old order predominated by the planters. Articles by Joseph L. Love, Verena Stolcke, and Mauricio Font analyze this issue in "Commentary and Debate," *Latin American Research Review* 24:3 (1989), 127–58.

30. Gifun, "Ribeirão Preto," 143 n. 20; Font, *Coffee, Contention, and Change*. See also Victor Nunes Leal, *Coronelismo: The Municipality and Representative Government in Brazil* (New York: Cambridge University Press, 1977).

The war itself caused a decline in the demand for coffee, weakening the economic might of the coffee bosses. The downturn also compelled some workers to move away from deteriorating coffee plantations, either into urban labor markets or onto parcels of wild or worn coffee lands then being sold off to generate capital. In the cities and towns of São Paulo, manufacturing gradually began to expand; in the countryside, smallholders planted foodstuffs, cotton, sugarcane, and even coffee, bringing social and crop diversity to the agrarian economy. In the Alta Mogiana, where coffee planting had an early start and trees on old estates, like those of Dumont, were at the end of their life cycle, the transition was especially noticeable. While the Alta Mogiana accounted for 44 percent of São Paulo coffee production in 1920, its percentage had declined to 16 by 1934, with the lost economic activity replaced by everything from peanut farming to textile and beer manufacturing. For Font, the diversifying economy gradually shifted the center of political power away from the traditional coffee elite, threatening the viability of *coronelismo* in São Paulo. Gifun made a related point about *coronelismo* in his study of Ribeirão Preto: "The physical and social mobility of the European *colono* during the Old Republic likely helped Ribeirão Preto avoid the rigid stratification [typical of *coronelismo*]. The accessibility of urban centers, the alternative of employment in industry, the railroads which lessened isolation, and the general economic health of São Paulo, combined to diminish the strength of such a system." From interior counties like Barretos to the state capital, the PRP found constituencies among an electorate growing ever more complex in its interests and needs. The party responded by gradually distancing itself from consistent support for pro-coffee policies, such as subsidized immigration and coffee price supports.[31]

By 1919, differences among planters had grown deep enough to inspire some to form new collective organizations. Whereas the Paulista Agriculture Society (SPA, Sociedade Paulista de Agricultura) had served as an effective advocate for planters since 1902, with many of its members serving in government, some of "the most prestigious and wealthy Paulista planters" came to believe it no longer represented their interests well and in 1919 founded the SRB. By 1921 the SRB was "the champion of large planter interests" at state and national levels; in 1930 the SRB became the planters' only lobbying organization when it absorbed members of the SPA and the Liga Agrí-

---

31. Percentages from Font, *Coffee, Contention, and Change*, 23; see also chaps. 2, 5, 6. Gifun, "Ribeirão Preto," 135.

cola Brasileira, which had been established around 1920.[32] To challenge the PRP locally, many planters formed political parties in their counties, and coffee interests eventually united these disparate opposition groups into the Democratic Party (PD, Partido Democrático), the Partido Republicano's first national challenger. Formed in 1926, the PD was designed primarily to oppose the presidential aspirations of Senator Washington Luís Pereira de Sousa, a lifelong PRP politician from the ranks of the São Paulo elite.

As the undercurrent of change identified by Font fractured the oligarchy's power and stimulated political conflict, rural workers became objects of political maneuvering for the first time. Washington Luís proved a pivotal figure. Font describes him as the quintessential "new *coronel*" of the period. Like traditional, landed *coronels,* the new ones had considerable authority, but they differed from their predecessors in that they had few direct connections to agriculture. Luís himself was a lawyer whose only career had been in politics. He attempted to balance the interests of coffee planters with those of a growing constituency linked to other economic activities. The Patronato Agrícola, established during Luís's tenure as state secretary of justice (1906–12), was one such measure. Often noted for his repressive policies, Luís was also one of the first leading politicians to compete for the votes of immigrants by promoting their political incorporation. Apparently, Luís subscribed to the modernist view that the ballot box was an effective means of suppressing radical politics. Despite the protests of some coffee planters, justice secretary Washington Luís ruled that all immigrants married to Brazilians, having Brazilian-born children, or owning property should themselves be considered Brazilian and thus eligible for citizenship rights. Ribeirão Preto's coffee king Francisco Schmidt, a PRP loyalist, used this ruling to register to vote 437 foreign-born *colonos* on his estate—an action that was unsuccessfully challenged by an anti-immigrant SRB front group, the Nationalist League (Liga Nacionalista), in 1920. Then, as governor (*presidente*) of São Paulo from 1920 to 1924, Luís aided the breakup of inefficient plantations, the growth of smaller farms, and crop diversification. He also enhanced the effectiveness of the Patronato Agrícola with the addition of new staff, professionalized the judiciary (taking de facto authority to appoint local judges out of the hands of the *coroneis*), instituted a system of rural labor tribunals (with Law 1,869 of 1922), and took possession of all untitled lands (once more alienating planters, who made claim to many such lands).

32. Font, *Coffee, Contention, and Change,* 56–60.

Selected national president in 1926, Luís continued to act in ways that exacerbated the fragmentation of São Paulo's coffee elite.[33]

The "coffee elite" are not easily defined. Font refers to the increasingly alienated group of coffee planters who organized in opposition to the government as "Big Coffee." Many of the individuals mentioned were owners of *fazendas* with huge quantities of trees, ranging from half a million to more than ten million producing coffee plants. By using size as a major criteria, Font contrasts this group with the immigrants who formed small to medium-sized farms, with anywhere from five thousand to one hundred thousand trees. As Font himself shows, however, significant discord marred the solidarity of the Big Coffee group. For example, coffee kings Francisco Schmidt and Geremia Lunardelli either backed the governing PRP system or remained aloof from politics. Both Schmidt and Lunardelli were foreign-born, and this seems to have been a dividing line between big planters. Font's Big Coffee group was vehemently nationalistic and occasionally anti-immigrant. And yet, the oppositional coffee group is not well understood as "traditional" either, for among them were some of the most enterprising and innovative of the São Paulo elite, including Antônio Prado and Júlio de Mesquita Filho. Both were planters, but Prado also owned factories, and Mesquita had been educated in Europe and was editor of the influential *O Estado de São Paulo* daily newspaper. In the end, the principal difference between coffee planters in the opposition and those comprising the governing party (*situação*) was the former's commitment to an agrarian future and the latter's attachment to industrialization. For Big Coffee, agriculture was seen as Brazil's "natural vocation," whereas industry was an "artificial pursuit."

While Big Coffee interests did not oppose industrialization per se, they saw agriculture—especially coffee—as the engine of economic progress and a proper social order. Industry could come only as an extension of agriculture—hence, in the form of textile mills, sugar mills, and coffee processors, each enhancing Brazil's agricultural wealth. The planters had a noble past and believed Brazil could have a noble future as long as measures were taken to strengthen the agrarian economy. They wanted the social pyramid of the plantation to be mirrored in Brazilian society because they felt confident that, as on the estates where they ruled to great profit, in society the planters could apply a unique array of skills and blessings, from education to authority, to guide Brazil forward. They claimed to be proud of the

33. See ibid., 133, 135, 147, 160, 304–5; and Holloway, *Immigrants on the Land,* 128.

success of those *colonos* who worked hard, saved, and lifted themselves up. In this regard, the plantation schooled the foreigner in what it meant to be a Brazilian. It was also a family, with the old planter patriarchs raising Brazil's children, both native and foreign-born, until they were strong enough to go out on their own. The planters were thus flattered by those who imitated their model of success by reaching farther and farther into Brazil's vast territory to open new lands to agriculture; the imitators need only remain deferential toward their former masters. Those planters who embraced this tradition-bound road to the future formed an increasingly powerful opposition movement.

The 1924 Revolt: Memory and Event

With *colonos* becoming landowners and Italian and other ethnic groups redefining *paulista* identity, the base of planter power dwindled during the 1920s, creating opportunities for rebellion as various interests sought to fill the void left by rulingclass fragmentation. The two most important revolts occurred in 1924 and 1930. In July 1924 retired army General Isidoro Dias Lopes led a conspiracy in revolt against the national government of President Artur Bernardes, a PR politician from the state of Minas Gerais. The month-long conflict began when troops under Lopes's command occupied the capital of São Paulo. This event has long been seen as a watershed in a multi-faceted, progressive assault on Brazil's rural oligarchy. But did the Bernardes government really represent this oligarchy? Mauricio Font says no. He offers a challenging alternative interpretation, one based on a systematic reading of newspapers published around the state. While some rebels may have advocated industrialization and denounced planters, many opposition coffee planters allied with the rebels. They used the opportunity created by the disruption of federal authority to oust local PRP governments and establish new ones. Police reports showed "positive acts of rebellion" not just in São Paulo but in eighty-seven interior counties, and support for the revolt in another thirty-seven. In Araras, Campinas, Jaú, and other *paulista municípios,* large planters with hundreds of thousands of coffee trees took the lead in toppling the local PRP power structure and establishing revolutionary juntas. One of the leading collaborators in the revolt proved to be Mesquita's *O Estado de São Paulo.* As a founding member of the SRB, an outspoken critic of PRP policies, a gentleman planter, and grandson of José Alves de Cerqueira César, one of São Paulo's historic coffee planters, Mesquita was the voice of the oppositionist planter elite. The revolt, which was decidedly anti-immigrant, was also backed by Mesquita's xenophobic Nationalist League. After loyal federal troops had turned the tide against the mutineers, the government jailed Mesquita for his betrayal, abolished the league, and closed his newspaper for three weeks. In contrast, Mesquita's senior opposition colleague, the planter Antônio Prado, had taken a wait and see attitude toward the revolt. Having graciously declined to accept General Lopes's request that he serve as revolutionary governor of the state, Prado suffered few consequences.[34]

As a young man living in the remote São Paulo frontier, Moraes witnessed the rebellion in the interior. Although he was only twelve in 1924, the episode remained a vividly exciting memory for him. Because his father had been hurt in a work accident, the family had traveled by train to a company hospital in Campinas when the revolt broke out that July. An important gateway to the interior and the state's second largest city, Campinas quickly became a rebel stronghold. Moraes remembers government planes flying overhead to leaflet and intimidate residents, crowds of refugees fleeing the fighting in the capital, panic in the streets, and interrupted train service that left his family stranded for several days.[35]

Back home in Barretos, Moraes was excited to encounter a rebel contingent of "fifty to a hundred" soldiers, led by Lieutenant Colonel Filogônio Teodoro de Carvalho, which had occupied the town: "When I heard tell that Filogônio had taken the city, I ran down to the police station. Revolt was a thing that attracted me, that I liked to be a part of. The lieutenant had taken Barretos and, as he was likable, the people applauded him and helped him out." Moraes remembers this incident in some detail, recollecting dialogues between Carvalho

34. See, for example, Anna Maria Martinez Corrêa, *A rebelião de 1924 em São Paulo* (São Paulo: Hucitec, 1976), esp. 155–77; and Font, *Coffee, Contention, and Change,* 166–72. Corrêa's evidence contradicts some of Font's arguments. Mesquita is shown to have remained aloof from the revolt and yet reports that his "Nationalist League played an outstanding role in the movement." Regarding the role of nationalism, she shows that General Lopes was accused of forming "foreign battalions" of recently arrived Hungarians, Germans, and Italians who were dissatisfied with Brazil. The formation of these units was used by loyalist forces to paint the revolt as an alien cause. Corrêa's sources are judicial records; this characterization may have arisen after the fact and played into the hands of Mesquita and other PRP opponents. Font, on the other hand, claims the rebels targeted the property of foreign — read "Italian" — industrialists for destruction. Matarazzo lost several buildings, and a factory was set ablaze during the fighting. For more on the 1924 rebellion, see Vilma Keller and César Benjamim, "Isidoro Dias Lopes," in Beloch and Abreu, eds., *DHBB,* 1918–22.

35. Welch and Geraldo, *Lutas camponesas,* 24–26; Corrêa, *Rebelião,* 124–26; and Font, *Coffee, Contention, and Change,* 170–71.

and the PRP sheriff (*delegado*) he had overthrown and specifics of Carvalho's assault on and retreat from Barretos.

> Lt. Filogônio managed to take the town with few men. He ordered two or three to the red-light district to cause a disturbance. They shot off their revolvers, taking pot shots at each other, not to hit anything, just to attract everyone's attention. Seeing the gunfight, a local vendor called the police and the sheriff sent three officers running for the zone. In the meantime, Filogônio and two or three other men hid out near the sheriff's office. They knew how many officers there were, and when only a sergeant remained in the station, they went in, and took him by surprise. They ordered the sergeant to take off his clothes and one of the lieutenant's men dressed in his uniform. After this, the other men dressed up like police. Thus, they also managed to capture the sheriff and dominate the city.[36]

What stands out in Moraes's recollection is how impressed he was with the ability of a few men under the command of a clever leader to take power. Although he seems to have kept a close watch on events during the "three days or so" that Carvalho occupied the town, it is unlikely that the young Moraes had the access required to make such observations himself. This is one of the questions that arises in assessing any memoir. Another question lies in a basic discrepancy between Moraes's memory and other accounts regarding the year of the event. Moraes thinks the occupation took place nearly two years after the 1924 revolt broke out: "I was already a lot bigger, nearly fourteen years old."

Although the story of Carvalho is not well documented, it most likely took place at the time of the revolt. Sources agree that from São Paulo, General Lopes tried to orchestrate the occupation of the entire state through allies and agents such as subordinate officers like Carvalho. Font sets Carvalho's story in 1924 and uses it to support his thesis of division within the ranks of the rural oligarchy. According to this version, the opposition Partido Popular enlisted Carvalho and a "battalion of 60 men . . . as soon as news of the rebellion arrived" to help them overthrow the PRP government and establish a new one. Although the attack on São Paulo had begun during the early morning hours of July 5, the first reports did not reach Barretos until late that same night, and it was July 8 before a copy of *O Estado de São*

---

36. Welch and Geraldo, *Lutas camponesas,* 24–26.

Paulo arrived, carrying enough detailed information to set off a dispute between the town's rival factions. Carvalho must have followed the news, and with his arrival, the Partido Popular's judge Belmiro Simões and Ricardo de Almeida Prado took power. Like many prominent families in São Paulo, the family of Almeida Prado had become rich by landgrabbing and intermarriage with the coffee elite.

Another perspective is offered by historian Anna Maria Martinez Corrêa. Her sources make no mention of Carvalho and show the PRP overruling the Popular Party's attempt to block the mayor (*governador*) from sending a telegram of support to the government. What is more, one of the sources cited by Font places the incident in May 1925, one year after the 1924 revolt and closer to Moraes's recollection of the event. However, both Font and Moraes agree that Carvalho worked to link the local rebellion to a wider movement by making contact with rebels in Araraquara (a larger town located nearer the capital), which had fallen into the hands of Lopes's allies. Carvalho's alleged ties to the opposition elite and Araraquara suggest his connections to Teodoro Carvalho, *coronel* of Araraquara at the turn of the century. According to historian Joseph Love, the elder Carvalho earned a reputation for butchery when he was tried in 1897 for having murdered several migrant workers from northeast Brazil. His acquittal came when the PRP assigned former governor Cerqueira César (Mesquita's grandfather) to lead his defense.[37]

Of equal interest is Moraes's fascination with a man who seems to have represented a faction of the São Paulo ruling class most committed to restoring the agrarian social order. Filogônio Teodoro de Carvalho earned Moraes's admiration not through his ideology but through his dramatic actions. Moraes recalled more than Carvalho's bravado in capturing the sheriff and escaping Barretos unharmed. He also remembered that the lieutenant colonel had stopped the trains and forced the Armour meatpacking plant to shut down: "The plant was paralyzed and the folks loved being allowed to stop work. It was, as they say, a wild time." Moraes, apparently, was not the only working-class individual who was attracted to the rebellion and confused by its politics. Moraes claims that this same event started the activist career of a childhood friend, Sebastião Dinart dos Santos, who later joined the PCB and became a rural labor leader much like Moraes. In

---

37. Font, *Coffee, Contention, and Change,* 156, 189 n. 53; Corrêa, *Rebelião,* 167–69; and, for Almeida Prado and the elder Carvalho, see Love, *São Paulo in the Brazilian Federation,* 73, 132. The key primary source on Carvalho is "Movimentos subversivos: Os acontecimentos de Barretos—pormenores das diligências da policia—o relatório da autoridade que presidiu o inquerito," *O Estado de São Paulo* (hereafter *OESP*), 26 July 1925, 8.

1929 Moraes would himself help shut down the Frigorífico Anglo for nationalist motives, quickly organizing a walkout to stop the company from replacing Brazilian workers with less costly Lithuanian immigrants. This too was a "crazy time" in which neither he nor his comrades "had a notion of politics or organization."[38]

Moraes prefaces his recollections about Carvalho and his links to the 1924 revolt with an oft-repeated reflection: "Today I notice that there's a tendency to underestimate that revolutionary movement." Moraes, who remembers himself bigger and older at the time of the Barretos occupations, also envisions the event as bigger in its potential for bringing to Brazil the revolutionary change to which he later dedicated his life as a Communist militant. The Italian oral history analyst Alessandro Portelli calls this a "motif of 'history that could have gone differently.'" It is a motif that constantly reappears in the memoirs of Communist rural labor activists. Moraes seems to blame himself for not grasping the significance of this event and self-consciously returns to the struggle by imprinting his vision of the moment's potential on the historical record, correcting the mistaken analysis of professional historians and leaving a guide for future militants to follow. The details that matter are tactical ones; the tone celebrates defiance in the face of power. Although the uprising appealed to Moraes and Dinart, Carvalho made no effort to gain mass support and form a rebel army. Ill prepared to articulate and defend his cause, the authorities overpowered Carvalho and his followers in a few days time. Still, the 1924 revolt and its aftermath lived on by inspiring the militancy of Moraes and others, a militancy soon reflected in the 1929 walkout.[39]

Prestes and the Worker and Peasant Bloc

Carvalho appears in the historical record of 1925 yet again when he is mentioned for his service as a messenger between General Lopes and Captain Luís Carlos Prestes. While Moraes's story provides some indication of how the 1924 revolt inspired teens and laborers in a frontier town, Prestes's story reveals how the revolt inspired the militancy of the man who would come to dominate the PCB and shape its rural labor policies for several decades. In July 1925, Lopes was in

38. Welch and Geraldo, *Lutas camponesas,* 130–35.
39. Ibid., 26–30. Portelli, "Uchronic Dreams," 147.

Argentina planning the revival of his movement, and Prestes, a muti-
nous comrade-in-arms from the southern state of Rio Grande do Sul,
was then leading hundreds of soldiers and supporters through the
interior state of Goiás, standing at the ready for Lopes's command.
Although the orders never came, Prestes and his column marched
for thousands of miles through the backlands of central and northern Brazil in a vain yet celebrated attempt to distract federal troops
and raise support for the rebellion against President Bernardes and
the Partido Republicano. Started in October 1924, the march ended
more than two years later in February 1927 when its leaders and more
than six hundred surviving combatants found refuge in Bolivia. The
march affected Prestes deeply: "I learned the misery of the people,"
he later told two journalists. "I saw people crawling on their knees,
breaking the soil with kitchen knives that had no handles. They
simply held the knives in their hands, working in a manner more
backward than the Indians. When I saw that, I was convinced that it
would be more than a simple change of Bernardes for another president that would resolve our problems." [40]

Prestes made this statement in the 1980s, nearly three generations after the Prestes column had repaired to Bolivia. The course
of time condensed events in his memory, as is invariably the case.
Clearly the experience of the march left him with genuine concern
for the poverty and despair of the rural poor and motivated him to
do something about it. The quote suggests he quickly embraced revolutionary Communism, but information from other sources reveals a
more gradual development of his ideology. Prestes's transformation is
the story of how the early PCB began to campaign among rural laborers. Court-martialed and hunted, Prestes fled to Argentina, where he
apparently gained his first exposure to Marx. But much of his time in
Buenos Aires was taken up by efforts to influence Brazilian politics
from a distance. The march and its recounting in the Communist and
mainstream press had made him a popular folk hero of mythic proportions, known to all as the "Horseman of Hope." While the ruling
Partido Republicano sought to smear his name, those who opposed
the PR hoped association with Prestes would enhance their popularity. Unsure of his own politics, Prestes flirted with visiting suitors
from both ends of the oppositional spectrum: the Partido Democrá-

40. See Lorenço Moreira Lima, *A coluna Prestes: Marchas e combates,* 3d ed. (São Paulo:
Alfa Omega, 1979); and Neill Macaulay, *The Prestes Column: Revolution in Brazil* (New York: New
Viewpoints, 1974). On Carvalho's presence, see Keller and Benjamim, "Lopes," 1920. Prestes
quoted in Dênis de Moraes and Francisco Viana, *Prestes: Lutas e autocríticas* (Petrópolis: Vôzes,
1982), 37, see also 18–21, 41–60; and Fernando Morais, *Olga.*

tico and the Worker and Peasant Bloc (BOC, Bloco Operário e Camponês), a front group for the PCB.

Although the PD and BOC represented different ends of the class spectrum, the two parties cooperated extensively until 1929, when their opposing class interests overwhelmed their common interest in ousting the PR. While the PD arose in 1926 from a ruling-class faction that distrusted Washington Luís, the BOC was formed when Luís's rebellion-wary government took away the PCB's legal standing at the beginning of 1927. The party hoped to use the BOC to overthrow the PR electorally by building a base of support among urban and rural workers and using it as leverage to broker alliances with other political parties. Some of its party-building campaign involved attacks on anarchists and Socialists who competed for the loyalty of workers. President Luís tolerated the BOC precisely because it seemed to channel working-class protest away from nonconformist and revolutionary rhetoric and toward legal activities such as electoral politics. By running worker-candidates for office in Rio de Janeiro and São Paulo, however, the BOC pushed to expand the political space in which workers could be heard, challenging Luís to accept the political mobilization of workers. His government's reformist policies—including a vacation law and regulations protecting the labor of women and children—had been meant to quell labor discontent. Through the BOC these policies became electoral planks, for the party's candidates demanded the law's application, extension, and expansion. The São Paulo BOC, for example, "envisioned the moral and physical regeneration of the rural laborer, the cleansing (*higienização*) of farm living and working conditions, and support for small farmers cooperatives." Overall, the BOC was pledged to obey one "fundamental principle . . . the realization of an independent class politics for the proletariat." Such goals, going well beyond the policies Luís had backed to address the needs of labor and immigrants, would be the cause of both friction in the oppositional alliance and its ultimate breakup. Although the PD was willing to support the BOC as long as it helped widen the base of the opposition movement, its leaders did not endorse the BOC platform. In toying with the BOC, elites in both parties assumed they could force the genie of working-class militancy back into the bottle should it become too threatening.[41]

---

41. Quotes from "Bloco operário e camponês de São Paulo," *O Trabalhador Gráfico* (7 February 1928), and "O programa do bloco operário," *A Nação* (17 February 1927), cited in Pinheiro and Hall, eds., *A classe operária*, 292–94. Edgar de Decca, *1930: O silêncio dos vencidos: Memória, história, e revolução*, 6th ed. (São Paulo: Brasiliense, 1994), 75–110; Mônica Kornis and

The BOC's focus on both industrial and agricultural workers was new to the PCB. Internationally, Communist revolutionary ideology spoke to the issue of uniting peasants and proletarians in struggle; in Brazil the revolt of 1924 and the Prestes march inspired the first homegrown version of this dogma. In a pamphlet entitled *Agrarismo e industrialismo,* a Communist journalist named Octavio Brandão portrayed rural workers as full partners in the Brazilian revolution.[42] Brandão's essay described a Brazil divided between an established rural oligarchy tied to imperialist nations through the export of agricultural products and a nascent bourgeoisie struggling to build a modern, industrial nation. Brandão forecast a role for urban and rural workers in first assisting the emerging middle class and later overthrowing it to establish socialism. "In Brazil," he wrote, "the revolution of the industrial workers against the regime of the industrial bourgeoisie, the wage regime, is going to coincide with an agrarian revolution of the rural laborers against the agrarian regime, the feudal regime, the regime of servitude. To fuse the two movements into one," he continued, "is to transform our 1789 into a permanent revolution, from which our 7 November 1917 will burst forth—such must be one of the fundamental tasks of Brazilian Communists." A united front of peasants and proletarians would catapult Brazil from the eighteenth to the twentieth century, overthrowing feudalism and capitalism and bringing about a socialist workers' dictatorship all in one fell swoop. When the BOC was formed, Brandão became one of its leading activists.[43]

Given Prestes's experience and repulsion toward the exploitation of rural workers, the BOC should have been the ideal organiza-

---

Dora Flaksman, "Bloco operário-camponês," in Beloch and Abreu, eds., *DHBB,* 400–402; and Joel Wolfe, *Working Women, Working Men: São Paulo and the Rise of Brasil's Industrial Working Class, 1900–1955* (Durham: Duke University Press, 1993), 49.

42. Octavio Brandão, *Combates e batalhas: Memórias,* vol. 1 (São Paulo: Alfa Omega, 1978), 284–301. On the origins and initial positions of the party, see also Michel Zaidan Filho, *PCB (1922–1929): Na busca das origens de um marxismo nacional* (São Paulo: Global, 1985). The unity of urban and rural labor was a classic Soviet-Communist representation, symbolized in the hammer and sickle motif emblazoned on Communist flags, walls, and monuments around the world. In the United States, the Communist Party formed the Farm Labor Party during the 1930s, envisioning it as a popular front for a revolutionary Leninist vanguard. See Nelson Lichtenstein, *The Most Dangerous Man in Detroit: Walter Reuther and the Fate of American Labor* (New York: Basic Books, 1995), 58–59.

43. Fritz Mayer [pseud.], *Agrarismo e industrialismo: Ensaio marxista-leninista sôbre a guerra de classe no Brasil e a revolta de São Paulo* (Buenos Aires: n.p., 1926), abridged version found in *O P.C.B. (1922–1943),* edited by Edgard Carone (São Paulo: Difel, 1982), 1:256–63; Brandão, *Combates e batalhas,* 343–81; Zaidan, *PCB,* 76–77; and Kornis and Flaksman, "Bloco," 401.

tion through which to channel his passion for revolution. Predict-ably, then, Prestes eventually rejected offers to align with the PD. But in May 1929, he also turned down BOC's nomination to run on its ticket for president of Brazil in the national election scheduled for March 1930. Prestes's rejection of the BOC offer came not long after the PCB had formalized a rural platform for the first time at its third congress, held clandestinely in late December 1928. Historians claim that Prestes then considered the party's call for the expropriation and distribution of *latifúndios* too extreme.[44]

Guided by the Soviet Union's Comintern, the PCB's new plat-form cast United States imperialism and the large landholdings of Brazil's rural oligarchy as the great enemies of working people. It also changed the party's stance on building alliances with the "national bourgeoisie." Veering from the collaborationist position articulated by Brandão, Brazilian Communists now viewed industrialists as im-perialist agents and allies of landlords. Influenced by the experience of Communists in China and India, the PCB characterized Brazil as a nation mired in feudalism from which an "agrarian revolution" would arise from social forces, led by "peasant soviets." Since "agricul-tural laborers throughout the country live[d] in conditions of near-slavery," it was incumbent on the party to organize among them. For some time after the III Congress, rural militancy became central to the party's agenda, and the goal of this militancy was revolutionary in nature: "land for those who work it."[45]

Curiously, the steps to attain this goal were quite pragmatic and specific. Emphasized were reformist measures, such as indexing wages to the cost of living, providing free and obligatory elementary education, abolishing the vestiges of slavery, controlling pests and the spread of disease, protecting free association, providing secret ballots, and encouraging rural workers to develop their own political leaders. Moreover, the third congress based additional resolutions on a regional analysis of the country, which offered even more par-ticular reformist demands, such as the "revision of contracts elabo-rated by the Patronato Agrícola" and the "right of elected agricultural workers' union representatives to oversee the work of the Patronato" in São Paulo. BOC efforts to turn *rural* labor issues into political cam-paign planks could potentially bring it closer to workers, even if

44. Alizira Alves de Abreu and Ivan Junqueira, "Luís Carlos Prestes," in Beloch and Abreu, eds., *DHBB*, 2816–17.

45. Zaidan, *PCB*, quotes lengthy segments of congress documents such as "O III Con-gesso do PCB" (76–93).

pivotal figures like Prestes dismissed the fundamental goal of land confiscation.[46]

By the time Prestes rejected the presidential nominations of the opposition, strains had developed in the relationship between the BOC and the PD, and the BOC's tendentious relations with the government were also stretched to the limit. At the end of April 1929, after a long campaign, the PCB had finally succeeded in establishing the General Confederation of Labor (CGT, Confederação Geral do Trabalho), uniting dozens of urban unions. In May the CGT sponsored a prolonged strike of some six thousand graphics workers in São Paulo, and the BOC used the event to build its credibility and experience. In this and subsequent incidents, the police cracked down on the BOC, arresting its leaders, and industrialists in the PD and the PR pressured their respective party elite to end their collaboration with the BOC. By promoting working-class militancy outside the electoral process, the BOC had "transgressed the norms of the political game," as Brazilian historian Edgar de Decca maintains. As the nation anticipated the March 1930 election, each party went their own way in choosing candidates. In this moment of political fragmentation, Prestes received one more offer from Getúlio Vargas, governor of Rio Grande do Sul and leader of the Liberal Alliance, which was also challenging the PR. Prestes rejected his embrace, as well.[47]

For many Brazilians, Prestes had come to symbolize a popular revolution against the landed oligarchy. His column's march through the backlands of Brazil had illuminated the unhealthy aspects of Brazil's agricultural economy. De Decca argues that support for Prestes and his followers, especially the "lieutenants" (*tenentes*), made it possible for all parties to be revolutionaries without engaging in a revolution. In time, this symbolic revolution became a way of characterizing politics in the era. If you were for Prestes, you were for revolution and against the rural oligarchy. For the PD—whose members included some of Brazil's wealthiest planters—verbal support for Prestes and accusations about the oligarchical nature of the PR government became a way of being revolutionary. The BOC almost fell into this trap, for it accepted the PD's support in 1927 and 1928, and

46. Zaidan, *PCB,* includes in its entirety the III Congress's "Resolucion sôbre la cuestion campesina" (139–43).

47. Moraes and Viana, *Prestes,* 43–45; Abreu and Junqueira, "Prestes," 2816–17; M. Fortus, "Le bilan de dix ans de mouvement ouvirier brésilien," *L'internationale syndicale rouge* (February 1929), reprinted in Pinheiro and Hall, eds., *A classe operária,* 297–396; Decca, *1930,* 183–205; and Kornis and Flaksman, "Bloco," 401.

this helped the Communists secure legislative seats for elected representatives such as Brandão. But PCB direction, and Soviet influence over the III Congress at the end of 1928, made it impossible for the front group to pursue a collaborationist course. "The BOC presents some of the dangers of electoral and opportunistic detours," the Congress concluded, warning that it should not be considered "the" party of the proletariat. "The BOC is," continued the Congress, "a united front political organization of the laboring masses which is under the hegemony of the Communist Party." It was up to people like Prestes, who might want to join the movement, to fit party doctrine, not the other way around. Michel Zaidan Filho, an analyst of the 1920s PCB, argued that this new rigidity in Communist theory isolated the party from other progressive forces, which is true, but it was based on sounder logic than the collaborationist ideas that had formerly oriented the party. The PD, with which the BOC was most entangled, was indeed compromised by its ties to large landlords and foreign interests. It may have been better off finding a way to work with the PR had the governing party not been so committed to repressing autonomous working-class political action.[48]

Snubbed by Prestes, in November 1929 the BOC chose Minervino de Oliveira to run for president. Oliveira, a skilled marbler and tireless BOC militant, had been elected along with Brandão to the Rio de Janeiro municipal council in 1928 and had become general secretary of the CGT in April 1929. He used his status as an elected official and working-class spokesman to lead strikes and organize assemblies of workers, activities that occasioned his repeated arrest. As the March 1930 election approached, the BOC organized more and more rallies in order to generate support and pressure for working-class causes, and many participants were attacked by police. Just prior to the election, hundreds of workers were arrested on one charge or another. In Ribeirão Preto in February, police broke into a BOC assembly of rural laborers, arresting Oliveira. Despite all this campaign activity, the PR political machine successfully delivered the election to Luís's handpicked successor, Júlio Prestes. Oliveira and other BOC candidates had a poor showing, as did Vargas, the opposition's leading candidate.[49]

48. On the PD, see Font, *Coffee, Contention, and Change,* 198–99, 207–10. On the BOC, see Decca, *1930,* 183–205. On the PCB, see Kornis and Flaksman, "Bloco," 402; and Zaidan, *PCB,* 91–92.

49. Report of Lester Baker, U.S. military attaché to Brazil (8 November 1929), quoted in Pinheiro and Hall, eds., *A classe operária,* 306–9; "O congresso dos colonos e assalariados agrícolas," in Carone, ed., *O P.C.B.,* 1:348–50; and Kornis and Flaksman, "Bloco," 401.

Following his defeat, Vargas reached out once more to the "Horseman of Hope." Presenting himself as Brazil's rightful president-elect, Vargas asked Prestes to serve as military commander in chief of a movement to overthrow the government, but Prestes rejected this offer too. In a manifesto written in April and first published at the end of May by the PD's *Diário Nacional* and the oppositional *O Estado de São Paulo*, Prestes wrote that "a simple change of men in power" would resolve nothing and be of little consequence to the great mass of people. The manifesto urged a "revolution by soldiers, workers, and fishermen" that would redistribute land and oppose imperialism. As a result of this publication, Vargas, the PD, and others in the opposition disavowed the famed revolutionary, underscoring the elitist nature of the mounting challenge against the government. These leaders denied the applicability of Communist ideology to Brazil, because the country was not capitalist, and "perverse oligarchies" not class conflict were at the root "the political problem." This distortion of reality came at a moment when coffee planters throughout the state had protected themselves from the ravages of the 1929 depression by cutting *colono* wages some 40 to 60 percent. After Vargas gained power in October 1930, following a brief revolt, Prestes intensified his critique of the ruling class, showing a firm grasp of socioeconomic if not political reality. In March 1931 he condemned the new government in a document that called for an anti-imperialist, agrarian revolution and the rise to power of the PCB, which had, since its poor showing in the 1930 election, disbanded the BOC, expelled Brandão, and reasserted its commitment to revolution. Thus, six years after the start of his famous march, Prestes had decided that an agrarian revolution led by the Communist Party was the only path to a better world.[50]

Rural Workers and the Vargas Revolt

Despite the 1930 oppositional movement's rejection of class analysis, the new government's policies betrayed a concern with workers as a class. From the start of the movement against Washington Luís, the mere presence of the BOC, of Prestes, and of striking and grieving

50. Newspaper and manifesto quotes from Font, *Coffee, Contention, and Change*, 260–62; and Abreu and Junqueira, "Prestes," 2817. See also Kornis and Flaksman, "Bloco," 402; and Brandão, *Combates e batalhas*. For *colono* salary cuts, see "Salários nominais médios nas fazendas de café, São Paulo," *RSRB* (December 1931), 556, reproduced in Stolcke, *Cafeicultura*, 101.

industrial and agricultural workers, as well as President Luís's own reformist policies, forced class issues into the political mix. The platform of Vargas's Liberal Alliance, announced 2 January 1930, included a section on "the social question" that recalled some of the reformist proposals put forward by the third PCB congress. It urged the government to develop a labor code that would apply to both "the urban and rural proletariat," and it suggested that the alliance would provide rural workers with improved educational, residential, nutritional, and health services. Vargas, like most of his colleagues in the alliance, was no common man, no *trabalhador rural,* but an elite, steeped in the patriarchal traditions of Brazil. A landholder, cattle rancher, lawyer, and former state governor of Rio Grande do Sul, he shrewdly gauged the party's rhetoric to attract supporters to his cause and dilute the influence of leftist opponents.[51]

Nevertheless, there was more to Vargas's rural labor proposals than pure political expediency. As leader of the Liberal Alliance, Vargas brought a fresh perspective from his experiences in Rio Grande do Sul—a state unlike São Paulo. As the historian Joan Bak has argued, Rio Grande do Sul produced a different political culture, one that looked to Italian corporatist models and saw benefits to enforcing cross-class cooperation, state intervention in the economy, and the creation of *sindicatos*—state-sanctioned economic interest groups, akin to trade unions, organized to represent owners as well as workers and dependent on government recognition to function legally. The *Riograndense* group that marched into Rio de Janeiro favored corporatism over both Communism and capitalism, rejecting the classconflict model of the former and the individualistic, competitive framework of the latter. As he occupied the presidential palace at Cateté, Vargas advocated "the need for social and economic organization, collaboration of class organs in modern government and . . . a controlled economy purged of conflict and competition." Within five months of taking office, labor minister Lindolfo Collor issued the first decrees regarding the organization of *sindicatos.*[52]

51. Decca (*1930,* 183–205) stresses the indirect influence of the BOC on the nature and character of the October revolution and the early Vargas administration. "A plataforma da Aliança Liberal," in Getúlio Vargas, *A nova política do Brasil,* vol. 1 (Rio de Janeiro: José Olympio, 1938), 26–28.

52. Joan L. Bak, "Cartels, Cooperatives, and Corporations: Getúlio Vargas in Rio Grande do Sul on the Eve of Brazil's 1930 Revolution," *HAHR* 63:2 (May 1983), 273–74. For more interpretations of the revolution, see also Boris Fausto, *A revolução de 1930: Historiografia e história* (São Paulo: Brasiliense, 1970). Angela Maria de Castro Gomes, "Confronto e compromisso no processo de constitucionalização (1930–1935)," in Fausto, ed., *História geral da civilização brasileira,* 7–75, discusses the early politics of the new regime.

The early alliance platform also revealed the modernizing, developmentalist logic behind Vargas's later statements about rural workers. The coffee export economy of São Paulo, which fueled the national economy, had been devastated by the 1930 depression. To get it going again, the platform borrowed ideas from the innovative coffee planter and PD founder Antônio Prado, who emphasized the control of production costs. To make coffee viable, planters needed cheap, efficient, and reliable labor. A shortage of "arms" (braços), as elites referred to workers, was one of the coffee economy's chronic problems. Contemporary conditions in Europe and Brazil made immigrant workers more costly to obtain and problematic to settle than in the past, and Vargas emphasized the need to rely instead on Brazilian manpower. He also professed a desire to comply with labor relations standards established by the International Labor Organization (ILO), for *his* Brazil aspired to be a member in good standing of the global community, and thus a more attractive recipient of foreign investment, with access to overseas markets. In fact, in 1926 Brazil had been criticized by the ILO—yet another grievance the opposition had filed against the former government. All of these influences added up to the conclusion that labor markets and the work process needed to be rationalized and that interventionist state regulation was the way to do it. As stated in the platform, Vargas promised labor policies "to initiate the valorization of human capital, for the measure of the social utility of man [was] given by his productive capacity."[53]

Increased productivity was the core of Vargas's interest in workers, and incorporation was the means by which they would be made capable of working harder. For the hundreds of thousands of rural Brazilians who lived on the political margins, social legislation was the tool that would bring them in. Vargas anticipated issuing labor legislation for all workers: "As the urban worker, so too the rural needs protective legal provisions, applicable to each, yet addressing the respective peculiarities of each." These thousands lived, according to Vargas, "without instruction, without good hygiene, poorly nourished and clothed, having contact with the state only through the high taxes they [were] forced to pay." Whether peasants or farmworkers, Vargas and other contemporary rulers grouped all rural workers together as rural labor (trabalho rural), zeroing in on their labor power rather than their humanity. What was new under Vargas, however, was the emphasis he placed on the self-motivation of peasants and

53. Quotes from Vargas, "A plataforma," 50–52, 29, 28.

farmworkers. He promised laws that would "awaken in them the interest, inculcating in them the habits of economic activity."[54]

Plans for the creation of rural labor policy took shape soon after the October 1930 revolt. Early in 1931, labor minister Collor articulated the government's syndicalist philosophy and sought the organization of rural labor syndicates: "Appearing certain that agrarian syndicates of employees do not exist, it will be indispensable to promote the formation of some, in various states." Meeting in assembly with syndicates of employers in agriculture, the two classes were to help design Brazil's farm policy. In the meantime, the labor ministry retained responsibility for regulating commercial and agricultural labor, for registering syndicates, for providing free legal assistance to rural and urban workers, for managing labor migration, and for overseeing homesteads or colonies established in frontier regions. By the end of 1931, the ministry had recognized 251 syndicates, 6 of them in the primary, agricultural sector. Only 6 out of 251 unions—even worse, only one additional rural syndicate—had been registered ten years later. In the early 1930s, the government clearly lacked a commitment to rural unionization.[55]

The government's attention to rural labor interests was partly motivated by the concerns and outlook of the most militant faction of the alliance. This was the lieutenants, a group composed primarily of junior military officers, many of whom had marched with Prestes through the backlands of Brazil. Comrades such as Miguel Costa, who had lead the march alongside Prestes, and João Alberto Lins de Barros adopted a pragmatic stance and broke with the "Horseman of Hope"—as Prestes was sometimes called—in order to participate in Vargas's provisional government. They organized a debating society called the Clube 3 de Outubro and distinguished themselves as the only group within the new government disciplined enough to prepare a comprehensive program for restructuring Brazilian society. Addressing the problems of the agricultural economy, the lieutenants' program demanded that rural workers be granted the same series of rights and benefits proposed for urban labor, such as mini-

---

54. Ibid., 28. The final quote reads, "despertar-lhes, em suma, o interesse, incutindo-lhes hábitos de atividade e de economia."

55. Collor's tenure as labor minister was influential, controversial, and brief. See Angela de Castro Gomes, *A invenção do trabalhismo* (Rio de Janeiro: Vertice/IUPERJ, 1988), 175–210; and Rosa Maria Araújo, *O batismo do trabalho: Experiência de Lindolfo Collor* (Rio de Janeiro: Civilização Brasileira, 1981). For the rural plan, see Lindolfo Collor, "Relatório ao chefe do govêrno provisório," 6 March 1931, appendixes. Ministério do Trabalho, Indústria e Comércio (MTIC), Lata 46, Fundo da Secretária da Presidência da República, Arquivo Nacional do Brasil (hereafter SPR/AN).

mum wages, compensation for unwarranted dismissal, and unions. The lieutenants also argued that rural workers deserved the right to share in both profits and control of the plantations where they worked.[56]

São Paulo became a test site for the *tenente* program, much to the dismay of the *paulistas,* especially those who had supported the October revolt expecting increased state autonomy, not less. PD leaders were dismayed when Vargas chose João Alberto Lins de Barros as state intervenor rather than one of their peers. As a *tenente,* João Alberto not only advocated the club's program of economic and social reform but also expressed resentment toward the *paulistas.* As a native of Pernambuco state, he, like many others from the northeast, believed São Paulo treated his region in imperialistic fashion, draining it of workers and raw materials, forcing residents to buy *paulista* manufactured goods, as if the northeast was a colony to São Paulo's "mother country." At the start of 1931, João Alberto issued a decree establishing a social services agency for the rural poor, many of them northeastern migrants. *Paulista* concerns were heightened when Miguel Costa, João Alberto's security chief, established the Revolutionary League to marshal working-class support for the intervenor. Even more irritating to coffee planters was a decree reorganizing the coffee institute, a state agency created in 1924 to guide the industry, placing it under the intervenor's personal control.[57]

Rural Workers in the 1932 Constitutionalist Rebellion

As it happened, these measures did little to excite the support of working people and much to galvanize *paulista* opposition to Vargas and his regime. Recent antagonists found they hated *tenente* rule more than each other. By July, the state's leaders had forced João Alberto to resign, and Vargas was struggling to repair relations with former allies in the state. He appointed a *paulista* as intervenor and promised to call elections for representatives to a constituent as-

56. Michael L. Conniff, "The Tenentes in Power: A New Perspective on the Brazilian Revolution of 1930," *Journal of Latin American Studies* 10:1 (1977): 61–82. Clube 3 de Outubro, *Esboço do programa de reconstrução política e social do Brasil* (1932), cited in Camargo, "A questão agrária," 135–36. Fausto, *A revolução de 1930,* 56–84, challenges the sincerity of the *tenentes.*

57. Jordan M. Young, *The Brazilian Revolution of 1930 and the Aftermath* (New Brunswick: Rutgers University Press, 1967), 85; Love, *São Paulo in the Brazilian Federation,* 119; and Font, *Coffee, Contention, and Change,* 72–77, 266.

sembly. But Vargas dragged his feet, and in February 1932, São Paulo Republicans and Democrats overcame their differences to form a united front in support of a rapid return to constitutional government. In May, Vargas finally scheduled elections for representatives to a constituent assembly. But the *paulista* elite distrusted him and fomented rebellion, building popular support for an armed revolt in the name of constitutionalism, a synonym for greater state's rights and less federal interference in their affairs.

On July 9, the *paulistas* appointed their own governor, declared themselves in opposition to the central government, and, mobilizing a force of more than one hundred thousand men, adopted a defensive military strategy, stationing troops along São Paulo's borders. Various factors weakened the rebels' chances. Like their planter forefathers, who resisted independence wars in the early nineteenth century fearing they might inspire a slave rebellion, the state's modern landlord class avoided actions that might similarly stir up urban militants. As the British consul reported, the *paulista* rebels, "obsessed with a fear of a communist uprising," recruited combatants primarily among interior residents. Apparently, they feared irritating their own number as well. The U.S. military attaché in São Paulo reported low morale among "young aristocrats" who enlisted with enthusiasm but, "unaccustomed to taking orders," soon "returned to the Paulista capital for a few days of rest and recreation," suffering no penalties for abandoning the front. Recruitment thus focused on working people in interior towns. In São Carlos, Ribeirão Preto, and other sizable towns in the coffee growing regions, monuments list the names of hundreds of local citizens who gave their lives for the cause of planter autonomy from the Vargas government. By September, when the uprising ended, total casualties were estimated at 2,100 killed and 7,600 wounded, making the 1932 conflict far bloodier than the 1930 revolt, in which there had been two thousand total casualties.[58]

Anecdotal information shows a curious pattern in the response of two agro-industrial workers from the interior. In Barretos, the *caboclo* Irineu Luís de Moraes responded favorably to the call of the constitutionalists. While in Batatais, Arlindo Teixeira, the son of Portuguese coffee *colonos,* did not join in. As a *camarada,* Moraes benefited from personal relations with landowners and overseers such as Bonifácio Ferreira, and the old order may have seemed preferable to the disruptive forces of change unleashed by economic depression and

---

58. Young, *The Brazilian Revolution,* 86; Love, *São Paulo in the Brazilian Federation,* 120–21; and Walker, "From Coronelismo to Populism," 148–52.

Vargas. As a *colono,* Teixeira had experienced recent events differently. The 1929 crash halved his family's earnings and forced them to give up the *colonato* and move to town, where they sought odd jobs. Eventually, Teixeira became a carpenter and returned to work as a skilled *camarada* on a number of plantations. The dependency and instability of the old order held no special charms for his family. Despite their contrasting responses to the planters' 1932 revolt, both men would soon join forces as Communist rural labor organizers.[59]

Moraes remembers his involvement in the revolt with vivid detail. He was working in a smokehouse when the movement began and recalls that he joined the revolt not for ideological reasons but because the talk of revolution excited him. "It was a thing I grabbed out of the air; given my vivacity and desires, I just signed up." Transferred to the border with Minas Gerais, along the banks of the Mogi Guaçu River, he exchanged gunfire with government troops and dodged "pineapples" (grenades) dropped from enemy planes. Only here did he begin to notice that the officers of his battalion were all planters and ranchers from Barretos. As in the case of his experience with Lieutenant Colonel Carvalho, he remembers overhearing conversations among officers that turned him against the movement:

> —No, but Getúlio is a Communist, one of them said.
> —Where did you ever see such a confused government? responded another.
> —Where is it that a rural laborer gets fifteen vacation days, like Vargas proposes?
> —It doesn't make any sense.

As in his tale of militancy on the Moreira ranch in 1930, Moraes spread the word to his fellow soldiers, raising their consciousness: this is a revolution against Vargas! "It was an armed movement to overthrow Getúlio and return to that which existed before 1930. They were against Vargas because he brought labor law, vacations, and the vote for women. Getúlio brought lots of things the planters didn't want. I listened to them complain about the intentions of the government . . . [and after awhile] about twenty soldiers and I decided to abandon that nonsense." Soon after he organized this desertion, "everyone was abandoning" the revolution. The whole thing was over in two or so months, he explained.

59. Welch and Geraldo, *Lutas camponesas,* 40–43; and Arlindo Teixeira, transcript of interview by author, Ribeirão Preto, 18 October 1988.

More than fifty years after the revolt, Moraes placed himself in the pivotal position of having unmasked the movement's reactionary character and exposed this fact to the troops, who then abandoned the field of combat, causing the movement to collapse. This episode, like other incidents he recounts, has an upbeat, empowering quality to it that transcends errors in fact. As he claims, the struggle pitted the old order against the government of Vargas, which stood for limited progressive reforms. But few of the measures Moraes mentioned had in fact become law—literate women, for example, gained the franchise only after the revolt was settled—and the extension of national labor laws to rural workers would be decades in coming. This raises questions about the importance of such policies to both planter-officers and worker-soldiers. In contradistinction to Moraes, most historians agree that the revolt had more to do with *paulista* hostility toward the centralizing trends of the new government, and when peace was negotiated at the end of September, the Vargas government was magnanimous in holding few accountable and in granting São Paulo greater autonomy. Nevertheless, Moraes's recollections show how the event was processed and remembered by grassroots militants; this memory—though mythic—was to shape future struggle in the countryside.[60]

The 1932 revolt symbolized the desperation of São Paulo's leaders to retain their status as rulers of their state, if not the entire nation. From World War I on, economic, demographic, and political change had assaulted their world, destabilizing the large-scale coffee industry on which their power was based. As the state's frontiers were settled, its land exhausted, and its trees and individuals aged, change inevitably came to the landlords' world. An influx of immigrant rural workers refused to accept an order based on slavery, and they grasped every opportunity to expand their freedom from dependency on the planters. As coffee prices rose and fell and retiring planters sold off tired lands, those who could bought them up. Where entrepreneurs created urban job opportunities, workers flocked to them, especially the Brazilian-born *camaradas,* who rarely enjoyed the acquisitive arrangements of land usufruct and contracts that immigrants gained as a right of passage to Brazil. The increasing diversification of the econ-

60. On myth verses reality in oral testimony, see Samuel and Thompson, eds., *Myths We Live By.* São Paulo's revolt is discussed in Castro Gomes, "Confronto e compromisso no processo de constitucionalização," 7–74; Angela Maria de Castro Gomes, Lúcia Lahmeyer Lobo, and Rodrigo Bellingrodt Marques Coelho, "Revolução e restauração: A experiência paulista no período da constitucionalização," in *Regionalismo e centralização política: Partidos e constituinte nos anos 30,* edited by Castro Gomes (Rio de Janeiro: Nova Fronteira, 1980), 237–337; Love, *São Paulo in the Brazilian Federation,* 240; and Walker, "From Coronelismo to Populism," 147–53.

omy, both in rural and urban contexts, fragmented the ruling class and dissembled their vision of progress. Ideological differences grew, and so did opposition groups who appealed to constituencies much broader than the traditional electorate of propertied men. These elite struggles opened channels for popular mobilization and protest. Although weak and ultimately ineffective, the movements signaled a shift toward populist politics, first in the city and then in the country. Rural workers had a difficult row to hoe as they sought fertile soil for their own political participation. The ruling class was committed to controlling their participation, and following the 1932 revolt, they tried to maintain a united front in this regard at least, letting few rural worker demands concern them as they composed rural labor policy.

2

Row upon row of leafy, dark green coffee trees followed the rolling contours of south-central Brazil. Each winter they yielded a rich harvest of plump shiny red fruit. Nearly every cherry and its precious seed had a long journey ahead as it was pitted, dried, shipped, roasted, ground, packaged, and brewed in a relentless series of steps taking it from the fields of Brazil to the suburban breakfast nooks and lunchroom coffee pots of the United States. At the start of this process was someone like João Francisco Thomaz, a self-described "agricultural worker" (*operário agrícola*), who cultivated twenty-three thousand coffee trees on the Fazenda Boa Vista in 1932 and 1933.

We know about Thomaz, unlike so many thousands of other agricultural workers, because he complained in writing when the owner of the plantation where he worked

BREAKING GROUND

Becoming a Bureaucratic Problem

treated him unfairly. As he explained in a 1934 letter to President Getúlio Vargas, the planter offered Thomaz no credit or payment even though he had delivered cartload upon cartload of harvested cherries for processing. In effect, the *fazenda* had robbed him, or so Thomaz claimed. He protested to Vargas that he had been victimized out of vengeance, because "I am always helping those who are loyal to you," while the planter always criticized the chief executive.

To confront the thieving planter, Thomaz sought the assistance of the local arbitration commission, but it claimed to lack authority to resolve rural labor complaints, and Thomaz's case was not heard. Although Thomaz probably had a contract to work the coffee and so had rights to sue the planter in court under the Brazilian Civil Code, Thomaz writes that the chief of the arbitration commission advised him to form a "league of workers" to pressure the planters to change their "barbarous" practices. So inspired, Thomaz agitated among the other workers and continued to confront *fazenda* managers until they evicted him from his plantation residence and kicked him off the property. Homeless and unemployed, he wrote Vargas personally, seeking assistance and urging the government to issue a rural labor code or statute, as "a clarification of our rights . . . , our duties, and how to proceed to act in accordance with [Vargas's] opinion." [1]

In his appeal, Thomaz addressed Vargas as the "precious chief and great [*grandiozicimo*] compatriot" of "mere laborers and the poor." He looked to Vargas for rules to live by, as children might turn to their father for guidelines and structure. Thomaz's choice of words and the characteristics he ascribed to Vargas must have pleased the president, for he, more than any Brazilian leader since the monarchs of the nineteenth century, sought to achieve a popular identity as "father of the poor." Thomaz's language shows how the discourse of the revolutionary administration of 1930 influenced his appeal and perhaps his thought. Vargas represented himself as a spokesman for the people (*o povo*), and Thomaz sought to generalize from his own case. When he expressed his demand for "a clarification of *our* rights . . . *our* duties," he broadened his personal misfortune to embrace other rural workers. His letter sought to represent a group rather than an individual appeal. As Vargas had addressed "the agricultural working class," Thomaz had adopted a class identity.

1. João Francisco Thomaz to Vargas, Processo No. (PR) 1926/34, 7 June 1934, MTIC, Lata 47, SPR/AN. (My thanks to Joel Wolfe for introducing me to this archive.)

Thomaz's letter was one among hundreds of pleas from rural workers and peasants that were submitted to Vargas between 1930 and 1945 and retained in the Brazilian national archives. Many contain heart-wrenching stories of brutality, dispossession, and destitution recounted in humble yet demanding tones. Written by rural workers and peasants or by intermediaries such as professional scribes, the letters to Vargas reveal a rural population informed about national politics and anxiously awaiting promised change in the countryside to match that in the city. On one level, the letters are consistent with appeals to authority throughout time: the clever prince has always known the wisdom of leaving a door open to his subjects, has always understood the authority-confirming value of a display of individual generosity and kindness. On another level, they reveal the unique discourse of Vargas's outreach to the Brazilian working classes and the peculiar dilemmas of the administration's efforts to reform rural society.

Although the appeals had no direct, formal connection to the development of rural labor policy, they helped break the ground during the late 1930s and early 1940s, preparing it for the seeds of rural unionization. Constituting the most immediate and vivid expression of rural worker concerns available to the administration as it initiated rural labor reform, the letters helped establish rural labor relations as a problem and provided a pretense for bureaucratic action. A desire to "satisfy" the "repeated and insistent appeals, requests, and queries arriving from . . . peasant laborers" influenced the president's Special Study Commission for Rural Syndicalization, which drafted the 1944 rural syndicalization decree.[2] As bureaucrats probed the inner life of Brazilian plantations and considered rearranging the relationship between workers and bosses, they encountered significant resistance from planters. By 1945, when Vargas was forced from power, what remained of this discussion was a revoked rural unionization law, a controversial organizational structure for rural employers, and a few rural labor laws. As long as reform depended on the idealism of elites rather than the real stimulus of a mobilized pressure group, meaningful change remained unlikely. As Thomaz had written, taking his lead from a government official, such laws would only prove influential once rural workers were organized to take advantage of them.

2. "O problema da sindicalização rural," *A Lavoura* (official journal of the Rio de Janeiro–based SNA) (April–June 1943), 4.

Handling Rural Worker Appeals

Given the variety of agrarian practices in Brazil and the diverse social origins of workers, the shaping of rural working-class identity was complicated and difficult. This is underscored by Thomaz's willingness to assume this identity when many would question his own status as a worker. Even the largest *colono* families rarely had the capability to care for more than eight thousand trees annually.[3] Thomaz, on the other hand, took responsibility for nearly three times that many trees, claiming to have counted on the help of four other families and two employees with the harvest. During the two-year period of his contract with the *fazenda,* he must have had significant help cultivating and weeding so many trees. His capable penmanship and syntax also challenge his self-ascribed identity as one among many "mere laborers" at a time when four out of ten landlords and nine of ten rural workers could neither read nor write.[4] In fact, it seems clear that Thomaz was of some middling class, neither a *colono* nor a plantation owner but a subcontractor (*empreteiro*) hired to organize the labor—and perhaps the capital—necessary to care for a vast number of trees.

Although Thomaz's letter, one of the earliest rural epistles found in the archive, clearly shows that the regime's populist rhetoric reached into the countryside, it also shows how ambiguously that message was received. Vargas claimed to be concerned about the "man of the country" (*homem do campo*). But was this man a peon, *colono, empreteiro,* planter, or all these and more? More striking still was the administration's response to Thomaz: don't worry, they said;

---

3. Holloway's *Immigrants on the Land* contains a clear description of the development of the labor process on coffee plantations. As he notes, the work of cultivating and harvesting trees was influenced significantly by the particular environmental and botanical features of the coffee trees themselves. In order to be the most fruitful, the base around each tree needed to be carefully cleared of weeds and grass through an operation known as the *carpa*. Despite the availability of machines, the *carpa* was mainly done by hand with a hoe (*enxada*) five times a year. Planters calculated that a single worker could care for two to three thousand trees a year. Depending on the size of a *colono* family, the age and gender of the children, and the fitness of each member, planters determined how many thousands of trees they could be contracted to treat (*trato*). Each family, as represented by the adult male, was to be paid a prearranged annual wage for each thousand trees. Whereas the *trato* required constant and consistent attention around the year, the harvest season occurred once a year between the months of May and September. During this time, even more workers were required to strip the cherries from the trees (*apanha*), clean them of twigs and leaves, and carry them to the processing plant where they were pulped, dried, hulled, and sacked for shipment (28–33).

4. Evaristo Leitão, Romulo Cavina, and João Soares Palmeira, *O trabalhador rural brasileiro* (Rio de Janeiro: Departamento de Estatística e Publicidade, MTIC, 1937), 75–76.

we're already drafting legislation to regulate rural labor.[5] It was true that labor minister Lindolfo Collor had drafted a plan for forming rural *sindicatos* in 1930 and that the 1934 constitution and enabling legislation included references to rural labor, but decades would pass before the ambiguities were resolved and the question of the legal rights and duties of the different parties had been clarified.

Until the 1940s when the administration finally began to generate a series of specific rural labor policies, most problems were dealt with haphazardly, with varied results for workers. It would be fair to say that most rural workers were forced to accommodate their exploitation, at least in the short term, resisting prolonged abuse by fleeing bad situations in search of slight improvements in wages and conditions within the national labor market. Some rural workers sought remedies with local authorities, in the courts, or—like Thomaz—through various channels ending with a direct appeal to the president. Each query sent to Vargas started an inquiry (*processo*) and opened a file. Down through the hierarchy of the bureaucracy to the local level, assistant ministers and local inspectors were asked to evaluate the merits of the worker's complaint, elaborate a case history, and make recommendations for Vargas's response. Despite the formality of official process, four out of five São Paulo rural workers and peasants who sent letters received curt notes from Vargas's secretary, José de Queiroz Lima, denying them assistance.

In contrast to Thomaz's eloquent letter, Benedito Camilo da Silva's 1935 letter to Vargas was so illegible that the president's secretary was unable to either route it or respond.[6] Silva's evidence, sent to document his indecipherable appeal for assistance, was routinely filed away. The evidence consisted of his *cadernetas agrícolas* for the years 1931 to 1935, a period in which he worked as a coffee and cotton *colono* on three plantations in the state of São Paulo. We can only speculate that Silva believed he had been inadequately compensated for his labor. It is also probable that he either trusted Vargas or saw the president as his last recourse, for his *cadernetas* must have been among his most precious possessions; without them he could have no case whatsoever. By sending them to Vargas, he surrendered his most valuable weapon to the "father of the poor."

Many rural workers turned to Vargas when their own patron

<hr>

5. Director General of the Secretaria de Estado dos Negócios do Trabalho, Indústria, e Comércio to Sr. Dr. Ronald de Carvalho, Secretária da Chefia do Govêrno Provisório, 28 June 1934, in PR 1926/34 MTIC, SPR/AN.

6. PR 13024/35, 8 October 1935, Ministério da Agricultura, Lata 29, SPR/NA.

abused them or violated their sense of justice. The coffee *colono* José Dário de Oliveira provides a case in point.[7] In 1940, after thirteen years of "obedient and thorough service" on the Fazenda São José in São José do Rio Preto, São Paulo, Oliveira wrote the president to complain about his boss. Contracting a scribe in Rio de Janeiro, the illiterate Oliveira was described as "one of the most humble of thousands of miserable pariahs that permeate the coffee *fazendas* of São Paulo." Informed that Vargas "had done much to benefit laborers," Oliveira hoped the president would defend him in a dispute with his former employer. In brief, Oliveira had contracted Chagas's disease (*molestia*), and it had caused him to fall behind in his work. The manager drove him off the plantation, confiscated his belongings, and withheld pay for his labor on three thousand coffee trees and unnumbered rows of corn. Following the orders of the plantation's "Syrian" owner, Moisés Miguel Haddad, the "perverse and barbarous" manager left Oliveira and his loved ones without clothes, cookery, and beds, "leaving a Brazilian family in a complete state of nature."

The administration jumped into this dispute, asking the Rio Preto district attorney to investigate and assigning a regional labor inspector to follow the progress of the case. After an inquiry in which Haddad, his manager, and Oliveira were interviewed, the majority of the *colono*'s belongings were returned to him. From start to finish, the case took a remarkably brief seven months. Oliveira, a migrant from the northeastern state of Bahia, nevertheless expressed displeasure with the outcome since a third of his possessions remained in Haddad's hands, and no compensation was offered for the coffee and corn he and his family had labored to produce. Despite this egregious oversight—one responded to with silence, as if to turn one's back on an ingrate—the intervention of the Vargas administration certainly left Oliveira better off than he would have been otherwise.

Of the complaints from agricultural workers to Vargas that tended to receive positive results, the majority were those of *colonos,* sharecroppers, tenants, and others who could document that they had been underpaid. Quite often, these cases were resolved administratively following a simple inquiry from the president's office. The case of José Dario de Oliveira, discussed above, exemplifies this tendency. By the late 1950s, when labor courts had opened in various rural districts, the vast majority of complaints filed by farmworkers

7. Oliveira to Vargas, 3 June 1940, PR 12437/40, MTIC, Lata 205, SPR/AN.

concerned wages, and court officials reconciled the parties to help them arrive at a settlement.[8]

Vargas presented himself as Brazil's superpatriarch, using an interventionist bureaucracy to restructure existing patriarchal systems. Sensing this, fathers turned to Vargas in desperation when they could no longer care for their families and uphold their own authority. Stricken by epilepsy, Miguel Turato, a lifelong rural laborer in São Paulo and the father of seven children, wrote asking for support from the state.[9] Appealing for Vargas's empathy, Turato trusted that the president cared about the "well-being of Brazilian citizens." As the "father of a country," Vargas would understand the pain Turato felt at his inability to provide for his children, especially the two who were also epileptic. But the ministries of labor and agriculture both claimed the case was outside their jurisdiction. The president's secretary considered no more alternatives and rejected the rural worker's request.

Since Turato was evidently too needy to help himself, and since his appeal to nationalism was not enhanced by a foreign exploiter, as Oliveira's complaint had been, Vargas ignored him. For those anxious to work but prevented from doing so by a lack of opportunity, Vargas tended to be more supportive. When a destitute Maria Bernadeth Castelo Branco wrote the president in 1937 asking for his help in paying for her family's trip from the northeastern state of Maranhão to São Paulo, seven one-way boat tickets to the state's port of entry, Santos, were provided.[10] Even though she was not a man, and her family was nontraditional—consisting of herself, her sister, and her five nephews—the government did not hesitate to honor her request. In her letter, Castelo Branco used jargon that recalled Vargas's public pronouncements. She called herself humble and fragile but "desperate to work for our prosperity and the enrichment of our fatherland."[11] She further elucidated her aspiration to work in São Paulo, which, unlike Maranhão, was the "land of industry, of labor, of progress."

Whether or not Castelo Branco chose her words intentionally,

8. Troy Spruit, "Ribeirão Preto Labor Court Analysis" (Grand Valley State University, 14 April 1993), mimeograph in author's possession.

9. "Central to Vargas's program of modernization and political centralization was the gradual expansion of the notion of public interest to encompass realms that had previously been regarded as private (thus helping to usurp the power of the rural oligarchy while establishing government control over the rising urban masses)." Susan K. Besse, *Restructuring Patriarchy: The Modernization of Gender Inequality in Brazil, 1914–1940* (Chapel Hill: University of North Carolina Press, 1996), 3–4. For Miguel Turato, see PR 12191/40, 25 May 1940, MTIC, Lata 207, SRP/AN.

10. PR 29603/37, MTIC (129), SPR/AN.

11. PR 29603/37, MTIC, SPR/AN.

her letter rang the right bells in Cateté Palace, Brazil's equivalent of the White House. Here were seven Brazilian nationals who had inculcated the desire to work and who wanted to enter the starved São Paulo farm labor market. Upon their arrival in Santos, the family was to be transported to the interior to work on one of the state's coffee plantations.

While the complaints of peasants fared a little better than those of rural workers, they too looked to Vargas to fulfill his promise of change. But the radical agrarian reform promised in 1930 became, in practice, a means of shifting human beings from poor agricultural zones and overcrowded urban centers to frontier regions. The most outstanding example of this was the Westward March (Marcha Para Oeste), organized in the 1940s to encourage migration to typically underfunded agricultural colonies in the northwest.[12] In regions that were not overcrowded or remote, Vargas's actions differed substantially. In São Paulo, where commercial cotton, sugar, and coffee farming predominated and export markets were within easy reach, peasants who took Vargas's promise of radical agrarian reform at face value met with disappointment. Dozens wrote the president in search of secure land titles.

In one case, Marciano Martins Nantes, an illiterate spokesman for twenty families of self-described *caboclos,* traveled more than six hundred miles to try to see Vargas personally. Hat in hand, he waited around Cateté Palace in Rio de Janeiro only to be told that the president was at his summer residence in Petrópolis.[13] Frustrated, Nantes returned home where he hired an intermediary to write his plea. In an April 1941 letter, Nantes explained that for a period of fifteen years, he and his fellow *caboclos* had cleared and cultivated an area of unsettled land near Presidente Prudente known as Fazenda Santa Guilhermina. Then, suddenly and inexplicably, engineer Eugenio Iecca appeared, surveyed the land, and declared Nantes and his neighbors trespassers. Nantes disputed this claim in court, but after eight months no decision had been reached, and the peasants faced expulsion from their land and homes.

Before Vargas responded, the court ruled against the Nantes collective. It said the land they had turned valuable with their sweat and toil belonged to someone else. Titled originally in 1854, the land passed through various hands until Nantes filed his case. Informed of the case, a descendant of the title holder decided to assert her inher-

    12. Alcir Lenharo, *Sacralização da política* (Campinas: Papírus, 1986).
    13. PR 13859/41, Secretaria da Justiça e Negócios do Interior do Estado de São Paulo, Lata 388, SPR/AN.

ited property rights rather than see the land turned over to Nantes or the state (as *terras devolutas*). As Nantes describes it, the peasants were violently kicked off the land by police and *capangas,* their homes torn down, their livestock killed, and their crops burned.

Sent a year later, Vargas's response carried, like all the others, the signature of Queiroz Lima. Cordial and brief, Queíroz Lima merely reiterated the court's decision. Through Nantes we learn that Vargas's idea of radical agrarian reform was very different from that envisioned by smallholders in São Paulo. In practice, usage rights were not nearly as important as the rights of the bureaucracy. The president seems never to have used his powers to overturn an earlier administrative ruling. Moreover, if the courts were involved, the secretary typically noted the president's inability to intervene in the judicial process.

Despite Vargas's dispassionate handling of these cases, his policy did not always favor the powerful at the expense of the weak. In 1942, for example, the manager of 11,283 acres of land near Santo Anastácio, São Paulo, complained that the state had unjustly acquired the area, and Vargas ordered a routine inquiry.[14] The government's title search found that no one had ever bought the land from the state. Federal authorities affirmed the state's decision: the land had been contracted to the manager, Elias Nascimento, by the Emprêsa Colonizadora "Irmãs Teixeira" on the basis of a false title. In this case and others, the Vargas administration defended procedure, regulation, and precedent, even if it meant disappointment for large interests such as Nascimento and the colonization company he represented. Largely concerned with establishing the legitimacy and autonomy of the state, Vargas had to confirm the value of the bureaucracy. A government that routinely ignores land titles and rides roughshod over local power structures cannot hope to succeed in fulfilling its programs. Treating precedent capriciously might delegitimate its own initiatives and set them up for reversal once a new government took office.

Incorporating Rural Workers

The Vargas administration's rural labor policy can be seen as a way of gradually inserting the federal government ever more deeply into rural social relations. This was a particularly controversial issue in São

14. PR 32442/42, Secretaria da Justiça e Negócios do Interior do Estado de São Paulo, Lata 388, SPR/AN.

Paulo, where the national government's intervention in both agricultural and industrial policy had contributed to the 1932 revolt. Although the issue was temporarily set aside thereafter, the letters to Vargas show the problems of rural labor had not dwindled. Demands were made on the government, as coffee *empreteiro* Thomaz's 1934 letter shows, to present a package of rights and duties that asserted Vargas's notion of how rural society should work. But the anti-statist tradition remained strong in the countryside, as did the custom of viewing coffee planters as master of their own domains. While the administration continued to assert its authority in the nascent industrial sector, with mixed results, its influence in the established Brazilian agricultural sector was minimal during the 1930s.[15] Even in 1937, when Vargas seized dictatorial powers and proclaimed the semifascist Estado Novo (New State), his government hesitated to grab the reins of rural society.

The corporatist 1937 charter, like the 1934 constitution, revealed the government's intent to foster the formation of rural unions. Decree Law No. 24,694 of 12 July 1934 instituted regulations for independent employee syndicates for those "that pursue the same type of agricultural, industrial or commercial activity." Although the decree had no practical effect, the 1937 charter persisted in lumping together agricultural workers with those of other sectors, suggesting the equivalence of all workers under the law. However, article 57 of the charter left room for the development of a unique law for the social organization of agriculture, and the legislature chose to interpret it that way. Thus, when a unionization law was decreed (Decree Law No. 1,402 of 5 July 1939), it specifically excluded the agrarian sector, stating that "the higher syndical associations of the agricultural and livestock sectors will be organized in conformity with laws that regulate the unionization of these professions." While the exclusion of

15. A lively debate continues among historians regarding the government's assistance to industrial workers during the 1930s. Scholars differ in their opinions regarding the extent to which Vargas's policies helped or hindered the effectiveness of labor unions as working-class organizations. The balance of evidence, if not opinion, supports those who claim Vargas's reforms—if unintentionally—helped workers. Some interesting and informed discussions can be found in John D. French, "The Origin of Corporatist State Intervention in Brazilian Industrial Relations, 1930–1934: A Critique of the Literature," *Luso-Brazilian Review* 28:2 (1991), 13–26; Castro Gomes, *A invenção do trabalhismo*; John D. French, *The Brazilian Workers' ABC: Class Conflict and Alliance in Modern São Paulo* (Chapel Hill: University of North Carolina Press, 1992); Wolfe, *Working Women, Working Men*; Yousef Cohen, *The Manipulation of Consent* (Pittsburgh: University of Pittsburgh Press, 1990); and Barbara Weinstein, *For Social Peace in Brazil: Industrialists and the Remaking of the Working Class in São Paulo, 1920–1964* (Chapel Hill: University of North Carolina Press, 1996).

rural workers continued, the issue would not die. In fact, it is clear that numerous agricultural leaders wanted a law for the sector that would enable it to be more connected to the state and thus more influential in national politics.[16] In the meantime, the social legislation committee of the federal house of representatives (*deputados*) commissioned a detailed study on rural laborers nationally. Published in 1937 by the labor ministry, the report contained elaborate wage and price statistics and specific recommendations for change.[17]

Although it is doubtful that rural workers read such reports, the letters rural workers wrote to Vargas show that ruling-class debate over the state's role in the countryside inspired individual workers to seek justice by writing to Vargas. Collective actions were either less frequent, unrecorded, or remain hidden in untapped archives. One event that surfaced during the research for this book demonstrates how workers in factories that processed agricultural products perceived of themselves as beneficiaries of the reforms and managed to prevent at least one rural worker from being excluded from the law.

In 1937, Irineu Luís de Moraes used his leadership of an agro-industrial syndicate to help an individual who had been defined as a rural worker in order to deny him the benefits of the law.[18] Moraes, who had joined the PCB soon after the confusion of the 1932 rebellion, was then president of the Professional Association of Laborers in the Cotton Seed Oil Fabrication Industry in Araraquara, a bustling agricultural town on São Paulo's central plateau. Even though the union was still awaiting official recognition from the government of its right to represent oil workers, Moraes risked using the organization to help a truck driver at the sugar mill, Usina Itaquerê. Federal labor law discouraged workers from forming organizations across industrial categories; one union could not service both oil processors and sugar mill hands. Despite the law and the precarious legality of the association itself, Moraes and the executive committee called a meeting of the membership and requested their support when the troubled worker approached him for help. Although the case put the union in conflict with one of the region's most powerful men—the Comendador Paulo Reis Magalhães, a statesman, cattle rancher, coffee planter,

16. The two decree laws are quoted in Pericles Madureira de Pinho, *O problema da sindicalização rural* (Rio de Janeiro: n.p.), 90, 94. Pinho, a young, educated, sugar producer from Bahia, expressed the enthusiasm of several planters for his class's incorporation under the law. How this should occur and how they saw it affecting farmworkers is further elaborated below.

17. Leitão et al., *O trabalhador.*

18. The following case is based on the account in Welch and Geraldo, *Lutas camponesas no interior paulista*, 49–55.

and owner of the Usina Itaquerê—members refused to appreciate formal distinctions between categories of workers and approved the union's involvement in the case.

The truck driver, his name now forgotten, had long worked for Magalhães when he was fired. To avoid regulations governing the dismissal of industrial employees, the mill designated the man an agricultural worker. According to the law, industrial workers had rights to annual paid vacations, prior notice of dismissal, and indemnity payments in cases of failure to fulfill these obligations, yet rural workers shared none of these benefits. Arguing the man had been wronged by denying him the status of industrial worker, the union sent a letter of complaint to the state labor department. Eventually a meeting was set up between the union and a state labor representative, Coutinho Sampaio Viana; the mill manager, Miguel Escavandela; and, of all people, the Comendador himself.

Seizing this unique opportunity to directly confront a powerful employer, Moraes encouraged a number of union members to attend in order to increase the pressure to settle in the employee's favor. Greeted by a crowd, the planter and his party tried to maintain authority by taking control of the meeting. Viana read the union's letter aloud and denied its allegations point by point. Satisfied with their presentation, Viana and Magalhães were preparing to leave the union hall when Moraes accosted them. "What's this!?" he asked. "Where do you think you're going?" Shocked by Moraes's bluntness, Viana defended himself by pulling rank: "Don't you know who you're dealing with?" he asked, for the Comendador was no common man. "Yes," said Moraes, "and he's the one I want to talk to." Laying out the case, Moraes claims to have silenced Viana and taken charge of the proceedings. When he was finished, Magalhães refused to acknowledge the merits of the complaint and agreed that it could only be resolved in court. Guarding his composure, he and the others left the union hall.

Soon afterward, a messenger arrived to ask Moraes to come quickly to meet the Comendador at his hotel. At the meeting, Magalhães offered to pay the truck driver what he asked in order to avoid further complications. This outcome was a great victory for the union and served as a catalyst for its involvement in numerous and varied complaints. It remained on Moraes's mind as a lesson of how powerful working-class organizations could be, and it also revealed the transition then unfolding in the rural social relations of São Paulo: workers who demanded respect now stood a chance of receiving dignified treatment, especially if they were organized.

The "Planter Clan"

For a variety of reasons—many related to the varied pressures of World War II—the early 1940s proved a propitious moment for Vargas to renew his effort to formally incorporate rural society. In May 1941, Vargas turned a spotlight on the "man of the country." Speaking at Rio de Janeiro's vast Vasco da Gama soccer stadium, Vargas revealed his preoccupation with the problems of rural workers to an audience of urban workers. He announced the government's intention to see that agricultural workers enjoyed the same structural and social improvements his administration had worked to make available to industrial and commercial workers since 1930.

> But our task is not yet finished. We have to confront, coura-
> geously, serious problems of the betterment of our people, in
> order that comfortable living conditions, education, and good
> hygiene shall not become the privileged situation of a few re-
> gions or zones. The benefits that you have conquered must be
> extended to rural workers, to those who, isolated in the back-
> lands, live far from the advantages of civilization. Moreover, if
> we do not take this step, we will run the risk of stimulating
> the exodus of the countryside and the overpopulation of our
> cities—causing an imbalance with unpredictable consequences,
> capable of diluting or annulling the effects of our campaign for
> the integral valorization of our people, to endow them with eco-
> nomic vigor, physical health, and productive energy.

Vargas was a clever orator. He spoke to the sense of justice and fairness of his audience as well as to their fears. His speech warned urban workers that if the standard of living in the countryside did not parallel that in the city, urban workers could expect to see their conditions worsen through competition from the in-migration of rural workers. Potential rural flight, Vargas said, threatened the government's goal of economically and physically strengthening the working class in order to enhance national productivity.[19]

19. Speech from Getúlio Vargas, *A nova política do Brasil,* vol. 3 (Rio de Janeiro: José Olympio, 1940), 255–63. In outlining the benefits won for urban labor, Vargas specified the creation of the labor department (Ministério do Trabalho, Indústria e Comércio); job preference to Brazilian nationals (*lei dos dois terços*); unions; social security; regulated industrial hours; standardized wage scales for women and children ("a regulamentação do salariado de mulheres e menores"); paid vacations; medical assistance; cafeterias (*restaurantes populares*); and the minimum wage (260). In an early part of the speech, Vargas announced the institution of the Justiça do Trabalho (261). This department of the judiciary eventually became an important instrument by which to achieve the objective of extending Brazilian labor law in rural areas.

A high-level conference on social legislation was held two weeks following the speech. In it, labor ministry officials, lawyers, and planters debated the extension of industrial labor law to agricultural workers. To many planters, Brazil's true vocation was agriculture, and urban industry introduced alien values, especially class relations. In the developing corporatist system of industrial relations, workers and bosses were required to define their own separate interests and, in the process of defending them before state mediators, both parties were to compromise in identifying their common interests. Landlords feared this system would stimulate class struggle in the countryside where, according to them, intimate relations between workers and bosses erased class barriers. They refused to see paternalism as an incipient system of class relations. Only syndicates that teamed planters and their workers in unitary interest groups gained support among landlords. But officials strenuously objected to this idea because it would have legitimized traditional rural social relations, strengthening agrarian elites who questioned Vargas's power and economic vision.[20]

Participants of the First Brazilian Social Rights Congress included São Paulo coffee planters and spokesmen for the powerful SRB, João C. Fairbancks and Francisco Malta Cardoso; and Pericles Madureira de Pinho, a lawyer and polemicist with links to sugarcane growers and millers in the northeast state of Bahia. Although they argued against the application of urban labor laws in the countryside, they did not oppose the concept of incorporating rural society within the Estado Novo's corporatist structure. Meeting in São Paulo for a week, these men joined other social reformers in the debate of a wide array of issues related to the corporatist reorganization of the Brazilian political economy. Agreeing that "rational" social organization was fundamental to Brazil's economic progress, they made their contributions in a cooperative rather than confrontational tone. Because the congress had been called by the Vargas regime, contributors concerned themselves with refining the corporatist system rather than criticizing it. "In an era so rich and abundant in social legislation applicable to urban commercial and industrial activities," Fairbancks asked, "why is it that so few laws, almost none apparently, have been made for the benefit of agricultural activity?"[21]

20. Contributions to the debate can be found in Instituto de Direito Social, *Anais do Primeiro Congresso Brasileiro de Direito Social*, 4 vols. (Rio de Janeiro: Serviço de Estatistico da Previdência e Trabalho, 1943–45). The conference is discussed in Clifford A. Welch, "Rural Labor and the Brazilian Revolution in São Paulo, 1930–1964" (Ph.D. diss., Duke University, 1990), 22–38.

21. João C. Fairbancks, "Tese oferecida ao primeiro congresso de direito social," in *Anais*, 3:191.

Agricultural spokesmen argued that the problems of rural society were unique and that problem-solving models developed for urban industrial and commercial society could not be applied to rural areas without careful study and adaptation.[22] Moreover, they took advantage of the ambiguity of Vargas's speech to emphasize general productivity problems rather than the specific problems and conditions of rural laborers. In his speech, Vargas had addressed not only the problems of rural workers (*operários rurais*) but also those of landless peasants (*camponeses sem gleba própria*). For the former, he called for the extension of urban labor law; for the latter, he offered a program of assistance to help them find and develop land in Brazil's considerable western frontier regions. This was part of the Westward March colonization scheme. "It is indispensable to raise the purchasing power of all Brazilians," said Vargas in referring to peasant productivity, "which can only be done by increasing the level of income of rural work."[23] Malta Cardoso and the other planters seized this idea, which Vargas had presented as a motive for stimulating peasant consumption levels, and applied it to plantation agriculture. Thus, the linkage between increasing peasant production and income became an argument for improving plantation productivity as well. In other words, they interpreted Vargas as saying that the critical problem was that of raising *agricultural* income, not necessarily the income of agricultural workers.

With no rural worker representatives on hand to advocate alternative interpretations, these tactics enabled planters to deflect attention from problems within rural society to the outside world. Whereas bottlenecks in industrial activity could be blamed on conflicts between capital and labor, this was not the case for agriculture. According to Fairbancks, the question of social rights was one of resolving the unjust exploitation of agriculture by industrial capitalists, merchants, and other speculators (*maquinistas*). As for inequality between planter and laborer within rural society, its existence was denied. Plantations were "formed through the great solidarity of economic interest and intimate contact between boss and worker." Fairbancks further claimed that far from being poorer than planters, rural workers often had more cash on hand than employers. For Malta Cardoso, coffee workers were not really wage laborers but the planter's

22. Francisco Malta Cardoso, "Aplicação das leis sociais as classes agrarias," *Anais,* 3:220–22.
    23. Vargas, *A nova política do Brasil,* 3:261–62. For a discussion of the marcha, see Lenharo, *Sacralização da política,* 53–74; and Alcir Lenharo, "A terra para quem nela não trabalha," *Revista Brasileira de História* 6:12 (March/August 1986), 47–64.

"work companions" (*companheiros de trabalho*). Moreover, rural labor was only a temporary stage on the road to landholding. "As for the 'rural worker' [*operariado rural*] in Brazil," wrote Fairbancks, "it has to be understood as a provisional situation, a preparatory and provisional status on the road to landowner." Labor laws appeared artificial in this setting; useful legislation was that which made it easier for workers to buy old coffee lands, becoming smallholders available to work on nearby plantations, and for planters to buy frontier territories, where "the tireless national laborer [*baiano*]" could be employed in "the grand spectacle" of founding new plantations.[24]

Planters at the meeting denied the role of market forces on relations between rural owners and workers, emphasizing instead the "convergent and complementary interests" of each.[25] By tying the earnings of both planters and laborers to the successful exploitation of the land, they denied the question of surplus labor expropriation. The planter spokesmen essentially argued that Brazilian agriculture was a hybrid capitalism: "The entire question rests in the 'possibility of economic exploitation' that will assure the boss or employer reasonable profits, capable of allowing each in his turn a portion equivalent to the well-being and security needs of the agrarian laborers and employees."[26] However, this concept did not lead them to argue for the exclusion of rural labor from the corporatist system. Rather, the profound cohesiveness of rural society provided the footing on which they rested an argument for agriculture's inclusion in the corporatist system of representative *sindicatos* established by the Estado Novo.

What concerned São Paulo planters was their perception of a relative lack of influence in the federal government. They did not want to see Vargas's ideas for the organization of rural society put into effect without their voice being heard. Better still, if new agrarian laws were to be decreed, they wanted to write them. Fairbancks protested the exclusion of *paulista* coffee representatives in the drafting of a rural syndicalization scheme that had been composed by planters from the northeast and the SNA, the Rio de Janeiro–based rival to the SRB.[27] "There's only one solution," Fairbancks stated at the congress:

24. Fairbancks, "Tese oferecida," 193–96, 200; and Malta Cardoso, "Aplicação das leis sociais," 214.
25. Fairbancks, "Tese oferecida," 193.
26. Malta Cardoso, "Aplicação das leis sociais," 218.
27. Pinho revealed at the congress that he and Arthur Torres Filho, president of the SNA (founded in 1897), had submitted a proposal regarding the formation of rural unions to the Ministry of Agriculture early in 1941. Although they had yet to receive a response, the fact that the government had asked the SNA rather than the SRB (founded in 1919) to compose a law on this sensitive issue clearly concerned the *paulistas*. For São Paulo coffee planters, agriculture's

"obligatory syndicalization." According to article 140 of the corporatist 1937 charter, all sectors of the economy were to organize themselves into product specific *sindicatos*. Within the agricultural sector, there would be separate syndicates for coffee growers, sugarcane planters, and so on, as well as parallel *sindicatos* of workers in each of these categories. "The *sindicatos* would have active lawyers," Fairbancks explained, "so active and energetic that . . . they will make a big push for the recognition of the *sindicatos* as organs of the state."[28]

In advocating syndical organization for agriculture, Fairbancks offered no reservations about the likelihood of the formation of rural worker *sindicatos*. He either believed his own rhetoric about the tranquillity and consensus of rural society or reasoned that the superior economic strength and organization of owners would guarantee their domination of the agricultural corporation. Quite possibly he envisioned agricultural *sindicatos* that joined both workers and bosses in one union, the so-called *sindicato mixto*. Pinho revealed that the SNA's draft rural syndicalization law followed this design. For balance, the proposed legislation required five members of each category of "employers, employees, and self-employed laborers" (*trabalhadores a conta própria*) to join together before a syndicate could win government recognition. This mixed syndicate would then arbitrate contracts between workers and bosses and between landlords and tenants. "It is that no division exists between rural classes," Pinho explained, coining the term "planter clan" (*clã fazendeiro*) to describe the familial nature of plantation labor relations. He reiterated Fairbanck's argument that agriculture was a victim of banks and speculators; to rebuild agricultural productivity, rural workers and bosses should be allowed to stand together to fight the capitalist pariah. Employers and landlords would lead the clan—a hierarchy the draft law codified by preventing illiterates, naturalized Brazilians, and the foreign born from serving as union officials of any kind. "These circumstances must be taken into consideration for any law that is going to unite in association, *sindicato,* and later in a 'corporation,' the economically debilitated employer and poor, almost starving employees."[29] These agricultural spokesmen seemed to tie their future to mandatory combination with workers.

---

inclusion was not only proceeding slowly but was being influenced by a group they could not accept as representative. Pericles Madureira de Pinho, "Fundamento da organização corporativa das profissões rurais," *Anais,* 4:76–77.

28. Fairbancks, "Tese oferecida," 202.

29. A copy of the draft legislation is printed as "Ante-projeto de decreto-lei para sindicalização rural" in "O problema," 11–30. Pinho quoted from "Fundamento da organização," 77, 79.

Divide, Conquer, and Develop

But it was just this sort of combination—workers in league with a revitalized planter oligarchy—that Vargas seemed most anxious to avoid. Part of the justification for the 1937 coup had included the need to keep rural laborers out of the manipulative hands of demagogues. "The false representation of the great rural mass—living in a near primal state with little comprehension of its rights—had turned frequent, and it had become impossible to counter this through electoral politics. This situation," a policymaker explained, "occasioned the advent of the Estado Novo." By speaking directly to workers at the Vasco da Gama stadium in 1941, Vargas wanted to bypass Communists, Fascists, and the Brazilian landlords, especially São Paulo planters. Similar ideas were behind the "Hour of Brazil" radio program his administration developed and his labor minister, Alexandre Marcondes Filho, used throughout the early 1940s. Talking directly to workers, the minister encouraged them to demand their rights while helping Vargas build a new Brazil by refraining from disruptive behavior such as strikes.[30] For Vargas, change would come not only through unionization but also through rural labor laws—social rights (*direitos sociais*)—that unions would give workers the power to secure.[31]

Vargas had both economic and political agendas behind his program for the reform of rural society. One aimed at stimulating the economy, the other at undermining the power of the planter oligarchy. By introducing measures to partially liberate rural workers from the singular dominance of the planters, he hoped both to stimulate the productive and consumptive capacity of this huge and diverse class and to weaken the hold of landowners on Brazilian agricultural policy. Perceiving this threat to their interests, the coffee planters of São Paulo played a unique role in Vargas's strategy. Their long experience with wage labor and regulation in São Paulo led them to accept the concept of rural labor law, yet their pride and interests led them to fight for laws that posed the least threat to their status and livelihood.[32] Their contest with Vargas began with the May 1941 social

30. Lenharo, *A sacralização da política*, 38–51; and Castro Gomes, *A invenção do trabalhismo*, 257–87. Estado Novo quote from Ben-Hur Raposo, "O problema," 39.

31. On the philosophy of the Brazilian labor justice system, see Waldemar Martins Ferreira, *Princípios de legislação social e direito judiciário do trabalho*, vol. 1 (São Paulo: Editorial Limitada, 1938), 27–57, 99–103; and Evaristo de Moraes Filho, *O problema do sindicato único no Brasil* (São Paulo: Alfa Omega, 1952).

32. On the social question and Brazilian modernization, see Angela Maria de Castro Gomes, Lúcia Lahmeyer Lobo, and Rodrigo Bellingrodt Marques Coelho, *Burguesia e trabalho: Política e legislação social* (Rio de Janeiro: Campus, 1979). On coffee planters and modernization,

rights congress and continued with their participation on two governmental commissions formed to draft rural social legislation. Francisco Malta Cardoso served the coffee planters on both commissions—one of which drew up a general rural code, and the other, a syndicalization law.[33]

In August, Malta Cardoso joined the Special Study Commission for Rural Syndicalization, headed by Arthur Torres Filho, who was president of the venerable SNA and head of the Rural Economy Service (SER, Serviço Economia Rural), an agricultural ministry agency. *A Lavoura,* the SNA's official journal, subsequently published a transcript of the commission's deliberations.[34] While Vargas's inspiration was duly noted, the transcript's introduction attributed some force of action for the commission's work to rural workers, for it remarks on the weight of their expectations for the fulfillment of the president's promise to bring their conditions in line with those of urban workers. This introduction, including an unsigned preface, consisted of a series of interviews with members of the commission reprinted from an October 1941 issue of *A Manhã,* a Rio daily newspaper. *A Manhã's* preface began with a populist claim: "The rural syndicalization law promised by the President of the Republic, a work that will place country laborers in a fraternal situation with urban laborers, not only opens a horizon of great dimension and promise for the laboring classes of the country. It also excites the masses who already enjoy the unmistakable benefits of the new syndical structure, who have anxiously followed the work and study of the Commission and, it is clear, await the advent of a work which will mark, without a doubt, an historic hour for the Brazilian proletariat." Evidently, the commission sought not only to satisfy the "appeals arriving from peasant laborers" but also the expectations of incorporated urban workers. This, at any rate, was the public face of the commission's work. Those who read this introductory material were left with the impression

---

see Warren Dean, "The Planter as Entrepreneur: The Case of São Paulo," *HAHR* 46 : 2 (May 1966), 138–52.

33. Malta Cardoso's membership on the syndicalization commission is reported in "Organização sindical para a lavoura brasileira," *RSRB* 24 : 286 (June 1944), 18–22. For the federal rural code commission, see Malta Cardoso's report to the 767th weekly meeting of the SRB, "Ante-projeto do codigo rural," *RSRB* 23 : 270 (February 1943), 7.

34. "O problema," 4–78. Other than Malta Cardoso and Torres Filho, the Special Study Commission for Rural Syndicalization included Luís Augusto do Rego Monteiro of the labor ministry; Campos Guimarães of the justice ministry; Ben-Hur Raposo of the SER; Mendes Baptista da Silva, representing the sugar industry of Pernambuco; Antônio Câmara of the agricultural ministry; Silvio da Cunha Enchenique, representing Rio Grande do Sul cattlemen; and Luiz Marques Poliano of the health and education ministry.

that the commission had designed a plan to bring the "benefits of the new syndical structure" to the countryside. Those who read further in the document would have been surprised to find something quite different.

The commission met for the first time in the afternoon of August 21 and continued to meet on a weekly basis until 25 September 1941. The group began its deliberations with a working draft of the law already provided by the SER.[35] They discussed it, identified points of agreement, and voted on matters of contention. While consensus was the rule, the commissioners did not shy away from controversy and agreed to disagree on some points in order to continue their work. One of the first disagreements concerned the wisdom of inviting a rural labor representative to participate in the discussion. The pros and cons were debated, with Malta Cardoso consistently opposed to the idea and certain that he could speak for the interests of all rural classes in São Paulo. While the idea was supported by representatives from the labor ministry and other government agencies, Torres concluded the discussion by observing that Vargas himself had appointed the commission as an intragovernmental body with additional, private sector members representing three significant agricultural zones and products: Rio Grande do Sul beef, São Paulo coffee, and Pernambuco sugar. "The commission was not set up to have a laborist character," said Torres. If Vargas had wanted a rural worker on it, he would have appointed one.

Another significant area of disagreement, one already debated in public, concerned the nature of the unions: whether there should be parallel or mixed syndicates of workers and employers. Although the workers' apparent "cultural deficiency" and other arguments were used to deny them the right to organize independently, a majority of the commission voted in favor of separate unions for each class. The case for parallel unions was first argued by Rego Monteiro, the sole labor ministry representative on the panel. A system of mixed membership syndicates, he said, was inconsistent with the "corporatist spirit of the constitution, where various articles recommend equality of representation between employers and employees." In a surprising development, Malta Cardoso spoke in support of Rego Monteiro. In seeming discordance with the position he, Fairbancks, and Pinho had struck at the recently concluded social rights congress,

35. This is the same draft indirectly discussed at the social rights congress in May, where the SRB had protested being excluded from its preparation.

Malta Cardoso described mixed syndicates as a "confusion incompatible with Aristotelian criteria." He advocated a system wherein employers and employees would have separate unions at the municipal level and join together to resolve their differences in federations organized in each state. To advocate separate syndicates, the agricultural ministry representative said, was to ensure inequality between workers and bosses. Since each union's membership was responsible for financing and operating their own union, employee syndicates would have been debilitated in many ways. But the representative of the Rio Grande do Sul cattlemen, Silvio da Cunha Enchenique, supported Malta Cardoso's opinion, and the justice ministry delegate supported Rego Monteiro's interpretation of the law. At day's end, the commission voted five to three in favor of separate unions for workers and bosses.[36]

Numerous additional issues divided the commissioners. While Rego Monteiro sought to expand the role of the labor ministry in agriculture, most other members resisted his amendments to the draft law. During the commission's third meeting, Rego Monteiro insisted that sugar refining and coffee processing were industrial activities that should be governed by industrial labor law, but Malta Cardoso and Mendes Baptista da Silva, who represented the sugar industry of Pernambuco, vociferously rejected this definition. Rego Monteiro also tried to win support for placing the unions under the umbrella of his ministry, but the commission resoundingly rejected that proposal, preferring the oversight of the agricultural ministry. A debate that would prove important in the near future involved a decision to excise the term *colono* from the law. Malta Cardoso argued that coffee *colonos* are both workers and bosses and thus could not rightly belong to either of the planned syndicates. Rego Monteiro protested, asserting that *colonos* were subject to the planters' will and hence clearly employees of the landlord. But the chair interrupted the argument, insisting it could not be resolved, since *colono* was a term used to describe rural workers in many different settings who perform a variety of functions. A majority agreed to drop the term. After a month's work, the members congratulated themselves on their efforts and sent a revised draft to President Vargas.[37] Three years would pass before it resurfaced.

36. "O problema," 33–42.
37. Ibid., 42–78.

The Agrarian and Industrial Roads

A fundamental disagreement between the coffee growers and the Vargas administration lay in how to attain the shared goal of national economic independence. Both agreed that agricultural export earnings provided the capital necessary for industrializing Brazil. Yet, while Vargas and other developmentalists envisioned the inevitable dominance of industry, the planters steadfastly held that agricultural products, and coffee in particular, would remain the cornerstone of Brazil's future.[38] Alberto Whately, an SRB leader and president of the Ribeirão Preto planters' group, showed how planters saw themselves at the heart of Brazilian modernization: "They are in the struggle, and they will continue in the struggle for the greatness of São Paulo and the wealth of Brazil. Coffee farming made the progress of São Paulo by a singular particularity: it is a permanent culture. Where it is planted, soon afterward comes progress: it attracts railroads, people, civilizing and enriching—enriching the state treasury above all, that has ruthlessly abused it."[39] Thus, for the coffee planters of Ribeirão Preto, the capital of Brazilian coffee production for several decades, coffee was the motor of national prosperity and expansion. Moreover, coffee's contribution was not temporary, for it served as both the catalyst of one stage of development and the permanent and perpetual engine of Brazilian progress. In Whately's view, the times called for a renewed appreciation of the contribution of coffee to Brazilian progress and the endorsement of tried and true methods rather than reform.

Central to Vargas's modernization strategy was a plan to improve rural living and working conditions through the institution of mandatory minimum wages and the expansion of labor ministry control over rural labor matters. While Vargas saw these measures as fundamental to the successful progress of Brazil, São Paulo coffee planters saw in them a threat to the stability of their enterprise and, through extension, Brazilian society. The question of minimum wage payments was one of the most difficult and prolonged battles the planters fought. As early as 1939, a decree specifically mandated the payment of minimum wages to rural workers. Despite the SRB's lengthy and convoluted judicial and legislative challenges to the

---

38. As one planter commented, without coffee, Brazilian progress was impossible ("sem as quais o progresso do nosso pais e impossivel"). Luiz Vicente Figueira de Mello, "Ante-projeto do codigo rural," *RSRB* 23:271 (March 1943), 40.
39. Alberto Whately, "Reunião dos cafeicultores de Ribeirão Preto," *RSRB* 23:277 (September 1943), 40.

measure, the Vargas administration did not relent.[40] Even after the fall of his regime in 1945, the 1946 constitution maintained the right of all workers to a minimum wage.[41]

In resisting minimum wages for agricultural workers, the SRB and individual planters followed a two-pronged strategy of delaying the composition of implementation regulations and refusing to comply with the law. Throughout this campaign, the SRB steadfastly maintained that forcing planters to pay their workers minimum wages would destroy Brazilian agriculture. In 1943, for example, the president of the SRB protested that such a measure would constitute "the complete subversion of relations between the agrarian boss and worker." It not only infringed on the rights of planters but threatened to provoke the "total disruption of labor."[42] This was neither the first nor the last planter protest against minimum wage laws.

While the wage question inspired the collective hostility of planters, Vargas's proposal to include agricultural workers in the industrial and commercial proletariat under the jurisdiction of the labor ministry awakened their darkest fears. According to SRB's legal advisor Malta Cardoso, grouping agricultural laborers together with industrial and commercial workers under the auspices of a single government ministry would create an uncontainable monster. Such a move established "a state within the state, stronger than the government's own armed forces, destroying the formidable equilibrium of governmental organs and functions built into the 1937 charter, a statute dignified of the ideas that feed the Estado Novo." Not even Mexican president Lázaro Cárdenas, with all of his radical sympathy for the working man, wrote Malta Cardoso, had been foolish enough to take such a step. Agricultural affairs, he concluded, should remain where they belonged: in the Ministry of Agriculture.[43]

Rural Workers in the CLT

Early in 1943, the battle over rural labor heated up when a government commission released the first draft of what became Brazil's Con-

40. The planter's argument against the minimum wage law can be found in A. P. Brasil, "O salário mínimo na lavoura paulista," *RLT* (October 1941).
41. Article 157 of the 1946 constitution preserved the extension of minimum wages to all workers.
42. Mello, "Ante-projeto do codigo rural," 39.
43. Francisco Malta Cardoso, "Trabalho agrícola na consolidação," *RSRB* 23:271 (March 1943), 14. For the draft law, see "O problema," 11–30.

solidated Labor Law (CLT, Consolidação das Leis do Trabalho). Since agricultural employers like the São Paulo coffee planters had not been invited to participate on this commission, they predictably reacted against the proposal. They called the law an "invasion of the field of rural activities" and argued that the law should not apply to rural labor.[44] But this was an argument they could not win. By 1943 the political context in Brazil and the world was changing. As the tide turned against the Axis powers in World War II, authoritarian regimes worldwide fell under increasing pressure to democratize. Brazil had allied with the United States and was the only South American nation to send troops into battle in Europe. Ironically, Brazilian troops fought in Italy, where Mussolini once reigned using the corporatist systems of governance that had inspired the Estado Novo. The contradictions of Brazil's fight against Fascism slowly eroded the ideological foundations of the Vargas regime. In 1943 a group of intellectuals in the state of Minas Gerais became the first to publicly challenge the regime when they issued a manifesto calling for Brazil's redemocratization. At the end of the year, Vargas responded to critics by openly promising to "readjust our political structure and devise ample and suitable formulas for the consultation of the Brazilian people" once the war had ended.[45] Although the 1943 CLT was a sublimely corporatist document, it also created a system for the "consultation of the Brazilian people," and part of the pressure for democratization included the pleas of agricultural groups to secure just such a place at the government's table.

The proposed general labor code included rural workers along with urban workers as beneficiaries of many of its provisions.[46] In February 1943, Malta Cardoso protested the reach of the proposal in a forum sponsored by the Social Rights Institute (Instituto de Direito Social), the organization of influential jurists, scholars, politicians, and bureaucrats that had sponsored the 1941 social rights congress.

44. Malta Cardoso, "Trabalho agrícola," 12–14.
45. Thomas E. Skidmore, *Politics in Brazil (1930–1964): An Experiment in Democracy* (New York: Oxford University Press, 1967), 48–49.
46. Malta Cardoso objected to the following articles: no. 5(d), defining ranch and plantation workers; no. 10, issuing a regularized union-type work register (*carteira profissional*) to rural workers, signifying regulation of rural labor relations by the labor ministry; no. 52, regulating the hours of the workday; no. 242, regulating time off and vacations; no. 342, providing special protections for minors; no. 491, stating that productive relations were to be defined by individual labor contracts, which would specify employer and employee obligations regarding services performed, methods of payment, advance notice, and fines and indemnification for noncompliance with contractual terms; and no. 492, stating that no more than 30 percent of rural worker wages could be paid in goods, such as coffee or food. Malta Cardoso, "Trabalho agrícola," 12–14.

This prolific and resilient advocate now argued that agricultural production differed fundamentally from commercial and industrial activity because it depended on the rhythms of nature rather than the rhythms of the clock: "How does one legislate the rain, the sun, the hard earth, the necessity to plant, the suitability to divide the fruits, the contingency of doing the work of a sick or even healthy *colono,* given Saturdays sacrificed for the justified closing of the market on Sundays, or holidays to honor the days of the Saints of each zone and sometimes of each plantation—in short, this infernally simple operation that in reality is the utilization of agricultural labor, in function of conditions that escape human control?" When so much agricultural production depended on nature, asked Malta Cardoso, how could one define the duration of the rural workday, regulate safety standards, or allow workers regular weekly days of rest or vacations?

Although nature mandated an unpredictable labor process, it demanded a very specialized response in the division of labor. In agriculture, Malta Cardoso argued, the problem of delimiting the division of labor into categories for the purpose of regulation was "infinitely more difficult" than in the industrial and commercial sectors. A preliminary and incomplete study showed that more than two hundred distinct job categories existed in rural labor. For Malta Cardoso, the study confirmed the absurdity of imposing an industrial union structure on rural labor. For these reasons, special norms and procedures had to be drawn up for rural society, and the implementation of these regulations had to be handled by specialized executive and judicial authorities. He pled for patience in the preparation of a specific rural code and labor law and the forestalling of plans to extend the social rights of urban workers to their rural counterparts.[47]

Concerns about the complexity of rural social relations and the need for specific policies concerned bureaucrats as well. A high-level economic council had proposed carrying out a massive survey of rural worker living standards in 1942. Inspired by a sociological study of sugarcane cutters and growers, and also mill workers and owners, that the Sugar and Alcohol Institute (IAA, Instituto de Açúcar e Álcool) had conducted, the federal Foreign Trade Council planned to survey thousands of rural workers in other important commercial and export areas—such as coffee and tobacco production—regarding their living, working, and physical conditions. The results were to be used in the development of policies that would help retain

47. Malta Cardoso's address, "Trabalho agrícola," was reprinted in the March 1943 issue of the *RSRB.* Quotes are from pages 12 and 14.

workers in the countryside, discouraging their migration to over-crowded cities by raising rural "standards of living."[48] The study was never undertaken, however—a victim of bureaucratic delays and obscure forces of resistance.

Given the dictatorial powers assumed by Vargas during the Estado Novo, the responsibility for halting the study certainly lies with him. Perhaps he saw it as a delaying tactic and believed in his own rhetoric: that some policies should be applied to all workers uniformly, no matter the sector. On the other hand, perhaps he feared the new information could help generate pressure for raising rural labor compensation to levels higher than he was willing to support. Rural wages had to be tied to productivity, not the cost of living, policymakers argued. Only in this way could the administration hope to increase the amount of money transferred from agricultural export earnings to the developing industrial sector.

The latter explanation of Vargas's motives fits the theory of authoritarian development in which agricultural and industrial elites are said to have formed an alliance to ensure that the rural working classes paid most of the costs of modernization.[49] Variously called the "oligarchic pact" (*pacto oligárquico*), "authoritarian capitalism" (*capitalismo autoritário*), "conservative modernization" (*modernização conservadora*), "agrarian pact" (*pacto agrário*), and "agrarian peace" (*paz agrário*), these unwritten ruling-class agreements are said to have offered landowners the freedom to deal with their workers and the workers' demands as they pleased.[50] Even though Vargas increased the tax on exported commodities such as coffee, planters could retain historic profit margins by squeezing more labor for less pay out of

48. Documents on the study are found in "Estudo do 'standard' de vida das populações rurais e operárias," PR 1210, Conselho Federal de Comércio Exterior, SPR/AN. Another broad-based study, though one that did not involve systematic rural worker interviews, had been conducted in the mid-1930s by investigators for a congressional committee. The authors of this study argued that knowledge of rural living costs and conditions were fundamental to improving the productivity of workers and, as a consequence, the overall prosperity of Brazil: "Our [national] liberation and economic prosperity will be realized when we have healthy and educated agricultural workers who are properly trained and equipped to apply their energy to the rational exploitation of the soils and climates of our immense country." Leitão et al., *O trabalhador*, 10.

49. The "agro-industrial block" concept is used by Azevêdo, *As ligas camponesas*. Azevêdo says he developed this idea of unity between an older agrarian elite and a new bourgeoisie from the Italian case as it was analyzed by Antonio Gramsci. See Gramsci's "Notes on Italian History: The City-Countryside Relationship During the Risorgimento and the National Structure," *Selections from the Prison Notebooks* (New York: International Publishers, 1971), 90–102.

50. See, for example, Aspásia de Alcântara Camargo, "Autoritarismo e populismo: Bipolaridade do sistema político brasileiro," *Dados* 12 (1976); Azevêdo, *As ligas camponesas*, 29–41; Otavio Guilherme Velho, *Capitalismo autoritário e campesinato* (São Paulo: Difel, 1979); and Bastos, *As ligas camponesas*.

their workers, assured that the state would not interfere in the process of exploitation. Whereas the state is said to have purchased industrial peace by providing urban workers with dispute conciliation machinery, wage adjustments, pensions, accident insurance, and other protections, rural workers were excluded from most of the benefits of corporatism. As one of the more subtle proponents of this argument has written, "this exclusion defines the precise place of peasants in the historical process" of Brazil.[51]

This place may not be as precisely defined as advocates of the theory contend. The persistence with which the Vargas administration attempted to endow rural workers with minimal rights and benefits challenges the notion of either an explicit or implicit oligarchic pact. The composition of the administration's most significant single piece of social legislation, the CLT, is a case in point. Malta Cardoso had sought to amend the draft by adding the sentence "This law does not apply to professional activities related to agriculture and livestock."[52] Instead, rural workers continued as beneficiaries of various provisions of the new general labor law, though not as many as originally proposed. Much to the displeasure of planters, the final version of the CLT applied to rural and urban workers alike general rules regarding minimum wages (art. 76–128), vacations (art. 129–31), labor contracts (art. 442–67), advance notice (art. 487–91), and limitations on payment in goods rather than in currency (art. 506).[53] These measures provided rural workers with a set of strictly limited basic rights. To this degree, the government interfered with the planter class and broke the pledge implied by the theory of authoritarian development.

Conflict between the state and the planters was as natural as their differing interests. The most outspoken group of São Paulo planters, the SRB, did not endorse the industrial development model pursued by Vargas. In the interest of that model, Vargas felt he needed to defend urban industrial centers from an invasion of discontented rural workers, and this pushed him to defy the planters, who protested every suggestion of equality between urban and rural worlds. Given their differences, each party wanted to gather rural workers to their own camp. The planters originally opposed parallel syndicates for workers and bosses as well as labor ministry influence over rural

51. Martins, *Os camponesas e a política no Brasil*, 25.
52. Malta Cardoso, "Trabalho agrícola," 13. The amendment was to read, "Está lei não se aplica as atividades profissionais relativas a agricultura e a pecuária."
53. See *Consolidação das leis do trabalho* (Rio de Janeiro: Imprensa Nacional, 1943), 12. The various articles are given on pages 12, 22–29, 76–78, 82, and 84, respectively.

syndicalization because these measures threatened to weaken their influence over rural workers. Vargas toyed with these two propositions for the opposite reason: they had the potential of strengthening his hand against the pesky but powerful *paulistas*.

But supporters of the pact theory can rightly claim that Vargas did little to help rural workers directly. A closer look at the CLT and subsequent campaigns to establish rural unions makes this clear. An important concession to Malta Cardoso's wishes for the total exclusion of rural workers appeared in article 7. Unless otherwise stated, the article read, the CLT would apply only to those rural workers whose "activities, when judged by the methods of labor or the results of their efforts, can be classified as industrial or commercial activity." [54] This group of rural workers most immediately came to include all those linked to the production of sugarcane and its by-products, as well as other agro-industrial workers, like the oil processors in Moraes's Araraquara union. Even where the CLT specifically included rural workers as beneficiaries, the administration did not promise to enforce the law's provisions. For workers to take advantage of them, they would have to file complaints against their employers in civil and labor courts. Despite the expense, duration, and frustrations of legal proceedings, some rural workers filed claims under the law.[55]

The best way for a worker to enjoy the law was by joining a syndicate, but the CLT excluded rural workers from the right to organize. When sanctioned through the labor ministry, the unions could demand equal benefits under the law for all members. Although the Vargas administration showed greater willingness to issue controversial social laws than had previous governments, it left the matter of enforcement in the hands of the people and the courts. This was how the rural incorporation process was to unfold in the years ahead. It was the hidden text of Vargas's populism. He was unwilling to extend this fundamental aspect of the incorporation process to rural workers. They could not mobilize, at least not legally.

Of the other specific complaints Malta Cardoso had expressed, two seem to have been taken to heart in writing the CLT. The law was silent regarding regulation of the length of the rural workday and week as well as the question of whether the labor ministry should issue a *carteira profissional* to rural workers. Had such a document

54. Ibid., 12.
55. The tendency to use law and the courts would grow over time and is explored in subsequent chapters. For the 1940s, evidence of rural worker legal proceedings can be found in "Jurisprudencia: Legislação social," *RLT* 7:69–70 (January–February 1943), 19–26; and J. A. Nogueira Junior, "Trabalhadores rurais," *RLT* 8:85–86 (May–June 1944), 121–24.

been issued—loaded as it was with labor laws, salary schedules, and income ledgers—workers would have had in their hands a powerful instrument to challenge capricious landlords. Vargas, however, was unwilling to entirely move rural labor matters out of the Ministry of Agriculture and into the hands of workers and labor bureaucrats. Advisors from the agricultural ministry contributed to this reluctance by arguing, "The intellectual and economic deficiencies of rural laborers warn against the formation of syndicates in the same pattern of the other laboring classes." [56]

The Rural Code and Rural Syndicalization

Despite gaining these substantial concessions, the agricultural elite continued their campaign to altogether exclude rural workers from the CLT by concentrating their efforts on the formulation of a rural code, the so-called Código Rural, which they hoped would supersede the CLT in the agrarian sector. When a draft code was published in January 1943, Malta Cardoso immediately began work on a revision. [57] As in many disputes between planters and the Vargas administration, the labor problem dominated the rural code debate. On May 4, three days after Vargas announced the institution of the CLT at the annual May Day rally, Malta Cardoso presented the SRB's official substitute code. [58] Malta Cardoso's document was a didactic, rambling, yet comprehensive proposal comprising three books, ten titles, and forty-nine chapters. The most extensive addition to the draft law was an eighteen-chapter book entitled "Do Trabalho Rural"—roughly, "On Rural Labor." The proposed code was preceded by a twenty-four-point commentary and justification that recalled the essence of the planter's attack against government interference, the labor ministry, and the application of "urban labor laws" in the countryside. At an April 1944 SRB meeting, Malta Cardoso read a letter from Dr. Luciano Pereira da Silva, chair of a commission working on the law, which

56. Ben-Hur Raposo, representative of the Rural Economy Service, speaking to his colleagues on the Special Study Commission for Rural Syndicalization, "O problema," 39.
57. Malta Cardoso's membership on the federal rural code commission was reported to the 767th weekly meeting of the SRB. "Ante-projeto do código rural," *RSRB* 23:270 (February 1943), 7. The SRB's general response to the commission's first draft is given in an open letter from SRB presidente Luiz Vicente Figueira de Mello to agricultural minister Apolonio Salles as "Ante-projeto do código rural" (36–43). The letter was dated 6 February 1943.
58. Vargas, *A nova política do Brasil*, vol. 3; and Castro Gomes, *A invenção do trabalhismo*. Malta Cardoso, "Ante-projeto do código rural," *RSRB* 23:274 (June 1943), 12–41.

suggested that many of his ideas had been included in a new proposal. "'Many of the provisions approved were consistent with the substitute adopted by the SRB,'" Silva wrote Malta Cardoso. The final version reached Vargas's desk in July. It seems to have died there, however, because little about the code appears in the record until 1951, when one observer claimed its chapters on rural labor were folded into another ill-fated rural labor proposal.[59] If there had been a pact between planters and bureaucrats, one might have expected the ready adoption of the code.

Instead, the rural syndicalization statute initially drafted in 1941 by the SNA resurfaced in this context, enduring various revisions before President Vargas finally signed it into law on the seventh anniversary of the Estado Novo, 10 November 1944.[60] While this law—Decree Law No. 7,038—like much social legislation, remained little enforced, it became an important organizing tool for rural labor militants during the 1950s, a subject explored in subsequent chapters of this book. Ironically, the measure's transformation into something rural workers could benefit from owed much to Malta Cardoso. As the coffee planter's chief lobbyist, he proved influential in shaping the measure. The final decree also shows that his opinions had been changed by years of negotiation with bureaucrats and colleagues in other agricultural sectors.

As a member of the Special Study Commission for Rural Syndicalization, Malta Cardoso had followed Rio Grande do Sul cattlemen in supporting the idea of separate municipal syndicates for workers and bosses. He worked to sway other members of the SRB to see this perspective. For the 7 June 1944 meeting of the SRB, Malta Cardoso invited Dr. Vasco de Andrade of the state labor department to speak. Andrade argued that parallel employee and employer unions could be beneficial for planters. "The *sindicatos* have normative functions,"

59. For the labor code, see Malta Cardoso, "Ante-projeto do código rural," *RSRB* 23:274 (June 1943), 24–35. The preamble is on pages 12–16. The legislative history of the rural code needs to be studied in order to discover exactly why it never became law. For the April meeting, see "Legislação sôbre trabalho rural e código rural," *RSRB* 24:287 (July 1944), 4. Its progress to Vargas is reported in "Lei da sindicalização rural," *RSRB* 35:295 (March 1945), 19. And for 1951, see José de Segadas Vianna, *O Estatuto do Trabalhador Rural e sua aplicação: Comentários a lei no. 4.214, de 2 de março de 1963*, 2d ed. (Rio de Janeiro: Freitas Bastos, 1965), 45–46. Segadas Vianna, who then worked in the labor ministry, claimed that some aspects of the 1951 legislation (Bill No. 606, introduced by Silvio Echenique) eventually found their way into the Rural Laborer Statute (ETR, Estatuto do Trabalhador Rural). See José Martins Catharino, *O trabalhador rural brasileiro (proteção jurídica)* (Rio de Janeiro: Livraria Freita Bastos, 1958), 38–39. As I show in Chapter 8, however, the ETR differed significantly from Malta Cardoso's treatise "On Rural Labor."

60. "Dispõe sôbre a sindicalização rural, decreto-lei no. 7038—de 10 de Novembro de 1944," *Revista de Direito do Trabalho* 7:6 (January–June 1945), 65–68.

Andrade explained, "in which there are two equal *sindicatos,* one for the employer and one for employees, that come to an agreement and adopt certain norms for the execution of labor contracts; and they have a representative function, in which the *sindicatos* represent not only their members but all the individuals that practice their respective professions." For these two reasons, planters could expect worker *sindicatos* to be instrumental to their own interests. Andrade assured the planters that the syndical law would "create an associative spirit among the men of the country" rather than one of class hostility.[61] For the final version, Malta Cardoso also supported the separation of labor and capital throughout the hierarchy of the corporatist system, in local, state, and national bodies.

In addressing a key controversial issue, that of ministerial oversight, Malta Cardoso unexpectedly approved of having the labor ministry control the entire structure of both employees and employers. In addition, *colonos* were specifically included in the measure, with employers and employees divided by a fairly simple definition: employers were those who worked for themselves, using the labor of others, and employees were those who worked for others, by themselves, or as heads of households. "Organization constitutes the modern imperative of all society," Malta Cardoso wrote. "Thus, responding to the appeals of the federal government and organizing itself in rural *sindicatos,* national agriculture will learn to present its class interests and great love of Brazilian land." [62]

The SRB was enthusiastic about the new law. In a November editorial entitled "Rural Syndicalization," SRB leaders reiterated "the importance of representation in rural syndicates" and emphasized the influence Malta Cardoso and other agriculturalists had on the measure.[63] An earlier editorial, appearing just after the April 1944 publication of a second draft of the law, also displayed the SRB's strong support for the concept of rural syndicates. Syndicalization was one of the best ways to make agriculture's voice heard: "The union of all those who work on the land today, under the flag of class association, within syndical organizations, beneath the dome of the rural federation, will be a factor for the successful attainment of measures beneficial to agriculture." The hierarchical structure of the *sindicatos*

61. For Andrade's comments, see "Sôbre a sindicalização rural," *RSRB* 24:288 (August 1944), 134, 136.

62. "Lei de sindicalização rural," introduced by Francisco Malta Cardoso, *RSRB* 24:290 (October 1944), 18–21.

63. "Dispõe sôbre a sindicalização rural, decreto-lei no. 7038—de 10 de Novembro de 1944," *Revista de Direito do Trabalho* 7:6 (January–June 1945), 65–68.

held a special appeal for *paulista* planters because they believed such a structure would allow them to retain their powerful influence in Brazilian society. "São Paulo farming," the editorial continued, "an endeavor that has dismayed the more civilized by its success in obtaining unparalleled wealth from the earth through individual and private initiative, is going to set out on a new path, turning itself, through the numbers it represents and the value of its product, into a ponderable factor in the national equation."[64]

The support of the SRB and Malta Cardoso was strictly self-interested, as a closer look at the details of the decree makes clear. Although *colonos* were mentioned in the decree, their status remained vague. Since the definitions of employers and employees centered on one's motives for work rather than one's relationship to the means of production, it was quite possible that planters continued to see *colonos* as partners rather than laborers. In the years ahead, many judges would be asked to rule in cases involving the rights of *colonos;* and nearly all rulings would hinge on interpretations of their status as employees. Those rural workers who were allowed to organize employee unions faced a daunting task, for members had to provide for the union's budget as well as accident insurance for members. Malta Cardoso had lobbied to specifically *exclude* rural employers from contributing to a union tax (*imposto sindical*) used to finance employee unions in urban settings. Although industrial employers often ignored the tax, it was designed to overcome the extreme economic inequalities between working and owning classes.[65] Insisting that rural workers pay their own accident insurance actually represented a step backward for workers, since Decree Law No. 24,637 of 1934 had established a state- and employer-financed fund to cover the expense of caring for disabled urban and rural workers. Organized rural workers could not expect to find help abroad either, since affiliation with international groups was illegal under the syndicalization decree. Whereas one of the union's duties was "to collaborate with the public powers in the development of social solidarity," the *sindicatos* were "prohibited from exercising economic activity."[66]

Finally, Decree Law No. 7,038 included a clause that guarded a special place for organizations such as the SRB in the Brazilian state. Article 20, which had not appeared in any previous versions of the law, specified that the president retained the power to license certain

64. "Organiza-se a agricultura em sindicato," *RSRB* 24:285 (May 1944), 15.
65. "Sôbre a sindicalização rural," *RSRB* 24:288 (August 1944), 16, 130.
66. "Dispõe sôbre a sindicalização," 67–68.

civil associations with some of the same rights the syndicates were being established to handle. The article would allow organizations like the SRB to "collaborate with the Government, as technical consultants, on the solution of problems" affecting agriculture without being held accountable for any other duties outlined in the law. The Ministry of Agriculture, mentioned only in this article, had the power to nominate organizations for this function.[67] In the end, the rural syndicalization law posed little immediate threat to coffee planters: worker unions would be impoverished, *colonos* would remain in a nebulous position, and the SRB would continue as a powerful lobby. How it would turn out depended on the Vargas administration. "We are waiting to see how the law is regulated," an SRB editorial explained, "to see what comes of the representative organ of Agriculture"—a reference to the planter group.

Four months later, in March 1945, the Ministry of Labor issued instructions necessary for the official recognition and administrative organization of the unions.[68] Nonetheless, as late as 1955 only five rural workers' unions *nationwide* had been recognized by the labor ministry, and by 1962 only one more had been legalized, despite the fact that twenty-nine official requests had been recorded, seven of them from the state of São Paulo. For that matter, no rural employer syndicates had been formed.[69] Contemporaries blamed the ineffectiveness of the law on its failure to fit rural socioeconomic realities. The law was "fatally tied up" by the near "impossibility of defining professional activity and the broad territorial dispersion of the agricultural class," editorialized the SNA's *A Lavoura*. It went unfulfilled, wrote José de Segadas Vianna, "for maladjustment with its times." Even before it was decreed, the jurist and legal scholar A. F. Cesarino Jr. anticipated that rural labor syndicalization was virtually impossible because of nomadism and illiteracy among rural workers and their relative isolation from one another. These drawbacks were compounded by the absence of adequate means of communication, Cesarino wrote.[70]

67. Ibid., 68.
68. "Portaria ministerial no. 14 de 19.3.1945," cited in José Gomes da Silva, *Noções sôbre associativismo rural (organização da classe rural brasileira)* (Campinas: Secretaria da Agricultura, Centro de Treinamento, 1962), 2. Some contemporary authors claim that enabling regulations were not issued for Decree Law No. 7,038: "The instructions were not elaborated and, consequently, the law of rural syndicalization, was never enforced." Dr. Admastor Lima, "Sindicalização rural," *A Lavoura* (July–August 1954), 29.
69. Azevêdo, *As ligas camponesas*, 55; and Silva, *Noções sôbre associativismo rural*, 4.
70. See editorial [unsigned], "A organização da classe rural," *A Lavoura* (October/December 1945), 2; Segadas Vianna, *Estatuto do Trabalhador Rural;* and A. F. Cesarino Jr., "Sindicalização rural," *Revista do Direito Social* 4:24 (September 1944), 1.

A "Fascist and Totalitarian" Decree

These obstacles were real, but so was the unwillingness of the Vargas administration to mobilize rural workers. Subsequent events confirmed, however, that the administration was equally unwilling to aid the SRB. In fact, as the pressure for democratization increased with the collapse of Fascism and the end of hostilities in Europe, weakening the SRB, which so forcefully defended the interests of the old rural oligarchy his government had overthrown, grew in importance to Vargas.[71] In April, he issued a new decree to regiment rural society geographically rather than by agricultural activity, as had been provided for in the 1944 rural syndicalization decree.[72] The SRB saw this new law as an attack on its prerogatives, holding up the 1944 decree as far more rational and preferable. In the SRB's calculation, the 1944 law gave coffee a substantial advantage because coffee growers were the most powerful and best organized agrarian interest group in Brazil. On the other hand, the new decree demanded that they subdivide and pool their resources with other interests to form municipal associations. As Malta Cardoso noted, this greatly diluted the power and influence of coffee planters.[73] Disregarding an onslaught of criticism from the SRB, Vargas revised and reissued Decree Law No. 8,127 with implementation regulations just five days before he was deposed in October 1945.[74]

For the *paulistas,* the new "organization of rural life" law was far worse than the rural syndicalization law had ever been: their complaints had obviously not been heard.[75] Malta Cardoso decried the law as "fascist and totalitarian" because it virtually delegitimized the SRB by allowing no provisions for the recognition of organizations not formed and registered according to the law. In contrast, under the syndical law, the SRB had retained the chance of official status in ar-

71. On labor in this transitional period, see John D. French, "Industrial Workers and the Birth of the Populist Republic in Brazil, 1945–1946," *Latin American Perspectives* 16:4 (Fall 1989), 6–28.

72. "Decreto lei 7.449 de 9 de abril de 1945, Dispõe sôbre a organização da vida rural," in Mario Penteado de Faria e Silva, ed., *Legislação agropecuária (relativa ao período de 1937–1947)* (São Paulo: Secretaria da Agricultura, 1952), 735–40.

73. Francisco Malta Cardoso, "Organização compulsoria e democracia," *RSRB* 28:306 (February 1946), 20.

74. "Decreto-lei no. 8.127 de 24 de outubro de 1945, altera e da nova redação ao decreto-lei no. 7.449 de 9 de abril de 1945, que dispõe sôbre a organização da vida rural" and "Decreto-lei no. 19.882 de 24 de outubro de 1945, aprova o regulamento a que se referem os artigos 13 do decreto-lei no. 7.449 e no. 24 do decreto-lei no. 8.127," in Faria e Silva, ed., *Legislação agropecuária,* 740–55.

75. Fernando Gomes, "A organização da vida rural do pais," *RSRB* 26:305 (January 1946), 18–19.

ticle 20. According to the new decree, however, the only organizations to play an official role were those built on the new structure with its geographical base. Adding insult to injury, Malta Cardoso noted, the law favored the Rio de Janeiro–based SNA with two slots for its representatives on the board of directors of the Brazilian Rural Confederation (CRB, Confederação Rural Brasileira)—the new, maximum organ of the regional rural employer associations and state federations. In article after article, Malta Cardoso and other planters demanded "the pure, simple, and immediate revocation of decree 8,127, that offends the democratic principles of Brazilian legislation."[76]

Despite SRB protests, however, the number of rural *employer* associations registered under Decree Law No. 8,127 grew. In February 1946 the government recognized a São Paulo federation of these entities, the São Paulo State Federation of Rural Associations (FARESP, Federação das Associações Rurais do Estado de São Paulo).[77] Shortly thereafter, FARESP established a monthly bulletin to promote the organization of other associations and to give voice to São Paulo's increasingly diversified community of farmers.[78] For the SRB, these associations represented an unacceptable challenge to its authority. In defending their position, planter spokesmen spared no words: "The SRB," one member proclaimed, "has incontestable authority to represent agriculturalists, and to defend their rights and interests, before the governors of the Republic."[79] But the SRB's position was highly contested.[80] The ineffectiveness of their support for the syndical law and their opposition to the association law revealed the internal struggle waging within the Brazilian elite. Intraclass rivalry and not class struggle shaped the composition of these laws. One can look back to the 1920s and see the beginnings of this trend with the diversification of São Paulo agriculture and the fragmentation of coffee planter solidarity recounted in Chapter 1.

Vargas was determined to whittle away at the power of the cof-

76. See Malta Cardoso, "Organização rural compulsoria," 20. See also, "Hierarquia e democracia," *RSRB* 26 : 307 (March 1946), 3–4; and "Pela revogação da lei totalitaria," *RSRB* 37 : 326 (October 1947), 2.
77. FARESP was recognized 8 February 1946 (Silva, *Noções sôbre associativismo rural*, 2).
78. By 1962 there were 181 associations organized in the state of São Paulo, with 45,219 members. This was a small number given the huge economically active rural population in the state. Silva (*Noções sôbre associativismo rural*, 3) says the associations accounted for only about 5 percent of farm owners.
79. Gomes, "A organização da vida rural," 18.
80. "Campanha de sócios," *RSRB* 27 : 322 (June 1947), 17. In this editorial, the editor reports that São Paulo had 268,238 rural properties, and if the SRB had 10 percent of these as members, it would be "one of the largest and most powerful class associations in the entire country."

fee planters and cattle barons who headed the SRB, yet he was not nearly so committed to empowering rural workers to do this for him. The fact that so few rural labor unions were formed demonstrates how various heads of state, from Vargas to Jânio Quadros in 1961, remained ambivalent toward the incorporation of rural workers. Politicians sought to contain the SRB by favoring competitors, not by mobilizing rural workers. When the SRB managed to turn the syndical law, intended to weaken them, into a tool to help them retain their faltering authority, Vargas produced the association law rather than a program of rural labor mobilization. Both sides had dismissed this option and excluded rural workers from participation in discussions regarding their well-being.

But common to both sides was a new assumption: rural workers had to be incorporated formally somehow, someday. The coffee contractor Thomaz had appealed for just that when he wrote of his need for "a clarification of our rights . . . , our duties, and how to proceed to act in accordance with your [Vargas's] opinion."[81] No consensus had been reached about including their voice in the formation of the political economy, yet resolving this issue posed a significant problem for bureaucrats. This question was at the heart of the debate over labor ministry recognition of rural workers and many other matters. When the Vargas regime collapsed and new political parties formed to compete for power, Brazil underwent significant political change. Just as Vargas and the SRB had tried to use rural workers to shore up their opposing positions during the Estado Novo, both politicians and planters now prepared to experiment with similar strategies as the new Populist Republic took shape. In the new democratic environment of the postwar era, rural workers would seize the opportunities created by these debates to sow the seeds of their own liberty tree.

81. João Francisco Thomaz to Vargas, PR 1926/34, 7 June 1934, MTIC, Lata 47, SPR/AN.

3

Approaching the hamlet by horse cart along the rough two-track from Ribeirão Preto, twelve miles to the northeast, Dumont appeared among the gentle hills only at the last moment. The low-profile village lay on a hillside, encircled by the area's ubiquitous coffee trees. Its most prominent building was the old plantation's big house (*casarão*), even though the massive, single-story structure boasted no regal columns and commanded a vista only of the central square. From the front porch, the village's twin-steepled chapel could be seen on the northeast corner of the plaza, the stores and *Cine Dumont* on its east end, and a row of squat, interlocked houses along its southern perimeter. The houses were so small, and the families so large—some with as many as twelve children—that the square was alive with people day in and day out. "It was like

PLANTING THE SEED

> ## Finding Opportunity in the New Policies

an ant hill," recalled Nelson Luís Guindalini, who moved to Dumont with his family in 1932, when he was nine.[1]

Around the plaza, the constant movement of people and vehicles flattened the tall grass and exposed a soil so rich in nutrients and color that it was called *terra roxa* (purple earth). Here and there, rising above the low, wooden shacks and outbuildings, could be seen a *cajamanga* tree, with its dark green leaves interrupted by flashes of small yellow fruit. During the day, most of the men and adolescent children left early to work in the fields. Outside of the harvest season, the women stayed close to their houses, chopping wood, gardening, doing laundry, cooking, watching after their youngest children. On the surface, Dumont seemed to be just another Brazilian town where farm people lived and raised their families. But, as everyone knew, Dumont had once been the central *colono* colony of the greatest of São Paulo's great coffee plantations, the Fazenda Dumont.

João Guerreiro Filho was born on Fazenda Dumont in 1916. Tall, lean, and energetic, he still worked the land in 1945, although no longer as a *colono*. An English company had bought the gigantic coffee plantation from the Dumont family, and in 1939 it had been sold again to a consortium of São Paulo's most renowned planters, including Antônio Prado Jr.—son of the planter Antônio Prado—and Celso Torquate Junqueira, who then broke it up in lots and sold it to speculators and former *colonos*. Guerreiro's father, João, had been one of the clever ones. With the help of his three growing boys, the family saved enough cash to buy about fifty acres. They uprooted nearly ten thousand unproductive coffee trees and planted cotton, castor-oil plant (*mamona*), rice, and corn. Thus, Guerreiro's father became a smallholder (*sitiante*), a member of the rural petty bourgeoisie. As the eldest son, the younger João shared in his family's pride of ownership.[2]

1. Nelson Luis Guindalini, interview by author, Dumont, 13 May 1995. The description of Dumont comes from personal experience, interviews with residents, and research in photographic evidence such as Cagno Carmen et al., *Ribeirão Preto: Memória fotográfica* (Ribeirão Preto: Colêgio, 1985).

2. The consortium was a land company, the Companhia Agrícola de Imigração e Colonização (CAIC), which was organized in the 1930s by the Paulista Railroad Company as a way of increasing commerce along its various routes. Its board of directors and principal shareholders were the elite of São Paulo planters. The existence of this company helps clarify some of the issues in a lengthy scholarly debate over the beneficiaries of the coffee economy. Participants in this debate are divided into camps, with one group arguing that coffee growers were virtually the only beneficiaries and the other group emphasizing the social mobility of *colonos*. The CAIC records show how the social mobility of many *colonos* was part of a strategy of landowners to sell off unproductive land and create a class of smallholders to produce foodstuffs to feed the cities,

Although Guerreiro had only one year of schooling, his Spanish-immigrant father encouraged him to develop his reading skills using newspapers. During World War II, he read the news to a German man who did not know how to read Portuguese. The newspapers brought word of Soviet daring in the war against Fascism, and, at war's end, news of Luís Carlos Prestes's PCB and its support of the rural labor laws Guerreiro had learned about in the government's "Hour of Brazil" radio shows.[3] By August 1945, Prestes had been campaigning for nearly four months, demonstrating how a new era of competitive politics had come to Brazil following eight years of authoritarian restrictions under the Estado Novo regime. On August 26, Guerreiro went to celebrate his birthday in Ribeirão Preto and saw a story in a recent *Diário da Manhã* announcing the opening of a PCB post in the hall of the Laborers' General Union (UGT, União Geral dos Trabalhadores) at 4 José Bonifácio Street.[4] He used the occasion to become a party member and registered to vote for the first time in his twenty-nine years. Leaving the building through its wide front doorway, he passed under the international emblem of labor solidarity, a relief of the united hands of agricultural and industrial workers.

Soon after joining the PCB, Guerreiro helped establish a Communist cell for Dumont. Eleven men came to weekly meetings at his house—among them rural workers and sharecroppers like Pedro Salla, Miguel Bernard, and Vitório Negre. Guerreiro's mother, Catarina, and two younger brothers encouraged him. Catarina made room for the group in her house, preparing bread and hot coffee for the men. Wanting to expand their membership, they decided to form a public organization. Toward the end of 1945, they rented the cinema auditorium, spread the word, and together with another fifty men and

---

where the elite were investing capital in industrial development. For *colonos* and planters, it was a win-win situation. See Honório de Souza Carneiro, "A CAIC: Companhia de Agricultura, Imigração e Colonização, 1928–1961" (master's thesis, Universidade do Estado de São Paulo, Araraquara, 1985); and the *Relatórios da diretoria da CAIC,* CAIC archive, Centro de Memórias, Universidade Estadual de Campinas (UNICAMP). For the social mobility debate, see Mauricio Font, "Coffee Planters, Politics, and Development in Brazil," *Latin American Research Review* 22:3 (1987), 69–90; and the commentaries offered by Joseph L. Love and Verena Stolcke as well as Font's reply in *Latin American Research Review* 24:3 (1989), 127–58. For João Guerreiro's proprietorship, see CAIC, *Livro com informações sôbre lotes e propretarios de terra do nucleo Dumont, area de terras,* Registro 3, Centro de Memórias, UNICAMP.

   3. João Guerreiro Filho, transcript of interview by author and Sebastião Geraldo, São Paulo, 11 July 1989, AEL/UNICAMP (hereafter Guerreiro transcript), p. 16. On the rally, see also "São Paulo a Luís Carlos Prestes," *Diário da Manhã* (hereafter *DM*), 17 July 1945, 1.

   4. "Partido Comunista Brasileiro: Foi empossado ontem o secretariado do comitê municipal, nesta cidade," *DM,* 14 August 1945, 8.

women founded the Dumont Peasant League (Liga Camponesa de Dumont) later that year.[5] Guerreiro became its political secretary, an important post in this political association of concerned *sitiantes, colonos,* rural wage workers (*camaradas, assalariados,* and *diários*), tenant farmers (*arrendatários*), sharecroppers (*parceiros* and *meeiros*), and teamsters (*carroceiros*). Together they confronted the municipal government, demanding a clinic, post office, bus service, and paved road for Dumont. Eventually, they established a cooperative in Dumont to buy and sell needed goods more cheaply than those offered by the local merchants who had once run the *fazenda*'s company stores.

Despite his mother's support, Guerreiro's militancy created a rift between him and his father. The elder Guerreiro said the league was unnecessary for smallholders like themselves, and he discouraged his sons from participating in PCB politics. The younger Guerreiro loved the work, though. He visited plantations in the region to speak at dances and weddings and found meaning in his role as a defender of peasant interests. "It's dishonorable to be a drunk or a thief. But to be a political prisoner," he said forty years later, "defending the interests of the oppressed class, isn't. It's an honor, something to be proud of." For Guerreiro, the Dumont Peasant League was the beginning of the movement toward freedom that linked a glorious past to the "Diretas já!" mobilizations of the 1980s. "The seed was planted," Guerreiro said of his time in the league, "and it's germinating." Following the suppression of the PCB in May 1947, however, the Guerreiro residence was raided by the police, and his father decided it would be better if young Guerreiro moved out. Still committed to his politics, Guerreiro relocated to Ribeirão Preto, where one of his brothers lived. He also married in 1947 and started a family. Ironically, his eldest son would one day become a police detective involved in suppressing a later generation of radicals.[6]

5. The exact date of this event remains obscure. Guindalini interview; and Pedro Salla, interview by author, Dumont, 14 May 1995. Guerreiro transcript. See also Geraldo, "Comunicação oral," 66–70. Another source claims that the "first peasant league" was established on lands now occupied by the University of São Paulo, in the heart of São Paulo city. See "A primeira liga camponesa," *Notícias de Hoje* (hereafter *NH*), 7–13 June 1963. (Thanks to John French for this clipping.)

6. Quotes from Guerreiro transcript, 5, 9. As I discuss in the Prologue, Guerreiro whispered these statements to us late that evening in the carport outside his son's house in a São Paulo neighborhood. His son's career as a policeman seemed to embarrass Guerreiro, and his use of the term *preso político* had more to do with the repression of leftists under the recent military regime than with his own experience in Dumont, for Guerreiro was never jailed. In other words, he identified his struggle in 1945 with that of the militants his son had helped suppress in the 1980s. The father was the rebel to the son's conformism.

Incipient Rural Labor Politics

Guerreiro's story raises interesting questions about the structure of democracy and the construction of rural citizenship in modern Brazil. The peasant league of Dumont was one among a number of unprecedented *camponês* political organizations that took shape in the country during the period of democratization that followed World War II. Yet the literature generally dismisses this story as insignificant and pays little attention to rural labor politics until 1959 when the so-called peasant league movement of Francisco Julião began to have a pronounced impact on the northeast and the nation. For these interpreters, rural workers were the pawns of the landed ruling class, helping to retain the dominance of this group by legitimating their hold on local government.[7] *Coronelismo,* the patron-client relationship between rural workers and landowners, was especially typical of the period known as the First Republic (1889–1930).[8] Because of proportional representation, Brazilian law gave the comparably populous countryside more federal and state deputies than the urban areas. These same election laws restricted the franchise to the literate, and because rural illiteracy was high, most rural workers remained outside the electoral process. The law counted them as bodies rather than voters. The literate rural elite naturally used high rural population statistics to elect legislators attentive to their interests.[9]

The illiteracy of rural workers has been coupled with the general increase in rural migration to the cities to explain Brazilian populism and the 1945 to 1964 "experiment with democracy," known by some as the Populist Republic. This argument has only reinforced a negative image of rural labor. Agricultural workers have been viewed not only as illiterate but also as ignorant and thus politically impres-

7. See, for example, Amaury de Souza, "The Cangação and the Politics of Violence in Northeast Brazil," in *Protest and Resistance in Brazil and Angola,* edited by Ronald Chilcote (Berkeley and Los Angeles: University of California Press, 1972); Linda Lewin, "The Oligarchical Limitations of Social Banditry in Brazil: The Case of the 'Good' Thief Antônio Silvino," *Past and Present* 82 (February 1979), 116–46; Shepherd Forman, *The Brazilian Peasantry* (New York: Columbia University Press, 1975); Robert W. Shirley, *The End of Tradition: Cultural Change and Development in the Município of Cunha, São Paulo* (New York: Columbia University Press, 1971).

8. The most thorough account of Brazilian politics at the municipal level remains Leal, *Coronelismo.* For Ribeirão Preto in particular, a detailed study of this system and its demise is Walker, "From Coronelismo to Populism."

9. Regarding planter manipulation of rural voters, see Robert Shirley, "Patronage and Cooperation: An Analysis from São Paulo State," in *Structure and Process in Latin America,* edited by Arnold Stricken and Sidney M. Greenfield (Albuquerque: University of New Mexico Press, 1972), 139–58; and Marcos Vilaca and Roberto Albuquerque, *Coronel, coroneis* (Rio de Janeiro: Tempo Brasileiro, 1965).

sionable members of the urban settings where they migrated in growing numbers in the 1940s, 1950s, and 1960s.[10] Their presumed lack
of political expertise made them blind supporters of populist demagogues. Their "false consciousness" led them to support such sup-
posedly non-ideological and inconsistent (nonprogrammatic) candidates as Adhemar de Barros, Getúlio Vargas, and Janio Quadros.[11]
Thus, the theory goes, in the country, rural workers justified the continued power of backward *coroneis* and *latifundiários,* while in the city,
they gave their votes away to corrupt opportunists or, worse still,
Communists.[12]

As Guerreiro's story reveals, however, the political history of
the rural working classes is somewhat more complex. Guerreiro supported the Communists not because he was gullible but because he
honestly thought their program fit his vision. Those who joined with
him in the Dumont Peasant League must also have found something
in its program that appealed to their interests. It was not out of ignorance and false consciousness that Guerreiro became politically active but out of compassion and identity with the oppressed. The PCB
appeared in Ribeirão Preto and offered a working-class discourse that
appealed to his sentiments and held out the possibility of resolving
some of the problems that afflicted rural workers and peasants. The
PCB seemed to him to be the best vehicle for expressing his concerns,
and he participated willingly in its activities, even at the cost of offending his father.

That Guerreiro's struggle was complicated by his family relations set him only slightly apart from the majority of the rural working classes. Like Guerreiro, many rural laborers in Brazil were put to
work by their parents, but unlike him, most were not smallholders,

10. For negative interpretations of rural migrant political and voting behavior in the city,
see Francisco Weffort, *O populismo na política brasileira* (Rio de Janeiro: Paz e Terra, 1978), 123–
44; José Alvaro Moisés, *A greve de massa e crise política (Estudo da greve dos 300 mil em São Paulo,
1953–1954)* (São Paulo: Polis, 1978); and Assis Simão, "O voto operário em São Paulo," *Revista
Brasileira de Estudos Políticos* 1 : 1 (December 1956), 130–41.

11. A critique of those who have found little ideological logic in the support workers gave
populists such as Barros can be found in John D. French, "Workers and the Rise of Adhemarista
Populism in Sao Paulo, Brazil, 1945–1947," *HAHR* 68 : 1 (February 1988), 1–43.

12. This argument found powerful evidence in the curious diary of Carolina Maria de
Jesus, *A Child in the Dark* (New York: E. P. Dutton, 1962). A migrant from rural Minas Gerais to a
São Paulo ghetto (*favela*) in the 1950s, Jesus became an overnight celebrity in 1960 when her
writings were published by an intrepid journalist. In no time, her angry and ultimately conservative views were published in English in the United States. She found nothing of value among
her fellow *favelados* and repetitiously recounted stories demonstrating their greed, pettiness, and
ignorance. She saved her harshest criticisms, however, for the politicians who came to the *favela*
to trade handouts and empty promises for votes.

so they had a more direct relationship with a planter or landlord. Guerreiro's most immediate disputes were with his father. As a blood relation, he could blame his troubles not on his parents but on forces beyond the family's singular control. His family was unable to succeed, he reckoned, due to market structures and the high cost of credit, farm implements, supplies, and transportation. He and the others formed the Dumont Peasant League as a pressure group to alter these structural problems. The majority of rural laborers were also made to work by their parents, but it was not the invisible hand of the market that seemingly forced these conditions on the family: it was the landlord or planter and his supervisors. These authorities, particularly the overseers, could be blamed for the laborer's misery. Of course, employers (not unlike Guerreiro) maintained that the state, market structures, and natural forces were the real terrorizers of them all. As discussed in Chapter 2, planters viewed workers as part of their "clan," and together worker and boss faced the costs and benefits of rural life.

In 1945, however, the rural working classes were in a somewhat transitional state, invited for the first time to challenge the hegemonic "clan" notion on a massive scale. They were being offered a chance to move from dependence on the plantation to a more independent identity as citizens of the nation. Under *coronelismo,* their political voice had traditionally been tied to the plantation, dependent on the will of planters. But now the nation sought their support, and political parties competed for their vote. Political participation was more open in 1945 than ever before. In preparation for the democratic transition of 1945, Vargas made two changes that had a profound impact on Brazilian workers, rural and urban alike. One was the legalization of the PCB, and the other was a change in the electoral law that facilitated voter registration, bringing many new voters into the system.

Both of these changes encouraged working-class political participation, especially in São Paulo, where coffee and immigrants had already combined to generate a more variegated polity.[13] The party's membership rolls exploded with thousands of new members signing up, many of them spontaneously, like Guerreiro. By the December 1945 presidential election, the party claimed sixty thousand members

13. See Francisco Weffort, "As origens do sindicalismo populista no Brasil (a conjuntura do após-guerra)," *Estudos CEBRAP* 4 (April/June, 1974); and Ricardo Maranhão, *Sindicatos e democratização (Brasil 1945/1950)* (São Paulo: Brasiliense, 1979).

in the state of São Paulo alone. The PCB's growth, moreover, was only part of a wave of expansion in the number of working-class voters set off by the new system of ex officio registration.[14] In 1930, 10 percent of all adults were registered to vote; in 1945 that proportion had risen to 33 percent. In urban and industrial areas such as Rio de Janeiro and São Paulo, electoral participation increased by 400 to 500 percent. As Brazilianist John D. French has commented, in 1945 the "electoral marketplace . . . was totally transformed."[15]

If the example of the Alta Mogiana region can serve as a case in point, then PCB activism and ex officio voter registration influenced rural politics no less than urban. The official party line identified the monopoly of land ownership as one of two obstacles preventing Brazil's democratic development. (The other was imperialist exploitation.)[16] Thus, from the moment the party was legalized in 1945 until it was repressed in 1947, the Communists established numerous organizing committees throughout the interior of São Paulo and other parts of Brazil.[17] A survey of PCB newspapers published between February 1945 and April 1947 revealed that committees in São Paulo sponsored the formation of some thirty-five local cells, professional associations, and leagues that appealed exclusively to the interests of rural labor.[18] The Dumont Peasant League was not among those re-

14. The ex officio registration method enabled employers and government officials to present lists of their employees to election judges. The lists could then be approved and each person named issued a voter registration card. Contemporary critics such as Virgílio de Melo Franco saw the ex officio as a strategy for Vargas to perpetuate Estado Novo corporatism because it provided a means for government-appointed union bosses to register their members. Franco, *A campanha da UDN* (Rio: Zelio Valverde, 1946), 27–28. John D. French has explored how astute critics like Franco were, proving that the ex officio led to the electoral participation of masses of workers who would not otherwise have participated in the elections. Although electoral regulations continued to exclude illiterates, the ex officio essentially eliminated this test by making it possible to register a new voter without so much as his or her signature. But whereas critics thought unions would be enlisting the majority of new voters, French found that a greater number were organized by factory employers who presented election officials with their payroll lists. French, "Adhemarista Populism in Sao Paulo," 6–8. See also Maria de Carmo Campello de Souza, *Estado e partidos políticos no Brasil (1930 a 1964)* (São Paulo: Alfa Omega, 1983), 121–24.

15. French, "Adhemarista Populism in Sao Paulo," 7.

16. Luís Carlos Prestes, "Situação do homen do campo," *Hoje,* 25 April 1946, 7, also published in Barriguelli, ed., *Subsídios à história,* 171–74.

17. Without citing sources, Azevêdo wrote, "These leagues and rural associations were founded in almost all Brazilian states, uniting in their turn some tens of thousands of rural workers and peasants." Azevêdo, *As ligas camponesas,* 56.

18. Barriguelli, ed., *Subsídios à história,* 2:127–267. This invaluable collection consists of articles on the rural labor movement taken from many São Paulo newspapers, especially those associated with the Communist and Socialist Parties. For the period 1945 to 1947, the editor consulted the São Paulo editions of *Hoje, Notícias de Hoje,* and *Tribuna Popular.* Unfortunately, some articles have been summarized rather than transcribed, and faulty proofing often makes it difficult to detect which is which. Nevertheless, the volumes provide an excellent topical guide and index to the subject in the original periodicals.

ported in the press, so the number of groups formed must have exceeded the amount reported.[19]

Cross-Class Alliances

The growth in rural labor voting did not depend solely on Communist converts like Guerreiro. In fact, the spread of the rural franchise in the Alta Mogiana owed a good deal to legwork sponsored by planters and the conservative parties. Interested in increasing local power through augmented voter rolls, the municipal political machines of the Social Democratic Party (PSD, Partido Social Democrático), the National Democratic Union Party (UDN, União Democrática Nacional), and the Brazilian Labor Party (PTB, Partido Trabalhista Brasileiro) registered new voters using Vargas's new ex officio regulation. With its strong planter class constituency, the PSD obtained permission from landowners to visit their plantations and prepare voter rolls of *colonos* in consultation with plantation foremen. This tactic easily tripled the number of registered voters in districts such as São Joaquim da Barra, located some forty miles north of Ribeirão Preto.[20] As postwar election results showed, however, this policy backfired on them. Workers were not convinced their employers knew what was best for them. The democratization of local politics is well characterized by the political scientist Thomas Walker's phrase, "from *coronelismo* to populism." As Walker shows, planter participation in the Ribeirão Preto municipal council dropped from 53 percent of the body to 9 percent between the periods 1910–28 and 1947–59.[21]

Vargas himself continued to contribute to the changing balance of power between owners and workers during this period. As a federal senator in 1947, he campaigned on behalf of candidates of the PTB, using his speeches to define a brand of politics that sought at once to both empower workers and pacify them. His speeches honored their achievements "on the vanguard of socialism" and subtly urged them to favor the PTB road of compromise over the road of confrontation imbedded in Communist rhetoric. In January, Vargas came to São

19. Guerreiro transcript; and Irineu Luís de Moraes, transcript of interview by author and Sebastião Geraldo, Ribeirão Preto, 27 May 1989 (hereafter Moraes transcript, pt. 3).

20. By 1 August 1945, PSD and UDN registration campaigns using ex officio lists had increased the number of voters in the district of São Joaquim da Barra from 748 to more than two thousand. "São Joaquim da Barra já fez dois mil eleitores," *DM,* 3 August 1945, 8.

21. Walker, "From Coronelismo to Populism," 220.

Paulo and celebrated the leadership of *paulista* workers in the fight
for the socioeconomic development of Brazil.

> Among all people, in all periods of history, the most violent
> transitions occur when the rural aristocracy is displaced by the
> dynamism of industry. When Brazil was still struggling to main-
> tain slavery, you [the workers of São Paulo] introduced free la-
> bor. When your agriculture was still at its apex, you launched
> great industries. And when the reactionaries united against the
> rise of social freedom, you were already in the vanguard of Bra-
> zilian socialism. . . . You know the path you are on and you know
> how to steer Brazil down this same path. . . . Your party [the
> PTB], workers of São Paulo, is the greatest political and social
> force of Brazil. It is the sum of all your energy, defending rights
> and the ideal of a future in which the worker has opened all the
> roads for government by the people and for the people.[22]

Vargas's message portrayed workers as the major force in Brazilian history, but not in the class struggle, which the Communists emphasized. This was the essence of the unique political currency Vargas
was then developing in preparation for his presidential bid in 1950.
Called *trabalhismo,* the approach honored workers not only for their
labor but also for their role in history—as historical agents in the
struggle against slavery and reactionary landlords and as individuals
pushing for industrial development and social and political democracy. The PTB was *their* heroic vehicle, and Vargas and other party
leaders were *their* humble public servants.[23]

The presence of this budding populist discourse, which offered
a critique of both communism and *coronelismo,* makes it difficult to
access the precise relationship between PCB organizing in the countryside and larger political developments. Electoral statistics demonstrate, however, that planters had lost their traditional grip on the
rural vote by the 19 January 1947 gubernatorial elections. That some
Ribeirão Preto planters later chose to ally with the PCB suggests that
this party had a more profound grip on rural workers than did the
PTB. Heading into the January election, planters divided their vote
between the PSD's Mario Tavares and Antônio de Almeida Prado, candidate of the laissez-faire UDN. The PSD candidate promised the best

22. Vargas, *A política trabalhista no Brasil* (Rio de Janeiro: José Olympio, 1950), 167–70.
    23. A sophisticated discussion of the origins and development of *trabalhismo* is Castro
Gomes, *A invenção do trabalhismo.* Further discussion of the PTB-PCB rivalry can be found in
part 1 of Glaúcio Ary Dillon Soares, *Sociedade e política no Brasil* (São Paulo: Difel, 1973).

chance of victory, especially since President Eurico Gaspar Dutra (of the PSD) could wield great influence through lingering Estado Novo machinery and personnel, which included the federally appointed governor, who appointed the mayors, and the mayors themselves, who presided over the local electoral process. But the election was lost to them (see Appendix, Table 1). Having openly accepted the endorsement and support of the Communist Party just twenty days prior to the election, Adhemar de Barros won a plurality on a ticket of his own making: his upstart Social Progressive Party (PSP, Partido Social Progressista).[24] The PCB, which could claim immense popularity among working-class voters, took justifiable credit for this victory.

For the planters and entrepreneurs of the PSD, an ominous message lurked behind the upset victory of a candidate who was not beholden to them and appeared to ally himself with the Communist "social disease."[25] Even though, as the son of a prominent family of coffee planters, Barros was someone the planters eventually found they could work with, the election results cut deeply into their bargaining power by showing that the São Paulo PSD could no longer deliver the rural vote. While the PSD's Tavares won a plurality (38 percent) in the interior, the majority (52 percent) of the votes had been split between two populist candidates whose campaigns appealed to rural labor. These two candidates were the PCB-backed Barros, who won 23 percent of the rural vote, and the Labor Party's Hugo Borghi, with 29 percent. A political disaster of historic proportions for conservatives, the election profoundly jolted the traditional conception of rural power relations.[26]

Throughout the Alta Mogiana, the center-left gubernatorial candidates polled better than those of the PSD or UDN (see Appendix, Table 2). In Ribeirão Preto and surrounding towns, candidates backed by planters (Tavares) and the commercial establishment (Almeida Prado) were overwhelmed by Barros and Borghi, who attracted 70 percent of the vote, considerably better than their rural, statewide av-

24. Regina Sampaio, *Adhemar de Barros e o PSP* (São Paulo: Global, 1982).

25. As Navy Commander Henrique Batista Silva Oliveira told two sessions of the Sociedade Rural Brasileira, "Communism is a social disease." See "Um fenomeno natural," *RSRB* 37: 320 (April 1947), 38; and "A questão Comunista," *RSRB* 37:321 (May 1947), 40–42. See also the reactions of various *fazendeiros* to Communist Party leader Luís Carlos Prestes's first São Paulo speech upon release from prison. "Uma campanha injusta e inconsequente contra os lavradores do Brasil e de Sao Paulo," *RSRB* 25:300 (August 1945), 14–24.

26. "The PSD's loss in the cities, however understandable, was accompanied by an electoral disaster in the interior where both the PTB and the PSP/PCB alliance outpolled it, a political revolution that deserves fuller study." French, "Adhemarista Populism in São Paulo," 25 n. 65. While French may have exaggerated the revolutionary proportions of the 1947 election, his comment does not overstate the need to look at this event more closely.

erage of 52 percent. In another important agricultural center, the adjacent Sertãozinho electoral zone, the center-left candidates also attracted a greater percentage (58 percent) of voters than represented in statewide averages.

It is difficult to attribute these results definitively to the rural labor vote, especially in the case of Ribeirão Preto itself. The 1950 census demonstrated that Ribeirão Preto had already become an economically complex regional center by the end of World War II. The survey showed that only 9,878, or 25 percent, of 39,102 working people were listed as agricultural.[27] However, much of the industry and commerce in Ribeirão Preto owed its existence to regional agricultural production, and so the planters' tentacles extended deep into the towns. Nevertheless, the clear electoral popularity of center-left candidates in Ribeirão Preto, then the most industrialized city of the region, suggests that proportionally more workers felt themselves to be out of range of those tentacles. At the very least, the January 1947 election results showed how difficult it had become to tell whether Ribeirão Preto's rural working or owning classes would have the most influence over politics during the Populist Republic.

Rise of the Alta Mogiana Working Class

By 1947, Ribeirão Preto's working classes had developed considerable autonomy. In the 1930s, Communists and labor activists founded the UGT, and workers successfully maintained working-class organizations from then on.[28] In June 1945, tired of wartime rationing and wage suppression, Ribeirão Preto workers demanded a wage readjustment over that promised by the legal minimum wage. The local

27. These figures themselves are extremely difficult to interpret. First, the census categories for workers, formally referred to as the economically active population (EAP), include all members of the workforce ten years of age and older. Knowing the ages of workers is essential when analyzing the eligible electorate because only adults (twenty-one or older) were allowed to vote. Moreover, I have already eliminated from the total EAP two additional legally excluded populations: military and police personnel, and unemployed women (primarily "housewives"). The basic figures themselves have been taken from the corresponding towns listed in the census and included in the various electoral zones. See table 43 in Instituto Brasileiro de Geografia e Estatística, *Censo demográfico: Estado de São Paulo,* Tomo I, vol. 25 (Rio de Janeiro: Instituto Brasileiro de Geografia e Estatística, Conselho Nacional de Estatística, Serviço Nacional de Recenseamento, 1954), 132–39.

28. Sebastião Geraldo, "Relatório para o exame geral de qualificação para obtenção do grau de mestre em ciências da comunicação" (Universidade de São Paulo, 1988, mimeographed), 22.

syndical hierarchy had been appointed by government officials, but dynamic militants such as Irineu Luís de Moraes organized pressure from below to force the union's leaders to negotiate wage hikes after the war.[29] When rallying workers faced armed resistance from the owners of the area's largest food distributor, the Casa Robin, some five thousand workers stormed the company warehouse and sacked it, carrying away everything but the walls.[30] Eventually, no fewer than nine unions and eight employer groups were represented in the settlement process, which brought not only increased wages but also the merchants' promise not to increase consumer prices corresponding-ly.[31] Then, stimulated by the strike's success, Ribeirão Preto served as the center of an unprecedented statewide strike against the U.S.-owned Power and Light Company (Companhia Força e Luz), genera-tor of electric power and operator of urban transit throughout the interior of Sao Paulo. Involving thousands of workers, the strike af-fected Força e Luz at its source—the company's hydroelectric plants. According to Moraes, the carefully orchestrated strike began with a phone call from the company's communication center in Ribeirão Preto, ordering all sixteen stations to turn off their generators.[32] The strike, opposed by both the PCB and the energy workers' official union, proved enormously successful. With broad popular support, in two days the strikers won a signed contract granting 100 percent

29. On a Monday morning when most workers would not be able to come, union bosses, or *pelegos* (a name used for government-appointed union officials or those otherwise compro-mised with bosses, such as scabs), called a public meeting at Ribeirão Preto's central square, Praça 15 de Novembro. The meeting was calculated to defuse working-class tension, and Moraes claims he helped organize a wildcat strike to make it possible for more workers to attend. Welch and Geraldo, *Lutas camponesas*, 59–82.

30. According to Moraes, the warehouse sacking was unplanned and came as a sponta-neous reaction of the rebellious mob. Although police were called to put it down, the mob was too big for the local police. In fact, police lent sackers a hand by organizing the chaotic assault on the Robin warehouse. An Army unit was sent from Pirassununga, seventy miles to the south, but everyone had gone home by the time the troops arrived. Irineu Luís de Moraes, transcript of interview by author, Ribeirão Preto, 22 August 1988 (hereafter Moraes transcript, pt. 1).

31. The unions involved represented printers, canners, and meatpackers, metalworkers, furniture makers, shoemakers, tailors, trolley car conductors, hotel and restaurant servers, beer-makers and bottlers, construction workers, and store clerks. See "Satisfeitas as justas reivindica-ções trabalhistas," *DM*, 14 June 1945, 8. Although the sacking had been spontaneous and the strike organized by militants such as Moraes, the fact that the strike was settled by *pelego* union bosses may indicate why Borghi did so well in the region (see Appendix, Table 2). As a central organizer of the PTB in São Paulo, Borghi could take credit for achievements of the official unions. See Maria Victoria Benevides, *O PTB e o trabalhismo* (São Paulo: Brasiliense, 1988), 41–45.

32. Moraes recalled the participation of hydroelectric plants and substations in the fol-lowing localities: Campinas, Bauru, Araraquara, Avanhandava, Marimbondo, Gavião Peixoto, Buriti, São Joaquim da Barra, and Dourados. Moraes transcript, pt. 1.

of the pay increase they had demanded and a month's extra pay at Christmas (*abono de natal*).[33]

On August 12, after the Força e Luz victory, Moraes and seven others opened the Ribeirão Preto office of the PCB and started to sign up new members.[34] Now a paid party organizer, Moraes devoted himself to building support for the party among rural workers of all categories: smallholders, sharecroppers, wage workers, and the area's ubiquitous coffee *colonos*. On August 26, when Guerreiro came to the office and joined the party, he became associated with Moraes. The Dumont league was the first one Moraes was involved in forming; the name, which later was popularized by Francisco Julião, had its origins in the times—numerous political organizations were then called leagues, such as the Liga Democrática—and Communist ideology, which fit rural workers as peasants into a theory about the semifeudal state of Brazilian agriculture.[35] Throughout late 1945 and 1946, Moraes traveled to other towns in the region and helped found rural labor organizations in Guará (November 1945), Viradouro (June 1946), and Barrinha (March 1947).[36] In Miguelópolis, in the far northern reaches of the Alta Mogiana, he also participated in founding another regional headquarters for the PCB among sharecroppers.[37] Thus, by the 1947 election, the PCB had extensively penetrated the Alta Mogiana, establishing itself as a major voice among the urban and rural working classes.

Different from Moraes's previous organizational efforts, these new groups were designed to galvanize the rural working classes as

33. Irineu Luís de Moraes, transcript of interview by Sebastião Geraldo, Ribeirão Preto, 20 February 1989 (hereafter Moraes transcript, pt. 2). See also Geraldo, "Comunicação oral," 89–102.

34. "Partido Comunista Brasileiro: Foi empossado ontem o secretariado do comité municipal, nesta cidade," *DM*, 14 August 1945, 8. Moraes was named general secretary, and Antônio Alagão became rural organizing secretary.

35. Welch and Geraldo, *Lutas camponesas*, 87. Guerreiro transcript, 1. Salla told me that Ciavatta had introduced the name, but Ciavatta never made this claim to us. Salla interview; and Natal Siviero and Nazareno Ciavatta, transcript of interview by author, Ribeirão Preto, 20 October 1988, AEL/UNICAMP. Medeiros, *História dos movimentos*, 26–27, discusses PCB ideology.

36. "Trabalhadores rurais e o PCB," *Hoje*, 21 November 1945, 6, "A miséria e fome os lares camponeses," *Tribuna Popular*, 9 March 1946, 8, "Organizam-se os camponeses do Viradouro," *NH*, 17 June 1946, 7, and "Fundado em Barrinha a associacao dos trabalhadores do campo," *NH*, 12 March 1947, 6, all in Barriguelli, ed., *Subsídios à história*, 138–39, 149–50, 205, 242.

37. While these organizations were legally constituted, they had no special identity within the Brazilian corporate structure. The PCB organized them with two goals in mind: (1) to gain control of an untapped voting block that would help either the party's electoral strength or that of allies and (2) to serve as organizing committees for *sindicatos* that did have a formal place in the Brazilian state. Moraes, "Peasant Leagues in Brazil," 103–5; and Moraes transcript, pts. 1, 3.

political pressure groups rather than as unions focused on economic concerns. "They couldn't properly be called syndicates," said Moraes of the leagues, "but political leagues that followed the elections and delivered votes for candidates backed by the party."[38] The Dumont league displayed its utility to the party in April 1946 when it brought some two hundred rural workers to the heart of Ribeirão Preto to hear a speech by Luís Carlos Prestes, the enormously popular general secretary of the PCB. On January 3, Moraes called on league members to attend a rally for PCB-PSP senatorial candidate Cândido Portinari, the world-renowned artist who was born a coffee *colono* in nearby Brodósqui. Through efforts such as these, the party soon claimed the loyalty of many thousands of rural voters in São Paulo and elsewhere.[39]

Repressing the Peasant Leagues

The outcomes of elections in 1945 and 1947 fully pleased neither the PCB nor the PSD, though the former generally advanced in status at the expense of the other parties. In fact, the growing popularity and electoral successes of the PCB led the government to outlaw the party in May 1947, and the leagues were gradually disbanded as well. On May 9, the police raided the party at the UGT building and confiscated a long list of political tracts and organizing material, including six red "Invitation(s) to the Country Laborers of Barrinha," a statute for "Agricultural Wage Laborers," and two monthly dues receipts for members of the Dumont Peasant League. Within a day, police raided Guerreiro's parent's house and carried away the league materials he had left there.[40] Six police officers sacked Salla's house, too, but they did not find any documents. Guerreiro had warned him of the im-

---

38. Welch and Geraldo, *Lutas camponesas,* 89.

39. Moraes and Guerreiro transcripts; Lindolfo Silva, transcript of interview by author, São Paulo, 16 August 1988, AEL/UNICAMP (hereafter Silva transcript, pt. 1); and João Batista Berardo, *O político Cândido Torquato Portinari* (São Paulo: Populares, 1983), 77–78.

40. On 7 May 1947, under pressure from President Dutra, the Superior Electoral Tribunal canceled the PCB's registry as a legal party. Fearful of the PCB-PSP coalition in São Paulo, Dutra threatened Governor Adhemar de Barros with intervention (permitted by the 1946 constitution) unless he ordered his police to crack down on the party and its labor organizations. Barros submitted to the pressure, and the police raided hundreds of offices of the party and affiliated groups, confiscating documents—including the *liga* records in Guerreiro's house—and arresting militants. A list of the documents and party papers confiscated by the police in Ribeirão Preto is provided in "Auto de Apreensão," 25 May 1947, Arquivo da Tribunal Regional Eleitoral do Estado de São Paulo (hereafter TRE/SP). I am grateful to John French for sending me a copy of this document. See also French, "Adhemarista Populism in São Paulo," 33–34; and Guerreiro transcript.

pending raid, and Salla claims his wife stashed everything under the hay in the manger. The close call with the police scared her, though, and she later burnt all of his papers, including a ledger of dues-paying members and PCB publications. "She scolded me a lot," Salla commented. "The work kept me away from the family too much and she was afraid I'd get arrested."[41]

While the repression of May was disruptive, it was not prosecuted wholeheartedly in the Alta Mogiana. The January election had shown the importance of the working-class vote, and local politicians were in no position to associate themselves with an unpopular attack on the local PCB.[42] At the party's suggestion, Guerreiro became a candidate for city council (*vereador*) in the election of November 9. With the party legally prohibited from electoral participation, the local PCB directorate chose to fuse its candidates with any legal party it could, save the PSP, whose leader had betrayed them by carrying out the repression orders of President Dutra. Since the PCB already had a relationship with the PSD, Guerreiro agreed to run on its ticket. Several other known members of the PCB joined him.[43]

On the surface, the PSD-PCB alliance was an odd one. The PSD was political home to many plantation owners and to President Dutra's ruling government, which had just canceled the PCB's registry. Although the PSD was technically a new party founded in 1945, it was built on traditional rural political structures such as *coronelismo*.[44] In São Paulo, however, the landed oligarchy remained divided over many issues, with some progressive planters supporting the PSD and more conservative ones joining the UDN. In the PSD, one was likely to find some old Partido Democrático (PD) members who recalled aligning with the PCB's BOC in the 1920s. In the mid-

---

41. Salla interview.

42. On repression, see the comments of Elias Chaves Neto, *Minha vida e as lutas de meu tempo* (São Paulo: Alfa Omega, 1978), 92–122, who reported the counterattack of Barros's police to be fierce in 1948 and 1949. For the region, see "Manobra diabólica das reacionários de Fernandópolis desmascarada pelo secretária de segurança," *Hoje*, 17 May 1947, 2, and "Arbitrariamente fechada a associação dos trabalhadores rurais de Rio Preto," *Hoje*, 24 May 1947, 3, in Barriguelli, ed., *Subsídios à história*, 258–60.

43. The PSD-PCB alliance was a matter of public record in Ribeirão Preto, one that did not go uncriticized. During the campaign, the city's leading newspaper, *A Cidade*, ran stories critical of the marriage of the two parties. See, for example, "Flagrantes de um 'casamento' político," *A Cidade*, 6 October 1947, which accused the PSD of delivering Ribeirão Preto to agents of the Kremlin. The documents are unambiguous in establishing the Communist membership of only a few of Guerreiro's co-candidates. They were José Engracia Garcia, Decio Fernandes, and Aparecido de Araújo. The other PSD candidates publicly endorsed by Prestes and accused of PCB-membership by opponents were Henrique Crosio, Albiono Tremschini Mioto, Antônio Pontim, Ofelio Russomano, Clemente José da Silva, and Salvador Trovato. PR 6337/209, 2 December 1947, TRE/SP.

44. Lucia Hippolito, *PSD: De raposas e reformistas* (Rio de Janeiro: Paz e Terra, 1985).

1940s, the Ribeirão Preto sections of the PSD and PCB apparently shared short-term assumptions about modernization, corporatism, and populism. Given these conditions, as well as traditional patron-client relations, Guerreiro straightforwardly accepted the tutelage of João Velloso, the chief bookkeeper of the Fazenda Santa Theresa and a known PSD leader in Ribeirão Preto. Velloso provided him with money and transportation and opened the door to various plantations. Invited to speak at weddings, dances, and soccer games, Guerreiro found himself the bearer of the rural equivalent of the key to the city.[45]

As the November election approached, however, Velloso issued Guerreiro a warning along with Cr$500 to rent a bus. "I'll give you the money," Guerreiro remembers Velloso saying, "but don't talk to the voters too much." In Guerreiro's view, Velloso seemed afraid he would alert the men to their rights and cause them to work less willingly and cheaply.[46] The peasant leader promised to refrain from giving electoral advice and merely to pass out the PSD ballot, which included Guerreiro's name as well as those of another ten city council candidates. Nevertheless, the campaign was marked by acrimony, as opposition parties tried to Red-bait the PSD. The Paulista Defense League (Liga da Defesa Paulista) ran ads warning voters to beware of the PSD: "Brazilian Fatherland to Bolshevik Fatherland! . . . The PSD donated Cr$30,000 to the local Communist chiefs. Alert!" Nevertheless, a few of these nominal PSD candidates ran openly as Communists, and all accepted the endorsement of Prestes, believing his support would appeal to voters.

In the countryside, Guerreiro was more cautious. He used the bus provided by Velloso to go from plantation to plantation in order to pick up rural workers and bring them to Ribeirão Preto where they could vote. In the end, however, Guerreiro attracted only 77 votes out of more than 13,492 cast.[47] His contradictory image as both a defender of rural working-class interests and a representative of the planter's party must have confused numerous voters. But in Brazil's partisan proportional distribution system, two other Communists on the ticket (Aparecido de Araújo and Décio Fernandes) and a sympathizer (Dr. Henrique Crosio) were elected to PSD seats; in fact, the

45. Details on Velloso were obtained from the historian José Pedro de Miranda, now with the Arquivo Público e Histórico de Ribeirão Preto. Guerreiro transcript.
46. Guerreiro transcript. More on this election can be found in Walker, "From Coronelismo to Populism," 191–96.
47. "Atas das juntas eleitorais do município de Ribeirão Preto," 9 November 1947, from PR 6337/209, TRE/SP.

Prestes candidates garnered a third more votes than the straight PSD candidates. Post-election legal challenges, however, saw the winners blocked from taking their seats in the council.[48]

For Guerreiro and the party the defeat was frustrating, but their campaign to wrest power from traditional groups continued to focus on democratic methods. For the PSD, however, the election weakened not only their power but also their self-esteem. They had allied with the Communists, faced embarrassment, and lost. Throughout most of the Alta Mogiana region, non-PSD candidates won mayoral and city council elections (see Appendix, Table 3). Try as it might, the PSD had failed to convince rural workers that it had their best interests at heart. The fantasy world celebrating the mythic harmony of rural life, the absence of classes, the *clã fazendeiro,* the vision the planters had concocted to defend themselves since 1941, proved ineffective against rural workers armed with ballots. The election put a temporary end to the planters' experiment with democracy and began a period of hardening rural social relations. Guerreiro and the workers he brought to vote had somehow deceived the planters.

An Ill-Fated Rural Labor Conference

Denied a seat on the city council, Guerreiro did not end his career as a rural agitator. Soon after the election, the PCB continued its negotiations with the state government and gained support for a rural labor congress, to be held in São Paulo in February 1948. The Ribeirão Preto executive committee picked Guerreiro to be the area's rural labor representative. But Guerreiro recalls that he refused to be appointed, asking instead to be elected by the remaining members of the now-clandestine league. "If the congress is hand-picked," he remembers saying, "it won't be a congress. Now, if it's a congress for folks to say what we think and talk about our problems, then it'd be a real congress."[49] Although Guerreiro did win the league's support, the congress was—as he suspected—largely manipulated from above. Called by Hugo Borghi, who had recently become the state secretary of agriculture, it promised to be a serious meeting, con-

---

48. After the election, three opposition parties—Social Progressive Party (PSP), Republican Party (PR), and National Labor Party (PTN)—united to demand that state election officials remove from office those successful PSD candidates presumed to be Communists. See PR 6337/209, 2 December 1947, TRE/SP. I thank John French for making this document available to me.
    49. Guerreiro transcript, 4.

ducted to generate ideas for reform from the rural workers themselves. After years of lofty elite debate regarding the problem of rural labor, this was to be a historic meeting, providing rural workers with their first official forum for participation. But the PCB's involvement made it a target of critics, and Borghi canceled it before it was held.[50]

The congress had been a product of this complex period of experimentation with democracy. Borghi was an aspiring politician who had run against his popular boss, Governor Adhemar de Barros, in the 1947 campaign for governor. Barros had benefited in the election from the PCB's endorsement. The PSD, no stranger to such alliances itself, painted the congress as a populist concession to the Communists. Influenced by his party's concerns, President Dutra also saw the congress as one part of Barros's strategy to expand his electoral popularity and had the São Paulo federation of rural associations, organized under Vargas's controversial Decree Law No. 8,127, put pressure on him to prevent the congress from taking place. Perhaps seeing the event as an opportunity to strengthen his National Labor Party (PTN, Partido Trabalhista Nacional), Borghi pleaded with Barros to let the congress go on, since it was not inconsistent with the governor's policies. As governor, Barros had already reduced interest rates for farm loans to smallholders and provided some tractors at low cost. The congress, after all, simply sought to unite fifteen hundred "farmer" (*lavrador*) representatives from all over the state to discuss the problems of credit, technical assistance, marketing, warehousing, and rural unionization.[51] Then the SRB joined the chorus of opposition to the congress. One SRB planter went so far as to say that the very debate about holding a congress would be dangerous if rural workers knew about it.[52] Barros gave in, forcing Borghi to resign and announcing that the congress would be postponed until Communist influence in the interior had been "neutralized."[53]

On one level, the Borghi congress itself provided the ruling

---

50. Sampaio, *Adhemar de Barros e o PSP,* 60–61.

51. Interview with Hugo Borghi, *O Dia* (São Paulo), 17 February 1948, 6. Borghi's defense of the rural congress reflected a durable commitment to an agrarian reform program. In his 1950 gubernatorial campaign, he returned to this theme by describing election day as "Man of the Country Redemption Day." A dramatic half-page newspaper ad appearing during the campaign promised that the election of Borghi would bring rural workers minimum wage increases and *colonos* higher pay for each one thousand trees contracted. It also promised benefits for smallholders, tenants, and those who wished to mechanize work processes. See "Redenção do homem do campo," *DM,* 1 October 1950, 3.

52. Virgílio Magano, in "Empreendimento perigoso," *RSRB* 27:300 (March 1948), 4. See also "Os propositos do congresso rural" and "A situação do trabalhador rural" in the same issue, 60, 74.

53. From *O Dia,* 27 February 1948, cited in Sampaio, *Adhemar de Barros e o PSP,* 61.

classes with an opportunity to neutralize Communist influence in the countryside. The intention was to use the congress to advance the process of incorporating rural labor in the Brazilian political economy. But the planters' vigorous resistance demonstrated how miserably they had failed at populist politics and how little faith they had in their ability to do better at it. Although the transition to the Populist Republic had been rocky and guaranteed few advantages for planters, rural workers had not gained many specific advantages either. Their new electoral strength was important, but backroom deals and repression had made the right to vote difficult to count on.

The PCB, repressed and alienated from the government, turned for the next several years to clandestine activity, including support for some armed conflicts. In doing so, the party left behind such once enthusiastic yet pragmatic followers as Guerreiro. While a new period in the construction of rural citizenship was about to begin, the years between 1945 and 1948 had brought significant change. For the first time, rural workers had broken away from political dependency on the plantation and had entered the realm of the nation.

4

The killer had to die. It was 1951, and Irineu Luís de Moraes had been led deep into the pine forests of northern Paraná state, to the secret night camp of a group of armed peasants. As the men planned to execute the killer—the chief hired gun of Geremia Lunardelli, one of the country's largest landowners—they could not know that the final chapter of their long battle of resistance against expulsion from their farmsteads was at hand. Their movement had never been stronger. Hundreds of families, each having committed considerable resources to clearing the thick woodland between the rivers Paranapanema and Bandeirante do Norte, had recently indicated their support for the rebels by signing a petition urging the federal government to affirm their small holdings and deny title to a handful of speculators like Lunardelli. But the messenger, just

SHIFTING TERRAIN

Resisting the Deadly Limits of Incorporation

back from delivering the petition to officials in Rio de Janeiro, had been butchered by Lunardelli's ruthless *jagunços*. It was *jagunço* chief José Celestino who had to die.[1]

After arriving in Londrina, the region's central city, Moraes contacted the peasant rebels through Celso Cabral de Melo, another PCB militant and a former Brazilian navy radio operator known by the nom de guerre "Captain Carlos." For Captain Carlos and the rebels, justice demanded the death of Celestino. By killing him, the revolutionary movement would be consolidated, and the impunity of the landlords' henchmen would be abolished.

Executing Celestino presented significant problems for the rebels, Moraes observed. None of them alone was his match, for Celestino had killed dozens of men, and several among the resisters had barely survived his attacks. Celestino, allegedly on orders from Lunardelli and his sons, appeared on their farmsteads accompanied by ten or more accomplices, each armed to the teeth and bound by a code of terror. Two bandoliers of bullets draped across Celestino's chest, two pistols dangled from his waist belt, and the handles of several knives, including one in the top of his boot, protruded from his lethal carriage. He was the image of the famous northeast bandit Lampião, or worse still, Cicero, Lampião's bloodthirsty lieutenant. Ordered to invade a peasant's homestead and rout the pilgrims, Celestino's gang acted with lusty intensity, raping women and girls, mutilating men, burning down buildings and crops, slaughtering livestock. Protected by the region's most powerful landlords, Celestino and his gang lived outside the reach of law and vengeance.

An opportunity for justice presented itself with the barbarous murder of João Berbardes, the peasants' emissary to the capital. To protect Lunardelli's interests, Celestino's henchmen captured Berbardes and beat him to death while he dangled upside down from a tree. Anxious for revenge, Berbardes's family learned that Celestino occasionally traveled alone to visit a lover who lived in a remote cabin. Armed with this intelligence, the rebels planned an ambush. One night that May, news came that Celestino had left to see his mistress, and the men laid their trap, quietly creeping into the woods surrounding the woman's cabin. In the morning, when Celestino left to mount his horse, a barrage of peasant rifle fire spurted from the shadowy forest and cut the *jagunço* down. "They set up an ex-

---

1. This account is derived from Irineu Luís de Moraes, transcript of interview by author and Sebastião Geraldo, Ribeirão Preto, 27 May 1989 (hereafter Moraes transcript, pt. 3); and Pedro Paulo Felismino, "Celestino, jagunço, espalhava o terror: Foi justiçado pelos posseiros," *Folha de Londrina* (hereafter *FL*), 6 July 1985, 11.

ecution," Moraes recalled, "and shot him eighteen or twenty times. They caught him and they killed him, the miserable thug [*jagunço desgraçado*]."[2] To intimidate other *jagunços,* they made a scarecrow of Celestino by tying his bullet-riddled body to a cross at the entrance of Centenário do Sul, a budding town in this frontier region.

The Struggle for Land

Contemporary press reports called it the "War of Porecatú," acknowledging the town of Porecatú as the hub of the conflict. The Communist-inspired combatants thought of it as a little Korea (*Coreinha*), making reference to the Cold War clash then unfolding in Asia. In any event, the conflict of peasants, landlords, and the state attained military proportions, for it included several pitched battles between soldiers and peasants and at least fourteen deaths and eighteen casualties before the fighting ceased on 21 June 1951.[3] The war was noteworthy not only for the lives lost but also as an example of the modern struggle for land in one of Brazil's richest agricultural belts, one contiguous with São Paulo's Alta Mogiana region and linked to it socially as well as geographically. Here were hardworking rural folk—many of them migrants from São Paulo's declining coffee producing areas—who, after having failed to resolve their grievances through peaceful means, had taken up arms to defend themselves against the terror of greedy landlords. Here was an elected state government struggling to maintain order against two militarized factions, finding itself, more often than not, fulfilling the bidding of the landlords. Here was a Communist Party closed out of electoral politics, anxious to recuperate a revolutionary image by backing the rebellious Porecatú peasants. Here, in the final analysis, was a nation anxious to capitalize on a strengthening world coffee market—a country politically divided, awash with underpaid and underemployed rural workers, and profoundly troubled by its agrarian problems.

2. Moraes transcript, pt. 3.

3. See, for example, *O cruzeiro,* 9 December 1950, cited in Pedro Paulo Felismino, "Revolta e traição," *FL,* 18 July 1975, 13. This article comes from a ten-part series written by Felismino, called "A guerra de Porecatú," that was published by *FL,* 14 July–28 July 1985. To write his story—the only attempt I know of to analyze and record the entire event—Felismino drew substantially on court records and oral history. This chapter draws extensively on Felismino's series. The reference to Korea is made by one of Felismino's informants, Manoel Jacinto Correia, in Felismino, "Memórias do Velho Mané," *FL,* 26 July 1985, 11. Thanks to Sebastião Geraldo for obtaining a copy of this series.

Brazil's agrarian problems were not easy to resolve. Small wonder that hundreds of Porecatú wars did not burst forth around the country. Each region had its own peculiarities. In regions like the Alta Mogiana, old coffee lands were subdivided and sold to better-off *colonos,* such as the Guerreiro and Guindalini families. The terms were often quite attractive. As Nelson Guindalini recalled, Dumont land purchasers required no down payment, and loans were interest free. In the northeast, however, a class of historic landowners dating back to the colonial era generally refused to sell land to their social inferiors. In distant frontier regions such as the Amazon forest, government assistance encouraged settlement of rubber tappers and small farmers. Underdeveloped lands near population and transportation centers, like those in Paraná, generated more conflict.[4] In the postwar era, some populist politicians tried to address these problems by noting that the 1946 constitution privileged "social utility" over ownership in the determination of land holdings. They sought electoral support by making proposals to appropriate and distribute unused or underutilized land to rural workers. A class of small farmers would be created whose self-interest would motivate them to use the land efficiently, thereby raising their standard of living and contributing to Brazil's progress.[5]

By and large, planters opposed such proposals. In their view, the politicians who advocated reform in the interior were opportunists, interested only in the rural worker's vote; their "demagogic promises" dangerously subverted agricultural productivity.[6] Luís Amaral, the SRB's delegate at a conference on immigration and rural labor problems in 1949, revealed the thinking of his fellow planters when he emphasized the issue of power. "The land is like a woman," he said; "if it comes easy, it has no value: it has to be conquered." Once conquered, the land presumably had value, and the planter could deal with it capriciously. "We will neither permit nor tolerate prejudicial interference over our sacred sovereignty [*soberania*]," commented

4. Nelson Luis Guindalini, interview by author, Dumont, 13 May 1995. For the northeast, see Manuel Correia de Andrade, *The Land and the People of Northeast Brazil* (Albuquerque: University of New Mexico Press, 1980). For the Amazon, see, for example, Márcio Souza, *A expressão Amazonense* (São Paulo: Alfa Omega, 1977).

5. Nestor Duarte, *Reforma agrária* (Rio de Janeiro: Ministério de Educação e Saude, Serviço de Documentação, n.d.), contains copies of Afranio de Carvalho's 1947 "Lei agrária" and Duarte's 1947 "Ante-projeto de reforma agrária," as well as other controversial reform projects voted down by congress. See the discussion in Camargo, "A questão agrária," 144–50.

6. Plinio de Castro Prado, 5 July 1950 regular meeting of the SRB, in "Ordem do dia," *RSRB* 30:357 (August 1950), 2.

SRB president Francisco Malta Cardoso.[7] Such imperious, not to mention sexist, statements became more typical in landlord discourse as the rights consciousness of rural workers and peasants grew.

Planters invited attack with such language, and the PCB obliged them with its own fighting words. As the self-appointed leader of the peasants' struggle, the party unquestionably influenced the evolution of rural social protest. Following the party's suppression in 1947, leaders adopted an increasingly revolutionary line that was shaped, like the anticommunism of Brazilian officials, by Cold War pressures. Embracing the Comintern analysis of colonialism, PCB theorists considered Brazil in a semicolonial relationship with so-called imperialist powers, especially the USSR's archenemy, the United States. Characteristically, the imperialists and their Brazilian collaborators, including SRB planters, were interested only in the production of export commodities like coffee and strategic resources like oil. In order to protect their interests, the imperialists and their collaborators conspired to hold the agricultural sector in a state of development so backward that it bordered on feudalism. Brazil could grow only if it broke its ties to the imperialists and restructured agriculture, favoring production of foodstuffs for the home market, foodstuffs essential to feed urban workers engaged in the industrial development of Brazil. It was a perception of reality not too far removed from the thinking that had oriented the BOC in the late 1920s, only now, forced underground by President Dutra, the party chose to fight force with force. "The masses want to struggle," declared Communist Party leader Luís Carlos Prestes in January 1948. "They have already demonstrated," he continued, "that they simply await direction from the Communists to confront police violence with decisiveness and courage." Driven by this logic, the party was to devote itself in theory to the revolutionary conquest of power by leading the masses in struggle from 1948 to 1954.[8]

On the first of August 1950, in what became known as the August Manifesto, Prestes called on party activists to struggle for the vio-

7. For the sexist remark, see Luis Amaral, "A reforma agrária: Aspecto econômico do projeto de reforma agrária apresentado a Assembléia Federal pelo Deputado Nestor Duarte," *RSRB* 37:326 (October 1947), 13. See also Luis Amaral, "Primeiro Conferência de imigração e colonização," *RSRB* 28:344 (June 1949), 26–30. Malta Cardoso quotes from "Relatório do Dr. Francisco Malta Cardoso, presidente da Sociedade Rural Brasileira," *RSRB* 30:353 (April 1950), 26.

8. Beatriz Ana Loner, "O PCB e a linha do manifesto de agosto: Um estudo" (master's thesis, Universidade Estadual de Campinas, 1985), 68–76, examines the alignment between postwar PCB policy and the resolutions of the Sixth Comintern of 1928. Luís Carlos Prestes, "Como enfrentar os problemas da revolução agrária e anti-imperialista," *Problemas* 9 (April 1948), 36.

lent overthrow of the government and the establishment of a popular revolutionary state. Framed by Cold War concerns, the statement was to guide party militants into the mid-1950s. Prestes condemned the "servile" Brazilian government for supporting the United States by signing military pacts and providing oil, coffee, and other products to allied troops in the unfolding Korean War. Only by standing with the Soviet Union could Brazil restore its traditions of peace, independence, and progress. To reverse the "reactionary fascist advance" of the country, "the only viable and progressive solution [was] the revolutionary solution." "We need to liberate the country from the imperialist game and take down the dictatorship of the large landlords [*latifundiários*] and big capitalists, substituting the government of treason, war, and terror against the people, with an effectively democratic and popular one." To accomplish this, "it is indispensable to liquidate the economic bases of the reaction, including . . . the confiscation of the great land holdings [*latifúndios*] that should be given freely into the hands of those who work and live on the properties." Echoing failed positions from the early 1930s, Prestes called for peasants and agricultural laborers to rise up and fight for land seizures without compensation to *latifundiários,* the end of sharecropping arrangements, wage payments in money rather than in kind, and the elimination of all debts. Finally, the manifesto called for the creation of a "popular army of national liberation" to free the nation from the imperialist grip of the United States and its Brazilian collaborators.[9] As part of the policy of building a revolutionary movement, Prestes urged party militants to be attentive to spontaneous forms of working-class rebellion. The first test of the party's commitment to revolutionary struggle and radical agrarian change came in northern Paraná. At the request of local militants and state leaders, the national executive committee sent men like Moraes and Captain Carlos

9. During this period, Brazilian Communists grew enthusiastic about a particular idea of the Chinese revolutionary experience. They came to identify Brazil with China and to envision Brazilian peasants rising up in armies to overthrow the government and kick out the imperialists. Obviously, their grasp of the Chinese situation was even less firm than their hold on Brazilian conditions. The nine principal objectives outlined in the August Manifesto were (1) a democratic and popular government; (2) peace; (3) the "immediate liberation of Brazil from the imperialist yoke [*jugo imperialista*]"; (4) distribution (*entrega*) of land to those who work it; (5) the independent development of the national economy; (6) civil rights (*liberdades democráticas*) to all people; (7) "the immediate improvement of living conditions for the mass of workers"; (8) support for the instruction and cultural development of the people; and (9) the formation of a popular army of national liberation. See Luís Carlos Prestes, "Manifesto de Agosto de 1950," in Moisés Vinhas, *O partidão: A luta por um partido de massas, 1922–1974* (São Paulo: Hucitec, 1982), 140–58; and Leôncio Martins Rodrigues, "O PCB: Os dirigentes e a organização," in Fausto, *História geral da civilização brasileira*, III: 3, 414–15.

Geremia Lunardelli, the Brazilian Coffee King who claimed ownership of disputed lands during the Porecatú War, was photographed in July 1952. Photo: courtesy Arquivo Fotográfico da *Última Hora* from Arquivo do Estado de São Paulo

to help the peasants. Through such men, the party supported, even stimulated, heightened levels of violence. There were moments when peace seemed at hand through negotiated means, but PCB militants, loyal to the precepts of the August Manifesto, opposed accepting these proposals. All authorities secretly conspired against the masses, the thinking went, and the era of cross-class alliance had ended with the party's suppression in 1947. Having squeezed the peasants into the party's theoretical framework, the party did not stand by their popular peasant army when the state police of Paraná and São Paulo massed to crush the rebellion. Facing defeat, the PCB abandoned the fight. The case provides an excellent opportunity to analyze the party's activities in the countryside, the application of

August Manifesto theory, and the complex dilemmas of rural social movements in the Brazilian coffee economy.[10]

The Extensive Coffee Frontier

The story of Porecatú is especially revealing because it makes up part of the particular history of Ribeirão Preto and the state of São Paulo in general. As São Paulo's coffee frontier reached the southern limits of the state, numerous coffee barons bought land in Paraná, awaiting favorable conditions to cultivate or sell it. Among those who did so were the Lunardellis. The family patron, Geremia Lunardelli, had been born in Treviso, Italy, in 1885 and moved to Brazil with his parents as a young boy. A Brazilian Horatio Alger, he grew to become a successful merchant and land speculator in Ribeirão Preto. With his brother Ricardo, Geremia invested in coffee agriculture and eventually earned a place in Brazil's club of coffee kings. As his nine children matured, they bought land all over São Paulo and expanded their holdings to the south into northern Paraná, as well as to the north, into Goiás state. "By 1943," the historian Joseph L. Love wrote of the elder Geremia, "he had ten thousand rural workers in his employ."[11]

Northern Paraná and Brazil's historic coffee-producing capital in the Alta Mogiana were related in other important ways. It can be argued that coffee cultivation in Paraná expanded in relation to the contraction of production in São Paulo's older zones. During the 1940s and 1950s, coffee production in Paraná outstripped that of São Paulo, and in 1960, Paraná was Brazil's leading coffee producer. Between 1940 and 1960, Paraná's proportion of Brazilian coffee output jumped from 5 to 47 percent, while São Paulo's share declined from 62 to 27 percent. In Paraná, 87 percent of the increase was in the north, where, by 1960, 50 percent of the region's land was under cultivation, 73 percent planted in mature coffee trees. In the meantime, in Ribeirão Preto county alone, the decline of the coffee

10. Prestes, "Como enfrentar os problemas da revolução agrária." On Porecatú, see Moraes transcript, pt. 3; Gregório Bezerra, *Memórias: Segunda parte, 1946–1969*, 2d. ed. (Rio de Janeiro: Civilização Brasileira, 1980), 126; and Felismino, "A guerra de Porecatú."

11. Biographical information on Geremia Lunardelli is from Love, *São Paulo in the Brazilian Federation*, 29; British Chamber of Commerce of São Paulo and Southern Brazil, *Personalidades no Brasil* (São Paulo: n.p., 1933), 365; and "Um pioneiro: Geremia Lunardelli," *A Lavoura* (March–April 1950), 17–19. Quote from Love, *São Paulo in the Brazilian Federation*, 79. Lunardelli died 9 May 1962. His given name is spelled "Geremias" in some sources. See "Lidadores agrícolas que desaperacerem," *A Rural* 42:494 (June 1962), 36.

economy manifested as a reduction in the number of producing trees. In 1940 there were thirteen million trees, in 1950 ten million, and in 1960 only eight million.[12] Thus, while the number of coffee trees in Ribeirão Preto dwindled by nearly 40 percent, the land devoted to coffee increased by nearly 50 percent in northern Paraná. In this way, the rise of coffee in northern Paraná was intimately related to the decline of coffee in São Paulo's Alta Mogiana region.

Various factors contributed to the contrasting development of each region, and among these one of the more telling contrasts was in the social relations of coffee production predominating in each area. The regional differences in the organization of work demonstrate the significance of time and place when analyzing the Brazilian rural labor movement.[13] As discussed in Chapter 1, the coffee economy of São Paulo based its success on the *colonato* system. Created in the nineteenth century as a means to replace slaves with free labor, this system depended on a constant influx of laborers. Its preconditions were the growth of the world coffee market between 1880 and 1930 and the simultaneous immigration of large numbers of Europeans to the New World. The *colonos* contracted annually to care for a given number of coffee trees in exchange for a fixed annual wage, rent, and a negotiated package of land usage rights, such as the right to plant corn or beans between the rows of coffee trees. This labor system was the central characteristic of the expanding plantations of São Paulo, and it lay at the heart of the high profits and longevity of the Ribeirão Preto coffee barons.[14]

In northern Paraná, on the other hand, the coffee economy produced a divergent set of social relations. Initial interest in the commercial exploitation of the region's fertile soils came in the 1920s. Coffee sales were booming, and because of its proximity to the transportation and commercial infrastructure of São Paulo, northern Paraná attracted the attention of investors. During that decade, various specu-

12. On São Paulo, see Constantino C. Fraga, "Resenha historica do café no Brasil," *Agricultura em São Paulo* (hereafter *ASP*) 10:1 (January 1963), 16. For Paraná, see William H. Nicholls, "The Agricultural Frontier in Modern Brazilian History: The State of Paraná, 1920–1960," in *Cultural Change in Brazil: Papers from the Midwest Association for Latin American Studies, October 30–31, 1969* (Muncie: Ball State University Press, 1969), 56. For the Alta Mogiana, see Walker, "From Coronelismo to Populism," 51. Although uniform comparative data are not always available, one of the best methods used to measure change in coffee production is to compare the number of trees being cultivated from one year to another.

13. For understanding the diversity of the African-American experience in the southern United States, the importance of time and place variables has been eloquently revealed in Ira Berlin's "Time, Space, and the Evolution of Afro-American Society on British Mainland North America," *American Historical Review* 85:1 (February 1980), 44–78.

14. On the development of the *colonato* system, see Chapter 1.

lators, (*grileiros*) bought land from the state under the stipulation that they would encourage homesteading. In 1925 an innovative Scottish land developer named Simon Joseph Fraser bought more than three million acres of land spreading east-west across nearly five thousand square miles of the northern frontier of the state. The land was cheap (U.S.$.50 an acre) but its development had barely begun when the 1929 crash dramatically depressed international commodity prices, underscoring the problems inherent in depending on a single export crop. Under depressed conditions, Fraser's land development corporation, the North Paraná Land Company (CTNP, Companhia de Terras Norte de Paraná), devised a colonization scheme requiring limited capital investment. Rather than continue the extensive monoculture model of São Paulo, the CTNP decided to foster the construction of an integrated regional economy based on smallholding, polyculture, and easy access to transportation. During the 1930s, the company sold only about 5 percent of its vast holdings to planters who could afford 30 percent cash down payments; the rest went to smallholders. In 1939, Geremia Lunardelli entered the market, buying properties in various districts, including Porecatú. Finally, with the end of hostilities in Europe and the notable postwar resurgence of the coffee market (see Appendix, Table 4), the settlement of northern Paraná took off. Although many rural workers earned wages in Paraná, frontier development itself was characterized by smallholder settlement rather than the *colonato*.[15]

Initially, much of the task of developing part of the Porecatú region had been assumed by the speculator Antônio Alves de Almeida.[16] During the 1930s, however, Almeida failed to colonize the area, and the state reclaimed the land. In 1942, some 720,000 acres (120,000 *alqueire*) was restored to the state and fell under the control of the Mixed Commission of Lands (CMT, Comissão Mista de Terras), established by Manoel Ribas, the state interventor appointed

15. On the development of northern Paraná, see the insightful study by São Paulo geology professor Nice Lecocq-Muller, "Contribuição ao estudo do norte do Paraná," *Boletim Paulista de Geografia* 22 (1956), 55–97; as well as Preston E. James, "The Coffee Lands of Southeastern Brazil," *Geographical Review* 22 (1932), 232; and Craig L. Dozier, "Northern Paraná, Brazil: An Example of Organized Regional Development," *Geographical Review* 46 (1956), 319–321. For Fraser, see Love, *São Paulo in the Brazilian Federation*, 79; Muller, "Estudo do norte do Paraná," 75–79; Nicholls, "The Agricultural Frontier," 45; and Dozier, "Northern Paraná, Brazil," 324. Fraser, who was better known as Lord Lovat, called his company the North Paraná Land Company (CTNP). It was one of two subsidiaries of the parent company, Paraná Plantations Limited, founded in 1924. The other company was the São Paulo–Paraná Railroad Company (Estrada de Ferro São Paulo–Paraná). Maxine L. Margolis, *The Moving Frontier: Social and Economic Change in a Southern Brazilian Community* (Gainesville: University of Florida Press, 1973), 21–23. For Lunardelli, see "Um pioneiro," 17.

16. Felismino, "A guerra de Porecatú," *FL*, 14 July 1985, 24.

by Vargas. That year, the CMT began a campaign to attract rural workers and smallholders from the more populous states of São Paulo and Minas Gerais by inviting any and all to settle, improve, and pay taxes on parcels divided out of the total. According to the plan, prospective farmers simply needed to comply with these minimal obligations for a period of six years in order to gain title to the land. In response to this call, hundreds of tenant farmers, *colonos,* and rural workers migrated to Paraná.

The New Settlers Get Organized

Among the first migrants to arrive was the family of José Billar. Born in Spain, Billar (called "the Spaniard" by his comrades) had immigrated to São Paulo to work as a coffee *colono.* He and his wife had five sons (José, João, Mario, Arlindo, and André), and with all this manpower the family earned enough money during the 1920s and 1930s to buy a sixty-acre farm in Regente Feijó, São Paulo—not far from the Paraná border—and to leave the *colonato* behind. When Billar heard Ribas's offer, however, he sold the farm on the chance of improving the family's circumstances and moved them to Agua de Tenente, an uninhabited area fifteen miles from Porecatú. Typical of *colono* families, Billar was "very authoritarian and decided everything for the entire family," his son João later told a *Folha de Londrina* reporter named Pedro Paulo Felismino.[17] Armed with a promissory note from the CMT, Billar commanded his fully grown sons to turn more than 240 acres of woodland into a rudimentary *fazenda.* Working hard for five years, they cleared the forest, planted eleven thousand coffee trees, prepared the soil for another nine thousand trees, raised eight hundred hogs, and built a dozen structures, including houses, a barn and corral, and a granary. Before the troubles began, they had also planted corn, rice, and beans for their subsistence.

The Billars were not alone in their hard work. As news of the land deal spread by word of mouth, more and more people moved to the area, and a generally disorganized settlement pattern resulted. Many new arrivals established farmsteads on land that would later be described as privately held. In the wild region of northern Paraná, the lines of demarcation between undeveloped public and private land were not only unclear but entirely absent. It may well be that such

17. Felismino, "A saga dos Billar," *FL,* 24 July 1985, 11.

lines did not exist, that none of the land areas was privately held until the work of peasants like Billar and rising coffee prices made the land more valuable to speculators and corrupt politicians. Nevertheless, the Ribas government allowed this state of affairs to germinate without intervening, and the migrant peasants put down roots. When the authorities did begin to demarcate the land and uproot them, defending the interests of the landlords rather than those who had settled and cultivated the land, the peasants became resentful and resistant. Transformed overnight from heroic homesteaders to land-invading squatters (*posseiros* in Brazilian terminology), war eventually came.

A hint of the troubles to come was already in the air before the end of World War II. Some *posseiros,* alert to potential political changes that might affect them, tried to document their proprietorship before the six-year trial period had come to an end. One peasant, Manoel Marques da Cunha, went so far as to appeal to President Vargas.[18] But none of the petitions had success, and the peasants began to worry. After the end of the war, with Vargas's downfall, the situation was thrown into further turmoil. Fearing the loss of their land, fifteen hundred *posseiros* rallied in the town of Guaraci in 1945. Their leader, Francisco Bernardo, was later arrested and died suspiciously while in police custody, reported Manoel Jacinto Correia, a Communist militant and politician from Londrina.[19]

Influenced by local Communists like Jacinto, the homesteaders reacted to the violence by organizing peasant leagues, not only in Guaraci but also in Porecatú, Jaguapitã, Centenário do Sul, and the agricultural districts of Agua das Pelotas and Agua do Mandacuru. One hundred and forty peasants participated in the Porecatú league, while two hundred joined the one in Centenário, and nearly four hundred belonged to the Jaguapitã league, said Hilário Padilha Pinha, then head of the Porecatú league.[20] Like the league in Dumont, however, these organizations had brief formal lives. Unlike Dumont, where grievances were soon channeled into politics, relations became more chaotic and violent in Paraná. Pinha—the son of a peasant who had migrated to the area in 1942, like the Billars—went from heading the league to leading a clandestine band of armed *posseiros* under the nom de guerre "Itagiba."

The *posseiros'* motives for forming the leagues were obviously defensive. They had occupied unoccupied land, cleared it, cultivated

18. Felismino, "A guerra de Porecatú," *FL,* 14 July 1985, 25.
19. "Memórias do Velho Mané," *FL,* 26 July 1985, 11.
20. Felismino, "Lembranças da guerra," *FL,* 23 July 1985, 17.

it, and, in their view, made it theirs. Staying in the house of a Porecatú *posseiro,* another PCB activist (the lawyer and journalist Elias Chaves Neto) described a "depressing scene . . . the reality of poverty in our country." The *posseiro* couple lived in a hut with an uneven dirt floor across which chickens moved freely, pecking and squabbling; the woman cooked over a wood-burning stove, whose sooty smoke had blackened the wall of the house. After a hearty supper, Chaves Neto's impression of the *posseiros'* material existence improved. He was particularly pleased to find his bed made with an "impeccably clean linen sheet." Later, Chaves Neto met some of the man's neighbors and learned how they had recently cleared the land and planted coffee. They all cooperated in the work and planted the rows of coffee trees together, as if in one big plantation. (This community labor sharing, typical of many frontier experiences in world history, was in Brazil called *mutirão,* a word of Tupi Indian origin.) One night, he amused himself by attending a dance and complimented the *posseiros* on the "spontaneity" of their lifestyle. He left appreciating their autonomy and their unwillingness to move or to satisfy anyone else's vision of development.[21]

But the *posseiros* had settled land without securing legal title to it, and their tenure was bound to be challenged. If legal questions were all that mattered, Brazilian law offered the *posseiros* numerous advantages. "The law regarding untitled lands in Paraná, as in the rest of Brazil," wrote Chaves Neto, "was quite reasonable and just. . . . The fact is, the law established that, up to a certain limit in acreage, he who worked the land would be recognized as its owner."[22] Article 141 of the 1946 federal constitution strengthened these measures by assigning a social value to land, specifying that landowners had a legal responsibility to develop their property and that, failing to do so, the state could legally take possession of the land.[23] By leaving their holdings in northern Paraná untouched, private owners had arguably forfeited their title to it. Constitutional article 156 further buttressed the peasants' position by ordering state governments to give preference

21. Chaves Neto, *Minha vida,* 123–24.
22. Ibid., 122.
23. Although the 1946 constitution, like the 1930 revolution and 1937 New State that preceded it, strengthened the authority of the federal government to intervene in state affairs, interventions in favor of *posseiros* were not common. Moreover, article 147 of the 1946 constitution specified that land expropriated by the state had to be paid for in cash. This measure generated much controversy until it was revoked in 1964. Fernando Pereira Sodero, *Direito agrário e reforma agrária* (São Paulo: Livraria Legislação Brasileira, 1968); and Ruy Miller Paiva, Salomão Schattan, and Claus F. Trench de Freitas, *Setor agrícola do Brasil: Comportamento econômico, problemas e possibilidades* (São Paulo: Secretaria da Agricultura, 1979), 212–17.

to the physical occupants (*"posseiros"* by definition) of land when issuing titles for *terras devolutas,* recognizing the customary rights of
those who had occupied and cultivated parcels up to sixty acres for
ten years or more.[24]

As British sociologist Joe Foweraker has documented, however,
the legal history of the land masks the nightmarish violence *posseiros*
encountered trying to fulfill their peasant dreams. Powerful land
speculators, frequently extracted a high price from *posseiros* rather
than let them obtain legal title to land they held in fact.[25] Porecatú is
a case in point, for the league's legal activities did not prevent the
struggle from becoming uglier. In 1946, Billar and more than one
hundred other *posseiros* had been urged to move by agents of
Lunardelli. They claimed Lunardelli owned the land, having bought
a ninety-thousand-acre territory near Porecatú from Escolástico Mel-
chert de Fonseca in 1942.[26] But the Billars had invested too much in
the region to move; not only had their property grown, so had their
family, for both the younger José and João had married the daughters
of neighboring peasants. When the Billars presented their note to
the CMT, and another to the CTNP, they got the runaround. An
unmistakably violent response came at the start of 1947. On January 4, Força Publica police under the command of Major Euzébio de
Carvalho raided at least two farmsteads, including those of Lázaro
Bueno de Camargo and José Billar. The police threatened the families
and assaulted José's young wife. On January 10, Carvalho returned,
arrested the elder Billar, and took him to the Porecatú jail. In the
meantime, a team of hired hands was sent to knock down their buildings, an act forestalled by the Billar brothers and their hunting rifles.

24. Caio Prado Junior, *A questão agrária,* 4th ed. (São Paulo: Brasiliense, 1987), 122. This
essay first appeared as "Nova contribuição para a análise da questão agrária no Brasil," *Revista
Brasiliense* 43 (September/October 1962).

25. Joe Foweraker details various cases of the speculators chicanery in chapter 4, "The
Legal History of the Land," in his *The Struggle for Land: A Political Economy of the Pioneer Frontier
in Brazil from 1930 to the Present Day* (New York: Cambridge University Press, 1980), 83–105. On
contemporary struggle in the Amazon, see Octavio Ianni, *A luta pela terra,* 3d ed. (Petrópolis:
Vôzes, 1981).

26. Felismino, "A guerra de Porecatú," 24. On Lunardelli's interests in Centenário, see
Moraes transcript, pt. 3; and "Caem os primeiros posseiros em defesa de suas terras," *NH,*
14 February 1950, 1–2, reprinted in Barriguelli, ed., *Subsídios à história,* 270–73. I was unable to
independently confirm Lunardelli's landholdings in Paraná, and one source contradicted the
others, stating that the government of Paraná owned and colonized the land in the disputed
areas of Centenário and Jaguapitã. See Bernardes, "O problema das 'frentes pioneiras,'" 38.
A Lavoura ("Um pioneiro," 17) listed several Lunardelli holdings in the vicinity of Porecatú,
including the Fazenda Cascata in Bela Vista do Paraíso, Fazenda Cascatinha in Porecatú, and
Fazenda Igarussú in Astorga. Geremia's brother Ricardo also owned considerable property in
Porecatú, including a sizable sugar mill (with an annual production of two hundred thousands
sacks) and land enough for more than one million coffee trees.

Billar was released from jail only after he had been coerced into signing an agreement to give up the land in exchange for Cr$28,000 and rights to the next harvest, an agreement that went unfulfilled.[27]

The Only Alternative: Armed Struggle

The growing intensity of the conflict followed on the heels of a change in state government. With the collapse of the Estado Novo, Ribas was out, and gubernatorial elections were scheduled for 1947. Large landowners and speculators gave their support to Moisés Lupion de Troya, the PSD's candidate for governor of Paraná. Analysts believe that Lupion's victory made it possible for speculators to count on state apparatus to get the *posseiro*'s land. Lupion was not only the speculators' tool but also a self-interested landowner. He was a coffee planter and head of a large land company called the Clevelândia Territorial e Agrícola Limitada (CITLA), which held substantial parcels of land in western Paraná.[28] Moreover, the state government owned and controlled hundreds of thousands of acres, making the state Paraná's largest single landholder.[29] Any serious landowner aimed to turn a profit through the speculative sale or exploitation of his or her land. As a landowner himself and as trustee of the state's landholdings, Lupion did not need to take orders from large, foreign landlords to take actions that served the interests of the large-propertied class.

Anxious to develop northern Paraná, Lupion established a commission to study the problems arising near Porecatú. He visited the area in April 1947, promising to resettle 250 families on sixty-acre lots near Paranavaí, in northwest Paraná. Still in the period of PCB legality and cooperation, Lupion's action drew the attention of *Notícias de Hoje,* a São Paulo–based Communist daily that challenged the commission to be realistic in its solution. "We must hope that the plan to be proposed establishes special conditions for the concession of land

27. On the Billars, see Felismino, "A guerra de Porecatú," 25 and "A saga dos Billar," 11.
28. In 1944 the CNTP was sold to a group of São Paulo capitalists. The new owners, who supported the Lupion candidacy, changed the name of the company to the Companhia de Melhoramentos Norte do Paraná, but they did not change the strategy of fostering the development of smallholding and integrated regional growth. On Lupion, see Maria Cristina Colnaghi, "Colonos e poder: A luta pela terra no sudoeste do Paraná" (master's thesis, Universidade Federal do Paraná, 1984), 45–65; and Renato Lemos and César Benjamim, "Lupion, Moisés," in Beloch and Abreu, eds., *DHBB*, 1956–57. See also Foweraker, *The Struggle for Land,* 90.
29. Acrisio Marques, *Relatório do Departamento de Terras e Colonização do Estado do Paraná em 1947* (Curitiba: DTC, 1947).

to the rural workers and poor peasants and that, at the same time, a companion plan offers them cheap credit and extended terms, as well as farming implements—everything, in other words, that they will need to add to the productivity of our countryside."[30] Investigating the area in 1948, the geographer Lysia Maria Cavalcanti Bernardes provided the commission with a less-favorable view of the *posseiros*. She found the region to be settled sparsely by "hicks and former *colonos*," who, as she put it, had been "kicked off land to which they held no title or who were fugitives from the law [despejados de terra ocupadas indevidamente ou foragidos da lei]." They had "spontaneously" and in a "disorderly" manner invaded and occupied portions of the northern frontier, and their presence had to be controlled to fit the plans of the state government and private landowners.[31]

As the more remote Jaguapitã area had not been sold to any private interests, the state government claimed title to the land. This gave the commission unfettered authority to recommend a solution to the problem offered by the *posseiros*. The commissioners decided to divide the area into parcels of about seventy-five acres each and invite the *posseiros* to buy the land they had already begun to develop. The town of Jaguapitã was also laid out with fifty smaller lots of about twenty-five acres each around its perimeter. Those *posseiros* who were able to meet the state's terms were on their way to becoming titled smallholders.[32]

The commission findings regarding the Centenário do Sul *posseiros* differed significantly. The land was owned by Lunardelli, they claimed, and it was nearer Porecatú and the São Paulo border than Jaguapitã. Moreover, Lunardelli did not endorse the colonization model of land exploitation, preferring to develop the land in the expansive style of his *paulista* plantations. Thus, the commission proposed the removal of the *posseiros* and their relocation to Lupion's CITLA lands along the southwestern frontier. The local courts backed the commission's conclusion and ordered the *posseiros'* expulsion.[33] Police came from Porecatú and Londrina to run them out, but some resisted. On 26 August 1947, Lieutenant Antônio Barbosa and a contingent of twelve men were shot at when they tried to expel *posseiros* from the Fazenda Otávio Faria in the village of Aguas do Rondon e Baiana. In the end, police corporal Antônio Alves and three *jagunços*

---

30. On Lupion's plans, see Felismino, "A guerra de Porecatú." Quote from "Terras devolutas no Paraná," *Hoje*, 6 May 1947, 2, reprinted in Barriguelli, ed., *Subsídios à história*, 256.
31. Bernardes, "O problema das frentes pioneiras," 29–30.
32. Ibid., 37.
33. "Terras devolutas no Paraná"; and Muller, "Estudo do norte do Paraná," 80.

lay dead.[34] The unnamed peasant defenders took refuge in the woods. In Porecatú, pressure continued to be placed on the Billars and others. Worried, Billar evacuated the family across the Paranapanema River to a friend's farm in São Paulo. He and his sons João, Mario, and Arlindo returned to the land, tending it by day and spending the nights in hideouts they had constructed in the forest.

In 1948, PCB involvement in the struggle deepened. To support the hounded *posseiros,* a group of PCB members in Londrina formed a solidarity organization whose core consisted of Jacinto, now an elected city councilman, the lawyer Flávio Ribeiro, and the physician Newton Cardoso. The group toured the conflict zone guided by Angelo Gajardoni, a pharmacist in Jaguapitã who became so enraged by the troubles that he sold his pharmacy to buy a forty-acre farm near Porecatú. Gajardoni's son Arlido eventually joined the struggle and became one of its most militant combatants, adopting the nom de guerre "Strogof." Oriented by this group, members of the old league elected Billar; Pinha's father, Hilário Gonçalves Padilha; and another *posseiro* who had moved to the area in 1942, Herculano Alves de Barros, to represent them in talks with the PCB central committee in Rio de Janeiro. In conversations with party executive Pedro Pomar, the PCB assigned the lawyer Rocha Faria to deliver their petition to the federal government and suggested the group contact José Rodrigues Vieira Neto, a party official in Curitiba, capital of Paraná.

During the final weeks of the year, PCB representatives visited with the *posseiros* on weekends, arriving at the Padilha house on Saturday and meeting with a group gathered to play soccer on Sunday. It was during these meetings, the Londrina journalist Felismino reports, that the *posseiros* agreed to mount an armed struggle in defense of their landholdings. This revelation was made by Barros, who abandoned the struggle when it took a violent turn and later cooperated with police interrogators. According to his 1951 testimony, the party used the Sunday meetings to distribute pamphlets and discuss the rights of rural workers. "Little by little," Barros said, "they started moving the discussion to the Communist side, insisting that the land belongs to those who work it and that everyone should join together to confront the *jagunços,* land grabbers, planters, and even the government, if necessary. From that, the idea of creating armed groups came out." Given the contemporary statements of Prestes and the party's revolutionary trajectory, Barros's recollections are quite plausible. Before the year was out, "PCB surveyors" made a geographical

---

34. "Caem os primeiros posseiros," 271.

study of the region, searching out its resources and military potential: through a network of observers and supply routes, the combatants would be kept informed, fed, and stocked with arms and munitions. In 1950, a young *posseiro* told a reporter, "We have no alternative but armed struggle."[35]

The Porecatú War

From the beginning of 1949 to June 1951, the Porecatú War raged. The land struggle was characterized by three basic types of conflict, each played out in random and overlapping order. Sometimes both landlords and *posseiros* appealed to judicial and governmental authorities; at other times, police and *jagunços* entered disputed areas and faced *posseiro* resistance. Finally, armed *posseiro* groups attacked workers hired to displace them. Throughout the war, both speculators and *posseiros* sought relief in court and from various executive and legislative authorities. In January 1949, for example, a group of thirty *posseiros* petitioned the court in Porecatú for a restraining order against Captain Manoel Alves do Amaral, the Força Publica commander assigned to enforce the terms of Governor Lupion's land commission. Amaral, who was sent to the area with a troop of one hundred soldiers from Curitiba, had himself been ordered to the scene through a chain of command that included the governor's landlord allies. One of Amaral's soldiers reported how dependent his squad was on the largesse of Jaguapitã planters. Ordered to "disarm the local population," the troop spent most of its time responding to the complaints of planters, eating, and traveling at the planters' ex-

---

35. Barros is quoted in Felismino, "Táticas de luta," *FL,* 16 July 1985, 13. The presence of "surveyors" is also discussed in this article. John French (personal communication, 8 May 1996) has noted that Pedro Pomar's appearance as a PCB representative at the outset of the struggle in Porecatú curiously parallels the role his Communist Party of Brazil (Partido Comunista do Brasil, founded in 1960) played as a catalyst of rural armed struggle along the Araguaia River in the state of Pará during the early 1970s. Both led to the tragic deaths of militants and bystanders, adding credence to Marx's famous observation that history repeats itself "the first time as tragedy, the second as farce." Pomar rose above this truism by urging militants to adopt a different course of action at Araguaia, yet hotter, less experienced heads prevailed, and more than fifty militants were eventually killed, including Pomar himself, who was executed by police when they broke in on a clandestine party meeting that had been called to discuss the Araguaia catastrophe and the death of Mao Tse-tung. See Jacob Gorender, *Combate nas trevas: A esquerda brasileira das ilusões perdidas à luta armada,* 2d ed. (São Paulo: Atica, 1987), 207–14; "Pomar, Pedro" in Beloch and Abreu, eds., *DHBB,* 2790; and Karl Marx, "The Eighteenth Brumaire of Louis Bonaparte," in *Surveys from Exile: Political Writings,* vol. 2, edited and introduced by David Fernbach (New York: Vintage Books, 1974), 146.

pense. "When one of the planters arrived in town to denounce a *posseiro*, he had to arrange transportation for us to go into the woods and kick the guy out," said former soldier Haroldo Francisco de Souza.[36] The captain received presents from planters and speculators and responded to their wishes. "Everyone that was a planter or speculator sought out the captain," Souza continued. As this example demonstrates, the democratic state apparatus typically sided with the more powerful interests, such as landlords, rather than the more numerous interests, such as those represented by the *posseiros*. In other words, the constituency of donors outweighed the constituency of potential voters.

Although the judiciary also tended to support planters over *posseiros*, many *posseiros* turned to the courts for relief throughout the conflict. The Billar family faced not only *jagunço* aggression but court action and police enforcement of the court's orders. Following unresolved court disputes in 1948, the Lunardellis sold Fazenda Tabapuã, the portion of "their" Porecatú land where the Billars lived, to José and Jerominho Inácio da Costa. To secure the Billars removal from the land, the Costas solicited an expulsion order from the court in Porecatú on 5 July 1950. To fight the order, Billar countersued, claiming the Costas owed him Cr$200,000 in compensation for land improvements. But on August 17, Judge Carlos Bezerra Valente ordered Billar's land "enclosed" (*sequestro das terras*). When a marshal arrived by jeep on the farmstead to deliver the expulsion order, the Billars refused to accept it and ordered the man to leave at gunpoint. Although the local judge continued to issue orders that favored the Costas, higher regional courts remained a recourse for Billar. At the conclusion of hostilities in 1951, Billar resubmitted his claim in Londrina and a judge finally found in his favor, ordering the Costas to pay Cr$300,000 for the family's work on Fazenda Tabapuã and to provide the Billars with twelve hundred acres of undeveloped land in another region.[37] This case exemplifies the contradictory role of the judiciary in Brazilian rural labor history. Judges like Valente felt the pressure of the local power structure, while regional tribunals acted more independently.

Long before this final, favorable settlement for the Billars, sol-

36. "Dias de medo," *FL*, 21 July 1985, 17.
37. Initial court cases reported in Felismino, "Táticas de luta." A discussion of the final resolution is in Felismino, "A saga dos Billar." According to José, the Costas refused to comply with the 1951 court order (issued in Londrina), and the Billars returned to their farmstead in Porecatú to confront workers there and prevent them from doing their jobs. Only after this confrontation did the Costas comply and the Billar saga end. Curiously, the elder Billar sold the land he received from the Costas and used it to buy rental houses.

diers and *jagunços* continued to invade the disputed area and attempt to dislodge the *posseiros*. Under constant attack, numerous *posseiros* agreed to unite in self-defense. Following the decision to initiate an "armed struggle," the PCB central committee sent José Ortiz to Porecatú. Ortiz was said to be an arms and first-aid specialist, and the party assigned him to train the *posseiros* in military tactics.[38] Two squads, each with a number of men varying from six to a dozen, were established to defend *posseiro* lands from attack and to carry out attacks on lands that had been taken by the police. Leading these squads were Itagiba (Hilário Padilha Pinha) and Strogof (Arildo Gajardoni), two *posseiros* closely linked to the PCB. By February 1950 the PCB's *Notícias de Hoje* spoke of these men as the "resisters" (*resistentes*) and reported on their confrontations with police and *jagunços*. The squads were equipped with carbines, food, and information by a network of supporters operated through Jacinto's Londrina solidarity group.[39]

Less numerous and well-armed than the Força Publica, a "handful" of the resisters used guerrilla tactics to defend their usage rights and autonomy.[40] They prepared a number of hideouts in the woods and located strategic points from which to mount ambushes. Their primary goal was to prevent the intrusion of soldiers into an area where a total of about fifteen hundred *posseiro* families had established farmsteads. Tuesday, 10 October 1950, proved to be the most violent single day, when four men and two boys were killed and eight soldiers and *posseiros* were wounded. The day of battles was set off when Porecatú's Judge Valente ordered state troops to uproot the families of Billar and Francisco Lourenço Figueiredo, who occupied a parcel that a land speculator named Antônio Angelo claimed as part of his estate, the Fazenda Palmeira.[41] Leaving Porecatú by truck after midnight, a brigade of twenty-two soldiers and three planter employees under the command of Lieutenant João André Dias Paredes hoped to take the *posseiros* by surprise. As the troop approached Figueiredo's property, Luís Menezes, administrator of the Palmeira plantation, went ahead to confront Figueiredo and his brother Cristovão. Within minutes, shots rang out, Menezes was hit three times and mortally wounded, and the Figueiredos ran off to

38. Felismino, "Lembranças da guerra" and "Táticas de luta."

39. "Caem os primeiros posseiros," 2; and Felismino, "Memórias do Velho Mané."

40. Bezerra referred to the resisters as "A handful of brave combatants (including some Communists) who showed the mass of homesteaders that, united and organized, peasants could resist and confront even as powerful a force as the Military Police." Bezerra, *Memórias*, 2:126.

41. Felismino develops the story in a two-page segment, "Sangue na primavera," *FL*, 17 July 1985, 11–12, explaining that all three incidents occurred on October 10.

warn other *posseiros* of the police presence. While Paredes failed to capture the Figueiredos, he did take prisoner a witness, a boy named Benedito dos Santos. Benedito's father, Valdomiro dos Santos, joined the brigade to accompany his son.

With the Figueiredos armed and on the run, the soldiers moved toward the Billar farmstead cautiously. Barricades of tree limbs and brush slowed their progress down the road. Along one stretch, it took more than two hours to go two miles. Passing near the Lote do Alemão, a farmstead ravaged by police in April, the soldiers on watch had to help the others clear the road. Suddenly, shots rang out from the forest around them. Caught off guard, three soldiers fell, wounded. Before the others fired back, a bullet shattered the truck windshield and killed Benedito dos Santos. Within a few minutes the soldiers' machine gun and rifle fire penetrated the resisters' hidden bulwarks. Screams from the woods forecast a wicked toll. Within ten minutes, the battle was over. Patrolling the brush around them, the police found the bodies of three men and a boy. With the bodies collected and the wounded men bandaged, the embattled soldiers planned to withdraw to Porecatú down the dangerous road that was their only alternative. As the woods closed in around them on yet another obstructed leg of the journey, the brush once again erupted in rifle fire. Soldiers on the ground, including Lieutenant Paredes, fled into the woods, while the truck driver floored the accelerator and forced the truck through the gauntlet. This ambush cost them five wounded men, including Benedito's father and the *jagunço* João Faustino. From their secret perches, the resisters watched the brigade's chaotic retreat.[42]

The Rural Working Classes

Several months of calm followed this stormy October day. Over the course of the next several months, the *posseiros,* landlords, and authorities regrouped. Politically, it was a sensitive moment of transition. Promising improvements for rural workers and peasants, Vargas was elected overwhelmingly as president in November, an event ex-

42. The three wounded soldiers were Corporal Ivair Ramos (shot in the stomach), Otávio de Oliveira Almeida (with a head wound), and Antonio Periera (shot in the arm). The three dead *posseiro* men were later identified as João Japão, Cassiano Coelho, Benedito Barbudo, and the boy was Pedro Vieira de Moraes. Felismino, "Sangue na primavera"; and "Caem os primeiros posseiros," 270.

amined in the next chapter. In Paraná the campaign for governor was under way, and in March 1951 the hated Lupion would be replaced by the populist Bento Munhoz da Rocha Neto. In the meantime, the PCB remained committed to its revolutionary line, having issued the August Manifesto only two months before the October firefights. It continued to support the resisters by funneling both munitions into the woods and more personnel to the area. In February 1951, Celso Cabral de Melo (Captain Carlos) was sent to replace José Ortiz (who had been killed in a training accident) as the resisters' military advisor. Captain Carlos would later be blamed for heightening the level of violence and for betraying the resisters to the police.[43] In March, *posseiros* in the São Paulo border town of Santa Fé do Sul sent the resisters a truckload of supplies.[44] In May, Moraes transferred to Londrina from Ribeirão Preto to help mobilize political support.

While the Paraná government recoiled from the resistance it encountered, the *posseiros* used the time to secure about sixteen square miles of farm and forest land west and southwest of Porecatú. This campaign was one of the more intriguing and politically astute of the *posseiro*-instigated conflicts described above. With each police and *jagunço* raid on disputed lands came a gang of laborers hired to tear down buildings, plant new crops, and tend existing ones. These workers presented the *posseiros* and the Communists with a dilemma. Communist theory unified the two groups as members of the rural working class. Yet for the laborers, the *posseiros'* ouster meant paid work, while for the *posseiros,* the laborers' activities meant the end of all they had worked so hard to build. In other words, the two groups of workers seemingly had more interests to divide than unify them. This dilemma would later trouble rubber tappers led by Chico Mendes in the Amazon rain forest who, in their struggle to defend the rubber trees that formed the basis of their livelihood, confronted gangs of workers hired by aggressive landowners to clear the woods to create cattle pastures. Perhaps informed by the mistakes of violent struggles like the Porecatú War, the rubber tappers chose to fight back nonviolently by tying themselves to trees or laying in the way of bulldozers.[45]

43. Felismino, "Revolta e traição" and "Os erros do PCB levaram o movimento à derrota," *FL,* 27 July 1985, 13. See also Welch and Geraldo, *Lutas camponesas,* 122.

44. "Organizam a solidariedade aos resistentes em Porecatú," *Hoje,* 30 March 1951, 3, cited in Barriguelli, ed., *Subsídios à história,* 279.

45. The rubber tappers can take credit for developing a form of struggle called the *empate,* or standoff. As described above, it was a variation on the theme of a sit-down strike—one especially suited to prevent "scabs" from working. See Revkin, *The Burning Season,* and Chico

Although PCB militants on the scene in Porecatú could not benefit from the hindsight afforded Mendes, they were not blind to the reality around them. We can now analyze social relations in northern Paraná with considerable precision and note that the *posseiros* accounted for one of the smallest portions of the regional labor force. Economist Martin T. Katzman made a useful study of employment in the region, distinguishing the economically active population on CTNP ("Company") lands from those on privately held ("Non-Company") lands. Although owner-operators, sharecroppers, and *posseiros* together constituted a substantial percentage of the labor force, wage earners were the largest single class of workers in the area.[46]

The postwar Paraná labor market was entirely different from that which had prevailed in São Paulo during the first coffee boom. The smallholding model of development established by the CTNP attracted more experienced, successful individuals from São Paulo and Minas Gerais, such as former *colonos* and peasants.[47] In the meantime, the flow of immigration to Brazil had slowed considerably since the 1920s, and the federal government remained undecided about resurrecting it despite constant pressure from planter groups such as the SRB to do so.[48] Thus, the possibility of resurrecting the traditional

---

Mendes, *Fight for the Forest.* The suggestion that Mendes somehow learned from the experiences of the Porecatú resisters is not as far-fetched as it seems. In fact, the idea that the seeds of contemporary rural labor incorporation were planted in the pre-1964 era is the thesis of this book. Mendes claimed to have been introduced to politics and popular militancy through a former PCB activist named Euclides Távora. Though no one claims Távora took part in the Porecatú War, the war had an impact on the party's behavior and must have influenced him. In addition to *Fight for the Forest,* see Kenneth Maxwell, "The Mystery of Chico Mendes," *New York Review of Books,* 28 March 1991, 39–48; and Peter Beatie, "Was Távora There?" *New York Review of Books,* 7 November 1991, 61.

46. Martin T. Katzman, "Social Relations of Production on the Brazilian Frontier," in *The Frontier: Comparative Studies,* vol. 1, edited by David H. Miller and Jerome Steffen (Norman: University of Oklahoma Press, 1974), 290–92.

47. Margolis, *The Moving Frontier,* 40, found that 37 percent of the inhabitants of Ouro Verde, the alias of a town she studied in northern Paraná, came from São Paulo, Minas Gerais, and older areas of Paraná. Dozier, "Northern Paraná, Brazil," 319, 323, also comments on the origins of migrants to the region.

48. São Paulo planters both in and out of the SRB believed São Paulo's coffee plantations would not survive without the annual influx of ten thousand foreign workers and their families (some fifty thousand people). Starting at the end of World War II, they pushed this argument relentlessly until 1952, when the *paulistas* were rewarded with a concession from the federal government to take over responsibility for the state's immigration program. See "A mão de obra italiana e a agricultura paulista," *Brasil Rural* 129 (April 1953), 14–19. See also "Primeira conferencia de imigração e colonização" *RSRB* 28:347 (September 1949), 36–40; and "Imigração e colonização para o estado de São Paulo: Memorial apresentado pelo sr. Manlio Agnese ao sr. governador do estado," *RSRB* 28:347 (September 1949), 40–41.

colonato system, as many planters would have preferred, grew ever more remote.[49]

Out of this cauldron emerged a contract system called the *empreitada*. Under this system, landowners signed contracts with *empreiteiros* (contractors)—or, as they infamously came to be known, cats (*gatos*), a term used because their job required them to be particularly cunning and crafty. *Empreiteiros* contracted with the landlords and then hired workers to fulfill the contract, keeping their expenses down and profits up by exploiting these men and women as much as possible. When virgin land was involved, the contractors were also called "coffee frontiersmen" (*formadores de café*), a term reflecting how they cleared away forest and formed coffee plantations in the wilderness. *Formadores* planted coffee in exchange for the full value of the sale of the yield over a specified period. In the case of uncleared land, contracts were commonly signed for four- to six-year spans because it usually took that amount of time for coffee trees to mature and produce beans. Thus, at first *empreiteiro* earnings did not come from coffee but from the sale of crops like rice and corn that could be cultivated while the coffee trees were maturing. Although terms varied from contract to contract, *empreiteiros* also earned income from selling the first one or two coffee harvests. To clear the land, plant the coffee trees, and make the harvest, the *gatos* called on their special skill: the ruthless extraction of surplus value from the labor of migrant workers.[50]

Anxious to make the land income-producing as quickly as possible, the contractor hired workers for short- and long-term projects, such as clearing the land or planting and harvesting cereals. Although many workers employed in the Porecatú area came in trucks from towns just over the border in São Paulo, the vast majority originated from northeast Brazil, an economically depressed region of the country. In response to news of wages two to three times higher than those paid on *paulista* plantations, they came to towns on the São Paulo–Paraná border, such as Iepê and Ourinhos. They soon discovered that contractors conspired with town merchants to charge outrageous prices for lodging and food. The PCB's Chaves Neto,

49. Defenders of the *colonato* were many, and they tended to be the same people who supported a return to subsidized immigration. Two of the more outspoken advocates were Alberto Whately and Antônio de Queirós Telles, past presidents of the SRB and prominent Ribeirão Preto coffee planters. See "Braços para a lavoura," *RSRB* 25:303 (November 1945), 11, an editorial published while Whately was the magazine's publisher; and Antônio de Queirós Telles, "A imigração em São Paulo," *RSRB* 27:329 (February 1948), 30–31.

50. See Margolis, *The Moving Frontier,* 33–41, for a colorful description of the work of the formadores.

who owned a small farm near Ourinhos, described how the system drove workers deeper and deeper into debt. The contractors paid the workers' bills, trapping them in a classic cycle of debt bordering on peonage. Those who tried to save money were sent away. Those who jumped from the trucks to escape the labor discipline of the contractors after their debts had been paid were "hunted by the police, arrested and thrashed [*surrado*]."[51]

Deceived, abused and underpaid, these contracted workers were obvious tinder for any union organizer's attempt to fire up the rural labor movement. Although the party remained committed to the *posseiros'* land struggle, their ideology oriented them to build solidarity between workers and peasants. In Londrina, Moraes and Jacinto sought to popularize the *posseiro* struggle as one common to everyone's interests. From the laborers' perspective, they argued that more dignified employment could be had on *posseiro* farmsteads than on the huge plantations of Lunardelli. Moreover, by protecting the *posseiros'* rights to the land, the workers protected the principle of smallholding, a principle they could benefit from in the long run. Meanwhile, Lunardelli resisted the denigration of his contributions to the region and defended the *empreitada* model. "Lunardelli is a great landholder, not a *latifundiário*," stated an *A Lavoura* profile of the coffee king. "He understands that the land ought to be productive. . . . where before there were vast tracts of land covered in forest or pasture, today they are extensive and prosperous fields of coffee, cotton, sugarcane, and more." Such productivity gains were not based on exploiting workers, the article claimed, for Lunardelli "speaks much about the necessity of assistance for rural laborers," and his *colonos* "live in large and comfortable houses."[52]

In Porecatú, the groups of Strogof and Itagiba developed a campaign of intimidation and persuasion against the hired workers. They disrupted the work of the *empreitada* gangs with arguments as well as gunshots. Since the resisters were nearly always outnumbered, they typically surrounded a worksite at dawn and began by firing their guns rapidly into the air to make it look like their ranks were swelled. They also shot at water buckets and food stores to make it impossible for the workers to sustain themselves in the woods. The resisters talked with the laborers, too, seeking their sympathy and support. The resisters claimed rights to the land and challenged the workers to consider the ethics of taking another man's livelihood. On several oc-

51. Chaves Neto, *Minha vida*, 122–23. Margolis, *The Moving Frontier*, 131–33, also reports on some of these abuses.
52. "Um pioneiro," 17.

casions, resisters arranged to bypass the *gato* and hire the men to help tend their crops. In these ways, they won adherents and slowed the absorption of their farmsteads into plantations. The potential for their work was seen in February 1951 when workers on the nearby plantations of Santa Lina, Santa Maria, Santa Terezinha, Flama, Quem Sabe, Palmeira, and Centenário went on strike for higher wages.[53] But such armed confrontations could also end badly. An attempt to stop work on a farmstead in May 1951 resulted in the death of a worker and the wounding of two men when the *empreiteiro* José Marques Teixeira returned the resisters' gunfire.[54]

The Petition of Fifteen Hundred

As late as April 1951, the government had hopes of negotiating a settlement with the *posseiros*. Lupion's term had ended, and the seemingly sympathetic Rocha was the new governor. Rocha had campaigned on the promise of settling the Porecatú War by distributing land to the *posseiros*. Soon after taking power, he acted on his promise by decree law, expropriating some conflicted lands in Porecatú, Jaguapitã, and Arapongas. Foreshadowing the famous 1959 expropriation of the Engenho Galiléia (a sugar plantation in Pernambuco), Rocha's act may have been the first time an elected official redistributed Brazil's patrimony, taking from the rich and giving to the poor. Enforcing the decree proved difficult, however, and the government appointed a commission to work out the details. One of the commissioners was Herculano Alves de Barros, one of the original Porecatú *posseiros* and representatives. Two years earlier, in March 1949, Barros had accepted an arrangement proposed by Lupion in which he gained title to his farm, and he thereafter distanced himself from the struggle.[55]

Having struggled so long by 1951, the *posseiros* viewed the governor's promises with skepticism. As the commission started to negotiate agreements between *posseiros* and landlords in Porecatú, the resisters suspected the commission would only serve to divide them if they failed to develop their own agenda. This concern prompted

53. Felismino, "Revolta e traição," *FL,* 18 July 1985, 13.
54. Felismino, "Cartada final," *FL,* 19 July 1985, 11.
55. Felismino, "Revolta e traição." The other commissioners were Renato Cunha, Oscar Santos, Herbert Palhano, Edgard Távora, Aldrovando Gançalves Magalhães, Pedro Nolasco, Clemente Vilela Arruda, and Francisco Oliveira.

Itagiba, Captain Carlos, and others to draft a remarkable document, a petition eventually signed by fifteen hundred *posseiros*. Entitled "For the Immediate Delivery [*entrega*] of the Land to the First Occupants: A Petition of 1,500 Signatures Sent to Federal and State Authorities by the Resisters of Porecatú," the document emphasized seven fundamental demands. As the title reveals, their principal demand was the return of lands to occupants who had been pushed off them since settlement began in 1942. The petition also requested compensation for property destroyed by authorities, discontinuance of all legal suits against the *posseiros,* withdrawal of the police force then amassed in the region, imprisonment of *jagunços,* prosecution of criminal kingpins Lupion and Lunardelli, election of a new land distribution commission, and official recognition of peasant leagues.[56] Tragically, it was the *posseiro* who delivered this petition to federal authorities in Rio de Janeiro—João Berbardes—who was tortured to death by José Celestino's gang on his return to Porecatú.

The evidence does not entirely reveal how this document was composed or details on the collection of the fifteen hundred signatures, a difficult task under the best of circumstances. Felismino, the *Folha de Londrina* reporter, presents Itagiba's account of the process. Apparently the seven points were drawn up in meetings of the resisters, but since the document was typed, it probably was prepared in more urban surroundings than a forest hideout. In all likelihood, Itagiba, Strogof, Captain Carlos, and members of the Londrina support group met to discuss it, and then someone like Jacinto or the pharmacist Gajardoni typed it and had it reproduced. Itagiba claims that the signatures were gathered in a series of meetings in various farmsteads throughout the region. He and other resisters made rounds of the area under their control, told the *posseiros* about the petition, and asked them to sign it.[57] While quasi-illiterate, most *posseiros* had enough education to sign their names. (Nearly all *colono* families of this generation had children who enjoyed a year or more of formal education at plantation schoolhouses). Even when the presence of some forged names and multiple entries for a few families is presumed, the petition loses little of its noteworthiness.

The petition's appeal for the return of land to "first occupants" reveals two important facts about the resisters: first, that they were dominated by original settlers from 1942, such as Billar and Padilha;

56. Felismino, "Revolta e traição."
57. Felismino, "Cartada final," 11, includes a facsimile of the petition; for the testimony of Itagiba, see Felismino, "Lembranças da guerra," *FL,* 23 July 1985, 17.

second, that the law granted special rights to such productive, long-time occupants. Although they tried to broaden their movement, resisters were motivated fundamentally by defensive interests based on an argument that their brief tenure in the area constituted a traditional right and that the work they had done to clear and plant virgin forest merited recognition and compensation. The document's call for the prosecution of *jagunços* and of Lupion and Lunardelli spoke to the resisters' sense of justice: these men were the outlaws, not the *posseiro* defenders. The final two demands may perhaps be the most interesting, though we cannot conclude that they represent the *posseiros'* thinking so much as that of PCB militants. Nevertheless, the fact that so many of them subscribed to the desire to elect a new commission and to select their own form of organization reveals a belief in local democratic practices and collective representation. While they distrusted the elected governor's appointed commission, they accepted the concept of forming a body to negotiate a solution so long as the *posseiros* had a say in its composition. Whereas the state insisted on dealing with each *posseiro* family individually, the *posseiros* themselves seemed to agree that they had enough interests in common to entrust their representation to an organization of their choosing. The petition itself was a fascinating blend of the frontier spirit of *mutirão* combined with the communist beliefs of their urban allies. At its core was the PCB objective of distributing "land to those who work it."

Despite the formality and thoughtfulness of the *posseiros'* appeal, the authorities did not take the petition seriously. The appointed commission continued its work until it became apparent that it would not be successful. Resisters threatened commission members and pressured *posseiros* to reject any agreements that failed to respect their collective demands. Such was the case on the Billar farmstead when Barros and another commission member arrived to negotiate a deal. Although the Billars had taken part in various resister actions, the family had emphasized its own self-defense. Only in February had José and his sons Mário, Arlindo, and João fully integrated themselves into the squad headed by Itagiba. But when Captain Carlos appeared on the farmstead and intervened in the discussion with commission members, the Billars agreed to follow the group rather than accept an individual settlement. Since the commissioners would not agree to accept the petition's conditions, Billar told them to leave.[58]

58. On the Billars and the commission, see Felismino, "A saga dos Billar" and "Revolta and traição."

The Role of Captain Carlos

Throughout these negotiations, the resisters' intimidation campaign against invading workers increased, with at least three more confrontations reported in May. In mid-month, the *jagunço* Celestino was ambushed and killed. In addition, the armed groups forced a halt to construction at the river port of Itaparica and along the region's only through road, Parallel 38. Frustrated by their ineffectiveness, the commission's chair telegraphed Governor Rocha on May 24, admitting defeat. The next day's response from Rocha reports that he "has already taken urgent measures [já tomei providências (sic) urgentes caso requer]" to resolve the conflict. In fact, he had requested more troops from the Paraná cities of Curitiba, Maringá, and Assai and, significantly, outside help from the infamous branch of São Paulo political police known as DOPS, Departamento de Ordem Política e Social (Department of Social and Political Order). His plan was to isolate and suppress the resisters by circling the Porecatú area with soldiers and by closing down their support group in Londrina.[59] The period of calm was about to come to an end.

As of June 1951, the resisters had not suffered a major setback since that bloody October day of the previous year, and their growth and apparent success fed their confidence. This confidence was also supported by the personality of Captain Carlos, the puzzling figure the PCB central committee sent to help them. Captain Carlos was instrumental in strengthening the armed groups throughout the first half of 1951 and seems to have been the main catalyst behind their aggressiveness. Interviews with participants brought Felismino close to accusing him of being a planted agent provocateur.[60] But Jacinto and Moraes painted him instead as a self-centered man of poor judgment. Eventually captured by the police and interrogated by DOPS, he claimed to have a long history of activism in the PCB. Born in 1915 in the northeast state of Alagoas, he was a Navy radio operator in 1935 when the party-led uprising took place, and he joined in. Imprisoned with Prestes, he became a confidant of the PCB leader and was assigned leadership positions after 1945 when the party reorganized openly. He also gained the resisters' confidence in Pore-

59. Felismino, "Cartada final"; facsimile copies of the two telegrams are reproduced in the article.

60. Felismino calls Carlos the "Cabo Anselmo of Porecatú," equating him with the Navy petty officer who provoked a revolt in Rio de Janeiro in 1964 on the orders of the conspiracy mounted against President Goulart. Felismino, "O Cabo Anselmo de Porecatú," *FL*, 18 July 1985, 13.

catú, but his drinking and philandering, once enchanting, ended up offending many *posseiros* and made him the worst violator of the resisters' code of conduct. Moraes believes that his behavior also attracted the attention of the police and compromised the security of the clandestine squads. "This guy, very loose for a situation like that," Moraes recalled. "He went to Londrina, hung out at the bars, places where he should not have been as someone responsible for such a serious movement. He had to stay in the houses of his comrades not in whorehouses."[61] But he would not be disciplined.

Captain Carlos has been blamed for bringing about the downfall of the resistance not only by his bad behavior but also by driving it into an offensive posture, beyond its essentially defensive mode, and into revolutionary fantasy. During the first week of June, Carlos convinced the squad led by Strogof to rob a bank. The details are not complete, but the idea seems to have been motivated by a desire to expand the struggle into one that could threaten the government, and this necessitated more money for supplies. At the same time, Carlos was accused of draining the resisters' financial reserves by spending money on alcohol and prostitutes. The robbery did not take place due to a variety of factors, including the difficulties Captain Carlos encountered when the entire Billar clan snuck out of the camp during the night of June 14, abandoning the armed struggle.[62]

The third week of June saw the end of the war. The resisters' shaky predominance collapsed quickly under the full weight of the state's repressive apparatus. The Billars' withdrawal was followed on June 15 and 16 by three more desertions. On Sunday, June 17, the Londrina solidarity group organized a morale boosting rally at Rocha Pombo Square, the second in four days. But as it disbanded, the police surrounded the organizers and arrested them. The political police of São Paulo had done their homework on the solidarity group. Only a few, such as Moraes, managed to escape, while key activists like Captain Carlos and Jacinto were arrested and jailed.[63] With the suppression of this group achieved, the police could now act with impunity in Porecatú, since they had control over access to the area. Supporters were isolated from the conflict zone, and the government closed

61. Manoel Jacinto Correia criticizes Captain Carlos in Felismino, "Os erros do PCB levaram o movimento à derrota," *FL,* 27 July 1985, 13. Moraes quoted from Welch and Geraldo, *Lutas camponesas,* 122.

62. Felismino, "Cartada final" and "Os erros do PCB."

63. Others arrested included Newton Camara, Flavio Ribeiro, Melciades Pereira da Silva, Almo Saturino, Bento Paiva, Gerson Monteiro de Lima, and Alberto Manoel. Felismino, "Cartada final"; and Welch and Geraldo, *Lutas camponesas,* 122–23.

in. São Paulo authorities placed soldiers along the Paranapanema to block the resisters' retreat across the river, and Paraná soldiers tightened their noose. Weakened from within and facing superior external forces, the resisters offered no resistance. While a few were captured, most managed to slip out of the closing circle. As late as August, Jacinto encountered a group of ten resisters hiding in the woods and told them the war was over.[64]

Most resisters scattered to the four winds, while the Billars eventually managed to resolve their dispute in the Londrina courthouse and resettle nearby.[65] Itagiba and the Padilha family moved to Rio Grande do Sul state, while Captain Carlos, after submitting to his interrogators, mysteriously escaped from the Porecatú jail and disappeared. Moraes and Jacinto blame him for betraying the struggle, but his recorded testimony of July 27 postdates the crucial events of June. The betrayal, if it can be called that, was much larger than the coerced revelations of one man, for the party itself abandoned the area, leaving hundreds of *posseiro* families behind to suffer the full brunt of *jagunços* and police. In fact, José Billar's son João blames them all: "a lot of outsiders wanted to get involved with our movement and I think they came at the end to betray us."[66] The suppression of resister defenses enabled the unfettered renewal of the state's campaign to convert the region from the model of smallholder production advocated by the party to the plantation model it abhorred. The Lunardellis secured possession of the huge Fazenda Umuarama, which remained in their hands into the 1990s.

History Takes a "Wrong Turn"

The resisters, oriented by the PCB, had rejected governmental solutions, and yet they also found the revolutionary option untenable. Many recognized the absurdities of the party's new line by abandoning the war once Captain Carlos pushed them to consider robbing a bank. The times were hardly ripe for the revolutionary call to arms of the August Manifesto. "In practice," wrote Eduardo Dias, a party organizer of rural workers in the interior of São Paulo, "the manifesto did not have any resonance, not a single condition existed for its

64. Felismino, "Cerco aos posseiros," *FL,* 20 July 1985, 11.
65. Felismino, "No rastro de uma guerra," *FL,* 28 July 1985, 17.
66. Felismino, "A saga dos Billar," 11.

application, especially not for the formation of a popular army." [67] When the manifesto was published, Elias Chaves Neto commented, "the scheme, as it did not correspond to the real situation within the country, was never understood by the people or even taken note of, for that matter." [68] Even the tension-filled situation in Porecatú, which seemed to legitimate the PCB line, actually belied its inadequacies. The resisters hardly constituted a popular army: they were homesteaders, defending their holdings, not revolutionaries. "The Communist Party, as the party of the workers," Moraes wryly commented years later, "always underestimated the agrarian problem." [69]

These assessments of what the party did wrong or what it could have done to change the course of history are typical products of the Communist philosophy of reflective self-criticism. They are means of searching for models of militancy that could serve future revolutionaries and put the train of history back on its proper track, chugging progressively forward to socialism. The comments of oral historian Alessandro Portelli are useful to this analysis: "The means of control embedded in . . . [the testimony of Italian Communists he interviewed] correspond to two major motifs: the wrong turn of history is traced to a single event; or the blame is laid on errors or failures of leadership. . . . Blaming the wrongness of history on 'our' side means, for one thing, that it is still our side that makes history. . . . The function of the uchronic motif is to keep up hope: if our past leaders missed their chance to 'shoot when the thrush was flying by,' better leaders in the future will not." [70] An alternative world of peace and equality for the Porecatú *posseiros* might have come about had Captain Carlos behaved better or had the party stayed on and provided them further support. This perspective allows Moraes, Jacinto, and other militants to take possession of the story and guide it to a more desirable conclusion. They know they cannot change the past, but their critique of it leaves open the possibility of changing the future. Hope is embedded in their observations, and it is a powerful stimulant. The notion that thorough analysis of the past will help the next generation do things right is a powerful myth not just for Communists but for most of Western culture.

Had party leaders kept the *posseiros'* interests at the forefront of their involvement in the region, these leaders may well have ad-

---

67. Eduardo Dias, *Um imigrante e a revolução: Memórias de um militante operário* (São Paulo: Brasiliense, 1983), 116.

68. Chaves Neto, *Minha vida,* 125.

69. Moraes transcript, pt. 3.

70. Portelli, "Uchronic Dreams," 155–56.

vocated a negotiated settlement along the lines of that which Governor Rocha decreed. The party could have played a positive role in resolving the conflict with the assistance of state mediators, helping the *posseiros* resettle as smallholders in a less desirable but more secure zone. Many resisters and *posseiros* seemed disposed to accept such agreements, and the party could have easily demonstrated how consistent such a step was with their staged theory of development toward Communism. But as a political entity, it is easy to see how difficult it would have been for the party to enter into a relationship with the government. After all, the government had rejected its cooperation in the late 1940s by declaring the PCB illegal. How could party leaders now feed this biting dog? Although it remains unclear why he thought so, even Prestes claimed the Porecatú War had been one of the party's greatest mistakes.[71]

Exactly what was the mistake, great or small? Was it to have demonized Lunardelli as an imperialist *latifundiário*? Was it the unwillingness to negotiate or see local politicians as sincerely interested in compromise, if only to enhance their own popular images? Was it the decision to pit different categories of rural workers against one another, fostering fights between *posseiros* and the employees of planters and contractors? Was it their support for any sort of armed confrontation? In Moraes's view, the party could have helped best by popularizing the *posseiro* struggle and attracting public attention to the concerns of the underdog peasants. This work should have continued despite the suppression of the resisters, he argues.[72] When the party stopped listening and orienting and started dictating according to its own interests, the moment of democratic leadership was lost, not only for itself but, what is far more important, for hundreds of *posseiros* who had accepted the party's patronage. The case shows a small number of rural folk taking their citizenship seriously and seeking alliances with those who were willing to support them. In their move from dependent plantation labor to independent proprietorship and political engagement, these wayward rural migrants had risked everything to gain a piece of the pie. A few succeeded, while the rest drifted on in their weary search for bread and dignity.

The emphasis of PCB militants on the shortcomings of party strategy neglects significant continuities in the history of land struggle in Brazil. The Porecatú War signified a dramatic encounter in a long history of extreme elite resistance to smallholding. Codified in the

---

71. Felismino, "A guerra de Porecatú."
72. Welch and Geraldo, *Lutas camponesas,* 123.

land law of 1850, subsequent land reform laws effectively restricted the growth of this class to isolated regions and otherwise undesirable lands. As late as the 1990s, violent conflicts like that in Porecatú, with landless workers suffering losses at the hands of authorities (both public and private) from whom they had seized undeveloped land, continued to make headlines throughout Brazil. Still today, *posseiros* find themselves kicked off land they have invested years of effort in improving. If, like the Porecatú resisters, they have local and national allies, they may find themselves rewarded with new plots of virgin land. But the pattern of having their efforts exploited only to be kicked out once they have made the land valuable is one that has been repeated untold times in Brazil. It is highly doubtful that the absence of Captain Carlos or a sudden change in the party's willingness to negotiate would have significantly altered the outcome of events in northern Paraná. For the party and rural militants generally, the Porecatú War would stand as a reminder of the deadly limits of the incorporation process and promote a return to more cooperative, less confrontational forms of rural labor struggle.

5

Dismayed by the Communist Party's inability to deliver on its promises, João Guerreiro Filho—the Dumont Peasant League leader—gradually backed away from PCB activities in the 1950s. He found that the party was only one of various political brokers trying to organize and lead rural workers in São Paulo. Its aim of fostering an anti-imperialist agrarian revolution had to compete with other approaches to bringing about change. In the 1950 presidential race, the hounded and hostile leaders of the PCB placed the party in opposition to the election, beseeching supporters to cast blank ballots. In the combative voice of the August Manifesto, Prestes called the leading candidate, Getúlio Vargas, a "feudal lord." To many workers, however, Vargas was still the "father of the poor," and they looked forward to voting for him and his Brazilian Labor Party (PTB). Although the

TENDING THE SOIL

> **Appropriating the Tools of Incorporation**

party branded Vargas an imperialist tool, Vargas strongly identified himself with nationalism and with those who called for the "emancipation" of Brazil from the control of foreign capital. In a calculated campaign to dilute the PCB's appeal to working-class audiences, Vargas called Communists "swindlers" (*velhacaria*) and their policies "suicidal."[1]

Back in 1945, Vargas had opened the road for Guerreiro's political incorporation just as he was becoming more aware of the world around him. Although the PCB had been his first companion on the journey toward citizenship, it had been Vargas's discourse of *trabalhismo*, praising Brazilian workers as the central force behind the country's modernization, that marked the way. Following his ouster from power, Vargas cultivated this popular image by emphasizing the paternalist elements of *trabalhismo*, such as the social security and minimum-wage laws he had introduced. His appeals to workers, no matter how shallow, stood it sharp contrast to the hostility President Dutra had shown workers and unions since 1947. When Vargas opened his 1950 campaign in São Paulo, he spoke to the agrarian reform issue, boldly proclaiming the federal government's right to expropriate unproductive lands and distribute them to rural workers. He also renewed his 1941 pledge to "extend *trabalhismo* to rural workers."[2] Inspired by the rhetoric and tired of ineffective PCB tactics, Guerreiro broke with the party line and used what he had learned as a PCB activist to campaign for Vargas. To prepare for Vargas's September appearance in Ribeirão Preto, Guerreiro spent many nights placing posters of the event around the city and Sundays sneaking onto area plantations to urge the *colonos* to attend.[3]

On the day of the rally, he recalled, Vargas's opponents tried to discourage attendance by littering nails on the streets to pop tires

1. Prestes and Vargas had concrete reasons to distrust one another despite the positive events of 1945. In 1935, Prestes masterminded the Intentona Comunista revolt against Vargas, which resulted in dozens of casualties within the armed forces. On the other hand, Vargas imprisoned Prestes and deported his German-Jewish wife, Olga Benario Prestes, delivering her to Hitler's torture chambers and eventual death. See Fernando de Morais, *Olga*, 13th ed. (Rio de Janeiro: Globo, 1986). On Prestes's opposition to Vargas's election, see Moraes and Viana, *Prestes*, 121; and Rodrigues, "O PCB," 416. For Vargas's comments, see his *A política trabalhista no Brasil* (Rio de Janeiro: José Olympio, 1950), 167; and Maria Celina Soares D'Araújo, *O segundo govêrno Vargas, 1951–1954* (Rio de Janeiro: Zahar, 1982), 41–43.

2. Getúlio Vargas, *A campanha presidencial* (Rio de Janeiro: José Olympio, 1951), 53. Of the 1950 election, the historian Ricardo Maranhão writes, "the triumphal return of Getúlio appeared out of a context in which the old chief, beyond his own populist charisma, promised the laboring class their citizenship at least, while Dutra's government had practically stripped them of it." Maranhão, *Sindicatos e democratização*, 114.

3. João Guerreiro Filho, transcript of interview by author and Sebastião Geraldo, São Paulo, 11 July 1989, AEL/UNICAMP (hereafter Guerreiro transcript), p. 13.

and by setting up barricades to keep vehicles away. But Guerreiro and many thousands of others remained undaunted as they packed the local soccer stadium. An unsympathetic local newspaper reported the presence of a crowd of forty thousand people—a surprisingly high number, representing nearly 15 percent of the county's population. Guerreiro felt rewarded at the rally when Vargas renewed his pledge "to extend to rural workers the same benefits that the labor laws give city workers." He applauded Vargas's statements that day, and as the October election results demonstrated, Guerreiro was not alone in his support for the cagey populist. Nationally, Vargas attracted 48.7 percent of the vote in a three-way race; in Ribeirão Preto, he amassed 60 percent of the vote. For the PCB, opposing Vargas proved to be as unpopular as enlisting recruits for the Porecatú peasant army: only 2.6 percent of the electorate followed the party's advice by submitting blank ballots. Vargas's *trabalhismo* also helped sweep into the governor's office Lucas Nogueira Garcez, a center-left candidate of an alliance between the PTB and Adhemar de Barros's Social Progressive Party (PSP). Garcez won 57 percent of the Ribeirão Preto vote.[4]

Placing his trust in the new Labor Party regime, Guerreiro moved to São Paulo in 1951 and gave up activism to pay closer attention to the needs of his growing family.[5] Urban migration was an increasingly attractive alternative for many rural workers as the 1950s unfolded. An unstable rural economy brought declining real earnings and the deterioration of rural living and working conditions.[6] Like Guerreiro, many workers recognized *trabalhismo* as an important potential ally in the struggle against capricious employers and the uncertainties of the marketplace. For urban workers, especially industrial and commercial employees, *trabalhismo* brought protective labor legislation, stable unions, specialized labor courts, and enfranchisement. Moreover, during his first year as president, Vargas granted union members greater autonomy by limiting state interference in union elections and eliminating the *atestado ideológico,* a loyalty oath all candidates for union office had been required to sign since 1947.

---

4. Vargas's speech is quoted from "Verdadeira consegração pública a Getúlio Vargas," *A Cidade* (Ribeirão Preto), 15 September 1950, 1. Cited in Walker, "From Coronelismo to Populism," 195. The PSD candidate, Cristiano Machado, scored 21.5 percent of the vote nationally, while General Eduardo Gomes, flag bearer of the conservative National Democratic Union Party (UDN), carried away 29.7 percent of the vote, despite his opposition to the minimum-wage law. Moraes and Viana, *Prestes,* 122. The 1950 census counted 270,293 people in Ribeirão Preto and its environs. On the governor's race, see "Terminadas as apurações no estado," *A Cidade,* 5 November 1950, 1, cited in Walker, "From Coronelismo to Populism," 195. See also D'Araújo, *O segundo govêrno Vargas,* 75, for a detailed tabulation of the 1950 election results.
    5. Guerreiro transcript.
    6. Paiva, Schattan, and Freitas, *Setor agrícola do Brasil,* 92; and Stolcke, *Coffee Planters,* 88.

This reinvigorated many *sindicatos* by allowing workers to oust inactive union officers, the so-called *pelegos,* who had collaborated with the Dutra government in repressing workers' demands. At year's end, under pressure from reenergized unions and PTB activists, Vargas fulfilled one of his campaign promises: he announced a 25 percent increase in minimum wages. "You can be sure," he reassured workers, "that the solutions to your problems are being handled by the government." The Communists, on the other hand, could offer workers no concrete benefits or measures. Their opposition to Vargas and evident attachment to armed conflict alienated the party from many workers. Only a few party militants distanced themselves from the central committee and rededicated themselves to working-class interests at the local level by agitating for the implementation or expansion of *trabalhista* promises.[7]

Having outmaneuvered both the left and the right with *trabalhismo,* Vargas initially turned most of his attention to other matters. His first, overall priority was economic development, putting the coffee economy under intense pressure to conform to government development strategies.[8] In the 1950s, an increasing number of groups and individuals advocated "economic development," believing economic growth to be the source of world peace and stability.[9] Despite wide differences of opinion among development advocates, dramatic change in the agricultural sector was viewed by all as a precondition for successful growth. Government planners looked to agriculture for the basic resources and raw materials needed to secure Brazil's economic independence through import-substitution industrialization. Large inflows of foreign capital were needed to finance the construction of modern industries. As in the past, officials considered coffee a natural source of necessary income because the sale of coffee abroad

7. Castro Gomes discusses urban labor support for Vargas in *A invenção do trabalhismo,* 328. The wage hike was issued in Decree Law No. 30,342 of 24 December 1951 and is presented by Vargas in "Mensagem de natal em 24.12.51," *O govêrno trabalhista do Brasil,* vol. 2 (Rio de Janeiro: José Olympio, 1954), 55–64. See also Timothy Fox Harding, "The Political History of Organized Labor in Brazil" (Ph.D. diss., Stanford University, 1973), 243–50, who notes contemporary criticism of the inadequacy of the 25 percent wage hike in light of the 100 percent increase in inflation that has occurred since 1943, when the last minimum-wage increase had been decreed. In addition to Maranhão, *Sindicatos e democratização,* see also Wolfe, *Working Women, Working Men,* 162–72; and French, *The Brazilian Workers' ABC,* 247–67.

8. Getúlio Vargas, "Convocação de todos os brasileiros á batalha da produção agrária, em 8.4.52," *O govêrno trabalhista do Brasil,* 2:429–40.

9. See, for example, Raul Prebisch, *The Economic Development of Latin America and Its Principal Problems* (Lake Success, N.Y.: United Nations, 1950); and W. W. Rostow, *The Stages of Economic Growth: A Non-Communist Manifesto* (New York: Cambridge University Press, 1960).

President Getúlio Vargas on a Rio Grande do Sul ranch in September 1952. On his
return to power in 1951, Vargas cultivated an image as Father of the Poor. The
original photo caption noted that he "made a point of greeting the ranch personnel, showing that, in his government, even the humblest friends are not forgotten." Photo: courtesy Arquivo Fotográfico da *Última Hora* from Arquivo do Estado de
São Paulo

generated more foreign exchange than any other export commodity.[10] Government economists sought to make coffee more profitable
than ever, while agronomists aimed to make agriculture generally
more efficient and productive. Nevertheless, both agreed that agricultural profits should be used to pay for industrial expansion. These
new policies thus encroached on the planters' interests by making
coffee the midwife for industrial growth nationally.[11]

10. United Nations Economic Commission for Latin America (hereafter ECLA), *Theo-
retical and Practical Problems of Economic Growth* (Santiago, Chile: ECLA, 1951). Publication No.
E/CN.12/221. These strategies were elaborated specifically for Brazil in Joint Brazil/United States
Economic Development Commission, *The Development of Brazil* (Rio de Janeiro and New York,
1954); and Brasil, Comissão de Desenvolvimento Industrial, *O problema da alimentação no Brasil*
(Rio de Janeiro, 1954).

11. Nathaniel Leff, *Economic Policy-Making and Development in Brazil, 1947–1964* (New
York: John Wiley & Sons, 1968), 19–34, states that decline in planter authority dates from the
1950s, when they were unsuccessful in defeating several aggravating governmental economic
policies, especially the "exchange confiscation" export tax.

Changes in the Coffee Economy

The trends and reforms that most concerned São Paulo coffee planters began with structural changes in the Brazilian and world coffee
economies. As late as 1945/46, Brazil supplied more than half (55 percent) of the exportable coffee produced in Latin America and nearly
half (48 percent) of all coffee exported worldwide. But with postwar
recovery under way, the United States gradually relaxed commodity
price controls, stimulating production by other nations. Convinced
that Brazil could not maintain its share of the market, Brazilian policymakers determined instead to protect the nation's coffee income by
manipulating world prices. Whereas Brazilian production had once
filled the lion's share of world coffee demand, now the nation's coffee
would simply top off world supply. Brazil would be a "residual producer," using its productive capacity to supply what other producers
could not.[12] Formed in reaction to rising competition in the world
coffee market, the policy took advantage of the "inelasticity of the
demand for coffee"—the stability of coffee consumption in the face
of increased costs—to force up world prices.[13] The government thus
attempted to overcome the volatility of the coffee market by controlling world supply.

As a result of government policy, coffee was the major source of
Brazil's foreign exchange income in the 1950s and 1960s. In 1948,
coffee provided 42 percent of the exchange Brazil obtained from its
exports; this figure increased to 74 percent in 1952 and averaged
55 percent throughout the 1950s and 1960s. Prices charged in national currency—the cruzeiro (Cr$)—for coffee exports rose dramati-
cally in the early 1950s. The price importers paid in cruzeiros for a
sixty-kilogram sack of coffee more than doubled between 1950 and
1954, jumping from Cr$1,223.58 to Cr$2,588.00. By 1961 the price
had more than doubled again, reaching Cr$5,549.00 per sack. Ironi-
cally, in 1954/55, just when prices reached their high point, Brazil's
share of world exports dropped to 43 percent. However, inflation
eroded the real value of export prices, and real prices declined after

12. Antônio Delfim Netto and Carlos Alberto de Andrade Pinto, "The Brazilian Coffee:
Twenty Years of Set-backs in the Competition on the World Market, 1945/1965," in *Essays on
Coffee and Economic Development* (Rio de Janeiro: Instituto Brasileiro do Café, 1973), 279–315,
esp. 283–91.
13. J. W. F. Rowe, *The World's Coffee: A Study of the Economics and Politics of the Coffee
Industries of Certain Countries and of the International Problem* (London: n.p., 1963); and Department of Economic and Social Affairs, Joint Working Group of the Banco Nacional do Desenvolvimento Econômico (Brazil) and the ECLA, *Analyses and Projections of Economic Development*,
pt. 2, *The Economic Development of Brazil* (New York, 1956), 98.

the 1954/55 fiscal year. Although the real value remained above 1940 levels until 1957, prices then dropped sharply, staying down until the end of the decade (see Appendix, Table 5).[14]

In the 1950s, planters felt singled out by the government for special punishment by what they derisively called the "exchange confiscation" (*confisco cambial*). Starting in 1951, the Vargas government began to sell coffee abroad at high free-market prices while paying planters in cruzeiros at lower, official rates of exchange. The policy amounted to an exchange tax. This strategy explains the obvious differences between export prices and prices received by planters (see Appendix, Figure 1). The method generated hard currency to fund the federal government's purchase of industrial imports and also provided money to maintain the valorization scheme itself. In order to protect high world-market prices, the government used these profits to buy and stockpile coffee surpluses, thus controlling world supplies. By manipulating foreign currency exchange rates, especially with regards to the U.S. dollar, and controlling coffee supplies, Brazil's coffee policy aimed solely to maximize exchange receipts. Until 1957, the policy generated an estimated 10 percent of the government's total revenue.[15]

In October 1953, the government compensated planters for reduced income by paying a "bonus" of five cruzeiros per dollar of foreign exchange income. Thereafter, the government eased the bite of exchange tax "confiscation" with periodic adjustments and bonuses. The heart of the problem was in the supply side. By protecting export prices, the government's policy encouraged new planting not only in Brazil but also in other Latin American countries and Africa. By 1958, world yields were predicted to be enormous, which pushed down prices. To protect the price in 1958/59, the Brazilian government

14. On government coffee policy, see Delfim Netto and Pinto, "The Brazilian Coffee," 283. Prices are reported in Constantino C. Fraga, "Resenha historica do café no Brazil," *ASP* 10 : 1 (January 1963), 21. Brazil's world share is analyzed in Department of Economic and Social Affairs, *The Economic Development of Brazil,* 102. Delfim Netto and Pinto claimed the share had fallen to 39 percent in 1953–54.

15. On the exchange scheme, see Delfim Netto and Pinto, "The Brazilian Coffee," 284. For the planters distaste of the government's coffee policy, including "exchange confiscation," see Gustavo Avelino Corrêa, "O problema cambial," *RSRB* 32 : 381 (October 1952), 66–67; Plinio de Oliveira Adams, "Café e cambio," *RSRB* 32 : 382 (November 1952), 35–41; the articles by José Bonifácio de Sousa Amaral (São Paulo's secretary of agriculture from 1957 to 1961), "Protecionismo industrial e depauperamento dos populações agrárias," *RSRB* 32 : 379 (August 1952), 22–29, and "O Brasil ainda e um pais essencialmente agrícola," *RSRB* 34 : 386 (March 1953), 48–49; and Plinio Cavalcanti de Albuquerque, "Política cafeeira," *RSRB* 35 : 413 (September 1955), 18. On the scheme's revenue generation, see Joel Bergson and Arthur Candal, "Industrialization: Past Success and Future Problems," in *The Economy of Brazil,* edited by Howard S. Ellis (Berkeley and Los Angeles: University of California Press, 1969), 33.

bought eleven million bags of coffee and withheld them from the market, paying planters a "symbolic price" that amounted to a 10 percent decline in their income, despite production levels that were 25 percent higher than before.[16] In the meantime, the government returned some of the difference between export and sale prices to planters, not only by buying their surplus production but also by subsidizing imports such as chemical fertilizer and tractors.[17] Some analysts held that these buybacks and subsidies reduced the planters' concerns over shrinking demand, falling prices, and the problem of the *confisco cambial*.[18] Between 1948 and 1958, in fact, no other crop provided an income matching that generated by coffee.[19] Thus, contrary to the planters' continual complaints, government interference helped coffee become more lucrative than any other crop, save sugarcane and onions. Until 1959, government policy so encouraged coffee production that in the state of São Paulo alone, 750,000 acres of land were newly planted in coffee.[20]

Impact on Coffee Workers

For coffee workers, however, the government's economic policy brought few rewards and plenty of distress. In the 1950s men, women, and children still performed the vast majority of work on Brazilian farms and plantations, significantly outweighing the con-

16. On the bonus, see Delfim Netto and Pinto, "The Brazilian Coffee," 283–87; and Stolcke, *Coffee Planters*, 77–79. Delfim Netto and Pinto discuss the symbolic price on pages 291–93.

17. Gordon W. Smith, "Brazilian Agricultural Policy, 1950–1967," in *The Economy of Brazil*, 277.

18. Fernando B. Homen de Mello, "A política econômica e a setor agrícola no período pôs-guerra," *Revista Brasileira de Economia* 33:1 (January/March 1959), 33–35, cited in Stolcke, *Coffee Planters*, 84.

19. *Conjunctura econômica* (Fundação Getúlio Vargas, Rio de Janeiro) 6:8 (August 1959), 67–73, cited in Stolcke, *Coffee Planters*, 84. Only in 1959 did planter returns fall by more than the decrease in world coffee prices. Werner Baer, *Industrialization and Economic Development in Brazil* (Homewood, Ill.: Richard D. Irwin, 1965), 103.

20. FAO, ECLA, Instituto Brasileiro do Café, and Secretaria da Agricultura do Estado de São Paulo, Divisão da Economia Rural, "Estudo de 33 propriedades cafeeiras tipicas do estado de São Paulo," *ASP* 9:6 (June 1962), 9. This detailed study of thirty-three selected coffee farms was part of a much larger investigation of the state's coffee economy jointly conducted by these agencies in 1958. The findings were published in English as ECLA, *Coffee in Latin America: Productivity, Problems, and Future Prospects*, pt. 1, *The State of São Paulo: Prospects for Production*, and pt. 2, (a) *Case Study of Thirty-three Coffee Farms*, and (b) *Analysis of the Functions of Production* (New York: United Nations, 1958) (E/CN.12/545, E/CN.12/490). FAO, ECLA, Instituto Brasileiro do Café, and Secretaria da Agricultura de São Paulo, Divisão da Economia Rural, "A indústria do café em São Paulo," *ASP* 8:3 (March 1961), 15.

tribution of animal and machine power. Workers contributed on average more than 90 percent of the inputs involved in producing coffee on existing plantations, while machines were used almost exclusively for transportation and processing.

This dependence on human labor had three sources. One was the high cost of machines, including tractors, many of which had to be imported. Another was a suspicion that machine and even animal driven tools could damage the coffee trees, that weeding devices would dig into the soil and destroy the coffee tree's system of hairlike roots that grew in the top layer of soil. But the third reason, labor control, was the most important. In a 1951 report on Brazilian coffee, U.S. foreign service officer Robert Elwood emphasized this factor: "The use of animal power for cultivation (the use of tractor power is probably not generally economical) would mean that the regular labor force would not be fully employed." In order to keep an adequate number of workers available on the plantation for the harvest season, the *colono* system occupied their time with the cultivation process, weeding thousands of trees with a hand-held hoe at least three times before the June and July harvest season. These matters interested U.S. diplomats because lower production costs could more readily translate into lower coffee prices for U.S. consumers. The key to lower prices, they argued, was to be found in greater labor productivity, and it was assumed that machine power could help produce these results. Nevertheless, as an exhaustive 1958 study concluded, no matter the size of the coffee plantation, the same labor-intensive cultivation methods tended to be used.[21]

Despite the importance of human labor power to coffee production, increased coffee income was not shared with coffee workers in the 1950s. To the contrary, planters successfully placed the burden of market fluctuation on the backs of workers. Whenever prices went down, so did wages, which shows how well planters managed to maintain their profit margin by taxing worker living standards. This trend varied only in the 1949 to 1951 period, when planters were forced to raise wages considerably in order to attract and retain workers during a period of heightened competition with the labor demand of cotton producers. In these years, coffee prices increased at the same

21. Robert B. Elwood, "Recent Developments and Trends in Brazilian Coffee Production," Despatch No. 1,118, American Embassy (hereafter AmEmbassy), Rio de Janeiro, 1951, cited in *Brazilian Coffee: Production and World Trade,* prepared by the Foreign Service of the United States of America (Washington, D.C.: U.S. Government Printing Office, 1953), 113, in Department of State Records, microfilm 1489-22, Department of State, United States National Archives (hereafter DS/USNA). The 1958 study, from which statistics used in the prior paragraph were taken, is FAO et al., "Estudo de 33 propriedades cafeeiras," 7–9, 52–75.

time that weather patterns varied, causing the cotton and coffee harvest seasons to overlap. By 1954, with *colono* wages in steady decline for two years, there was nearly an inverse relationship between planter profits and worker wages. Thereafter, *colono* income suffered greater losses than planter income (see Appendix, Figure 2).[22] The price received for two to three 60-kilogram sacks of coffee paid for the yearlong upkeep of one thousand trees—a statistic that reveals the extent of the imbalance between *colono* wages and planter income (see Appendix, Table 6). Each of these trees yielded an average of 540 kilograms, or nine such sacks. Thus, *colonos'* basic wages cost planters less than 1 percent of the price they were bound to make selling their coffee. *Colonos* also earned piecework payments for their labor during the harvest and for odd jobs throughout the year, which significantly increased their income. All together, labor absorbed less than a third of the total cost of coffee production, according to a 1953 study of four diverse São Paulo coffee plantations.[23] Under these conditions, plantation life became increasingly difficult for coffee workers during the 1950s.

That wages on São Paulo coffee plantations fell so far below the cost of living index indicates that planters had little trouble attracting labor in the 1950s. This evidence contrasts sharply with planters' repeated claims of the labor shortages they suffered in the period. Shortly before the government's coffee policy was introduced, planters maintained that São Paulo's coffee economy could not be sus-

22. The base salary of coffee *colonos* (used to prepare this analysis and Figure 2 in the Appendix) was the compensation paid for weeding and caring for coffee trees. Negotiated annually, *colono* contracts established a fixed salary for every group of one thousand trees cared for (*tratado*) by the *colono*. Generally, the total annual sum was negotiated in October or November and paid out every two months in six equal portions. From sparse data, it is known that the rate varied from plantation to plantation, but the extent of the variation is unknown. Of course, the coffee economy was not nearly so simple as this. In addition to the base *trato* wage, *colonos* also received wages for the volume of coffee beans they harvested, occasional chores, and whatever marketable food or livestock they raised on lands provided for their use.

The rising wage trend and the unique circumstances of 1949 to 1951 are reported and analyzed in William T. Briggs (American Vice Consul, São Paulo) to AmEmbassy, Rio de Janeiro, "Labor Conditions in the São Paulo Consular District" (for January, February, April, and June 1950), Record Group (hereafter RG) 84, Post File 560, Box 84, DS/USNA; and Elwood, "Recent Developments and Trends in Brazilian Coffee Production," 99–101.

23. On yields, see FAO et al., "A indústria do café," 67. The 1953 study is "Estudo sôbre o custo de produção," *Brasil Rural* 137 (December 1953), 40–45. Directed by the São Paulo secretary of agriculture, this study examined the costs of coffee production on four different plantations, one considered small, one medium, and the other two large. (These terms were not defined.) The smallest was found to make the most efficient use of labor, which accounted for 23 percent of the cost of production. Labor cost factors were highest on the largest two plantations: 33 percent for one, and 42 percent for the other. On the medium-sized plantation, the use of a tractor reduced the cost of labor to 16 percent of total production expenses. The average of these four percentage figures is 29 percent.

tained without the annual influx of ten thousand foreign workers and their families—a total of some fifty thousand people per year. When planters decried the "exchange confiscation," they claimed it caused workers to abandon the countryside, leaving them short-handed. By 1954, coffee's economic strength was no longer in doubt, yet in January the prominent SRB representative Antônio de Queirós Telles, commented on how "immensely planters feel a shortage of labor that will only be made up for by the arrival of great waves of foreign immigration." In March, planters used the labor shortage argument to win a blanket exemption for rural workers from the army draft, a privilege at least one planter found shamefully unpatriotic.[24]

In the 1950s, however, the number of new immigrants to Brazil did not fulfill the desires of São Paulo planters (see Appendix, Table 7). In a reversal of Estado Novo policies, the new Vargas administration began supporting subsidized European immigration. But of the 370,000 Italian, Dutch, and other Europeans who came to work in Brazil during the decade, the portion directed to *paulista* coffee plantations was very low. In 1952 fewer than 6,000 subsidized immigrants were farm laborers, and by the period 1958–60, only 205 of nearly 20,000 Italian immigrants—once the most numerous of all immigrant groups engaged in coffee production—fell into this category.[25] As some planters speculated, declining agricultural wages made it difficult to attract immigrants.[26]

What the planters would not admit was how internal migration

24. On labor and immigration, see "Falta de braços para a lavoura," *RSRB* 27:320 (April 1947), 4; and "Braços para a lavoura de café," *RSRB* 28:347 (September 1949), 4. The link between the exchange tax and rural exodus is drawn in "Memorial da Federação das Associações Rurais do Estado de São Paulo (FARESP) a Osvaldo Aranha, de 22.06.53," Document No. 58, in *Impasse na democracia brasileira, 1951/1955: Coletânea de documentos,* edited by Adelina Alves Novaes e Cruz et al. (Rio de Janeiro: Centro de Pesquisa e Documentação, Editora da Fundação Getúlio Vargas, 1983), 185. For Telles, see Antônio de Queirós Telles, "Instituto Nacional de Imigração e Colonização," *RSRB* 34:396 (February 1954), 54. On the draft, see "Dispensa de incorporação de trabalhadores agrícolas nas fileiras do exército," *Brasil Rural* 140 (March 1954), 54; and José A. Viera, "Participação do exército na recuperação agrícola do país," *Brasil Rural* 168 (July 1956), 55–57.

25. On Vargas's immigration policies, see Joint Commission, "Bases do govêrno brasileiro para a negociação da Comissão Mista," Document No. 27, in Cruz et al., eds., *Impasse na democracia brasileira,* 73. As one of Brazil's fourteen points of negotiation in the Joint Commission—which was organized to discuss economic relations between the two countries in 1952—financial support for the "transportation and establishment of European immigrants, principally Italian," was listed as item 9. In response, the United States used its Intergovernmental Committee for European Migration to subsidize and place some 43,456 Italian immigrants in Brazil between 1952 and 1957. The small number of immigrants working in agriculture is examined by Gloria La Cava's "As origens da emigração italiana para a América Latina após a segunda guerra mundial," *Novos Cadernos* 2 (1988), 49–77, esp. tables 3, 5, 6. (Thanks to Jeff Lesser for drawing my attention to this article.)

26. Antônio de Queirós Telles, "Imigração," *RSRB* 35:410 (July 1955), 68.

to the state of São Paulo supplied them with an abundance of laborers. In the 1950s more than 1.25 million Brazilians migrated to São Paulo from the northeastern states of Bahia, Paraíba, Sergipe, Pernambuco, and Alagoas, as well as from Minas Gerais, which abuts São Paulo along its northern and eastern borders (see Appendix, Table 7). The vast majority of these northeasterners (*nordestinos*) sought work in São Paulo agriculture during periods of peak demand, such as the harvest months of January, February, March, and July. Thereafter, many returned home or left agriculture in pursuit of urban-based employment. Despite high turnover, the flood of migrants increased at the start of the 1960s with more than 120,000 people entering São Paulo in 1961.[27] Still, coffee planters were not satisfied.[28]

The planters' pleas for increased European immigrant labor had less to do with labor shortages than with labor control. Some may also have clung to lingering prejudices about the cultural superiority of Europeans over Brazil's mixed-race majority. Important sectors of the Brazilian ruling class viewed national laborers as restive, undisciplined, and opportunistic, while they looked on Europeans, especially "the Latins" of Italy and Portugal, as stable, self-motivated, and ambitious. "We must receive the bulk of our immigration from races which, like the Latins, present the greatest similarity to us," said Queirós Telles. An "example of immigration that we do not care for is the immigration of people from other states in our own country," said another commentator referring to *nordestinos:* "this is not the solution for Brazil."[29]

Planter opinions had some basis in fact. Although the migration of Brazilian families was encouraged by the agricultural ministry's Department of Immigration and Colonization (DNIC), the bulk of the *nordestinos* came spontaneously. Between 1952 and 1961, only 35 percent of the migrants claimed to be married, and 64 percent of those who came to São Paulo were single men or boys. In a revealing study sponsored by the São Paulo Department of Agriculture, the so-

27. Santa Helena Bosco and Antônio Jordão Netto, *Migrações: Estudo especial sôbre as migrações internas para o estado de São Paulo e seus efeitos* (São Paulo: Setor de Estudos e Pesquisas Sociológicas, Departamento de Imigração e Colonização, Secretaria da Agricultura do Estado de São Paulo, 1967), 32–33. On the migratory patterns of *nordestinos* see pages 18–19 and 24.

28. Octávio Teixeira Mendes Sobrinho, *Planejamento da fazenda de café: Separata do Boletim de Agricultura* (São Paulo: Diretoria de Publicidade Agrícola, 1962).

29. Translations of interviews given to the press by Queirós Telles and Flavio Rodrigues of the Union of Cotton Planters, in Cecil M. P. Cross (American Consul, São Paulo), Report No. 16, "Attitude Toward New Immigration Law," 12 January 1945, RG 84, Post File 560, Box 77, DS/USNA.

ciologists Santa Helena Bosco and Antônio Jordão Netto concluded that the *nordestinos* came south primarily for financial reasons: to earn as much as they could as fast as they could. They had few compunctions about shopping around for the best conditions and wages. While immigrant *colonos* were no less interested in money, the government sponsored the travel only of selected nuclear families who were then contracted to specific coffee plantations for periods of a year or more. While many immigrants longed to go home, and many did, a good number settled down in São Paulo and sought to advance themselves there.[30] For these reasons, planters believed immigrants were less mobile, less demanding, and thus more disciplined and controllable than migrant Brazilian workers.[31]

Mobilizing Rural Workers

The movement of workers to São Paulo did not meet planter preferences. In the populist political climate of the 1950s, the spontaneous and autonomous flow of workers further complicated the effectiveness of planter authority. The more mobile and independent rural workers were, the more difficult it was for planters to influence their behavior and political allegiances.[32] High rates of labor turnover helped erode the traditional bases of planter paternalism and pave the way for the deepening appeal of rural populism. Vargas had long

30. The principal ideologue of European superiority at this time was Fernando Bastos d'Avila, whose *L'immigration au Bresil: Contribuition a une theorie generale de l'immigration* (Rio de Janeiro: AGIR, 1956) was influential. See La Cava, "As origens da emigração italiana," 55–56. On migrant behavior, see Bosco and Jordão Netto, *Migrações,* 64–75, 219–24. Holloway analyzes *colono* mobility in *Immigrants on the Land.*

31. Mendes Sobrinho, *Planejamento da fazenda de café.* The assumptions of Italian immigration advocates received a serious blow in September 1952 when one of the first of the new groups of Italian *colono* families brought to Brazil revolted. Employment agencies in Italy had attracted six families by promising they could return home once their contracts had been fulfilled. But when the Italians arrived on a large coffee plantation in Guatapará, situated near Ribeirão Preto, they found they had been misled and demanded to be returned to Italy. The case attracted the attention of the press, and soon other cases of dissatisfaction came up. Alarmingly, of the six thousand rural labor immigrants who came to São Paulo in 1952, two thousand demanded repatriation to Europe by March 1953. This situation brought the entire immigration program under question. See Henrique Doria de Vasconcelos, "A mão-de-obra italiana e a agricultura paulista," *Brazil Rural* 129 (April 1953), 14–19.

32. On local boss rule (*coronelismo*), see Chapter 1 and Leal, *Coronelismo.* See also Linda Lewin, *Politics and Parentela in Paraíbá: A Case Study of Family-Based Oligarchy in Brazil* (Princeton: Princeton University Press, 1987); and Darrell E. Levi, *The Prados of São Paulo: An Elite Family and Social Change, 1840–1930* (Athens: University of Georgia Press, 1987).

identified himself as rural labor's compassionate protector, but his administration placed economic development before the specific needs of rural workers. Endorsing the trickle-down doctrines of the day, Vargas argued that a strong economy uplifted *all* who participated in it, including rural workers. In fact, the president's policies brought greater hardship to rural labor. Thus, despite the government's rhetoric on behalf of rural workers, Communist militants found plenty of discontent in the countryside and capitalized on Vargas's apparent incapacity to practice what he preached. In the process, the party eventually replaced its emphasis on agrarian revolution with a reformist outlook.

In the Barretos region, the northern portion of the state, the party assigned Eduardo Dias to clandestinely organize tenant farmers, peons, and meatpackers under the nom de guerre "Vitor." His efforts paid off in 1951, when he claimed that hundreds of meatpackers at the Frigorífico Anglo challenged their *pelego* union president to call a strike for better working conditions and pay. The radicals, oriented and supported by Dias, formed an independent workers' union, called Unidade dos Trabalhadores de Barretos, and expanded the strike movement to other employee groups in the company, including cattle hands and tenant farmers (hired to clear land and plant grass for pasture) located throughout the region. It was a far more successful mobilization than the one Irineu Luís de Moraes had initiated at the start of his rebellious career in 1929. In the end, workers won half of what they demanded.[33] During the same period, Moraes remained active. He and his family moved from Porecatú to Araçatuba, which lay to the west of Barretos, where he infiltrated several coffee plantations and organized *colonos*. In Ribeirão Preto, former peasant league member Pedro Salla continued to agitate among coffee *colonos*. In the southwest, another party recruit, José Alves Portela, organized cotton sharecroppers and pickers.[34]

Like thousands of other rural workers in São Paulo, Portela migrated south from the northeast in search of higher agricultural

33. Dias, *Um imigrante e a revolução*, 116–20. In mid-1947, the government of President Eurico Gaspar Dutra not only suppressed the PCB but also intervened in hundreds of unions, forcing out elected officers and appointing leaders sympathetic to his administration, who were known as *pelegos*. Apparently, the Barretos meatpackers union was one Dutra interfered with, for Dias's memoir reports Dutra's involvement with a strike movement there that lasted from January to May 1947, the month of the crackdown. See Dias, *Um imigrante*, 97–106.

34. Irineu Luís de Moraes, transcript of interview by author, Ribeirão Preto, 22 August 1988 (hereafter Moraes transcript, pt. 1); Pedro Salla, interview by author, Dumont, 14 May 1995; Guerreiro transcript; and José Alves Portela, transcript of interview by author, São Paulo, 23 August 1988, AEL/UNICAMP.

wages.[35] With the end of World War II, his brothers migrated to join him, and they tried tenant farming cotton near a southwestern town called Santo Anastácio. He paid no attention to politics until 1949 when he joined other tenants in a march on the town hall. Organized by local Communists, the tenants protested high rents and demanded distribution of a large expanse of undeveloped land, but the mayor responded by ordering the march repressed. As Portela remembers the event, the police killed one of their leaders, a popular physician, and severely beat other participants: "It was a massacre."[36] It was not the first conflict between Communists and authorities in the town. In 1946, Sheriff Roque Calabrese had forced the closure of a PCB peasant league, arguing that "the Brazilian people needed a whipping not democracy."[37]

Blacklisted by local landlords and outraged by the brutality of the Santo Anastácio police, Portela entered the PCB and accepted an assignment to go to Martinópolis, a town some thirty miles away, to try to organize five hundred families of cotton sharecroppers. "The people were easy to organize," he recalled. "They weren't influenced by the press or the radio, and no other political groups were out to mobilize them. We were the only alternative." But Portela kept his party affiliation to himself and used a defensive social justice argument to inspire the sharecroppers to rally in town protesting an increase in rents arbitrarily imposed by the landlord. Descending on the small-town courthouse with more than one thousand people, the

35. In 1941, at seventeen years of age, Portela traveled by truck from Sergipe, some two thousand miles away. Like many others, he earned money as a cotton cultivator and sent part of his earnings home to his mother and six siblings. Portela recounted how advertisements proclaiming the high wages paid in São Paulo caused him to migrate. (If this is true, the ads were not very successful, since only another 133 people migrated from Sergipe in 1941. By the end of the decade, however, Portela would find nearly twenty thousand additional compatriots working in São Paulo. See Bosco and Jordão Netto, *Migrações,* 54a.) The region Portela moved to was being developed for the first time, and much of his work involved clearing away large trees and shrubs with an ax and scythe. From 1941 to 1945 he sent money home to help support his family, but with the war over, Portela's wages fell along with cotton prices, and his family decided to join him in São Paulo. With his brothers he became a tenant farmer, raising mint and later cotton in Santo Anastácio. Portela transcript, 1–3.

36. Local Communists organized the event when they learned rents had escalated to rates too high for tenants to pay. Meeting in the town's central square, they demanded the distribution of a huge area of unclaimed land, but local authorities would not hear of it, and the police broke up the meeting. The group reacted to police brutality by counterattacking the police. Portela's participation in the protest became known, and the landlord broke his contract. He remembers this experience as transformational: it drove him to join the PCB and dedicate himself to fighting for other rural workers. Portela transcript, 5–6. For more on Portela's activism in the era, see "Em marcha para a Conferência Nacional de Trabalhadores Agrícolas: Grande concentração em Presidente Prudente," *NH,* 23 July 1953.

37. "Fechamento da liga camponesa de Santo Anastácio," *NH,* 28 June 1946, 5, quoted in Barriguelli, ed., *Subsídios à história,* 211–12.

sharecroppers chose Portela to negotiate for the group. Agreeing to meet alone with a judge and the landlord's two lawyers, Portela suddenly felt the gravity of the situation ("a dureza deles") and agreed to postpone negotiations for eight days. As it turned out, the delay gave the judge time to call in a police squadron. "We were just children," Portela said. The movement was repressed, and Portela became a fugitive. In 1951, however, he returned to Santo Anastácio, now a full-time rural labor organizer and clandestine revolutionary.[38]

The activities of Communist militants like Dias, Portela, and Moraes were significant enough to come to the attention of President Vargas. In September 1952, Vargas's labor minister, José de Segadas Vianna, reported that his spies had secured a secret PCB memorandum on the distribution and discussion of a Prestes communiqué regarding revolutionary strategy in São Paulo. The document revealed that rural militants had succeeded in meeting with several hundred "peasants" (*camponeses*) in the interior, including two hundred in Santo Anastácio, forty in Araçatuba, and twenty in Ribeirão Preto, the very places organized by Portela, Moraes, and Salla. Vianna's memo contrasted these rural successes with an anecdote about an industrial city on the outskirts of the capital where Communist activists reportedly failed to unite any workers at all. The minister emphasized the "gravity of Communist infiltration of the rural masses" and asked the president to instruct PTB leaders to promote worker-marches and other popular manifestations to build support for the improvement of agricultural working conditions and living standards.[39]

The New Rural Labor Populism

With his memorandum, Segadas Vianna alerted the administration to a resurgence of Communist rural activism and urged increased government activity in support of agrarian reform in order to help weaken the appeal of militants.[40] This was a key function of the labor

38. On ease of organization, see Portela transcript, 7. On the meeting with landlords, see page 10. On Martinópolis and Portela's return to Santo Anastácio, see pages 6–10.

39. "Carta de José Segadas Vianna a Getúlio Vargas, de setembro de 1952," Document No. 62, in Cruz et al., eds., *Impasse na democracia brasileira,* 202–5.

40. Vianna himself came under fire in 1952 for not moving fast enough to save the country from "Communist dangers" and "demagogic adventurers" by putting the government's *trabalhista* measures in place. Under pressure from left and right, he submitted a letter of resignation in January. But Vargas refused to accept it, retaining Vianna in the post until June 1953. D'Araújo, *O segundo govêrno Vargas,* 111.

minister, to help dilute the influence of leftists and appease workers with reforms, or at least the appearance of progress toward reform. Throughout 1952, Vargas spoke about the need to improve the lot of rural work ers. In January, the high-level National Agrarian Policy Commission (CNPA, Comissão Nacional de Política Agrária)—created in July 1951 by Decree Law No. 29,803—began to study and compose legislative solutions to the problems of Brazilian agriculture. Vargas also ordered the National Commission on Social Welfare to propose legislation to include rural workers in the social security benefits system. In April, Vargas addressed the fifth conference of the American member na tions of the ILO in Rio de Janeiro, convened to establish international rural labor law standards and to debate the problem of implementing them. On May Day he broadcast the news that the labor ministry had just completed work on a special rural labor code, and in June he sent a bill establishing the Rural Social Service (SSR, Serviço Social Rural) agency to congress.[41] After the winter holidays, Segadas Vianna's September memo, suggesting that the appearance of progress toward reform had not succeeded in satisfying the rural working classes, arrived on the president's desk.

Until the pivotal year of 1953, Vargas limited agrarian reform actions to tax and tariff manipulation, skimming profits off coffee exports with the exchange tax. With substantial political power still resting in the hands of the rural ruling class, a broader concept of agrarian reform remained taboo. The exchange tax alone had inspired the wrath of planter organizations. As João Soares Maciel Filho, one of the president's closest aides, commented, "São Paulo will not permit Brazil to grow beyond São Paulo itself." The state "defends its hegemony," he added, "a hegemony that is measured by the greatest number of cruzeiros paid for coffee." Elected to the presidency for the first time, Vargas preferred to take a conciliatory position toward these powerful interests, knowing full well what political suicide it could be to advocate legislation that threatened rural property rights and meddled in productive relations—two essential bases of the rural elite's power and prestige.[42] In 1953, however, Vargas took

41. Vargas, O govêrno trabalhista, 2:57, 422–28, 433, 439–40, 461–62; Segadas Vianna, O Estatuto do Trabalhador Rural, 39–43; Walter Godfrey, Brazil: Economic and Commercial Condition in Brazil Overseas Economic Survey, October 1953 (London: Her Majesty's Stationary Office, 1954), 58; and Camargo, "A questão agrária," 148–51.

42. On Vargas's actions, see D'Araújo, O segundo govêrno Vargas, 96. Maciel Filho quoted from "Trechos da carta de J. S. Maciel Filho a Vargas," in Cruz et al., eds., Impasse na democracia brasileira, 157–61. René Armand Dreifuss, 1964: A conquista do estado. Ação política, poder e golpe de classe (Petrópolis: Vôzes, 1981), 31–32, noted the continuing political strength of planters in the 1950s despite growth of the urban and industrial bourgeoisie.

several controversial steps that planters found threatening to their privileges.

It was a difficult year for the former dictator. Persistent inflation and a negative balance of payments forestalled the success of the government's economic development strategy. Although Vargas claimed to represent Brazil's struggle for economic emancipation from foreign interests, he lost control of one of the most explosive issues to mark his term of office: the "oil is ours" campaign to nationalize Brazilian oil reserves and the refinement process. By 1953 the streets were alive with calls to nationalize the oil industry, and the PCB was closely associated with this popular movement.[43] Vargas also claimed to have built his return to politics on a pact with workers, but his actions as president had shown him unwilling to deliver his side of the bargain. His one substantive act, raising the minimum wage to 1944 levels late in 1951, had done little to enhance urban living standards, while the agricultural economy had continued to deteriorate in the absence of an agrarian policy, prompting thousands of rural workers to enter urban job markets—a phenomenon that further damaged the precarious lifestyles of industrial and commercial employees. The rising cost of living had grown so intolerable that in March and April, more than three hundred thousand industrial and commercial workers and craftsmen in São Paulo and Rio de Janeiro walked off their jobs in an unprecedented series of strikes known as the "Strike of the 300,000." Here again, the PCB and not Vargas's PTB could claim significant participation in this popular mobilization.[44] In May, more trouble came to the president when a committee of specialists from the left-leaning United Nations Economic Commission for Latin America (ECLA), met in Campinas, São Paulo, to discuss agrarian reform. Joined by agronomists from the Food and Agriculture Organization of the United Nations (FAO) and the Brazilian and São Paulo governments, the ECLA committee urged Vargas to act on his stated goals.

In June, Vargas took several significant steps in response to mounting pressure from the left. In response to the ECLA report, Vargas sent an agrarian reform measure to congress. Prepared by the CNPA, the bill was modeled on a position paper composed the year

43. Responding to legislation proposed by Vargas at the end of 1951, the PCB played a significant part in the "o petróleo é nosso" movement that resulted in the creation of Petrobrás, a government-owned industry that coordinated all aspects of the exploitation of Brazil's oil reserves into the 1990s. On Petrobrás and the PCB, see Rodrigues, "O PCB," 416; and John Wirth, *The Politics of Brazilian Development* (Stanford: Stanford University Press, 1970), 189–206.

44. For a general discussion of the politics of the time, see Skidmore, *Politics in Brazil,* 112–27. On the Strike of the 300,000, see Moisés, *A greve de massa,* 67–94; and Wolfe, *Working Women, Working Men,* 176–88.

before by commission member Pompeu Accioly Borges. The bill paved the way for the government to appropriate and distribute land deemed underutilized by its owner. It was, in essence, a land reform bill that combined articles 141 and 147 of the 1946 federal constitution to legitimize fair compensation for seized land on the basis of the price originally paid for the land, its so-called historic value, plus adjustments for inflation. The concept of historic value was rejected by most landowner groups, who argued that fair compensation had to be based on current market prices. As the appropriation and distribution of unproductive land was constitutional (art. 147), the debate centered on the issue of compensation.[45]

In the middle of June, Vargas reconstructed his government by replacing six of the seven civilian members of his cabinet. Troubled by the predominance of Communist militants at the head of the strike movement of March and April, he replaced the moderate Segadas Vianna as minister of labor with the more dynamic and popular João Belchior Marques Goulart, the gaucho heir apparent of Vargas and *trabalhismo*. His nomination was "one of the measures taken by Vargas to block the growth of independent mobilizations," such as those represented by the "Strike of the 300,000" and the "oil is ours" campaign. "The doors of my cabinet are open to all true representatives of the laboring classes," announced the new labor minister, alluding to the newfound willingness of the PTB to work in collaboration with the PCB in order to strengthen the former party and weaken the latter. In October, Vargas took the lead in the oil campaign, too, by establishing a state oil monopoly through the creation of Petrobrás.[46]

In spite of these reforms, or perhaps because of them, opposition to Vargas grew, causing some to recall the tensions that drove

---

45. The agrarian reform bill was numbered 3.406-53 and sent to the congress in June 1953, accompanied by presidential message number 289.53. See Pompeu Accioly Borges, "Diretrizes para uma reforma agrária no Brazil," in Duarte, ed., *Reforma agrária*. See planter commentaries in "Sôbre as 'diretrizes de uma reforma agrária' da Comissão Nacional de Política Agrária, aprovados pelo presidente da república," *RSRB* 32:383 (December 1952), 28–30; and Raul Renato Cardoso de Melo Filho, "Diretrizes para uma reforma agrária no Brasil," *Brasil Rural* 6:122 (September 1952), 9–14. Landowners believed they should be compensated at current market prices, and they submitted a draft law including this language to the CNPA, which voted eight to five in favor of historic value on June 2. Curiously, CNPA member Alkinder Junqueira, president of the CRB, voted with the majority and against the position of his organization, the SRB, and FARESP. See "Reforma agrária," *Brasil Rural* 128 (March 1953), 22–37; "Inconstitucional a indenização pelo custo historico," *Brasil Rural* 133 (August 1953), 20–24; and "Atividides da Sociedade Rural Brasileira em 1953," *RSRB* 34:401 (August 1954), 22–24.

46. On the strike and cabinet changes, see Moisés, *A greve de massa*, 67–94; and D'Araújo, *O segundo govêrno Vargas*, 113–26; for Goulart quote, see Armando Boito, *O golpe de 1954: A burguesia contra o populismo* (São Paulo: Brasiliense, 1982), 85; for Petrobrás, see Skidmore, *Politics in Brazil*, 97–100; and Lucilia de Almeida Neves Delgado, *PTB: Do getulismo ao reformismo (1945–1964)* (São Paulo: Marco Zero, 1989), 148.

him from office in 1945.[47] The appointment of Goulart only seemed to aggravate the president's conservative opponents, and the peace it bought from organized labor did not promise to be of long duration unless real measures were taken to satisfy the needs of workers.[48] The pressures on the government were many, and since most concerned the economy, the demands of coffee planters had to be treated with sensitivity. The use of coffee as a source of government revenue angered planters and caused FARESP, a federally registered interest group, to unite an assortment of agricultural organizations in São Paulo in June.[49] The meeting included representatives of the coffee planter–dominated SRB who sought to join with FARESP in opposition to Vargas's land reform bill and in condemnation of the ECLA's "socialist" Campinas conference.[50] A final, joint petition side stepped the land reform issue and emphasized elimination of "unjust exchange confiscation."[51] Sent to finance minister Osvaldo Aranha, the petition argued that confiscation was making coffee less attractive as

47. John W. F. Dulles, *Vargas of Brazil: A Political Biography* (Austin: University of Texas Press, 1967).

48. Some leaders of the UDN accused Goulart of using the labor ministry to establish a "dangerous sindicalist republic," while others saw him as a Communist agent, bent on the absolute subversion of the Brazilian political economy. See Maria Victoria de Mesquita Benevides, *A UDN e o udenismo: Ambiguidades do liberalismo brasileiro (1945-1965)* (Rio de Janeiro: Paz e Terra, 1981), 83-87. To appease labor's economic demands, early in 1954 Goulart backed a minimum wage hike of 100 percent, a ludicrous proposal in the eyes of the new finance minister, Osvaldo Aranha. D'Araújo, *O segundo govêrno Vargas,* 123-24.

49. On 8 February 1946, FARESP registered with the minister of agriculture under Decree Law No. 8,127 of 1945, decreed by Vargas to the consternation of the SRB shortly before his downfall (see Chapter 2). The law sought to create a competitor to the voice of the SRB. According to a brief history printed in FARESP's official organ, *Brasil Rural,* the Federação das Associações de Pecuária do Brasil Central (founded in Barretos in 1942) and the União dos Associações Agropecuárias de Brasil Central (founded in 1945) joined together to form the new entity. *Brasil Rural* 128 (March 1953), back cover. Contrary to Vargas's wishes, events in 1953 fostered greater unity within the rural ruling class and its organizations—a trend encouraged by the First Brazilian Rural Conference of October 1952, which saw the founding of the CRB, the umbrella group of all state federations like FARESP. See "Primeira Conferência Rural Brasileira," *Brasil Rural* 123 (October 1952), 19-20. Iris Meinberg, "Mobilização efetiva da classe agrícola," *Brasil Rural* 129 (April 1953), 26-28. Meinberg was then president of FARESP.

50. At Campinas, agronomists from around the world discussed the need to expropriate large landholdings and then distribute the land for the establishment of small farms. The SRB delegates saw the seeds of Communism in these discussions and denounced the conference in "A FAO e a reforma agrária: Revolução social tramada nos planos internacionais," *RSRB* 33:391 (August 1953), 30-32. While the meeting was still going on, the SRB voted to ask FARESP to condemn Vargas's land reform bill. See "Atividades da Sociedade Rural Brasileira em 1953," 22-24.

51. The attacks different planter and landowner groups focused on the land reform law were already proceeding smoothly, if on separate fronts. See "Reforma agrária," *RSRB* 33:389 (June 1953): 14-17; Alvaro de Oliveira Machado, "Reforma agrária," *RSRB* 33:390 (July 1953), 60-62; "A FAO e a reforma agrária," 30-32; and Melo Filho, "Inconstitucional a indenização pelo custo historico," 20-24. With all this pressure against the bill, congress shelved it until the early 1960s. Camargo, "A questão agrária," 150-51.

an investment because the policy caused inflation, which drove up the cost of fertilizers and other supplies needed to make improvements in productivity. At the same time, the *confisco cambial* put a lid on the profitability of coffee. Investment capital was more profitably put into real estate, industry, and frontier areas where the virgin soil was still naturally rich and did not require special care. Coffee planters in the traditional coffee zones, meanwhile, were forced to lay off workers and abandon old crop land because of a lack of capital. The results were tragic, the SRB-FARESP petitioners complained: the pace of the rural exodus quickened and aggravated urban food shortages. These conditions demanded drastic corrective measures.[52]

Declining Conditions, New Strategies

Conditions certainly had worsened for coffee in 1953, but it was the workers and not the owners who urgently needed help, as comparative income figures demonstrate (see Appendix, Figure 2). Although planter incomes varied with inflation, the wages of *colonos* sank at an alarming rate. While the planters' petition secured the concession of a Cr$5.00 per dollar bonus from the government in October, *colonos* received neither readjustments nor bonuses.[53] Along with the attractions of urban life, poor wages drove rural workers away from the plantations, only to be replaced by hundreds of thousands of *nordestinos* attracted by the comparative strength of São Paulo's economy. Over the course of these decades of supposed rural exodus, the number of people employed in agriculture actually increased (see Appendix, Table 8). But the declining quality of rural life must have been unpalatable for all rural workers—old hands and newcomers alike. When coffee was king, some planters invested in their plantations: they built schools for workers' children, provided medical services, maintained and improved buildings, and sponsored dances and other social events. If in the past these attractions were not universally provided, in the 1950s they became increasingly scarce.[54]

52. "Memorial da FARESP a Osvaldo Aranha," in *Impasse na democrácia brasileira*, 184–88.
53. Delfim Netto and Pinto, "The Brazilian Coffee," 289; and Stolcke, *Coffee Planters*, 80.
54. A striking example of an "ideal" plantation is offered by Oscar K. Moore, U.S. agricultural officer in São Paulo, who toured Fazenda Iracema near Ribeirão Preto in 1950. Planter Thomas Alberto Whately endeavored to impress upon Moore the steps he was taking to improve the quality of life for his *colonos*. Growing enough coffee to saturate the consumption needs of 36,400 U.S. coffee drinkers annually, Whately hoped his plantation would serve as a model for other planters. All *colono* residences had electricity, and each was provided with a radio; clothes

In the 1940s, for example, João Geraldo's family of Italian immigrant *colonos* moved from Fazenda Dumont to Fazenda São João near Jardinópolis, a large town to the north of Ribeirão Preto. They had a standard *colono* contract, with rights to graze livestock, for the family had managed to acquire a number of beef cattle, hogs, a milk cow, and some work animals. But in 1947 the owner (Paulo Prado) complained of low coffee prices and eliminated the family's grazing rights in order to rent the land they had been using. Unable to find another arrangement with land usage rights, they sold the animals and moved to Ribeirão Preto, dividing the burden of caring for their eight children between various relatives.[55]

Among migrants from the northeast, Zildete Ribeiro do Desterro's story is equally revealing. She recalled living on Fazenda Santa Cruz in Colina in the early 1950s. Conditions were good on this plantation, located some fifty miles northwest of Ribeirão Preto. Their house was kept in good repair, furnished, and painted. They could come and go from the *fazenda* as they pleased. They ate well from the pigs, chickens, and cows they raised on a lot near their house. Around 1956, however, an illness in the family caused them to move back to their state of origin, Bahia. After a two-year absence, they returned to the *fazenda* and found that the houses had not been kept up, and *colono* land usage rights had been restricted. As the years went on, conditions worsened: they had to ask the planter's permission to come and go from the plantation; they were prohibited from eating or meeting with the other families; and no materials were provided for maintenance of the buildings. They moved to town in 1963.[56]

The mounting grievances of rural workers like Geraldo and Desterro kept the avenue open for Communist agitation in the countryside. This situation encouraged militants like Dias, Portela, and Moraes to move away from strict adherence to the August Manifesto. In light of pragmatism like theirs, the failure of past policies, and the political opening fostered by Vargas, party leaders finally endorsed a

---

washing shelters allowed women to fulfill this task away from the river's edge; a library featured North American magazines; planned recreational activities included a social hall with a phonograph and space for dancing; a physician and a dentist visited regularly; and three years of schooling were provided. Like Henry Ford, who was also famous for providing model accommodations for his workers, Whately's paternalism was not entirely a magnanimous gesture. He imposed on *colonos* standards of cleanliness and personal conduct and enforced them with fines and the threat of expulsion. In addition, he docked each *colono*'s salary to pay for the electricity and medical services. See Moore to United States Department of State (hereafter USDS), "A Modern Sustained-Production Coffee Fazenda," 13 January 1950, RG 59, Decimal File (DF) 832.2333 (Microfilm 1489/21), DS/USNA.

55. João Geraldo, interview by author, Ribeirão Preto, 7 July 1989.
56. Zildete Ribeiro do Desterro, interview by author, Ribeirão Preto, 5 July 1989.

strategy of working with existing unions. Support for this shift grew stronger when Goulart became minister of labor. "For the first time since 1946," two Brazilian scholars noted, "the Communists came to enjoy a margin of unofficial but obliging liberty in which they could pursue their true calling: influencing the laboring classes." While the law had always been an important organizing tool for the PCB, its importance grew as Goulart moved to institutionalize Vargas's repeated promise to extend urban labor laws to rural workers. When Goulart broached the topic of welcoming rural syndicalization, planters and their allies reacted with hostility. A 30 July 1953 *O Estado de São Paulo* editorial called Goulart's proposal a "dangerous . . . frank and deliberate appeal to collaborate with Communist forces," and the paper "denounced" such talk "without hesitation." [57] The more hostile conservatives became, however, the more it seemed to Communists that the law itself had the capacity to turn the planter's world upside down. The potential power of unions, coupled with deteriorating working and living conditions, inspired some rural workers to leap from the stage of quiet resignation and the endless, migratory search for a better fate to concerted action with their fellow workers. The very right to form a union to advance collective interests, overheard on the radio, discussed by those who could read the newspapers, and occasionally debated by politicians, sounded good to Natal Siviero, an itinerant rural worker in the Alta Mogiana, who approached the PCB in 1953. [58]

Some would say that Siviero started down a path toward communism early in his life. "I broke with religion early," he recalled in a 1988 interview, "because if you put God in a thing, it was already sorted out two thousand years ago. I saw people suffering, carrying the cross, praying for rain, and I figured it was a big lie." [59] At forty-five years of age, much of Siviero's life had passed when he decided he had found something better than religion in the Communist Party. The head of the regional committee in Ribeirão Preto, Antônio Girotto, asked him to go to first one and then another nearby sugar plantation to find work and initiate unionization campaigns if he found support. Siviero was unable to find work on the large plantations in São Martinho and Sertãozinho, where Girotto hoped to

57. Angela Maria de Castro Gomes, Maria Celina D'Araújo, and the 30 July 1953 *O Estado de São Paulo* editorial are quoted in Delgado, *PTB*, 148–49.
58. Natal Siviero and Nazareno Ciavatta, transcript of interview by author, Ribeirão Preto, 20 October 1988, AEL/UNICAMP (hereafter Siviero/Ciavatta transcript).
59. Natal Siviero and Nazareno Ciavatta, transcript of interview by Sebastião Geraldo, Ribeirão Preto, 1988, tape 2, side 1, p. 9 (hereafter cited in the following form: Siviero/Ciavatta, interview by Geraldo, 2/1:9).

organize workers. But he was soon employed on the Fazenda Marti-nópolis—a sugar plantation situated in Serrana, on the outskirts of Ribeirão Preto, that was owned, along with a sugar processing plant, by Jamil Cury.[60]

Siviero found the workers at Fazenda Martinópolis troubled by numerous grievances. The plantation paid male cane cutters (*corta-dores de cana*) less than half the minimum wage mandated by law; women earned even less than men.[61] Moreover, rent was deducted from the pay of workers who stayed in the plantation's "dirty, old tumbledown shacks [casebres, casas muito sujas, imundo]," and the plantation store sold the "worst goods" at high prices. Confronted by this situation, Siviero began to talk with other workers about forming a union. The discussion grew to include townspeople and workers from a neighboring sugar mill (*usina de açucar*), the Usina da Pedra. He sent word to Girotto for help and received a packet of materials specifying the steps needed to form a union.

Before these plans were realized, however, the police appre-hended him and took him to São Paulo to be interrogated by DOPS, the notorious "social and political" division of the state law enforce-ment apparatus. His interrogators intimidated him, claimed he was a Communist agitator, and pressured him to confess his subversive ac-tivities. Siviero denied the accusations, saying he "understood noth-ing of Communism." This may very well have been true, given his quick introduction to the party through Girotto. Siviero recalls ex-plaining his activities to the police by telling them he "was forming unions because it was a request from Mr. Getúlio Vargas. He told us rural laborers to form unions where we worked," Siviero continued, "and things would be a lot better." The interrogators pressed on, de-manding to know Siviero's religion. "If I told you I believed in God, I'd be lying," he responded. "He's a Communist, alright," concluded the DOPS agents.[62]

It is revealing that, as Siviero remembers it, theological ques-tions concerned the police more than political ones. During the

---

60. Siviero/Ciavatta, interview by Geraldo, 4/2:1–2.
61. According to Siviero, when the legal minimum was Cr$64.00 per day, Martinópolis paid the men Cr$45.00 and the women Cr$40.00 for a day's work. Siviero/Ciavatta transcript, 1. Siviero's memory may have failed him. Decree Law No. 30,342 of 24 December 1951, established a minimum hourly wage of Cr$3.46 and a daily wage of Cr$27.66 for eight hours work. Even under the worst conditions, few *cortadores* worked more than fourteen hours a day. This would give a maximum daily wage of Cr$48.00. In 1954, however, minimum wages were raised on May 1 with Decree Law No. 35,450. From then on, wages were more like those referred to by Siviero. The hourly rate was Cr$7.92, giving a total of nearly Cr$64.00 for an eight-hour day.
62. Siviero/Ciavatta transcript, 3; and Siviero/Ciavatta, interview by Geraldo, 2/1:6.

Dutra years, DOPS agents aggressively repressed rural militancy, including peasant mobilization in Porecatú. But with the election of Vargas, the lines seemed to blur between proper and improper behavior of the rural proletariat. DOPS officers told Siviero they had investigated his charges about the Fazenda Martinópolis and found them to be true. The planter was violating labor laws. They decided to categorize Siviero as a *sindicalista* (union organizer) rather than a *comunista*, concluding that there was nothing illegal about his activities. This was a remarkable change from their past behavior, indicating the transitional nature of the period. The reforms Vargas instituted in 1953 may have underscored the twilight of the rural elite and the dawn of a new hegemony based on *trabalhismo*. Who and what was right or wrong was no longer certain. In their handling of Siviero, DOPS eventually acted in a way that supported the *trabalhista* worldview. After a two-month process of interrogation and investigation, they let him go. A new day had seemingly arrived. Siviero was not so sure of all this, however. Following his release, he returned to Ribeirão Preto determined to lay low for the time being.[63]

A National Rural Workers' Conference

Siviero's efforts to organize *cortadores* on the Fazenda Martinópolis fit into a larger party plan to institutionalize a national rural labor movement, one that both responded to the announced intentions of Vargas and Goulart and offered opportunities to push beyond the boundaries of formal incorporation. In mid-1953, for example, activists used their contacts on plantations throughout the state to gather signatures in homage to Joseph Stalin, the Soviet dictator who had recently passed away. By the end of June, more than fourteen thousand signatures had been gathered, hundreds from plantations in Araçatuba, Valparaiso, Guararapes, Miguelópolis, Marília, and other São Paulo towns. As the year unfolded, party militants around the country started to build support for the First National Conference of Agrarian Laborers. Two meetings were to be held clandestinely on September 6 and 7, one in São Paulo and one in Recife—the former seating representatives of rural labor organizations from central and southern states, and the latter serving north and northeastern state representatives. The inspiration for these events was the PCB's deci-

63. Siviero/Ciavatta, interview by Geraldo, 2/1:4, 7.

Geremia Lunardelli (center) receives the Perseverance Medal from Vargas (right) in July 1952. Barely a year had passed since Lunardelli and state troopers managed to "persevere" over squatters resisting expulsion from land he claimed to own in Paraná; in 1953, he faced another PCB organizing campaign on his coffee plantation in Valparaiso, São Paulo. Photo: courtesy Arquivo Fotográfico da *Última Hora* from Arquivo do Estado de São Paulo

sion to elect delegates to attend the International Conference of Agricultural Laborers, scheduled to meet in Vienna, Austria, in October. To meet this deadline, rural labor mobilization was stepped up all over the country.[64]

In São Paulo, Moraes was one of the more successful organizers dispatched to generate support for the conference. On party orders, he moved west from Araçatuba, capital of the state's Alta Paulista re-

64. On Stalin, see "Assinaturas em homenagem a Stalin," *NH,* 24 June 1953. (Thanks to John French for a copy of this article.) According to Brazilian rural labor specialist Leonilde Sérvolo de Medeiros, the meeting was called the Primeiro Encontro Nacional dos Trabalhadores Agrícolas. Both Lindolfo Silva, a top PCB rural labor bureaucrat, and Lygia Sigaud, an anthropologist specializing in rural labor matters, called it the I Conferência Nacional de Trabalhadores Agrícolas. See Medeiros, *História dos movimentos,* 30; Silva transcript, pt. 1, p. 9; and Lygia Sigaud, "Congressos camponeses (1953–1964)," *Reforma agrária* 11:6 (November/December 1981), 3.

gion, to Valparaiso, where a greater number of rural workers could be found. Like Porecatú in Paraná, Valparaiso was part of the coffee frontier. As coffee prices improved in the 1950s, the Alta Paulista was the setting of more than 30 percent of the new trees planted in São Paulo.[65] There, Moraes engaged in a revealing and risky organizing campaign among *colonos* on the Fazenda Aguapeí, a large coffee plantation owned by Geremia Lunardelli, the land baron he and the *posseiros* had confronted only a few years before.[66]

In Paraná, Lunardelli cleared the squatters off his property; on his Valparaiso plantation, the laborers he employed wanted access to the land. They had been contracted under the new *empreitado* system, and unlike traditional *colonos*, Lunardelli's workers had no land usage rights. The provision of this contractual right, a defining feature of the *colonato* system in São Paulo, became the centerpiece demand of a flyer (*boletim*) Moraes eventually printed to distribute around the plantation.[67] Getting to a stage of defining demands like this took several months. Moraes claims that when he arrived in Valparaiso, his main contact was a poor custodian who looked after the town hall. A native of the state of Bahia (*baiano*), he invited Moraes to share his shack in the municipal barnyard. It seems, however, that more ground had been broken by earlier organizers than Moraes remembers, for by June someone had managed to gather signatures in honor of Stalin from 64 Valparaiso residents and 133 workers on nearby Fazenda Santa Helena. Nevertheless, Moraes tells a story that characteristically emphasizes his solitary, heroic fight to organize area laborers. He did this by frequenting the dusty bars called *botecos*, located around the periphery of Valparaiso, sharing shots of *pinga*—a strong, cheap, sugarcane-derived alcohol—with rural workers as he dug for information, sympathizers, and insights on the local situation. Little by little, returning to the same bars, he recalls developing their trust as they began confiding in him, recounting stories of the conditions under which they worked. Little by little, he urged them to demand their rights to unite, form a union, and fight for what was rightfully theirs—just as workers in the city were doing. The base of the movement slowly grew as workers brought friends with them to the *botecos* to hear what Moraes had to say.[68]

65. FAO et al., "A indústria do café," 19.

66. For an account of the Valparaiso episode of Moraes's militancy, see Welch and Geraldo, *Lutas camponesas,* 125–39. See also Moraes transcript, pt. 1, pp. 17–18.

67. Ibid., 19. The flyer was printed by party supporters in Araçatuba. Evidence of prior Communist success in Valparaiso is to be found in "Assinaturas em homenagem a Stalin."

68. Ibid., 23–24. The example urban workers had set with their strikes of March and April was important to the success of Moraes's efforts.

Despite the involvement of a substantial number of rural workers, Moraes remembers them as reluctant to take the initiative for themselves. This disappointed Moraes. In his view, the job of a professional agitator was fairly limited. When entering a new area, he liked to think of himself as serving to help people identify their problems, define their demands, select their own leaders, and establish their own organizations before he moved on to the next assignment. In general, he kept his affiliation with the PCB hidden from everyone but a core group or trusted cell. In Valparaiso, he succeeded in forming a cell of three coffee workers, but they did little work without his being there personally to urge them on. Frustrated, he formed an alliance with an unlikely class warrior: Joaquim Quirino, captain (*capataz*) of Lunardelli's *jagunços*. "He stopped me on the street one day and asked me if I was the fellow talking about a union," Moraes recalled. "I didn't know who he was but I admitted it." Moraes was scared when he learned about Quirino's reputation as a vicious enforcer for Lunardelli, but it was too late: he had already scheduled a rendezvous with the *jagunço* in the house of a worker-activist. Quirino brought his gang, adding to Moraes's concern. "All of them came armed with pistols, knives, and clubs," he recalled. Moraes sought to ingratiate the *capataz,* but it was hardly necessary. Quirino was sympathetic to the workers' problems and supported the idea of forming a union. In a later meeting with other supporters, Moraes brought the flyer, and when he suggested they distribute it secretly at night, the *jagunço* said no. "From then on he took charge," Moraes said. "He was so dictatorial even the administrator was afraid of him, so he got things done." At Quirino's command, the flyer was circulated openly.[69]

Moraes's achievements attracted the attention of Lindolfo Silva, the PCB's national representative for rural labor, who pressured Moraes to provide support for the upcoming national conference.[70] The Valparaiso workers gladly complied. In a noteworthy strategy, Moraes and Quirino gathered more than a thousand rural workers in the town's central square, quickly taking their photo and dispersing the crowd before the police had time to react to the illegal gather-

69. Ibid., 18–25.
70. Silva transcript, pt. 1, pp. 2–3, 9. Born in 1924 in Barro do Pirai in the state of Guanabara (today's Rio de Janeiro), Silva joined the party in 1947; in 1952 the central committee asked him to work full-time on the development of a national rural labor movement. It was then he began his career as a "professional revolutionary," a career that continued into the 1990s. In his memoir, Moraes contradicts Silva, claiming it was Heros Trench, Silva's superior, who contacted him in Valparaiso. See Welch and Geraldo, *Lutas camponesas,* 134.

ing.[71] Moraes had prepared banners calling for the legalization of rural unions and proclaiming the Valparaiso workers' support for the first national rural workers conference. The photo was published in the Communist press as solid proof of the depth of the party's penetration in the countryside. "The assembly confused the authorities: 'how was it that we let the Communists take over a city like Valparaiso?' The town isn't big but it was big enough to have police," Moraes said. "After that, the legality of rural unions had to be taken seriously." [72]

Evidently, the formal recognition of rural unions was not a key demand of the September meeting of agrarian laborers. Organized by the PCB, the conference was a show of urban labor support for rural labor, based on the party's conviction that an alliance between peasants and proletarians was essential for the conquest of power and the construction of state capitalism. Influenced by theoreticians and its Porecatú experience, the party directed the conference toward an emphasis on radical land reform, the confiscation and distribution of *latifúndios* and foreign-owned land, the abolition of feudal sharecropping arrangements, and credit to help small farmers. But documentation for this clandestine event has yet to surface, and its full story remains hidden from history. The rural labor specialist Leonilde Medeiros claims that the central purpose of the 1953 meeting was to elect delegates to attend the Vienna conference.[73]

The method of delegate selection was less than democratic and resulted in some telling misadventures, if Moraes's recollections can serve as a guide, for one of the Vienna delegates turned out to be Quirino, the *jagunço* captain from Valparaiso. Moraes remembers how impressed he was with Quirino's enthusiasm for leading workers, but he was far from ready to trust the gunman with secrets about the PCB. Nevertheless, party higher-ups needed delegates for the international conference, and the dramatic and public successes of Moraes and Quirino made Valparaiso a likely source for representatives. "One day

71. Moraes transcript, pt. 1, p. 16. Rather than gather in the square, the workers met in small groups in nearby bars or otherwise spread out in the area. At the appointed time, they united in the square, opened the concealed banners, waved to the camera, and quickly walked away.

72. Ibid., 17.

73. The best sources for the conference are newspaper stories regarding preparatory organizing. See, for example, "Grande concentração em Presidente Prudente" and "Em marcha para a Conferência Nacional dos Trabalhadores Agrícolas: Juros de agiota cobram os tatuiras," *NH*, 25 July 1953. Medeiros has a paragraph on the 1953 meeting, though she cites no sources. See *História dos movimentos*, 30.

the party sent Heros Trench to Valparaiso to get a name for someone" to go to the conference, Moraes recalls. None of the workers was ready, Moraes protested, since only a few knew anything about the Communist Party. "It was very difficult and time-consuming to bring up the question of Communism with them. They understood very little, and still thought in religious terms, in God and the Virgin Mary." But Trench, a pharmacist who served as national director for the PCB rural campaign, insisted, and Moraes explained that only Quirino was anywhere near ready for such an experience. "He's the one who has to go," said Trench. Although Quirino himself resisted, Moraes convinced him to go, assuring him that his family would be well cared for in his absence. In preparation for the trip, Quirino spoke to a group of "doctors and small bourgeoisie" in Araçatuba, who donated money for his journey. But the trip by ship from Rio de Janeiro went badly for him. Trench made all the rural labor delegates attend meetings and study groups throughout the voyage, and Quirino, used to having his own way on the range of Valparaiso, felt suffocated and trapped. He turned his frustrations on Trench, threatening to kill him with a knife. By the time they reached port, Quirino had been stripped of his mandate as a conference delegate, and he was sent back to Brazil. Though angered, Moraes claims he calmed down when he saw how well his family had been treated, and he remained faithful to his early commitment to organize coffee workers.[74]

The September meeting also established a commission to begin preparations for a much larger, second national conference. This conference would not only issue a slate of "peasant demands" but also create a broad peasant and rural worker organization that would get the rural union movement started on a national scale once and for all. Held a year after the first conference, from 17 to 19 September 1954, the second gathering also took place in São Paulo. According to one observer, nearly "five hundred directors from more than one hundred of the most important unions in the country" signed a final petition. Even this source may have exaggerated the number of delegates. More attention is given to the 1954 conference in Chapter 6.[75]

74. Welch and Geraldo, *Lutas camponesas,* 134–37.

75. Sigaud, "Congressos camponeses," 3, makes the claim that five hundred attended the second conference. The 1954 conference is reported in Oto Santos, "O programa do partido, a questão agrária, a organização e a luta dos camponeses," *Problemas* 50 (December 1954), 244–54; and "Trabalhadores da cidade e do campo reafirmam unidade—Dirigentes sindicais de São Paulo apoiam a realização da II Conferência Nacional dos Trabalhadores Agrícolas," *NH,* 14 July 1954, reprinted in Barriguelli, ed., *Subsídios à história,* 294. Founded at the meeting was ULTAB.

Furor over Rural Unionization

Whatever the exact number of participants at the 1953 meeting, the growth of the party in the interior alarmed the Vargas administration. On 6 January 1954, Gilberto Crockett de Sá, director of the government's national labor department, announced that "the syndicalization of rural laborers will begin immediately in São Paulo, seeking to neutralize Communist influence and bring under government control all the farmers' (*lavradores*) representative organizations." Crockett de Sá set a goal of founding 250 rural labor unions in the state beginning in Monte Aprazível, where Communists had allegedly infiltrated the government. Soon after this announcement, the pages of the SRB journal vented the planters' opposition to the project in no uncertain terms. They called the plan a thinly veiled scheme for the "regimentation of force for the triumph of a future syndicalist republic, or perhaps even a Soviet republic." Behind the project, they argued, was a plan to organize rural worker votes in support of the Labor Party, led by Goulart. As evidence, SRB president Luís de Toledo Piza Sobrinho pointed out that the announcement occurred on the eve of state gubernatorial elections and that the initiative for the law had come from the *trabalhista* government, not from any "necessities resulting from relations between bosses and employees."[76] Indeed, the SRB's analysis was entirely consistent with the Vargas administration's long history of conflict with São Paulo planters and Vargas's efforts to strengthen the PTB at the expense of both planters and radical militants, such as those in the PCB.

In the following few weeks the SRB's technical office, the Rural Economy Institute, elaborated these arguments, and on February 11 it lodged a formal protest with General Aguinaldo Caiado de Castro, head of the government's National Security Council. This peculiar administrative routing—through the general rather than the ministers of labor or agriculture—was justified by claiming the unionization plan posed a national security threat: "In an epic of monetary inflation and escalating living costs, the Federal Government is initiating the agitation of the rural laboring masses as a political movement of syndicalist character that could carry the nation to uncontrollable economic disorder."[77] But General Castro downplayed the

---

76. Crockett de Sá quoted in "Sindicalização rural," *RSRB* (February 1954), 11; and "A sindicalização rural apontada como manobra para fins eleitorais," *RSRB* 34:397 (March 1954), 13. For Piza Sobrinho, see "Sindicalização rural," *RSRB* (February 1954), 6.

77. "A sindicalização rural apontada," 12–17. Rural unionization was also maligned in the press. An editorial in São Paulo's *Folha da Manhã* (20 March 1954) argued that the illiteracy,

threat and sent the petition to the minister of agriculture for "careful study."[78]

One of the most intriguing aspects of the planters' attack against Crockett de Sá's proposal was the admission that all workers had the right to organize unions, a right recognized by the federal constitution and supported by history that "could not be put in doubt." But in order to be legitimate, unions had to come out of the day-to-day needs of the workers themselves. São Paulo rural workers were not motivated to take this step, the protest stated, because labor shortages had made it necessary for planters to provide decent working and living conditions. "There are no conflicts that cannot be resolved by the contracting parts," the petition said, "because, in reality, the scarcity of rural workers has caused landowners to accept demands for higher wages even when the price of the product does not assure he can cover the increased cost." Capitalist market mechanisms worked, making state intervention unnecessary and dangerous, argued the SRB.[79]

These nods in the direction of rural syndicalization softened the SRB's unequivocal opposition to the government's plan to sponsor the formation of unions. The desire to have it both ways recalled their response to Vargas's drive to organize rural workers in the early 1940s, when a tactic of supporting corporatist ideology enabled them to transform the 1944 syndicalization law into toothless propaganda. In fact, the SRB's retired legal counselor Francisco Malta Cardoso reappeared to argue for this strategy, saying the government's plans were perfectly legal. This position was readily accepted by the society's new leaders. Nothing about the petition, said SRB president Toledo Piza, was meant to be "contrary to government measures which pragmatically seek to favor the rural laborer." But, he went on, "the ruralist class of São Paulo disagrees with the execution of this dictatorial decree; under the present emergency . . . it would be catastrophic and destructive to *paulista* agriculture." The main objection was political, Toledo Piza explained. The petition's "single, exclusive preoccupation," he continued, "was timely combat against the demagogic and electoral form of the rural worker syndicalization campaign to be launched in the state, under the aegis of the president of

---

"nomadism," and diseases of rural workers would cause them to be apathetic toward their unions, thus allowing the organizations to fall into the hands of "false leaders" (*pelegos*).

78. "Sindicalização rural," *RSRB* 34:397 (March 1954), 54.

79. The influence of labor shortages is emphasized in "A sindicalização rural apontada," 13.

the republic and minister João Goulart." They protested the combination of rural workers under the direction of Goulart. In the present "circumstances of political antagonism and inflation," the petition said, the unionization scheme would only serve to "alert social unrest in the richest region of Brazil." Only unions that were truly independent and "free of any intromission of political powers" could serve workers properly. As in 1944, the SRB wanted to forestall the transference of worker deference from planter pockets to the state while keeping the door open to a union structure that might allow them to restore some of their declining influence as patrons.[80]

By the end of February, the furor over rural unionization had died down, quieted by Vargas's willingness to offer the planters and other opposition groups a gesture of appeasement. On February 22 the controversial minister of labor resigned. Attacked for agitating the rural masses and fraternizing with union members, accused of being a Communist dupe, and lambasted for supporting a 100 percent rise in minimum wages, Goulart resigned in protest against the "forces of reaction" that had frustrated his efforts to help workers in the struggle for their rights.[81] In resigning, the future Brazilian president (1961–64) left a lingering legacy. Along with his letter of resignation he included a plan for freezing prices and raising wages as well as a draft rural labor code. As an unapologetic supporter of *trabalhismo,* he would never shake the hostility of factions within the elite, particularly those of landed interests whom he had seemingly betrayed.[82]

On the first of April 1954, Vargas placed his administration behind the rural labor legislation Goulart had drafted by sending the bill to congress. Despite the hostility toward Goulart and the defeated unionization drive, Vargas pushed the bill, further antagonizing rural employers in the name of his *trabalhista* campaign promises. Visiting the São Paulo town of Agua Branca on April 3 to inaugurate an agricultural exhibit, Vargas restated what was already known: he had sent Goulart's bill to congress. The same issue of the SRB journal that reprinted the president's speech also carried two articles denouncing him as a "demagogue" and calling the law "grotesque." It proved to

80. Planter pros and cons on unions are presented in "Sindicalização proletária rural," *RSRB* 34:397 (March 1954), 11; and in "Sindicalização rural," *RSRB* 34:397 (March 1954), 64, where Malta Cardoso and Toledo Piza's views are recorded.

81. "Carta a Getúlio Vargas de 22.02.54," in *Impasse na democrácia brasileira,* 210–12.

82. Goulart, who so effectively rallied working-class support at various times in his career and who had become a charismatic leader of the masses, was born the son of a wealthy cattle rancher in the state of Rio Grande do Sul and was himself a large landowner.

be one of the reforms most vigorously resisted by congress, lingering in the legislature until 28 June 1957, when it was voted down, 102 to 62, with 54 abstentions.[83]

Well before this defeat, however, the drama that had caused Vargas to reform his cabinet in June 1953 and accept the resignation of Goulart eight months later was far from over. Conservative congressmen continued to block many bills as the government entered a period of constitutional crisis. The issues of inflation, resource nationalization, land reform, rural unionization, and the *confisco cambial* continued to excite the passions of powerful interests, from unions to coffee planters. On 3 June 1954, the government satisfied some planter complaints by setting a minimum price of 87 cents a pound for coffee, nearly 30 cents higher than the minimum established in 1951. Later in the month, Vargas faced impeachment proceedings, charged with engaging in treacherous intrigues with Argentina's Juan Perón, but the vote went against his opponents. Chief among these was Carlos Lacerda, a Rio de Janeiro–based journalist and head of the UDN, which had been founded in 1945 as the leading anti-Getúlista party. On August 5, an assassination attempt against Lacerda resulted in the death of Lacerda's bodyguard and an investigation that reached the presidential palace, implicating a loyal presidential aide and uncovering massive corruption. This news greatly embarrassed the president. In the meantime, the administration's efforts to maximize profits from coffee exports backfired. Outraged buyers in the United States had organized a boycott of coffee consumption, and it cost Brazil dearly. By August only 145,000 sacks of coffee had been exported, earning U.S.$14 million as compared to the U.S.$66 million earned on the sale of 860,000 sacks one year earlier. Mired in scandal, economic collapse, and pressured to resign by diverse individuals and interests, including the air force hierarchy and his own vice president, the beleaguered president wrote a final message to the people of Brazil on the morning of August 24, put a gun to his heart, and killed himself.[84]

83. For Vargas's Agua Branca speech, see "Exposição de animais," *RSRB* 34:398 (April/May 1954), 25–26. Planter reaction is expressed in Antônio de Queirós Telles, "Demagógico o discurso do presidente da república," *RSRB* 34:398 (April/May 1954), 88; and J. V. Marcondes Freitas, "E agir com ma fé estender ao campo as leis para operários," *RSRB* 34:398 (April/May 1954), 92–93. On the reform's legislative history, see Camargo, "A questão agrária," 159–60; and Benevides, *A UDN e o udenismo*, 190–91.

84. For the UDN, see Benevides, *O UDN e o udenismo*, 81–87. Although planters protested against the policy, higher prices stimulated new planting in Brazil and other producer countries—an event that was to have grave long-term implications for Brazil's coffee economy. Delfim Netto and Pinto, "The Brazilian Coffee," 289. Skidmore, *Politics in Brazil*, 136, offers data on coffee earnings. The suicide and its context are further discussed in D'Araújo, *O segundo go-*

The suicide brought a shocking end to the "father of the poor," but it reignited *trabalhismo,* infusing it with the power of martyrdom. Vargas's final declaration was read aloud over the radio an hour after his death, bringing the masses into the street in a spontaneous salute to their fallen patron. Vargas had cast himself as the victim of an "underground campaign of international groups joined by national groups" that worked against his unceasing efforts "to defend the people . . . especially the humble." He had tried to defend the value of coffee so as to protect the value of the work that went into producing it, but these measures were violently opposed. "They do not want the worker to be free," he went on. "They do not want the people to be independent." With his death he declared, "I was a slave of the people, and today I am freeing myself for eternal life. But this people whose slave I was will no longer be slave to anyone." These bold remarks, the authenticity of which have been debated, rang true for "the people" Vargas claimed to lead.[85]

Vargas's enemies rejoiced at the death of this tenacious politician, but with the public reading of his testament, the clever conciliator seemed to have the last laugh. Vargas had evidently chosen sides in the age-old balancing act between economic growth and social reform, between capitalists and laborers. After the suicide, Vargas's legacy belonged to those who could make the most of it, and Vargas's mantle passed from one politician to the other. Notably, those who advocated rural labor laws became *trabalhismo*'s most radical proponents and the clearest inheritors of the Vargas legacy. Depending on the political winds, these spokesmen included Adhemar de Barros, future president Jânio Quadros, the Christian Democratic Party (PDC, Partido Democrata Cristão) leader André Franco Montoro, and Goulart. In the immediate aftermath of the suicide, however, it was the Communist Party that took the greatest advantage of Vargas's popularity. In shifting from Communist militancy to *trabalhismo,* João Guerreiro Filho had anticipated this transition several years before it happened.[86]

---

vêrno Vargas, 122–26; Cruz et al., eds., *Impasse na democracia brasileira,* 273–323; and John V. D. Saunders, "A Revolution of Agreement Among Friends: The End of the Vargas Era," *HAHR* 44:2 (May 1964), 197–213. A good narrative of Vargas's final months is found in Dulles, *Vargas of Brazil,* 313–33.

85. Vargas cited from Dulles, *Vargas of Brazil,* 333–35. The book recounts the events of the suicide and includes a translation of Vargas's declaration. See also Skidmore, *Politics in Brazil,* 142.

86. Some conservative reaction is found in Benevides, *A UDN e o udenismo,* 89–91. Rodrigues, "O PCB," 417. On changes in the party, see Raimundo Santos, *A primeira renovação pecebista: Reflexos do XX Congresso do PCUS no PCB (1956–1957)* (Belo Horizonte: Oficina de Livros, 1988), 69–81.

6

The tie fit uncomfortably around Nazareno Ciavatta's neck. The son of Italian immigrant *colonos,* Ciavatta was born and raised on the giant Dumont coffee plantation. Unlike Pedro Salla and João Guerreiro Filho, however, Ciavatta's family had left the plantation in 1933. Thereafter, Ciavatta lived and worked in various places, including São Paulo, where he eventually joined the PCB, impressed by its campaigns in favor of rural unionization and oil nationalization. In 1954, Ciavatta accepted a party assignment to return to the Alta Mogiana to organize rural workers. Now, in September, he appeared before an audience of hundreds of men assembled to attend the Second National Conference of Agrarian Laborers and Farmers in São Paulo. He was one of many workers of rural background who had been cultivated by the party to take

SHAPING THE TREE

> **Mobilizing to Enforce Rural Labor Law**

part in the rural labor movement. Despite the urban experiences of many delegates, the press called them "hicks" (*caipiras*) and made a spectacle of their country ways.

At forty-four, Ciavatta had a certain authority about him. He "comes from the country [vem da roça]," as many would say when proudly describing a man with deep roots in Brazilian soil. Like Irineu Luís de Moraes and João Guerreiro Filho, Ciavatta valued militancy and fought long and hard to defend the dignity of rural workers like himself. He accepted the job of helping to form a union with enthusiasm, contributing his entire savings of about U.S.$300 to it. "Country folk didn't have anything," said Ciavatta. "They didn't have *trabalhista* law like city workers, no vacations or anything." Ciavatta believed rural workers deserved the same benefits as their counterparts in the city. He worked hard for the union, traveling throughout the region to talk with workers, certain it could help them gain access to labor laws. Salla, interviewed in 1995, said he was proud to have known Ciavatta and regularly offered his small house as a place of refuge for the class warrior. Even when Ciavatta appeared late at night, Salla and his wife welcomed him with coffee, food, conversation, and a bed. "He'd be in town talking with workers, gathered from different plantations in the bars," Salla recalled. "It was Ciavatta who built the union here." In July, two thousand people attended a rally declaiming the poor treatment of the area's rural workers and peasants. Then, on August 29, thirty workers gathered to found the organizing committee of the Ribeirão Preto Syndicate of Colonos and Agrarian Wage Workers, and Ciavatta was assigned to attend the São Paulo conference as a delegate.

From the podium, Ciavatta looked out at the gathering to see dozens of men in wide-brimmed hats, many cloaked in poor-fitting dark blazers—a sweaty auditorium full of men dressed awkwardly in their Sunday best. He was more comfortable talking around a kitchen table with country folk like Salla than addressing an auditorium full of people, but his passion for workers' rights inspired him to fire off a list of grievances experienced by agricultural workers and tenants in the Alta Mogiana. For the former, the pay was too low; for the latter, rents were too high and credit too difficult to obtain. The men of the country toiled relentlessly yet saw little to no gain for their labors. Worse still, a conspiracy of planters and police prevented them from improving their lot. "The peasant was dealt with by the police, only the police. Any dispute he had on the plantation, the planter just delivered him to the cops," said Ciavatta. "It was necessary to form

Nazareno Ciavatta, photographed in Ribeirão Preto in October 1988. Photo: author

a union to change this state of things." In Ribeirão Preto, "the duty fell to me."[1]

More than three hundred rural labor representatives attended the conference from Bahia, Minas Gerais, Paraná, Pernambuco,

1. Ciavatta's conference appearance is reported in "Debatem os trabalhadores agrícolas seus problemas e reivindicações," *Última Hora* (hereafter *UH*), (São Paulo) 21 September 1954, 8. Ciavatta quotes from Nazareno Ciavatta, transcript of interview by author, Ribeirão Preto, 20 October 1988, AEL/UNICAMP, p. 1. On organizing in Ribeirão Preto, see "Duas mil pessoas presentes ao comício de Ribeirão Preto," *NH,* 23 July 1954; "Conferências regionais," *Terra Livre* (hereafter *TL*), 15–31 August 1954, 1; and "16 Sindicatos Foram Criados," *TL,* 15 September–

Ceará, Goías, Rio de Janeiro, Rio Grande do Sul, São Paulo, and other states and territories. From Sunday to Tuesday, 19–21 September 1954, they met in the Cabana dos Bandeirantes, an auditorium in São Paulo's Ibirapuera park, a huge public recreation area located in the center of the expanding metropolis. Seven workers captured the attention of the popular press for having walked barefoot hundreds of miles from Mato Grosso in order to attend. An *Última Hora* reporter toyed with three of the men by offering them shoes, but their wide, calloused feet rejected the footwear. A photo of them—smiling, waving, and barefoot—appeared on the front page of the paper. Another rural worker, Telesforo Correia do Amaral, was shown statuelike as a more urbane conference participant knotted a tie around his neck. Numerous urban supporters attended, making a show of their solidarity and charity toward rural workers by giving them "mountains" of presents. These images underscored the privileged status of city life and expressed a belief that city workers had to extend a helping hand to country workers to lift them up to equal status. While the historic conference joined city and country as one, the press coverage reassured spectators that the proper order of things, the urban above the rural, was still intact, and the world was not about to be overturned.[2]

The conference marked a new stage in the growth of rural labor's liberty tree. The seed planted after World War II had become a small tree, and in the wake of Getúlio Vargas's suicide, many contenders wanted to prune it into shape. *Última Hora,* a newspaper chain owned by one of Vargas's close associates, Samuel Wainer, used every opportunity to emphasize the former president's influence on the conferees. "One year ago," an *Última Hora* headline read, "Getúlio Vargas was already telling us: 'Rural laborers should organize themselves.'" With the conference, *Última Hora* explained, rural workers demonstrated their desire to fulfill Vargas's order. "The demand for the syndical regimentation of country laborers constitutes a right based in a decree signed by President Vargas in 1944," proclaimed Sebastião Dinart dos Santos, a conference organizer and São Paulo

15 October 1954, 6. Salla quotes from Pedro Salla, interview by author, Dumont, 14 May 1995. For Girotto, see Antônio Girotto, transcript of interview by author, Ribeirão Preto, 19 October 1988, AEL/UNICAMP (hereafter Girotto transcript), pp. 3–5.

2. Images from "Caipiras de todo o mundo encontram-se no Ibirapuera," *UH,* 20 September 1954, 1, 2. A more detailed account is "Cercada do carinho dos operários e do povo a 2.a conferência," *TL,* 15 September–15 October 1954, 2. Without citing sources, the Brazilian anthropologist and rural labor specialist Lygia Sigaud incorrectly recorded that the conference was held in August 1954, the month of Vargas's suicide. Sigaud, "Congressos camponeses," 3.

rural labor activist. It was time to focus mobilization on the enforcement of existing law.[3]

Organizing the 1954 Conference

Vargas's death had created a political vacuum in the Populist Republic. With São Paulo's gubernatorial election approaching in October, many politicians wanted to be associated with Vargas's appeal. These circumstances created a unique context for the budding movement. Just six years before, in 1948, opposition from the SRB and the state federation of rural associations had led to the cancellation of a similar rural congress and forced the resignation of state agriculture secretary Hugo Borghi, who had proposed the conference. Now, in 1954, politicians vied with each other to demonstrate their attachment to the cause of rural labor rights. São Paulo's governor and the city's mayor, who fought each other on many other issues, reached out to delegates with free food, transportation, and housing. Three politically engaged retired military officers, Edgar Buxbaum and the brothers Felicissimo and Leônidas Cardoso, addressed the assembly and extended their support. State legislators and congressmen also appeared. Media outlets like *Última Hora, O Dia,* and the radio station 9 de Julho covered the event prominently. It was, as the historian and rural labor specialist Leonilde Medeiros writes, "a fundamental step for overcoming localism and the isolation of struggles developing in the country."[4] Demonstrating concern for peasants and rural laborers had started to become both newsworthy and politically appealing.

This turn of events marked a sharp change for the PCB. Operating clandestinely, the party had laid the groundwork for the conference long before Vargas's death and was quite reluctant to give all credit to the former president. In contrast to *Última Hora's* reporting of the event, the PCB's *Notícias de Hoje* and *Terra Livre* barely men-

3. For the headline and Dinart quote, see "Caipiras de todo o mundo," 2.

4. See "Debatem os trabalhadores agrícolas seus problemas e reivindicações," *UH,* 21 September 1954, 8. An early announcement of the September conference is "Trabalhadores da cidade e do campo reafirmam unidade," *NH* (São Paulo), 14 July 1954, reprinted in Barriguelli, ed., *Subsídios à história,* 294. On Borghi, see Chapter 3 and Jorge Miguel Mayer and Ivan Junqueira, "Borghi, Hugo," in Beloch and Abreu, eds., *DHBB,* 420. The presence of various media and politicians and their roles is found in "Cercada do carinho"; "Moções aprovados na II Conferência," *TL,* 15 September–15 October 1954, 2; and "Josué de Castro e o governador prestigiam os trabalhadores do campo," *UH,* 20 September 1954, 2. Medeiros, *História dos movimentos,* 30.

tioned Vargas and certainly refrained from crediting him with inspiring the rural labor movement. On the other hand, party leaders
recognized the political capital of the rural labor movement and did
not want to squander it. The presence of individuals from outside the
party demonstrated the PCB's desire to broaden the base of the movement. Conference resolutions signaled the party's shift to coalition
politics. Gone was the emphasis on achieving land reform through
violence that had so typified the party's thinking since 1947. Although agrarian reform was the key demand of the conference, it was
to be consolidated "with legal guarantees." Moreover, demands for
the enforcement of rural labor law, a theme barely mentioned in the
revolutionary August Manifesto of 1950, constituted the vast majority of items in the conference's final "Charter of the Rights and
Demands of Farmers and Agrarian Laborers."[5]

The success of the conference depended on the help of urban
labor unions, and for this reason, it demonstrated urban labor's interest in the agrarian question. Vargas and other *trabalhista* politicians
had long stressed the negative impact of rural labor out-migration to
the city, the way poor conditions in the countryside tended to push
rural workers into the urban labor market, weakening the bargaining
position of unions. Thus, urban labor unions were well represented
on the organizing committee for the conference, which had been established in June. As one of the principal means of building support,
members of the organizing committee hosted union meetings to discuss rural labor issues, the extension of urban labor rights to rural
workers, and the linked interests of urban and rural laborers. The
unions opened their meeting halls to rural labor activists such as
José Alves Portela, who addressed industrial workers in various locations, asking for their help and pledging the solidarity of rural workers.[6] Eventually, PCB analyst Oto Santos wrote, "innumerable cara-
vans of labor leaders went to the country, carrying with them not

5. Oto Santos, "O programa do partido, a questão agrária, a organização e a luta dos
camponeses," *Problemas* 64 (January 1955), 244–54. On the August Manifesto, see Chapter 4.
For the emphasis on *trabalhista* laws, see "Carta dos direitos e das reivindicações dos lavradores
e trabalhadores agrícolas do Brasil," *TL,* 15 September–15 October 1954, 4.
6. "Conferência dos Trabalhadores Agrícolas: Sindicatos e entidades membros da comissão central promotora," *NH,* 25 June 1954, n.p., lists forty organizations that were believed to
serve on the conference organizing committee. Of these, twenty-one were industrial, commercial, or service workers' unions. (Thanks to John French for a copy of this clipping.) In July, for
example, Portela spoke before the Interunion Unity Pact (PUI), a multi-union solidarity committee formed in São Paulo as a consequence of the general strike of 1953, requesting its assistance and promising rural labor solidarity with urban workers in demanding the payment of
minimum wages, salary increases, and a price freeze. In offering the solidarity of rural workers,
Portela claimed to speak for the unions of the *colonos* and *camaradas* of São João da Boa Vista
and Monte Aprazível as well as the sugar workers' union of Capivari. See "Trabalhadores da

only their solidarity but also their experience of urban struggle and organization."

According to the Santos report, nearly five hundred leaders (*dirigentes*) from one hundred "of the most important" labor unions in Brazil attended the conference and joined rural delegates in signing the charter. More than one hundred of the industrial workers' representatives came from the "largest factory unions" in metropolitan São Paulo. PCB journalist Lindolfo Silva, who was covertly assigned the task of advancing the PCB's position within the rural labor movement, confirms the large presence of urban labor. "Some five hundred union directors from São Paulo, Rio de Janeiro and Recife" met at the conference and signed the charter of demands, Silva recalled in a 1988 interview. Given the presence of urban labor leaders, the conference reflected some of the preoccupations ascribed to organized urban workers, including fears of a "rural exodus" and higher food costs.[7]

While urban workers were a significant presence, the vast majority of official conference delegates hailed from the countryside. Of the 303 delegates present, only 48 listed urban occupations. Like Lindolfo Silva, many of them may have had rural backgrounds, for it was only in the late 1940s that Silva moved off his family's farm to apprentice as a tailor, entering the PCB in 1947 and becoming a full-time activist in 1952. Of the 255 rural delegates, 119 described themselves as wage-earning rural workers, while the remaining 136 were identified as squatters, peasants, tenants, and farmers. Delegates were said to have come from fifteen states and the federal district of Rio de Janeiro. With 156 delegates, São Paulo contributed more representatives than all the other states combined. Minas Gerais sent the next largest amount, with twenty-three delegates. São Paulo also sent the largest number of female delegates to the conference: five representatives out of the seventeen women who attended officially. The presence of so many *paulistas* reflected the strength of the state's labor movement generally and underscored the influential role São Paulo had on the early rural movement.[8]

---

cidade e do campo reafirmam unidade—Dirigentes sindicais de São Paulo apoiam a realização da II Conferência Nacional," *NH,* 14 July 1954, n.p., quoted in Barriguelli, ed., *Subsídios à história,* 294.

7. Santos quoted in ibid., 249–50. For Silva, see Lindolfo Silva, transcript of interview by author, São Paulo, 16 August 1988, AEL/UNICAMP, pt. 1, p. 9.

8. See "A composição social da II Conferência," *TL,* 15 September–15 October 1954, 3; and Medeiros, *História dos movimentos,* 31. Without citing a source, Lygia Sigaud reported the presence of "303 representatives of rural labor" from more than fifteen states. Sigaud, "Congressos camponeses," 3–4.

Founding ULTAB

The mixture of rural laborers and peasants, broadly speaking, was reflected in the title of the organization founded by the conference on Tuesday, September 21: the Farmers' and Agricultural Laborers' Union of Brazil (ULTAB, União dos Lavradores e Trabalhadores Agrícolas do Brasil). For nearly ten years, ULTAB was to be the only organization of national scope in the rural labor movement. Although its effectiveness can be criticized, ULTAB helped end the isolation of local struggles and shape a national agenda for reform. Its founding president was Geraldo Tibúrcio, a peasant from the state of Goiás. The PCB had groomed Tibúrico for the post and prepared delegates for his ascension by narrating his life story in picture-book fashion in a pre-conference issue of *Terra Livre*. According to the story, Tibúrcio was born to peasant parents in 1924, worked as a mason's helper in town as a young man, traveled widely in Brazil as a cowboy and miner, got involved in the "PCB directed" strike movement of meatpackers after World War II, and finally returned to farming on a government-subsidized colony, from which he launched his career as a rural labor organizer, first as founding president of the peasant union of Goiás. In 1953 the PCB sent Tibúrcio to Chile to represent Goiás at the 1953 conference of the Confederation of Latin American Laborers (CTAL), which was affiliated internationally with Soviet Union labor organizations. His election in absentia to head ULTAB reflected either the effectiveness of this profile or the party's control over the São Paulo conference. Several other ULTAB officers also belonged to the PCB. These included José Alves Portela, who was named general secretary; Lindolfo Silva, who became first secretary for organizing; and, as first treasurer, Sebastião Dinart dos Santos.[9]

These four joined six other men to compose ULTAB's executive

9. Of these four, only Silva claims to have been a paid PCB functionary. Tibúrcio, Portela, and Dinart, on the other hand, earned ULTAB funds that had been generated from dues, fund-raising, newspaper subscriptions, and the donations of urban unions. Despite these distinctions, the policies of ULTAB rarely diverged from those of the PCB. Although ULTAB could claim to be independent, the newspaper through which its positions were expressed was controlled entirely by the party. This is a point of some confusion in the literature, but *Terra Livre*, a tabloid published periodically from 1954 to 1964, was directed by Heros Trench, head of the PCB's rural labor committee, the Secção do Campo. "It was directly sustained with the money of the party," said Silva; "ULTAB didn't have a journal." Silva transcript, pt. 1, pp. 9–10, 19. See also Nestor Vera, *"Terra Livre* e a luta dos camponeses," *TL*, May 1963, 3. On Tibúrcio and ULTAB, see "Vida e luta do camponês Geraldo Tibúrcio," *TL*, 1–15 August 1954, 3; and "Geraldo Tibúrcio eleito presidente." Dinart had been a childhood friend of Moraes in Barretos and a longtime companion in the party's rural labor campaigns in São Paulo. See Chapter 1 and Welch and Geraldo, *Lutas camponesas no interior paulista*, 29. Curiously, Tibúrcio's narrative also includes stops in Barretos, where he rested after trailing cattle there from Goiás.

commission. In terms of their occupations, three were listed as tenant farmers, two as rural wage earners (*assalariados agrícolas*), two as farm owners (*proprietários*), two as urban workers, and one as a squatter (*posseiro*). ULTAB also had a fourteen-member consultative council, of which five members were listed as wage workers, three as farmer-owners, two as tenants, one as a *colono,* and one as a *posseiro,* with the occupations of two left unrecorded. In addition to the diversity of rural occupations represented, officers of ULTAB's two directive bodies came from thirteen different states, with nine members from the state of São Paulo and no other state having more than two representatives. How many other officers were Communist remains unknown, but clearly the PCB retained significant clandestine control over ULTAB. In fact, São Paulo's secret police may have underestimated the party's influence when they later noted that "a Communist cell directed by Lindolfo Silva functioned" in a second-floor room of the ULTAB office at 36 Direito Street, São Paulo.[10]

The conference and its charter reflected traditional PCB ideology in at least five particulars. One was the emphasis placed on solidarity between urban and rural workers. For Communism, this was as old as the hammer and sickle; for the PCB, it had antecedents in the BOC of the late 1920s. The feudal nature of Brazil's land tenure system was a second theme peculiar to the PCB and imposed by them on the conference. Following this assumption came two additional PCB stances: a critique of greedy "imperialists" and "*latifundiários*" who controlled far more land than they needed, and a demand for the end of "all forms of semi-feudal exploitation, such as sharecropping," with this land distributed "to those who worked it."[11] Finally, the decision to headquarter ULTAB in São Paulo was based on the sort of political calculations that were fundamental to most PCB decision-making processes. It was a strategic political decision, said Portela. "The masters of coffee were also the masters of power," he said. "This was the motive, the principal impulse behind the formation of ULTAB."[12] Despite this continuity with the PCB's

10. On the composition of ULTAB's directorate, see "Geraldo Tibúrcio eleito presidente da ULTAB," *TL*, 15 September–15 October 1954, 2. On the police and Silva, see "Serviço secreto: Lindolfo Silva," Secretaria da Segurança Pública, DOPS, 14 May 1965, B:NM, Box 144, Vol. 11, 1848, AEL/UNICAMP.

11. "Carta dos Direitos," 4.

12. On the influence of the Comintern in Brazil, see Manuel Cabellero, *Latin America and the Comintern, 1919–43* (New York: Cambridge University Press, 1986). On exports and trends in paulista agriculture between 1948 and 1962, see "Estado e tendências da agricultura paulista," *Agricultura em São Paulo* 10:5/6 (May/June 1963), 1–61, esp. 46–47. For Portela, see José Alves Portela, transcript of interview by author, São Paulo, 23 August 1988, AEL/UNICAMP, p. 11.

revolutionary past, the general tenor of the conference was decidedly reformist.

With regard to the basic issue of the inequality of the Brazilian land tenure system, the conferees opted to pressure the government to create conditions for restructuring land ownership. In the name of "social justice," they wanted the state to expropriate unproductive *latifúndio* and to distribute surplus land to landless peasants and rural workers. This was called "democratic agrarian reform," and the conferees agreed to pursue political means of implementation. They drew up a petition and started a national campaign for agrarian reform to gather five million signatures in support of agrarian reform from rural workers and peasants. The petition, including the name and location of each signer's plantation, was to be submitted to the president. Santos described the campaign as an opportunity to educate both urban and rural dwellers about this fundamental Brazilian problem and to rally support for the peaceful but radical resolution of the agrarian question.[13] That most rural workers barely knew how to read or write was noted by the conferees: the petition could be read aloud and people's "marks" produced. For organizers, it was important that the petition help rural labor adopt a moderate look and broaden its appeal to well-to-do farmers, the so-called "rich peasants" (*camponeses ricos*). In June 1956, ULTAB reported having collected 100,902 signatures, with nearly 40,000 coming from São Paulo.[14]

The conferees' resolve to widen the rural labor movement beyond the confines of the forgotten revolutionary manifesto hardened with the endorsement of rural *trabalhismo*—the resolution of rural workers' problems through the legal and administrative channels initiated by Vargas. Militants in attendance criticized themselves for having underestimated the importance of the workers' "immediate demands" for the payment of minimum wages, the enjoyment of annual vacation periods, weekly days off, shorter hours, the fulfillment of contract obligations, and the legitimacy of their organizations. The

13. On the petition and reform, see Santos, "O programa do partido," 246, 249; and Sigaud, "Congressos camponeses," 3–4.

14. In 1950, illiteracy in Brazil was 57.2 percent. The figure for rural São Paulo at that time was rising, for nearly 90 percent of rural labor migrants who entered the state between 1952 and 1961 could neither read nor write. See Armin K. Ludwig, *Brazil: A Handbook of Historical Statistics* (Boston: G. K. Hall, 1985), 132; and Bosco and Jordão Netto, *Migrações*, 71. On the program and rich peasants, Santos wrote, "The program of the party thus corresponds to the yearnings and the interests of the totality of the peasant mass. Giving substance to the fundamental demands of millions of poor, middle and rich peasants, the program establishes and demarcates a broad, united front line, excluding only the minority of large landholders [*latifundiários*]." Santos, "O programa do partido," 246. The petition's progress is reported in "Cresce o numero de assinaturas na campanha pela reforma agrária," *TL*, 1–15 June 1956, 2.

charter went beyond demands to win the enforcement of existing laws by specifying demands for the creation of pension plans for rural workers, the provision of education, electoral rights for the illiterate, freedom of speech, and the abolition of payment in kind, particularly counting residential rents as part of a worker's wage. The charter was quite elaborate in shaping specific demands for Brazil's major export crops, with separate programs prepared for sugarcane, coffee, and cacao workers. Each crop-specific program included items that addressed different categories of workers, such as the *colonos* and *camaradas* engaged in coffee production. Subsequently, the emphasis of ULTAB-directed militancy was to turn on the day-to-day needs of rural wage workers in these strategic commercial crops.[15]

Perhaps no better justification for the party's reformism existed than the almost relentless decay of rural worker livelihoods (see Appendix, Table 6 and Figure 2). More than anything else, the loss of income justified the decision to draw the first line of defense in the enforcement of existing laws. One must be careful to avoid generalizing for all Brazil, however. In truth, *trabalhista* legislation had little influence in such frontier regions as northwest Paraná and the far off territories of the Amazon, but the party consciously chose to headquarter ULTAB, and thus the rural labor movement, in São Paulo rather than the frontier or Rio de Janeiro, the nation's capital. While far from ideal, the judicial bureaucracy in São Paulo took pride in its relative independence and professionalism.[16] In this way, São Paulo was not a representative Brazilian setting but, in the eyes of many, a representation of Brazil's future.

Political Competition for Rural Workers

São Paulo also seemed to be a good political setting for ULTAB. The weakness of *coronelismo,* the strength of urban unions, and the level of literacy in São Paulo helped make politics there more dynamic

15. "Carta dos direitos," 4–5. An earlier indication of the stress to be placed on immediate demands is "A importância da luta pelas reivindicações imediatas," *NH,* 1 June 1954, 3, reprinted in Barriguelli, ed., *Subsídios à história,* 289–91. On the commercial crop strategy, see Santos, "O programa do partido," 250–52.

16. The decision is discussed in Lindolfo Silva, transcript of interview by author, São Paulo, 18 July 1989, AEL/UNICAMP (hereafter Silva transcript, pt. 2), p. 20. On the unique autonomy and professionalism of the São Paulo judiciary, see Robert W. Shirley, "Law in Rural Brazil," *Brazil: Anthropological Perspectives,* edited by Maxine Margolis (New York: Columbia University Press, 1979), 343–62.

and fluid than in most other Brazilian states. The PCB was one of many rivals for the electoral allegiance of workers. The names alone of the many parties tell this story: Labor Republican Party (PRT), Social Democratic Party (PSD), Social Progressive Party (PSP), Popular Representation Party (PRP), Social Labor Party (PST), National Labor Party (PTN). The São Paulo branch of Vargas's Brazilian Labor Party, the PTB, was one of the greatest potential contenders. Yet the PTB remained "electorally weak, politically disjointed, and ideologically inconsequential," as the analyst Maria Victoria Benevides has written. It tried to be nationalistic by supporting the popular Petrobrás campaign, yet anticommunist in order to appease Catholic, elite, and foreign interests. It also remained hierarchical from its inception, proving far less effective than the PCB at becoming a "party of the workers" rather than one "for the workers." Most of its leaders did not spring from labor's rank and file, a charge that was much less true of the PCB, despite its own elitist tendencies. A close association between the PTB and government labor agencies also earned the party an ambiguous reputation, for neither delivered on their promises. The rise of several populist leaders, chief among them the PSP's Adhemar de Barros and the independent Jânio Quadros, further aggravated the weaknesses of the São Paulo branch of the PTB. Each of these politicians catered to workers and curried the favor of unions, and the force of their personalities regularly overwhelmed any sense of party loyalty among both the electorate and PTB leaders. In the meantime, the illegal PCB aspired to reaffirm its position as a power broker of the São Paulo labor movement through backroom deals and the achievements of organizations like ULTAB.[17]

Illustrating this swirling constellation of forces was the 1954 São Paulo rural labor conference, which reflected the PCB's reluctant acceptance of *trabalhismo* and efforts by other politicians to attract the support of workers. In this election year, Governor Lucas Nogueira Garcez (elected in 1950 as a PTB-PSP candidate, with the blessings of Vargas and Barros) fed more than three hundred delegates two meals a day for three days in order to help his chosen successor, Francisco Prestes Maia, in the October 3 gubernatorial election.[18] The conference also depended on the largesse of mayor Quadros, who directed the city's blue-ribbon IV Centennial Festival Commission to make

17. This thesis is argued by Benevides in *O PTB e o trabalhismo;* see esp. 9, 20–21, 43–76. On the PCB's aspirations, see Moisés, *A greve de massa.*
18. On Garcez and politics, see "Josué de Castro e o Governador prestigiam os trabalhadores do campo," *UH* (São Paulo), 20 September 1954, 2; Silva transcript, pt. 1, pp. 16–17; and Benevides, *O PTB e o trabalhismo,* 53.

the main auditorium of the park facility open to the group. Even though Quadros had just been elected mayor in 1953, he too was running for governor on a coalition ticket supported by a PTB faction and the PTN and Brazilian Socialist Party (PSB). To further ingratiate himself with conference delegates, he had the city provide them with transportation to the conference on special buses. Yet another complication was generated by the conference appearance of retired Brigadier General Leônidas Cardoso, who worked with the PCB on the League for National Emancipation—an organization pushing for more nationalizations like Petrobrás—who was himself a candidate for the state legislature on the gubernatorial ticket of Vladimir de Toledo Piza, an unofficial PTB-PCB candidate. Among politicians, only Cardoso and Euzébio Martins de Rocha Filho, a PTB leader, congressman, and rural labor lawyer, were reported to have addressed the assembly of rural labor delegates, which suggests the other candidates' uncertainty about the value of being *too* closely linked to the rural labor movement.[19] The rivals for Vargas's legacy were sharply divided among themselves, with each struggling to define a proper level of engagement with the rural labor movement. It seems, in fact, that all of these delicate arrangements were finalized in the first two weeks following Vargas's suicide, for the date and place of the long-scheduled conference suddenly changed during this period.[20]

A politician's association with the conference did not guarantee him electoral success. Euzébio Martins de Rocha Filho, for example, lost his race to be reelected to congress, while Cardoso won with the second highest number of votes ever received by a PTB legislative candidate. Rural workers had become political players, but their votes belonged to no single individual or would-be broker like the PCB.

19. Quadros's cultural affairs director, Professor Valerio Giuli, provided transportation, and the Comissão de Festijos do IV Centenário da Cidade de São Paulo was thanked for providing the auditorium. See "Moções aprovadas na II Conferência," *TL,* 15 September–15 October 1954, 2. On Cardoso, Toledo Piza, and Rocha, see "Cercada do carinho," Benevides, *O PTB,* 56; and entries on each in Beloch and Abreu, eds., *DHBB,* 627–28, 2773–74, 2993. Cardoso, who died in 1965, was the father of Fernando Henrique Cardoso, who was first elected president of Brazil in 1995. Rocha, who was first elected to congress in 1946, was followed by DOPS, apparently because of his pro-labor sympathies. In March 1954, for example, DOPS reported him offering legal services to the Professional Association of Agricultural Laborers of Guararapes, São Paulo, one of the groups established to send delegates to the September conference. See "Euzébio da Rocha Filho," DOPS Processo 3 J (1958), in TRE/SP. (Thanks to John French for this reference.)

20. The September issue of *Terra Livre* announced the dates and place of the conference, noting the festival commission's kindness in making the rooms available. "No Ibirapuera a II Conferência," 1. The name of Adhemar de Barros, a leading gubernatorial contender, was conspicuous by its absence from news reports of the conference—a circumstance that may have stemmed from the PCB, which scorned Barros due to the way he betrayed the party in 1947, or because of Barros's own desire to make himself unique by rejecting the Vargas legacy. However, the newspaper supportive of him, Rio de Janeiro's *O Dia,* covered the event.

This became clear to Natal Siviero when the PCB treasurer in Ribeirão Preto, Antônio Girotto, asked him to campaign for Prestes Maia. Since his release from police custody in 1953, Siviero had found work as a fireman at a sugar mill in the Alta Mogiana town of Santa Rosa de Viterbo. Siviero believed that Girotto's order had originated with the PCB state central committee, but this could not be confirmed by a second source. At any rate, the party was far from the disciplined machine former Captain Luís Carlos Prestes wanted it to be. At a Sunday campaign rally in Santa Rosa, Siviero refused to speak for Prestes Maia because he sensed that the audience was "inflamed with Jânio." Many brandished brooms, Siviero recalled, the signature symbol of incorruptibility used by the bespectacled and charismatic Quadros. Girotto and others in his entourage that day discovered the truth of Siviero's warning when one of them denounced Quadros as a fraud who would forget their interests when elected. The crowd shouted them down and a group rushed the stage, threatening Quadros's opponents with their broom handles.[21]

As the Santa Rosa de Viterbo incident suggested, Prestes Maia did not do well in the October election. Like Siviero and Girotto, the PCB itself was divided, with some supporting Toledo Piza and few enthusiastic about Prestes Maia. More than any of the candidates, Toledo Piza played up his ideological and practical links to Vargas. Prestes Maia was a more conservative figure, though one with a sound repudiation from his days as appointed mayor of São Paulo in the late 1940s. But when the election was over, Jânio Quadros had won the statehouse with a plurality of 34 percent of the vote (see Appendix, Table 9). A good portion of his lead came from the capital city, but he also garnered much support in rural districts where he had campaigned vigorously. His greatest competition came from Barros. Yet, although Barros played to the crowds and skillfully used the rural dialects he had learned in his life as a *fazendeiro,* he had far less credibility than Quadros as a *trabalhista.* In January 1954, Barros had publicly denounced Vargas and distanced himself from *trabalhismo.* In the meantime the PTB adopted a platform that identified rural unionization and labor rights as one of its top three priorities, and Quadros, as a PTB candidate, could add to this priority his known record as

---

21. Natal Siviero and Nazareno Ciavatta, transcript of interview by Sebastião Geraldo, Ribeirão Preto, 1988, tape 4, side B, pp. 3–4 (hereafter cited in the following form: Siviero/ Ciavatta, interview by Geraldo, 4/B:3–4). See also Girotto transcript, 11. In the mid-1950s, Jânio Quadros was the new political phenomenon who figuratively made way for the common man in the halls of power by sweeping away political corruption and privilege with a broom that became the symbol of his campaign.

a critic of *latifundiários* (like Barros) and a defender of northeastern migrants, union leaders, and, in constant refrain, "the poor and humble." Quadros's running mate—São Paulo's *"getúlista numero um,"* vice gubernatorial candidate José Porfírio da Paz—added still more *trabalhista* appeal to the winning ticket. A postelection statement from Quadros revealed the ambiguous meaning of his victory: "The laborer of the city and the country who elected me, humble and long suffering, did not subject me to any party, to any group, to any individual. He subjected me only and exclusively to the common welfare." The PCB lent no formal support to either of the top two candidates, but its grassroots work mobilizing rural workers had certainly contributed to the growing influence of populism in the São Paulo interior.[22]

At first glance, the results of the October 1955 presidential election offer an interesting contrast to this trend. The ticket with the candidate who had the greatest record of supporting agrarian reform and rural labor legislation finished third in São Paulo, despite PCB support. This candidate was vice presidential contender João "Jango" Goulart, the PTB leader who had backed controversial rural labor legislation when he served as Vargas's penultimate labor minister. Running for president on the same ticket was the PSD's Juscelino Kubitschek, former governor of Minas Gerais. This coalition ticket combined two beneficiaries of Vargas's tutelage, one from the conservative party Vargas had created to serve business and agrarian leaders, and one from the populist party he had formed to attract the votes of labor leaders and ordinary folk. Internal politics and the tested appeal of populism necessitated the seemingly contradictory alliance between these two parties and their leaders. As a supporter of Vargas, Kubitschek was on the left wing of his party, and many of his more conservative partisans opposed his candidacy. Goulart had also supported Vargas but was perceived as having pushed the former president further to the left, and for this many in the ruling class hated and feared him more than any other politician. Sharing a basic faith in the developmentalist and corporatist policies of Vargas, Kubitschek and Goulart came to believe they needed one another to win the election. In negotiating the alliance, the PTB demanded the opportunity to select the ministers of labor and agriculture in the

---

22. On the 1954 contest, see Sampaio, *Adhemar de Barros e o PSP,* 80–85; Jorge Miguel Mayer and César Benjamim, "Barros, Ademar de," in Beloch and Abreu, eds., *DHBB,* 316–21; Benevides, *O PTB,* 55–59, 116; and Walker, "From Coronelismo to Populism," 198–200. For Quadros's quote, see Jorge Miguel Mayer e César Benjamim, "Quadros, Jânio," in Beloch and Abreu, eds., *DHBB,* 2848.

new government. Kubitschek accepted this deal and took his campaign one step further toward embracing populism by reaching out
to the PCB. In a secret meeting later reported by one of his secretaries,
Kubitschek promised PCB leaders that his government would reward
their support by promising to let the party (though illegal) operate as
freely as any other (legal) party. He also would not reject their support
publicly, arguing that in a democracy even Communists had a right
to vote, and he offered to channel state resources through the PCB as
well as the PTB. These alliances underscored how times had changed.
Not only had the PCB become more reformist, but the PSD had become more liberal.[23]

Nationally, Kubitschek and Goulart narrowly won election.
However, in São Paulo, Adhemar de Barros took the lead, and even
second-place Juarez Távora, a conservative (though historically popular) army general running on the PDC and National Democratic
Union (UDN) ticket, swamped Kubitschek by nearly four hundred
thousand votes. Moreover, Távora's running mate, UDN president
Milton Campos, easily out-polled Goulart in the state. This pattern of
defeat for the PTB-PSD ticket was repeated from district to district
statewide (see Appendix, Table 10). It seemed like the populist, *trabalhista* forces had been routed in São Paulo.

Although these election results need further study, especially regarding events in São Paulo's interior, several known circumstances
raise questions about the overall meaning of the Kubitschek-Goulart
loss in the state. First, neither candidate had roots in São Paulo, a state
whose electorate traditionally favors native sons. In fact, both came
from states that historically had competed with São Paulo for national influence: Minas Gerais and Rio Grande do Sul. The state victor, the PSP's Barros, had deep roots in the state and had lost to
Quadros in the just-completed governor's race by fewer than twenty
thousand votes. His 1954 campaign had helped his party gain control
of many municipalities in the state, providing him a formidable political machine, with more than twice as many PSP mayors, vice mayors, and councilmen than any other party. A PSP mayor took office in
São Paulo, too, during a May 1955 special election. Barros used his
influence over local governments to earn the support of a significant
faction of the state PTB. In return for his support of PTB mayoral can-

<hr/>

23. Negotiations between Kubitschek and the PTB and PCB are discussed in Robert J.
Alexander, *Juscelino Kubitschek and the Development of Brazil* (Athens: Ohio University Center for
International Studies, 1991), 121–44; and Maria Victoria de Mesquita Benevides, *O govêrno Kubitschek: Desenvolvimento econômico e estabilidade política (1956–1961)* (Rio de Janeiro: Paz e Terra,
1976), esp. 95–103. See also "Manifesto eleitoral do partido," in Carone, ed., *O P.C.B.,* 136–39.

didates, Barros gained PTB leader Danton Coelho as his vice presidential running mate. This hurt Goulart's candidacy severely and led the national party to formally oust Coelho. Thus, by October 1955, Barros was well positioned to correct the mistakes of 1954 and secure a victory in the presidential contest, at least in São Paulo state.

The second-place ranking of Távora and first-place victory of his running mate, Campos, is more difficult to explain. These results only make sense in light of the support Távora and Campos received from Governor Quadros and President João Café Filho, who had replaced Vargas upon his death. In an April 1955 deal known as the Jânio-Café Accord, Quadros agreed to back the UDN ticket and not run for president if he was allowed to select members of a Távora-Campos cabinet. By June, Quadros lent his charisma to Távora, and Campos and put his machine to work for the ticket. Campos also benefited from votes for the fourth presidential candidate, São Paulo native son and cryptofascist Plinio Salgado, who lacked a running mate. Thus, in some ways the 1955 election was a repeat of the 1954 contest between Barros and Quadros, and all other candidates, especially non-*paulistas,* were mere bystanders. As in 1954, nearly all of the candidates and their supporters ran populist campaigns, differentiating themselves by the degree of their support for protectionism and government intervention. They all promised to support the man of the country. Távora's campaign posters featured positive images of rural workers.[24]

Rather than repudiating rural populism, these two elections demonstrated the staying power of appeals to working-class interests. Rural workers soon felt the effects of the Kubitschek-Goulart victory because the administration supported reform and opened the door to PCB freedom, both of which encouraged the party to step up its rural activism. One symbol of this new relationship was the presence of ULTAB president Tibúrcio at the inauguration of President Kubitschek. Determined to prove it could play by the political rules of the game, the party sought to build its credibility in the interior in order to more effectively broker the rural labor vote. In the meantime, rural elites reflected the national alliance by seeking the support of rural labor for their own political purposes. The willingness of both

24. Barros's municipal victories are analyzed from "Resultados das eleições municipais de 3 de outubro de 1954," *Boletim Eleitoral da Tribunal Regional Eleitoral do Estado de São Paulo* 9 : 119 (January 1956), 2173–79. The importance of municipal power in this election is discussed in Hippolito, *PSD: De raposas e reformistas,* 157–59; and Alexander, *Juscelino Kubitschek,* 143–44. See also Benevides, *O PTB,* 60–62; Benevides, *A UDN e o udenismo,* 92–96; Sampaio, *Adhemar de Barros e o PSP,* 87–90; Skidmore, *Politics in Brazil,* 143–66; and in Beloch and Abreu, eds., *DHBB,* on Quadros (2848–49), Barros (321), Távora (3322), and Coelho (819).

parties to cooperate with a reformist agenda helped secure the space for militants to operate more openly than they had in more than a decade. It also helped keep rural labor questions on the national political agenda.[25]

The Production March Alliance

A striking example of the new alliance came between 1956 and 1958 when some planters bargained and others competed with local militants in order to gain rural worker support for the Production March (Marcha da Produção), a planned coffee-producers march on Cateté Palace, the presidential residence in Rio de Janeiro. The coffee economy had entered a new cycle in 1956, with trees planted during the postwar boom gradually generating capacity yields, forcing coffee prices to drop. Only a devastating frost in northern Paraná contained yields and thus prices in 1955, though at great cost to that region's planters and workers. From then until 1959, when coffee workers harvested an unprecedented forty-four million sacks, supply outstripped demand. To recoup losses of income, planters focused on the exchange tax, the *confisco cambial* examined in the previous chapter, as the source of their troubles. In preparation for an assault on governmental policy, planters organized numerous rallies to attract worker and farmer participation. Hoping to benefit from a unified display of rural community support for the elimination of coffee exchange taxes, planters eventually agreed to include rural unionization and labor legislation in their list of demands.[26] Although the planters and their workers were momentarily joined in a common cause, the terms were far different from the paternalism that shaped the "planter clan" (*clã fazendeiro*) concept that had animated planter spokesmen in earlier political debates. The "march joined farmers, planters, and agricultural laborers . . . to defend their interests" against "the masters of the situation, those that construct fabulous fortunes, or that live with all the comfort in the great cities." It was a rising of the moral country

25. The new sense of liberty enjoyed by the PCB under Kubitschek-Goulart and its consequences is discussed in Benevides, *O govêrno Kubitschek*, 97–103. See also "Presente a ULTAB a posse de Juscelino e Jango," *TL*, 1–15 February 1956, 1.

26. Silva transcript, pt. 1, pp. 14–18; "Marcha da produção: Possibilidade de paralisação total dos trabalhos agrícolas. A luta tenaz contra o confisco cambial," *Brasil Rural* (journal of FARESP) 170 (September 1956), 6–19; "Milhares de lavradores irão ao Rio," *TL*, 1–5 September 1956, 4; and Benevides, *O govêrno Kubitschek*, 168–69. On the coffee economy, see Alexandre Beltrão, "Café," in Beloch and Abreu, eds., *DHBB*, 523.

against the immoral city.[27] In this case, however, cooperation was negotiated on political rather than paternalist ground.

In August, September, and October 1956, coffee *colonos* and planters united in production march rallies in Cafelândia and Bauru in São Paulo; and Jacarézinho, Rolândia, and Apucarana in Paraná. Another rally, this one exceptional for its rejection of rural labor participation, was held at an exclusive tennis club in Marília, São Paulo. Speaking at the Marília event, a Paraná coffee grower attacked Communist infiltration among coffee *colonos* and alarmed his audience with the news that a Communist-inspired rural labor union in his area had more than twenty thousand members. But a tone of cooperation between workers and bosses typified the other rallies. In Cafelândia, where more than three thousand planters, smallholders, and *colonos* rallied, the *colono* Catálino de Oliveira spoke for workers when he demanded the protection of their traditional rights to cultivate their own crops. While planters expressed sympathy for the coffee workers' plight, they ignored their own responsibility and claimed that the situation of *colonos* could only be improved with elimination of the export tax.[28]

The largest and most dramatic rally of 1956 took place in São José do Rio Preto, capital of the Alta Araraquarense region of São Paulo, located immediately to the west of Ribeirão Preto's Alta Mogiana region. Some thirty-five hundred *colonos,* sharecroppers, and other agriculturalists—the majority of them organized by Communist militants— amassed in the town center November 10 to hear the speeches of planter representatives such as Clovis de Salles Santos, president of

27. Clovis de Salles Santos quoted in "Fala o presidente da FARESP sôbre a 'Marcha da Produção,'" *TL*, 1–15 October 1956, 4.

28. "Marcha da Produção," 6–19. The Marília rally was particularly influenced by events in Paraná due to its proximity to the state. Following the 1954 rural labor conference, Paraná delegates such as Antônio Gondim de Alencar had just returned to the state when the 1955 frost greatly worsened conditions for coffee workers. Operating out of Londrina, he and such seasoned militants as Manoel Jacinto Correia (who had participated in the Porecatú War) organized several rural labor unions, attracting an estimated fifteen thousand members by mid-1956, when the year's heavy rainfall further afflicted workers. This story had received extensive press coverage in three major newspapers in August, just before the Marília rally. Apparently, planters felt the tables had turned too far in the direction of the PCB to now compromise with militants—or at least the publicity embarrassed them into taking a hard-line anticommunist stance. In the meantime, public officials in Londrina sought to reduce tensions by offering a helping hand to suffering workers, and the zealous district attorney Paulo d'Assumpção shut down the union and tried to prosecute its leaders. His actions were frustrated by Judge Hercules de Macedo Rocha, who found "no evidence of a criminal act" in the defendants' behavior. Reports of these developments in *O Estado de São Paulo, Diário de São Paulo, Notícias de Hoje,* and *A Gazeta* caught the attention of the American consulate in São Paulo. See Philip Raine, American consul, São Paulo, to USDS, 21 August 1956, Despatch Nos. 23 and 29 (28 August 1956), Post File 732.001, M1511/5, DS/USNA.

FARESP, and Luís Duarte da Silva, president of the local planter association. Addressing the group, Duarte asserted that rural unionization
was "a pressing necessity" and the "first step of a new era" marking
the final end of the incomplete abolition of slavery.[29] Here was a
prominent planter adopting the precise discourse rural militants had
been using against landlords since World War I.

To organize such an impressive event, Duarte arranged the presence of more than two thousand rural workers with Communist rural
labor organizers, including Irineu Luís de Moraes. Moraes guaranteed
a large turnout so long as workers were allowed to carry banners
demanding unionization, salary hikes, and other measures. Duarte
spoke with members of the rural association, and they agreed to
Moraes's terms, asking only that no mention be made of the Soviet
Union. The workers' demands became bargaining points when São
Paulo mayor Vladimir de Toledo Piza—appointed spokesman for the
rally—presented the planters' demands to officials in Rio de Janeiro.
"It is the rural laborer who produces what the Brazilian people eat,"
said Toledo Piza. And yet, "the labor regime for the men of the
country is still what it was" in colonial times. To end this situation
and improve the lot of rural workers, the exchange tax had to be
eliminated.[30]

The day of the march on the presidential palace, continually
delayed by negotiations with the government, drew nearer after another group of rallies was held in May 1958. Convinced that the future of coffee rested in the hands of workers, planters selected May
Day to hold enormous public assemblies in Birigui, Osvaldo Cruz,
Guariba, and Jaboticabal, an important Araraquarense town located
some thirty miles west of Ribeirão Preto.[31] With ten thousand people
at the Jaboticabal rally, FARESP leaders urged their audience to support
a nonpartisan platform of twelve reforms that included eliminating
the exchange tax, organizing rural unions, and composing protective
laws for rural workers. The threat of instability and rebellion seemed

29. On the Rio Preto rally, see "Condenada a ação dos políticos profissionais no setor
rural: Concentração rural da Alta Araraquarense," *Brasil Rural* 173 (December 1956), 4–6; and
"Marcha da Produção," *TL*, 1–15 December 1956, 1. Duarte's speech is reprinted in "São Jose
do Rio Preto: Reforma cambial e reforma bancária, pontos basicos," *Brasil Rural* 174 (January 1957), 27.

30. Irineu Luís de Moraes, transcript of interview by author, Ribeirão Preto, 22 August
1988, pt. 1, pp. 33–34. For Toledo Piza quote, see "Concentração rural da Alta Araraquarense," 5–6.

31. "Enxada contra Cadillac: Os homens do campo festejam o 1 de maio—Luta o homem
do campo pela sua emancipação econômica—Lavradores de barriga vazia representam uma revolução em marcha—Esclarecimento do interior—Arregimentação política em bases partida-
rias," *Brasil Rural* 190 (May 1958), 6–11.

to motivate some rally organizers. "Men with empty stomachs represent a social revolution in march," warned Silvio Borsari, president of the Jaboticabal farmers' association. Speaking for the farmers' federation, Toledo Piza said FARESP had "called together the workers of the city and the country to unite in a white revolution in order to avoid a bloody one." [32]

The planters' Marcha da Produção never took place. The organizers planned to join rural bosses and workers in a march down the highway linking São Paulo with Rio de Janeiro. They wanted to tie-up traffic on this major commercial artery by filling it with slow-moving tractors, farm vehicles, and marchers. Anticipating a crisis, the government threatened FARESP with military intervention and the violent suppression of the march, and the planters abandoned their plans. With a tone of sarcasm, Lucas Lopes, the federal finance minister, thanked the planters for providing the tax revenue needed to buy the arms used to halt the march. [33] As the production march incident showed, rural social and political relations had clearly undergone considerable change since 1945, when planters confidently but mistakenly took the support of workers for granted. This time a number of planters included rural workers and their demands when organizing rallies and fashioned themselves as political rather than patriarchal leaders.

"This Here's the Law"

To build on these events and ensure the party's position as the defender of rural labor, ULTAB organizers Portela and Silva traveled throughout the interior preaching the gospel of rural unionization

32. On the twelve-reform platform, see "Arregimentação rural política apartidaria," *Brasil Rural* 189 (April 1958), 68–73. Listed on page 72 are the twelve policy demands: (1) combat the rise of taxes; (2) struggle against the "exchange confiscation" and the price tables that harm producers and consumers; (3) alter the revenue distribution system to the benefit of municipalities; (4) lower the cost of living; (5) heighten the standard of living of the rural population; (6) improve access to credit for agriculturalists, lowering interest rates and lengthening terms; (7) provide medical, dental, hospital and maternity care to the rural population; (8) put an honest and meaningful electoral system in place; (9) select better political candidates to represent the interior; (10) rural unionization, by legitimate farmers; (11) agrarian reform that is a true "organization of agriculture"; and (12) adequate protection law for rural laborers, and respect for the rights of rural property owners. For Borsari and Piza quotes, see "Enxada contra Cadillac," 8, 10.

33. On the plans to block traffic, see Oliveiros S. Ferreira, interviewed by Maria Victoria de Mesquita Benevides and cited in Benevides, *O govêrno Kubitschek,* 168. For Lopes, see *Maquis* 73 (1 November 1958), cited in ibid., 169.

as they secretly struggled to deepen the party's rural base. In the coffee and sugarcane zones of São Paulo, Silva discovered the practical utility of the law. "Peasants and rural wage-workers were men that put a lot of faith in the law," he said. "They were educated that way. What's outside the law scares them." In São Paulo, the law made a powerful impression on workers as well as authorities. Silva recalled occasions when local police desisted in their attempts to break up rural labor union organizing meetings once they were presented with a copy of the rural unionization law, Decree Law No. 7,038, issued by Vargas in 1944. Such visible displays of the power of the law helped fend off repression and embolden rural workers. "In the countryside most workers were illiterate and they had few sources of information," Silva explained. "Some didn't know what world they were in and the great place they turned to for help was the church." Traditionally, the priests sided with the planters and "told the man to have patience and to wait for God to work things out." But as rural workers became informed about the law, an alternative vision emerged in rural society. Workers learned they had legal rights that could be defended in court. "They had their own expression for it," explained Silva: "This here's the law [Isso aí é de leis]." Although the impartiality of judges could not be counted on, the existence of the law "encouraged them to defend themselves."[34] Rural workers had begun to make the law and its promises their key to a counterhegemonic assault on injustice. To help this process along, Silva began to publish a regular labor law column in *Terra Livre* called "Know Your Rights."

Some analysts of the labor movement in Brazil have criticized the emphasis the party came to place on the law. It channeled protest into defined categories that strictly contained workers in capitalist relations of production. But Silva believed that real conditions in Brazil justified the new policy, at least for rural society. The party interpreted the unpaid obligations of resident farmworkers—fire fighting, road construction, and other duties demanded by the planter or overseer—as vestiges of feudalism. To use the law to put a price on these obligations and set a minimum wage was to lift rural workers into the modern era.[35] On their own initiative, Silva explained, rural

34. Silva transcript, pt. 1, pp. 25–30. Silva recounted how the decree helped turn back police in the cities of Monte Azul Paulista, Tabatinga, and Nissen. See also Lindolfo Silva, Premeiro Secretário da ULTAB, "E ilegal o desconto de aluguel de casa," *NH,* 16 March 1956, 4.

35. "The Party started from the principle that Brazil was a semifeudal country," said Caio Prado Junior, a PCB member who criticized party policies. "For the Party," he continued, "we were living in a semifeudal country that needed, therefore, a democratic bourgeois revolution to get rid of this situation. In my view, all of this was fantasy. . . . The problem is capitalism itself. The problem is that we've always had a deformed capitalism, a backward one, but capitalism,

workers had turned to the stipulations of the law well before the founding of ULTAB, proving its progressive character. As discussed in Chapter 2, the 1943 CLT provided rural workers legal rights to a weekly day of rest, annual paid vacations, standardized individual labor contracts, and advanced notice of dismissal (or compensating severance pay). Moreover, the 1946 constitution stated that minimum-wage laws applied to all workers, including those in agriculture, mandating the payment of wages that met the criteria of regionally specific "living wage" tests and limiting the amount of compensation that could be paid in goods such as food and clothing rather than in cash.[36] Starting with the wage adjustment of December 1951, a copy of the minimum-wage schedule was included in the *caderneta agrícola,* the pocket-sized ledger distributed to São Paulo *colonos.*[37] Chapter 1 shows how the *caderneta* literally put the law into the hands of *colonos.* Judging by the particular cases discussed in the SRB journal *Revista da Sociedade Rural Brasileira* and the legal journal *Revista Legislação do Trabalho,* the question of *colono* vacation pay generated one of the most prolonged judicial disputes in the early history of rural labor law.[38]

The dispute over paid vacations helped to establish *colono* eligibility for those articles of the CLT that specifically applied to rural

---

capitalist extortion of surplus labor. The Party never comprehended this." Quoted in *A história vivida: Documetos abertos,* vol. 1, edited by Lourenço Dantas Mota (São Paulo: O Estado de São Paulo, 1981), 314–15.

36. For the CLT, see Chapter 2 and articles no. 76–141, 442–67, 487–91, and 506 of *Consolidação das leis do trabalho,* 12, 22–29, 76–78, 82, 84, and article 157 of the 1946 federal constitution.

37. São Paulo state Decree Law No. 6,405 of 19 April 1934 required property owners to distribute *cadernetas agrícolas* to their workers at no charge after purchasing the booklets from the state department of labor for the nominal fee of Cr$5.00 (see Chapter 1). The schedule of rates from the 1951 minimum-wage law were printed in the booklet, but the previous minimum-wage adjustments of 1 May 1943 (Decree Law No. 5,452) were not. The *cadernetas* also included a copy of most of the articles of the consolidated labor code that applied to rural workers. Most important was the account ledger, which took up some thirty-five pages of the book. Federal laws 1,150 of 5 January 1904; 1,607 of 29 December 1906; 6,437 of 27 March 1907; and 2,400 of 9 July 1913 initially ordered and regulated the distribution of an accounts ledger to all rural employers and employees. As with any such law, enforcement was uneven; in all likelihood a limited number of workers received *cadernatas,* and an even smaller number had their *cadernetas* properly maintained. For a brief, contemporary review of the laws that applied to rural workers, see Oscar J. Thomazini Ettori, "Mão-de-obra na agricultura paulista," *ASP* 8:12 (December 1961), 13–39.

38. See, for example, "Férias, empregados rurais: Processo TRT/SP 577/48," *RLT* 12:139 (November 1948), 456; "Colono, férias: Processo TRT/SP No. 1,033/52," *RLT* 17:196 (August 1953), 310; and "Férias de colonos de cafe: Processo No. 6,535/51," *RLT* 18:201/202 (January/Februray 1954), 70–73. See also Dr. Edras Pereira Gerbello, "O colono e o direito as férias," *RSRB* 31:365 (April 1951), 32–33; Dr. Virgílio dos Santos Magano, "Férias aos colonos," *RSRB* 31:370 (October 1951), 28–31; and Dr. Eduardo de Carvalho, "Férias aos colonos," *RSRB* 32:374 (March 1952), 60–61, and "Férias aos colonos," 32:375 (April 1952), 48–52.

laborers. The vacation issue stimulated a legal debate that prompted the composition of broadly worded decisions.[39] Generated randomly and independently, these and other cases demonstrated the workers' interest in the law and the courts' interest in applying the CLT to rural workers.[40] Various factors limited and weakened both interests. The courts had no independent policing power, and although precedent-setting decisions could not be ignored, nothing prevented local judges from turning these precedents on their head by reinterpreting the jurisprudence. Appeals might ultimately overturn their decisions, but this was a long, costly, tiresome process well beyond the means and patience of most rural workers. For the law to be effective and meaningful for the majority of rural laborers, it needed to be regularly and definitively enforced. Moreover, little of the labor code applied to rural workers, and for the law to bring even short-term benefits to them, its provisions needed to be expanded and elaborated. To accomplish these goals, pressure needed to be applied on the courts, planters, and the state. With these motives in mind, ULTAB militants like Silva and Portela put most of their energy into forming rural labor organizations.

In the months before and after the September 1954 rural labor conference, PCB regional councils in the interior started to form rural labor organizations. In some areas they were called rural associations and formally registered with the Ministry of Agriculture under Decree Law No. 8,127 of 1945. ULTAB reported that 108 embryonic organizations in seventeen states had been established by 1956; fourteen

39. See, in particular, Doutor Humberto de Andrade Junqueira, "Férias de colonos," *RSRB* 31:371 (November 1951), 70–76; and "Férias, colono de fazenda: Processo TST 5.176/51," written for the majority by Dr. Geraldo Montedonio Bezerra de Menezes, 2 September 1952, and printed in *RLT* 17:189 (January 1953), 21–32. Medeiros (*História dos movimentos,* 24) argues that a 1951 São Paulo regional labor tribunal decision recognized the right to paid vacations of *colonos* and other rural wage workers and suggests that this case helped "to create a jurisprudence that guaranteed [rural workers] some rights." The above-cited Superior Labor Tribunal case set the national standard, but it was still quite common, as discussed below, for local judges to disregard such precedents.

40. Measuring rural labor's use of the law presents an impossible task of quantification that would require thumbing through hundreds of thousands of local court records. A rough indication of the intensification of labor's use of the law can be taken from counting the number of precedent-setting cases published in the *Revista Legislação do Trabalho,* an independent journal associated with the prestigious São Paulo School of Law. Between 1942 when the journal began publication and 1950, eleven rural labor cases were published. In the following period, 1951 to 1960, the number of published cases doubled. Labor disputes in São Paulo generated the majority of cases in both periods: 64 and 73 percent respectively. The earlier period seems to have been a time during which the justice system came to terms with the concept of adjudicating rural labor relations. See, for example, Mozart Victor Russomano, "Os direitos trabalhistas do empregado rural," *RLT* 13:145 (May 1949), 247–49; and Wellington Brandão, "Salário mínimo e outros direitos fundamentais do trabalhador rural," *RLT* 14:149 (September 1949), 419–28.

more had been formed by 1959.[41] When authorities permitted, the word *"sindicato"* would replace *"associação,"* and the organization would register with the labor ministry. Organizers further claimed their activities were within the law—as in the anecdote recounted by Silva above—noting the existence of the 1944 rural unionization law.[42] In the meantime, official recognition was difficult to obtain. Even though ULTAB claimed the number of *sindicatos* had grown from thirty to fifty between 1956 and 1959, only six rural labor unions had received official labor ministry recognition by 1961.[43] In some areas, such as the Alta Mogiana, the PCB nevertheless established agrarian laborers' unions (*sindicatos dos trabalhadores agrícolas*), dodging the law by dubbing them unions "in formation." In addition to founding a union in the regional capital of Ribeirão Preto, the party helped establish *sindicatos* in several other important area townships, including Franca, São João da Boa Vista, Igarapava, Batatais, Morro Agudo, Sertãozinho, Pontal, and Altinópolis.[44]

Founding the Ribeirão Preto Labor Court

The case of Ribeirão Preto and the Alta Mogiana reveal some details of how the rural labor movement developed during this period. When Ciavatta returned to the field from his speaking debut at the September conference, he took off his tie and rolled up his shirt

41. For law 8.127, the "organization of rural life" decree, see Chapter 2. Under this law, anyone engaged in agriculture could form a rural association and use the association to represent the members' "class interests." Only one association was allowed for each municipality, and so, where large landowners and planters had already established an association, the party was more likely to form a parallel rural workers' union than to attempt to influence the policies of existing, planter-dominated rural associations. The ULTAB report is "Relatório sôbre a organização dos lavradores e trabalhadores rurais," cited in Medeiros, *História dos movimentos,* 51.

42. Interview with Sebastião Dinart dos Santos in *Ultíma Hora*'s "Caipiras de todo o mundo encontram-se no Ibirapuera."

43. SUPRA, Sindicatos Rurais. Relação No. 1 (Rio de Janeiro, 31 December 1963), 18, cited by Robert E. Price, "Rural Unionization in Brazil," Land Tenure Center, University of Wisconsin, Madison. Study No. 14 (August 1964), 68. ULTAB's statistics from "Relatório sôbre a organização." Azevêdo, *As ligas camponeses,* 55, reports that five rural unions had been recognized under law 7.038 by 1955. He identified only two of these unions, one in Campos, Rio de Janeiro, and one at the Usina Barreiros in São Paulo, both uniting sugar mill workers. Of the remaining three, two more were in São Paulo, and one was in the northeast state of Bahia. Unlike sugarcane-field workers, the rights of sugar mill workers were regulated by the CLT, which allowed them to organize unions. See "Artigos 19 a 26 do decreto lei no. 6.969 (19 October 1944): Dispõe sôbre o Estatuto da Lavoura Canavieira," *RLT* 16:181 (May 1952), 261–62.

44. Antônio Girotto, transcript of interview by Sebastião Geraldo, Ribeirão Preto, 28 November 1988, p. 5.

sleeves to pursue the delicate task of union organizing. Having lived the first twenty-two years of his life in the region, he knew that confrontations promised to inspire solidarity among workers only until they stood at risk of losing their jobs or being arrested. Thus, it was with great reluctance that in March 1955, he agreed to sign a document authorizing the coffee *colonos* of Quintino Facci's Fazenda São Sebastião do Alto to go on strike. The *colonos* had approached him repeatedly asking the union to support them in a strike to get Facci to pay the minimum wage. When they did strike, Facci called the police, who responded by promising to take the strikers to the regional office of the department of labor. Some *colonos* were taken there, but the police unloaded the leaders at the jailhouse and locked them up. Coming to their aid, Ciavatta organized the twenty-five or so *colonos* at the Ribeirão Preto labor department in a sit-in protest until the leaders were released and Facci promised to raise wages. When the pressure was off, however, Facci fired the presumed strike leaders and, according to one worker, held other participants "like slaves" on the plantation. Ciavatta and Luiz Anaconi, a *colono,* went to jail, where Ciavatta was held until May.[45]

After his release, Ciavatta followed his instincts in pursuing a more conciliatory course of action. In July the union filed suit on behalf of an Usina da Pedra worker, protesting the deduction of 33 percent of the man's salary to pay for his housing on the plantation. Deduction of rent was to become a key bone of contention in many labor law disputes in the years ahead. Near the end of the year, Ciavatta applied to the regional office of the labor ministry for recognition of the Ribeirão Preto union—another matter of great dispute in the middle years of rural labor movement history. In January 1956, seven hundred members attended the union's formal (though unofficial) founding ceremony and confirmed Ciavatta as

---

45. Siviero/Ciavatta, interview by Geraldo. According to a newspaper recap of the incident, the São Sebastião *colonos* eventually won an unspecified wage hike, and their victory spurred nearly one thousand other rural workers in the region to demand and win a Cr$5.00 a day increase in wages from the *fazendas* Santa Luiza, Matão, Santa Adelaide, Monte Vistos, and Conquista. "Ribeirão Preto: Mais de mil trabalhadores tiverem aumento de salarios," *TL,* January 1956, 4. A contradictory report came from a letter to *Terra Livre* signed by Silva Oliveira. He claims that most of the strikers were fired, despite their "great unity," and that his daughter was fired as Facci's maid to punish him for participating in the strike. Although he wanted to leave the plantation, Facci "did not permit" him to leave. Conditions had deteriorated greatly, with no rights, slavelike treatment, and no diversions allowed, neither dance nor soccer. "Quintino Facci proibiu até futebol em sua fazenda," *TL,* 1–15 October 1956, 2. These two stories are compatible if one concedes that the victory negotiated in 1955 expired with the new agricultural year. In June 1991, Facci declined to be interviewed about this event. Author's field notes, 25 June 1991.

president. He was also voted a salary, drawn from dues, equivalent to the standard minimum wage for the region. Whatever he was doing, Ciavatta's success as a rural labor leader only seemed to grow. Within fifteen months of the São Paulo conference, the Alta Mogiana was easily the best organized region in Brazil, with members on more than 250 plantations and with collective actions reported at more than a dozen of them.[46]

As Ciavatta tells the story, one of his greatest achievements came toward the end of January. On a trip to Rio de Janeiro organized by ULTAB, Ciavatta joined four additional rural labor leaders from the Alta Mogiana to ask Minister of Labor Nelson Omegna to officially recognize their syndicates. "I explained to him what was happening in Ribeirão, that the police had closed the union, arrested me, that they had invaded the plantations, arrested the workers who were in the union and," continued Ciavatta, "that the planters' persecution of workers was great." But Omegna, a sociology professor active in the São Paulo branch of the Labor Party, insisted that it was not a union that Ciavatta and the rural workers of Ribeirão Preto needed but a labor court (*junta de trabalho*). "I thought that was a pretty shabby excuse [*desculpa esfarrapada*]," Ciavatta recalls.[47] In fact, Ciavatta was lucky to be speaking to the minister. Omegna, who represented the more liberal wing of the São Paulo PTB, had been appointed to his post during the crisis that followed the election of Kubitschek and Goulart. He served only a few months, but during this brief interregnum, his liberal views influenced policies that created openings for grassroots activism throughout the labor movement. And yet, he also fell victim to the need to protect his anticommunist credentials. Just

46. See, "Na região Mogiana, em São Paulo: Colonos sindicalizados em mais de 250 fazendas," *TL*, 1–15 July 1955, 1; "Notícias breves," *TL*, 15–30 November 1955, 1; and "Ribeirão Preto: Mais de mil trabalhadores."

47. Ciavatta's recollection of these events is from his transcript, 7; and Siviero/Ciavatta, interview by Geraldo, 1/A:10–11. See also Silva transcript, pt. 1; and "Uma comissão," *TL*, 1–15 February 1956, 1. In addition to Ribeirão Preto, this article lists Franca, Morro Agudo, Igarapava, and Batatais as having sent representatives. On Omegna, the São Paulo organization of the PTB, and party's relationship with the São Paulo union movement, see Benevides, *O PTB e o trabalhismo*.

On 1 May 1939, Vargas created the labor judiciary, a special branch of the federal justice department that would be charged with mediating disputes between labor and capital. On 1 May 1941, the dictator finally established the branch. Two years later, in May 1943, Brazil's wide-ranging labor laws were consolidated, giving the labor justice system a legal basis on which to resolve class conflicts. In 1943 the government created four regional tribunals (Tribunal Regional do Trabalho), with eight local juntas divided between them. The city of São Paulo was headquarters to the second regional tribunal, which had jurisdiction over labor disputes in the states of São Paulo, Paraná, and Mato Grosso. See Castro Gomes, *A invenção do trabalhismo*, 255; and "Decreto lei 5.926," *RLT* 7:78 (October 1943), 370–71.

before meeting with Ciavatta and the rural labor militants, Omegna made a public statement protecting the corrupt leader of the industrial laborers confederation, Deocleciano Holanda de Cavalcanti, arguing that to punish him for stealing pension funds "would mean giving credit to the Communist cause."[48]

According to Ciavatta, Omegna argued that legalizing the Ribeirão Preto rural workers' union would only bring trouble for Ciavatta and other militants, whereas the special court would help put an end to abuses of power on the part of authorities. This was not Ciavatta's point of view: he thought a legalized *sindicato* would help keep the police from harassing militants. But the minister was in charge. "Look, son," the elder Omegna told Ciavatta; "if I legalize your union and the other rural workers' unions you have around there—that are all leftist, I know—the police are just going to go in there and kill you people, and track you down and destroy what you've built, even within your own homes." Alta Mogiana rural workers would fare better, the minister continued, with a Junta de Conciliação e Julgamento. "With that established, all your problems will be handled there and the police won't be able to mess with you any longer," Omegna said.[49] In the context of the moment, the court was an advance for rural labor, even though it fell short of Ciavatta's interest in institutionalizing a union. It was the result of a convergence of forces in conflict for decades: the mobilization of rebellious rural workers demanding change, government and planter efforts to harness their discontent and energy, and the political leadership of the PCB anxious to help rural workers and strengthen the party's credibility.

According to Ciavatta, then, his meeting with Omegna resulted in establishing a labor court in Ribeirão Preto. However, no written records of Ciavatta's conversation with Omegna have come to light, and there are two problems with his story. Records show that the decree establishing the court was issued on Christmas eve 1955, while Ciavatta's meeting came one month later, at the end of January.[50] The motif of the narrator's heroic role survived the decades between the event and the recounting. For that matter, Ciavatta may never have

48. Omegna quoted in Benevides, *O PTB,* 109. See also "Miscellaneous Notes by John French on the Book Manuscript: 'And the Seed Was Planted'" (8 May 1996, manuscript in author's possession), 18–19. Cavalcanti (whose name is sometimes written as Deocleciano Hollanda de Cavalcanti) was a highly visible *pelego* who enjoyed the favor of the U.S. embassy and the AFL-CIO's Latin American labor ambassador Serafino Romualdi. See Cliff Welch, "Labor Internationalism: U.S. Involvement in Brazilian Unions, 1945–1965," *Latin American Research Review* 30:2 (1995), 61–89.

49. Quotes from Siviero/Ciavatta transcript, 7.

50. The court was created with Decree Law No. 2,695 of 24 December 1955.

known that the court had already been decreed; it may have been in Omegna's interest to let the militants think their meeting had had immediate results. A photographer caught Omegna smiling in a jovial moment with three members of the delegation. In important ways, Ciavatta could take credit for the court. The level of mobilization he and others had achieved in the Alta Mogiana made the region stand out, clearly drawing the authorities' attention to the need to find a way to stabilize the area. It was collective action, channeled by rural labor leaders like Ciavatta, that caused authorities to establish a labor court in Ribeirão Preto.

In the Alta Mogiana in the latter half of the 1950s, the labor court became the principal focus of the rural labor movement. When it finally went into operation in May 1957, it joined eight other local juntas within the jurisdiction of a regional tribunal in São Paulo. Invariably underfunded and understaffed, these nine juntas oversaw a massive three-state area with a diverse laboring population that included nearly one million people in the primary sector. Thus, counting only rural employees, each court had a potential clientele significantly exceeding one hundred thousand workers, not to mention significant numbers of industrial and commercial employees, some of them tied to agro-industrial activity.[51] Swamped as they were, the courts came under increased pressure as rural workers turned to them in ever greater numbers in the late 1950s and early 1960s. Ciavatta found more and more of his time devoted to advising workers how to file court claims, sending those with complex problems to see Holanda Noir Tavella, a lawyer the party had supported in his failed attempt to be elected to the city council the year before. With Tavella's help, he prepared a brochure for distribution that outlined the rights of rural workers and listed minimum wages for the region. In June 1956, Ciavatta once again appealed for official recognition of the union, delivering a letter to President Kubitschek, who was making an official visit to Ribeirão Preto. The letter also asked the president to help ensure the application of labor laws on local plantations and protested continued police pressure against the union, including repeated "invasions" of its office. In September, he accompanied other rural labor representatives on a trip to Rio de Janeiro to lobby

51. "Anda a passo de jaboti a justiça do trabalho!" *DM* (Ribeirão Preto), 2 March 1957, 6. Figures from table 4:5, "Evolution of the Economically Active Population of the Agricultural Sector (persons 10-years-old or older)," in Tomas Szmrecsanyi, "O desenvolvimento da produção agropecuária (1930–1970)," in *História geral da civilização brasileira*, Tomo III, *O Brasil republicano*, vol. 4, *Economia e cultura (1930–1964)*, edited by Boris Fausto, 2d ed. (São Paulo: Difel, 1986), 201.

congressmen such as Fernando Ferrari and Nestor Duarte, both of whom contributed significantly to the formulation of rural labor and land laws.[52] Rural workers like Ciavatta were becoming a part of the process, showing how much the situation had changed since Vargas's rural syndicalization study commission rejected the inclusion of rural labor representatives in its deliberations.

Imposing Party Discipline

In the midst of these developments, Silva traveled to Ribeirão Preto and in a revealing display of the party's institutional preoccupations, disciplined Ciavatta, expelling him from the party and the union. The circumstances of this event remain confused by memory and inadequate documentation. When interviewed in the late 1980s, Ciavatta remembered having been in a long-running dispute with Antônio Girotto. (Ciavatta was not alone in his criticism of Girotto, who also came under attack by Siviero and Moraes.) "He's a rascal. Of the party! So, I saw I was in the middle of a gang of bandits. They weren't Communists, they were a gang of thieves, of vagabonds," Ciavatta proclaimed. "Communism is a society where the wealth is divided, but these guys made it a society where my property was to be divided." In addition to ideological protest, Ciavatta condemned Girotto for using him for the benefit of the party rather than the union and its members.

> So, this Antônio Girotto was only interested in seeing that I was always in jail because with me there he could raise money from the people and make himself look good in the eyes of the party's central committee, showing them the local party was working. But it was working with me in jail. . . . I only figured this out later. . . . But I never distributed the "overthrow the government" stuff. I explained to him that the party had contracted me to found the union and put labor law in the hands of country folk, not to overthrow the government. If he wanted to overthrow the government, he could perform this service himself.

---

52. Siviero/Ciavatta, interview by Geraldo, 2/B:5. On lobbying the president and congress, see "Os sindicatos rurais da Mogiana pediram diretamente a Juscelino o seu reconhecimento," *TL*, 1–15 July 1956, 2; and "Não permitir que acabem com os direitos que os trabalhadores da roça já possuem," *TL*, 15–30 September 1956, 1.

Between 1955 and 1957, Ciavatta was consistently harassed by police and twice jailed, once for two months. When he was in jail, Girotto raised money to "liberate" Ciavatta and to care for his family. Ciavatta claims Girotto never gave him any money, though, and throughout the time Ciavatta worked on the union, it was necessary for his wife to wash clothes—a disagreeable, low-status job—in order to make ends meet. In running these liberation campaigns, Girotto made a point of describing Ciavatta as a Communist, "to show that the party was big." When Ciavatta was free, Girotto wanted him to use the union to distribute the party newspaper, *Notícias de Hoje*. Ciavatta thought this would complicate his work, attracting repression and alienating workers. He took to heart news reports about crackdowns on plantations where copies of these newspapers were found. Just such a story had appeared on a recent cover of Ribeirão Preto's *Diário da Manhã*.[53]

For his part, Girotto saw Ciavatta as a PCB appointee and expected the union boss to fulfill his party duties. Indeed, Ciavatta had campaigned for party-backed candidates in 1954 and 1955, but he claims he always refused to circulate copies of party newspapers. When Girotto left him papers to distribute, Ciavatta threw them in the trash. "I was a dead duck," said Ciavatta. "I pass out the paper, the workers read it, it falls into the hands of the planters, and the planters (who were already suing me in court) would just have proof I was out to overthrow them and the government." Finally, in October, Silva and other PCB officials (Ciavatta also identified Rui Facó, a journalist) came to town, and when Ciavatta again refused to carry out party orders, Silva dismissed him from the union and the party. Do you know whose union it is? Silva asked him. "Yes," said Ciavatta, "I know. The union belongs to the workers that support it, they pay for the union and, good or bad, the union is there for them." No, responded Silva: the union belongs to the party.[54] Four days later, as Ciavatta tells the story, he handed over the union office key to Sebastião Lopes, the new party-appointed union president.

The story, and Ciavatta's critique, seems credible insofar as it reveals the hierarchical nature of the rural labor movement in the late

---

53. Siviero/Ciavatta transcript, 1–7; and "Infiltração Comunista nos meios agrícolas de São Paulo," *DM*, 15 January 1957, 1.

54. This dispute, which reveals the level of PCB interference in the rural labor movement at the local level, is described by the participants in Siviero/Ciavatta, interview by Geraldo, 3/A: 7–8; and Siviero/Ciavatta transcript, 7–10. See also Siviero/Ciavatta, interview by Geraldo, 1/B:16–20; and Silva transcript, pt. 2, pp. 33–35.

1950s. In Ciavatta the party had an experienced rural worker who had spent several years fighting to improve the lives and expand the rights of *colonos,* cane cutters, and other rural laborers. But his success also owed a lot to ULTAB, the PCB, and their state and national alliances. Although Ciavatta called his organization a union, it had marginal legal standing.[55] Only the labor court existed as a legal recourse. This is the interesting sidelight Ciavatta fails to recall in his account of expulsion. The labor court had a very rocky beginning and quickly came under attack by local militants. Within three months of its May inauguration, dozens of local labor activists distributed a petition calling for the removal of Alfredo de Oliveira Coutinho, the court's first chief judge (*presidente*). Conspicuously absent from the petition campaign, which criticized Coutinho for bias in favor of rural employers, was Ciavatta. This campaign received support from the PCB, which gave it substantial press coverage in September issues of *Notícias de Hoje.*[56] This may well have been the campaign to "overthrow the government" that disturbed Ciavatta. "The party wanted me to go against the judge," Ciavatta recalls, "to say he was a reactionary, an enemy of the laborers, and in the service of the planters, but it was just a way to get me thrown in jail again." He refused to participate.[57]

It is difficult to find other examples of rebellious behavior on the part of the PCB at this time. From top to bottom, the party now seemed committed to reformism, alliance building, and united-front politics like the coalitions built between landlords and rural labor organizations in support of the Marcha da Produção. At the same time, popular suspicion of Communism ran deep, and the party's eagerness to build its credentials caused *Terra Livre* and *Notícias de Hoje* to play up the PCB and the achievements of its members. It seems clear that Ciavatta, who had already experienced tremendous hardship, wanted to avoid additional confrontations. His perspective may also have been shaped by the era in which we interviewed him. The late 1980s was a moment of international assault on Communism,

55. A letter to city councilman Luciano Lepera from Alta Mogiana regional labor ministry chief Celsus Pimenta Requejo, reprinted in *Terra Livre,* interprets Decree Law No. 7,938 of 1944 and enabling rule 14 of 1945 as legitimating the union. Requejo wrote that "*sindicatos rurais* . . . can function so long as they are not denied recognition because this [recognition] always presupposes the prior existence of a syndicate already founded." See "Grande vitória dos trabalhadores: Confirmado pelo ministério o direito de organização dos sindicatos rurais," *TL,* April 1957, 1.

56. See, for example, "Como trabalha a junta de conciliação e julgamento de Ribeirão Preto: Justiça de trabalho ou agência de fazendeiros?" *NH,* 26 July 1957, n.p.; and "Trabalhadores de Ribeirão Preto: Voltam a reclamar a remoção do pres. da junta de conciliação," *NH,* 26 September 1957, 4.

57. Siviero/Ciavatta, interview by Geraldo, 3A:2.

and Ciavatta's tendency to blame his troubles on a corrupt party while portraying himself as a man of integrity was somewhat typical of the period. Without questioning anyone's integrity, it seems possible to consider that Girotto and Silva each had a different yet sincere vision. They both felt Judge Oliveira Coutinho needed to be ousted if the court was to be of assistance to workers. As the petition read, "The laborers, through many struggles, attained a labor court, but the bosses' class, with its unity, obtained the judge." Ciavatta played a major part in the struggle to gain a court, but his reluctance to push for the judge's removal may have made the party hierarchy believed a change of leadership was necessary. The fact the Ribeirão Preto rural workers' syndicate was not a registered union made it easier for the party to make this change in an authoritarian manner, one that left Ciavatta feeling bitter thirty years later.

The new union president, Lopes, put more pressure on the court. Unlike Ciavatta, Lopes himself filed cases for rural workers in addition to passing many along to Tavella and another pro-labor lawyer named Said Issa Halah.[58] In fact, from the day the court held its first hearing (*audiência*) on 13 May 1957, the junta attracted many aggrieved rural workers anxious to resolve their problems.[59] Its jurisdiction was the largest geographically of any junta in Brazil, covering more than three thousand square miles and serving some 335,000 people.[60] Looking closely at the record of the court and the experi-

---

58. Although Ciavatta died in 1992, Lopes was reported to be alive in Ribeirão Preto as late as 1994. Unfortunately, I was unable to locate him. A sample of one of the claims he filed was *Benedito Bertoldo de Oliveira v. Sítio Santa Maria (Luiz Gonzaga Lellis)*, PR 21 (1960), Packet No. 118, in the archive of the Junta de Conciliação e Julgamento de Ribeirão Preto (hereafter, the *processos*, or cases, will be cited in the following manner: names of the parties, case/year and (packet) numbers, JT/RP). Tavella and Halah's advocacy for the union and the party was confirmed in an interview with Irineu Luís de Moraes. See Moraes transcript, pt. 3, 22–23.

59. The following observations of the court's business are based on several months' research in the archive of the Ribeirão Preto junta. Then stored in the back room of the labor court building in central Ribeirão Preto, the junta archive consists of thousands of dusty file folders containing complete records—including evidentiary documents, such as the workers' *cadernetas agrícolas*—of all class disputes mediated by the court. These records were moved to the Arquivo Público e Histórico de Rébeirão Preto in 1996.

60. In 1967 the Ribeirão Preto Chamber of Commerce (Associação Comercial e Industrial) contracted Maria Therezinha de Vasconcellos, secretary of the labor court, to write a history of the court on the occasion of its tenth anniversary. This unpublished manuscript contains valuable data about the court, including the number of the decree law that authorized its establishment and the population and area under the court's jurisdiction. It had authority over labor disputes arising in seventeen *municípios* in the Alta Mogiana: Altinópolis, Barrinha, Batatais, Bonfim Paulista, Brodósqui, Cravinhos, Dumont, Guatapará, Jardinópolis, Luís Antônio, Pontal, Ribeirão Preto, São Antônio D'Alegria, São Simão, Serra Azul, Serrana, and Sertãozinho. See Vasconcellos, "Transcurso do primeiro decenio da Junta de Conciliação e Julgamento de Ribeirão Preto" (Ribeirão Preto, [1967?], mimeographed).

ence of rural workers who filed cases, one can more precisely evaluate the labor movement's turn to legal and administrative methods to resolve what were essentially conflicts of opposing class interests.

Rural Workers Go to Court

Court records from the establishment of the junta through the end of 1964 reveal that rural workers—*colonos,* sugarcane cutters, farm-hands, and livestock handlers—accounted for fully one-third (33.8 percent) of those who went to court to claim their rights under Bra-zilian labor law (see Appendix, Table 11). The 5,523 workers who filed these claims made up more than one-fifth (22.5 percent) of the num-ber of rural workers permanently employed within the court's juris-diction, according to the 1960 census.[61] These claimants accused 386, or nearly 15 percent, of the area's 2,897 agricultural establishments of violating the law and denying them their rights.[62] Together, they filed more than three thousand claims, accounting for more than 30 per-cent of the labor court's activity during the period.

Most of the complaints filed by rural workers sought relief in the form of time and money. They wanted a weekly day of rest, vacation allowances, compensation for overtime, and income parity with ur-ban workers. Fundamentally, they saw the law as a way to acquire more leisure time and more power to consume the products that make life enjoyable.[63] As time passed, perceived improvements in ur-ban life came to be the standard by which rural workers judged their living and working conditions. Rural electrification and transporta-

61. Using totals for permanent male and female employees listed in "Quadro 16: Pessoal ocupado, distribuido por sexo e categoria," Instituto Brasileiro de Geografia e Estatística, *Censo agrícola do estado de São Paulo recensamento geral de 1960* (Rio de Janeiro: Instituto Brasileiro de Geografia e Estatística, 1963), 145, 149, I estimated that 24,590 rural workers were permanently employed in the areas served by the Ribeirão Preto junta. At harvest time, seasonal workers tem-porarily quadrupled the number of rural workers in the region.

62. Of the 386 agricultural establishments identified, 282 were *fazendas;* 94, *sitios* or *cha-caras;* and 10, agro-industries. These numbers are based on distinctions between names of the establishments, owners, and addresses as they were related in the court ledgers (*protocolos*) from 1957 to 1964. The identifying information was not always complete in the *protocolos,* and some names, such as São Sebastião and São João, were popular and used by more than one *fazenda* or *sitio.* Thus, my figures are no more than estimates. The total of 2,897 agricultural establishments is calculated from the sum of the numbers listed in "Table 18: Atividade predominante dos es-tabelecimentos de agricultura e agropecuária," *Censo agrícola: 1960,* 196, 200, for the seventeen *municípios* under the jurisdiction of the Ribeirão Preto junta.

63. For an inspiring debate on this theme, see Gary Cross, "Time, Money, and Labor History's Encounter with Consumer Culture," and responses by Michael Rustin and Victoria de Grazia, in *International Labor and Working Class History* 43 (Spring 1993), 2–30.

tion developments since World War II had steadily enhanced the quality of life in Ribeirão Preto and other interior towns. Moreover, the rationale behind the labor laws that applied to rural workers emphasized the need for balance between town and country. "As the urban worker, so too the rural needs protective legal provisions," said Vargas as early as 1930.[64] The reforms he initiated culminated in 1963 with the creation of the ETR. To this day, São Paulo farmworkers credit Vargas for sponsoring a hiatus in the normal grind of their burdened lives. "Getúlio was good to the poor," a coffee picker told the anthropologist Verena Stolcke. "He left those laws, that the poor were not dogs, that the workers could not be dismissed, that bosses had to pay compensation."[65]

Stolcke found that coffee workers experienced the 1950s and 1960s as a downward slide from the "age of plenty to the time of money." Others have characterized this period as a transition from *colono* to *bóia-fria,* where *colonos* were the typical permanent workers up to the late 1950s and *bóias-frias* were the temporary wageworkers who replaced them from the 1960s on. *Colonos* resided in plantation housing and had guaranteed wages and the use of garden plots to grow subsistence and cash crops. Some enjoyed considerable social mobility. On the other hand, *bóias-frias,* whose nickname refers to the cold lunch they ate while away from their homes working in the fields, faced daily shape-ups, grueling commutes to the job site, and depressed wages.[66] Inherent in this shift was a loss of status—of dignity—as rural workers went from near self-sufficiency as *colonos* to total wage dependency as *bóias-frias.* Some have explained the shift of workers off the plantations as a consequence of the application of rural labor law: that planters reacted to the interference of the law by firing their *colonos* and rehiring them as temporary workers. Although this happened, the majority of the force behind this transition came from the opposite direction—from planters who, tight for cash, let conditions for their *colonos* deteriorate so far that the workers had no choice but to sue and flee.

Although the number of cases handled by the court made it difficult to evaluate each dispute, the vast majority—more than 80 percent of rural claims filed—involved workers on *fazendas* (see Appen-

---

64. See Chapter 1 and Vargas, "A plataforma," 27.
65. Quote is from an informant named Da Maria (possibly a pseudonym for Dona Maria, with no last name given), cited in Stolcke, *Coffee Planters,* 193.
66. Vinicius Caldeira Brant, "Do colono ao bóia-fria: Transformações na agricultura e constituição do mercado de trabalho na Alta Sorocabana de Assis," *Estudos CEBRAP* 19 (January/March 1977), 37–91; and Holloway, *Immigrants on the Land.*

dix, Table 12). While no rules governed the naming of agricultural establishments, *fazenda* was the word most often assigned to large and medium-sized plantations. A fair guess can be made that most of these claims involved coffee and sugar *colonos,* for coffee production predominated in the region, and commercial sugarcane production was simultaneously increasing in importance.[67] Another example of this tendency can be documented by some unscientific sampling. Fifty rural case files from the shelves of the archive revealed that thirty claims concerned disputes on plantations. Of these thirty, six-teen were lodged by coffee *colonos* and eleven by sugarcane *colonos.*[68]

One of the central issues in disputes brought by coffee and sugar *colonos* was residency on the plantations. In the western regions of São Paulo, residency had begun with the immigration of European labor to the coffee plantations of the area. These immigrants lived in housing colonies provided by the planters, which they left each day to go out to the fields. Living on the job site, *colonos* were also avail-able to fulfill many other job assignments: road maintenance, har-vesting, construction, livestock husbandry, and fire fighting.[69] The lack of transportation and the structure of the local rural economy

67. In 1959, coffee trees covered 49 percent of the farmland devoted to "permanent cul-tures," and coffee production was the principal activity of 45 percent of agricultural establish-ments in the Alta Mogiana. Likewise, a sea of sugarcane inundated 21 percent of farmland de-voted to "temporary cultures" and occupied 14 percent of all establishments. *Censo agrícola de São Paulo: 1960,* 296, 400.

68. While sugar and coffee *colonos* shared residency and similarly enjoyed access to gar-den plots, their situations differed in one central detail. Whereas coffee *colonos* were paid for a task—caring for so many thousands of trees—sugar *colonos* were paid a percentage of the market value of the cane they cut. This difference had various ramifications for the rural labor move-ment. See João Marcos Beraldo et al., *O colono paulista e o Instituto de Açucar e Álcool* (São Paulo: Revista dos Tribunais, 1945), 5–40; and A. J. Cesarino Junior, "Situação dos colonos paulistas em face do Estatuto da Lavoura Canavieira," *Revista de Direito Social* 4:19 (April/June, 1943), 70–91.

69. An example of the services *colonos* were obligated to fulfill for no pay can be found in the following clause from the coffee *colono* Augusto Leoncini's 1940/41 contract with the Companhia Agrícola Junqueira, owner of the *fazendas* Conquista, Santa Adelaide, and Santa Luiza—all in the Ribeirão Preto area. The clause, the tenth of thirteen, read,

Obligations—The *colono* obliges himself to perform the following services without addi-tional pay:

1. To maintain farm roads, lanes, corridors, and drainage ditches.

2. To clear all roads just before the harvest.

3. To cut down and bury common jack beans from the ruts of the coffee fields where they were planted, on the determination of the Plantation Administrator.

4. To respond to calls to extinguish forest, pasture, house, and other Planta-tion fires.

Leoncini not only had to worry about the planting, weeding, and harvesting for which he was paid but also these additional duties—duties he was obliged to fulfill at the behest of the plantation administrator. *Caderneta agrícola* 160,83 from *Leoncini v. Conquista,* 29/64 (199), JT/RP. Such duties were traditional to the *colonato* system, as Holloway shows in his *Immigrants on the Land.*

compelled them to buy goods on the *fazenda*. Meanwhile, they provided for many of their basic needs by growing vegetables and raising animals in lots provided by the planter. Residential shelters and allotment of land were essential features of the *colonato* system. Ideally, the system allowed planters to keep a labor force constantly at hand at minimal expense while creating a means for *colonos* to reproduce themselves and hoard their wage income by spending little money on the basic maintenance of their family. The system also allowed planters of both coffee and sugar unmatched flexibility to respond to socioeconomic trends and thus to protect and increase their power and profits. As we have seen, planters generally protected themselves from slumps in commodity prices mainly by reducing wages, confident that *colonos* would remain resident on the plantations and available to work at reduced rates.

While the flexibility of the system was good for planters, it often alienated *colonos,* driving them to defend themselves through work slowdowns, strikes, abandonment, and contractual disputes.[70] One coffee *colono* who lost patience with the *colonato* system was João Anunciato.[71] When Anunciato signed a contract with Fazenda Lagoa in October 1956, he clearly calculated that he could improve his income by hiring himself out occasionally for day work; by growing beans and corn between the rows of coffee; by counting on the labor of his wife and two young sons; and by saving money on rent, firewood, and coffee, as these items were to be provided at no cost (*gratuitamente*) by the plantation. But Anunciato's calculations proved misleading. The plantation owner, Ihigayochi Nagayochi, docked his pay for the tools he needed to work the coffee and paid him only once every three months. Falling behind with his creditors, in desperation he sought out the agricultural workers' union in Ribeirão Preto, where he was referred to the union's attorney, Holanda Noir Tavella, who wrote out Anunciato's claim, filing it in June 1957, eight months after the *colono* had signed a yearlong contract.

The first hearing occurred 26 August 1957, but Nagayochi failed to appear, and the court rescheduled the *audiência* for October 10, four months after Tavella filed the claim and ten days after the expiration of Anunciato's contract. As a *colono* on Fazenda Lagoa, Anunciato had contracted to care for 5,458 coffee trees at the pay rate of

---

70. Labor relations in São Paulo agriculture have long been regulated to a limited degree. For the pre-1930 history, see Chapter 1; Rocha, "Conflito social e dominação"; Decree Law No. 6,405 (19 April 1934); and Stolcke, *Coffee Planters*, 35.

71. *João Anunciato v. Fazenda Lagoa,* 354/57 (9), JT/RP.

Cr$2,500 annually per one thousand trees. According to the claim Anunciato filed in the Ribeirão Preto court, this rate needed to be raised more than five times to Cr$13,600 per one thousand trees in order to provide Anunciato with a salary equivalent to the minimum wage mandated by Decree Law No. 36,604A of July 1956. Anunciato asked the court to order Nagayochi to raise his wages accordingly to equal Cr$3,200 per month.

Nagayochi's lawyer argued that Anunciato's claim was groundless. Fazenda Lagoa owed him nothing, because in addition to the money he was paid for caring for the coffee trees, Anunciato also received payment "in kind" totaling the mandated regional wage. These "in kind" payments included the house, coffee beans, firewood, and the product of nine rows of beans and one row of corn Anunciato had planted between the coffee trees. From the perspective of Nagayochi, goods offered to attract and hold *colonos* were privileges that had a specific money value. The court, in this instance, accepted the planter's argument and rejected Anunciato's claim, ordering him to pay court costs.[72]

Awarded nothing, Anunciato's case typified the plight of rural workers. As a rule, they received only about 25 percent of the value they claimed to be owed.[73] Moreover, the junta's decision meant that goods that had once been taken for granted as an obligation of the planter came to have cash value that could be deducted from the *colono*'s pay. Anunciato was surprised because none of these items had been assigned a monetary value in his labor contract. Moreover, he had taken it upon himself (*em proveito próprio*) to plant the beans and corn. The goods and foodstuffs cost Nagayochi next to nothing and had been the traditional footing for *colono* social mobility. Calculated in this way, Anunciato, and other *colonos* like him, had to evaluate the costs and benefits of continuing to live in remote rural areas where their options, as well as those of their wives and children, were generally restricted. Anunciato's fate is not known, but if he was like many thousands of other rural workers in his position, he gave up residency and moved to a town or city from where he continued to work in agriculture on either a day-to-day or seasonal basis.[74]

72. Ibid.

73. In the period June to December 1962, the first period for which both *valor pedido* (amount requested or sued for) and *valor da solução* (amount sentenced to pay) figures were available, workers asked for Cr$86,968,000 and were awarded Cr$21,264,000. In 1962 U.S. dollars (U.S.$1 = Cr$390.52), these figures were equivalent to $222,700 and $54,450. Thus, in this period, workers received 25 percent of what they requested.

74. Between 1950 and 1970, the number of permanent resident rural laborers in the Alta Mogiana decreased by 65 percent, while the number of temporary workers, commuting daily

A passionate orator, the Peasant Leagues' Francisco Julião (left, addressing a São Paulo metal workers union meeting on 31 March 1962) became Brazil's most well known supporter of radical agrarian reform. Photo: courtesy Arquivo Fotográfico da *Última Hora* from Arquivo do Estado de São Paulo

Despite such disappointments, rural workers turned to the court with much greater frequency from 1961 to 1964. As the next chapter recounts, rural militancy exploded in this period, further narrowing the gap between rural workers and the judicial and political systems and encouraging more and more workers to become active in the defense of their interests. From 1960 to 1961, the number of rural claims more than doubled. At the beginning of 1961, a greater number of workers, often filing complaints collectively, started to appear before the Ribeirão Preto labor court. In 1963 the rate of growth slowed a little, but the actual numbers of claims and claimants continued to grow. In 1964, however, the quantity of rural cases fell back even while the total number of claims filed remained steady. Despite a 22 percent drop in the number of rural cases filed, the number of rural workers filing these claims exceeded the 1963 level. While the number of workers in other economic sectors who filed continued to grow apace, rural workers were responsible for much of the growth in the

from town to country, increased by 15 percent. Remaining labor requirements were absorbed largely by the use of more labor-efficient farming techniques and machines. São Paulo, Secretaria da Economia e Planejamento (hereafter SEPLAN), *Trabalho volante na agricultura paulista* (São Paulo: Estudos e pesquisas, No. 25, 1978), 220–25.

activity of the junta. In 1962, 1963, and 1964, they accounted for more than one-third of the number of workers who turned to the law for help (see Appendix, Table 11).

The Revival of Rural Labor Mobilization

The seeming institutionalization of rural labor militancy in the Alta Mogiana partially reflected the attractions of legal recourse, the hopes of earning the favor of national authorities, and exhaustion in the face of local repression. The subdued climate also reflected a crisis in the PCB nationally. In 1956 and 1957, the revelation of Stalin's crimes embarrassed the party, leading many supporters to question their own idealism. Party leaders also lost some of their self-assurance and began a debate over PCB policies and structures.[75] The first national ULTAB conference scheduled for September 1956 was ultimately postponed for three years, "to guarantee a better prepared conference, beginning from the plantations and sugar mills." Lacking funds, Tibúrcio and Portela, ULTAB's president and secretary, abandoned their activities and returned to farming, and only Lindolfo Silva remained active nationally. *Terra Livre,* which had been coming out as often as twice a month, started to appear irregularly in 1956, publishing only eight issues in the following two years. Nevertheless, the movement continued to grow, with large, first-ever rural labor conferences held toward the end of 1956 in the states of Alagoas, Mato Grosso, Minas Gerais, Espirito Santo, Goiás, and Maranhão. In addition to spreading the movement outside its base in São Paulo and Paraná, ULTAB continued to lobby in the nation's capital for rural labor legislation and the election of more sympathetic congressional representatives. In the few issues of *Terra Livre* that did appear during this period, many articles were devoted to a campaign to gain passage of a new rural labor law, proposal 4264-A, which sought to end the exclusion of rural workers from all CLT provisions. In June 1957, however, a Chamber of Deputies still dominated by landlord interests voted it down by a forty-vote margin. In September, *Terra Livre* de-

---

75. On the impact of Stalin's death in Brazil, see Raimundo Santos, *A primeira renovação pecebista: Reflexos do XX Congresso do PCUS no PCB (1956–1957)* (Belo Horizonte: Oficina de Livros, 1988). Medeiros (*História dos movimentos,* 53–54) notes that in response to the "destalinization" of the Partido Comunista, the PCB central committee resolved in 1958 to pursue legal forms of struggle in order to build a united front against North American imperialism. From the point of view of rural labor organizers, this official change merely confirmed ongoing, cross-class cooperation, such as that reflected in the Production March campaign.

nounced labor minister Fernando Nobrega, an appointee of João Goulart, who had approved a decision to deny recognition to a rural union in the town of Bragança Paulista. This decision angered the editors, since it supported a position argued by the SRB's Francisco Malta Cardoso and showed how PTB allies could not be trusted. These developments gave impetus to a campaign to elect "nationalist" candidates—those critical of U.S. imperialism and supportive of agrarian reform and rural *trabalhismo*—in the October 1958 state and local elections.[76]

In the midst of the campaign, Luís Carlos Prestes emerged from more than ten years of hiding. The press, if not the public, proved to be fascinated with his narrative of struggle for Brazilian socioeconomic progress and national dignity. Candidates such as Adhemar de Barros and Luís Tenório de Lima, a Communist labor leader, accepted his endorsement as allied members of the "patriotic, democratic, and nationalist forces." Barros, who was running again for governor of São Paulo, appeared on the cover of *Terra Livre* under the heading "For the Application of Labor Laws in the Country." While some PCB-supported candidates won election, Barros came in second behind Carlos Alberto Alves de Carvalho Pinto, outgoing governor Jânio Quadros's chosen successor. In the cooperative spirit of the time, Prestes sent Pinto a telegram of congratulations on his inauguration in January 1959. Other victors in São Paulo elections included anticommunist supporters of rural labor reform. Two state legislators and a federal deputy were elected from a new political party created in 1958 by the longtime courter of rural worker votes, Hugo Borghi. It was called the Rural Labor Party (PTR, Partido Trabalhista Rural), demonstrating the increased value of incorporating rural labor themes and symbolizing the growing number of political options available to rural workers. Into the early 1960s, the number of PTR representatives in the state legislature and national congress grew.[77]

76. On the ULTAB conference, see "Em setembro a primeira conferência da ULTAB," *TL,* April 1956, 1; "Adiada a conferência da ULTAB," *TL,* 15–30 July 1956, 1; and "Convocada para setembro: A conferência da ULTAB," *TL,* March 1959, 1. On the state conferences, see "Realizadas importantes conferências de lavradores e trabalhadores agrícolas em varios estados," *TL,* January 1957, 4. On internal ULTAB changes, see Silva transcript, pt. 1, pp. 21–22; and Portela transcript, 20–22. On the rural labor proposal, see "É preciso defender o projeto de Getúlio: Milhares de cartas e telegramas poderão fazer a balança pender a favor dos trabalhadores rurais," *TL,* 1–15 September 1956, 1; and Woodruff Walker, Rio de Janeiro, to USDS, Despatch No. 20 (5 July 1957), RG 59, DF 732.001, DS/USNA. On the labor ministry, see "Ministro do Trabalho (PTB) cria embaraços à sindicalização rural," *TL,* November 1958, 1.

77. On Prestes's return, see, for example, "Prestes a *Última Hora:* 'A carta de Vargas foi um grande legado ao Brasil!'" *UH,* 26 March 1958, 2. On Barros and the campaign, see, for example, "Dez mil trabalhadores do campo no comício de Ademar de Barros," *TL,* September 1958, 2; "Por

Not only was the national context for reform greatly improved by the end of the 1950s, but the international situation changed dramatically with the victory of Fidel Castro's revolutionaries in Cuba at the beginning of 1959. This event helped make agrarian reform seem a fundamental necessity to help prevent revolutions by peasants and rural workers in places as far away as Vietnam and Kenya. In Brazil, citizens read sympathetic treatments of the Cuban guerrillas in the popular press and, in February, learned about the dramatic expropriations program carried out there.[78] Later in the year, media attention shifted to the long-abandoned Engenho Galiléia, in Pernambuco. There, thirty miles west of Recife, a group of peasants and tenant farmers forced the state government to take their side in a dispute with the landlord. In a close vote, a majority of the legislature joined the governor, Cid Sampaio, in agreeing to expropriate the unproductive sugar mill and the surrounding land. In February 1960, the state took possession of the land and distributed it to members of the tenant group, the Engenho Galiléia peasant league, presided over by the charismatic lawyer Francisco Julião. In short order, other states and the federal government stepped up their efforts to compose new agricultural land and labor laws, many of them assisted by a U.S. government anxious to forestall more Cuba-like revolutions in the hemisphere.[79]

The rise of the Julião's peasant leagues and political parties like the PTR meant that by the end of the 1950s, the PCB was far from

medidas de reforma agrária, pela aplicação das leis trabalhistas no campo," *TL*, October 1957, 1; and "Telegrama de Prestes aos novos governadores," *TL*, February 1959, 4. A list of winners is "Candidatos nacionalistas eleitos em nosso estado," *TL*, November 1958, 1. On Borghi and the PTR, see "Borghi," in Beloch and Abreu, eds., *DHBB*, 421; and Quadros V and VI in Sampaio, *Adhemar de Barros e o PSP*.

78. See, for example, "Fidel Castro inicia a distribuição de terras a milhares de campo-neses," *UH*, 1 February 1959, 4.

79. The press covered these events extensively. In an unusual bow to populism, the staid *O Estado de São Paulo* solicited and published a series of articles by Julião himself. See Francisco Julião, "As ligas camponesas I: A tragédia do agricultor sem terra," 8 December 1959, 8; "As ligas camponesas II: Organizam-se os arrendatarios," 9 December 1959, 4; "As ligas camponesas III: O papel das ligas nas eleições," 10 December 1959, 6 — all in *OESP.* Other examples of contemporary press coverage include Gonçalo Duarte, "Ligas camponesas," *O Observador: Econômico e Financeiro* (Rio de Janeiro) 24:286 (December 1959), 29–32; and Antônio Callado, *Tempo de Arraes: A revolução sem violência,* 3d ed. (Rio de Janeiro: Paz e Terra, 1980), originally published as a series of articles in Rio de Janeiro's *Jornal do Brasil* between 7 December 1963 and 19 January 1964. Recently published evaluations of the leagues and Julião are Bastos, *As ligas camponesas,* and Azevêdo, *As ligas camponesas,* 69–73. Julião's life story is provocatively recounted in a 1977 interview transcript. "Francisco Julião," transcript of interview by Aspásia Camargo, Yxcatepec, Mexico, December 1977, CPDOC/FGV—História Oral. The most recent analysis is found in Pereira, *The End of the Peasantry.* For U.S. interest, see Joseph A. Page, *The Revolution That Never Was: Northern Brazil, 1955–1964* (New York: Grossman Publisher, 1972).

the only organization seeking to attract rural worker participation and resolve their concerns, a situation that would help enliven and enlarge the rural labor movement in the 1960s. During the 1950s the PCB had helped give shape to a diversity of rural worker grievances and demands. The party had united militants from around the country and facilitated the creation of rural labor organizations. It had nurtured the seed and shaped the tree more than any other single entity in Brazil. In September 1959 the party momentarily revived its place at the vanguard of the movement by hosting ULTAB's first national conference. Held in São Paulo, the conference brought together delegates from 122 unofficial rural unions affiliated with ULTAB. Seventeen states were represented. Despite these numbers, a tone of concern about the weakness of the movement characterized the proceedings. Given that the majority of Brazilians still worked the land, thousands of unions should have been organized since the 1954 conference. The delegates discussed this challenge, and Sebastião Dinart argued for the necessity of accepting the guidance of organized industrial workers to overcome the difficulty of identifying "natural leaders" among rural workers themselves. But the conference was better at analyzing the problem than at identifying solutions, and the final charter called for yet another conference. Most of this went unreported, however. Due to financial difficulties, the PCB was not able to publish another issue of *Terra Livre* until January, nearly four months after the conference had ended.[80]

Sebastião Lopes attended the 1959 meeting from Ribeirão Preto. Since his expulsion from the union and the party, Nazareno Ciavatta had bounced from one job to another, demonstrating the difficulties confronted by rural labor activists during this moment of relative stability for the movement. He worked as a sugarcane cutter on various plantations but found that he could only hold a job for a week or a month before he was identified as a labor militant and fired. "I was persecuted because I was marked as a Communist," he said. In 1958, however, Judge Oliveira Coutinho ran into him in front of a café called "A Única" and offered to help him get a job with the Department of Transportation (DER, Departamento de Estradas de Rodagem). The judge appreciated Ciavatta's role in opposing the petition to have him removed from the court. This job eventually helped Cia-

80. On the conference, see "Convocada para setembro: A conferência da ULTAB," 1, Sebastião Dinart dos Santos, "O problema da organização rural," 1, and "Decidido no conselho de representantes da ULTAB organizar a luta por medidas de reforma agrária," 4—all in *TL*, March 1959; "Carta Pela Reforma Agrária," *TL*, January 1960, 10; and Medeiros, *História dos movimentos*, 51–52.

vatta secure a patronage position at city hall, where different politicians called on his record as a defender of rural worker rights to help
them attract votes. These politicians had helped him escape the grip
of Girotto and the PCB, he believed. "Girotto wanted me to keep
working in the cane fields, agitating among the workers, so I would
be jailed again and again, giving him a chance to demonstrate how
active the party was in the region, even though I'd already been
kicked out of the party!"[81] Fact or fiction, this kind of corruption lore
was also a legacy of the PCB. As the 1960s began and competition
grew for predominance over the rural labor movement the PCB itself
had done so much to shape, such images influenced ULTAB's
behavior.

81. Siviero/Ciavatta, interview by Geraldo, 3B:3.

7

Toward the end of 1959, Irineu Luís de Moraes returned to Ribeirão Preto after a ten-year absence. At forty-seven years of age, Moraes was a seasoned veteran of the rural labor struggle in São Paulo and Paraná. He felt at home in Ribeirão Preto, fondly remembering the 1945 Power and Light Company strike and his time organizing peasant leagues in Dumont and other towns throughout the Alta Mogiana region. Despite this groundwork, he remembers finding little evidence of the organizations he had so painstakingly helped build in the postwar period. In town and country, the party had grown inactive. "Nothing was organized," Moraes recalled. Former comrades he encountered in Ribeirão Preto complained that a PCB agent flew around the area collecting dues but "didn't do anything"; worst of all, Moraes added, "no one knew where he lived." Local Com-

FIRST FRUITS

► Harvesting Rural Labor Unions

munist leaders had grown comfortable with the status quo, Moraes concluded, "and let the party go to the devil." On area plantations, Moraes heard about Nazareno Ciavatta and the Ribeirão Preto rural labor union but found no sign of the syndicate and never met Ciavatta. "In my opinion, Ciavatta, as president of the union, made no headway with the masses, advanced nothing, because when I got [to Ribeirão Preto], there was no mark left of his existence." Disgusted with the moribund state of the local party, Moraes resolved to rebuild it.[1]

Expressions of despair aside, Moraes's new start in the Alta Mogiana benefited greatly from the dramatically different context he now faced. In fact, since he last lived in Ribeirão Preto, his own actions had helped create a much more favorable situation for rural labor mobilization. By organizing peasant leagues, squatters in Porecatú, and *colono* actions in Valparaiso, Araraquara, and other towns, Moraes had contributed to the success of the 1954 conference in which Ciavatta added his voice to the rural labor movement. Before Ciavatta fell by the wayside, ousted from the movement, his activism helped establish the Ribeirão Preto labor court, an institution that may well have contributed to the decline of militancy in the region (see Appendix, Figure 3).[2] By the end of the decade, the collective efforts of these men and others had helped make rural unionization a popular issue for idealistic students, professionals, industrial workers, and politicians across much of the ideological spectrum. Moraes himself had shown how mainstream the cause had become when he formed an alliance with *fazendeiros* in São José do Rio Preto. In a perfectly characteristic yet ideologically troubling way, Moraes's narrative of single-handedly rebuilding the party emphasizes his *individual* role in reviving the *collective* spirit of wayward militants. Yet, even his very return to Ribeirão Preto, explained in the narrative by his wanderlust, may in fact be better explained by the resurgence of ULTAB at its September 1959 conference. Since the state central committee had sent Moraes almost everywhere he went for the past fifteen years, it seems more than likely that he had been ordered to Ribeirão Preto to do exactly what he set out to do: revive the party.

1. Welch and Geraldo, *Lutas camponesas,* 159–62.
2. Coincidentally, *TL* (February 1960, 2) celebrated the empowering influence of the court on rural workers at the moment that Moraes found "nothing" going on. In the first six months of 1959, the paper reported, the Ribeirão Preto syndicate had helped many workers win numerous cases against fourteen different Alta Mogiana plantations. "Without doubt, these victories, lived by the workers themselves, teach the great lesson that only through organization and struggle is it possible to defend one's rights, interests, and demands."

Given his reputation as a militant in the area, Moraes claims to have had little trouble gathering together a few old allies to help plan a barbecue to unite supporters behind the party's revival. Party members such as Antônio Girotto and Luciano Lepera, a Communist state assemblyman running for reelection on the Brazilian Labor Party (PTB) ticket, opposed the picnic. Satisfied with the party's quiet electoral and courtroom advances, they were disturbed by Moraes's gruff, street-fighting ways. But times had changed, and preparations for the picnic went ahead. Although the PCB was technically illegal, the tolerance shown the party by President Kubitschek and Vice President Goulart gave militants more room to operate above ground, especially in cities like Ribeirão Preto, where there lived a sizable industrial working class, student population, and independent middle class. Shopkeepers and butchers who knew and trusted Moraes donated meat and other supplies; other expenses were covered by ticket sales to the event. On the chosen day, comrades and friends gathered under the mango trees on a vacant lot in the Vila Tibério neighborhood to eat roasted meat, drink beer, and talk politics from ten in the morning until five in the evening.[3]

For Moraes, the barbecue was a success. He had set out to rejuvenate the party "from below or above," and by the picnic's end, a provisional directorate and new organizing committee had been selected from a group of eager backers. Dr. Clarimundo Soares, a physician, became first secretary. Other directors included university students, such as Pedro Alves de Azevêdo and his wife, Marisa, and some teachers. According to Moraes, he was the only member of working-class origins. "Of workers there was only me," he said. "The rest were petty bourgeois: there were physicians over here, professors over there. But they were an enthusiastic and jovial group." The only sour note came when supporters of Lepera argued with him that the affair should be turned into a campaign benefit. Moraes knew little about Lepera but opposed giving the proceeds of picnic ticket sales to someone who had opposed the event and now seemed interested only in taking advantage of the large turnout. After the picnic, the new committee communicated its formation to state leaders and began an intense round of meetings, many held at Moraes's house. The committee's success led the party hierarchy to sever its ties with Girotto's inactive group in order to recognize the new movement. Angered,

3. Irineu Luís de Moraes, transcript of interview by author, Ribeirão Preto, 22 August 1988, AEL/UNICAMP (hereafter Moraes transcript, pt. 1), p. 39; Girotto transcript; and Luciano Lepera, interview by author, Ribeirão Preto, 18 October 1988.

Girotto stimulated factional fights that discouraged Moraes and led him to focus his energy less on the local committee and more on rural labor organizing. "I went to work in the country to avoid a confrontation with them," he recalls.[4]

This, too, may be a misleading recollection. Logic suggests that, given Moraes's skills and interests, he went to work organizing rural laborers with the full support of local, state, and national PCB bureaucrats. The rural labor movement's most active period was about to begin, and ULTAB's leaders were better positioned to recognize this than was Moraes. Following the apparent success of the Engenho Galiléia Peasant League in Pernambuco, leader Francisco Julião encouraged the formation of leagues in many northeastern states and became a national spokesman for radical agrarian reform. The more Julião's movement grew, the more threatened the Catholic Church became: Julião's quasi-messianic style compelled the church to demonstrate that it, rather than the leagues, was the institution the rural poor could trust and count on. Thus, it was not long before the Catholic Church, with an established national presence, began to invest in rural labor organizing. With such formidable competitors on their hands, the PCB could no longer take its predominance in the movement for granted. From place to place, bitter rivalries developed between these three forces; from time to time, uneasy alliances formed, as well. In response, the federal government sought to wield control over the movement by passing rural labor legislation and instituting a program of rural union formation.

In a context of organizational rivalry and official acceptance, the rural labor movement blossomed as never before. Finally, the seeds rural labor militants like Moraes had so painstakingly cultivated bore fruit as an unprecedented number of rural unions gained official recognition by the Ministry of Labor. At the grassroots level, Moraes found he was no longer alone in harvesting the first fruits of a long struggle. In Celso Ibson de Syllos, a Catholic priest who became involved in the local movement at the start of 1962, Moraes found a worthy rival. Moraes and Padre Celso were the two most influential activists in the Alta Mogiana until the Populist Republic collapsed with the military overthrow of President Goulart in March 1964. Using Ribeirão Preto as their center of activities, the party, the church, planters, and politicians—representatives of all national players save the peasant leagues—sought the favor of rural workers and the right to broker the power of this significant sector. In the ferment, the goals

4. Welch and Geraldo, *Lutas camponesas,* 161–62; and Girotto transcript.

of rural labor mobilization shifted from Moraes's rural proletarian revolution to the state's emphasis on rural worker incorporation, revealing tendencies that help explain the perseverance of the movement after the military came to power.[5]

Mobilizing Sugar Workers

Before Padre Celso became active and before the drive to form rural unions overwhelmed all other concerns, Moraes began to mobilize sugarcane field and mill workers near Sertãozinho, Barrinha, and Pontal, a cluster of towns located to the west of Ribeirão Preto. Despite the proximity of the two areas, this pocket of the Alta Mogiana differed substantially from that of Ribeirão Preto. Like the rest of the region, coffee predominated in Sertãozinho until the 1930s. Thereafter, exhausted land was sold to former *colonos* and investors who planted cotton, marking the end of coffee's preeminence. Following World War II, the profitability of cotton declined, and sugarcane grew in importance as several *usinas de açucar* (sugar mills) were constructed in the area. Looking for greater economies of scale, the mill owners (*usineiros*) bought land in order to increase their control over cane yields to ensure the efficient use of *usinas* around the clock. In 1944 the area planted in cane was greater than that planted in coffee; ten years later, sugar covered nearly three times the amount of land devoted to coffee and cotton combined. By 1956, pungent, black smoke billowed from the chimney stacks of seven large sugar mills. Ironically, the success of the socialist revolution in Cuba stimulated yet another round of growth in sugar production, for the United States boycott of Cuban sugar created opportunities for other suppliers. Brazil found that its quota of the U.S. sugar market went from 0 percent in 1960 to 6.4 percent in 1962. The *usinas* thus pushed production to the limit. A typical response was made by Sertãozinho's Usina São Geraldo: annual production there jumped from about 150,000 sixty-kilogram sacks in 1954 to more than 400,000 in 1964. By 1974 output had more than doubled again.[6]

5. Moraes transcript, pt. 1; and Celso Ibson de Syllos, transcript of interview by author, São Paulo, 19 January 1989, AEL/UNICAMP.
    6. The expanding fortunes of sugarcane in this period helped speed the abandonment of coffee and the growth of sugar production throughout the Alta Mogiana. See Roberto Ferreira do Amaral, ed., *Diagnóstico: Sexta região administrativa: Ribeirão Preto* (São Paulo: SEPLAN, August 1972), 4/15–4/23. See also José Jorge Gebara, "A estrutura agrária do município de Sertãozinho: Evolução, caracterização e efeitos" (master's thesis, Escola de Administração de Empresas

The phenomenal development of the region's sugar economy depended on a large labor force, and the dense rural labor population attracted Moraes to the area in 1960. "There was a great concentration of peasants, wage workers, mill hands," said Moraes, "so I headed over there." In 1959, census takers counted nearly ten thousand rural employees living and working in the area of the three towns within this subregion. In Sertãozinho alone, 97 percent of its rural labor force was considered to be permanently employed in 1940. By 1960, however, the percentage had dropped to under 40. During the same period, the rural laboring population of the town almost doubled, increasing from 3,979 to 6,268. A high proportion of rural laborers were now considered temporary employees; they numbered 3,835 workers, more than 60 percent of all rural employees. During the 1960s, both the total number of rural workers and the ratio between permanent and temporary workers remained fairly constant. The story was similar in sugar zones throughout the state. Between 1958 and 1968, the ratio of permanent workers to temporary workers changed little, while the overall number of workers engaged in sugar production climbed from 26,240 to 48,843, imitating the experience of Sertãozinho in the 1950s.[7]

For Moraes, the size and diversity of the sugar production workforce presented problems he had not encountered before. He had spent most of his recent career organizing coffee *colonos;* now he prepared to agitate sugarcane cultivators, cutters, and mill hands. The modern sugar industry he confronted was a product of the 1940s. Many of the *usinas* were heavily capitalized, holding huge tracts of land and hiring sugar *colonos* who farmed cane for the mills. In contrast to coffee *colonos,* sugar workers earned wages based on the current market price of a percentage of what they produced. While sugar *colonos* were much like sharecroppers, those employed in the sugar mills labored as industrial workers, earning cash wages and falling under the provisions of the CLT. This system gradually changed after 1944, when an amendment to the 1941 Sugar Cane Farming Statute

---

de São Paulo, Fundação Getúlio Vargas, 1976), 20–31; Octavio Ianni, *Origens agrárias do estado brasileiro* (São Paulo: Brasiliense, 1984), 41–49; and Francisco Ribeiro da Silva, "A lei americana sôbre o açucar—'Sugar Act'—seus propositos e como funciona," *Brasil Açucareiro* (Rio de Janeiro) 4 (April 1971), 10.

7. Moraes transcript, pt. 1, p. 40. More on Sertãozinho is found in table 6 in Instituto Brasileiro de Geografia e Estatística (IBGE), *Censo agrícola do estado de São Paulo: Recenseamento do 1960* (Rio de Janeiro, 1963), 144–49; and Ianni, *Origens agrárias*, 64. Comparative national trends are discussed in José Cesar Gnaccarini, *Estado, ideologia e ação empresarial na agroindústria açucareira do estado de São Paulo* (São Paulo: n.p., 1972, mimeographed), 194.

specified that São Paulo sugar *colonos* had the same legal rights as their brothers and sisters in the sugar mill because the product of their labor, cane, went through immediate industrial processing. In labor disputes, the courts generally recognized the amended law during the 1950s. When the Superior Labor Tribunal in 1957 unanimously upheld an interpretation of the CLT that said a field worker had the same rights as an industrial worker so long as both worked for the same employer and the product of the farm labor was destined to be processed, *Terra Livre* argued that sugar field and mill workers could organize actions together, since they had equal legal standing. But the journal also lamented that most sugar industry workers were unaware of their rights. Worse still, *usineiros* tried to evade the law by passing formal ownership and management of the fields to third parties, who quite often were their business partners.[8] Some planters experimented with new technologies to reduce the full-time labor dependency of both the plantations and the mills. Except for a few labor-saving innovations in transporting the cane from the field to the mill, however, the harvest continued to depend on manual labor into the 1990s. In 1959 a conference of the São Paulo State Federation of Food Industry Laborers' Unions (FESTIAESP, Federação dos Sindicatos dos Trabalhadores nas Indústrias de Alimentação do Estado de São Paulo), headed by the Communist ally Luís Tenório de Lima, made securing full labor rights under the CLT a top priority for sugarcane cutters. As a consequence, Tenório de Lima and the union participated in dozens of cutter labor actions.[9]

8. Labor law applying to the sugar industry in São Paulo is succinctly discussed in Luiz Roberto de Rezende Puech, *Direito individual e coletivo do trabalho (estudos e comentários)* (São Paulo: Revista dos Tribunais, 1960), 184–96. (Thanks to John French for this citation.) See also A. F. Cesarino Junior, "Situação dos colonos paulistas em face do Estatuto da Lavoura Canavieira," *Revista de Direito Social* 4 : 19 (April–June 1943), 70–91; and Beraldo et al., *O colono paulista.* The amendment is recorded in "Artigos 19 a 26 do Decreto Lei No. 6.969, de 19 de octubro de 1944," *RLT* 16 : 181 (May 1952), 261–62. Attempts to evade the law are exemplified by the following cases: "Propriedade rural—finalidades, Processo TST No. 4.823/51," *RLT* 17 : 189 (January 1953), 17–18; and "Carpa da cana, Processo TRT/SP No. 3.634/58," *RLT* 22 : 245/6 (January/February 1958), 59–60. The TST (Tribunal Superior do Trabalho) decision of 14 November 1957 is analyzed in "Trabalhador da lavoura de cana tem iguais direitos que os operários da usina de açucar," *TL,* February 1959, 4. See also Gebara, "A estrutura agrícola do município de Sertãozinho," 34–36.

9. "Already in the 1950s, the growing instability of labor and *trabalhista* demagoguery provoked the first isolated attempts at mechanization." See Luis Antonio Ribeiro Pinto, "Colheita da cana-do-açucar," *Brasil Açucareiro* (April 1977), reprinted in *Diário de Manhã* (Ribeirão Preto), 13 September 1977, 7. However, due to soil conditions and the fear of damaging second- and third-cut harvests, manual labor predominated into the 1990s, when the introduction of new mechanical harvesters threatened the livelihoods of thousands of seasonal workers. See the Epilogue. On FESTIAESP, see below and Fatima Regina de Barros, "A organização sindical dos trabalhadores rurais: Contribuição ao estudo do caso do estado de São Paulo, entre 1954–1964"

Full understanding of these conditions and their implications for organizing shaped Moraes's strategy in the region. Initially he acted as he usually did when arriving in a targeted town for the first time: he tracked down people he knew to be Communists, former Communists, or sympathizers; queried them to learn about local conditions and concerns; and then patronized the *botecos* frequented by rural workers. He drank shots of *pinga* and glasses of beer with them, slowly developing a familiarity with both the place and the people. Eventually, the bar atmosphere outlived its utility, and he met with small groups of workers at prearranged times and locations. "Later, with a lot of work, a lot of sacrifice, a little organization started to develop with five, ten, twenty workers getting together every month," said Moraes. "But you have to sleep with them, eat together with them, and suffer the consequences with them, everything, to live with them, to earn their confidence because *camponeses* are very suspicious people." When he had gained legitimacy in Sertãozinho, he moved to Pontal, where he went through much the same process. In Barrinha, Moraes got help from a popular local Communist who pulled together a meeting of two hundred *usina* workers. "Now, that was nice," he said, "but building a union was more difficult than that." Mill workers had clear legal rights to form unions, but employers thwarted their efforts as much as possible, firing known union sympathizers and blacklisting them at other mills in the area. "In that situation," said Moraes, "a man could do nothing but move out of town." [10]

The following year, 1961, Moraes continued to talk with a diversity of rural workers, temporary and permanent, employed in the field and mill. He thought the informality of their organization bothered the workers and kept them quiet. "I talked with them about their rights and I tried to convince them they could improve their situation if they all worked together," said Moraes. "They listened, but they did not talk. When they start talking on their own, offering their own opinions, that is when you got something going." He tried a new tactic. He formally registered the group in Sertãozinho with a notary public. An announcement appeared in the local paper: "Association of Agrarian Laborers of Sertãozinho Formed." He did the same thing in Barrinha. "It did not have any legal value," said Moraes, "but we

---

(master's thesis, Universidade de Campinas, 1986), 111 n. 37; and Ibiapaba Martins, "Proletariado e inquietação rural," *Revista Brasiliense* 42 (July–August 1962), 62–81. (At the time, Martins was a federation lawyer.)

10. Moraes transcript, pt. 1, pp. 42–43.

thought it would help." Still, it did not seem to make any difference. "There were still a lot of sad, silent faces around the room."

When he saw them on the street, Moraes asked those who stopped coming to the meetings to explain their absences. Some failed to appear for personal reasons, but others told him they had given up the group because they did not share the same problems as the others. Moraes reflected on the diversity of those who attended, the different types of work they performed, and the variety of ways they related to the *usina*. Some simply cut cane, living in the towns and moving from one field to another during the June to September harvest season; others lived on the *usina* property and worked year-round at a variety of tasks, including industrial work in the mill; still another group farmed the cane on shares. Each group had its own set of needs and demands; some positions had distinct definition in law. "With laborers, you need to talk vacation pay, eight hour days, and wage hikes," said Moraes, "but sharecroppers and small farmers had no interest in such things. With them, you need to talk about increasing sale prices and obtaining cheap credit." In this situation, the only answer was to divide the association into categories, a fundamental point that had not been lost on the 1954 or 1959 ULTAB conference organizers.[11] On May 7 a group of five hundred workers gathered in Pontal to re-form as the Association of Laborers in Sugar Mills, Cane Farms, and General Agriculture. Named president was Antônio Paulo Dias, a rural laborer tailored for the post by Moraes. Similar associations were formed in Sertãozinho and Barrinha.[12]

For Moraes, the association was to help workers defend and advance their workplace interests. After success in the economic field, the party might call on them to help advance the political revolution that oriented PCB policy. This step-by-step principle gripped Moraes so strongly that, years later when he recalled events in the Alta Mogiana, he was sure the associations had led successful strikes before

---

11. Ibid., 42. Conference participants had been assigned to nine distinct working groups, including commissions examining the specific problems of sugar mill workers, wage-earning farmworkers (*assalariados agrícolas*), contract workers such as *colonos*, squatters (*posseiros*), tenants and sharecroppers, and cacao workers. "Debatem os trabalhadores agrícolas seus problemas e reivindicações," *UH*, 21 September 1954, 8.

12. Moraes transcript, pt. 1; and "Assembléia de Fundação da Associação dos Trabalhadores Agrícolas de Ituverava," *TL*, March 1961, 2; "Fundada a Associação dos Trabalhadores Agrícolas de Igarapava," *TL*, May 1961, 2; "Pontal: Criada a Associação dos Trabalhadores em Usinas de Açucar" and "Sertãozinho: Fundação da Associação de Trabalhadores em Açucar," *TL*, June 1961, center section; "Lavoura Canavieira: Convite dos trabalhadores," *TL*, July 1961, 7; and "Associação dos Trabalhadores em Usinas de Açucar e da Lavoura Canavieira: Reuniões em Sertãozinho e em Ituverava," *DM*, 19 August 1961, 6.

they became involved in politics. But, as fate would have it, the first substantive action of the Sertãozinho labor association was politically motivated, offering another example of how entangled economic and political issues had become in the Populist Republic era.

The Succession Crisis of 1961

On the morning of 25 August 1961, only a few short months after the Sertãozinho rural labor associations were founded, Jânio Quadros renounced the Brazilian presidency. Within twenty-four hours he had returned to his home in São Paulo, jumped into his white Volkswagen beetle, and gone on vacation.[13] The president's sudden, dramatic action caught the nation by surprise. Constitutionally, power passed to the vice president, who was to serve out the presidential term, but the vice president elected along with Quadros in October 1960 was João Goulart, the Labor Party leader reviled as a Communist "fellow traveler" and *getúlista* by conservatives. When Quadros resigned, Goulart was out of the country conducting official business in the People's Republic of China. Three influential military ministers opposed to Goulart's succession took advantage of his absence to challenge the constitutional process. Federal troops were mustered in Rio Grande do Sul, São Paulo, Santa Catarina, and Guanabara, but their loyalties were uncertain. The tide turned against the challengers when the Third Army, based in Rio Grande do Sul, joined the governor of the state—Goulart's brother-in-law, Leonel Brizola—in defending the constitution. Broadcasting his pro-legality stance over the radio, Brizola called on the people to mobilize in defense of the constitutional process. Answering the call, the PCB encouraged militants to mobilize the public, defying the ministers and displaying popular support for Goulart and the legal transition of power.[14]

In the end, Goulart's opponents failed to rally sufficient support to block his succession, but they forced the vice president and his allies to accept a compromise. Reversing decades of strong executive tradition, the constitution was amended to create the position of

---

13. For a detailed account of the renunciation, see John W. F. Dulles, *Unrest in Brazil: Political-Military Crises, 1953–1964* (Austin: University of Texas Press, 1970), 114–56; and on the resulting political crisis of 1961, see also Amir Labaki, *1961: A crise da renuncia e a solução parlamentarista* (São Paulo: Brasiliense, 1986).

14. See, for example, "Luta pela legalidade!" *NR*, 1–7 September 1961, 1; and "Jango é o presidente de fato e de direito," and "Janio aprovou a reforma agrária e foi obrigado a renunciar," *TL*, August 1961, 1, 6. *Novos Rumos* is the Rio de Janeiro–based PCB weekly.

prime minister. Nominated by the president and confirmed by congress, the prime minister selected cabinet members and governed the country through them. Reluctantly accepting this arrangement, Goulart was inaugurated president on September 7. Tancredo de Almeida Neves, a moderate PSD politician from the state of Minas Gerais, was named prime minister.[15]

Despite these machinations to inhibit Goulart's power, the popular movement for legality went ahead full force. In Ribeirão Preto, on the very day Goulart was sworn in, several thousand people amassed in historic Praça XV de Novembro in the center of town for a "Mass Rally for Legality." In photos of the rally published in *Terra Livre,* banners of the rural worker associations of Sertãozinho, Pontal, and Barrinha predominated. As evidence of the breadth of support for Goulart and the Communist's success in helping to rebuild a popular front, city hall became the headquarters of the Democratic Legality Front. The photographs suggest that the cane harvesters and mill workers organized by Moraes in the Sertãozinho area constituted a fair portion of the new front.[16] Once Goulart's position seemed secure, Moraes mobilized sugar workers yet again in order to ensure that the new administration was aware of their needs and demands and that it also remembered their support of Goulart's succession. On October 15, more than a thousand cane cutters and mill workers, including about one hundred female field hands, gathered in the center of Sertãozinho supporting a telegram Moraes and Nestor Vera, another PCB rural labor organizer, had prepared to send to Goulart. Coming from neighboring towns, they listened as Moraes read the telegram, which called on the president to help them end unemployment, secure the minimum wage, and transform their associations into recognized unions. A final demand was abolition of a practice recently adopted by rural employers—deducting rent from their pay.[17]

Events such as these encouraged Goulart to resist the strictures of the new parliamentary system. While the new cabinet quickly adopted a reformist program of government, Goulart challenged the cabinet to be more far-reaching in its proposals and aggressive in their

15. Labaki, *1961: A crise da renuncia,* 102–33; and Moniz Bandeira, *O govêrno João Goulart: As lutas sociais no Brasil, 1961–1964,* 6th ed. (Rio de Janeiro: Civilização Brasileira, 1983), 43–53.
16. "Alta Mogiana desenvolve grandes lutas camponesas: Comício pela legalidade," *TL,* September 1961, 3; and Moraes transcript, pt. 1, pp. 42–43.
17. "Alta Mogiana desenvolve grandes lutas camponesas," *TL,* September 1961, 3; and "Usineiros desrespeitam salário mínimo," *TL,* October 1961, 2. In the latter story, rural labor associations were named for the following towns: Pradópolis, Guariba, Pitangueiras, Pontal, and Barrinha. The rally counted on the support of established urban industrial unions, especially the food processors' union of Ribeirão Preto and state federation president Luís Tenório de Lima.

realization. The congress, where conservative representatives predominated, resisted change, and while Neves preferred to negotiate and compromise with the legislature, Goulart tended to advocate faster action and broader change. This was a risky business, for similar behavior had led Quadros to his resentful resignation. Just two days before Quadros resigned, a controversial agrarian reform bill he had been pushing died in congress, contributing to his frustration. Goulart calculated that in order to govern, he needed to expand his base of support, and he looked to a package of basic reforms to help him accomplish this goal. The *reformas de base,* as they were known, were first introduced by Neves. They included vague intentions to reform Brazil's agrarian structure, banking, administrative, financial, and electoral systems. These ideas had their origins in ECLA studies arguing that successful Latin American development required fundamental reform in the basic structure of each nation's economic and political systems. In Brazil, where agriculture played such a prominent role in the political economy, the question of agrarian reform became the most controversial issue of the time. Eventually, nearly all political factions supported agrarian reform, but few of them agreed on the means of achieving it, let alone the goals of policy.[18]

The Agrarian Reform Debate

One of the most divisive questions of the entire agrarian reform debate was whether or not the 1946 constitution needed to be amended. Under constitutional article 147, a standard of "social well-being" applied to all land use, enabling the government "to promote the just distribution of property, with equal opportunity for all." Yet article 141 recognized private property rights and, in paragraph 16, mandated that property owners receive "prior, just compensation [*indenização*] in cash" for any land expropriated by the state for "social interest or public utility." Informed by Catholic and capitalist idealism, the article affirmed a contradictory rule of law: that land was a fundamental *community* resource subject to *individual* domain. At ULTAB's 19 September 1959 conference, revoking paragraph 16 had emerged as a top priority for the movement. The conference recommended replacing it with clauses setting land prices at the (generally

18. The best treatment of the elite agrarian reform debate, especially in the Quadros and Goulart eras, is found in Camargo, "A questão agrária," 168–224. See also Marta Cehelsky, *Land Reform in Brazil: The Management of Social Change* (Boulder, Colo.: Westview Press, 1979).

low) tax assessment value paid by property owners and allowing compensation to be paid in interest-gathering public bonds rather than cash. Given inflation and public debt, ULTAB activists argued, the government would never be able to afford cash payments at "just" rates. Moreover, government entry into the land market might set off an inflationary spiral of land speculation that could further damage reform efforts. These concessions to market forces and bourgeois rights may have strained the ideological framework of the Communists who ran ULTAB, but the PCB's commitment to coalition politics demanded such concessions.[19]

Within two weeks of his inauguration, two years to the day after the ULTAB conference, Goulart vaguely reflected the ULTAB line by hinting that constitutional modification would be required if congress failed to find in the constitution's "larger dimension of social conquest" the wherewithal to compose a meaningful agrarian reform statute, reflecting the "people's aspirations." Differing from ULTAB and Goulart, the Neves cabinet refrained from engaging the issue publicly, preferring a pragmatic stance in the face of traditional congressional hostility toward any reform more ambitious than technical and regulatory adjustments. Nonetheless, Neves joined the chorus of those who saw agrarian reform as a popular issue. "The integration of the man of the country to our national economy [is] one of the items of absolute priority in the agenda of the government."[20] In Neves's mouth, Vargas's vague approach to the problem of "the man of the country" took the place of Goulart's emphasis on agrarian reform.

In the early 1960s, such equivocation pleased few listeners. By this time, the dual challenges of enhancing agricultural productivity and improving rural workers' quality of life had blended into a single concern. The peasant league's honorary chairman, Francisco Julião, deserved much of the credit for this trend. He spoke of radical agrarian reform: land seizures by landless workers. The revolutionary nature of his position, along with the recent success of the Engenho Galiléia Peasant League, shifted the agrarian reform debate to the left. After Julião visited Cuba in 1960, he advocated the immediate distribution of land to those who worked it. The example of land expropriation in Pernambuco inspired him to propose this model as ideal

19. Evaristo Giovanetti Netto, *O PCB na Assembléia Constituinte de 1946* (São Paulo: Novos Rumos, 1986), 162–68; and "Carta sôbre a reforma agrária," *TL,* January 1960, 10.

20. "Discurso do President João Goulart por ocasião do 15 aniversário da constituição de 1946," *Jornal do Brasil,* 19 September 1961; and "Discurso do Primeiro-Ministro Tancredo Neves na câmara dos deputados para apresentar o plano de ação político-administrativo do govêrno," *Jornal do Brasil,* 29 September 1961, quoted in Camargo, "A questão agrária," 190.

for all Brazil. Where governments failed to respond to peasant demands for expropriation, he urged direct action. These choices gave birth to a phrase that became popular among militants: land distribution "by law or by force [na lei ou na marra]." Unlike PCB theorists, Julião—who was a member of the PSB—believed peasants and not industrial proletarians had the greatest potential to lead a people's revolution in Brazil. He distrusted the PCB's propensity to form alliances with the middle class, certain a properly organized peasant class would be strong enough to overthrow the bourgeois regime. In practice, however, most league organizations tried to work within the law, as did Julião. After all, he was a lawyer. As an elected state assemblyman (*deputado*) and (from 1962) federal congressman, he defended the legislature as Brazil's highest symbol of democratic process. Nevertheless, his fiery rhetoric earned him increasing attention from Brazilian and U.S. authorities, while his charisma and quasi-messianic style attracted the support of many desperate rural workers and squatters.[21]

One of the most touted conservative agrarian reform measures was the so-called "agrarian revision" put in place in São Paulo by Governor Carvalho Pinto and his secretary of agriculture, José Bonifácio Coutinho Nogueira, at the end of 1960. The reform proposal went through eight months of debate and modification. Although FARESP opposed its final passage, objecting to a progressive tax on uncultivated land, the new law satisfied many landlord interests. It not only conformed to constitutional article 141 but defined "just" payment as market price, requiring the state to pay for any improvements on the land as well as all costs related to the sale transaction. The progressive tax objected to by FARESP posed little threat to the vast majority of landowners, since only those owning four thousand or more

21. "Francisco Julião," transcript of interview by Aspásia Camargo, Yxcatepec, Mexico, December 1977, CPDOC/FGV—História Oral (hereafter Julião transcript); Julião, "Carta de emancipação," *Novos Rumos* (special supplement) (8–14 December 1961), 6–7; Medeiros, *História dos movimentos,* 54–56. Some of the decline in Julião's popularity can be traced to the ineffectiveness of his organizing strategy. Soon after land was expropriated on Engenho Galiléia, the American vice consul visited the site and reported a dismal scene, with government agronomists monitoring the movements of peasants and little productivity: "The members of the ligas, now being helped and led by the state, were losing their interest in the radical programs of their leaders." Moreover, the consul quoted Governor Sampaio as telling him, "'I was actually doing the owner a favor. The state worked out a way to purchase the farm from him, an old man whose children had deserted the Engenho for the luxury of city living. The plantation was bankrupt; the owner sick and tired after battling the league for years; and although the children—absentee landlords—objected, we really did them a favor.'" Edward T. Walters (Recife) to USDS, Despatch No. 9, "The Ligas of Pernambuco and Brazil," RG 59, DF 832.062/9-760, DS/USNA (2417).

hectares had to pay higher annual taxes at the 5 or 6 percent rate. A 1956 census showed that only 0.3 percent of landlords held property exceeding three thousand hectares, while nearly 95 percent of São Paulo's proprietors had holdings under 300 hectares. These owners would be subject to a 2 percent tax. The money would be used to purchase land for distribution to needy peasants. Decisions about these purchases and redistributions were to be made by the Agrarian Revision Council. No rural labor or peasant representative was invited to sit on the council, whereas the FARESP, SRB, and every other major landowner group in the state had the right to send a representative of their choosing. Naturally, the São Paulo–based ULTAB condemned the new law. When first proposed, however, *Terra Livre* published a summary of the draft legislation and asked readers to comment on it. Once the law was in place, tenants and squatters from the state's eastern seaboard to its western frontier reported that the law encouraged land speculators, who responded to its passage by driving residents off their lands. By 1961, *Terra Livre* described the law as a "trap" designed to "trick" peasants into believing the governor was on their side while really helping "land grabbers." [22]

The 1961 Belo Horizonte Congress

In November, the rural labor position on agrarian reform received unprecedented attention when more than fifteen hundred rural labor delegates gathered in Belo Horizonte, the capital of Minas Gerais state, to participate in the First National Congress of Farmers and Agrarian Laborers. Organized by ULTAB and held in a public building furnished by Governor José de Magalhães Pinto, the congress marked a transcendent moment in the long struggle of rural workers for political legitimacy. Here gathered hundreds of representatives of rural

22. An authoritative copy of the law is "A Revisão Agrária de São Paulo," *ASP* 8:4 (April 1961), 1–20. For the land census, see "Quadro II: Propriedades e divisão das áreas que ocupam—1956," *Revista Brasileira de Estudos Políticos,* reproduced in Moisés Vinhas, *Operários e camponeses na revolução brasileira* (São Paulo: Fulgor, 1963), 79. On FARESP and ULTAB opposition, see American Consul General (hereafter AmConGen), São Paulo, to USDS, "São Paulo Quarterly Review—Fourth Quarter 1960," Despatch No. 252, RG 59, DF 832.00/1-361, DS/USNA (2412); "Debate com urgência do projecto de lei sôbre loteamento de terras," *TL,* April 1960, 7; and "Camponeses desmascaram a 'Revisão Agrária' de Carvalho Pinto," *TL,* September 1961, 8. An incisive contemporary critique is Caio Prado Junior, "A reforma agrária e o momento nacional" (originally published in 1960), in *A questão agrária,* 4th ed. (São Paulo: Brasiliense, 1987), 126–41.

unions, rural worker associations, peasant leagues, student organizations, and Catholic Church groups from all over the country. Despite decades of speeches about attending the needs of the "man of the country," no president or senior official had ever faced an assembly of rural workers. This time, in Belo Horizonte, both President Goulart and Prime Minister Neves, as well as Governor Magalhães Pinto, made appearances. After the congress, as rural labor specialist Leonilde Medeiros stresses, "it was no longer possible to respond to the agrarian question with local measures" like São Paulo's agrarian revision or Pernambuco's Galiléia expropriation. After the congress, "profound transformations of the agrarian structure appeared to be an essential national development question." [23]

At the conference's conclusion on November 17, before a crowd estimated at seven thousand people, Goulart veered from his prepared text to acknowledge a proposal by Julião to amend the constitution. "On the one hand," said Goulart, "our constitution recognizes the social function of the land while, on the other, making expropriation for social interests impossible to apply in practice [due to market rate, cash payment demands]. To put an agrarian reform plan in place that really attends to peasant interests, we must, as Deputy Francisco Julião said a little while ago, seriously consider the reform of our constitution." In his prepared text, Goulart praised the rural labor movement, called the organization of rural laborers the "cornerstone of the democratic regime," and pledged himself to do everything possible "to transform [the delegates'] just demands into reality." In conclusion, he invited congress directors to visit him in the capital to discuss "the results of this memorable gathering of rural laborers." [24]

Leaders of the PCB-directed rural labor movement believed their actions in support of Goulart's inauguration—with rallies such as the one organized by Moraes—proved the movement's worth to officials

23. Medeiros, *História dos movimentos,* 60. Details on the conference can be found in a special twelve-page supplement of the PCB weekly, *Novos Rumos* (8–14 December 1961) (hereafter *NR*-ss); *TL*, November 1961; Nestor Vera, "O congresso camponês em Belo Horizonte," *Revista Brasiliense* 39 (January–February 1962), 94–99; José Chasin, "Contribuição para a análise da vanguarda política do campo," *Revista Brasiliense* 44 (November–December 1962), 102–29; Sigaud, "Congressos camponeses," 6–7; and Medeiros, *História dos movimentos,* 56–60. Reports on the number of delegates present vary between a head count of 1,038 for a single day's attendance (Chasin, 105) and general figures of 1,600 (*Novos Rumos*) and 1,800 (*Terra Livre*), a number undoubtedly exaggerated for political effect by the newspaper's headline writers. Although Chasin's head count was lower, he presented the higher number of "over 1,500 delegates" as accurate for the entire conference. Given the scientific nature of his analysis (discussed below), I accept it as a reasonable figure.
24. Goulart's speech is reproduced as "Reforma da constituição para a reforma agrária," *NR*-ss, 8.

and initiated a new era in the struggle for democracy. H. Sosthenes Jambo, executive director of *Terra Livre,* wrote, "The new stage, that was born in the overthrow of the recent coup by the people's struggle in defense of democratic legality, is well represented by the first national congress of peasants that forced Prime Minister Tancredo Neves to sink in his chair and cover his face with his hands under the weight of the responsibility he assumes for the forty million peasants there represented." Rural labor's mobilization on behalf of the constitutional succession process helped rural workers reach a new level of collaboration and incorporation with the state, Jambo argued. The congress itself reaffirmed this alliance, Julião later insisted, claiming that it had moved the president "to immediately decree rural unionization." Actually, Goulart did not formally "decree" rural unionization until he signed the ETR in March 1963, yet his government did quicken the pace of rural union recognition within a few months of the November 1961 congress. Thus, Goulart's transformation seems to have been more gradual than Jambo and Julião remembered. As time passed and Goulart's political position weakened, the president may have looked back on Belo Horizonte for inspiration, seeing an opportunity to turn this growing social movement into a political ally.[25]

Jambo's comments reveal his confidence in the power of rural worker militancy as an addition to discourse. The image of a balding Neves covering his face in sudden realization of the enormous challenge agrarian reform presented the government offers a vivid representation of the point. In the setting of the congress, rural laborers and their concerns swirled around Neves, enveloping him in an alternative worldview of discontent and struggle. In a series of tribunals, hundreds of workers gave testimony on their perspective of the reality of rural life across the nation's great expanse. Their stories of abuse, exploitation, infant mortality, hunger, and exhaustion contrasted dramatically with the paternal niceties of the planter clan. Dozens of commissions examined this testimony and proposed solutions, granting the complaints of the rural poor unprecedented legitimacy. It was almost as if the survey of rural workers entertained by the Vargas administration in 1942 had finally been conducted. But Jambo was wrong to think this web of evidence was strong enough to ensnare Neves. He left the conference as opposed to radical agrarian reform as he had been on his arrival. Seeing him slip through the

25. Sosthenes Jambo, "Uma nova etapa no process revolucionário brasileiro," *TL,* November 1961, 1; and Julião transcript, 124, 130–32.

net, *Terra Livre* turned on Neves, demanding his ouster and "substi-
tution by a democratic and popular cabinet, that represent neither
the interests of the reactionary bourgeoisie, nor the interests of the
latifúndio."[26]

The final declaration of the congress demonstrated considerable sophistication. Divided into three parts, it called for the "radical
transformation of the agrarian structure" and for "improvements in
the living and working conditions of the peasant masses," and it presented specific strategies for accomplishing these goals.[27] Most commentators have made much of the first item, arguing that it over-
shadowed the second and demonstrated the predominant influence
of Julião at the congress and his displacement of the PCB as leader of
the rural labor struggle. Medeiros has questioned the latter impression, arguing that the Belo Horizonte declaration on agrarian reform
"did not differ substantially from the proposals the Communist Party
had already advanced" at its 1959 conference. In both cases, radical
agrarian reform was defined by the elimination through expropriation of large private holdings of idle land (*latifúndio*) and the free distribution of these and unutilized public lands "to those who work it
[para os que nela trabalham]" and to landless peasants in general. As
in 1959, the Belo Horizonte declaration demanded a constitutional
amendment setting assessed value as the sales price of expropriated
land and allowing for payment in "long-term, low-interest treasury
notes." Although Julião does not seem to have significantly altered
the PCB line on agrarian reform, Medeiros does agree that pressure
from peasant league delegates ensured that the call for radical agrar-

26. Jambo, "Uma nova etapa," 1; and, against Neves, "Reforma agrária radical só com
govêrno popular e nacionalista," *TL,* November 1961, 2.
27. In outline, summary fashion, the declaration pledged the rural labor movement to
fight for the following: (I.) Radical transformation of the agrarian structure; (a) liquidation of
latifúndio; (b) maximization of laborers' access to land. (II.) Improvement of living and working
conditions for the peasant masses; (a) respect for independent, free, and democratic class organizations; (b) extension of existing labor laws to rural workers and the elaboration of a specific
rural labor statute; (c) guarantee of union liberty and immediate recognition of existing associations; (d) provision of economic assistance to peasants. (III.) Achievement of radical agrarian
reform through a joint strategy; (a) modify article 141, paragraph 16 of the 1946 constitution;
(b) conduct a census of all properties larger than 500 hectares; (c) expropriate unutilized land on
properties larger than 500 hectares, starting with those nearest urban areas and transportation
routes; (d) compensate expropriated owners with long-term, low-interest treasury notes, buying
land at a price established by its declared taxable value; (e) conduct a census of all unclaimed
public land; (f) revert all untitled land to public possession; (g) introduce a progressive territorial
tax, exempting smallholders; (h) regulate land sales and rents; (i) freely distribute unclaimed
public land; (j) prohibit land speculation on distributed lands; (k) grant titles to squatters and
defend them from land-grabbers; and (l) establish peasant cooperatives. From "Reforma agrária
radical com destruição do latifúndio," *NR*-ss, 3–4.

ian reform "filled the bulk" of the declaration and kept demands for incremental measures and *trabalhista* reforms to a minimum.[28]

It is true that three-fifths of the document deals with agrarian reform, but more than half of this discussion is on strategy, much of it devoted to reformist steps that could be immediately put in place. Two-fifths consists of specific demands for "organizational liberty," the extension of labor laws to rural workers, the composition of a rural labor law, recognition of existing rural labor organizations, and other reformist measures intended to enhance the rural labor movement. Sitting shoulder to shoulder with Julião, ULTAB's newly elected secretary, Nestor Vera, closed the conference by stating, "We judge it necessary to pledge unwavering struggle for the conquest of all the partial measures, as small as they might seem to be, not only because they open the way to achieving complete and radical agrarian reform, but also because they bring improvements to the terrible conditions of life and work that the great mass of country laborers presently face." Vera's speech does not provide evidence for the assertion of sociologist Fernando Antônio Azevêdo that the league "managed to take charge of the closing plenary, routing the proposals elaborated by the PCB."[29]

What is most inaccurate in scholarly writing on the subject is the impression of the congress as a boxing ring for an ULTAB versus *liga* match, the "authentic peasants' bickering would-be leaders," as historian John W . F. Dulles put it. There were philosophical and tactical differences between the leagues and the Communists, such as the debate over whether peasants or proletarians were the ideal revolutionary vanguard, but the remarkable thing is how collegial the left was in discussing these issues, and in doing so publicly.[30] Nevertheless, scholars resurrected the match concept years later, apparently under the impression that it revealed insights about the failure of the

28. "Reforma agrária radical"; and Medeiros, *História dos movimentos,* 59.

29. Nestor Vera, "Mobilizar, esclarecer, e organizar as massas camponesas," *TL,* November 1961, 8; Azevêdo, *As ligas camponesas,* 90.

30. Dulles, *Unrest in Brazil,* 161. In a contrasting show of solidarity and exchange, both PCB papers, *Novos Rumos* and *Terra Livre,* regularly published articles by and about Julião and the peasant leagues. See, for example, Julião, "Organização dos assalariados agrícolas nova etapa das ligas camponesas," *NR,* 15–21 December 1961, 8; Giocando Dias, "Francisco Julião: Os Comunistas e a revolução brasileira," *TL,* August 1962, supplement; and Julião's reply, "Giocondo Dias, os Comunistas, e a revolução brasileira," *NR,* 10–16 August 1962, 3. Cooperation extended from the abstract to the concrete. In March 1962, for example, Silva and other PCB leaders joined Julião in celebrating the opening of a *liga* office in São Paulo. See "Ligas Camponeses Come to São Paulo," in AmConGen to USDS, "Weekly Summary No. 14," Despatch No. 334, RG 59, DF 732.00/4-462 (1577), DS/USNA.

left to prevent the military *golpe* of 1964. The philosopher Marilena Chaui, for instance, sees Vera and Julião fighting to make their differing representations of the congress prevail as ultimately destructive gestures. Given the pro-labor sympathies of analysts such as Chaui and Azevêdo, it is worth noting that their representation of the congress as a battleground mirrors the negative image the movement's enemies advocated. In December 1961, for example, a U.S. embassy official wrote Washington about the congress using the following language: "Francisco Julião played a prominent role at the Congress, but he had competition from Lindolfo Silva, president of the Communist-controlled ULTAB." Yet, in the very same dispatch the official noted that a special congress supplement of the PCB weekly *Novos Rumos* "devotes as much space to ULTAB as to Julião." Critics seemed incapable of recognizing the congress's spectacular success at bringing together for the first time "all the currents in Brazil that were interested in agrarian reform," as Julião later remarked. At the final plenary, Julião expressed his confidence that radical agrarian reform would soon be put in place, now that "the most humble and exploited of the fatherland, the peasant without land, [had] come face to face with the highest powers of the Republic." The evidence shows Julião, Silva, and many others ending the congress embracing unity. "The peasants are united from the north to the south until the final victory against the *latifúndio,*" said Silva during the closing ceremony.[31]

The more significant disagreement revealed at the congress is not to be found among groups vying for leadership of the rural labor movement—all of whom proved perfectly capable of engaging the give and take of intellectual combat—but between leaders and followers, between rural worker delegates and the Communist, socialist, governmental, and religious chiefs of the congress. In this regard, *Terra Livre*'s Jambo provides a succinct statement of the main image ULTAB leaders hoped the congress conveyed: "The disposition to struggle and the political consciousness demonstrated by the delegates of rural Brazilian men, shoulder to shoulder with working-class leaders and students, and the support of a broad range of progressives, initiated in Belo Horizonte a new stage in the democratic process in which the people discuss their problems, deliberate over them,

31. Marilena Chaui, *Seminários*, 2d ed. (São Paulo: Brasiliense, 1982), 68–73; Harry Weiner (Second Secretary, AmEmbassy, Rio de Janeiro) to USDS, "First National Congress of Farmers and Agricultural Workers," Despatch No. 495, RG 59, DF 832.062/12-1961, DS/USNA (2417); Julião transcript, 133; and Lindolfo Silva, "Camponeses estão unidos de norte a sul até a vitória final contra o latifúndio," *TL*, November 1961, 7. A good part of Chaui's confusion about the significance of the congress comes from mistakenly dating it as occurring in November 1962 rather than 1961.

From 1959 to 1964, Jofre Correa Neto (center) enjoyed notoriety as a peasant organizer in São Paulo, especially after he was shot during a struggle in Santa Fé do Sul. He worked closely with Lindolfo Silva (to Jofre's right), the PCB's leading rural worker advocate. On 28 December 1960, Silva led the delegation of rural and urban workers shown here on a well-publicized campaign to win Jofre's release from the Mirassol, SP, jail. Three days later, he was free. Photo: courtesy Arquivo Fotográfico da *Última Hora* from Arquivo do Estado de São Paulo

and force the government to respond to the demands of the great mass of Brazilians." Jambo alleges that the congress's final declaration came about in a bottom-up fashion, with delegates expressing their concerns and concocting measures to resolve them. As mentioned above, delegates had a chance to articulate their problems in a series of "tribunals"; subsequently, "commissions" analyzed the data. It is the last step—the process of building the declaration from the evidence—that lacks support in the record. On the same page where Jambo's article appeared, another story contradicts his narrative of a bottom-up process by claiming that the final declaration was "based on theses presented by ULTAB." Moreover, a survey of congress participants showed little direct correlation between the declaration and delegate concerns.[32]

The survey, conducted during the Belo Horizonte congress by José and Hanna P. Chasin, offers a revealing glimpse of the event from

32. Jambo, "Uma nova etapa," 1; "1,800 delegados camponeses exigiram em Belo Horizonte a reforma agrária," *TL*, November 1961, 1; and Chasin, "Contribuição para a análise."

the perspective of its rural labor participants. The Chasins were members of a São Paulo student group linked to the PCB. Called the Centro Popular de Cultura, it reminds one of New Left activist organizations such as Students for a Democratic Society in the United States. The Chasins and others pursued two projects in Belo Horizonte. One was to perform a play based on the a dramatic confrontation between tenants and authorities in Santa Fé do Sul, São Paulo; the other was to conduct an opinion and background analysis of the "political vanguard of the country." The survey stands without equal in the documentary record of the early Brazilian rural labor movement. Although the authors apologize for the survey's faults as a scientific study, their very acknowledgment of these difficulties gives readers the contextual information needed to extract a portrait of rural labor leaders from fifteen different states and varied occupations. Although nearly 10 percent (120) of the 1,500 delegates were interviewed, the Chasins felt that only 90 were reliable, so the results are based on interviews conducted with 90 delegates on 16 September 1961.[33]

The Chasins found that 92 percent of this group worked in agriculture, with only 14 percent owning their own land. Of those interviewed, 34 percent were wage workers, 28 percent tenants, and 31 percent earned their living through some sort of sharecropping. Based on their findings, the Chasins offered a preliminary sketch of the rural labor vanguard. Most worked more than ten hours a day and earned less than half the minimum wage. Most were men in their forties, married to women in their thirties, with an average of seven children. Three-quarters were literate, though little educated, and this same percentage were registered voters. Although the Belo Horizonte congress was called the first such meeting, the Chasins found that their ninety subjects tended to have considerable experience in the rural labor struggle. Around thirty of the fifty delegates interviewed from the central and southeastern states, including São Paulo and Minas Gerais, claimed to have had more than five years of experience as militants. Out of ninety interviewed, only twenty-seven were newcomers with less than a year's experience, while half had been activists for five or more years. Despite the relatively high level of past involvement, only half of these delegates described them-

33. The center and its publication *Cadernos do Povo Brasileiro* are the main subjects of the Chaui essay criticized earlier. The essay is not, as she admits, a social or political history of the era but a discursive analysis of the period in which she tries not to "attribute to the past a sense that it, while it was present, did not have." In this context, she was accurate in preserving the rivalry perspective then generated by opponents of the movement. *Seminários*, 11–12.

selves as officials of rural labor organizations. One comes away from the Chasin survey impressed by its demonstration of the maturity, experience, and occupational fit of most delegates.

The collective biography offered by the survey provides a frame of reference for a second group of figures regarding the steps delegates saw as necessary to "immediately correct the situation in rural areas." This group of responses offers a challenge to Jambo's contention that the proceedings unfolded in a democratic manner. The survey shows fifty-eight of ninety informants listing "agrarian reform" as their top priority. Although this is consistent with the congress's final declaration, such a measure was on everyone's lips. In fact, a common name for the conference was the Agrarian Reform Congress. More revealing is a second group of numbers reflecting what some of these informants meant by reform. Only sixteen of ninety defined agrarian reform as "obtaining land and making use of abandoned and untitled land," a phrasing generally consistent with radical agrarian reform. As noted above, the attack on "*latifundiários*" and "imperialists" was crucial to the perspectives of ULTAB and *liga* leaders. Yet only four delegates mentioned abolishing the *latifúndio* and land ownership by foreigners. Informants made slight mention of another priority of the declaration: the right to organize. "Promoting the unity of the man of the country and joining the struggle for their demands" was mentioned thirteen times, Chasin reports. "Forming cooperatives" was mentioned by nine delegates. But "unionization" came up only three times, and only one delegate believed "holding new peasant congresses" would help change rural life. Among the least frequently mentioned measures was "making revolution" (three times), "obtaining the right to vote" (one time), and "creating female departments within class associations" (one time). In other words, only a minority of those delegates interviewed articulated demands like those central to the congress's concluding declaration.

One demand for which there was considerable support—government assistance—received far less attention in the congress declaration. The survey showed forty-three informants naming some form of governmental technical, financial, educational, or legal assistance as important goals for the rural labor movement. For many interviewees, assistance was concrete, recognizable, and practical. It was also consistent with paternalist cultural norms and decades of corporatist practice. Another question showed how most informants believed that providing assistance was and should be a top priority of existing rural labor organizations. While support for organization did not rise to the surface as an "immediate measure," the delegates had specific ideas about what "the peasant movement could do to transform the countryside." In this case, thirty-one of the ninety informants placed an emphasis on "uniting the laborers of the country," while another eleven thought "organizing class associations" was most important. Here again, a relatively large number—twenty-seven of ninety—felt the movement should emphasize government implementation of their demands. In this regard, Chasin notes some regional trends, with delegates from the north and northeast stressing assistance and those from the south and east (including São Paulo, Paraná, and Minas Gerais) emphasizing autonomous demands, such as the right to organize. All in all, there is little support in this survey for either the general or specific measures of the Belo Horizonte declaration.

The question of leadership has puzzled students of the Brazilian rural labor movement. It also vexed contemporary activists. Jambo and the PCB believed that "working-class leaders" were necessary; Julião and the church, as we will see, believed "natural leaders" of peasant background were best suited to the task. To the contrary, argued a Dutch social scientist in a contemporary analysis, the most decisive factor in explaining the actions of Brazilian rural labor organizations was not the class background of its leaders but their ability to manipulate a network of connections to local, state, and federal sources of power. A study of the movement from 1964 to 1985 corroborates this view, listing external connections as one of five key factors determining the nature of a rural labor organization. It is not who the leader is but his or her network of connections and what these connections can accomplish, they say. This point of view seems to fit the situation in Belo Horizonte. For most of the delegates interviewed, pragmatic and concrete measures held more interest than lofty goals. Nevertheless, they showed considerable interest in developing a relationship with the industrial working class and students. Both groups could benefit the rural labor movement by uniting with peasants and lending support. What kind of support? According to Chasin, the peasants most wanted political education from urban workers and intellectual education ("the clarification and propagation of ideas") from students such as Chasin himself. Thus, perhaps the evident distance between leaders and followers is less troubling than first thought. The delegates seem to have accepted the idea that congress leaders had a better idea of the exact measures needed to accomplish common goals. This is the way political work proceeds: sometimes leaders get too far ahead of followers, sometimes they fall behind, sometimes their goals conflict, sometimes they fail to listen, and sometimes the two work well together. The Belo Horizonte congress seems to be an example of the latter two syndromes.[34]

Reactions to the Belo Horizonte Congress

President Goulart left Belo Horizonte impressed with the leadership displayed there by Julião. At the conclusion of his speech, he publicly invited Julião and other congress directors to meet with him. In December, as Julião recalls, Neves invited to Brasília a commission including Julião and at least two other key organizers of the congress: Padre Francisco Pessoa Laje, of Minas Gerais, and José Porfírio da Paz, an influential peasant leader who in 1957, with PCB help, had managed to create the ten-thousand-square-kilometer Trombas e Formosa peasant domain within the state of Goiás. After a group conversation with Neves regarding the conclusions of the congress, Julião met privately with Goulart at the presidential residence, Granja do Torto. At the meeting, as Julião recalls it, the two men discussed agrarian reform, politics, and unionization. Goulart wanted Julião to assist him in forming an alliance—between the Socialist and Labor Parties—to help elect sympathetic legislators to congress in the November 1962 elections. But no commitments were made, and Julião says that although the idea of joining others appealed to him, he realized that Goulart's goals were fundamentally different from his own. Goulart was not a Socialist, and his idea of agrarian reform was much more limited than Julião's. Julião supported wide expropriation and land distribution, whereas Goulart "wanted fiscal reform and more democratic relations between peasants and landlords, and moderate land distribution in areas of conflict." Julião believed that Goulart wanted him to follow the president's directives, to help his political plans, in exchange for transforming the leagues into unions and using them to distribute government assistance. But Julião rejected this step, fearing he would become a government lackey (a *pelego*) and abandon the larger cause of radical agrarian reform.[35]

34. Galjart, "Class and 'Following' in Rural Brazil," 3–23; and Biorn Maybury-Lewis, *The Politics of the Possible: The Brazilian Rural Workers' Trade Union Movement, 1964–1985* (Philadelphia: Temple University Press, 1994).

35. At the time, journalist Antônio Callado reported of Julião that João Goulart "wanted to transform him into a rural *pelego*," but that Julião had refused. Later, Julião offered this elaboration: "I saw the union movement as substantially controled and what I most feared was just this, that this phenomenon of *peleguismo* might spread to the country, falling into the middle of the great peasant mass that so desperately needed land. This was my fear, my reason for distancing myself from Jango." Callado, *Tempo de Arraes*, 85–86; and Julião transcript, 142.

This was a crucial meeting in the history of the Brazilian rural labor movement. Communist militants were willing to compromise with Goulart, to accept half measures in hopes of achieving more profound change in the future. Church militants like Padre Laje were similarly inclined; however, more conservative Catholics, as we will see, found some of Goulart's measures too radical for their taste. On the other hand, Julião's attachment to his principles set off a series of conflicts with Goulart's broad network of allies. Although Julião won election to the congress later that year, his political star had already begun to fade. The tactical debates he had with ULTAB and PCB strategists like Giocondo Dias were a sign of this struggle to either pull Julião into the fold or isolate him. Influenced by the government's new willingness to recognize rural unions, the center of struggle gradually shifted away from Julião's concerns and toward the regimentation of rural workers under a hierarchical system of unions, federations, and a national confederation, each tied to the Ministry of Labor. The consequences were disastrous for the peasant leagues. While maintaining his distance from the corrupting influences of politics and the bureaucracy, Julião proved himself a leader too principled to do his followers much good. In his unwillingness to compromise, he became irrelevant to the rural labor struggle by 1963.[36]

All of these events caught the attention of the rural owning class. As Goulart and rural delegates in Belo Horizonte made front-page news of agrarian reform, the planters scheduled their own national congress. Gathered together in the associational structure the SRB condemned as fascist when first decreed by Vargas in 1945 (No. 8,127), landlords were, by 1962, better organized and more homogenous in their views then ever before. On January 24 and 25, the CRB held the landlord's sixth national conference in Rio de Janeiro. In the words of CRB president Iris Meinberg, the conference had the "singular objective" of making the public and government officials aware of the views of "the Classes directly responsible for the so-called primary production of the country." In a veiled reference to the rural labor congress, he criticized the "purely demagogic use"

36. A key event in the process of isolating Julião was the April 1962 murder of a peasant league leader named João Pedro Teixeira in the state of Paraíba. Goulart attended a protest rally to condemn the killing, carried out to suppress the league by a landlord's gunman. Since Julião would not compromise with the administration, the government used the occasion to enhance the position of Communist militants in and around the movement. See Bernardete Wrublevski Aued, *A vitória dos vencidos (Partido Comunista Brasileiro—PCB—e Ligas Camponesas, 1955-64)* (Florianópolis: Editora da UFSC, 1986), 51-72; and Vilma Keller and César Benjamim, "Julião, Francisco," in Beloch and Abreu, eds., *DHBB*, 1659-60.

Labor minister Franco Montoro (center) meets with union leaders in September 1961. Montoro favored Catholic organizers when he opened the door to rural labor union recognition in June 1962. Photo: courtesy Arquivo Fotográfico da *Última Hora* from Arquivo do Estado de São Paulo

to which "the highly emotional content" of agrarian reform had recently been put. He nevertheless pledged the CRB to support agrarian reform so long as it was carefully planned and expropriated property owners appropriately compensated. As an example, he endorsed São Paulo's agrarian revision, especially its prudent implementation— "preventing the annual creation of one thousand smallholders, since such a move would generate elevated costs of a million cruzeiros." In contrast to the Belo Horizonte declaration, Meinberg upheld the 1946 constitution and insisted it needed no amendment. In a concession to the times that recalled the maneuvers of the SRB in Vargas's day, Meinberg also declared the CRB "entirely favorable to the syndicalization of the country laborer." Rural unionization like urban unionization, said Meinberg, "will be a powerful instrument of social peace." In contrast, the rural labor declaration had emphasized independent and autonomous rural unions as a source of liberation for rural workers. In another contradistinction, Meinberg rejected the idea of extending CLT provisions to the countryside, recommending instead the creation of a body of law specifically attuned to the peculiarities and complexities of Brazilian rural life. In the published proceedings of the conference, a number of regional landlord representatives—including FARESP president Clovis de Salles Santos—offered similar remarks.

President Goulart's address at the conclusion of the CRB conference skillfully capitalized on the planters' profession of support for these two major reforms. Not unlike John F. Kennedy, he congratulated his audience "for thinking more of your country than your immediate personal interests." The best agrarian reform, he alleged, was a rational exploitation of agriculture that engendered growth and uplifted the laborer with better wages and conditions. While skirting the sensitive issue of constitutional modification, he emphasized how thoroughly a "literal reading" of the law would trammel meaningful land redistribution. "To expropriate just 10 percent of the land would cost nearly two trillion cruzeiros." Although the land question remained a touchy one, Goulart sensed the consensus building around rural unionization. "To obtain these laws, that I hope to see put in place during my term in office, we can already count on the valiant contributions of our nation's farm leaders and on the good will, so often made manifest, of rural laborers." For him, as for the planters, rural unionization was a way to "regiment" agricultural workers. It would enable the state to "discipline" rural labor relations and would be "one more instrument of effective social peace."[37]

In February, the Neves cabinet began in earnest to debate agrarian reform proposals. As expected, constitutional amendments received much attention. Some ministers supported modifications akin to those proposed in Belo Horizonte. But consensus built around amending another constitutional article—that referring to a rural land tax (*imposto territorial*). Under the 1946 constitution, the tax went to support municipal governments; under the proposal of agricultural minister Armando Monteiro Filho, a well-known northeastern sugar mill owner, the money would be collected by the federal government and used to pay for expropriated land. To administer the funds and the entire agrarian reform agenda in general, a new agency was to be established: the Superintendência da Política Agrária (SUPRA). In this context, labor minister André Franco Montoro, the São Paulo–based leader of the PDC, proposed issuing regulations that would finally activate both the rural unionization law decreed by Vargas in 1944 (No. 7.038) and administrative support for Bill No. 94/61, a comprehensive rural labor law then under consideration by the congress.

37. Iris Meinberg, "Discurso," in *A Reforma agrária na VI Conferência Rural* (Rio de Janeiro: Ministério da Agricultura, Serviço de Informação Agrícola, 1962), 25–33. Six additional speeches and Goulart's address (9–14) are reproduced in this volume.

Lindolfo Silva saw Montoro's proposal to issue new regulations as disingenuous given the fact that regulations needed to implement Decree Law No. 7,038 had been issued in March 1945. "The minister's decision smells like another capitulation to the *fazendeiros*," Silva wrote. "What the workers want is IMMEDIATE recognition of their unions." Even the cabinet's mild proposals ran into significant congressional resistance, however. It would take continued pressure from mobilized rural workers and their leadership networks to hasten the process and turn plans and proposals into concrete actions.[38]

In São Paulo, as in other states, the pace of rural labor mobilization picked up considerably after the Belo Horizonte congress. In 1962, dozens of new rural labor associations were founded, many intended to convert to official rural unions. Around the country, different vanguard organizations took command of the movement. In São Paulo, ULTAB quickly established a leading presence; in Minas Gerais, Catholic activists succeeded in forming most of the incipient unions; and in Rio Grande do Sul, Governor Brizola backed the Landless Farmers' Movement (MASTER, Movimento dos Agricultores Sem Terra), giving it the upper hand. As the likelihood of formal recognition grew, competition for the hearts and minds of rural workers *and* the support of state and federal labor apparatuses intensified. While the peasant leagues spread south from the northeast into Rio de Janeiro, São Paulo, and Paraná, their strongest base of support remained in Pernambuco. As Julião's star waned, and peasants lost this interlocutor to the corridors of power, the influence of the leagues declined in relation to that of Communist- and Catholic-connected groups. The church soon established itself as the richest, best organized, and most effective of the competitors. Driven by anticommunist ideology and Christian social doctrine dating from the nineteenth century, it aggressively confronted the leagues, ULTAB, and MASTER. In states such as São Paulo, where the Communists had historically been most active, the Catholic Church stimulated a period of intense rivalry.[39]

38. Camargo, "A questão agrária," 158–71, 194–201, details the debate among ministers and legislators. For further background information, see also Segadas Vianna, *O Estatuto do Trabalhador Rural;* Mozart Victor Russomano, *Comentários ao Estatuto do Trabalhador Rural,* 2 vols., 2d ed. (São Paulo: Revista dos Tribunais, 1969), 3–14; and Price, "Rural Unionization in Brazil," 8–12. SUPRA was commonly known as the Superintendência da Reforma Agrária, but the law establishing the agency, issued in October, called it the Superintendência da Política Agrária (SUPRA). See below and Chapter 8. ULTAB knowledge and reaction to these developments is reported in Silva, "Querem dar um golpe contra a sindicalização rural" and "Reconhecimento dos sindicatos rurais," *TL,* February 1962, 2, 6.

39. A summary of the national context can be found in Medeiros, *História dos movimentos,* 75–79.

Catholic Rural Labor Activism

In the Alta Mogiana, the activist church came in the person of Padre Celso Ibson de Syllos. From the Belo Horizonte congress until Padre Celso arrived early in 1962, the region's top militant—Irineu Luís de Moraes—had shifted the focus of his activities from protest rallies to quiet organization. In the agricultural sector, the best time for workers to act was always at harvest time. In sugar, in the state of São Paulo, this period ran from June through September. In coffee, the harvest season was longer, starting in March or April and running through September. In both sectors, the need for harvest labor peaked in July and August. As sugar workers knew, the best time to make demands was just when the cane was tall, mature, and ready to cut. If cutting did not proceed then, the syrup trapped inside the stalks would begin to spoil, decreasing the value of the crop with every passing hour. Similar crucial moments existed in coffee harvesting. If the cherries were not picked when ripe, trees reduced rather than augmented fruit production, diminishing the quantity of future crop yields.[40] The months of October through April presented few opportunities for effective strikes and other labor actions, but this did not mean rural organizing had to come to a complete halt. In fact, Moraes was busy building support for a March rally to demand payment of minimum wages on Sertãozinho, Pontal, and Barretos sugar plantations when he first heard about Padre Celso.[41]

In early February, Padre Celso returned to Ribeirão Preto after an absence of eighteen months. Born in 1929, the priest was a native of the Paulista interior, one of nine surviving children born to two primary school teachers in São José do Rio Pardo. Influenced by an older brother, Padre Celso entered the seminary located in Campinas, São Paulo, when he was fourteen years old. At twenty-five, he became a parish priest in Ribeirão Preto, but the provincial archbishop, Dom Luís de Amaral Mousinho, had other plans for the bright and compulsive young man. In August 1956, Dom Luís assigned Padre Celso to work on *Diário de Notícias,* the daily newspaper of the archdiocese. Named editor in December, Padre Celso's tenure brought a noticeable shift in the focus of the paper. Long the repository of family news and religious propaganda, with front-page stories on Nossa Senhora

40. "Estudo de 33 propriedades tipicas do estado de São Paulo," *ASP* 9:8 (August 1962), 10–11; and FAO et al., "Estudo de 33 propriedades cafeeiras," 66–67.
41. On Moraes's activities in this period, see "Pontal: Usinas de açucar não pagam salário mínimo aos trabalhadores," *TL,* January 1962, 7; and "Camponesas de Barretos vão lutar para não morrer de fome," *TL,* February 1962, 1.

Aparecida, Brazil's patron saint, and back-page items on knitting and other homemaking crafts, the paper gradually began to cover local news and advocate greater public awareness and responsibility for the affairs of the day. In his New Year's Day editorial of 1959, Padre Celso proudly wrote, "during 1958, *DN* [*Diário de Notícias*] struggled shoulder to shoulder with Ribeirão Preto workers, defending their just causes." Starting in 1959, Padre Celso expanded the coverage of the paper to world events, with special attention given to the Cuban revolution. In 1961 he went to Europe, where he received intensive training in union-organizing techniques, journalism, propaganda, and Marxism at the Gregorian University in Rome and labor schools in West Germany.[42]

During his absence, *Diário de Notícias* continued, under the direction of Padre Angélico Sandalo Bernardino and with the clear blessings of Dom Luís, to take the side of the oppressed. But it was the reappearance of Padre Celso that moved the diocese from advocacy journalism to political agitation. "We will struggle with all our forces for social justice," editorialized Padre Celso upon retaking the helm of *Diário de Notícias* in February 1962. "We will do everything," he continued, "to be on the front line, commanding campaigns, decisively collaborating for the solidification of populist and Christian theses." Central to these doctrines were the political education and unionization of rural workers. "The Catholic Church became afraid [of the influence of the peasant leagues and the Communists on *camponeses*] and there began a reaction of [union] formation," the bespectacled former priest explained some twenty-five years later. "The church began to have an influence among the *camponeses*."[43]

Following the rise of the peasant leagues in Pernambuco, church officials in the nearby state of Rio Grande do Norte started a rural unionization team in 1960. The team's ability to prevent the spread of the leagues in Rio Grande do Norte inspired church officials in Paraná, where the leagues began to appear, and Rio Grande do Sul, where MASTER stimulated rural class conflict, to organize "agrarian fronts" (*frentes agrárias*) in August 1961. With growing agitation for agrarian reform and increased Communist activism in the country-

---

42. Syllos transcript, 1–3; "P. Celso Retorna ao Brasil," *Diário de Notícias* (hereafter *DN*), 27 January 1962, 6; and "O ex-padre Celso lembra sua experiência jornalistica," *Jornal de Ribeirão*, 21–27 August 1988, 9. Editorial, *DN*, 1 January 1959, 2. By early 1962, the paper had decided to condemn the Cuban government in a mock, educational tribunal in which Padre Celso served as prosecutor. See "Tribunal julgou problema cubano," *DN*, 15 February 1962, 6.

43. See the useful, concise history of *DN* in "Um jovem padre muda a feição do jornal" and "Apesar dos pesares, chega-se ao fim 63," *Jornal de Ribeirão*, 21–27 August 1988, 3. Editorial, *DN*, 6 February 1962, 2. On Julião and Padre Celso's training, see Syllos transcript, 3.

side, the central commission of the National Conference of Brazilian Bishops (CNBB, Conferência Nacional dos Bispos Brasileiros) met in Rio de Janeiro on October 5 and issued a declaration urging the formation of a national network of *frentes agrárias*. In a veiled reference to Communists, the bishops said it was proper for these organizations' rural unionization campaigns to be "extended to all rural centers, above all when just demands are agitated by those with hidden intentions." With a few exceptions, the church's campaign led to the formation of rural labor associations that easily accommodated employer interests. Typically, priests began to organize these unions-information by contacting local planters, asking them to select likely participants from their labor force and to subsidize worker social services. For most priests and Catholic laymen, the practice fit Catholic ideology, with its rejection of class struggle and emphasis on community.[44] In São Paulo, a scenario like this preceded Padre Celso's return, setting the stage on which his unique brand of militancy would later appear.

In the context of ULTAB's upcoming Belo Horizonte congress, the church moved quickly to establish a presence in the São Paulo interior. In September and October 1961, the church's São Paulo State Federation of Workers Circles (FECOESP, Federação de Círculos Operários do Estado de São Paulo) founded rural laborer associations in seven cities, including Presidente Prudente, Marília, and São José do Rio Preto—all settings of significant ULTAB activism. Presiding over the federation was José Rotta, a former merchant from Presidente Prudente who later collaborated with the military regime that ousted Goulart. On November 9, Rotta founded the São Paulo State Federation of Rural Laborers and Others (FTRSESP, Federação dos Trabalhadores Rurais e Similares do Estado de São Paulo), becoming its president. The next day, a long-planned, preannounced ULTAB conference of 189 São Paulo rural labor organization delegates met to

44. CNBB quoted from "A igreja e a situação do meio rural brasileiro: Declarações da Comissão Nacional dos Bispos do Brasil," *DN,* 14 November 1962, 2. On the agrarian fronts, see AmConsul, Curitiba to USDS, "Rural Workers in Paraná," Despacho No. D-14, RG 59, DF 832.062/8-3061 (2417); and AmConsul, Porto Alegre, to USDS, "Establishment of Local Agrarian Front," Despacho No. 50, RG 59, DF 832.401/3-0262 (1577), both DS/USNA. Underscoring the confrontational nature of the church's efforts, the Curitiba consul wrote, "When it became evident that the [league-ULTAB] Congress of Paraná Rural Workers would, in fact, be held, the Catholic bishops of four of the largest cities in northern Paraná decided to create a rural organization of their own, and to bring the organization into existence at the same time and in the same place that the [congress] was being held [Maringá, 12–15 August 1961]." A useful chronology of national events is Abdias Vilar de Carvalho, "Cronologia dos fatos da igreja católica no meio rural," in *Igreja e questão agrária,* edited by Vanilda Paiva (São Paulo: Loyola, 1985), 104–9. See also Carvalho's essay on the period, "A igreja católica e a questão agrária," esp. 92–101.

elect representatives for Belo Horizonte and to found the São Paulo State Federation of Agrarian Laborers' Associations (FATAESP, Federação de Associações de Trabalhadores Agrícolas do Estado de São Paulo), with José Alves Portela as president and Irineu Luís de Moraes as secretary. Neither federation had any legal standing, but they did improve the position of both Catholics and Communists in the rivalry for eventual recognition. On November 14, the day before the Belo Horizonte congress, Rotta traveled to Ribeirão Preto to found the Professional Association of Rural Laborers. The founding ceremony, held in a public amphitheater, featured speakers such as the mayor, city councilmen, the planters' association leader, the head of the merchants and industrialists' association, and a few industrial union leaders. Workers and a "great number of planters" from Sertãozinho, São Joaquim da Barra, Franca, Brodósqui, Batatais, and other Alta Mogiana towns were also present. As a story of the event explains, the new association's bylaws were "read aloud and approved by the assembly without discussion." Councilman Said Issa Halah, the lawyer of ULTAB's as yet unofficial local rural labor union, asked to address the crowd, but "Rotta denied him a chance to speak due to the late hour."[45]

In December, the two groups came into conflict when the Usina Perdigão, located near Ribeirão Preto, went bankrupt owing six months of back pay to more than two hundred field and mill workers. While ULTAB and foodworker president Tenório de Lima called for expropriating the *usina* and giving it to workers, the church's rural association lawyer, Edmur Gonçalves de Oliveira, joined with Padre Angelo Pino and planter leaders to form the Christian Social Front

45. On the Catholic FTRSESP, see Araguaya Feitosa Martins, "Alguns aspectos da inquietação trabalhista no campo," *Revista Brasiliense* 40 (March/April 1962), 132–41. Regarding ULTAB's FATAESP, see "Federação das associações de campo é o proximo passo dos lavradores," *TL*, October 1961, 3; and "Conferência de lavradores paulistas propõe desapropriação da grande propriedade agrícola: Interêsse social," *TL*, December 1961, 6. The Ribeirão Preto founding event is reported in "Trabalhadores rurais se unem para conquista da justiça," *DN*, 14 November 1961, 1. The timing of these events and articles sharply contradict the allegation of political scientist Neale J. Pearson, who claimed that Julião and Silva planned the Belo Horizonte congress as a response to the success of Catholic organizing efforts. Just the opposite was true. Pearson conducted an impressive amount of research in Brazil in 1965, soon after the military coup, when the conservative Rotta had taken over the national movement. While Pearson's dissertation is extremely valuable, it is tainted by the context of the time—the repression that made contact with ULTAB activists and documents impossible and necessitated his dependency on Rotta and other conservative informants. One of these informants told him that Portela had no rural background but was a "stevedore in Rio de Janeiro" and that Rotta's federation was the only one with "direct access to the State Assembly," because Rotta had been elected an "alternate" in 1962. Deputy Luciano Lepera, among others, gave ULTAB and its organizations far more direct representation in the assembly. Neale J. Pearson, "Small Farmer and Rural Worker Pressure Groups in Brazil" (Ph.D. diss., University of Florida, 1967), 245–65.

President João Goulart (right foreground) tried to preserve Vargas's populist republic by building a political base among rural workers. In the 1963 May Day speech depicted here, Goulart told an assembly of industrial unionists that "a country's social peace can no longer be constructed on the misery of the working class and much less on crushing the rural class." Photo: courtesy Arquivo Fotográfico da *Última Hora* from Arquivo do Estado de São Paulo

(FSC, Frente Social Cristão). Foodworker attorney Ibiapaba Martins, who participated in the negotiations, marveled at the willingness of Padre Angelo to provide moral and intellectual cover for the *usineiros*. Apparently, labor court judge Décio de Toledo Leite found the priest's presence repellent, for Martins claims that the judge dismissed Padre Angelo from the hearing. But the FSC had powerful allies in the labor ministry and the IAA, and they used their connections to work out a deal for the laid-off employees that was far better than anything the ULTAB team had been able to offer. By the middle of January, the front announced that labor minister Montoro and officials of the IAA had obtained a settlement for workers. The workers not only received back pay, but the mill owners' cooperative agreed to find jobs in the region for them. By any measure, the church's top-down strategy of problem solving had produced remarkable results, eclipsing nearly two decades of Communist militancy in the short span of three months.[46]

Padre Celso arrived in Ribeirão Preto soon after the settlement was announced. The superficial, paternalistic method seemed to work well, and Padre Celso supported it for a while. At the end of February he published a statement by Frei Celso Maria, a FECOESP director, that offered an interpretation of Pope John XXIII's "Mater et Magistra" encyclical consistent with the FSC's paternalist approach. "Those most interested," wrote Frei Celso, "must be the protagonists of the socioeconomic progress and the cultural uplift of the countryside." These protagonists were to be united teams of Christian planters and workers, ensuring that the "reign of anarchy" would end with the church's neutral guidance. Until the end of April, the pages of *Diário de Notícias* featured stories on FSC efforts to help rural workers in Cravinhos, a town several miles south of Ribeirão Preto. Padre Celso was strangely absent from these stories, while his peer Padre

---

46. On the Perdigão case, see "Trabalhadores da Perdigão serão pagos: Importante decisão do Instituto do Açucar e do Alcoól—Frente Social Cristã mereceu os elogíos dos representantes do IAA—Trabalhadores receberam a visita do procurador geral—Outros detalhes sôbre o rumoroso caso da Usina Perdigão," *DN*, 16 January 1962, 1; and "Ribeirão Preto: 1000 trabalhadores querem a posse da Usina Perdigão," *TL*, December 1961, 1. Both the church and PCB stories present representations of worker consciousness: the Catholic's "applauding workers" and the Communist's laborers "wanting possession" of the mill. Martins's comments are in his "Proletariado e inquietação rural," 76 n. 8. The labor court route advocated by the union—the labor movement's fingerhold on power—offered a slow alternative solution to the traditional patron-client methods employed by the FSC. Labor court records show that several collective complaints involving more than three hundred individuals and millions of cruzeiros were not resolved until March 1964 . See Processos 911/61, 944/61, 945/61, 964/61, 970/61, all in packet 139 (hereafter listed in parenthesis following the case number), and 926/61 (81), 985/61, 986/61 (140), 1027/61 (140), and 1011/61 (99), in the archive of the JT/RP. This dramatic and interesting case warrants further study.

Angelo remained the archdiocese's representative in the front. In Cravinhos, the FSC founded a professional association of rural laborers in February. Its reported activities included establishing a tennis club, denouncing the condition of local roads, and providing a forum for local political candidates. The list reflected the predominant influence of urban-based planters, liberal professionals, and politicians among the so-called rural labor association.[47]

Around the middle of 1962, in a rush of events, Padre Celso broke with the FSC and its conservative approach. As he recalls, he became disgusted with the group's reluctance to form unions and decided to reject the aid of planters altogether. He remembers suddenly refusing to continue discussing his ideas with them. "Let's quit this," Padre Celso remembers telling the group. "One day soon enough we'll face-off out there in the fields because I am going out there to organize workers." In contrast with local church practice, Padre Celso started to see that the interests of workers and planters differed and that for the former's interests to be heard, workers would have to organize themselves. Repelled by this argument, the planters accused him of advocating Communism. They were outraged, Padre Celso remembers, and they went to the archbishop, asking him to restrain the impetuous priest. But Dom Luís stood firmly behind Padre Celso, declaring the FSC defunct and supporting Padre Celso in the formation of a new, more radical group, the Paulista Agrarian Front (FAP, Frente Agrária Paulista). As Padre Celso tells it, from then until the repressive military coup of 1964, he dedicated himself to the rural labor struggle.[48]

There are several things wrong with Padre Celso's recollection. The first is that Dom Luís died at the end of April, months before any sign of the FAP appears in the record and while stories of the FSC continued to appear in *Diário de Notícias*. In fact, it seems more likely that Dom Luís's death influenced Padre Celso's change of heart. For one thing, the archdiocese was left without a new archbishop until September, leaving a vacuum of power in the local hierarchy. In addition, Padre Celso claimed to have been at the prelate's bedside upon his death. As the favored son of the beloved leader, Padre Celso saw

47. Syllos transcript, 5. Frei Celso [Maria], "Procuram-se líderes Cristãos para o campo," *DN*, 25 February 1962, 4. (Frei Celso further elaborates his views in *Os Cristãos e o sindicato na cidade e o campo* [São Paulo: Saraiva, 1963].) On Cravinhos, see, for example, Gilberto Bellini, "Fundada associação profissional dos trabalhadores rurais," *DN*, 8 February 1962, 5; and "Trabalhadores rurais fundam clube," *DN*, 1 April 1962, 7.

48. Syllos transcript, 7–8.

himself as the inheritor of Dom Luís's commitment to social change. In an editorial honoring the archbishop's life, Padre Celso wrote that Dom Luís had told him his next campaign should be to bring order to the church's multiple social initiatives in the region. The priest also reported being urged to continue to pursue a crusading, evangelical line.[49]

Recognizing Rural Unions

So inspired, Padre Celso met the next month with labor minister Montoro. As president of the PDC, a São Paulo congressman, and a member of the Neves cabinet, Montoro was Brazil's most influential and prominent Catholic politician. Given the pragmatic idealism of Christian Democrats, it is not surprising to find Montoro advocating rural unionization during cabinet discussions. The issue resurfaced following President Goulart's May Day address. For the first time, Goulart publicly committed the administration to radical agrarian reform, including amendment of the constitutional stipulation regarding prior, cash payment for expropriated land. Goulart's new aggressiveness alarmed the Neves cabinet, which stood opposed to amending the constitution. Afraid that Communist gains among rural workers might give the president the backing he needed to force his reforms through congress, the Council of Ministers met on May 11 to discuss their reactions to Goulart's new initiative. Montoro showed himself to be at once perturbed by the seeming anarchy caused by Communist and peasant league actions in the countryside and yet willing to deal with the problem constructively. He bemoaned the unofficial unions "that without any juridical aspect, without any responsibility and without any right to represent the professional category, promote movements, demands which serve more as agitation than as demands for effective rights." Rather than press for the movement's suppression, Montoro advocated the cre-

49. Syllos transcript, 9. Editorial, "Dom Luís e nós," *DN,* 26 April 1962, 3; and "Trabalhadores rurais ingressam no sindicato: Estão dispostos a conseguir justiça social," *DN,* 29 May 1962, 6. Another sign of Padre Celso's radicalization during this period is his editorial "Igreja contra capitalismo," *DN,* 22 May 1962, 2. The unique progressivism of Dom Luís was also an inspiration for Waldemar Rossi, a sugarcane cutter, born in Sertãozinho, who served as the director of the activist Catholic Worker's Youth brigade (JOC) in Ribeirão Preto (1959) and for the tristate region (1960–64). Waldemar Rossi, transcript (by John D. French) of interview supervised by Ralph Della Cava, Universidade de São Paulo, 31 May 1983.

ation of a controlled rural labor movement through the introduction of state-sanctioned unions.[50]

One Sunday later in May, the forty-seven-year-old Montoro called the young priest to his home in São Paulo to discuss the rural labor problem. As Padre Celso remembers it, Montoro explained that the government planned to authorize rural labor unionization but did not know quite how to do it. Given his links to the Catholic Church, Montoro wanted to know if he could count on activist priests like Padre Celso to register unions before the Communists did. In addition, Montoro asked Padre Celso for his reaction to a Workers Circles' proposal to define the territory of rural unions in accordance with diocesan boundaries. Padre Celso knew the diocesan-based union idea to be José Rotta's. He explained that Rotta tended to promote the formation of urban centered, bourgeois-dominated associations, not unions. Like the efforts of the FSC in Cravinhos, Padre Celso argued that these associations held few appeals for workers. Since all other official unions registered in accordance with municipal boundaries, Padre Celso recalls advising Montoro to follow the same rules in establishing rural unions. Otherwise, he argued, they would not withstand legal challenges and would be too fragile to offer much to those most in need of assistance. The priest urged the minister to go ahead with the unionization regulation but avoid setting his hopes too high on a church-dominated labor movement in São Paulo. By following Rotta's strategy, the church's role among rural workers had not advanced significantly.[51]

Stimulated by his meeting with Montoro and confident that union recognition rules would soon be issued, Padre Celso visited

50. On Montoro, see Syllos transcript, 58; Labaki, *1961: A crise da renuncia*, 130; and Jorge Miguel Mayer and Ivan Junqueira, "Montoro, Franco," in Beloch and Abreu, eds., *DHBB*, 2266–68. Camargo ("A questão agrária," 198) claims that Goulart gave his support to a constitutional amendment at the Belo Horizonte congress, but the record does not support this view. On the May date, see Marieta de Morais Ferreira and César Benjamim, "Goulart, João," in Beloch and Abreu, eds., *DHBB*, 1513. The May Day address is summarized in AmEmbassy to USDS, "President Goulart Continues to Agitate for 'Basic Reforms,'" Airgram 489 (hereafter cited in the following form: A-489), RG 59, DS 732.00/5-1962 (1578), DS/USNA. Quote from Council of Ministers, Brasília, 11 May 1962, transcripts, 3:14–16, cited in Anthony Pereira, "The Unions Under the Ancien Regime," 30 November 1989, 17, mimeograph in author's possession. Montoro's support for rural social legislation found expression during the Kubitschek presidency when Montoro was named vice chair of the Rural Laborer Assistance Commission set up in 1957 by labor minister Parsifal Barroso and Rio Grande do Sul congressman Fernando Ferrari. At a weeklong hearing in São Paulo, regular testimony was offered by Lindolfo Silva, of ULTAB, and José Eduardo Reis, of the Franca (SP) rural laborers' union. See, "Reuniu-se novamente a Comissão de Assistencia ao Trabalhador Rural," *NH*, 26 July 1957.

51. Syllos transcript, 34–35, 58–59. For more on Rotta, see previous references to him in this book; see also Martins, "Alguns aspectos da inquietação trabalhista no campo," 132–41; and Barros, "A organização sindical," 104–21.

Cravinhos at the end of May. Bypassing the FSC, Padre Celso took the lead in transforming the rural laborers professional association into a *sindicato*. Meeting Sunday, May 27, with "innumerable laborers, from the diverse plantations of the region," Padre Celso and city councilmen Fioravante Manelia of Cravinhos and Welson Gasparini of Ribeirão Preto took credit for establishing the area's first rural labor union. "We will be a powerful force in the struggle for Social Justice," Padre Celso told the unnumbered crowd. "Already we are in open struggle to conquer the sacred rights conceded to us by human nature and law." The union's founding marked Padre Celso's first reported public engagement with the rural labor struggle, and his words of struggle rang a far more militant tone than any previously ascribed to the FSC. Although the men were not rural workers themselves, they placed themselves in solidarity with the laborers by using a first-person plural discourse. "United we will represent such a great force," said Gasparini, "that we will be capable of gaining that which we have always had as an ideal and a dream. Within democratic principles, the laborers of the rural zones will know how to construct a better world." (Gasparini, who was an energetic young lawyer, broadcast journalist, and frequent contributor to *Diário de Notícias,* was the only personality who made the transition from the FSC to the FAP.) With the founding of the Cravinhos union, Gasparini and Padre Celso distanced themselves from more conservative elements in the archdiocese. Reading between the lines of these statements, one can see continuity in the urban initiative and patron-client nature of the new union, but also evident is significant change: the end of planter-dominated Catholic worker associations and the beginning of working-class unions.[52]

Still, Padre Celso's break from the conservative approach was not yet complete. It was July before *Diário de Notícias* included any references to the FAP, and only thereafter did the paper reveal increased rural labor activity on the part of the archdiocese.[53] Before this, in June, a serious confrontation between the church and Communists arose that influenced Padre Celso's turn to more aggressive social action. The key event, which Padre Celso entirely overlooked in narrating the story of his transition to militancy, was a Sertãozinho

52. "Trabalhadores rurais ingressam no sindicato: Estão dispostos a conseguir justiça social," *DN,* 29 May 1962, 6.

53. "Hoje haverá reunião de trabalhadores: Frente agrária estará em Jardinópolis," *DN,* 8 July 1962, 6, is the first story to mention the agrarian front, and it was not until August 8 that Padre Celso published an editorial explaining the front's radical program. See below and "Frente agrária paulista e sindicatos rurais, duas realidades," *DN,* 8 August 1962, 11.

strike organized by Irineu Luís de Moraes. For the first time, the two men came into direct conflict with each other, putting Padre Celso's organizing skills and knowledge to a severe test.

Padre Celso was still in Europe when Moraes started to organize workers from the Sertãozinho sugar mills in defense of Goulart's succession to the presidency. Upon Padre Celso's return to Ribeirão Preto, however, *Terra Livre* published an article protesting the low wages paid at the *usinas* in Sertãozinho and Pontal. By midyear, with the cane standing tall and impenetrably dense in the fields, talk of a strike was rampant. On June 9, the crushers, furnaces, and vats of the mills anxiously waited the first delivery of raw, freshly cut cane, but instead of going to the fields, the cane cutters from Sertãozinho, as well as Barrinha, Pontal, Jaboticabal, and Guariba, amassed in the center of town. Filling the plaza in front of Sertãozinho's city hall, they demanded a wage hike and the abolition of the rent deduction. A commission formed of four rural workers, Moraes, and Councilman Halah went inside to meet with the owners of *usinas* Santa Elisa, Albertina, Santo Antônio, São Francisco, São Geraldo, and Bela Vista. They struck a deal: wages were to go up 45 percent, and the housing deduction would be eliminated if the owners secured a comparable increase in prices from the IAA. This pattern of collaboration between workers and *usineiros* soon became an industry standard.[54]

The final stipulation eventually created an ugly situation. The IAA was not obliged to abide by the settlement made in Sertãozinho; nor were workers obliged to return to the fields without fulfillment of the new terms. A waiting game ensued that cost all parties dearly as the cane stood uncut in the field, losing its value day by day and putting off the all-important harvests of the second and third growths. As the days wore on, the day-to-day existence of the strikers grew problematic, and some broke ranks. On June 17, a second altercation occurred in Sertãozinho when three to six hundred families of workers protested in front of city hall, demanding that the *usinas* start operation and begging for immediate public assistance to hold back

54. "Pontal: Usinas de açucar não daram salário mínimo aos trabalhadores," *TL,* January 1962, 7. Moraes transcript, pt. 1, pp. 43–44. According to the report contained in "Alta Mogiana: 6 mil trabalhadores em greve derrotaram império dos usineiros," *TL,* August 1962, 5, the settlement brought hourly wages of Cr$65.10, daily wages of Cr$520.60, and monthly wages of Cr$15,610.00, or Cr$203.00 per ton of cane cut during normal, daylight hours. Since piece rates, that is, payment by ton, offered employers many opportunities to underpay workers, the strikers insisted that cutters be paid for hours worked rather than by the piece. Further confirmation of these events was gained in an interview with Halah. Said Issa Halah, interview by author, Ribeirão Preto, 28 June 1991. Sigaud reports this pattern of negotiation in the northeast sugar industry in *Greve nos engenhos,* as does Pereira, *The End of the Peasantry.*

their hunger. Fully aware of the dependency of the *usinas* and the community on these seasonal workers, the mayor and city council agreed to provide each family with vouchers worth up to Cr$1,400 that could be used to buy goods in local stores. Within a day, more than Cr$250,000 had been distributed by police chief Ruy de Biagi.[55]

In this battle, which eventually resulted in higher wages for workers, Padre Celso chose to Red-bait the strikers. He argued that workers were the victims of Communist agitators, not greedy mill owners. He named "declared Communist elements," such as Moraes, in *Diário de Notícias* and accused them of stirring up trouble among the cane cutters by "promoting meetings . . . , inciting them to engage in strike movements and protests." "Lamentably," a councilman quoted by the paper said, "the unemployment and consequent starvation of the people had been effectively exploited by elements of the extreme left that infest the region, using the humility and simplicity of the laborer as an instrument to accomplish their desire to subvert the social order."[56] This may have been true, but no matter how conniving the "Communists" were, their method of organizing and leading workers had proved more effective than anything the church had thus far attempted in the region. The power grab of the Usina Perdigão settlement had not proved to be reproducible for Padre Celso. In Sertãozinho, the priest had cast the workers' demands for pay and sustenance as a confrontation between the church and "Communist elements," and the church had lost. It was only after this event that Padre Celso threw himself wholeheartedly into a rivalry against Moraes and FATAESP. Over time, he developed organizing strategies that proved more enduring than those of the other groups.

Padre Celso's transition to rural labor activism could not have come at a better time. Toward the end of June, Minister Montoro issued Portaria No. 209-A, detailing the rural union recognition process under the rural labor decree of November 1944. The new regulation

55. José Teodoro, "Usinas de açúcar começaram a funcionar," *DN*, 23 June 1962, 3; and "Sertãozinho e Pontal: Levanta-se o povo contra a carestia," *TL*, July 1962, 8. With Cr$1,400, a careful homemaker could buy enough food to feed a family of five rice, beans, and meat for three days to a week. For a list of average annual retail food prices, see table xxv-5 in Ludwig, *Brazil: A Handbook of Historical Statistics,* 450.

56. Teodoro, "Usinas de açúcar"; Geraldo Paulo Nardelli of Sertãozinho is the councilman (*vereador*) quoted in the story. Another significant June strike, which seems to have involved neither Padre Celso nor Moraes, occurred at Fazenda Amália in Santa Rosa de Viterbo, an Alta Mogiana town located to the southeast of Ribeirão Preto. With the help of Tenório de Lima of the foodworkers' federation, twelve thousand wage workers of the huge Matarazzo complex, incorporating the *fazenda* and two *usinas,* won a 50 percent wage increase and elimination of a 33 percent salary deduction for housing on the plantation. "Greve derrotou império Matarazzo em 'Santa Rosa de Viterbo,'" *TL*, July 1962, 1.

intensified the race to legalize all of the various rural worker organizations then established. Two years later, after the military came to power, José Rotta bragged to U.S. officials that his rural labor federation had been in a far better position than ULTAB when this regulation was issued because the Catholic Workers Circles had concentrated on establishing "unions-in-formation," while the Communists had set up "civil associations." Rotta further claimed that Communist strength in the countryside stemmed from their ties to the labor ministry and SUPRA, not their appeal among rural workers. Rotta might just as well have been talking about himself, however. So long as the Christian Democrat Montoro controlled the ministry, church-related organizations stood the best chance of being recognized by the government. This was Montoro's plan, as shown by his meeting with Padre Celso and a May Day rally appearance with Rotta in São Paulo.[57]

Non-church groups criticized Montoro's *portaria*. ULTAB's Silva believed regulation 209-A served the interests of rural employers rather than workers. It required the formation of separate unions for each of various categories of production—distinguishing coffee workers from cotton pickers, for example, even though they might work on the same plantation. This diluted the influence they might have as workers organized within a single union. Ironically, the SRB attacked the *portaria,* too, demonstrating either a fissure in the recent solidarity of the rural owning class or the SRB's traditional strategy of verbally supporting proposed reforms—as they did at the CRB conference in January—and then opposing actual implementation. Planter-lawyer Virgilio dos Santos Magano lambasted Montoro, claiming his regulations ignored the fact that Decree Law No. 7,038 had been replaced by Decree Law No. 8,127, which granted organizing rights only to rural employers and placed these associations under the umbrella of the agricultural ministry. As labor minister, Montoro had no legal rights to unionize workers, Santos Magano argued. Moreover, rural workers lacked the necessary maturity and education to run their own unions. These were old arguments, recalling SRB protests from the 1940s. Santos Magano concluded his attack on

57. "Portaria 209-A do Ministério do Trabalho" was published 29 June 1962. Montoro joined Rotta in a church-sponsored May Day celebration in front of Sé Cathedral. Many speakers called for the extension of labor rights to rural workers, and Montoro promised unions for them. U.S. labor attaché Jack Liebof emphasized that ten thousand workers attended this event, while only one thousand appeared at a labor rally sponsored by the PCB. AmConGen, São Paulo, to USDS, "May Day 1962 in São Paulo," Despatch No. 280, RG 59, DF 732.00/5-2462 (1580), DS/USNA. Acting labor officer Richard E. Ginnold interviewed Rotta in São Paulo on 4 August 1964. See AmEmbassy to USDS, "Rural Workers Reaction to Alliance for Progress Program," A-370, 20 October 1964, LAB 10 BRAZ (1283), DS/USNA.

Montoro by calling on fellow planters to block application of the regulations. Criticism of regulation 209-A contributed to growing tensions between the president and his cabinet as Goulart became more insistent on implementing basic reforms and restoring full powers to his office. Montoro and the rest of the Neves cabinet finally resigned on July 12, but the minister made good use of his last weeks in office. Although Lindolfo Silva urged the ministry to recognize all "rural unions without discrimination on the basis of ideology, politics, or religion," during his last twenty-three days in office, Montoro's ministry recognized eleven rural unions in the state of São Paulo alone, nearly all of them organized by the Rotta wing of the church.[58]

The Paulista Agrarian Front

In the Alta Mogiana, Montoro's chief assistant was João Carlos de Souza Meireles, the son of a prominent Batatais planter and UDN political chief. On June 29, Meireles traveled to Ribeirão Preto from his São Paulo office to help Padre Celso organize unions in the Alta Mogiana towns of Orlândia and Bonfim Paulista. Joined by a representative of the church-linked National Labor Front (FNT), Souza Meireles urged a crowd of more than two thousand "men of the country" to "join the labor class to demand" their rights to vacations, overtime pay, and an end to "insufferable" conditions. One week later, the words "Frente Agrária Paulista" appeared in *Diário de Notícias* for the first time. From then on, the FSC disappeared from the news, and all the credit for the church's rural labor organizing campaign went to the FAP. Padre Celso held the post of FAP president, and João Carlos Caio Magri, a young lawyer with a car, drove the priest on many FAP missions into rural communities. Two other regular participants were

58. Silva's criticisms are in "A portaria 209-A e a unidade dos trabalhadores," *TL*, November 1962, 2. Santos Magano's are in "A sindicalização rural," *A Rural* (June 1962), 71. An editorial formalized Santos Magano's complaints as the official SRB line. See "Proletariado e política," *A Rural* (August 1962), 3. *Sindicatos* formed in Presidente Prudente, Assis, Guariba, Juquia, Lins, Matão, Porto Feliz, Marília, Piracicaba, São João da Boa Vista, and Rio das Pedras. They were all affiliated with groups headed by Rotta: FECOESP, and the São Paulo State Federation of Agricultural Laborers (FETAESP, Federação de Trabalhadores Agrícolas do Estado de São Paulo). ULTAB organizers had long been active in most of these settings, showing how important it was to have connections in the labor ministry. During the remainder of 1962, only five more São Paulo rural unions were recognized by the ministry. These were the *sindicatos dos trabalhadores rurais* of Capivari, Santa Barbara d'Oeste, São Pedro, and Jaboticabal. The first four were associated with Rotta and the last with Moraes. See Barros, "A organização sindical dos trabalhadores rurais," 114–16.

Gasparini and Dr. Antônio Duarte Nogueira, a physician. Like Gasparini, who already sat in the city council, Nogueira had political aspirations. (Beginning with Gasparini's election in October 1963 and lasting until 1992, Gasparini and Nogueira were elected mayors of Ribeirão Preto, serving consecutive back-to-back terms.) The diverse, professional background of many FAP leaders shows how the church's rural labor campaign, like that of the Communists, built on the assumption that broad economic and political links were necessary. As a leader, Padre Celso sought to build networks he could use to attract followers and handle their concerns. He found them in Souza Meireles, Gasparini, and Nogueira.[59]

Several days after the first mention of the FAP, an explanation for the organization appeared in the pages of *Diário de Notícias*. On July 10, an editorial described it as an organization of "democratic and Christian leaders," including "some planters and landlords that are coming to understand the . . . necessity to join together to demand policies of support for farming that will reestablish the equilibrium between the city and the country." Only one statement marked the subtle divergence between the FAP and the FSC: "The unity of rural laborers in syndicates is a large step forward for agriculture." (The FSC had resisted unionization.) A few weeks later, Caio Magri sharpened the FAP's cutting edge, writing that the "politicization of the rural laborer" is essential for "wrenching the country out of the medieval phase in which it finds itself," adopting a perspective similar to the PCB's historic attack on feudalism. Caio Magri also came close to endorsing class struggle. He wrote that the FAP promoted the formation of unions "not to avoid conflict between the classes" but to help workers "defend their rights." In a line aimed directly at the patron-client conventions of Rotta and the FSC, Caio Magri claimed that the FAP "leaves behind 'the standard style of organizing' to struggle for rural unions free of Marxist mercenaries and the corrupt bureaucrats [*pelegos*] of liberal capitalism."[60]

Under the direction of Padre Celso, the FAP was easily among the most militant of the agrarian fronts formed by the church in other states. The fronts in Paraná, Rio Grande do Sul, and Goiás

59. On Meireles, see Bellini, "Trabalhadores rurais respeito" and "Organizou-se frente agrária estadual," *DN*, 29 January 1963, 6. The first mention of the FAP is in "Hoje haverá reunião de trabalhadores." On Gasparini and Nogueira, see also "E Ribeirão escolheu Gasparini," *Jornal de Ribeirão*, 20–26 November 1988.

60. On the FAP, see Padre Celso, "Problemas do campo," *DN*, 10 July 1962, 5; Magri, "Frente Agrária Paulista."

were started by bishops and saw themselves as rural social assistance organizations similar to the FSC. Following Montoro's lead, however, they eventually supported the formation of rural labor unions. On the other hand, the FAP maintained an anticommunist perspective that distinguished it from the most radical wing of Catholic politics: Popular Action (AP, Ação Popular), a youth group that broke away from the socially conscious but church-controlled Catholic Action (AC, Ação Católica) in 1961. According to political scientist Neale Pearson, AC and Rotta allies saw Padre Celso as "an opportunist who wished to dominate the rural organizations he associated with." Soon after the *golpe,* one of these informants described Padre Celso as "a rather shallow thinker in the matter of rural organization; all he thinks about are strikes and land division; he does not think about cooperatives, rural credit, and marketing." These criticisms reveal the regional as well as institutional biases working against the FAP. The Alta Mogiana was a region where rural wage earners predominated; rural credit and marketing held little appeal for them. The criticisms were also ideological, showing the kind of cutthroat internal politics that confronted the FAP. The only real way to describe the FAP is to examine its historical experience of engagement with rural workers and partisans of both the right and left in the Alta Mogiana.[61]

Catholic and Communist Conflicts

The first confrontation for the FAP came in Pradópolis, located to the southeast of Ribeirão Preto, just to the east of Cravinhos. Pradópolis had just been incorporated in 1960, declaring its independence from its established neighbors, Sertãozinho and Guariba. Named in honor of the enterprising Prado family, which developed a huge coffee plantation there in the late nineteenth century, the town was the setting of one of the first transitions from coffee to sugar recorded in the region. The first sugar mill was built there in the late 1940s, producing 2,694 tons of sugar and 150,350 liters of alcohol in 1948. In the 1950s, the plant and plantation were sold to Nelson and Orlando Ometto—brothers and pioneering sugarcane entrepreneurs

61. Pearson, "Small Farmer and Rural Worker," 247–48. For more on the agrarian fronts, AP, and AC, see ibid., 79–83, 223–48; Thomas C. Bruneau, *Católicismo Brasileiro em época de transição* (São Paulo: Loyola, 1974), 139–93; and Scott Mainwaring, *The Catholic Church and Politics in Brazil, 1916–1985* (Stanford: Stanford University Press, 1986), 64–66.

from Piracicaba, São Paulo. They retained control of the *usina* and surrounding plantation as well as the town, where they exchanged duties as mayor into the 1970s. Under their management, the Usina São Martinho saw more than a thousandfold increase in production by 1977, when output reached three million tons of sugar and one hundred million liters of alcohol. From 1950 to 1977 only one serious challenge befell the Ometto empire: a strike organized by Moraes in 1962.[62]

Moraes organized the strike in July, soon after the dispute in Sertãozinho had been resolved. As in Sertãozinho, the bulk of Moraes's followers were seasonal cane cutters who lived outside the confines of the *usina*. During the harvest season, an *usina* the size of São Martinho had an average of five hundred mill workers and three thousand field hands, with the cutters the most numerous group. Moraes also had some success among those who worked inside the mill because of their status as industrial workers under Brazilian labor law. Although the Sertãozinho victory gave workers a powerful argument for matching wage and conditions adjustments, in Pradópolis, Moraes's plan faced opposition not only from the Omettos and the police but also from the competition of workers allied with Padre Celso.

Padre Celso recalls that he had anticipated the spread of Moraes's strike movement in the regional sugar industry. The FAP responded by organizing workers at the São Martinho site. The FAP wanted to help the workers improve their conditions but at the same time keep PCB influence from growing stronger in the region. Political expediency and lack of experience led the FAP to form alliances with labor contractors—known as *gatos* (cats)—rather than with the workers they employed. While some of the field hands were permanent employees and lived on the *usina* property, most cane cutters were transported to the fields each day by these *gatos*. As owners of trucks used in hauling cut cane from the field to the *usina*, *gatos* organized and commanded the gangs of workers they brought to the fields from neighboring towns. Although closer to workers than owners in background, *gatos* nevertheless filled the role of middle-level management in the Brazilian sugar industry. The church developed influence

---

62. The sale was reported in "Vendida uma das mais famosas fazendas de cafe em São Paulo," *OESP,* 11 April 1950, 6. More elaborate histories are found in "História da Usina São Martinho" and "Pradópolis, um município integrado" in "Usina São Martinho: Elo da integração regional," 2, 11. On the strike, see Irineu Luís de Moraes, transcript of interview by author, Ribeirão Preto, 22 August 1988 (hereafter Moraes transcript, pt. 1), pp. 44–47; and Moraes transcript, pt. 3, pp. 25–29. See also "Alta Mogiana: 6 mil trabalhadores."

among this managerial group, while Moraes claimed to represent the interests of the cutters themselves.[63]

Oriented by Padre Celso, *gatos* cautioned their workers to wait for the Omettos to offer competitive wages and conditions. If the Omettos refused, Padre Celso counseled filing claims for fair wages in the Ribeirão Preto labor court. Moraes, however, was typically impatient with such tactics. From his point of view, when the moment for collective action came, it had to be seized quickly and decisively. Thus, he was not surprised when a group of nearly a thousand cutters staged a work stoppage, but another group loyal to the labor contractors continued cutting. The strikers turned militant and stormed the fields, forcing the others to stop work and either join the strike or flee. "The masses were thrown against the masses," said Moraes. "The strikers entered the fields with clubs in their hands, everybody went and the others started running. They made them abandon their jobs at the point of their machetes." From the fields, the mob marched on the mill itself, and the mill workers stopped processing the cane in solidarity with the cutters. Some three thousand men, women, and children armed with machetes and self-righteous confidence filled the central yard of the mill. Despite the arrival of police from several regional towns, the Ometto brothers were in no mood for a confrontation. According to Moraes, neither were the police, who seemed convinced of the rightfulness of the workers' cause.[64] Faced with these dramatic developments, Orlando Ometto was especially anxious to negotiate a settlement. When Moraes, Halah, and a commission of workers met with him, he agreed to match the Sertãozinho settlement and wrote a contract to back up his words. Significantly, Ometto also agreed to abolish the *gato* system by hiring cutters directly through the *usina* personnel office. This was a remarkable development, representing the abolition of one of the most exploitative aspects of the sugar industry.[65]

For Padre Celso, the defeats faced in the sugar wars of Sertãozinho and Pradópolis meant the FAP needed a change in strategy. Padre Celso reasoned that the organization would need to build support among workers slowly and carefully in order to counteract the

63. "História da Usina São Martinho." On *gatos* in Pernambuco, see Lygia Sigaud, *Os clandestinos e os direitos: Estudo sôbre trabalhadores da cana-de-açucar de Pernambuco* (São Paulo: Duas Cidades, 1979), 49–82. See also Moraes transcript, pt. 3, pp. 28–29.

64. Syllos transcript, 23–25; and Moraes transcript, pt. 1, p. 45.

65. Moraes transcript, pt. 1, pp. 46–47, pt. 3, pp. 26–28; and "Alta Mogiana: 6 mil trabalhadores." Halah interview; and Tulio Marco Rampazzo (counsel for Usina São Martinho, 1950–1972), interview by author, Pradópolis, 23 July 1991.

influence of Communists. In August, the group reoriented their work toward the development of "natural leaders." Certain forms of behavior identified such leaders, said Padre Celso. "The person who, all of a sudden, speaks out, asks questions, argues with you and tries to explain things to others. He's the one who comes back to your second and third meetings; the others fail to show up, but he comes always." Padre Celso imagined it would take one year to find and train such leaders and another year to institutionalize rural unions and prepare the ground for struggle. Natural leaders would help establish "authentic and not mutilated unionism," he wrote. Authentic unions "promoted the whole man of the country and his integration into the world of work, school, civilization, and culture." This kind of union began with the "whole politicization of fieldhands," not with the formation of unions concerned only with struggling for higher wages. In other words, Padre Celso intended to de-emphasize unionization, favoring instead rural worker consciousness-raising, community building, and sociopolitical incorporation. Such a strategy reflected the repudiation of standard wisdom and the union-forming trend of the times.[66]

Padre Celso presents an idealized narrative of how the FAP put this change of direction in place. Unlike Moraes, Padre Celso says he avoided corner bars. Instead, FAP organizers met with rural workers at crossroads where some had a tendency to gather on Sundays to sell and exchange goods and news. As Caio Magri and Padre Celso addressed crowds of rural workers, they assumed the laborers were in despair and tired of their lives as they were. The FAP activists stressed this discontent, describing and analyzing the sorry circle of poverty in which they and their ancestors had lived. "Nothing changed in all this time," he remembers telling them. "Working from sunrise to sunset is your life. You do not even have official documents and the planter does what he wants with you," he went on. They returned to the same places, rotating from week to week, talking to workers in towns throughout the Alta Mogiana. Stories in *Diário de Notícias* show Padre Celso and Caio Magri repeatedly visiting Cravinhos, Brodósqui, Batatais, São Joaquim da Barra, Igarapava, Franca, Jardinópolis, and still other towns. As Padre Celso tells it, it was only after he and Caio Magri had gained the trust of listeners that the subject of *sindicatos* was broached. "And so," Padre Celso remembers saying, "you have to unite because unity is power."

66. Syllos transcript, 6. Gilberto Bellini, "FAP administrará cursos a camponeses: Trabalhadores serão recepcionados dia 9," *DN*, 23 August 1962, 8; and Padre Celso, "Sindicalização rural," *DN*, 13 October 1962, 2.

Newspaper accounts reveal a different story, however. The head-line of a report of the FAP's first appearance in Jardinópolis, for ex-ample, reads, "Rural Laborers in Search of Advancement, Women of the Soil Also Want Unions." In the body of the story, four hundred workers reportedly sought out Padre Celso, "vibrating with excite-ment unleashed [*desencadeado*]" by the subject of unionization that the priest had broached. (Among the most anxious to form a union among the four hundred was "a lady" who worked as a processor of picked cotton.) Apparently, it was not as necessary to avoid talking about unions as the priest remembered. It was certainly easier for Padre Celso than it was for Moraes. Moraes tended to avoid the sub-ject of unions, speaking instead about the advantages of solidarity, and he rarely felt secure enough to reveal his affiliation with the PCB. Padre Celso's high collar announced his affiliation with a higher au-thority, assuring workers that as a Catholic priest, he could not be a Communist, even if he did talk about unions. The church constantly associated communism with the devil; planters did the rest, associat-ing union organizers with Communists. Hence, for many rural work-ers—Padre Celso and Moraes explained—union organizers were do-ing the work of the devil, and many workers consequently avoided them. "The worst problem was overcoming their fear," said the priest. "They were afraid of their bosses and afraid of communism. But since I was a priest, it made it easier to overcome [the latter] objection."[67]

Politicization Circles

During these road trips, Padre Celso and Caio Magri identified a group of individuals seemingly endowed with natural leadership abilities. On Sunday, September 9, the FAP invited them to gather at the orga-nization's headquarters at 716 São Paulo Street in Ribeirão Preto to study ways to change their situation by forming rural unions. During the remainder of the year, an ever growing number of rural workers attended nine additional Sunday "politicization circles" at the FAP office. As part of the first session, the leaders received health care services—from physicians and dentists who donated their time to

67. Syllos transcript, 1–3, 89; and Antônio Crispim da Cruz, transcript of interview by author, Ribeirão Preto, 31 March 1989, AEL/UNICAMP. For Jardinópolis, see "Trabalhadores rurais buscam sua promoção: Mulheres da roça tambem querem sindicato," *DN,* 11 July 1962, 5. On the reception of Communists and Catholics, see Moraes transcript, pt. 1, pp. 47–65; and Syllos transcript, 7–9.

the FAP—and attended lessons on Catholic social doctrine, labor law, and rural unionization. The emphasis given unionization in the day's training challenges Padre Celso's remembrance of the FAP's plan. Although he remembered a staged process—first leaders, then unions—the two actually seemed to have developed hand-in-hand. The story announcing the FAP's first meeting reveals another misleading idea, insisting that the FAP school "would tolerate no interference from political parties or candidates, or anybody directly interested in the elections." The presence of city councilman and state assembly aspirant Gasparini contradicted this claim. Nevertheless, it is interesting to consider the ironic intent of these contradictions. On the one hand, the FAP wanted contemporaries to see the organization as pure and uncorrupted by partisan politics—even though it was "politicizing" workers. On the other, the former Padre Celso—turned corporate executive by 1989—wanted to keep a foreign interviewer from thinking him too pro-union.[68]

Despite these well-considered steps and increasing federal support for rural unionization, Padre Celso's work followed unpredictable paths in late 1962 and 1963. Confrontations of various intensity cropped up around the region, with one of the more publicized incidents occurring in Jardinópolis. As Padre Celso had discovered in July, a mixed group of *colonos,* cane cutters, cotton pickers, and ranch hands there were anxious to organize a union. Padre Celso may have hoped to put off establishing one until leaders had been identified and trained, but other groups did not share his priorities, and they forced the FAP to act more quickly than it may have wanted. Confrontations marred many of the meetings FAP organizers attended in Jardinópolis, including the first, which was made difficult by the suspicious appearance of two "powerful earthmovers." Even though it was a Sunday, the two machines worked furiously, making "a tre-

68. Syllos transcript, 82–84. The first local meeting was announced in Gilberto Bellini, "FAP administrará cursos a camponeses: Trabalhadores serão recepcionados dia 9," *DN,* 23 August 1962, 8. Representatives from the following nineteen towns reportedly attended the meeting: Cravinhos, Bonfim Paulista, Orlândia, Serra Azul, Guaira, Sales Oliveira, Brodósqui, Guatapará, Dumont, Domingos Vilela, São Simão, Luís Antônio, Altinópolis, Santo Antônio de Alegria, Jardinópolis, Sertãozinho, Pontal, and Batatais. The last meeting of 1962 was reported in "Frente Agrária reuniu camponeses: Dom Angelo prestigia o movimento," *DN,* 25 December 1962, 8. Participating in the fourteenth "circle," held 21 April 1963, were thirty-four rural leaders from seven different towns: Batatais, Cravinhos, Sales Oliveira, Bonfim Paulista, Jardinópolis, São Simão, and Ribeirão Preto, a new addition to the group. See, "FA esta em plena ação lutando pela promoção do trabalhador rural," *DN,* 23 April 1963, 5–6. A Ribeirão Preto *sindicato* loyal to Padre Celso had been organized in the interim and had affiliated with the front on Saturday, 2 March 1963. See "Insalou-se Frente Agrária regional: A primeira diretória foi empossada," *DN,* 5 March 1963, 8.

mendous noise" in the otherwise tranquil setting. A *Diário de Notícias* report did not identify those responsible for the noise but speculated that the fault may have lain with "landowners unwilling to conform with our campaign" or with city officials who opposed the FAP's activities. Two months later, on the FAP's third reported visit to the town, *Diário de Notícias* named names. City council president Olímpio Freiria Filho and lawyer Holanda Noir Tavella, formerly legal aide to Nazareno Ciavatta's ULTAB-affiliated Ribeirão Preto union, seemed to be at the bottom of FAP's difficulties in Jardinópolis.[69]

The FAP claimed to have initiated the movement for rural unionization in Jardinópolis, but at the Sunday, September 2, meeting scheduled to elect officers for the budding union, Freiria and Tavella took charge and tried to displace the FAP activists. Despite Tavella's earlier links to the PCB, he and Freiria appear to have been acting independently. Tavella had experience in the movement and as much right to be present as Padre Celso. Since the FAP chose city hall as the venue, it was not unreasonable for Freiria to be on hand. Sitting together at a long table, Padre Celso, Caio Magri, FAP lawyer Eréas de Oliveira Vianna, Freiria, and Tavella faced some two hundred rural workers, most of them standing. Tavella presided over the proceedings, accepting nominations for union president and secretary. *Diário de Notícias* correspondent Gilberto Bellini wrote that "Two gentlemen, rural laborers, were placed in the two posts. There they stood, mute and impassive while Dr. Tavella gave a rambling explanation about the union." Thereafter, Freiria began to read aloud the union bylaws, but "after about twenty minutes, almost no one continued listening. Some workers left the room, others sat, while some moved about the room, chatting with their colleagues." Finally, Padre Celso spoke out, denouncing the bylaws read by Freiria as outmoded and urging the assembly to elect an interim board of directors. As Bellini wrote, "When Padre Celso started to speak, all the laborers who were seated got up, those hanging around outside returned to the room, all moving closer to hear the orator." They applauded his motion, but Tavella and Freiria blocked it. Familiar with the workers, Freiria protested that they lacked a quorum of those who had signed the FAP-sponsored petition calling the meeting. At this, Caio Magri called for a recess and reassembly on September 23 at a local church where the Union of Farm, Livestock, and Rural Industry Laborers

---

69. The July 8 meeting is reported in "Trabalhadores rurais buscam sua promoção," and Tavella appears in Gilberto Bellini, "Camponeses querem sindicato em Jardinópolis: FAP continuará apoiando movimento iniciado," *DN,* 5 September 1962, 6.

would be founded. When Tavella moved to table this motion, "those present started to protest so loudly" that Tavella desisted. Three weeks later, the FAP carried out Caio Magri's plan without interference.[70]

The Jardinópolis story shows the interworkings of several forces. News of the rural labor movement and its successes had spread throughout the Alta Mogiana. Padre Celso appeared in town and offered workers the support and protection of the church in founding an organization. A significant number of rural workers, some thirty men and two women, applauded the idea and showed enough interest, courage, and literacy to sign a public notice—published in the local press and *Diário de Notícias*—announcing their desire to form a union. Local politicians tried to take it over but proved inept, and so the church accomplished its plans. In the narrative, the desires of workers seem to shape the story, and yet for the most part they appear only as spectators, applauding here, standing speechless there. The names of a brave group of petitioners is documented, but the main record left behind is one of followers in search of a trustworthy leader who would speak for them.

Planter Opposition Grows

While FAP and ULTAB struggled to overcome elitist images and put rural workers in charge of the movement, the SRB cultivated the image of rural workers as ignorant followers. From the first discussions of rural unionization under Vargas, the SRB maintained that rural workers were too uneducated, illiterate, and ill-prepared to run their own organizations. The Cold War context of 1962 merely intensified the planter's attacks. Rural workers were so indiscriminate in their choice of leaders that unions would simply serve the purpose of giving Communists an opportunity to generate class struggle, promote "rural anarchy," and create a state of chaos out of which power could quickly be seized. To support these arguments, the SRB developed a convenient if inaccurate story about U.S. experience. Articles in the SRB claimed that "not even in the U.S.," with "a low percentage of illiterate rural proletarians . . . is agrarian unionization permitted." The "pragmatic North Americans" were smart enough to realize that

---

70. Bellini's account of the meeting is in "Camponeses querem sindicato em Jardinópolis." FAP's initiation of the meeting, showing the public notice and the names of those who signed it, is in Gilberto Bellini, "Camponeses elegerão diretória: FAP apoia criação do sindicato," *DN,* 31 August 1962, 6. Paulo Freitas da Silva was the first president of the Jardinópolis union.

unions could have a destabilizing influence on the agricultural sector, the basis of their national economy. In this light, it was all the more absurd for Brazil to consider unionizing its rural workers when their lack of education made them susceptible to manipulation by "subversive agents." Of course, rural unionization was not prohibited in the United States so much as it was left out of such early labor laws as the Wagner Act—a situation not unlike the general exclusion of rural workers from Brazil's CLT. After many decades of struggle and the rise and fall of many organizations, the U.S. farm labor movement was, in the 1960s, about to enter its most active and successful era. Coincidentally, César Chávez founded the National Farm Workers' Association in 1962, just as the SRB was denying the existence of such a movement in the United States.[71]

SRB opposition to rural unionization seemed particularly forceful in late 1962 due the growing power of President Goulart and SRB fears of losing influence in the upcoming October election of governors and legislators. In September, congress relented to Goulart's demand, supported by organized labor, to hold a plebiscite on presidentialism. They also granted him the right to appoint an interim prime minister and cabinet without subjecting his candidates to senate approval. This turn of events deeply concerned and offended leaders of the SRB, for their former president, Renato da Costa Lima, had no sooner been named minister of agriculture by Prime Minister Francisco de Paula Brochado da Rocha, who took over from Neves in July, than he was forced to step down when the cabinet disbanded in September. In one confrontational gambit after another, Goulart threatened to use his executive powers to put aspects of his program of basic reforms in place, forcing congress to take concrete steps toward approving legislation, including a variety of agrarian reform measures. The pressure on congress grew with the October elections, which resulted in a strong showing for left-nationalist candidates. The planter leaders of the SRB called those politicians who supported land reform and rural unionization demagogues. They were the subversives who dangerously manipulated the uneducated rural masses. The hostility expressed toward populist politicians in 1962 contrasted sharply with the coalition-building tactics adopted by FARESP and

71. The SRB critique is gleaned from Ellen Bromfield Geld, "Sindicalização dos operários rurais," *A Rural* (August 1962), 12; editorial, "As classes productoras e a situação política," *A Rural* (November 1962), 3; and editorial, "Sindicalismo e anarquia rural," *A Rural* (January 1963), 3. For a brief history of farm labor organizing in the United States, and California in particular, see Cletus E. Daniel, "César Chávez and the Unionization of California Farmworkers," in *Working People in California,* edited by Daniel Cornford (Berkeley and Los Angeles: University of California Press, 1995), 371–404.

some SRB members in the context of the 1958 Production March. Their changed posture reflected the increased independence of pro-labor politicians. At least in some parts of São Paulo—the Alta Mogiana included—populists no longer depended on alliances with the established conservative power structure to win. This was especially true in São Paulo, where rural labor defenders Luciano Lepera and Luís Tenório de Lima won election to the state assembly on the PTB ticket. These victories and others, including the gubernatorial election of rural labor supporter Miguel Arraes in Pernambuco, promised significant governmental support for rural labor demands and less need for compromise between labor and conservatives in the PSD and UDN.[72]

As in the United States, a combination of social pressure and public policy change was important to the Brazilian rural labor movement and, at the end of 1962, the two converged to inspire another series of reforms that defied SRB protests. In November, for example, Minister of Labor João Pinheiro da Silva Neto issued new rural union formation regulations, replacing those of his predecessor with rules both Padre Celso and Silva found easier to implement. A Minas Gerais politician and Goulart confidant, Pinheiro Neto, became a key figure in the agrarian reform debate from this time until the military coup. While U.S. embassy officials saw Pinheiro Neto as naive and easily duped by Communists, Pinheiro Neto himself believed the PCB to be an important and useful ally in Goulart's drive to make structural reforms that would ultimately reduce the mass appeal of revolutionary rhetoric. His *portarias* pleased the PCB by eliminating those parts of Montoro's regulations that required workers to form separate unions for each specific type of agricultural activity. Instead, Portaria No. 355-A of November 20 implemented Decree Law No.

72. Unfortunately, opponents challenged Lepera and Tenóriode Lima's mandates along with those of two federal and two additional state deputies. On November 21, the Superior Electoral Tribunal declared their elections null. All were accused of being PCB members and ineligible for election, even though they had run on the PTB ticket. See "Eleitos os candidatos populars," *TL*, November 1962, 4; and AmConGen, São Paulo, to USDS, "Communist Candidates Barred from Office," A-160, RG 59, DF 732.00/11-2962, DS/USNA. In Goiás, ULTAB's first president, Geraldo Tibúrcio, was elected city councilman in Anápolis, and José Porfirio da Paz was elected to the state assembly. See "Barolomeu reeleito em Amaro Leite," *TL*, February 1963, 6. The United States was concerned about the leftist tilt of politics in Brazil but believed the Brazilian government would "continue . . . to be one the United States [could] work with." Am-Embassy, Rio de Janeiro, to USDS, "Some Election Results and First Thoughts Thereupon," A-508, RG 59, DF 732.00/11-562, DS/USNA. For changes in the fortunes of Goulart and agrarian reform, see Ferreira and Benjamim, "Goulart," 1513–14; Camargo, "A questão agrária," 202; "Renato da Costa Lima no ministério de agricultura," *A Rural* (August 1962), 4–6; and "Discurso do sr. Renato da Costa Lima," *A Rural* (April 1963), 8–9.

7,038 of 1944 by subdividing rural labor into four broad categories: extractive industries (lumbermen and miners), livestock handlers, farmworkers, and autonomous producers (sharecroppers and tenant farmers). In an implied criticism of the regulations issued by former minister Montoro, Padre Celso wrote, "now, with the new Portaria, everything seems to be simplified and the evident intention of the government is to facilitate the organization of the rural classes." A second *portaria,* No. 356-A of November 21, included step-by-step instructions for holding a first meeting, advertising the meeting, holding an election, registering members, composing bylaws, and submitting the paperwork for official recognition by the labor ministry, including model forms and sample scenarios. A special four-page supplement to the February 1963 *Terra Livre* included copies of all these documents, with blanks to fill in the names of people, places, and dates, as well as summary instructions for the entire process. After so many years of obstacles, the new rules left the barriers wide open to anyone who could gather together a minimum of fifty rural workers living and working in the same municipal area. Under these rules, which stayed in effect until June 1963, more than one hundred unions were recognized nationally, with twenty added to the rolls in São Paulo alone. In the meantime, hundreds more began to organize by following the formal recognition procedures. The new rules brought the first big harvest from the seedlings João Guerreiro Filho and others had planted in the 1940s.[73]

SUPRA Gets Established

The year ended with additional advances on the rural labor front. December saw the creation of two new bodies, one a government agency and the other a civic organization, each destined to play major roles

73. See a copy of Portaria 355-A in "Regulamenta a sindicalização rural," *TL,* December 1962, 4; and Portaria 356-A, in "Instruções para a organização de sindicatos rurais," *TL,* February 1963, special supplement. U.S. attitudes toward Pinheiro Neto are recorded in Am-Embassy, Rio de Janeiro, to USDS, "Conversations with João Pinheiro Neto" and "Evaluation of Minister of Labor," A-505 and A-506, 5 November 1962, RG 59, DF 832.06 (2416), DS/USNA. Pinheiro Neto's reflections on the era are found in his *Jango: Um depoimento pessoal* (Rio de Janeiro: Record, 1993). See also Mônica Kornis and Leda Soares, "Pinheiro Neto, João," in Beloch and Abreu, eds., *DHBB,* 2738–40. For Padre Celso, see "Sindicatos na roça," *DN,* 23 November 1962, 2. Barros, "A organização sindical," 158–65, contains useful tables of rural labor associations and unions formed and recognized between 1955 and 1964.

in the São Paulo rural labor movement. To hasten the pace of the basic reforms, the Goulart administration asked for increased executive powers to decree laws related to rural labor legislation, the control of rural rents, land expropriation, and the creation of an executive agency to administer these projects. Fearing a loss of control over the agrarian reform process, the congress moved to accommodate Goulart by, among other measures, legislating the creation of SUPRA, an agency first promoted by the Neves cabinet in February. In December, Governor Brizola's nationalistic, former secretary of agriculture, João Caruso, became SUPRA's first superintendent. The SRB journal warned planters that the "most important and dangerous" aspect of SUPRA was its duty to encourage "social equality" by "promoting the just distribution of property, tying its use to the social welfare." With congress continuing to procrastinate over land reform, however, Goulart directed Caruso to set up the Department of Promotion and Rural Organization (DEPROR) in order to encourage the growth of peasant associations and rural workers' unions, groups he hoped to use to build support for the basic reform package. Within the coming year, SUPRA would come to play a central role in Brazil's rural labor movement.[74]

December also saw FAP making a bold move to place itself in direct competition with Rotta's Federation of Workers Circles. On Christmas day, Souza Meireles, Padre Celso, and a group of like-minded priests, sympathizers, and rural labor leaders met at the Colégio São Bento in São Paulo to initiate the formation of a statewide organization, modeled after the Ribeirão Preto FAP. Souza Meireles, who had political aspirations, became president of the statewide group. They hoped a statewide presence would position the FAP to take part in the newly sanctified rural labor movement. Neale Pearson claims the FAP was "never able to build up a strong organization," blaming personality conflicts and a small staff. This may have been true for other parts of the state, but at its Alta Mogiana base, the FAP was extremely strong. To help the statewide organization, Padre

74. SUPRA had been created on 11 October 1962 by Delegated Law No. 11, which was activated by Decree Law No. 1878-A of December 13. It combined departments from various ministries, including the SSR, the National Institute of Immigration and Colonization, the National Council of Agrarian Reform, and the Tapajós Rural Establishment (formerly Ford's vast rubber plantation). Starting in 1963, DEPROR worked closely with the labor ministry's National Rural Unionization Commission (CONSIR) to foster rural unionization. See Camargo, "A questão agrária," 202–7; and Leonilde Sérvolo de Medeiros and Brás José de Araújo, "Superintedência da Política Agrária (SUPRA)," in Beloch and Abreu, eds., *DHBB*, 3284–85. The SRB warning is in "Leis Delegadas no.s 8, 9, 10, e 11," *A Rural* (December 1962), 5.

Celso's local group changed its name to the Ribeirão Preto Regional Agrarian Front in March 1963, installing a new board of directors. The new directors reflected the increased polarization of rural labor and owner groups, for only Souza Meireles—a planter's son—had any direct links to the landed class. All the same, not a single rural worker sat on the board. There were academics, journalists, students, politicians, and, as honorary president, Archbishop Angelo Rossi, the prelate who replaced the deceased Dom Luís. Tactfully, the board also included a representative from the regional sheriff's office, Zenon Batista Sitrangulo. In a photograph of the meeting, a wall poster proclaims, "Peace is the Fruit of Justice." Thus, by early 1963, Padre Celso was poised to take advantage of a spate of new laws, institutions, and political forces favoring a dramatic expansion of the rural labor movement.[75]

Not so Moraes and ULTAB. As the fortunes of the church group grew, those of the Communists seemed to decline. A March headline in *Terra Livre* boldly announced that the police threatened to imprison the "Peasant Leader Irineu de Morais." Moraes accused DOPS, now directed by newly elected governor Adhemar de Barros, of hounding him. He told a story of having to disguise himself whenever he traveled by bus from one meeting of workers to another because the state police had begun stopping buses on the road to capture him. When he was in town or with the workers, "the peasant masses protected him." Indeed, in February the SRB reported having asked Barros to "stop the disorder brought to this state by agitators . . . on numerous estates . . . and to prevent the actions of those extremist revolutionary elements who are . . . provoking tensions among workers." Mario Bugliani, a cane cutter who became president of the Pontal union Moraes had helped found, faced similar threats. The sheriff of Pontal, Italo Pachioni, threatened to arrest forty-two families who marched on the courthouse to protest being fired from the Usina Bela Vista for union activity, and he called in a contingent of Ribeirão Preto police armed with rifles and machine guns to help him. Thus, while a Ribeirão Preto deputy sheriff sat with Padre Celso on the board of the FAP, other police officials moved to suppress ULTAB activists. "Only the

75. On founding the statewide FAP, see "Lideres sindicais rurais chegaram a diversas conclusões classistas," *DN*, 11 November 1962, 12; Gilberto Bellini, "Cria-se em São Paulo a FAP (Estadual): Interior está participando das reuniões," *DN*, 4 December 1962, 6; and "Organizou-se Frente Agrária estadual," *DN*, 29 January 1963, 6. On the regional FAP, see "Instalou-se frente agrária regional: A primeira diretória foi empossada," *DN*, 5 March 1963, 8. According to Syllos, little became of Souza Meireles's political career, although he did eventually become a successful land baron in the state of Amazonas. Syllos transcript, 82–83.

priests' rural unions will be forming in my jurisdiction," *Terra Livre* quoted the sheriff of Altinópolis as saying. "The peasants themselves are Communists, they don't have a right to form unions."[76]

To a considerable extent, this turn of events transpired as forecast by reformers. The reformist path to structural change in the countryside was the "white" revolution that would help stop a "red" revolution from occurring. As the unionization campaign became more official and formalized, Communist militants became outsiders and targets for repression. All the same, times had changed, for the repression seemed sporadic rather than systematic, as in the past. It is notable that Moraes felt safe in town and among the workers, for DOPS was reduced to operating on the open road, outside the jurisdiction of local authorities. Moreover, it had been the unique circumstance of Barros's election and his allegiance with planters that activated DOPS. Bugliani's story of confrontation in Pontal ended not with mass arrest but with the Ribeirão Preto police recognizing the plight of the fired families and "helping them to get services, carrying them by truck back to the plantation, totally unmasking the reactionary sheriff." Apparently, deputy sheriff Sitrangulo saw himself on the side of justice rather than simply as a partisan of the FAP. A sea change had come to social relations in the São Paulo interior since Moraes reappeared in Ribeirão Preto. The tide could turn either way, washing the radical movement to safety on the shore or out to sea to drown.[77]

76. On the hounding of Moraes and the situation in Pontal and Altinópolis, see "Ribeirão Preto: Líder camponês Irineu de Moraes ameaçado de prisão," *TL*, March 1963, 8. On Barros and the SRB, see *A Rural* (February 1963), 32, cited in Stolcke, *Coffee Planters*, 113.

77. On the Pontal incident, see "Policia protegé camponeses da furia feudal," *TL*, March 1963, 8.

8

On 26 December 1963, Otávio Sampaio da Silva appealed to President Goulart for help in solving the plight of desperate rural workers in the Alta Mogiana town of Batatais. Sampaio presented himself as director of the Batatais Professional Association of Rural Laborers, "a technical and consultative organ of the State in the study and resolution of problems" affecting rural workers. A coffee *colono* from Batatais, Sampaio had been trained as a rural labor leader by Padre Celso's *frente agrária*. He could have been president of a union but, as Sampaio explained in his petition to Goulart, "the intervention of outsiders" had complicated the process of obtaining official recognition from the labor ministry. Still, he felt obliged to speak up for rural workers in the area.

Sampaio explained that 150 of 500 association members had been fired and ex-

CUT BACK HARD

Facing the Repression of a Growing Movement

pelled from their plantation employment for daring to ask for the minimum wage, vacation pay, a weekly day of rest, and other "elementary rights of laborers." By dismissing these 150 contracted *colonos*, the planters had thrown 650 additional family members out on the road, too. Sampaio noted that his unfortunate associates joined as many as 2,500 other unemployed rural workers in Batatais. All had gone without income for several months and now lived in "unhealthy and precarious" conditions. Sampaio described the landlords' reaction to workers' "just and fair yearnings" as "base and violent," contributing to the "aggravation of social tension with irreparable damage done to the equilibrium of relations between labor and capital." Even though the association had filed complaints against planters in the labor court, settlements were "systematically frustrated by interminable actions and made weak by inflation." Sampaio warned Goulart that his fellow workers were so afflicted by despair that little kept them from turning to criminal behavior in order provide for their families. Only the charity of good neighbors and funds raised by the Ribeirão Preto Regional Agrarian Front prevented these thousands of starving workers from exploding in revolt. Wouldn't it be wise, wrote Sampaio, for the president to have his agrarian policy agency (SUPRA) investigate and resolve the rural labor problem in Batatais?[1]

This was not the first time a rural laborer had appealed to a Brazilian president for help. Nearly three decades earlier, as Chapter 2 reports, the *colono* contractor João Francisco Thomaz had helped urge on the composition of rural labor law when he wrote Vargas to ask for "a clarification of our rights . . . , our duties, and how to proceed to act in accordance with" the president's wishes. In 1934, Thomaz had presented himself as a spokesman for other rural workers; in 1963, Sampaio *was* a spokesman for other *colonos*. While Thomaz had appealed for the president to *create* laws, Sampaio asked Goulart to *fulfill* existing laws. Moreover, by Sampaio's day, a special executive agency—SUPRA—had been established just for that purpose. Times had changed. And yet, as Sampaio's frustrations attest, much remained unchanged. The planters continued to behave with impunity, firing *colonos* when they asked for their rights, defying the authority of outsiders, capriciously abandoning their own paternalist values by rejecting the demands of their "uppity children" and kicking them out of the Big House to fend for themselves. These continuities of the past must have left workers feeling as vulnerable as be-

1. "Líder rural adverte João Goulart contra perigos da revolta popular," *DN*, 28 December 1963, 6.

fore and doubtful about the benefits of the corporatist legal apparatus of unions and labor codes then being constructed in their names.

Sampaio's petition and the story of his rise to labor leadership reveal both achievements and shortcomings of Brazil's rural labor activists in the fifteen months before the military overthrew Goulart's government and tore through the rural labor movement like a gardener pruning trees with a hatchet. Sampaio was an extraordinary leader, one of the most honest and enduring created by the explosion of activism that preceded the twenty-one-year military takeover. The move from his role as head of a large *colono* family to that of rural labor militant had been dramatic and deliberate. Along the way he attracted the support of hundreds of rural workers by fighting intransigent landlords, corrupt officials, and rival Communist rural labor organizers. He not only wrote President Goulart but visited him in Brasília with a church-labor delegation. His appeals helped convince Goulart to plan his ill-fated April visit to Ribeirão Preto to inaugurate the SUPRA office.

By mid-1963, the movement had been fully legalized by the ETR; in December, rural labor delegates from around Brazil met in Rio de Janeiro to found CONTAG; by the start of 1964, SUPRA's supportive intervention had nearly eliminated factional rivalries and had set off a period of rapid union formation and recognition. These developments brought Sampaio and other rural labor activists of the period unprecedented influence and prestige.

As Sampaio and others knew, however, rural employers were deeply disturbed by labor's new status, and few rural workers had experienced real gains, despite all the legal and institutional progress. In April 1964, when conspirators of the *golpe* descended on the Alta Mogiana, they cut away at the rural labor tree, hacking off branches, leaving only nubs and the rooted trunk, hoping to use this base to cultivate a rural labor union structure that would quell social unrest and direct rural labor problems away from politics. Sampaio and his Batatais union were among the few trees left standing.[2]

2. Other important individuals could be discussed, such as Antônio Crispim da Cruz of Cravinhos. Whereas Sampaio died in the early 1980s, after leading the Batatais union for more than two decades, Crispim—who was born in 1934—was still active into the 1990s. For Crispim, see, for example, Gilberto Bellini, "Trabalhadores rurais estão unidos no sindicato lutarão pela justiça," *DN*, 10 April 1962, 6; and Jorge Martins, "Trabalhadores rurais ingressam no sindicato: Estão dispostos a conseguir justiça social," *DN*, 29 May 1962, 6. Padre Celso called Crispim "very radical." Syllos transcript, 45. Antônio Crispim da Cruz, transcript of interview by author, Ribeirão Preto, 31 March 1989, AEL/UNICAMP (hereafter Crispim transcript). Quite by intention, Sampaio's story was exceptionally significant at the time.

Making a Rural Labor Leader

The story of Sampaio's development as a local leader shares qualities with accounts of the deliberate selection of U.S. civil rights pioneers such as Jackie Robinson and Rosa Parks. Intending to gain ground on the Communists, retrograde planters, political opportunists, and conservative clergy, Padre Celso and his colleagues in the *frente agrária* tried to identify a single focal point presenting the greatest opportunity for success on all fronts. In consultation with agrarian front participants, including the political hopeful João Carlos de Souza Meireles, organizers decided to place special emphasis on gaining recognition for a rural workers' union in Batatais. They calculated that one union formed and solidified from above, with strong natural leaders, and from below—with the active, willing participation of the rural working class—would be as a "City on a Hill," a beacon to use in guiding and promoting the formation of other rural unions.[3]

The selection of Sampaio and Batatais, a town located thirty miles to the northeast of Ribeirão Preto, was not made idly. As an employee on the nearby Fazenda Boa Esperança, Sampaio had long complained of unfair labor practices in the area. Souza Meireles could surely confirm this, for his father, Antônio Josino Meireles, owned the *fazenda* and had a reputation as a reactionary landlord and union opponent who mistreated his workers.[4] Thus, the targeted planter and plantation epitomized evil, while Sampaio represented good. Married to Elvira Maria Sampaio da Silva and the father of twelve children, Sampaio was a struggling coffee *colono* when he first encountered the strident Padre Celso in August 1962. On Saturday, August 4, the priest rode into Batatais's central Praça Pio XII on the back of a big truck. As he made clear to Sampaio and some four hundred other listeners in the plaza, the setting had been selected not only because of its centrality but also because of the opportunity it gave to challenge the local cleric. At the head of the plaza was the São Sebastião church, an ornate edifice with an imported marble altar and a series of striking panels depicting the Crucifixion. The renowned artist Cândido Portinari—a native of neighboring Brodósqui who was also a Com-

3. On Batatais and Sampaio, see below and "Fazendeiro desacatou líder rural," *DN,* 26 May 1963, 6; and Syllos transcript, 56.

4. *Notícias de Hoje* condemned Souza Meireles's father in 1953 for getting a priest to use confessions to secretly interrogate workers on the Fazenda Boa Esperança (Good Hope) about their activities and politics. "Um padre a serviço do tatuíra," *NH,* 27 August 1953, n.p. The article refers to Meireles by an insulting local nickname relating him to a small armadillo species. (Thanks to John French for this citation.) The younger Souza Meireles must have resented his father deeply to have consented to this campaign.

munist and a rural labor movement sympathizer—had painted the panels in 1954, and yet, ironically, the local priest allied himself with the planters whose contributions had paid for the construction of the church, a stone-cold monument to the suffering Jesus. By appearing atop a dirty farm truck stationed defiantly before the church, Padre Celso highlighted the differences between his kind of Catholicism and that being preached to the planters inside. As Sampaio listened, Padre Celso decried the "tremendous injustices committed in the name of Christ against the worker."[5] The demonstration had a considerable impact on workers gathered in the square, and two weeks later, on Sunday, August 19, Padre Celso and the others returned to Batatais to offer an alternative mass to still larger numbers of workers dispersed among two humble, neighborhood chapels and a crossroads gathering point.

Dr. Vicente Tassinari, the agrarian front coordinator in Batatais, had made arrangements for the August rallies and service. During the mass, Tassinari surveyed those in attendance and identified *colonos* from several area plantations, including Fazenda Boa Esperança. In the following weeks, he continued to try to stimulate local interest in forming a rural union.[6] Not surprisingly, the Communist Party had already formed a rural association in Batatais. In 1954 party militant Arlindo Teixeira had even applied to the labor ministry for formal recognition of his association as a union. This was just as Padre Celso wanted it to be. The agrarian front generally opted to organize workers in areas previously agitated by the party. One of the fundamental goals of the church, after all, was to neutralize the Communist rural labor movement. The success of the "pacification program" of the *frente agrária,* Caio Magri told an assembly of seventy rural workers,

5. See Syllos transcript, 47–48. The central plaza rally was announced in Gilberto Bellini, "Campanha sindicalismo rural continua: Batatais e Guaira receberão FAP," *DN,* 1 August 1962, 7. It was reported in Gilberto Bellini, "FAP quer redenção do camponês: Camponeses querem seu sindicato," *DN,* 7 August 1962, 2, 11. In addition to Syllos and Caio Magri, Dr. Vicente Tassinari and the college students Terezinha Gasparini and Fernando Vidal Martin de Melo also spoke. For more on the paintings and Portinari, who died 6 February 1962, see "Mestre Candinho: Farda filosófica," *Tribuna Ribeirão,* December 1996; and Gerson Knispel, "Portinari," *Revista Brasiliense* 40 (March/April 1962), 18–25. As the region grew and coffee gave way to sugarcane, the church was renamed the Matriz de Bom Jesus da Cana Verde (Cathedral of the Good Jesus of Green Cane).

6. Workers from the following *fazendas* attended mass at the Batatais chapels, Capela da Santana do Estreito and Capela da Limeira: Boa Esperança, São Pedro, Santana do Estreito, Limeira, Santa Tereza, dos Enganos, da Mata, Boa Vista, Santa Helena, California, Floresta, and Batatais. At the crossroads, or Beco do Macaco, Tassinari found workers from *fazendas* Santo Antonio da Ilha, da Mata, and Santana. See "Em Batatais e Orlândia: Camponeses cerram fileiras em torno da FAP; Nada imperdirá a criação de sindicato rural," *DN,* 21 August 1962, 6. Further activities were reported in Tomaz Roberto Rodrigues, "Sindicato de Batatais recebe mais adesões," *DN,* 27 September 1962, 3.

"will depend on unmasking Communist elements who come provoking the laborer to adopt drastic positions, with anarchy and violence." The training for this began in the politicization circles, where
Otávio Sampaio became a regular student of courses on Catholic social doctrine, unionization, and rural labor law.[7]

Sampaio's transformation from *colono* to rural labor leader occurred in a context of significant national change. In early December,
Goulart raised the minimum wage for 1963 and created the *abono de
natal,* a Christmas bonus equal to one month's salary that all employers had to pay.[8] On 6 January 1963, a plebiscite restored full presidential powers to Goulart. On January 21, ULTAB held an assembly in São
Paulo in which delegates from nine states learned how to use the new
union recognition regulations, celebrated their numerous victories,
and reaffirmed their commitment to "the struggle for the application
of" the Belo Horizonte declaration.[9] In February the new populist majority in the chamber of deputies passed the Rural Laborer Statute
(ETR), and on March 2, Goulart signed it into law. Once it went into
effect on June 18, the ETR symbolized the culmination of more than
two decades of elite debate, legislative wrangling, and rural labor mobilization in support of the formal incorporation of rural workers.
The fruit of many limbs, the basic statute remained in place through
the end of the century, shaping rural workers' lives and making Brazil
the home of the largest rural labor union movement in the Western
Hemisphere.[10]

7. Arlindo Teixeira, transcript of interview by author, Ribeirão Preto, 18 October 1988, 10–
11, revealed the early PCB campaign. Syllos transcript, 15, 57, discusses the church's confrontational tactics. Caio Magri is quoted in Gilberto Bellini, "FAP exige justiça social para roça: Camponeses lutarão por sua promoção," *DN,* 22 August 1962, 7. The announcement and program of
the circles was given in Bellini, "FAP administrará cursos a camponeses." Sampaio apparently
missed the first two circles, held in September, but he was listed as present at the third meeting,
held Sunday, 21 October 1962. See "Camponeses da FAP ouviram diretor do HC," *DN,* 23 October
1962, 8. Of the remaining thirteen organized sessions, Sampaio missed only the sixth (18 November 1962) and twelfth (3 May 1963) circles; he sent his eldest son, Sebastião, in his place.

8. ULTAB stressed the law's applicability to rural workers in "Direitos dos trabalhadores
da roça," *TL,* February 1963, 2. The SRB called it "one more onus on the economic life . . . of
business, already so overloaded with obligations imposed by public authorities." R. Shalmer, "O
que representará o 13 salário para seu negócio," *A Rural* (November 1962), 57.

9. "Assembléia da ULTAB: Intensificar a luta pela reforma agrária e pela sindicalização
rural" and "Plano de trabalho para 1963 da união dos lavradores e trabalhadores agrícolas do
Brasil," *TL,* February 1963, 8. Rural labor federations or associations from the following states
are mentioned: Pará, Ceará, Goiás, Espírito Santo, Minas Gerais, Rio de Janeiro, São Paulo, Mato
Grosso, and Paraná.

10. The ETR has been the subject of several legal studies (discussed below) but no social
or legislative histories of the law have been written, despite its importance. By 1995 there were
3,200 unions representing ten million workers formally integrated into the movement. See
CONTAG, *Anais do VI Congresso Nacional dos Trabalhadores Rurais* (Brasília: CONTAG, 1995).

The Rural Laborer Statute

By the time the ETR became law, rural labor legislation per se had few opponents. Nearly everyone pronounced their support for rural labor law, yet different groups and individuals had different sorts of law in mind. These camps can be divided usefully into three categories. Among elites, the most popular and least controversial form of legislation was that which dealt with rural labor as an object of concern. These laws set standards for the health and welfare of some rural workers through means such as specifying sanitation codes for rural labor residences. Clean and healthy workers performed better, the lawmakers assumed. The most notable of these measures was a 1934 decree (No. 24,637) offering compensation to rural as well as urban workers who were injured on the job. But this and other such laws presented few threats to rural social relations and had little impact on rural workers' lives. A second category of rural labor law sought to make rural living and working conditions more like urban ones and thus "fix" rural workers in the countryside, discouraging their migration to towns and cities. The rights to a minimum wage and time off that were written into the 1946 constitution and the CLT fall into this camp. Even the profoundly anticorporatist Rio de Janeiro politician Carlos Lacerda (of the UDN) had authored a rural labor bill along these lines as a congressman in 1955.

The ETR fell into the third category, which was the most controversial. These proposals integrated features of the former categories with a structure for incorporating and empowering rural workers through syndicalization. By early 1962, as noted above, the corporatist landlord body, the CRB, had endorsed this category of law, seeing a controlled official union structure as better than the anarchic mobilization then presumed to be afflicting many plantations. As we shall see, however, groups like the SRB, which sat outside the corporatist structure, vehemently opposed the ETR.[11]

The legislature itself had been dealing with the matter of rural labor reform since the era of slavery abolition. Examining progress made in the twentieth century, analysts of the ETR routinely tied the statute to a long history of proposals and counterproposals, beginning with the 1903 rural unionization law (No. 979), passing through Vargas's 1944 Decree Law No. 7,038 and ill-fated 1954 bill

---

11. A brief description of different group's stances on rural labor legislation can be found in Stolcke, *Coffee Planters*, 108–10.

(No. 4,264), and extending up to the draft version of the final ETR, Project No. 1,837, proposed in May 1960 by Rio Grande do Sul representative Fernando Ferrari. From his first years in congress under President Vargas until his last under Goulart, Ferrari developed a reputation for advocating rural labor legislation. A book of his speeches on the subject, *Escravos da terra* (Slaves of the land), published posthumously (he died in a May 1963 airplane crash), showed him to be the recipient of appeals from rural workers and rural labor leaders such as Benedito Pereira Serra, president of ULTAB's Pará state organization. A skillful spokesman, his arguments reflected nearly all of the motives for passing such a law. Like Vargas, he believed it would stop the rural exodus; like developmentalists, he saw it as a way of strengthening industrialization by creating a new class of rural consumers; like landlords, he considered it a means of ensuring social peace and disciplining rural production processes; like other politicians, he hoped it would expand his constituency, circumventing traditional clientelistic power networks; like the CNBB, he expected it to uplift the rural poor and fight Communism; and like the Communists, he saw it as an approach to empowering rural workers and erasing the legacies of slavery. These many branches carried varied ideas and structures into the legislative debate over the ETR.[12]

Despite Ferrari's efforts, no single law could satisfy all of the contradictory expectations of such diverse objectives. In 1944 the SRB supported the rural unionization decree, so long as it left rural workers no way of funding their organizations. But the ETR included the *imposto sindical* (union tax), which funded unions through the deduction of one day's pay for all workers in the union's jurisdiction, whether or not they belonged to the entity (art. 135). The ETR also made it easy for rural employer associations organized under the CRB, through Decree Law No. 8,127 of 1945, to convert into syndicates (art. 141)—which they soon did, creating another source of irritation for the SRB. For workers, the new law grouped together and expanded a variety of existing rights and duties, making them fit agricultural realities more specifically than they had previously, as provisions of the CLT. These matters included rights to paid vacations (arts. 43–48), no-

12. On Lacerda's bill, see Catharino, *O trabalhador rural brasileiro*, 40–41. For the legislative history, see ibid. (which includes a detailed analysis of Ferrari's 1956 proposal, No. 1938); and Segadas Vianna, *O Estatuto do Trabalhador Rural*, 35–47. For more on Ferrari, see *Escravos da terra* (Rio de Janeiro: Globo, 1963)—the ULTAB letter is on pages 107–8—and Renato Lemos and Elias Fajardo, "Ferrari, Fernando," in Beloch and Abreu, eds., *DHBB*, 1256–57. Another glimpse into the legislative process is provided by Marta Cehelsky's study of the ET, which was up for discussion in the same period as the ETR but not adopted until mid-1964. See her *Land Reform in Brazil*, esp. chap. 3.

tice of dismissal (arts. 90–94), weekly days of rest (art. 42), and individual contracts (Title IV). Planters had successfully kept earlier laws from requiring workers to have a "work booklet" (*carteira profissional*), but the ETR mandated their distribution free of charge to all workers fourteen years old and older (arts. 11–24). With the booklet in hand, all workers would be armed with copies of their labor contract and those general laws applying to them, as well as a work history—something like the *cadernetas agrícolas* issued to *colonos* since the 1920s. The ETR also included new rights for rural workers such as the eight-hour day (arts. 25–27) and prohibitions against dismissing pregnant and married women (arts. 54–56) and assigning minors to physically demanding and unhealthy work (arts. 57–61). Significantly, article 179 extended those provisions of the CLT not covered in the ETR to rural laborers. Thus, in 1963 the long-promised proposal of extending urban law to rural workers and creating a special law to regulate rural labor relations became a reality. A lengthy and complex law, it was not long before jurists and legal scholars began to analyze it word by word, subjecting the law's every phrase to multiple interpretations.[13]

While many aspects of the law deserve attention, the clauses that caused the most conflict related to compensation. The ETR established new compensation parameters that could potentially put more cash in workers' pockets. As in the recent past, rural workers were to receive at least the regional minimum wage, which was adjusted periodically by government commissions and presidential decree. But the ETR limited the discounts that could be deducted from wages before their payment in cash. Whereas food, clothing, and the costs of health care and transportation had been routinely deducted in the past, now only rent and food costs could be deducted. As discussed in the last chapter, planters typically responded to worker demands for minimum-wage payments by deducting rent from their salaries. Until the ETR, employers could deduct up to one-third of a worker's wages to cover rent. Under the ETR, however, rent deductions were capped at 20 percent of the minimum wage—not 20 percent of the worker's salary—and landlords could not double- or triple-charge a household where two or more members might be contracted workers (art. 29). If the housing was not decent and functional, no rent could

13. The copy of the law used here is in Ferrari, *Escravos,* 167–216. Among the most thorough and early legal examinations are Segadas Vianna, *O Estatuto do Trabalhador Rural;* and Russomano, *Comentários ao Estatuto do Trabalhador Rural.* Russomano takes the discussion back to Brazil's first constitution and an 1837 law, No. 108, which regulated contract labor and includes copies of the ministerial *portarias* and decrees issued from 1963 to 1967 to regulate or modify the ETR.

be charged at all (art. 32). Besides rent, planters had also begun to consider the product of *colono* food crops and livestock husbandry as part of their pay, but the ETR disallowed this practice, unless spelled out in a separate sharecropping contract (art. 41). In other words, those values of rent and land usufruct that planters had traditionally used to compensate and retain *colonos* now, under the ETR, either had limited or no compensatory value. This law would have made a big difference for João Anunciato, whose case was discussed in Chapter 6. Finally, the ETR granted "stability"—protection against dismissal—for all workers with more than ten years employment on the same farm (art. 95–102). When unions formed and workers struggled, adjusting compensation to at least match the ETR topped the list of demands. When planters united, however, they sought ways to reduce their dependency on resident employees, thereby escaping the law's application to "employees." As both classes became familiar with the new rules, the ETR intensified the rural exodus long under way, in ironic contradistinction to the intentions of its authors, all of whom imagined the law would "fix" rural workers in the countryside.[14]

Reactions to the ETR

The allegation that planters responded to the ETR by firing permanent employees bothered the SRB. In an August polemic, SRB president Salvio de Almeida Prado rejected the allegation. It was not the law that led planters to fire workers, he said, but the economics of coffee production. Lacking access to cheap credit and suffering from price regulation and trade taxation, it was only natural for planters to let unnecessary workers go in order to protect the viability of their estates. Planters had nothing to fear from the ETR, he claimed. "We know it would not be worthwhile to dispense with our longtime rural laborers to escape the obligations of the ETR because it is certain that agricultural work has to be done by someone and who better is there to do it than those who remain on the plantation for a long period." By virtue of their longevity on the plantation, Almeida Prado said, these are the "good" workers. "If they're good laborers, there's noth-

14. In addition to contrasts gathered from previous chapters, insights about how workers were treated by the courts before the ETR have been drawn from Luiz Roberto de Rezende Peuch, *Direito individual e coletivo do trabalho (estudo e comentários)* (São Paulo: Revista dos Tribunais, 1960), 178–83. (Thanks to John French for the reference.)

ing more just and intelligent than to keep them around." By the following year, however, *A Rural* published a series of studies of the ETR that emphasized ways to avoid its provisions, especially by reconfiguring a labor force into categories not covered by the law. "All of the Rural Laborer Statute was structured around attending the needs of the rural labor employee, that is the laborer retained by a labor contract," wrote SRB lawyer João Batista Camargo. "Autonomous workers . . . such as those retained by contractors, share arrangements, and as tenants . . . are not referenced by the ETR." Subsequent issues of the magazine provided planters with sample contracts that could help them minimize the impact of the law on their operations. One sample contract had workers attest to the structural soundness of plantation housing and promise not to complain about their huts.[15]

When the ETR came into effect on June 17, São Paulo and Paraná planters were in the midst of a campaign to attract government attention. The early 1960s were difficult years for Brazilian coffee. Overproduction of mediocre coffee had contributed to declining world prices, and to combat this trend, the Brazilian Coffee Institute (IBC, Instituto Brasileiro do Café) and the Goulart administration invested in a program of production regulation known as the Executive Group on the Rationalization of Coffee Growing (GERCA, Grupo Executivo de Racionalização da Cafeicultura). From mid-1962 to 1967, GERCA paid coffee planters to eliminate low-yield trees, diversify land usage, and plant higher-quality coffee varieties. The most intense period of eradication was from June 1962 to the end of 1963, when millions of trees were uprooted. Financing for this program came from a coffee export levy that planters resented. Suspicious that the government was diverting the funds to other purposes, planters ridiculed the levy as the "confiscation quota." In June 1963, when the government announced levy and exchange rates for the 1963/64 harvest season, planters rose up in protest, demanding relief from the quota and the tax. They mimicked radical labor by forming a group to coordinate their protest called the General Coffee Command (CGC, Comando Geral do Café). When Goulart rejected their demands, planters throughout the region paralyzed commercial activity in the countryside. The U.S. consul in São Paulo saw this dispute over regulatory issues as "one of the most important factors

---

15. Almeida Prado, "A situação da lavoura em face do Estatuto do Trabalhador Rural," *A Rural* (August 1963), 47; and Camargo, "Campo de aplicação do Estatuto do Trabalhador Rural," *A Rural* (August 1964), 24–26; and subsequent issues under the same title.

in the rapid growth of the rightist, anti-Goulart movement in São Paulo." After a few days, however, the CGC negotiated a settlement with GERCA that finally secured the relief planters sought, and in September, the administration further pleased them by raising domestic prices by 25 percent and promising to entirely eliminate the 1964 contribution quota. In this same period, international demand strengthened, and prices climbed. As the anthropologist Verena Stolcke writes, "coffee planters, especially in São Paulo, had no further grounds to complain." [16]

Yet complain they did once workers began to demand application of the ETR. In an August editorial, Almeida Prado saw the ETR as the product of "electoral demagoguery" and lambasted the law for thoughtlessly applying inappropriate urban standards to rural settings. "The diploma approved for farming is a loyal copy of the labor regime of the cities, presenting itself as one of the most grave and difficult problems to be resolved in the present context," Almeida Prado concluded. Even though the specific bill that became the ETR had been under review since 1960, Almeida Prado complained that inadequate study had gone into the measure, and it had been passed too quickly. Stolcke argues that it was not the speed with which the ETR passed but the fact the SRB had so little influence in writing it that bothered Almeida Prado. This is entirely consistent with past behavior, for few issues had outraged former SRB activist Francisco Malta Cardoso more than being excluded from the process. Despite improved economic indicators for coffee, SRB spokesmen maintained that their profit margins were too narrow to enable them to comply with the law. Because they were "subordinated" and "dependent" on "economic happenings" outside their control, planters had to "lower their responsibilities" by converting their "dispensable fund of manual labor." In other words, they had to fire workers to protect their profits.

The planters' position was strengthened by the effects of coffee eradication, said SRB secretary Arnaldo Borba de Moraes. In uprooting so many trees in such a short span of time, the planters claimed to have no alternative but to lay off *colonos*, producing the first labor surplus in São Paulo admitted by the SRB since the Great Depression. "There is a colossal mass of unemployed men of the country, wander-

16. The ETR enabling regulations were Portarias No. 346 and 347 of 17 June 1963. Stolcke, *Coffee Planters*, 111–12; and AmConGen, São Paulo, to USDS, "Coffee Prices Become Political Issue," Airgram 3 (hereafter cited in the following form: A-3), 6 July 1963, RG 59, Inco-Coffee BRAZ (3510), DS/USNA.

ing from here to there with their families," Borba de Moraes said. "If the government doesn't improve coffee prices, there's nothing planters can do beyond hiring these people during the harvest period, as they always have, because coffee no longer supports the maintenance of workers during the entire year." Since the ETR itself was not the problem, however, the situation could be resolved by increasing the income of planters. With their income up, planters would have no incentive to let workers go, Almeida Prado argued. In fact, when FTRSESP president José Rotta criticized planters for responding to the ETR by firing employees, Almeida Prado responded by urging Rotta to join with the SRB in pressuring the government to fulfill the "rights of the rural class, of which [you] are a part." In the years ahead, Rotta would prove a better ally than Communist militants had been for the planters.[17]

Soon after the law went into effect, social commentators submitted the ETR to intensive examination. Despite years of discussion and the drafting of numerous versions of such a law, many sympathizers were as dumbfounded as São Paulo planters by the final shape of Brazil's long-awaited rural labor code. When the ETR was publicized, the renowned Brazilian historian and editor Caio Prado Junior remarked that its promulgation had taken "many by surprise." Although it was "the most important event relative to [Goulart's] much touted basic reforms," he felt that "disinterest . . . surrounded [its] elaboration." He thought the public's fascination with agrarian reform, especially land distribution, led observers to discount the utility of the ETR. Although later analysts such as Leonilde Medeiros argued that passage of the ETR symbolized the failure of the popular movement to succeed in achieving more fundamental change through land distribution, for Caio Prado the ETR would bring about land reform by helping workers on Brazil's largest plantations pressure their employers for improved conditions and better wages. Applying the terms of liberal political economy, he saw mobilized rural labor as a force for generating happier, healthier workers, greater agricultural efficiency, and an expansion of the land market, bringing

17. In April 1965, with the military in power, Rotta became president of the National Confederation of Agriculture Laborers (CONTAG). Almeida Prado, "Legislações trabalhistas," *A Rural* (August 1963), 3; and "A situação da lavoura." Arnaldo Borba de Moraes, "Os agricultores e o Estatuto do Trabalhador Rural," *A Rural* (July 1963), 55. Stolcke, *Coffee Planters,* 110. One specialist on *boiás-frias,* Maria Conceição D'Incao, agrees that those who blame the ETR for causing out-migration are wrong; she claims it was the availability of a labor surplus that made it possible for employers to reduce their dependency on resident workers from the 1960s on. See her *O "boia-fria": Acumulação e miséria* (Petrópolis: Vôzes, 1975), 117.

down prices and making it possible for workers to become proprietors and producers.[18]

Caio Prado was no stranger to rural society; he wrote of it regularly, and his magazine—*Revista Brasiliense*—covered rural issues often. Moreover, Caio Prado had grown up on a São Paulo plantation, and despite descending from one of Brazil's great landed families, he had become a Communist, though an undisciplined one, and committed himself to studies that could help engender radical social change. His comments on the ETR reflected the informed view of an independent leftist intellectual. He thought the law important—"the true completion of the abolition of slavery"—yet problematic. For him, its definition of the rural laborer left out too many forms of rural employment: not all rural laborers "render services to rural employers . . . in exchange for a salary paid in money or in kind, or partially in kind and partially in money," as the law read. (As noted above, planters would soon learn to use the ETR's narrow definitions to their advantage.) In addition, the law failed to account for the local and regional diversity of Brazilian agriculture, favoring universal rules and regulations that would prove impractical in many settings. Despite these failings and others, the law's chapters on unionization caused Caio Prado to urge workers and their advocates to use the ETR to organize and to marshal their new power to urge enforcement of the best parts of the law and revisions of the worst. The *sindicato* provisions constituted the heart of the law, the piece that allowed free workers to legally participate in the corporatist system. If they used this power correctly, said Caio Prado, their pressure would eventually destroy the concentrated landholdings that were a legacy of the slave era and that continued to place enormous burdens on Brazil's progress.

Caio Prado's analysis differed from official PCB theorists in various respects. He disagreed that sharecropping was a vestige of feudalism and saw it instead as an arrangement far superior to wage earning for most rural workers. In other words, he contested Marxist doctrine on proletarianization, believing those who avoided dependency on wages more free than wage earners. For Caio Prado, rural unions promised to serve as vehicles for articulating the collective voice of various segments of the rural working classes. The party's position on

18. Caio Prado Junior, "O Estatuto do Trabalhador Rural," in *A questão agrária*, 142–60. Two additional contemporary sociological studies are J. V. Freitas Marcondes, "O Estatuto do Trabalhador Rural e o problema da terra," *Cadernos Brasileiros* 5 : 4 (1963), 55–59; and Price, "Rural Unionization in Brazil." See also, Medieros, *História dos movimentos*, 81.

João Pinheiro Neto (right foreground) received a warm welcome from peasants in Sapê, Paraiba, soon after he was named head of SUPRA in July 1963. Photo: courtesy Arquivo Fotográfico da *Última Hora* from Arquivo do Estado de São Paulo

unions was more ambiguous. Most leftist theorists supported the idea of "land for those who work it," while simultaneously promoting the proletarianization of sharecroppers and *camponeses* in general. For the party as for Caio Prado, the organizational aspects of the ETR became its most important features, and ULTAB, through *Terra Livre,* argued that "without syndicates [the ETR] will be a dead letter."[19]

In the ETR, the process of forming unions (Title VI) was made easier than that spelled out in the November 1962 *portarias* of labor minister Pinheiro Neto. Rural workers across the nation used the 1962 rules to unite in four broad occupational categories, gaining official recognition for more than one hundred unions, with twenty added to the rolls in São Paulo alone. The June 1963 ETR rules eliminated the constraint of unifying workers by job categories and emphasized location instead. Now, a single union in each municipality could form to serve all rural workers, so long as they qualified as "rural employees . . . paid in cash or in kind," a qualification that excluded the broad category of "autonomous producers." Still, union organizing proceeded apace, such that 270 Rural Laborers' Unions (STRs, Sindicatos dos Trabalhadores Rurais) had been recognized by the end of

19. Cicero Viana, "Sem sindicatos a lei será letra morta," *TL,* July 1963, 2.

1963, with 555 additional groups awaiting recognition. Robert Price of the Wisconsin Land Tenure Center calculated that by the end of 1963, rural labor unions had been recognized or were in the process of seeking official recognition in 22 percent (827) of Brazil's 3,719 *municípios*. In July, Pinheiro Neto was named to head SUPRA and, as its superintendent, pledged the agency to help organize rural labor unions in 2,000 of these municipalities. By April 1964, 1,604 unions had been founded and recognized, with dozens more in formation.[20]

The organization of recognized rural labor unions eventually caused some of the changes Caio Prado had envisaged. The ETR was only as good as the unions it legitimized. In response to organizing, rural employers eventually altered their production methods and modernized their plantations. Many did not want to deal with demanding workers who questioned their authority and paternalism. At the time, a São Paulo agronomist surmised that the most important aspect of the law was its potential for altering rural power relations. It put more "decision making" authority in the hands of workers, he wrote, redistributing power away from proprietors. This would add "flexibility" to the "rigid social stratification" of Brazilian agriculture and accelerate social and technological change, such as the "outmigration" of workers and greater landlord investment in machine over human "inputs."

But the power given workers by the ETR would not be strong enough to support their "*fixação*" in the country: it would not stop the economic forces that were calling workers to the cities and spurring employers to reduce their dependency on resident labor. "The sum of these forces are more powerful than the Statute itself," the agronomist wrote, "yet, it is opportune to recognize that the Statute will also contribute to the intensification of this process." Indeed, in the later half of 1963, the law and courts contributed to the formal

20. Pinheiro Neto was named president of SUPRA in July. The agency had been created in October 1962, and João Caruso became its first president. Composed of agricultural ministry departments such as the SSR and labor ministry units such as the Rural Unionization Commission, SUPRA became a significant player in rural politics under Pinheiro Neto's guidance. See Chapter 7; Mônica Kornis and Leda Soares, "Pinheiro Neto, João," in Beloch and Abreu, eds., *DHBB,* 2738–40; and Leonilde Sérvolo de Medeiros and Brás José de Araújo, "Superintendência da Política Agrária (SUPRA)," in Beloch and Abreu, eds., *DHBB,* 3284–85. For the ETR regulations, see "Como fazer eleição no sindicato rural," *TL,* October 1963, special supplement. Barros, "A organização sindical," 158–65, consists of useful tables of rural labor associations and unions formed and recognized between 1955 and 1964. For Price's table, see "Rural Unionization," appendix 2; and for other union numbers, see table 18 in Pearson, "Small Farmer and Rural Worker," 257–58. See also Dulles, *Unrest in Brazil,* 220–75, passim; and Camargo, "A questão agrária," 203–22.

expulsion of nearly two hundred workers from sixteen *fazendas* in the Alta Mogiana. The two most dramatic cases dated from October through December and involved 140 resident sugarcane workers dismissed by Matarazzo from the Fazenda Amália in Santa Rosa de Viterbo and fourteen coffee *colono* families fired by Meireles from the Fazenda Boa Esperança. As we have seen, both plantations were settings of considerable class conflict, with the former agitated by ULTAB and the latter by the FAP.[21]

As Caio Prado and the agronomist had foreseen, the ETR affected a change in relationships on Brazilian plantations. Where the workers were organized, where they demanded their rights under the ETR, their demands resulted in an inversion of the intended objectives of the law. "Until 1963," stated FAP protégé Antônio Crispim da Cruz, "no law existed for the laborer, the law determined nothing, it gave no rights to the rural laborer." Despite the error of Crispim's observation, it is clear that the advent of the ETR was a turning point in the history of the rural labor movement. It is also worth emphasizing, however, that this was a gradual process. In 1963 relatively few workers on a small proportion of the region's thousands of agricultural establishments fell victim to the ironic potential of the ETR. Thus, the Alta Mogiana experience supports the agronomist's preoccupations. In several cases, the ETR did hasten the shift from the *colonato* to the temporary wage labor system known as the *volante* (mobile, or flying) system. *Volante* workers were later ridiculed as "cold lunches" (*bóias-frias*). On the other hand, the ETR itself merely shaped this transition: it was the planters' greed and hostility toward the law and those who invoked it that led them to abolish the *colonato* by 1970.[22]

21. Antônio Dinaer Piteri, "O Estatuto do Trabalhador Rural: Problemas de aplicação e prováveis conséquências sócio-econômicas," *ASP* 9 : 1–2 (January/February 1964), 3–4. The dismissal cases discussed stem from a thorough examination of the records of the Justiça do Trabalho, Ribeirão Preto, conducted by the author and Vilma Welch in 1991. The cases counted were those in which the workers' dismissal was *homologado* (formalized) by the court, a procedure that terminated the worker's right to make further claims against the employer in exchange for a one-time severance payment. Article 179 of the ETR made this procedure available to employers by extending CLT provisions to rural labor cases. The Matarazzo and Batatais stories are discussed later in this chapter.

22. Crispim transcript, 10. Stolcke argues that the ETR "aroused the intense hostility [of planters] against the Goulart government" and that it was "a genuine threat to their traditional privileges." But I am arguing that the law did little unless workers organized to insist on its enforcement. Stolcke, *Coffee Planters,* 112. From 1958 to 1970, the proportion of *colonos* and sharecroppers with families working on São Paulo coffee plantations dropped from 67.4 percent to 8.2 percent of the labor force. See Cliff Welch, "Rural Workers and the Law in São Paulo, Brazil, 1930–1970," in *Identity, Consciousness, and Class Action: New Approaches to the Study of Latin American Workers,* edited by John D. French and Daniel James (Durham: Duke University Press, forthcoming).

Organizing in Batatais

These national developments significantly influenced local labor organizing in 1963. Although most efforts continued under the provisions of the 1944 decree and Pinheiro Neto's *portarias,* the organizing atmosphere improved as militants awaited the ETR's activation. Soon after Goulart signed the law in March, the FAP campaign in Batatais moved into high gear. The story of Otávio Sampaio's efforts in this town offers a case study of the problems workers and leaders faced in preventing the law from becoming a "dead letter." By stimulating the formation of a union in Batatais, Padre Celso invited trouble from reactionary coffee planters and Communist militants. In the agrarian front's campaign to make an example of Batatais, the town was chosen to initiate a regional campaign for the payment of minimum wages and the provision of written contracts. In the blazing heat of a Sunday afternoon in March, Sampaio took the microphone for the first time, addressing three thousand rural workers gathered in the square in front of city hall. Only two hours earlier, he had placed his name as president on an application to the federal labor ministry petitioning the registration of the rural laborers' union of Batatais. Although many others also spoke that day, the occasion marked the "coming out" of native son Sampaio.

Shortly after the rally, *Diário de Notícias* interviewed Sampaio and his wife regarding their heightened public profile as union leaders. Elvira Sampaio, forty-six years old and the mother of nineteen children, admitted to fearing the vengeance of the planters so much that she had "horrendous nightmares" and had almost "lost her way from so much worry." Sampaio placed his trust in Jesus, in a curt reference to the ideas that would soon form the core of liberation theology. "Could it be that He enjoys seeing us suffer like slaves?" asked Sampaio rhetorically. "I don't believe it and for that we struggle for our liberty, our rights and for social justice."[23] The first test of his faith in the struggle for justice came soon enough.

In the weeks following the rally, Sampaio, Padre Celso, and Tassinari met with *colonos* in a half dozen places to prepare for action. Then, in the late afternoon of May 24, Sampaio stopped work and,

23. The initiation ceremony was announced in "Frente Agrária promoverá concentração. Dois novos sindicatos serão criados," *DN,* 24 February 1963, 7. Workers and speakers came from Jardinópolis, Sales Oliveira, Altinópolis, Brodósqui, Ribeirão Preto, Dumont, Guatapará, Bonfim Paulista, and of course, Batatais. See "Frente agrária estará amanhã em Batatais: Cria-se sindicato e realiza-se concentração," *DN,* 2 March 1963, 3. The Sampaios were interviewed in "Batatais: Agita-se a roça com assombroso movimento sindicalista. Presidente do sindicato prestou oportunas declarações," *DN,* 16 March 1963, 9.

President Goulart signs SUPRA regulations in October 1963 as a smiling Pinheiro Neto (center) looks on. Photo: courtesy Arquivo Fotográfico da *Última Hora* from Arquivo do Estado de São Paulo

accompanied by a group of fellow *colonos,* approached the plantation office, where they encountered Antônio Bartolomeu Sobrinho, administrator of Fazenda Boa Esperança. Sampaio presented himself as president of the Batatais union, placing a sheet of paper before Sobrinho listing his group's demands. They wanted payment of minimum wages, on a monthly rather than bimonthly basis, and provision of written contracts that conformed to the legal standards set forth in the law. But Sobrinho would hear none of it and castigated Sampaio, shouting at him in front of the others. Less than two days later, planter Antônio Josino Meireles stripped Sampaio and his family of essential work privileges.[24]

Blocked from harvesting and prevented from cultivating the ten thousand coffee trees the family had contracted to treat, some of Elvira Sampaio's worst fears were turning real. Nevertheless, Sampaio threw himself into a struggle with Meireles. Within a few days, he traveled to Ribeirão Preto, and with FAP lawyer Caio Magri's help,

24. Preparations were reported in "Camponeses de Batatais receberão frente agrária hoje e amanhã" and Gilberto Bellini, "Camponeses de Batatais: Unam-se que a vitória esta proxima," *DN,* 11 May 1963, 5. The events of May 24–26 are reconstructed from "Fazendeiro desacatou líder rural" and the defense brief written by Divo Marino and submitted to the regional labor tribunal of São Paulo in the case *Otavio Sampaio c. Fazenda Boa Esperança,* Processo 854/63, Packet 175, JT/RP (hereafter cited as Marino brief).

he sued Boa Esperança for his reinstatement and what the law said was owed him: minimum wages, compensatory back wages, and the "thirteenth month bonus" Goulart had introduced. Urged on by Padre Celso and the front, he also filed a request to secure the state's mediation in contract negotiations with eight additional Batatais *fazendas*. Called a *"dissidio coletivo,"* Sampaio and Padre Celso claimed that because *colonos* on the nine *fazendas* were "collectively dissatisfied" with the terms of their employment, they wanted the regional labor delegate to mediate contract negotiations. One hundred and seventeen *colonos* and family workers had their names listed on the motion. The ETR was not due to go into effect for another month, and so the agrarian front grounded its complaint in Decree Law No. 9,070 of 1946, which regulated strikes and collective disputes. The complaint stated that Batatais *colonos* wanted daily wages raised from Cr$150 to Cr$400, written contracts, their right to assembly honored, and their living conditions improved.[25]

While Sampaio and Padre Celso awaited the action of the court and labor ministry, Meireles and the other planters united to suppress the work stoppage. On nearby Fazenda Boa Vista, planter Irineu Marques persecuted seven *colono* families, known members of the association, by prohibiting them from working on the harvest and freezing their credit at the plantation store. As the *dissidio coletivo* came before the labor court in June, the planters fought back on a broad front. Administrators on *fazendas* California and Floresta blocked the entrance of agrarian front activists sent to gather information for the hearing, threatening them until they backed away. Then, at the scheduled June 7 hearing, planters from eight of the nine plantations ordered to appear failed to show up, effectively scuttling the contract negotiations. In the meantime, Sampaio was singled out for special treatment. Prevented from working and earning a salary in the harvest, Sampaio's contract nevertheless did not expire until October, which allowed him to continue living temporarily on Fazenda Boa Esperança, but Meireles punitively impeded his mobility by prohibiting him from going to town on the milk truck that came to the *fazenda* each day. Thus, Sampaio had to make the nine-mile trek on foot. Protected from worse treatment by his high profile and his association with Meireles's son, he faced the ultimate indignity when his contract expired. On October 8, local police forcibly evicted Sampaio, his family, and four other families suspected of supporting

---

25. "Fazenda Boa Esperança declara guerra a frente agrária," *DN*, 31 May 1963, 6. The other plantations were Boa Vista, Capão Grande, California, Floresta, Bela Vista, Caridade, Limeira, and Moradinha. "Fazendeiros decepcionaram trabalhadores," *DN*, 8 June 1963, 6.

the association and contract talks. With the collusion of a local judge, the planters then blacklisted them from working in the area.[26]

While the collective bargaining dispute and Sampaio's suit slowly made its way through the labyrinth of the labor justice system, the episode produced several effects Padre Celso had anticipated. Like a beacon indeed, the *frente agrária* used the conflict in Batatais to rally support for reform from the public and reformist politicians. A municipal election was scheduled for October 13, and the front decided to run a candidate for mayor of Ribeirão Preto. Selecting the popular thirty-six-year-old journalist, city councilman, and agrarian front activist Welson Gasparini, Padre Celso and the others hoped to capitalize on their work in the countryside. In June, a caravan of the front's rural labor leaders, including Sampaio, traveled to the nation's capital in Brasília to meet with President Goulart. On June 5, in the Granja do Torto presidential residence, they told Goulart about rural labor developments in the Alta Mogiana, inviting him to come to Ribeirão Preto.[27] Although the meeting resolved nothing, *Diário de Notícias* made the most of the agrarian front's association with the popular president. Two weeks later, on June 18, the ETR went into effect, making it appear as though the FAP visit had resulted in this historic legislation. In the following months, Gasparini identified himself increasingly with the president's package of reforms and appeared in public with Sampaio and other rural leaders. Studiously organized and developed by Padre Celso, Gasparini's campaign aimed to win the mayoralty by a thin margin based on solid support from the city's rural wards. In the communities of Guatapará, Bonfim Paulista, and Dumont, the *frente agrária* worked diligently to secure the loyalty of smallholders and rural workers.

Just two days before the election, the regional labor tribunal ruled in favor of Sampaio, and *Diário de Notícias* published the successful defense brief written by front attorney Divo Marino. Making use of the ETR, Marino had argued that as a union activist, Sampaio was protected from unjustified dismissal. He and the other workers also had rights to prior notice of dismissal and indemnity payments for not receiving such notice. The court ordered Meireles to pay

26. The deepening conflict was reported in "Fazendeiro desacatou líder rural"; "Colonos tiveram liberdade cercada," *DN*, 9 June 1963, 6; and "Fazendeiros decepcionaram trabalhadores." The church started implicating authorities in "Lei funcionou (de novo) contra justiça: Fazendeiro Josino consumou reintegração," *DN*, 8 October 1963, 8; "Fazendeiro Josino quis ver casebre vazio: Aparato policial na explusão do camponês," *DN*, 11 October 1963, 6; and "Juiz de paz faz guerra contra camponeses," *DN*, 25 October 1963, 8. See also Marino brief.

27. "Jango recebeu CGT e a frente agrária," *DN*, 7 June 1963, 8; and "JG recebeu convite de camponeses," *DN*, 16 June 1963, 1.

Sampaio the minimum wage, the thirteenth month salary, and back pay for unpaid vacation time. Since the other workers were union members, Meireles was also ordered to pay the court fines for firing them. News of this decision as well as the front's hard campaigning helped bring Gasparini a narrow victory over more established candidates. To acknowledge the symbolic significance of Sampaio's struggle, Gasparini visited Batatais on the day of his election.[28]

Candidates supported by the Communists had as poor a showing in the election as they were having on the rural labor front. Mayoral candidate Antônio Carlos Santana, editor of Ribeirão Preto's *Diário da Manhã,* ran on a joint PTB-PSB ticket and placed a distant fifth behind Gasparini. The left's vice mayoral candidate, Guilherme Simões Gomes, came in sixth. Both Gomes and Santana supported the rural labor movement, with the *Diário da Manhã* carrying an eight-part series on the ETR in July and sponsoring public debates on national problems for "students, workers, peasants, and people." But this decidedly PTB newspaper and its editor did not capture the affection of these groups. The party's activities had shifted away from Ribeirão Preto toward other Alta Mogiana towns and regions. Demonstrating the party's base of strength among agro-industry workers, most of the rural organizing successes of 1963 involved sugar mill workers and, by extension, field workers. At Matarazzo's Fazenda Amália in Santa Rosa de Viterbo, six thousand workers threatened to strike once again in April. In May, twelve strikes affected São Paulo sugar mills, and in July, Luís Tenório de Lima's federation of food industry workers and the mill owners' association signed the state's first industry-wide wage accord. (A more well-known general strike of some two hundred thousand Pernambuco sugar workers, masterminded by legendary PCB-organizer Gregório Bezerra, occurred later in October.) But in Ribeirão Preto and its rural suburbs, where coffee and small producers remained important, ULTAB had lost the lead to Padre Celso's FAP.[29]

28. The church's strategy was revealed in Syllos transcript, 25–26; and Welson Gasparini, interview by author, Ribeirão Preto, 25 July 1991. See the election summary, "Povo consagrou Gasparini," *DN,* 17 October 1963, 1. The second-place candidate, Paulo Gomes Romeo, who enjoyed the support of the planter's social democratic and republican parties, lost by only 322 votes. "Resultado final das eleições em Ribeirão Preto," *DN,* 20 October 1963, 3. Marino brief.

29. On disappointments regarding the election, see "Como podem os ribeirãopretanos votar em candidatos de partidos que não apoiam as reformas de base (agrária, urbana, bancária, etc.), quando as esperanças de melhoras dias estão justamente nestas reformas?" as well as other articles in *A Tarde,* a special election supplement of *DM,* 5 August 1963, 3; "Resultado final das eleições"; and Guilherme Simões Gomes, interview by author, Ribeirão Preto, 22 May 1991. For the eight-part series on the ETR analysis, see Rafael Raya Junior, "Estudos do Estatuto do Trabalhador Rural," *DM,* July 1963. On the sugar strikes, see Stolcke, *Coffee Planters,* 111; "Fazenda

Changes in the national government also influenced local militancy in 1963. Since Goulart's presidential powers had been restored, the party and not the church had gained friends in high places. While *Terra Livre* reports the founding of many rural organizations around the country, it is also clear that in the months leading up to the *golpe militar,* the PCB enjoyed a closer relationship to power than ever before. Naturally, party leaders including ULTAB president Lindolfo Silva sought to use these connections at least as much as popular mobilizations to spur along the Brazilian revolution. In his memoir, Pinheiro Neto reports on the regular encounters between Goulart and leftist labor leaders such as Tenório de Lima. On one occasion, PCB chief Luís Carlos Prestes asked Pinheiro Neto to deliver a message to the president, which he did. In January, Goulart had appointed Almino Monteiro Alvares Afonso, a popular Labor Party congressman from Amazonas, as head of the labor ministry. As leader of the PTB in Congress in 1962, Almino Afonso had supported the government's controversial condemnation of the U.S. blockade of Cuba, and as labor minister, in April 1963 he granted legal standing to the PCB-dominated CGT, a move that distanced him from the administration. Under Almino Afonso, Sérgio Luís Rocha Veloso was made chief of the National Rural Unionization Commission (CONSIR, Comissão Nacional de Sindicalização Rural). CONSIR took responsibility for administering the formation and recognition of new rural unions. Impressed with the organizing capabilities and national presence of ULTAB, Veloso later reported how that influenced the commission's work. "I felt that they worked more efficiently than other groups," Veloso told a U.S. historian in 1968. Concerned about the mounting political power of the FAP-linked PDC in the Alta Mogiana, Veloso sent the party regional committee a packet of rural union registration materials, including a *carta sindical* (official union recognition certificate) for the Batatais union the party had first attempted to register in 1954.[30]

Amália: Seis mil trabalhadores irão à greve em defesa de seus direitos," *NR,* 19–25 April 1963; "Santa Rosa do Viterbo: Trabalhadores farão nova greve contro o império Matarazzo," *TL,* May 1963, 4; and "Trabalhadores paulistas do açúcar conquistam 80% de reajuste salarial," *NR,* 28 June–4 July 1963.

30. On this period of rising PCB fortunes in the government, see Pinheiro Neto, *Jango: Um depoimento pessoal* (Rio de Janeiro: Record, 1993), 80–85; and Mônica Kornis and Leda Soares, "Afonso, Almino," in Beloch and Abreu, eds., *DHBB,* 28–29. Velozo is cited in Dulles, *Unrest in Brazil,* 220–21. Moraes claimed that the ministry sent "ten to twelve *cartas,* all filled out, ready to go, but for the signatures of at least fifty members." Irineu Luís de Moraes, transcript of interview by author and Sebastião Geraldo, Ribeirão Preto, 27 May 1989 (hereafter Moraes transcript, pt. 3), p. 30.

The Batatais charter had been issued officially on July 16, and according to the law, ULTAB had four months (120 days) to hold a union meeting and elect officers. But no one took action until the November deadline was approaching. Then, in early November a commission of eight men lead by Arlindo Teixeira, who lived in Batatais and worked as a carpenter on various *fazendas,* tried to negotiate a deal with Padre Celso. They had the necessary documents to legalize the union, Teixeira said, and if Padre Celso agreed to a compromise, they would leave the paperwork with him. The compromise was to split the direction of the union between the church and the party. They proposed allying to endorse a joint slate of candidates for union officers, three from FAP and three from the party. By legally transforming the association into a union, everyone would benefit from the federal protections and financial resources provided by the ETR. Padre Celso balked at Teixeira's offer, however. Sensing the strength of the FAP movement, he opted for a winner-take-all posture and demanded that Teixeira hand over the *carta.* Teixeira refused, saying that the party needed only fifty signatures to have the document accepted by the labor ministry; this would give to the party the union, taking it away from the church. Pursuing this course, the party placed an advertisement in the Batatais newspaper on November 24, calling all rural workers to attend a meeting of the "Rural Wageworkers and Colonos Union" on Sunday, December 1.[31]

Incensed, Padre Celso wrote a scathing *Diário de Notícias* article denouncing the Communist power play. In the December story, the priest revealed the problems Sampaio and the front had encountered for over a year in trying to gain recognition for their Union of Laborers in Agriculture, Animal Husbandry, and Extractive Industries—a name befitting the era of Decree Law No. 7,038 more than the ETR. Padre Celso blamed the problems on the favoritism labor ministry officials showed ULTAB. Sampaio's association was the only legitimate labor organization in Batatais, Padre Celso asserted. Teixeira's group had been idle since 1954, and few of its original members now

---

31. Official issuance was recorded in "Demitido a carta sindical do Sindicato dos Assalariados Agrícolas e Colonos de Batatais, 10 de maio de 1963," *Diário Oficial da União* (16 July 1963), 6159. Some unresolved confusion about this date comes from the union recognition lists developed by Barros, in "A organização sindical," where page 164 shows a recognition date of 15 March 1963 for the Sindicato de Trabalhadores Rurais de Batatais (Batatais Rural Labor Union). Under the ETR, only the latter organizational name was permissible. The dispute between the PCB and the church was revealed in Teixeira transcript, 19; Syllos transcript, 11–12, 57–58; and "Camponeses armam expectativa em Batatais: Auxiliares do PC tentam 'golpe' sindical. Graves denuncias apresentadas a reportagem pelo atual president da Frente Agrária regional de Ribeirão Preto," *DN,* 1 December 1963, 8.

lived in the region. To add insult to injury, the man whose signature appeared on the newspaper announcement for the meeting swore he had no knowledge of the advertisement or union and claimed his name had been used without his knowledge. As Padre Celso revealed these discoveries, he urged Batatais workers to appear at the meeting to reject unanimously the Communist impostors.

That Sunday, more that a hundred workers converged at 417 Dr. Amador de Barros Street, the site of the meeting. Hearing Moraes and Padre Celso exchange accusations, the question was called to disband the meeting as unrepresentative and illegitimate. With the motion made, a group followed Padre Celso, Sampaio, and Tassinari out of the hall. Teixeira's band tried to constitute a quorum again on December 15, but with Padre Celso and Sampaio heckling them from outside, only three workers attended. The Communist attempt to influence the rural labor movement in Batatais had been a fiasco. Padre Celso had blocked their every move. Apparently, their time in Batatais had come and gone. Since ULTAB's charter had expired, Sampaio prepared a labor ministry petition for union recognition of his five-hundred-member association.[32]

The public display of hostility and rivalry characterizing the Batatais dispute masked a grudging respect between the two groups. In his angriest attack on the party for interfering in the Batatais labor association, Padre Celso addressed Moraes not only by the usual preface—"the known Communist"—but also as "the authentic leader." Years later, Padre Celso reflected that the Communist Party's "work was very difficult. They had to do it clandestinely. Any slip and they'd wind up in prison; many virtually lived in jail. They were heroic pioneers of the rural labor movement in Brazil." Despite bitter competition from the FAP, Moraes later admitted that he admired the Batatais union. "They had a strong link in Batatais," Moraes said. "The president there was very Catholic and he stayed impenetrable to any ideology that was not his and for this he built a grand union. They made demands for the rights of members, and they worked the system hard." After the fracas over recognition, Antônio Girotto of the regional committee went to see Padre Celso to appeal for an end to the divisive confrontation. Girotto offered to hand over the party's ex-

32. Padre Celso vented his frustrations in "Camponeses armam expectativa em Batatais." On the dispute, see also "Confirman-se dununcias da Frente Agrária: Camponeses não permitirão nenhum 'golpe.' Presidente da FA expôs manobras divisionistas preparadas por elementos diretamente ligados a ULTAB (pro-Comunista)," *DN*, 3 December 1963, 1. Sampaio's 16 December 1963 petition is reprinted in "Camponeses repudiam 'golpes' sindicais: Elementos do PC continuam abusando," *DN*, 17 December 1963, 6.

pired union document and to leave the Batatais union in the front's hands. "Don't give it to me," Padre Celso recalls saying. "Give it to Sampaio, it belongs to them in Batatais."[33]

While the record shows that both Padre Celso and Moraes emphasized union-forming activities, both privileged consciousness-raising in their memories of the time, and some documentary evidence supports this view. In rivalry with ULTAB, Padre Celso and the agrarian front put considerable energy into gaining control of unions. Yet, all the same, the front's main, continuous activity was the series of "politicization circles" it sponsored one Sunday after another. At the time, Moraes was known for organizing workers in syndicates, but he protested later that consciousness raising had to precede institution building. Working-class consciousness of the essential kind came through struggle, he thought. If the struggle caused workers to decide to form a union, all the better. As Moraes saw it, however, the fundamental work of the militant was to stimulate conflicts to help develop a working-class identity. To build unions first and use them to resolve disputes in the labor courts was futile, in Moraes's opinion. Padre Celso made similar comments at the time, claiming the important thing was working-class political education to help "the man of the country integrate into society." The similarities between the two men and their movements seem surprising given the emphasis the literature places on tensions between the church and the party.[34]

Forming State and National Organizations

While left-leaning priests like Padre Celso and Communist militants like Moraes could find enough common ground to work through their rivalries on the local level, a cold war raged between the party and more conservative Catholic elements at the state and federal levels. At these levels, the ETR set off a race between the two groups to establish and control state and national labor organizations.

The Catholic Workers Circles leader José Rotta continued to press the church's anticommunist agenda in São Paulo. As in 1961, when

33. On the dispute's resolution and the participants later assessments, see "Camponeses armam expectativa em Batatais"; Syllos transcript, 14–15, 58; Moraes transcript, pt. 3, p. 22; and Antônio Girotto, transcript of interview by author, Ribeirão Preto, 19 October 1988, pp. 20–21.

34. The two organizers discussed their differences in Syllos transcript, 14, 22; and Moraes transcript, pt. 3, p. 24.

Rotta tried to take public attention away from ULTAB, in 1963 — as militants prepared to establish a national confederation under ETR rules — Rotta positioned himself to challenge the party. The new organization, something like an AFL-CIO of rural workers, was to be called CONTAG, for the National Confederation of Laborers in Agriculture. Given the increasing role of federal legislation in rural society and the ongoing debate regarding land reform, the presence of a fully recognized, national, representative rural labor body was of intense interest to all those engaged in rural labor politics and organizing. CONTAG offered them their first opportunity to become an official part of the policymaking process. Planter lobbying groups were already well organized, and their official civil association, the CRB, was preparing to transform itself under ETR rules into the National Confederation of Agriculture (CNA). This would be the one employer group incorporated through labor ministry recognition. Simply to catch up with planters, rural labor advocates needed to build their movement through a series of essential steps now required by the ETR. To form CONTAG, they needed at least three state federations and to establish these federations, they needed at least five recognized *sindicatos* in each state. Thus, the potential power of CONTAG raised the stakes of the campaign to form unions and federations.

In June, soon after the ETR went into effect, ULTAB's José Alves Portela announced plans for an 8 September 1963 conference of FATAESP, which, though founded in 1961, was as yet unrecognized. One month later, in a replay of the events that preceded the Belo Horizonte congress, Rotta scheduled a rival conference for the end of August, just a week before Portela's meeting. Rising to the bait, *Terra Livre* called Rotta a *pelego* and a "failed merchant who resolved to be a 'peasant leader.'" The paper ran Rotta's photograph and told readers to "watch out for the *pelegos* of rural unionization!" Rotta shot back at ULTAB, Red-baiting FATAESP as "*comuno-jangista*" (Goulart-oriented Communists) and accusing the Goulart government of favoring leftists and ignoring "Christian unions." After Rotta's São Paulo State Federation of Agricultural Laborers (FETAESP, Federação de Trabalhadores Agrícolas do Estado de São Paulo) met in the São Paulo town of Araraquara, *Terra Livre* devoted a full page to ridiculing the meeting as illegitimate and undemocratic. Only eighty people appeared, the stories claimed, and photographs showed that well-dressed participants — allegedly planters, priests, and lawyers — composed most of the audience and leadership of the meeting. (Of course, the party was also known to have allies among planters, lawyers, and even the clergy.) *Novos Rumos* claimed Rotta denied the twenty-three FATAESP and ULTAB representatives who attended the meeting credentials and the opportunity to speak. Supportive news accounts told the story differently, saying that in addition to nine priests, eight agronomists, and several lawyers, 189 delegates from 69 recognized and unrecognized rural labor unions attended. Both reports were probably inaccurate. But the sources agree that members of the SRB, including Francisco Toledo Piza, played prominent roles at the congress. This was quite consistent with Rotta's collaborationist ideology and the church's condemnation of class struggle.[35]

The party's hostility toward the FETAESP conference may have been a case of sour grapes, for on August 17, the labor ministry surprised everyone by formally recognizing Rotta's federation as the maximum rural labor union body in São Paulo. The reasons for this development were complex. Technically, the ETR allowed multiple federations to form in each state so long as they represented clearly delineated categories of rural labor and grouped together five or more *sindicatos* in a given category. However, the ETR did not specify any categories, and since it was so new, no one was sure what to call their federations and unions. The church had the advantage with FETAESP—a federation of "agricultural laborers"—because it used the same broad and general words used in the ETR, while ULTAB's FATAESP—a federation of *associations*—represented no specific category and had no place in the corporatist structure. From a political perspective, the month of August was an interesting time in national affairs. Goulart had just replaced the radical Almino Afonso with the moderate Amaury de Oliveira e Silva as minister of labor, hoping to reduce Communist influence, which had grown under Almino Afonso's tenure in the post. The badgering of Rotta may have seemed a welcome opportunity to show support for the church. By recognizing FETAESP, Silva marked a clear distinction between his administration and that of Almino Afonso. The U.S. labor specialist in São Paulo, Jack Liebof, speculated that FETAESP earned recognition by cooper-

35. ULTAB's satirical attacks on Rotta are featured in "Camponeses em Araraquara desmascaram o 'congresso' do Rota [*sic*]" and "Camponeses de batina motorizados," *TL*, October 1963, 2. See also "Mais de 40 sindicatos rurais exigem: Expulsão já do pelego José Rotta," *TL*, October 1963, 4. See also "Comerciante falido negou credencial a legítimos trabalhadores da terra," *NR*, 13–19 September 1963, 6; and Lindolfo Silva, "Congresso particular de Araraquara," *NR*, 18–24 October 1963, 6. A summary of mainstream press accounts is in item 11 of AmConGen, São Paulo, to USDS, "Weekly Summary No. 88," 6 September 1963, RG 59, Pol 2-2 BRAZ (3834), DS/USNA. For Rotta's accusations against ULTAB and the government, see Rotta, "Discriminação contra sindicatos Cristãos," *OESP*, 8 August 1963, 7. Of course, there was some truth to his allegations. Of the forty-seven São Paulo rural unions registered in 1963, only four were determined to be affiliated with Rotta's conservative federation. Barros, "A organização sindical," 117.

ating with the ministry in shutting Communist delegates out of its conference. True or not, Goulart's ministry switch earned him important points with a key foe. To retain legitimacy among workers, Liebof warned that the "generally conservative Rotta will have to adopt a more militant stance in favor of improved working and living conditions for rural workers." By the end of September, however, Rotta still had not allowed any of the ULTAB-organized official unions to affiliate with FETAESP. As the consul had warned, to do so would risk tipping the balance of delegates against him. In fact, Rotta also kept out rival Catholic unions, forestalling the affiliation of any Alta Mogiana unions organized by the FAP.[36]

The United States encouraged such hardball politics on many levels and in various places. The worst area for this was the northeast, where the popularity and radicalism of the *ligas camponesas* and the exceptional growth of ULTAB-oriented sugar workers' unions motivated the United States to establish one of the first Alliance for Progress programs. Under the alliance umbrella, numerous Cold War agencies went to work in the region, including the Central Intelligence Agency, the American Institute for Free Labor Development (AIFLD), and the Food for Peace program. To offset the appeal of the leagues, the United States funneled money to church groups, especially the Pernambuco Rural Orientation Service (SORPE, Serviço de Orientação Rural de Pernambuco), which was headed by Padre Paulo Crespo. In São Paulo, the AIFLD- and CIA-financed Cultural Institute of Labor (ICT, Instituto Cultural de Trabalho) sponsored various projects, including training for Rotta and a Food for Peace project in Marília that, according to U.S. documents, "helped the [rural labor] union in its organizing efforts." Soon after Pinheiro Neto took control of SUPRA, U.S. labor attaché John Fishburn pressured him to favor Catholic over Communist unions in the official recognition process. At first, Pinheiro Neto told Fishburn that SUPRA funds "would be made available to all who request them." Pinheiro Neto also said that he planned to "recognize all unions organized by the Communists or by the church" and that his office could "make no distinctions" between them. But Fishburn made his displeasure with this answer

36. On the recognition of FETAESP and its Araraquara meeting, see also item 7 in Am-ConGen, São Paulo, to USDS, "Weekly Summary No. 86," 23 August 1963, RG 59, POL 2-1 BRAZ (3833), DS/USNA. A list of union affiliates is in AmConGen, São Paulo, to USDS, "List of Labor Federations in São Paulo State," RG 59, LAB 3-2 BRAZ (3576), DS/USNA. It may also be that FAP unions did not want to associate with Rotta. "I didn't participate in [Rotta's] congress and neither did a single of my leaders," Padre Celso recalled, "because we didn't agree with the federation's line. They were true reactionaries, in close accord with the planters, they didn't have any fight in them." Syllos transcript, 34.

Former U.S. labor attaché in Brazil John Fishburn, near his retirement home in Woodstock, Virginia (27 April 1985). Photo: author

known, and by the end of the meeting, Pinheiro Neto had "changed his stand and stated that while he would recognize rural unions by whomever organized, he would withhold funds if it were clear that those requesting them were Communists." Nevertheless, Fishburn doubted Pinheiro Neto's sincerity as an anticommunist and did what he could to strengthen the church-oriented movement. It was a frustrating business, though. For the United States, the church's movement was too diffuse and weak to competently challenge the Red Menace.[37]

Fishburn had tried to impress on Pinheiro Neto the importance of recognizing only church federations so that Communists would be shut out of a role in founding CONTAG. When the two met at the end of August, five federations had already been recognized. Pinheiro Neto accepted Fishburn's characterization of the federations of Pernambuco, Rio Grande do Norte, and São Paulo as church-oriented and the Paraná and Rio de Janeiro groups as Communist-directed. No

37. On SORPE and the United States, see Joseph Page, *The Revolution That Never Was,* 74, 129–34; and Moniz Bandeira, *O govêrno Goulart,* 70. U.S. State Department records show that Padre Crespo was a regular visitor to the consulate in Recife and the embassy in Rio de Janeiro. On the ICT and AIFLD in São Paulo, see AmEmbassy to USDS, "Labor: Rural Workers Reaction to the Alliance for Progress Program," A-370, 20 October 1964, RG 59, LAB 10 BRAZ (1283), DS/USNA. For Fishburn, see AmEmbassy to USDS, A-301, 30 August 1963, RG 59, LAB 3-2 BRAZ (3576), DS/USNA. For comments on the church movement, see AmConsul, Recife, to USDS, "Weekly Summary No. 3," A-7, 26 July 1963, RG 59 POL 2-3 BRAZ (3835), DS/USNA.

more ULTAB federations should be recognized, Fishburn insisted. When negotiations were held to plan the CONTAG ceremony, however, an ULTAB-*liga* alliance had earned the recognition of a new federation for Paraíba state. Although Pinheiro Neto had assured Fishburn that SUPRA had responsibility for providing 80 percent of the budget assigned to promote the rural labor movement, the labor ministry had all the responsibility for officiating the movement. Fishburn was no doubt upset to learn that labor minister Amauri Silva met on November 23 with ULTAB representatives Lindolfo Silva, Antônio Mendonça Conde (Paraná), and Everaldo Silveira (Rio de Janeiro state), as well as representatives of the church-related federations of Rio Grande do Norte and São Paulo, to plan the CONTAG founding convention. In a long and rancorous meeting, which also included the presence of CONSIR's Sérgio Veloso and presidential cabinet official José Augusto, the labor minister elaborated on ETR regulation no. 346 by deciding that the ministry would recognize five categories of federations: those for agricultural wage earners (*trabalhadores na lavoura*); livestock handlers (*trabalhadores na pecuária*); processors (*trabalhadores na produção extrativa rural*); groupings of independent sharecroppers and tenants (*trabalhadores autônomos*); and small farmers (*pequenos proprietários*). Thus, a maximum of five federations would be recognized for each state. The minister also decided to allow the participation of all delegates from federations that had submitted applications for recognition to CONSIR by the time of the conference, which was then scheduled to be held in the state of Rio de Janeiro on December 20–22. If applications for two federations in the same category were submitted, the votes of neither delegation were to be counted. A rush of federation formation activities followed.[38]

To accommodate the new categories, FATAESP disbanded, and its activists worked hard to reconfigure ULTAB's rural labor associations to ensure its militants had federations that conformed to regulation no. 346's guidelines for representation at the CONTAG meet-

38. For Fishburn and Pinheiro Neto, see A-301. Development of the allied *liga*-PCB union federation in Paraíba is discussed in Aued, *A vitória dos vencidos*, 56–68; and in "Francisco de Assis Lemos (depoimento, 1978)," the transcript of the interview conducted by the CPDOC/FGV. On planning the CONTAG meeting, see "Federações de todo o país integrarão a 'CNTA,'" *TL*, December 1963, 5. November also brought the creation of a rural workers' social welfare fund, which was to provide medical and retirement benefits to laborers. A U.S. diplomat saw Goulart's support for the law, which merely elaborated on ETR measures, as a sign of his demagoguery. "The decreeing of the regulations at this time," wrote acting labor attaché Harold Shapiro, "serves as a further indication of Goulart's interest in building up and mobilizing a more articulate rural political base." The law, which received little press attention, was not to take effect until January 1965. AmEmbassy Rio de Janeiro to USDS, "President Signs Decree on Rural Social Welfare," A-636, 22 November 1963, RG 59, LAB 5 BRAZ (4205), DS/USNA.

ing. For example, the São Paulo Federation of Autonomous Rural Laborers (FTRAESP) was recognized by the labor ministry on December 16, just four days before the CONTAG congress was scheduled to begin. In the first reference to FTRAESP to appear in the press, a January *Novos Rumos* report claimed the group's origins went back to 1960, when tenants and sharecroppers first started to organize. In October 1963, the story continued, eleven *sindicatos dos trabalhadores autônomos* received ministry recognition and founded the federation. By December, nine more unions had joined them, and the twenty *sindicatos* submitted to the labor ministry their application for recognition, which Silva signed on December 16. Two of FTRAESP's delegates to the CONTAG conference were Nestor Vera of ULTAB and João Bistaffa, a longtime Communist rural labor militant from Bragança Paulista who had also been a FATAESP director.[39]

CONTAG's Founding Congress

When the CONTAG meeting was finally held in Rio de Janeiro, twenty-seven to twenty-nine federations from at least nineteen states sent delegates. Although it is unclear how many of these federations belonged to ULTAB, two-thirds were later declared "ghost federations" by the military regime that overthrew Goulart. CONSIR's records have not yet surfaced, so it is difficult to chart these developments. But it is important to note in relation to FTRAESP that in São Paulo and other states, the PCB had long been active in supporting groups of tenants and sharecroppers who were highly exploited by landlords. At least one member union of FTRAESP had considerable experience and could not be called a "ghost" union at all. The Santa Fé do Sul union of autonomous workers had taken shape in a land dispute that began in 1959. In 1960, the conflict intensified when peasant leader Jofre Corrêa Neto was shot and dozens of tenants were run off their land by stampeding cattle set loose by the landowner. In other words, though FTRAESP may have been hastily formed, the PCB-linked autonomous workers' movement had a substantial history in São Paulo, and for that matter, in Paraná, where participants of the Porecatú War had joined with other disgruntled *posseiros* to form another federation. In fact, the labor minister's

39. A history of FTRAESP is "São Paulo: 518 mil trabalhadores rurais autônomos já têm sua federação," *NR*, 31 January–6 February 1964, 6. For Pernambuco, see Pearson, "Small Farmer and Rural Worker," 269 n. 4.

guidelines for the formation of foundations were purposefully made easy in order to "enlarge the composition of CONTAG," *Terra Livre* reported. Given the spread and duration of ULTAB's investment in the rural labor movement, it was no surprise that they were able to take advantage of these new rules by quickly forming numerous federations. Indeed, Fishburn's concerns about the influence of Communists proved well-founded, for party members came out on top by the conclusion of the CONTAG conference.[40]

There are only a few secondary accounts of CONTAG's foundation meeting. In general, they relate how ULTAB and the Catholic AP formed an unholy alliance that enabled a slate of candidates led by Lindolfo Silva to gain control of the organization. Historian John W. F. Dulles, for example, tells the story this way:

> Ação Popular had nine *federações;* the Communists (ULTAB), with the most *sindicatos,* also had nine; and the non-AP Christians had nine. Although the AP and the Communists had shown keen rivalry in forming *sindicatos,* they reached an agreement at the summit. . . .This agreement gave CONTAG's top posts to Communists.

Writing soon after the event, the analyst Robert Price offered a similar description:

> In the December 1963 elections for direction of [CONTAG], the communist "ULTAB" group secured control of the confederation. The participants in the election were the delegates of 29 federations from 19 states and directors of 743 rural unions, 263 of them then recognized, composed of political elements representing "ULTAB," a radical Catholic "Popular Action" group, and "democratic-christian" elements. It appears that an alliance of the "Popular Action" group with "ULTAB" was able to defeat the church group, apparently representative of only two federations.

Neale Pearson adds that the São Paulo and Rio Grande do Norte Catholic "reformist groups . . . were outmaneuvered by the Commu-

---

40. The organization included a Santa Fé do Sul union headed by Olímpio Pereira Machado, who had long been active in the tenant movement in this far-west São Paulo town. See Cliff Welch, "Jofre and the Brazilian Revolution: Peasant Mobilization, Land Reform, and History in São Paulo, Brazil," paper presented at the thirteenth annual Latin American Labor History Conference, Duke University, 19–20 April 1996. For the decertification of "ghost federations," see Dulles, *Unrest in Brazil,* 222 n. 8.

nist ULTAB allied with leftist MEB leaders." The MEB was the Grassroots Education Movement, an activist Catholic group founded in
1960, many of whose participants belonged to the AP. In other words,
while commentators differ on some details, most agree that the Communist and leftist Catholic movements collaborated to take control
of CONTAG.[41]

These accounts leave the impression that Communist militants
were especially conniving and manipulative in gaining control of
CONTAG. As one might expect, the *Terra Livre* correspondent saw
things differently:

> All of the currents that work on the organization of peasants
> were present and took part in the study and debate of the ques-
> tions, in a tranquil and secure meshing of the gears. This re-
> sulted in the presentation of a single slate of candidates for offi-
> cers of CONTAG, elected without any restriction, unanimously
> by the plenary, which not only acclaimed the slate, but con-
> firmed their unity in support of the slate by depositing their
> votes in the ballot box.

Like Price, *Terra Livre* said that delegates from 29 federations in 19
states were present in addition to representatives of 263 unions that
were recognized and 480 still in the process of being recognized. Neither *Terra Livre* nor *Novos Rumos* had anything to say about the "currents" each federation represented. Yet these mouthpieces of the victors agree with critics that only one slate was presented for delegates

41. Dulles, *Unrest in Brazil,* 222; and Price, "Rural Unionization," 64–65. Both Pearson
and historian Thomas Bruneau allege that a July 1963 meeting of Catholic rural labor federations in Natal, Rio Grande do Norte, led to the founding of a rural labor confederation that
predated CONTAG. Goulart refused to recognize this organization, they claim, because the Communists had been closed out of the meeting. The July meeting did occur, and Communists were
closed out, but so were reactionary Catholic movements such as Rotta's and the Rio Grande do
Sul Agrarian Front (Frente Agrárian Gaúcho). The meeting seems to have been poorly planned
and poorly attended, a perspective shared by the U.S. consulate in Recife, which otherwise supported the gathering. Rather than having founded a confederation, the Natal meeting concluded by calling for the foundation of such a body. Pearson, "Small Farmer and Rural Worker,"
267–69; and Bruneau, *Católicismo Brasileiro em época de transição* (São Paulo: Edições Loyola,
1974), 178. For the consulate's view, see item 2 in AmConsul, Recife, to USDS, "Weekly Summary No. 3," A-7, 26 July 1963, RG 59, POL 2-3 BRAZ (3835), DS/USNA. However, Consul
General Edward Rowell filed a detailed report on the October 25 founding of CONTAG in Recife by Catholic-oriented rural labor groups, an event not mentioned by any other sources.
AmConGen, Recife, to USDS, "The National Confederation of Workers in Agriculture: Background, Formation, and Struggle for Control," A-63, 12 December 1963, RG 59, LAB 3-2 BRAZ
(3576), DS/USNA.

to vote on, a sign of either unanimity—as ULTAB claimed—or a packed hall—as the anticommunists alleged.[42]

As we have seen, fierce rivalry for control of the organization characterized the latter half of 1963. Each side played politics and dirtied themselves. Yet, from the present perspective, ULTAB looks the cleanest of all partisans. As was typical of the Cold War, anticommunists generally had more resources to draw on and used them to contain progressives as well as Communists whenever they could, completely contradicting their democratic discourse by their authoritarian actions. Rotta, for example, refused to recognize FAP unions in FETAESP and denied credentials to ULTAB at the Araraquara conference. In contrast, ULTAB and the PCB could claim a tradition of leadership in the movement and, despite financial hardship and constant harassment, of conferences open to all applicants. Rotta, Padre Crespo, and other conservative church activists and their rural labor allies were all invited to participate at the CONTAG conference. Although party militants and leaders welcomed alliances with sympathetic elites, they sought to build the strength of the rural labor movement through horizontal alliances. Ruling-class alliances had all too often proved fragile and ephemeral. In 1963, however, ULTAB enjoyed unprecedented access to the Goulart administration.[43]

The PCB's links to the government enhanced ULTAB's ability to negotiate with rivals, especially those its militants had worked with before, and this included many Catholics. Padre Francisco Pessoa Laje of Minas Gerais had taken a leading role alongside the Communists at the Belo Horizonte congress of 1961, and at the CONTAG conference in Rio, he continued to play a prominent role. In the days leading up to the founding of CONTAG, *Terra Livre* ran a feature article on Padre Laje and other priests that stressed progressive currents within

42. "Foi conquistada com lutas a Confederação Nacional dos Trabalhadores na Agricultura," *TL* (January 1964), 5. In addition to Silva, who was named president, the new officers of CONTAG, their affiliations (if known), and their bases of activity were First Vice President Manoel Gonçalo Ferreira (Church-SORPE, Pernambuco); Second Vice President José Leandro Bezerra da Costa (ULTAB, Ceará); Third Vice President José Gomes Novaes (unknown, Alagoas); Secretary General Sebastião Lourenço de Lima (Church-AP, Minas Gerais); First Secretary José Rodrigues dos Santos (ULTAB, Paraná); Second Secretary João de Almeida Cavalcanti (*Ligas* and SORPE, Paraíba); General Treasurer Nestor Vera (ULTAB, São Paulo); and Second Treasurer Manoel Lito Muniz (unknown, Bahia). CONTAG was formally recognized by Goulart on 31 January 1964, through Presidential Decree Law No. 53,517. See CONTAG, "Trabalhadores criam confederação," *CONTAG: 30 anos de luta* (Brasília: Gráfica Sindical, 1993), 10.

43. Accounts of the conference are "CONTAG: Poderoso instrumento de luta nas mãos dos trabalhadores do campo" and "Foi conquistada com lutas a Confederação Nacional dos Trabalhadores na Agricultura," *TL*, January 1964, 1, 5; and "CONTAG: Acontecimento marcante," *NR*, 17 December–2 January 1964.

the church. The other priests mentioned included Padre Arquimedo Brunos of Ceará, Padre Alípio de Freitas, Bishop Jerónimo de Sá Cavalcanti of Bahia, and Brother Carlos Josephat of São Paulo, who was a sponsor of the FAP. "If Christ returned to the earth," Padre Laje was quoted as saying, "he would be accused of being a Communist."[44]

As the outcome of the CONTAG meeting demonstrates, ULTAB also had friends among Catholic laymen in the AP group. At least two of the nine CONTAG officers and five of nine substitute officers elected at the December congress belonged to this group. Rotta himself later accused a third director, second secretary João de Almeida Cavalcanti of Paraíba, of being a tool of Padre Crespo's SORPE. Of the AP directors, one was Sebastião Lourenço de Lima, from Minas Gerais, who became CONTAG's secretary general, and the other was Manoel Gonçalo Ferreira of Pernambuco, who became first vice president. Before the meeting, Gonçalo—who was president of the state's rural workers federation—accepted a position as first vice president of a church-dominated confederation—the CNTA—hastily founded without government support on October 25 in Recife. When the futility of this effort became apparent, Gonçalo entered into negotiations with ULTAB. In exchange for ULTAB support of his election as an officer of CONTAG, Pearson alleges that Gonçalo agreed to make the Communist rural labor union president from the town of Igaraçu the first vice president of his federation. The U.S. consul in Recife tells a slightly different version of this story, alleging that Gonçalo had "never been known for his strength of convictions" and that he was lured to support the ULTAB-AP slate "with political favors and [the] exorbitant salaries offered to whomever would accept them." In any event, the superior bureaucratic connections of ULTAB helped Gonçalo decide to collaborate with the party. Even if this alienated him from conservative sectors of the church, the alliance between priests like Padre Laje and ULTAB must have given him some comfort.[45]

44. For Padre Lage, see "'Se Cristo voltasse à terra seria acusado de Comunista,'" *TL*, October 1953, 8.

45. Rotta's comments on Cavalcanti are from AmConGen, São Paulo, to USDS, "Elections in National Confederation of Agricultural Workers (CONTAG)," A-191, 7 January 1965, RG 59 AGR 9 BRAZ (467), DS/USNA. The Igaraçu president was Antônio Guedes, a peasant leader like Gonçalo who had risen from rural worker to *sindicalista* in recent years. Pearson, "Small Farmer and Rural Worker," 269 n. 4, 270, tells the behind-the-scenes story without citing any sources; A-63 discusses the October 25 conference. The analysis by consul Edward Rowell is in AmConGen, Recife, to USDS, "Recent Changes in Rural Union Structure and Leadership in Pernambuco," A-88, 4 February 1964, RG 59, LAB 3-2 BRAZ (1282). Raising questions about both accounts is a contemporary report by Rowell that purports to be a thorough overview of Communist and Catholic rivalries in rural labor in Pernambuco but offers no corroborating evidence of Pearson's account. AmConGen, Recife, to USDS, "The Current Contending Forces in Rural Union Activity in Pernambuco," A-60, 4 December 1963, RG 59, LAB 2 BRAZ (3576), DS/USNA.

That priests offered comfort and protection to Communists greatly concerned a growing segment of the Catholic hierarchy in 1963. Among an expanding group of influential critics of priests like Padre Laje was Ribeirão Preto's Archbishop Angelo Rossi. Even though Rossi had been a principal author of the CNBB's progressive Emergency Plan of 1962, he and other church leaders were increasingly alarmed by the growing influence of Communists. They came to fear that the social agitation of radical priests "inevitably favored the implantation of communism in the country" by helping to cause a deterioration in the social order that created opportunities for the better-organized Communists. The example of CONTAG's founding congress, which evidently demonstrated the party's ability to outmaneuver the church, underscored these concerns. In fact, a myth arose among clerics that all currents of the church had been entirely shut out of CONTAG, even though this was not true. For Padre Celso, Rossi's conservative turn threatened to bring an end to much of his work with the Frente Agrária Paulista. Toward the end of the year, Padre Celso began to develop an indirect response to Rossi's heightened conservatism by publishing a variety of surprisingly argumentative articles in the pages of the *Diário de Notícias*. In October, a series of ten articles appeared under the heading, "Laborism Without Disguise." They argued that recent church social doctrine, such as Pope John's "Pacem in Terris" and Rossi's own "Plano de Emergência," gave shape to Brazil's most sincere social movements. "We demonstrate," the article series preface declared, "that in obedience to ecclesiastical guidance the Agrarian Front of Ribeirão Preto has promoted rural unionization, the formation of leaders, and raised the laborers' consciousness according to the dictates and teachings of Christian social doctrine." [46]

After CONTAG's founding congress, tensions within the archdiocese grew. They became so well known that Ribeirão Preto's other large daily newspaper, the PTB-allied *Diário da Manhã,* interviewed Rossi about the problems. In a nuanced critique of Catholic militants, Rossi said that Padre Celso had his complete confidence. Rossi looked forward to having Padre Celso become a member of his new initiative, the Social Action Secretariat, which would absorb the *frente* and

---

46. Mainwaring, *The Catholic Church and Politics,* 50–59; and "Rossi, Angelo," in Beloch and Abreu, eds., *DHBB,* 3019. In November 1964, after the military overthrow, Rossi was promoted to archbishop of São Paulo and invited to sit on the CNBB. On closing out the church altogether, see Abdias Vilar de Carvalho, "Cronologia dos fatos da igreja católica no meio rural," *Igreja e questão agrária* (São Paulo: Loyola, 1985), 109; and Bruneau, *Catolicism brasileiro,* 178. For Padre Celso, see "Trabalhismo sem disfarce," Texto No. 8, "Frente agrária negam trabalho e fomentam miséria," *DN,* 15 October 1963; and Syllos transcript.

welcome Padre Celso as a board member, while handing over day-to-day operations to laymen. Rossi argued that priests should focus on the spiritual rather than temporal world. In other words, Padre Celso was being demoted, and his prize creation—the FAP—disbanded. Defiant to the end, Padre Celso wrote a Christmas Eve editorial that bordered on the sacrilegious. "Who is a Communist?" the editorial's title demanded. "We are, in fact, under the threat of Communism," he wrote, "but not due to the evangelical line of many bishops and priests; not because the Church may have betrayed its mission; not because the workers join together in unions to defend their rights." The blame for this state rested with the "liberal capitalists who stir up anticommunist sentiments in order to generate the confusion and anarchy that justify the implantation of a fascist state." The fact that the liberals failed to resolve Brazil's serious social and economic problems left the door open for Communist agitation and made it necessary for the church to become enmeshed in the real world. On that Christmas Eve, with a repressive military takeover less than one hundred days away, few could have recognized the accuracy and prescience of Padre Celso's epistle.[47]

United Under SUPRA

This time Moraes traveled to Dumont in a Volkswagen van. The dirt two-track hugged the hillside above a long ravine, and the air had the sweet aroma of sugar processing. It was a sign of how sugarcane had come to displace coffee growing in the twenty years since Moraes last came to Dumont—by jumping a small freight train—to help start the peasant league. The hills were a duller green in those days, but now the wind washing through the stalks of young cane set off waves of sharp contrast between the bright green blades and the royal-purple earth. It was a beautiful sight, and more beautiful yet was his reason for driving to Dumont that March day in 1964. An envelope carefully guarded on the bench seat beside him carried all the documents needed to found Dumont's first STR. It had been a long time coming, but Moraes could finally see some results from all the hard

47. See the editorial "Nosso comentário: Quem é Comunista?" *DN*, 24 December 1963, 4; and Raul Machado, "D. Angello Rossi: A militância política social dos sacerdotes existe por falta de quadros leigos," *DM*, 5 January 1964, 7.

and dangerous work he and so many others had devoted to creating formal organizations for the rural working classes.[48]

This time Moraes came to Dumont as an agent of SUPRA, the executive branch agency assigned to implement Goulart's agrarian policies. At the beginning of the year, several federal government officials had arrived in Ribeirão Preto to establish a regional office of SUPRA. While the agency had a broad mission—including identifying underutilized property for expropriation and arranging health care services for rural workers—rural unionization was its first priority in São Paulo. The state director of SUPRA, the writer and free-speech activist Mario Donato, set a goal of forming 252 rural labor unions in 1964, with each of the nine regional offices of SUPRA in São Paulo state expected to meet a quota of 28 unions. SUPRA head João Pinheiro Neto had appointed Donato—who was born in Campinas in 1915—because of his politics rather than his knowledge of farm labor. As a writer, Donato became involved in politics defending the rights of prisoners of conscience in Brazil, a cause that brought him into close contact with Communists and made him, in the eyes of DOPS, a Communist himself. But, like Pinheiro Neto, Donato saw SUPRA as a way of ameliorating the problems of rural workers before misery and despair drove them to rebellion. In this regard, Donato also directed his staff to "reorganize and stimulate existing unions," inform and educate workers and labor leaders about the law, and teach workers how to read using the methods of Paulo Freire, the innovative Brazilian educator.[49]

Political goals also oriented SUPRA's emphasis on rural unions. Following ideas developed by Vargas-era policymakers, the Goulart administration wanted the new rural unions to register laborers as

48. Moraes transcript, pt. 3, p. 30; and "Fundado o Sindicato dos Trabalhadores Rurais de Dumont pela SUPRA e ULTAB: Grande numero de camponeses presentes—um minuto de silêncio pela morte de agente da SUPRA—diretoria," *DM,* 5 March 1964, 8. The union directors included Vitório Negre, president; Pedro Salla, first secretary; Nobre José Lorenzato, second secretary; Argemireo Polegato, treasurer; Antônio Bovo; and João Quintana.

49. "O superintendente da SUPRA, João Pinheiro Neto falará hoje no salão nobre da associação comercial," *DM,* 31 January 1964, 1; and Pinheiro Neto, *Jango,* 72–81; passim. "Plano de trabalho da delegacia estadual da SUPRA em São Paulo para o ano de 1964," São Paulo, n.d., Arquivo do Projeto "Brasil: Nunca Mais," vol. 7, archive 144, AEL/UNICAMP (hereafter cited in the following form: B:NM volume number/archive number). Donato had been an officer of the Brazilian Writers Union (UNE), which the police considered a PCB front group. See "Copia autentico do relatório reservado do DOPS no. 6: Quem é Mario Donato?" B:NM 7/158; and Defense Brief of Dante Delmanto to the Superior Tribunal Militar, 29 November 1971, B:NM 12/160. Besides the office in Ribeirão Preto, eight other regional offices were established, in São Paulo, Taubaté, Campinas, São José do Rio Preto, Araçatuba, Presidente Prudente, Bauru, and Itapetininga. "Plano de trabalho da delegacia estadual da SUPRA," B:NM 7/144.

voters to help erode the influence of the rural elite. Whereas the lack
of a viable rural labor movement made it difficult for Vargas to implement this plan, the presence of an increasingly autonomous and demanding rural labor movement in Goulart's time generated greater
pressure on the state to intervene and regiment the movement under
government control. The issue of land reform still fiercely divided
legislators, frustrating the administration's attempts to put this key
"basic reform" in place. Using his executive powers, Goulart applied
further pressure to Congress on January 24, when he signed a statement of understanding between three military ministers and SUPRA
to cooperate in expropriating and redistributing land along Brazil's
rights-of-way: highways, railways, and waterways. The more small
farmers that were created, argued the president, the more productive
and democratic the country. (When press reports of the proposed
decree indicated the government planned to expropriate a twenty-
kilometer swath of land, Luís Carlos Prestes called Pinheiro Neto to
recommend a ten-kilometer band. Too many smallholders would be
affected by the larger number, he said, a critique Goulart readily accepted, Pinheiro Neto claims.) In the view of policymakers, rural labor unions would be natural proponents of agrarian reform. Thus,
SUPRA had a broad and demanding range of responsibilities, from
forming unions and educating workers to locating, appropriating,
and distributing land.[50]

Heading up the broad SUPRA effort in the Alta Mogiana was
Hans Alfred Rappel, an agronomist from Rio de Janeiro. Assigned to
the post by Donato, Rappel sought to centralize all regional activities
related to the rural labor movement under his orientation. To these
ends, he reached out to both Moraes and Padre Celso, in addition
to student organizations, politicians, and journalists. The advent of
SUPRA promised to alter dramatically the dynamics of rural struggle
in the Alta Mogiana. It threw federal government support behind
those persecuted as subversives only months before. As Padre Celso
commented in an editorial on SUPRA, "Never before have we seen a
single governmental measure that presented Brazilian society with
such promising possibilities." SUPRA, he wrote, "gives new impulse
to the march of the Brazilian revolution." It also helped keep Padre

50. Before the end, in January 1965, of Goulart's term of office, labor minister Amauri
Silva wanted SUPRA to set up two thousand rural unions, establish five hundred additional regional labor courts, stimulate pressure for the implementation of rural labor laws, and register
three million new voters. "SUPRA: Maquina de corrupção e subversão," OESP, 3 March 1964, 3.
See also Price, "Rural Unionization in Brazil," 68–70; and Goulart's March 13 speech, reproduced
in Pinheiro Neto, Jango, 185–202. For the January 24 agreement, see telegram 1554, AmEmbassy,
Rio de Janeiro, to USDS, 25 January 1964, RG 59 E 12-2 BRAZ (695), DS/USNA.

Celso in the game, making him less dependent on the church and Archbishop Rossi. From the very start, socially concerned young people and rural labor activists welcomed the agency enthusiastically. Numerous activists wrote the agency to request literature, workshops on the law, and union-formation documents. Dozens of young professionals and students like Sidney Vassimon, a medical intern at Ribeirão Preto's prestigious Hospital das Clínicas, and Vanderlei Caixe, a young law student, voluntarily offered their services to SUPRA.[51]

As Moraes discovered, the trade of the rural labor organizer changed after SUPRA appeared in the region. Significantly, the agency unified and coordinated the efforts of the two wings guided by Moraes and Padre Celso, bringing the rural labor movement under one aegis. Moraes took full advantage of the agency's help. "Things were a lot better for me," he recalled. In addition to Volkswagen buses, SUPRA provided guides to the law and rural union formation. These included the *Guia para organização de sindicatos rurais,* which came with all the paperwork needed to register a union, and *O catecismo do trabalhador rural,* a summary introduction to the ETR that answered common questions about the law. Both were more accessible than any previous discussions of the law in either the partisan or the mainstream press. Although neither he nor Padre Celso became employees of the agency, both served as SUPRA consultants, and when Moraes traveled for the agency, he accepted a daily stipend 20 percent higher than minimum wage. Intending to exploit their diverse expertise, Rappel believed Moraes more suited to agitation and the registration of workers and unions and Padre Celso and former-FAP volunteers more qualified to train leaders and strengthen the unions as institutions. "Each had their own field of influence," Rappel said. With SUPRA in existence, coordinated activity was now more prevalent than the rivalry of the past.[52]

On Wednesday, March 4, when Moraes returned from founding the Dumont union, SUPRA checked one union off its annual quota.

51. "Inquirição: Depoimento do sr. Hans Alfred Rappel," 30 June 1964, B:NM 2/144. Padre Celso, "SUPRA: Rendenção da roça," *DN,* 14 October 1963, 4. After the military takeover, the police interrogated Vassimon and asked if he had been forced to work for SUPRA. Quite to the contrary, Vassimon responded, it was he who had sought to volunteer. "Têrmo de declaração do Sidney Gomes Vassimon," 26 June 1964, B:NM 9/144. For Vanderlei Caixe, see interview by author, Ribeirão Preto, 11 June 1997.

52. Moraes transcript, pt. 3, pp. 29–30. "Têrmo de declaração do Adhemar Teixeira de Morais," 10 June 1964, B:NM 9/144. Moraes was the administrative chief of SUPRA's Ribeirão Preto office. See B:NM 7/144, 12/144, for copies of the pamphlets. Rappel quoted in "Depoimento," B:NM 2/144.

Over the years, the Dumont union helped strengthen the bargaining position of members, gaining wage adjustments and administering health programs, particularly for those who worked in the nearby cane fields. But the transitional period from founding a union to making it effective was often long and hard. Just as Moraes submitted paperwork for the new Dumont union, word came from Fazenda Boa Fé that ten resident sugar *colonos* had been summarily fired when they asked for a raise on March 3. Suddenly, the men were not only jobless, but they and their families were homeless as well.[53]

Sugar workers in the region had become troubled by the return of sharp inequities in the two years since the victorious Pontal strike of 1962. While this successful mobilization had encouraged workers at the Usina São Martinho to strike for parity with their neighbors, by 1964 wages and conditions at São Martinho far exceeded those found at other area sugar mills and plantations. São Martinho workers earned a minimum of Cr$1,259 daily, while Sertãozinho sugar lords such as João Marchesi, owner of Fazenda Boa Fé, paid less than half that amount. Marchesi was a very prominent man. In December, he had been given the honorific title of "Ribeirão Citizen." In addition to Boa Fé, he owned the *fazendas* Aparecida and São João and the Usina Barbacena, as well as his own bank (Banco Marchesi). Yet labor problems on *usinas* in this region were common enough. In February, a gang of some three hundred workers, hired to plant cane for the Usina São Geraldo, walked off the job and made their case public by rallying in the center of Ribeirão Preto. According to newspaper reports, they too wanted parity with São Martinho workers and elimination of the *gato* contract system, a cherished concession won by São Martinho workers two years before. All of these difficult cases prompted union leaders in Pontal, Barrinha, Ribeirão Preto, and Sertãozinho to beg SUPRA's intervention and assistance in the form of training sessions.[54]

53. For Dumont, see "Fundado o Sindicato dos Trabalhadores Rurais de Dumont"; and Nelson Luis Guindalini, interview by author, Dumont, 13 May 1995. On the Boa Fé dispute, see *Euripedes Resende e outros 8 c. Fazenda Bôa Fé*, 422/64 (264), JT/RP.

54. For Rappel, see "Inquirição: Depoimento da Srta. Miriam Di Salvi," B:NM 2/144. For Marchesi, see "Marchesi denominado cidadão da cidade," *DN*, 29 December 1963, 5. Di Salvi was Rappel's executive assistant. The labor leader request letter was signed by Mario Bugliani of Pontal, Manoel da Silva of Barrinha, Sebastião Lopes of Ribeirão Preto, and Antônio Conte of Sertãozinho. See Bugliani et al. to Donato, "Curso com os dirigentes sindicais da Alta Mogiana," Ribeirão Preto, 3 February 1964, B:NM, Anexo 4971. Of the four, at least Lopes and Bugliani were linked to ULTAB. On Ribeirão Preto, see "Centenas de camponeses invadiram a cidade reclamando contra dispensa maciça em um usina de açucar," *DM*, 1 February 1964, 8; and "Camponeses desejam equiparação á São Martinho: Advogados prestam informações sôbre o assunto," *DM*, 2 Februray 1964, 8.

The Military-Landlord Counter Revolt

While Rappel busily prepared a response for union leaders, a massive public event that was to serve as a tragic pretext for the military takeover eighteen days later took place in Rio de Janeiro's Cristiano Otoni Square. At eight o'clock on Friday evening, March 13, Goulart addressed a crowd estimated at nearly two hundred thousand people, many of them federal employees. In dramatic oratory, Goulart attacked article 141 of the Brazilian constitution, claiming it legalized an "unjust and inhumane socioeconomic structure" and insisted on its amendment. Standing at his side were Communist rural labor spokesmen Lindolfo Silva and Luís Tenório de Lima. For some, their presence added an ominous note to the president's announced intention to fight for the elimination of constitutional language that required the government to pay cash for expropriated land. "The use of land is conditioned by the well-being of society," he said. "No one has the right to hold land without using it just by virtue of the concept of 'property rights.'" It was the hour of reform, he said; to reform is "to peacefully resolve the contradictions of an overwhelmed economic and legal order." Before a cheering crowd, Goulart announced having just signed the much-anticipated decree ordering SUPRA to confiscate *latifúndio* from a ten-kilometer band along the right-of-way and distribute it to landless rural laborers. Moreover, Goulart promised to send congress an agrarian reform bill fundamentally redirecting agricultural production away from export commodities and toward the cultivation of food crops for internal consumption. Finally, he called for the legalization of the Communist Party and promised to reform the electoral code by eliminating literacy requirements.[55]

While supporters of radical agrarian reform cheered the president, the March 13 rally and speech offered Goulart's detractors the symbolic and emotional material they needed to uncoil their attack on the administration. One of the key figures so affected that day was General Humberto de Alencar Castelo Branco, who watched the assembly from his office in the war ministry building that bordered the square. A moderate among military men, Castelo Branco claims he was moved by the rally's radical demeanor to participate in the move-

55. Details of the event have been gleaned from Dulles, *Unrest in Brazil*, 269–72; Moniz Bandeira, *O govêrno João Goulart*, 163–65; and "Personagem 7: Luís Carlos Prestes," in Denis de Moraes, *A esquerda e o golpe de 64* (Rio de Janeiro: Espaço e Tempo, 1989), 264–65. Goulart's speech is quoted in Carlos Castelo Branco, *Introdução á revolução de 1964*, vol. 2 (Rio de Janeiro: Artenova, 1975), 262–66; and Pinheiro Neto, *Jango*, 187–202.

ment against Goulart. But the conspiracy against Goulart had been long in the making, and Castelo Branco was a frequent caller at the U.S. embassy, where Ambassador Lincoln Gordon had drawn up a "contingency plan" outlining U.S. support for a Brazilian coup d'état as early as December. Still, March 13 proved an unlucky day for Goulart, for events on that day fed the rancor of his opponents. In São Paulo, Governor Adhemar de Barros called Goulart a hypocrite, noting the president's large landholdings in Rio Grande do Sul and denounced the proposed agrarian reform measure as "confiscation, in violation of the most sacred juridical constitutional traditions."[56]

Although Goulart skillfully deflected the hypocrisy charge by handing over five areas of his two *fazendas* for immediate distribution, he must have sensed how little time such action could buy. The very day he took this bold step, March 19, a protest march of nearly half a million people swamped downtown São Paulo. Called the March of the Family with God for Liberty, the rally had been thrown together remarkably fast. In less than six days time, speakers were mustered to accuse Goulart of plotting a palace coup to turn himself into a dictator. Their inflammatory speeches appealed to enthusiastic listeners, some of whom carried signs alerting people to an imminent Communist takeover and demanding the president's immediate resignation or impeachment. In the tension of the moment, Goulart went to congress to assure legislators that he had no intention of prolonging his term or of operating outside the law. "If there is anyone in this country who will never accept the role of dictator, it is I," he said. "Those who speak of a *golpe* or of 'continuism' do so on their own account, out of their own political immaturity, or an insidious desire to impede the great reformist debate in which all the nation is involved and push it off its pacific and democratic track."[57]

Not apparent at the time was how long the right had been working behind scenes to produce a political crisis. As recent scholarship has made clear, a military-civilian conspiracy led by the army and conservative organizations such as the Brazilian Democratic Action Institute (IBAD, Instituto Brasileiro de Ação Democrático) had been

56. On Castelo Branco, see Phyllis R. Parker, *Brazil and the Quiet Intervention, 1964* (Austin: University of Texas Press, 1979), 59–61. "A Contingency Plan for Brazil," memorandum to the undersecretary from Mr. Martin, American Republics Administration, 11 December 1963, RG 59, POL 1-1 BRAZ (3836), DS/USNA. Barros is quoted in Dulles, *Unrest in Brazil*, 275.

57. On the president's land distribution, see "Terras de propriedade do presidente João Goulart começarão a ser divididas dentro de quinze dias," *DM*, 20 March 1964, 1. On the march, see Dulles, *Unrest in Brazil*, 274–78. In Ribeirão Preto, Goulart's speech was covered in "Enganam-se os que pensam ter o chefe do executivo qualquer objectivo golpista, continuista ou personalista," *DM*, 21 March 1964, 1.

plotting against Goulart since he took office in 1961. Enlisting media magnates such as the Rupert Murdoch–like Assis Chateaubriand Bandeira de Melo (owner of the scandal-mongering Diários Associados newspapers and radio and television stations) and prestigious publishers like Júlio de Mesquita Filho of the *O Estado de São Paulo,* the conspirators first sought to influence public opinion. They decided to ignore the positive achievements of the government and emphasize its failures. At the same time, they gave extensive coverage to Goulart's opponents while ignoring all but the most embarrassing stories of his allies.[58]

Landowner groups such as the Rio Grande do Sul Federation of Agriculturalists (FARSUL, Federação dos Agricultores de Rio Grande do Sul) and São Paulo's SRB became early supporters of the conspiracy. One of the leading conspirators, Porto Alegre–based Third Army chief General Olympio Mourão Filho, consulted with FARSUL's president, A. Saint Pastous, in drafting the movement's "Protocol of the Defense of Democracy in Brazil." In this analysis of the national political economy in 1962, the recent spate of rural labor mobilization was identified as a principal threat. "Isolated movements in the rural zones" and "meetings of pseudo-peasants without land," wrote the conspirators, served "as the first phase of a revolutionary war." Pastous and Mourão Filho determined that it was in their best interests to solidify the ties between military and civilian elites from all sectors of the society in order to avoid a civil war. If they failed and a civil war ensued, the enemy would intensify its subversive tactics in the countryside, stimulating strikes among rural workers and peasant movements for land. Such actions would prolong the takeover and generate conflicts too costly in lives and lost production.[59]

The SRB was deeply involved in the plot. In 1963, Mourão Filho's aide in São Paulo, General Sebastião Dalysio Menna Barreto, was in regular contact with Salvio de Almeida Prado, president of the SRB. For their own reasons, members of the society had grown impatient with Goulart. Unlike the CRB (the official national representa-

---

58. In addition to Parker's *Brazil and the Quiet Intervention,* see also the minutely detailed and well-documented story of the conspiracy against Goulart in René Dreifuss, *1964: A conquista do estado,* 3d ed. (Petrópolis: Vôzes, 1981), and the provocative biography of Assis Chateaubriand by Fernando Morais, *Chatô, O Rei do Brasil* (São Paulo: Companhia das Letras, 1994). Insights on the conspiracy come from Mourão Filho, *Memórias,* 162–97; Dreifuss, *1964,* 192–96, 244–52, 373–96; and Maria Celina D'Araújo, Glaúcio Ary Dillon Soares, and Celso Castro, *Visões do Golpe: A memória militar sôbre 1964* (Rio de Janeiro: Relume Dumará, 1994).

59. Mourão Filho, *Memórias,* 25–47, 158, 162–63. For more on the motives of FARSUL, see Eckert, "Movimento dos Agricultores Sem Terra no Rio Grande do Sul." The thesis examines the movement of rural workers and landless peasants for the redistribution of land in Rio Grande, where the sympathetic Leonel Brizola, the brother-in-law of Goulart, was governor.

tive body of the landowner's rural associations), the SRB continued to oppose government support for rural labor unionization. Whereas the CRB openly supported unions, the SRB persisted in associating them with "rural anarchy." "As we have long held," an editorial read, "the object of national agrarian unionization is not the defense of the just interests of the rural proletarian class but the institution of provisions of political manipulation, designed by federal officials, that constantly push the country into greater social distortions." Mounting aggravations such as these prompted Almeida Prado to join the conspiracy against Goulart, and in April 1963 he offered to share the SRB's elegant new, wood-paneled offices in downtown São Paulo with the Independent League for Liberty, which ultimately organized the crucial March 19 protest rally against Goulart.[60]

While capital cities such as Porto Alegre, São Paulo, and Rio de Janeiro received primary attention from the conspirators, their preoccupation with the rural labor struggle induced them to develop the conspiracy in the interior as well. Since the first stage of the opposition to Goulart emphasized propaganda, the conspirators labored to establish groups that could articulate a legitimate ideological position that contrasted sharply with the popular movement. The male leaders of the conspiracy enlisted their wives and sisters in this campaign, many of whom became outstanding critics of Goulart. The SRB's Almeida Prado was one of the first to initiate this strategy, urging his wife Sebastiana do Amaral Almeida Prado to form the Christian and Rural Friendship Fraternal Institution (FACUR) in December 1962. In important interior centers like Ribeirão Preto, the opposition movement was especially well prepared. There, FACUR combined with the Feminine Regimentation Movement (MAF, Mo-

60. On Barretos and Prado, see Mourão Filho, *Memórias,* 183. Officially, the CRB held that employer and employee unions would help discipline rural labor relations and stimulate greater social harmony and economic productivity. See the speech of CRB president Iris Meinberg in *A reforma agrária na VI Conferência Rural,* 28–29, 53. "Only beneficial results can result," the CRB journal editorialized in 1962. "For planters, they will see better returns for their capital investments. For workers, they will sense the fair compensation for their efforts and dedication. For the country, that, without inglorious and unproductive struggles between classes that ought to walk together like brothers, will have its agricultural potential fully exploited." "Sindicalização rural: Não há o que temer," *O Dirigente Rural* 1:7 (April 1962), 5; and "SUPRA agradece a CRB," *O Dirigente Rural* 3:4 (January 1964), 13. The SRB, on the other hand, seemed more opposed to rural unions than ever before. See, for example, Virgílio dos Santos Magano, SRB counsel, "A sindicalização rural," *A Rural* 42:494 (June 1962), 71; and editorial, "Proletariado e política," *A Rural* 42:496 (August 1962), 3. Editorial quote from "Sindicalismo e anarquia rural," *A Rural* 43: 501 (January 1963), 3. See also the signed editorial, Salvio de Almeida Prado, "Legislações trabalhistas," *A Rural* 43:508 (August 1963), 3. Mourão Filho, *Memórias,* 183, discusses the use of SRB offices, as does "Pronunciamentos da SRB durante a revolução redentora do país," *A Rural* 44:517 (May 1964), 28–30.

vimento de Arregimentação Feminina). Headed by the sister of a member of the "revolutionary commission" that directed the *golpe* in São Paulo, MAF built public animosity toward Goulart and helped justify the military's intervention. For this reason, shortly before the *golpe,* Mourão Filho, shipped a trainload of arms to the Alta Mogiana along the zone's extensive railroad network.[61]

The *Golpe* Unfolds in Ribeirão Preto

Although the press in Ribeirão Preto closely monitored the president's rally in Rio de Janeiro and the spectacular opposition march in São Paulo, few had an inkling of the elaborate web being spun to change their lives forever. Even in the case of the mass rallies, several days passed before they had local repercussions. One of the first controversies that arose involved the training course area labor leaders had asked SUPRA to organize for them. On March 17, Rappel went to SUPRA headquarters in São Paulo to collect a requisition check. Taking away Cr$700,000, he returned to Ribeirão Preto and gave Moraes Cr$270,000 (about U.S.$150) to cover the costs of the meeting. Two days later, on the evening of March 19, Donato tried to reach Rappel with an urgent request. Disturbed by the opposition rally, Donato called Rappel at home before finally reaching his assistant, Miriam Di Silva, at the office. The SUPRA director urged them to cancel the training classes in order to avoid further controversy until the crisis passed. But Rappel, who got the message on March 20, wired back that it was too late to cancel. The training session was already scheduled for March 21 and 22. And besides, he wrote, the rally had not affected local politics. Everything was calm, he assured his boss.[62]

61. "FACUR: Movimento de redenção dos trabalhadores do campo," *A Rural* 43:510 (October 1963), 45. In Portuguese, FACUR was the Instituição Fraterna Amizade Cristã e Rural. On Ribeirão Preto, see Mourão Filho, *Memórias,* 219; and Dreifuss, *1964.* Dreifuss reveals details about the MAF. Its chief, Antonieta Pellegrini, was the sister of *OESP* publisher Júlio de Mesquita Filho. Mesquita was one of four civilian members of the military-civilian general staff (*estado-maior civil-militar*) that planned the *golpe* in São Paulo. The predominantly male conspirators encouraged their sisters, wives, and daughters to establish organizations like MAF to organize middle-class and conservative Catholic resentment against the "syndicalist state" of Goulart. See Dreifuss, *1964,* esp. 294–95, 373–77. On the arms shipments, see Mourão Filho, *Memórias,* 216; and "Projetam um golpe nacional as forças da reação: Vagãoes de armas teriam sido vistos em São Simão," *DM,* 5 February 1964, 1.

62. Readers in Ribeirão Preto followed national events in a steady stream of front-page articles, such as "Será assinado no dia 13 de março próximo o decreto de desapropriações de terras," *DM,* 16 February 1964, 1; and "Todas as atenções do país voltadas para Rio com a realização do comício de reformas de base," *DM,* 13 March 1964, 1. Police interrogators extensively

In contrast to the caution urged by Donato, the pace of SUPRA activities in Ribeirão Preto actually intensified. While volunteers offered courses in labor law and union management for labor leaders from all over the Alta Mogiana, Rappel left for Altinópolis to register yet another rural union. SUPRA's biggest day was still to come: on Tuesday, March 24, dozens of people attended the first general organizing meeting of the regional office. Editors such as Antônio Carlos Santana of *Diário da Manhã* attended, as did lawyers, urban labor leaders, medical and dental college students, and more. As Rappel explained, the medical students were to assist the health needs of rural workers; the dental students, their oral hygiene; the liberal arts students, their educational and literacy needs; and the editors, the promotional needs of the movement The trade unionists provided the strategical and political support; and the lawyers saw to the workers' labor law claims and other legal matters. Seemingly undaunted by national events, the group planned to time the formal inauguration of the local SUPRA office with Goulart's visit to Ribeirão Preto scheduled for April 12. To pay for a massive rally of rural workers in honor of Goulart, Padre Celso asked Rappel for Cr$2,500,000 (about U.S.$1,400).[63]

While the pace of national events seemed to both quicken and to alter SUPRA's agenda, those aligned with the conspiracy against the president simultaneously stepped up their activities. After the success of the March of the Family, they solidified their plans and secretly scheduled April 1 for the *golpe*. With the military takeover prepared, civilian groups were directed to intensify their pressure on authorities loyal to the president. The situation reached a head in Ribeirão Preto as elsewhere toward the end of March. "By the eve of the *golpe*," said Padre Celso, "the bourgeoisie and the planters had already laid all their plans to organize a movement against the left."

---

questioned Rappel and his assistant about the training session and the dispute with Donato. This account was reconstructed from the Rappel and Di Salvi testimony found in B:NM 2/144.

63. Rappel depoimento, B:NM 2/144. Twenty-eight rural labor activists attended the course. Although no record of their names survives, it was possible to learn that at least four who attended were from Bonfim Paulista; three from Franca; four from Ituverava; four from São Joaquim da Barra; three from Pontal; three from Barrinha; five from Sertãozinho; and two from Guatápara. The budget receipt for the course showed expenses for the respective number of bus tickets from each of these towns. The receipt, which Moraes signed, showed that Cr$79,620 of the Cr$270,000 requisitioned for the course was spent on it. "Recibo das despesas do curso com os dirigentes sindicais da Alta Mogiana, 21–22 de março de 1964," B:NM, Anexo 4932. For details on the Tuesday meeting, see Rappel depoimento, B:NM 2/144; and "O presidente da república viria dia doze de abril a Ribeirão Preto para inaugurar agência da SUPRA," *DM*, 25 March 1964, 8. Planning for Goulart's visit is discussed in Syllos transcript, 67–70; and Rappel depoimento, B:NM 2/144.

The first battle fought came on Saturday, March 28, at the Colégio Maristas. In a debate sponsored by MAF, Padre Celso faced the enemy. To stimulate a confrontation, MAF invited Padre Masueto, a reactionary priest from São Paulo, to put Padre Celso and his allies, including Mayor Welson Gasparini, on the defensive. Speaking from the podium, Masueto accused Padre Celso of being a "paid agent of Moscow." The radical priest had fended off such charges before, but he did not expect what followed when provocateurs attempted to draw Mayor Gasparini into a fight. They shouted down the mayor's talk, calling him "stupid" (*burro*); wielding clubs, they started to attack those who defended the mayor and the progressive cleric. Only the arrival of the police ended the conflict.[64]

The next day's religious activities took Padre Celso's mind off Saturday's events. Moraes, on the other hand, only learned of the events that Sunday. Relaxing in his simple, cinder block home on the outskirts of Ribeirão Preto, Moraes was listening to a report of the confrontation on the radio when a telegram arrived from São Paulo ordering him to attend a hastily called meeting of the Communist Party state central committee. At five o'clock the next morning, March 30, he left Ribeirão Preto by car with another member of the party, Dr. Clarimundo Soares. Arriving in the capital city, they went directly to the party's state headquarters, which was located on the fourteenth floor of the Martinelli building on São Bento Street in the center of the commercial district and disguised as an "electoral office." When they walked in, the hall was nearly full with about seventy comrades—party delegates from all over the state. But the meeting had barely begun when a young man rushed into the room yelling for attention. He warned everyone to flee immediately because the police were getting ready to invade the building. He claimed to have learned the information from a government official, São Paulo's secretary of justice. "With that, we all rushed out of the building. The elevator filled up fast," Moraes recalled, "so most of us ran down the stairs, all fourteen floors of them." On the way down, Moisés Vinhas, a journalist and activist, told Moraes and Soares what they would have heard in the meeting. "Stock up on gasoline, he told us," recalled Moraes. "Prepare the resistance!"[65]

64. The incidents of March 28 were reported in "O prefeito Welson Gasparini violentamente ofendido em reunião ontem a noite, sendo-lhe negada palavra!" *DM,* 29 March 1964, 8; and Syllos transcript, 41–42. See also "Os acontecimentos lamentaveis de sabado: Exposição ampla do Prefeito Welson Gasparini," *DM,* 31 March 1964, 8.

65. Although Padre Celso continued to guide the agrarian front, Ribeirão Preto archbishop Angelo Rossi had ordered him to hand direction of the organization over to a layman,

Once they reached the street, the group split up, and small pockets of men waited to see if the young man's information proved accurate. From a safe distance, they watched as the police swarmed the tall, stately building. Moraes remembers his anger. At the eleventh hour, the party now expected its cadre to reverse years of strategy. "Until yesterday they were against it, now they order us to fill up on gas," he cried. "How? Where? And from today to tomorrow?" Considering the predicament on their return to Ribeirão Preto, they decided to talk with Padre Celso. It was now March 31, and Moraes found the activist priest at the office of *Diário de Notícias,* at 67 Visconde de Inhaúma Street. Moraes told him what had happened in São Paulo, and for the first time revealed that he and about thirty *"camponeses"* and other militants had been engaged in military training on a farm near Altinópolis for several weeks. With a right-wing coup happening around them, Moraes appealed for Padre Celso's cooperation in planning the resistance. If Padre Ceslo used his influence to prepare a general strike in Ribeirão Preto, Moraes and his guerrilla band would attempt to neutralize the police in the neighboring towns.[66]

Padre Celso was astounded by what he heard. Although reactionary newspapers like Carlos Lacerda's *Tribuna da Imprensa* and Assis Chateaubriand's *Diários* regularly scandalized readers with talk of revolutionary peasant armies training in the backlands, Padre Celso ignored the cry of alarm, convinced that if such armies existed, they would be ineffective. After all, Brazil was no island nation like Cuba. But Moraes confirmed the accounts and, what was more, asked for his help. Rather than argue about the guerrillas, Padre Celso remembers saying that it was preposterous to think he could prepare a general strike overnight. The labor movement simply was not cohesive enough. Moreover, popular support for their work was still too superficial. "What am I supposed to do," he asked. "Start a movement in the middle of the morning with everybody sleeping or listening to the radio, quiet, inside their houses, scared?" But Padre Celso's sup-

Duarte Nogueira, earlier in the year. Since that time, the priest had moved out of the agrarian front office and begun to live at his parish in Ribeirão Preto's Vila Seixas neighborhood. Syllos transcript, 73; and "O *DN* circulará a partir do dia l de março pleno exito nas gestões de domingo ultimo," *DM,* 25 February 1964, 8. On Moraes's activities, see Moraes transcript, pt. 1, pp. 91–92; and Moraes and Viana, *Prestes,* 177–81. For quote on Vinhas, see Moraes transcript, pt. 1, p. 92.

66. For Moraes's revelations about the guerrilla training camp, see Moraes transcript, pt. 1, pp. 65–66, 89–90, and pt. 3, p. 32. More on the camp can be found in Girotto transcript, 22; and Arlindo Teixeira, transcript of interview by author, Ribeirão Preto, 18 October 1988, pp. 22–23. "It was asinine [*besteira*]," Teixeira said of the camp. "It only served to prejudice us. I participated there too. But it was foolish [*bobagem*], complete rubbish [*porcaria*]."

port for Goulart's reforms and the long-running Brazilian revolution was unyielding. Alert to the risk he was taking, he nevertheless decided to follow his principles and publish and distribute a newspaper that opposed the *golpe*. With a police guard keeping an eye on the newspaper from outside the office, he and his staff printed an eight-page edition. While the police were distracted, they threw several hundred copies over the back wall of the building. But few were distributed before the authorities discovered them. The chief of police must have been outraged when he read the bold headlines emblazoned across the front page: "FIGHT FOR PEACE!" and "GENERAL STRIKE DECREED!"[67]

The April 1 edition was the last Padre Celso edited. By the early morning hours, the right wing's coordinated attack on various strategic targets around the nation had taken its toll. Facing minimal resistance, the *golpe* was complete; Goulart was deposed in two days. In São Paulo, ten thousand civil guardsmen under the control of Governor Barros invaded newspaper and electronic media offices, arrested labor leaders, and tracked down Communist militants. In Ribeirão Preto, the police occupied the offices of *Diário de Notícias,* preventing the paper from publishing a new edition until May 12; they also closed down *Diário da Manhã* before their April 1 edition went to press and did not allow it to resume publication until May 31. At the *Diário de Notícias* office, they took all copies of the newspaper from February and March, leaving no trace of the periodical record during those critical months.[68]

Cutting Back a Growing Movement

The SUPRA office was also invaded, closed, and its staff interrogated. Here, too, the police confiscated everything. The new regime used the documents taken from the SUPRA office to discredit the agency and the rural labor movement in the press; officials also used them to initiate a criminal indictment against the agency and its staff. All involved were accused of subversion under the national security law, and for eight years, the military government hounded Donato and

---

67. Syllos transcript, 72; and *DN,* 1 April 1964, 1.

68. The military-civilian conspiracy in São Paulo is detailed in Mourão Filho, *Memórias,* 169–288; Sampaio, *Adhemar de Barros e o PSP,* 103–5; and Dreifuss, *1964,* 376–96. For Ribeirão Preto, see "Em 64, um paralisação indesejável," *Jornal de Ribeirão,* 21–27 August 1988, 4; and *"Diário da Manhã," DM,* 31 May 1964, 1.

the others. In São Paulo and other states, SUPRA was singled out for the harshest repression because in a short time it had managed to quell the rivalry between many factions of the rural labor movement, helping them attain an unprecedented level of unity. Such an increasingly consolidated movement threatened to become ever more powerful and effective, raising the anxieties of the rural ruling class. While many developments inspired landowners to oppose the Goulart regime, SUPRA's potential for unifying the workers' protest movement truly frightened them. Whoever controlled the federal government controlled SUPRA, and the landed elite wanted that control.[69]

As the SRB's participation in the *golpe* shows, São Paulo coffee planters in particular felt threatened by state intervention in their sociopolitical affairs. The threat of such intervention had always inspired their most strenuous criticisms of the government. But the last straw was the activation of SUPRA. Given the extraordinary independence of executive branch agencies under the 1946 constitution, SUPRA threatened to tip the balance of power against Brazil's most traditional privileged class. Under these circumstances, democracy itself had subverted the social order and disrupted the proper path of political and economic progress. They repudiated SUPRA and then they repudiated the system that gave birth to it. Standing against a system that extended back thirty years to the time of Vargas, they characterized themselves as revolutionaries. Victorious in the field of battle and determined to establish a government that would protect their property and privileges, they seized power.[70]

In June 1972 the Superior Military Tribunal unanimously ruled the government's case against SUPRA groundless. According to the court, officials and staff had merely been carrying out the directives of the law. They had executed the law, not violated it.[71] By then, how-

69. On SUPRA's vilification, see B:NM 144; and Camargo, "A questão agrária," 203–5.

70. "A lavoura paulista repudia o decreto da SUPRA e 'reafirma seu pensamento em favor de uma reforma agrária justa e real,'" *A Rural* 44:515 (April 1964), 6. "Victorious in two days," wrote the SRB's Almeida Prado, "the military battle that constituted the first phase of the revolution . . . has a complete program of demands to fulfill." From the signed editorial, "Da Marcha da Familia a revolução vencedora," *A Rural* 44:517 (May 1964), 3. Other clear examples of how the conspirators saw themselves as revolutionaries are represented in the titles of their memoirs. See, for example, Mourão Filho's *Memórias*; and Hernani D'Aguiar, *A revolução pro dentro* (Rio de Janeiro, 1976). For more on the SRB's expectations, see "Pronunciamentos da SRB durante a revolução redentora do pais," *A Rural* 44:517 (May 1964), 28–30.

71. The tribunal's opinion merits recording here. "Considering SUPRA, the organization that the accused served," wrote Dr. Waldemar Torres da Costa, vice president of the military tribunal, "was an official institution, created by the federal government, and that the creation of rural unions, intended to support the workers of the interior, was one of its mandates . . . and that the accused limited themselves to fulfilling orders sent from above . . . the ministers of the

ever, the damage had already been done. The new rulers understood that if different outcomes were desired, the law had to be changed and new people found to execute it. In April 1964, João Pinheiro Neto was replaced by Colonel Vital Queiróz and eventually arrested as one of 102 enemies of the state under the first of what would become a series of "institutional acts." Due to his elite connections, Pinheiro Neto was soon released. He faced three indictments but was ultimately absolved of one, while the others were dropped. One punishment was served, however: the regime prohibited him from pursuing a political, journalistic, or academic career. SUPRA was also dismantled. One of Colonel Queirós's first acts was to rescind the right-of-way expropriation decree of March 13. In November, SUPRA was transformed into two new agencies, the National Agrarian Development Institute (INDA, Instituto Nacional de Desenvolvimento Agrária) and the Brazilian Agrarian Reform Institute (IBRA, Instituto Brasileiro de Reforma Agrária), neither of which promoted rural unionization. Under the new Land Statute (ET, Estatuto da Terra) issued that month, IBRA and INDA encouraged the colonization of lands far in the interior. Here began official support for the migration and settlement that would eventually be blamed for engendering ecological disaster and human tragedy in the Amazon Basin in the 1980s.[72]

Many of the unions SUPRA officials created in the first trimester of 1964 were denied recognition by the military and destroyed. The tree of the rural labor movement, planted in the 1940s as a seed and nurtured through years of struggle, was cut back hard by the military regime, with whole branches hacked off at their base. All of CONTAG's officers were judged subversives, and all but six of the twenty-nine state federations that had founded the confederation were eventually ruled "paper" or "phantom" organizations and erased from the labor ministry register. Within a year, the regime closed 2,381 rural labor unions for the same reason, leaving the country with about 490 functioning unions in August 1965. The people involved with the closed organizations were imprisoned or forced into hiding or exile. Lindolfo Silva, Nestor Vera, and Luís Tenório de Lima each escaped capture but had their political rights suspended by the regime. Silva went into

---

Superior Military Tribunal, unanimously agree to reject the appeal of the military prosecutor." "Apelação No. 39.067—Estado de São Paulo," Superior Tribunal Militar, Rio de Janeiro, 2 June 1972, B:NM 12/144.

72. Tomás Pompeu Acióli Borges, "Estatuto da Terra," in Beloch and Abreu, eds., *DHBB*, 1203–5; Medeiros et al., "Superintendência," in Beloch and Abreu, eds., *DHBB*, 3284; Kornis and Soares, "Pinheiro Neto," in Beloch and Abreu, eds., *DHBB*, 2740; Medeiros, *História dos movimentos*, 85–88; and Octavio Ianni, *A luta pela terra* (Petrópolis: Vôzes, 1978).

exile, but Vera—as well as José Alves Portela and others—went underground. Accustomed to living clandestinely, Irineu Luís de Moraes escaped capture when the *golpe* occurred by confining himself to a farm in Altinópolis for three months. The rural labor associations and unions he had helped found in Pontal, Sertãozinho, Cajuru, and Altinópolis had all been closed. Mario Bugliani, the Pontal union president Moraes had helped along, also escaped capture. He hid in far-off Ituverava. Like many militants, Moraes and Bugliani soon became frustrated by the military regime, which suppressed all forms of collective action. In 1967, Bugliani joined forces with other disgruntled activists, such as Vanderlei Caixe and Aurea Moretti, to found the National Liberation Armed Front, a particularly ineffective guerrilla band that was wiped out by a police dragnet in 1969, resulting in the imprisonment of both Moraes and Bugliani.[73]

Padre Celso Ibson de Syllos and his compatriots in the agrarian front suffered significantly different fates. After the *golpe,* Padre Celso spent the month of April hiding in a Franciscan sanctuary: a mountain resort above Rio de Janeiro, in Petrópolis. In May he reluctantly returned to Ribeirão Preto and found, to his surprise, that the police had no outstanding order for his arrest. Police Captain Antônio Ribeiro de Andrade warned Padre Celso, however, that armed vigilante groups might be after him, and advised the priest to stay at the archdiocesan curia for the time being. Defiant as ever, Padre Celso refused to stay off the streets and demanded he either be arrested or left alone. Thus, on May 3 the military police seized him and confined him in their barracks along with all of the other supposed agitators and Communists. This pleased Padre Celso. He opposed the *golpe* and wanted to be treated like all other enemies of the new regime. As it turned out, he was treated better than expected. For all the conspiratorial discipline and military leadership of the *golpe,* the crackdown also had its inefficient and soft sides. "I was very well in-

---

73. Statistics on the repression of unions are not readily available. These numbers come from table 18 in Pearson, "Small Farmer and Rural Worker," 258, which cites "Govêrno fecha os sindicatos do peleguismo," *Tribuna da Imprensa,* 30 March 1964; and from Dulles, *Unrest in Brazil,* 222, who has a footnote about the closing of federations. Moraes transcript, pt. 1, pp. 89–93. Lindolfo Silva, transcript of interview by author, São Paulo, 16 August 1988, AEL/UNICAMP. José Alves Portela, transcript of interview by author, São Paulo, 23 August 1988, AEL/UNICAMP. See also AmConGen, São Paulo, to USDS, "The Revolution's Impact on São Paulo Labor," A-8, 10 July 1964, RG 59, LAB 2 BRAZ (1282), DS/USNA. On the National Liberation Armed Front (FALN, Frente Armada de Liberação Nacional), see "Processo contra a Frente Armada de Libertação Nacional de Ribeirão Preto," B:NM 65; Irineu Luís de Moraes, transcript of interview by Sebastião Geraldo, Ribeirão Preto, 20 February 1989, pt. 2, pp. 39–49; Aurea Moretti Pires, interview by author, Ribeirão Preto, 11 June 1997; Caixe interview; "Anos de Chumbo," *Folha de São Paulo* (Ribeirão Preto section), 25 May 1997, 1–22; and Gorender, *Combate nas trevas.*

stalled," he said of the makeshift military prison. "It was a month of fraternization among the left of Ribeirão Preto. A party of sorts."[74]

The party ended for Padre Celso on June 4. One of the last political prisoners captured, he was among the last to leave captivity and enter the altered world of post-Goulart Brazil. The new government had severely restrained political and labor activities, and any notion of expanding the rural labor movement or agitating outside the labor-law justice system met with swift resistance. The priest tried to adjust to the new situation but was particularly frustrated because Archbishop Rossi refused to let him return to his former duties as editor of *Diário de Notícias*. Padre Angélico Sandalo Bernardino now filled that post, as he had when Padre Celso went to Europe. Restricted to the activities of a parish priest in Ribeirão Preto's Vila Seixas, Padre Celso rebelled. On June 26, *Diário da Manhã* published his "Sermon on the Mount." In it, he skillfully used the words of the disciple Matthew to condemn the military government and all those who accommodated to it. "Concretely," the sermon concluded, "in the Brazil of today, the Christian who *conforms* with the current order and social structure, who does not struggle for profound modifications in favor of the less fortunate, is the Christian who may not *yet* participate in the Holy Sacrament" (emphasis in original). Frustrated, Padre Celso also found subtle ways to speak out and to act until abandoning the priesthood in 1967.[75]

The military harassed agrarian front leaders Otávio Sampaio of Batatais and Antônio Crispim da Cruz of Cravinhos but eventually let them continue as presidents of their respective unions. In fact, while the military destroyed SUPRA, closed hundreds of unions, and forced all known Communists into hiding, it did not entirely uproot the rural labor tree. Significantly, some local unions and state federations were left intact, the ETR was not abolished, and CONTAG was not eliminated. In Crispim's recollection of the *golpe,* the fundamental legitimacy of the movement stands out. On April 1, the police arrived at his house guided by his employer, the owner of the Fazenda São José de Colônia Preta. Since his house served as the union office, the police tore through it, collecting papers and breaking furniture in search of hidden documents, weapons, or explosives. They took Crispim to police headquarters in Ribeirão Preto where several DOPS

74. Syllos transcript, 75–76.

75. On the church newspaper, see *"Diário de Notícias comemora 37 anos, sob a direção do arcebispo de Ribeirão Preto," DM,* 1 July 1964, 4. For Padre Celso's sermon, see Padre Celso I. de Syllos, "Crônica religiosa; Momento de Deus; Confusão de revisão," *DM,* 26 June 1964, 2. Early in 1998, the former Padre Celso was killed in an automobile accident in Brazil.

agents interrogated him. For every accusation, he protested that he had done nothing illegal, that it was the planter who "fingered him" who had violated the law by treating his workers poorly, underpaying them, and "even prohibiting priests to come onto the plantation to help a family that was dying of hunger." In Crispim's memory, this accusation transformed the police from his inquisitors to his advocates. "The army captain, representing DOPS, turned around and asked the planter if what I said was true and he admitted it." Apparently, the police found Crispim's accusations both compelling and legitimate because, after a few hours, they let him go home.[76]

This anecdote opens a window on why rural workers did not rise up to defend the Goulart administration or reject the military regime. On the one hand, the repression was selective, allowing activists like Crispim and Sampaio to return to their duties while cracking down on radicals and figureheads like João Pinheiro Neto, Francisco Julião, and Lindolfo Silva. Apparently, the military was after a few select leaders, not the entire movement. On the other hand, the military ran an effective campaign, having confused, divided, and surprised their populist enemies. The *golpistas* moved so fast that Moraes did not have time to organize protest rallies, as he had done to support Goulart during the 1961 succession crisis.

It is difficult to say how workers would have responded to such a call. The petition Sampaio sent Goulart in December 1963 shows just how difficult life had become for so many workers. Goulart may have helped create the rural unionization structure, but it had delivered ambiguous results, and workers cannot be blamed for being ambivalent in their attitude toward his government. The laws legalized unions, but what powers did the unions have to help them when they were thrown out of work? Filing labor court claims was only a partial answer. In fact, the unions must have looked quite powerless, for the planters routinely defied them, the law, and the courts. Goulart wanted to break the old patron-client ties of traditional rural society, but by March 1964, his unions offered little to replace these once reliable, if abusive, ties. Many unions had barely got off the ground when the military offensive began. Perhaps there were not so many "ghost" unions as the military claimed, but in the campaign to gain control of CONTAG, the grassroots had certainly been neglected. The emphasis turned from years of clandestine, grassroots struggle to a top-down strategy based on gaining the support of SUPRA and CONTAG. When Goulart fell, these organizations fell with him, leav-

76. Crispim transcript, 15–20.

ing a short supply of well-rooted unions. Perhaps the strongest among them were those left out of the CONTAG struggle. This was the case of the FAP unions of the Alta Mogiana.

While Crispim and Sampaio may have thought that the military let them return to their activities because they were doing good works, it is clear that each side had different ideas about the task of rural labor leaders and unions. Crispim and Sampaio wanted to help workers improve their lives, a task they dedicated themselves to serving. But the military regime gradually developed a policy that established as a priority developing the most effective and economically rational means of exploiting Brazil's resources, both human and natural. In their view, the rural labor movement could help achieve greater efficiency by containing strikes, channeling complaints through the courts, training workers to operate machinery, and dispensing social services that could ameliorate some of the worst abuses of the transition from an agricultural sector dependent on manual labor to one dependent on machine power. In February 1965 labor minister Arnaldo Sussekind, a longtime informant to U.S. labor attachés, reformed the ETR to eliminate the five categories of rural professional activity that had earlier been established. This forced workers with different problems and perspectives to join together in a single union per *município,* pitting the workers against themselves and causing untold internal problems for the labor movement. To their credit, Crispim and Sampaio tried to remain true to their vision of a union leader's duty by working from within to change the system.[77]

Not so José Rotta. He became the military's favorite rural labor leader after they overthrew the Goulart administration. With all of its directors on the run, CONTAG was handed over to the care of Rotta, who continued to receive training and financing from the United States. In April 1965 Minister Sussekind allowed Rotta to engineer his transition from appointed trustee to elected president of CONTAG. Even though only eleven recognized federations could participate, Pearson alleges that Rotta ensured delegates from those federations he did not trust were unable to participate by waiting to inform them of the meeting when it was already too late. Through this intrigue, Rotta excluded the more progressive Catholic federations of Rio Grande do Sul, Minas Gerais, Bahia, and Ceará and bought himself two more years as president of CONTAG. Under his reign, the rural labor movement fragmented. Local union leaders became disgusted with the confederation and broke their ties with it until a campaign was launched

77. Syllos and Crispim transcripts. Medeiros, *História dos movimentos,* 92–95.

to vote Rotta out of office. The old *frente agrária* alliance of Padre Celso, Crispim, and Sampaio reunited and, joining with other progressive forces from Rio Grande do Sul and Pernambuco, mounted a challenge to Rotta's leadership. In the 1967 election, Rotta was defeated by a slate led by Pernambuco federation president José Francisco da Silva. From then on CONTAG gradually grew in strength, and the union and federation structure became more meaningful to members.[78]

Rural workers needed a structure of support after the military takeover. The miserable conditions of chronic underemployment, which Sampaio described in his December petition to President Goulart, affected an ever growing number of workers, for more and more planters took advantage of the law and a labor surplus. It became much more efficient and economical for planters to lay off resident workers and expel their families, rehiring them through labor contractors as seasonal and casual labor. As noted above, by 1970 the *colonato* system was all but extinct in São Paulo, as were the related *cambão* and *morador* arrangements typical of northeastern plantations. As a consequence, millions of workers moved to the cities, flooding service and commercial labor markets when they were unable to find day jobs as *bóias-frias* on area farms. These conditions allowed some families to progress by gaining access to urban services, such as schools for their children. For others, the move to the city exposed them to colonization schemes and labor recruiters from the Amazon region, and they joined a steady stream of migrants to the wilderness. For most, irregular urban and rural employment provided just enough income to allow them to stabilize at a subsistence level. Good union leaders like Sampaio continued to do all they could with the resources at their disposal to provide workers with health and legal services, nurturing the tree of rural unionization as the years of military rule slowly unfolded.[79]

78. Medeiros, *História dos movimentos,* 88–95; Pearson, "Small Farmer and Rural Worker," 271–73; AmEmbassy, Rio de Janeiro, to USDS, "Rural Workers Reaction to Alliance for Progress Program," A-370, 20 October 1964, RG 59, LAB 10 BRAZ (1283); and AmEmbassy, Rio de Janeiro, to USDS, "Labor Developments Since New Regime Installed," A-295, 25 September 1964, RG 59, LAB 2 BRAZ (1282), both DS/USNA; and Syllos transcript, 65–66. The federations that collaborated with Rotta in 1965 were those of Pernambuco, Rio de Janeiro, São Paulo, Paraíba, Sergipe, Rio Grande do Norte, and Paraná. After his defeat, Rotta resurfaced as president of the Capivari, São Paulo, rural labor union.

79. On the recent history of rural labor in Brazil, see, for example, D'Incao, *O "bóia-fria": Acumulação e miséria,* 8th ed. (Petrópolis: Vôzes, 1975); Juarez Rubens Brandão Lopes, *Do latifúndio á empresa: Unidade e diversidade do capitalismo no campo,* 2d ed. (Petrópolis: Vôzes, 1976); Moacir Palmeira, "The Aftermath of Peasant Mobilization: Rural Conflict in the Brazilian Northeast Since 1964," in *The Structure of Brazilian Development,* edited by Neuma Aguiar (New Brunswick: Transaction Books, 1979), 71–97; Maybury-Lewis, *The Politics of the Possible;* and Pereira, *The End of the Peasantry.*

Irineu Luís de Moraes briefly returned to the São Paulo rural labor struggle with its reawakening in 1984. Times had changed significantly since 1970, when DOPS agents brutalized him. Brazil was now nearing the final stage of a transitional process of gradual democratization called the "opening" (*abertura*). A general amnesty in 1977 had allowed former activists like Lindolfo Silva and Francisco Julião to return from exile and cautiously reenter political life. State governors and legislators had been elected directly by voters in 1982 for the first time since 1965, and a handful of new political parties had replaced the rigid bipartisan structure formerly imposed by the regime. Mass "Diretas Já" rallies had demanded direct elections for president, too, but the military resisted this demand. Instead, they scheduled an indirect election for January 1985, after which the

EPILOGUE

São Paulo Rural Workers and Brazil's Democratic Transition

regime planned to withdraw from power. The election was to result in the selection of Brazil's first civilian president in twenty-one years: the opposition leader Tancredo de Almeida Neves, Goulart's first prime minister, from 1961 to 1962.[1]

Life had changed for rural workers, too. The military's modernization project affected few rural workers more than those of the Ribeirão Preto region. The military responded to the energy crisis of the 1970s by mandating the development of automobiles that could run on sugarcane-derived alcohol, encouraging a shift away from dependency on imported oil. Through subsidies and guaranteed markets, the program catalyzed the Alta Mogiana sugar industry, and the region soon became Brazil's greatest single producer of sugar and alcohol. Over the course of the decade, sugarcane monoculture seized the region, and towns doubled in size with the migration of hundreds of thousands of workers, especially seasonal cane harvesters and mill hands. To capture its prosperity, rooted as it was in an agro-industrial complex of sugarcane plantations and highly efficient mills, some called the region the "Brazilian California." Others called it the "rural ABC," in a reference to Brazil's chief industrial complex, located in three São Paulo suburbs (Santo André, São Bernardo, and São Caetano). It was out of the ABC that metalworkers revived Brazil's industrial labor movement in 1979—giving birth to the country's innovative, grassroots Workers' Party (PT, Partido dos Trabalhadores)—and out of the rural ABC of the greater Alta Mogiana that Brazil's rural labor movement began a new life, challenging not only the military but new civilian structures of power as well.[2]

1. Irineu Luís de Moraes, transcript of interview by Sebastião Geraldo, Ribeirão Preto, 20 February 1989, pt. 2. Neves, who had long been ill, died the day he was to be inaugurated as president, and his running mate, José Sarney, became Brazil's first post-*golpe* civilian president in April 1985. While Neves had inspired the public and represented change from the military regime, Sarney had been a supporter of the military government and his elevation to the presidency represented continuity with the past and disappointed the public. See Skidmore, *The Politics of Military Rule in Brazil.*

2. On the Alta Mogiana, see Maria Conceição D'Incao, "O movimento de Guariba: O papel acelerador da crise econômica," *Política e Administração* 2 (July–September 1985), 201–22; Medeiros, *História dos movimentos,* 133–35; and Mayla Yara Porto, "De bóias-frias a cortadores de cana: O direto ao progresso com desordem na região de Ribeirão Preto" (master's thesis, Faculdade de Direito, USP, 1993), 8–12. For the ABC and the PT, see Margaret Keck, *The Workers Party and Democratization in Brazil* (New Haven: Yale University Press, 1992). Under the direction of CONTAG, sugar workers in Pernambuco started a series of annual strikes in 1979 that are normally associated with a rise in rural labor militancy. Although these strikes were of great significance, involving tens of thousands of workers, they took place within legal parameters and did not have the same long-term influence that the São Paulo cycle of strikes, begun in 1984, have had on society and the rural labor movement. Almost the opposite argument is made by Anthony Pereira in his 1996 book *The End of the Peasantry,* which highlights the Pernambuco case as "exemplary" (6). See also Cândido Grzybowski, "Rural Workers' Movements and Demo-

The Guariba Strike of 1984

Moraes was seventy-three years old in 1984. Weakened by decades of struggle and demoralized by Communist factional disputes, he was pleased to see an explosion of militance among sugarcane cutters in Guariba, a town of twenty-five thousand people located some twenty-five miles southwest of Ribeirão Preto. On May 15, Guariba became a household name around Brazil as the media arrived to document a bloody conflict between thousands of seasonal cane cutters and dozens of officers from the Military Police (PM, Polícia Militar). That morning, the cutters attacked the local water and sanitation agency, SABESP, burning down its office and destroying the city water tank. The crowd had just started to sack a grocery store when a contingent of PMs fired on them, killing a bystander and wounding thirty others. A police attack dog set lose on the crowd was torn apart by angry strikers, and three officers were injured by rocks. Authorities quickly blamed outside agitators, but the media, labor leaders, and the new political activists knew the responsibility lay in the horrendous living and working conditions of the sugar workers.

Workers had gone two frustrating harvest seasons without receiving any response to their protests against a 1982 change in the labor process that caused their pay to be reduced and their labor increased. They rejected their exclusion from the legal protections extended to permanent rural workers by a 1973 law (decree 5,889). They also condemned the housing arrangements hundreds were forced to accept—arrangements that had them living crowded together in stables and bathing in water troughs used by livestock. In addition, their low pay quickly left them indebted to local merchants and service providers. Their 1984 protest had begun with the start of the harvest season on Monday morning, May 14, when sixteen gangs of cutters stopped work on Usina São Martinho lands. The next morning, they set up pickets on the roads leading out of Guariba in order to stop the *gatos* from carrying new loads of workers to the plantations. Support grew quickly among *bóias-frias,* but so did the opposition of *usineiros.* They had SABESP and the supermarket cut off the workers' water supply and credit, angering the strikers and making these institutions strategic targets. Burning down the SABESP meant destroying records of their debts with the agency; the same was true of their attack on the store. The police came to protect both the prop-

cratisation in Brazil," in *The Challenge of Rural Democratisation: Perspectives from Latin America and the Philippines,* edited by Jonathan Fox (London: Frank Cass, 1990), 35.

erty of *usineiros* and their prerogative to run their fields and mills however they pleased. The police assault showed how little tolerance authorities had for "uppity" *bóias-frias*. The name was used pejoratively, reducing them to an unappealing inanimate object ("cold lunch") and calling into question their very humanity.[3]

Few had anticipated the ability of *bóias-frias* to initiate such a shocking series of events. No unions or recognized groups had been involved in organizing the action that day. Yet, within twenty-four hours nearly ten thousand workers adhered to the strike. Inspired by the Guariba example, nine to twelve thousand orange pickers in nearby Bebedouro struck on May 15, and by the time the Guariba dispute was settled on May 18, cutters from another five towns in the region had gone out demanding similar adjustments. As of the end of June, twenty-four conflicts had been reported—including nineteen strikes—involving nearly fifty thousand workers. Over the course of the next decade, tens of thousands of temporary rural wage workers throughout the region mobilized for new demands as well as the enforcement of old agreements. In 1987, for example, more than one hundred thousand workers from forty-two *municípios* went on strike. They made it clear that in the new democratic era, the *bóias-frias* of São Paulo expected to be considered equal in status to registered permanent workers, showing their determination to define democracy as a rejection of the marginal status the military regime had condemned them to suffer. Their insistence on equality forced profound changes in the rural labor movement and the sugar industry and fed a still more radical movement for redistribution of land, the Landless Laborers' Movement (MST, Movimento dos Trabalhadores Rurais Sem Terra).[4]

Only the workers themselves and a few old militants like Moraes knew the *bóias-frias* had the capacity to act and shape history. Harbored in the memories of some of the older strikers was the pre-1964 history of mobilization in the region. They recalled a victorious strike

3. This account is derived from details provided in "Um morto e 30 feridos num dia de muito violência em Guariba," *A Cidade* (16 May 1984), 16; D'Incao, "O movimento de Guariba"; Maria Conceição D'Incao and Moacyr Rodrigues Botelho, "Movimento social e movimento sindical entre os assalariados temporários da agroindústria canavieira no estado de São Paulo," in *Movimentos sociais na transição democrática,* edited by Emir Sader (São Paulo: Cortez, 1987), 53–81; and Francisco José da Costa Alves, "Modernização da agricultura e sindicalismo: Lutas dos trabalhadores assalariados rurais da região canavieira de Ribeirão Preto" (master's thesis, UNICAMP, 1991). (Thanks to Michael Hall for mailing me a copy of this thesis.)

4. Medeiros, *História dos movimentos,* 132–209; and Porto, "De bóias-frias a cortadores de cana," 10.

from 1961 and told social scientist Maria Conceição D'Incao about it. "Although fragmented," D'Incao wrote, "the memory of this strike was a significant presence among the oldest laborers." The recollection "had an important role in the Guariba events" of 1984, D'Incao concluded, because it proved their ability to carry out a successful collective action. It was the only memory of militancy she encountered during a 1981 to 1984 field study of seasonal labor in the area.

Finding more detailed information unavailable, D'Incao reconstructed the 1961 event from the bits and pieces her informants remembered. They said that some leaders in a Barrinha rural union had called the strike to demand a wage hike following a rise in the market price of sugar, that pickets had been posted along the roads, and that all the workers of Guariba and Barrinha participated in it. Two generations of rural workers had helped to keep the memory alive until 1984. Remarkably, many leaders of the 1984 action were older workers who remembered the 1961 event and projected an image of the past as better than the present. "The oldest men, heads of families," wrote D'Incao and a collaborator, "are those responsible for the construction of the code which has oriented the struggle of these laborers." These older workers were "the principal ones responsible for the elaboration of nearly all of the demands the laborers presented to their employers." They were "strengthened by the memory of a time when they lived better." Younger leaders, such as Elio Neves of the Araraquara STR, carried memories of militancy from their parents. "I'm accustomed to calling myself an extension of my father," said Neves, who remembered well the persecution his father suffered for his activities as a Communist rural labor militant in late 1950s and early 1960s.[5]

5. The workers' nostalgia recalls the "time of plenty" (*tempo da fatura*) phrase the anthropologist Verena Stolcke found common among São Paulo cane cutters during her research in the early 1970s. She saw it as a way workers identified the pluses of the *trabalhista* era as compared to the military years, which they characterized as the "time of money" (*tempo de dinheiro*). The cutters did not mean that they *had* money but that the values of a market culture had taken over and turned their labor—*their very being*—into a commodity. See Verena Martinez-Alier (Stolcke) and Armando Boito Junior, "The Hoe and the Vote: Rural Labourers and the National Election in Brazil in 1974," *Journal of Peasant Studies* 4:3 (April 1977), 151–54. D'Incao's Ford Foundation field study report, carried out while she worked at the CEDEC (Center for the Study of Contemporary Culture), is entitled "Participação social e trabalhadores assalariados temporários da agricultura." Her 1985 article, "O movimento de Guariba," discusses her findings about the 1961 strike on page 214. For the role of old timers, see D'Incao and Botelho, "Movimento social e movimento sindical," 61–66. For Neves, see Elio Neves, interview by author, Araraquara, 22 July 1997.

The Seed Was Planted

Moraes had more specific memories of the early 1960s. He had been one of the key instigators of labor mobilization in the area before the military came to power. In fact, Guariba's rich rural labor history underscores the central thesis of this book: that the seed of the contemporary rural labor movement was planted earlier in the century. Surprising continuities connect Guariba to the past. Guariba was one of the towns Moraes visited as he worked in 1960 and 1961 to establish organizations among sugarcane cutters at Sertãozinho, Pontal, Barrinha, and Pradópolis mills. At the time, the heterogeneity of the regional economy fragmented his efforts, but gradually the cutters proved the most interested in what he had to say. Moraes found willing leaders in Jorcelindo de Souza and Mario Bugliani who became presidents, respectively, of the Barrinha and Pontal "associations of sugar mill and farm laborers." Following the succession struggle for Goulart in September, Guariba's workers joined a crowd of one thousand rural workers from Pitangueira, Pradópolis, Pontal, and Sertãozinho in an October protest rally for higher wages and the right to organize rural unions.

The area's real strike wave came in 1962, not 1961. In June, cutters living in Guariba were among six thousand field and mill hands who stopped operations in the fields and factories of the Santa Elisa, Albertina, Santo Antônio, São Francisco, São Geraldo, and Bela Vista agro-industrial complexes. By July, word of their success had spread to workers on the plantations of the Usina São Martinho, and they too went on strike. As Chapter 7 reports, both strikes succeeded in gaining salary increases and promises of improved working conditions. In both 1962 and 1984, workers residing in Guariba struck the São Martinho and Santa Elisa mills.[6]

The Guariba strike of 1984 was exceptional for the number of seasonal workers involved, their solidarity in the face of harsh repression, and the independence of their initial action. Still, it was not the first time workers in this category had acted collectively on their own. In 1962, Moraes was lounging at his house in Ribeirão Preto when São Martinho owner Orlando Ometto came to get him to help

6. See Chapter 7 and "Usineiros desrespeitam salário mínimo," *TL*, October 1961, 2; "Alta Mogiana: 6 mil trabalhadores em greve derrotaram império dos usineiros," *TL*, August 1962, 5; and José Teodoro, "Usinas de açúcar começaram a funcionar," *DN*, 23 June 1962, 3. Moraes passed away in December 1996, and Bugliani died in September 1989. One of his comrades in the FALN, Aurea Moretti Pires, claims that Bugliani served as a reference point for Guariba militants. "They used to gather at his house in Sertãozinho to discuss strategy and tactics," Moretti told me. Aurea Moretti Pires, interview by author, Ribeirão Preto, 11 June 1997.

Araraquara rural employees union president Elio Neves, photographed during a July 1997 interview, became a leader of militant migrant sugar harvesters during the 1984 Guariba strike.
Photo: author

control the cutters' self-initiated strike. Moraes and Said Issa Halah soon took control of negotiations. The 1984 Guariba strike had a similar start and was soon under the control of union leaders. On the evening of its first full day, May 15, FETAESP treasurer Elio Neves and Jaboticabal rural labor union president Benedito Guimarães Magalhães hosted a strike assembly in the Guariba municipal stadium. Workers voted formally to strike and accept a plank of negotiating demands that had been prepared by union officials. Although both actions appeared spontaneous and autonomous, both had been preceded by intensive contact with rural labor organizations: ULTAB, in 1962; and FETAESP, in 1984.

Negotiations followed in both cases, with professional union administrators and lawyers taking charge, but the cutters of 1984 were more involved in the process than those of 1962. The May 15 assembly elected a strike committee of representative workers, something Moraes had not seen fit to do twenty-two years before. When May 16 ended with the *usineiros* demanding more time, the cane fields started to burn, apparently set afire by cutters in order to prevent the mill owners from prolonging the negotiations. State labor relations secretary Almir Pazzianoto Pinto then worried aloud that "the cane cutters . . . were a mass without a head and without direction." But putting fire to cane to intimidate the master class has been a time-tested mode of resistance among agricultural workers since commercial sugarcane harvesting was first developed in the Mediterranean nearly seven hundred years ago. Once the *usineiros* conceded to their demands, the workers voted to approve the "Guariba Accord" and return to work.[7]

Whereas the 1984 Guariba strike included a broad plank of money, conditions, and labor process issues, the demands of the 1962 strikers were less complicated but comparable. Their concerns overlapped in three key areas: measuring productivity, prohibiting deductions, and gaining representation. The seasonal workers of 1984 were credited with making demands that pushed beyond institutional and legal parameters. They asked to be allowed to change key aspects of the labor process and to be considered regular rural employees with full legal rights and benefits, despite their seasonal work patterns. In the 1962 strikes, the cutters similarly shaped the composition of demands and expected changes in the labor process and their legal standing. In 1984 workers wanted to restore a system of assigning each cutter five, five-foot wide swathes of cane to harvest. They complained that the seven-swathe system, imposed in 1982, exhausted them and lowered their daily output. It required them to carry armloads of cut cane an additional 10 feet in order to stack it in a central row for pickup and delivery to the mill. In 1962 workers wanted to be paid by the hour rather than the ton, and they demanded the elimination of *gato* middlemen and the abolition of rent deductions. These were demands the workers themselves had defined and fought to put in place.[8]

It is not clear how committed each group of strikers was to the idea of forming unions. Comments from delegates at the 1961 Belo Horizonte congress suggested shallow attachment to unions as such. But worker delegates seemed to appreciate the benefits of organization and desired the incorporation promised by unions. With ULTAB's Moraes articulating the interests of workers in the 1962 strike wave,

7. Pazzianoto quoted from *Folha de São Paulo,* 17 May 1984, and cited in Costa Alves, "Modernização da agricultura e sindicalização," 146. For the Guariba Accord, see ibid., 133–40; and D'Incao, "O movimento de Guariba," 215–16. The president of the employer group, São Paulo State Agrarian Federation (FAESP, Federação Agrícola do Estado de São Paulo), was Fabio de Sales Meireles.

8. Restoring the five-swathe system had become such an issue in the region that FETAESP had already added the item to the list of demands it brought to annual negotiations with FAESP and the state labor relations secretary.

the demand to form unions was certainly present. In 1984 the seasonal workers of Guariba similarly demonstrated pragmatic ambiguity in regard to the question of forming a union. Technically, their town sat within the territorial jurisdiction of the Jaboticabal STR headed by Magalhães. Magalhães had been active in the labor movement from the pre-*golpe* days, but he had done nothing for migrant workers. His involvement in the Guariba strike had been forced on him by the forward-looking Neves, who took responsibility for the region as a FETAESP officer from his base in the Araraquara STR. In all likelihood, Magalhães had risen through the ranks as a protégé of José Rotta, for Rotta's Workers Circle had been active in the region before the *golpe*. In fact, before Franco Montoro stepped down as labor minister in June 1962, Rotta gained recognition for a Guariba rural labor union. In any event, the Guariba strikers accepted sympathetic union direction. It was not until after ratifying the accord, when the question of ensuring its enforcement became a primary concern to them, that the seasonal workers seriously took on the challenge of forming a union.[9]

One of the problems inherited from the past was the territorial restriction of union action. Under the ETR, both employer and employee unions were assigned to specific *municípios*. Within this space, only one workers' union was to operate, handling the needs of all laborers. This was called "uniqueness" (*unicidade*). This policy had its roots in the Vargas era for it was embedded in the 1943 CLT. It became an issue in the 1944 rural unionization decree, which, as Chapter 2 describes, the SRB criticized. They wanted the *sindicatos* to be organized by crop categories or agricultural activities, just like their society of coffee planters and beef growers. But Vargas sought to weaken such single issue interest groups, preferring the corporatist model of segmentation into community interest groups. In this context, leaders of the rural labor movement recognized benefits in *unicidade,* for it helped level the playing field with their richer and better-organized opponents. But they also realized the debilitating factionalism that could result from forcing one union to represent the interests of such diverse groups as salaried farmhands and family-based tenant farmers. By the end of 1963, as Chapter 8 discusses, the labor ministry had allowed unions to specialize in four categories, so long as they each limited their activities to defending the interests of their

9. For Moraes, see Chapter 7. On Neves, see D'Incao and Botelho, "Movimento social e movimento sindical," 70; and Costa Alves, "Modernização da agricultura," 138–40. For Magalhães and Rotta, see Costa Alves, ibid., 111 n. 11; and Barros, "A organização sindical dos trabalhadores rurais," 115 n. 45.

defined categories within the boundaries of assigned territories. From the perspective of leaders like Lindolfo Silva, this ruling by Minister Amauri Silva promised to help strengthen the movement by allowing workers with similar interests to unite and by preventing rival organizing groups from setting up competing unions, which would weaken the PCB's predominance.

The singular jurisdiction of Magalhães's STR for the Jaboticabal *município,* which included Guariba, came out of reforms the military regime put in place in order to weaken the rural labor movement and make it especially difficult for organizers to represent the growing class of seasonal workers. Some examples are Portaria No. 71 of February 1965, which eliminated the categories that had formerly allowed the movement flexibility in dealing with Brazil's complicated rural employment structure; Decree Law No. 761 of August 1969, which created a special law for seasonal harvesters that further set the migrant workers apart from other rural workers; the 1971 law of labor cooperatives (Decree Law No. 5,764), which defined members as nonemployees, despite the reality of their seasonal employment by sugar growers; and 1973's Decree Law No. 5,889, which defined rural workers eligible for participation in union activities as those who worked in agriculture full-time on an annual rather than seasonal basis. Slowly but surely the military regime divided the rural working class, turning the unions into relatively privileged domains and *bóias-frias* into outsiders. This was not something the pre-*golpe* movement had wanted. To the contrary, Moraes and other leaders had worked hard to maintain categories that could accommodate seasonal workers, even as they accepted the territorial limitations imposed by the concept of *unicidade.*[10]

In the years leading up to the founding of CONTAG in 1963, several groups fought for the allegiance of rural workers. In São Paulo, as we have seen, two church groups and the Communist Party were especially active. By the time of the Guariba strike, new groups had appeared on the scene. The *abertura* and aloof official unions combined with the self-evident problems of migrant workers and their obvious capacity for struggle to bring several organizations to the Ribeirão Preto region. A leading Catholic group was the Pastoral Land Commission (CPT, Comissão Pastoral da Terra), founded in 1975.

10. The laws are summarized from Medeiros, *História dos movimentos,* 95–100, 132; D'Incao and Botelho, "Movimento social e movimento sindical," 56–57; Porto, "De bóias-frias a cortadores de cana," 58; and Costa Alves, "Modernização da agricultura," 168. Copies of laws and regulations dated before 1970 can be consulted in the appendix of Russomano, *Comentários ao Estatuto do Trabalhador Rural.*

Although a land reform agenda animated the CPT, its activists in Ribeirão Preto soon adjusted to the proletarian ambitions of seasonal workers. Most of these workers initially rejected the idea of becoming peasants and dreamed of finding decent, stable, and adequately paid work in agriculture or industry. The rural labor activists of the Unified Laborers' Central (CUT, Central Única dos Trabalhadores)—a radical new national labor organization with strong links to the PT—also appeared on the scene. After the May strike, these two groups developed significant followings among the Guariba workers. By the end of the year, when union elections were called, each fronted a slate of candidates. The CPT slate, headed by José Laurents Junior, won, but this did not stop the leader of the CUT faction, José de Fatima Soares, from taking the initiative while the labor ministry considered the union application. Thus, on 3 January 1985, just two days before the national presidential election, the Guariba militants started an unprecedented interharvest strike for job stability and full-year employment.[11]

Despite the apparent appeals of the CPT and CUT, the official unions had not entirely withdrawn from the scene. From the *golpe* until 1979, CONTAG had become a creature of the military regime, though not an entirely tame one. It was destined to become Brazil's largest labor confederation, representing ten to thirteen million members, more than three thousand unions, and twenty-four state federations. It owed much of its phenomenal growth to social welfare duties first assigned to the unions under the ETR but put in place by the military regime with the initiation of the Rural Laborer Assistance Fund (FUNRURAL, Fundo de Assistência ao Trabalhador Rural) in 1971. With funds for medical, dental, legal, and retirement services, FUNRURAL allowed unions to serve as the principal social service agency for the rural poor. Unfortunately, it also allowed some to become corrupt fiefdoms, as payroll deductions obliged workers to contribute to FUNRURAL while the unions themselves banked the money and decided who was eligible for services. It was a purely corporatist system, a perfect fit for the hierarchical union structure the pre-*golpe* labor movement had helped build.[12]

But *assistencialismo,* as the tendency to turn unions into wel-

11. On the CPT and CUT in general, see Medeiros, *História dos movimentos,* 111–14, 150–55. For the groups' entrance into Guariba, see Costa Alves, "Modernização da agricultura e sindicalização," 119–23. On the January strike, see D'Incao, "O movimento de Guariba," 217–18.

12. On FUNRURAL and *assistencialismo* (also called the unionism of *aparelhismo* and *dos resultados*), see Maybury-Lewis, *The Politics of the Possible,* 63–98. A critical view of this tendency is offered by Medeiros, *História dos movimentos,* 92–111.

fare agencies became known, did not please everyone. By the late 1970s, a reformist faction from Pernambuco became dominant within CONTAG. In 1979 they organized Brazil's first major rural strike since 1964, gaining the support of one hundred thousand workers and idling dozens of sugar mills in an action carefully tailored to fit within the parameters of Brazil's restrictive strike laws. This action, which proved successful, was followed by others, and the experience inspired a resurgence of rural labor militancy in other regions of Brazil. In São Paulo, various radical unionists such as Elio Neves traveled to the northeast to support and learn from militants there. They were "socialized" by contact with the Pernambuco strikes, but vast differences in conditions prevented the experience from turning into a model approach to activism. Nevertheless, the Pernambuco strikes inspired a series of meetings to discuss the problems of sugar workers and to disseminate a proactive discourse. Because of these meetings, FETAESP officers were ready to intervene in the Guariba strike. But the organization's corporatist origins and institutional inertia prevented it from remaining at the forefront of the migrant workers' struggle.[13]

Instead of supporting the January strike, FETAESP played a role in suppressing it. While the CUT sought to build up Fatima, FETAESP worked with the government and Guariba's mayor to end the conflict by passing out baskets of food, unemployment checks, and promises to study the problem. Uncertain what to do, the CPT faction leaned in favor FETAESP's position. Politics entered the picture, with the PT supporting Fatima and denouncing the deal makers, and FETAESP aligned with the Brazilian Democratic Movement Party (PMDB, Partido do Movimento Democrático Brasileiro), which was getting set to rule Brazil with the election of Tancredo Neves and had little interest in getting bogged down in regional labor disputes. As the Guariba strike began to inspire stoppages in Barrinha, Jaboticabal, São Joaquim da Barra, Sertãozinho, and Monte Alto, putting thirty

13. For the Pernambuco strike, see Sigaud, *Greve nos engenhos;* and Pereira, *The End of the Peasantry.* Some FETAESP union presidents resisted the changes inspired by the Pernambuco strikes because their permanently employed and small producer members were more or less content. In 1982, however, FETAESP joined the CPT and members of the PMDB—whose candidate, André Franco Montoro, was then seeking election as São Paulo's first directly elected governor since the *golpe*—to begin reaching out to *bóias-frias* in a meeting held in Ribeirão Preto. After Montoro was elected, the state labor secretary hosted another Encontro dos Volantes in Ribeirão Preto in September 1983. Like ULTAB conferences in the 1950s, these meetings included the participation of *bóias-frias;* unlike those conferences, the 1980s meetings took more of their direction from grassroots activists and the seasonal workers themselves. D'Incao believes the meetings allowed the Guariba harvesters and Bebedouro pickers to coordinate their strikes. See D'Incao, "O movimento de Guariba," 212; and Porto, "De bóias-frias a cortadores de cana," 84–86. See also Neves interview.

thousand people out of work, the owners of the region's thirty-seven sugar mills demanded military intervention. On January 12, the government obliged them with a vicious attack on the Guariba strikers. The PMs raced through worker neighborhoods with their guns blazing, invading the houses of picketers and bombing them with tear gas to intimidate and break the strike. Assaulted by one hand and soothed by the other, the strikers' solidarity gave way, the strike collapsed, and the sugar industry returned to normal. There is little doubt that struggles among the CUT, CPT, and FETAESP contributed to the defeat of the strike, just as rivalries between Catholic activists, Communists, and populist politicians in an earlier era had helped strengthen the hand of the *golpistas*.[14]

The pre-1964 rural labor movement left both negative and positive legacies for the democratic transition of the 1980s. A memory of struggle had been bequeathed to the next generation, as had a body of law and a system of representation. In a moment of crisis and opportunity, the memory proved most enduring, transcending the limits of the law and the inertia of the unions, inspiring seasonal workers to fight against exploitation and for better lives. Although the military regime had modified the law to exclude them, the cutters still saw value in many of its provisions. They wanted the law to see them as workers, just like any other, despite the seasonal rhythms of their work. More than anything else, they wanted to fit into the sugar industry on a regular basis, employed year-round renewing the soil, planting crops, and doing odd jobs between the harvests; this was the chief goal of the January strike. While some unions ignored seasonal workers, others search for ways to address the needs of the *bóias-frias*. Elio Neves's union, for example, was ready when the May strike came. But the flowchart of FETAESP, like CONTAG, was strictly top-down. This helped labor bureaucrats justify suppressing a regional strike in order to strengthen the organization's ties to the newly elected civilian government. The PCB—with such examples as the Porecatú War and the Production March—had already fully developed this tendency. By the time ULTAB's Lindolfo Silva became CONTAG's first president in 1963, a populist authoritarian tradition had been well established. Perhaps unwittingly, CONTAG president José Francisco

14. This is not to say that FETAESP betrayed the workers. In the evaluation of some observers, the CUT and PT were wrong to have supported the leadership of Fatima, who soon revealed his opportunism and the shallowness of his commitment to the struggle. Moretti and Neves interviews; and Lilian Arruda Marques (CONTAG wage policy assistant and former FETAESP staff member), interview by author, Brasília, 17 July 1997. For the interseason strike, see D'Incao, "O movimento de Guariba," 217–18; Costa Alves, "Modernização da agricultura e sindicalização," 180–89; and Porto, "De bóias-frias a cortadores de cana," 89–90.

da Silva made a bow toward both the good and bad legacies of the past when he welcomed Lindolfo Silva to help celebrate his reelection in April 1980 to the directory, where he ruled for twenty years (1968–89).[15]

Rural Workers as Historical Agents

The 1962 and 1984 strike waves engaged specific individuals at specific times and places. These strikes occurred primarily because of the convergence of particular forces and motivations that are best found in the immediate locale. To the extent that history played a part in these events, we can trace a long line of antecedents for the behavior of the Guariba *bóias-frias* from the enslaved Africans, who contributed to the abolition movement, to striking immigrant *colonos,* who supported socialist and oppositionist movements in the 1910s and 1920s; to the corporatism of the 1930s, which began the process of formalizing the participation of rural workers in the political economy. Rural workers had become an object of ruling-class rivalry, and the new regime of Getúlio Vargas contoured the field of rural labor struggle in a way that was to affect the lives of rural workers for generations to come. In the CLT of 1943 and the rural unionization decree of 1944, Vargas began to establish the parameters of struggle as ones in which being unionized meant being incorporated, and being incorporated meant being *somebody.* In conditions of limited opportunity, smallholders like João Guerreiro Filho and rural workers like Pedro Salla seized the promise of incorporation by forming peasant leagues. These men made themselves historical agents. Increasing numbers of rural workers would follow their initiative through the 1950s—using the law, the courts, and the promise of incorporation to enhance their opportunities and overcome bad work environments. This trend continued to develop until, by the early 1960s, one could speak of a national rural labor movement in Brazil. In 1962 and 1963, the movement bore its first fruit in the rapid recognition of rural unions, in the creation of the ETR, and in the formation of CONTAG. These actions, laws, and organizations rooted the Guariba struggle in a substantial past.

This history of continuity in struggle, institutions, law, and per-

15. On Silva, see *O Trabalhador Rural* 1 (May–June 1980), 1–27.

sonalities contradicts some of the conclusions of those who study "new social movements," as the 1984 Guariba strike has been categorized. Although D'Incao heard her informants' memory of the 1961/62 labor actions and recognized this memory as playing an "important role," she argues that the 1984 strike arose *in spite of* the labor movement's history. Like many analysts, D'Incao associates the ETR, CONTAG, and the whole rise of the movement in the early 1960s with the peasant leagues of Julião and not with ULTAB. The historical rural movement she describes was, like the peasant leagues, rooted in a resistance to proletarianization. "The ideal peasant, which has historically characterized Brazilian rural unionism, has impeded the definition of labor policies and practices adequate to the specific situation of pure wage earners." Thus, she argues, the ETR privileged permanent agricultural workers like *colonos,* while marginalizing temporary workers like *bóias-frias.* Similarly, the ET, "conquered by the just born rural labor movement," emphasized the needs of workers who depended for their livelihood on land usage rights as much or more than they depended on wages. Excluded from the rural labor movement, the ever expanding population of temporary and seasonal workers like the *bóias-frias* of Guariba had no one to depend on but themselves. In 1984 they suddenly became historical agents on their own terms, a transition to "subjectivity" unprecedented in the modern history of Brazilian rural workers.[16]

This book demonstrates some of the problems with the new social movements theory by carefully examining the old social movements. By the time the ETR and CONTAG were set up, Julião's leagues had been marginalized, and, as a Communist organization, ULTAB had little reason to oppose proletarianization when its directors took control of CONTAG. With its base in São Paulo and its strengths among sugar mill and field hands, ULTAB brought a working-class bias to CONTAG. Whatever happened to drive unions away from temporary wage workers happened under military rule. The regime replaced the Communists with many Catholic activists, especially those connected to Rotta, who most certainly did bring a petty bourgeois perspective to CONTAG. Thereafter, the regime modified the ETR in a series of ministerial edicts and laws to isolate the growing category of seasonal workers from the corporatist structure. To the extent there was a *bóias-frias* problem before the *golpe,* the rural labor

16. D'Incao, "O movimento de Guariba," 206; and D'Incao and Botelho, "Movimento social e movimento sindical," 55. Passed into law in November 1964, after the rural labor movement had been smashed by the military, the ET was far from a conquest of the movement.

movement attempted to address it. The military regime, however, tried to sweep the problems under the rug, even as they grew in size and complexity.

By 1984, São Paulo rural workers had memories and structures they could use to make their needs known. They influenced the democratic transition by insisting that their concerns be heard among the cacophony of newly mobilized, rights-conscious civil groups. Their protests helped make the call for agrarian reform a central issue the new civilian government would have to confront, and their demands for representation began a grassroots challenge to the corporatist union structure. As early as September 1984, a regional meeting of rural laborers held in Sertãozinho produced the Sertãozinho Manifesto. The document was meant to strengthen the hand of grassroots organizers and their perspectives in debates scheduled for CONTAG's fourth national congress, held in May 1985. They demanded a commitment from CONTAG for the creation of worker commissions to help enforce contracts, greater liberty for local unions in mobilizing workers to strike, and the direct election of both union and government officials. The manifesto joined others from around the country in an effort to democratize CONTAG just as Brazil was being democratized. But much like the military had resisted direct elections for president, the leaders of CONTAG put off critics by taking the initiative. They proposed the solidarity of all militants behind a CONTAG-led campaign for a National Plan of Agrarian Reform (PNRA). This move successfully divided supporters for change within CONTAG.[17]

In the 1988 constitutional convention, however, CONTAG was outmaneuvered. A reenergized landlord lobby called the Rural Democratic Union Party (UDR, União Democrática Ruralista) defeated the PNRA and eliminated central achievements of the 1946 constitution such as articles limiting property rights to those whose agricultural practice benefited the social welfare, and clauses of the 1964 ET, which allowed for expropriation in bonds rather than cash. While CONTAG succeeded in advancing some labor law reforms, such as gaining retirement benefits for rural workers, the insiders game pursued by CONTAG leaders largely failed the rural poor. These mixed results led to the ouster of longtime CONTAG president José Francisco da Silva and strengthened competing groups. In 1989, CUT formed a rural labor department under the direction of Avelino Ganzer, a small producer from Santarém, Pará, intending to use the depart-

17. CONTAG, *Anais: IV Congresso Nacional dos Trabalhadores Rurais* (Brasília: Gráfica e Papelaria Tipogresso, 1985); and CONTAG, *CONTAG: 30 anos de luta* (Brasília: Gráfica Sindical, 1993).

ment to build a parallel rural labor movement that might prove popular enough with workers to drain and destroy CONTAG. Increasing numbers of rural labor unions affiliated with the CUT but did not leave CONTAG, and so, by 1995, CUT leaders allied with progressives within CONTAG, and Ganzer and other CUT supporters gained election to the confederation's directory. In the meantime, Elio Neves and other union leaders, such as the FAP's aging activist Antônio Crispim da Cruz, pursued the pluralist strategy of the CUT at the grassroots. They insisted on ending the monopoly of *unicidade* by founding Rural Employee Unions (SERs, Sindicatos dos Empregados Rurais) to better accommodate wage earners like *bóias-frias*. In 1989 these union leaders helped found the São Paulo State Federation of Rural Employees (FERAESP, Federação de Empregados Rurais Assalariados do Estado de São Paulo), a separate state federation for the rural employee unions, and unlike the CUT's rural labor department, FERAESP leaders refused to merge with FETAESP. Through grassroots pressure, the corporatist system of the past was gradually giving way to a pluralist one.[18]

São Paulo rural workers also hastened changes in the agricultural history of the state. The enslaved Africans helped bring down slavery and the contracted free laborers helped design the *colonato* that replaced the slave system on São Paulo coffee plantations. In the early twentieth century, *colono* protests and planter needs converged to begin a process of formalizing rural labor relations in ways that strengthened plantations as profitable capitalist enterprises. A symbiosis then developed among successful *colonos,* planters interested in selling land, and a state interested in diversifying the agricultural economy. As the *colonos,* along with their descendants and dependents, grew in number, they formed a new constituency for those who sought to further diversify the state's economy. This helped São Paulo respond to the Great Depression by turning more land to cotton, sugarcane, and other uses.

After World War II, coffee and sugarcane competed for laborers during the harvest season, and the migratory labor market grew. In this context, workers began to take advantage of the few legal benefits extended to them, helping to break patron-client bonds, weaken the *colonato* system, and lead planters to invest more in mechanization.

18. On the late 1980s, see Porto, "De bóias-frias a cortadores de cana," 86–94; Medeiros, *História dos movimentos,* 169–209; Costa Alves, "Modernização da agricultura e sindicalismo," 280–87; and D'Incao, "O movimento social e movimento sindical," 74–80. For the 1990s, see Avelino Ganzer, interview by author, Taguatinga, 18 July 1997; Neves interview; and Airton Faleiro, interview by author, Brasília, 18 July 1997.

The place of machines in Brazilian agriculture stimulated many conflicts between *bóias-frias* and *usineiros*. From sugar mills to tractors, machines became a regular feature of life in the agro-industrial complex of São Paulo sugar production. The Sertãozinho Manifesto had asked for a moratorium on investments in new labor-saving devices, but the trend was in the opposite direction. The more migratory workers protested their conditions and demanded job security, the more large mill owners invested in machines. "The great impulse for mechanization was the strikes, labor indemnities, the whole social problem of working with cutters," an Usina da Pedra manager reported. "We ended up throwing all those problems into the hands of the government." By 1996, 65 percent of the harvest on the São Martinho estate was being done by machines the owners themselves had developed into world-class harvesters. One such apparatus replaced the work of a hundred men. With no jobs to replace those lost to machines, the displaced harvesters became frontline militants in the fastest growing social movement of the 1990s: the MST, an effort to force the government to provide every interested family with a homestead. With so many members suffering deprivation around them, union leaders like Neves became organizers of MST-like camps of hundreds of jobless workers who came to occupy six different areas in the Alta Mogiana in an effort to force the government to redistribute underutilized land.[19]

The years 1962 and 1984 were unusual historical moments for Brazil. Goulart's rise to power in 1961 created a significant opening for labor mobilization, as did the 1980s process of transition to civilian rule. Rural workers in both settings acted in ways that generated reaction. We have seen how the rise of the rural labor movement inadvertently helped inspire the participation of planters in the conspiracy to overthrow Goulart in 1964. The mobilization of *bóias-frias* similarly influenced historical processes in the late 1980s. But rural workers have also made their interests a part of other historic moments in Brazil's modern saga. They helped shape the transition from slavery to freedom in the nineteenth century and from authoritari-

19. On mechanization, see José Graziano da Silva, *Progresso técnico e relações de trabalho na agricultura* (São Paulo: Hucitec, 1981); Porto, "De bóias-frias a cortadores de cana," 15–19; and Costa Alves, "Modernização da agricultura e sindicalismo," 288–307. On the MST, see Costa Alves, ibid., 307–9; Medeiros, *História dos movimentos*, 147–50; and Jack Hammond, "The Landless Workers' Movement of Brazil" (paper presented at the Latin American Studies Association Congress, Guadalajara, Mexico, April 1997, mimeographed). See also Sérgio Luís dos Santos (Usina da Pedra mechanization manager), interview by Sebastião Geraldo and Cliff Welch, Serrana, 11 July 1997; and Neves interview. Geraldo and Welch conducted further interviews on the MST with rural workers and leaders in the region during June and July 1997.

anism to populism in the twentieth. Over time, their organizational capacity and influence grew, but these individuals had long been there, working in cross-class alliances as well as for themselves, to participate in the process of making history. Until the enormous contradictions of Brazil's capitalist system are resolved, rural workers and militants like Irineu Luís de Moraes will continue to challenge the nation's ruling interests.

APPENDIX: FIGURES AND TABLES

FIGURE 1. Deflated indices of export prices and prices received by São Paulo planters, 1948–58

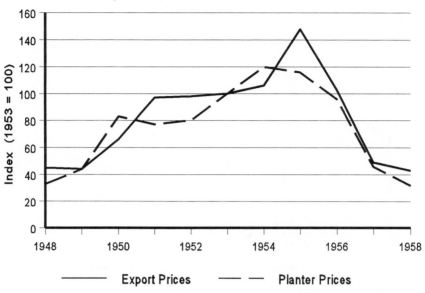

Export Prices   — — Planter Prices

FIGURE 2. *Colono* wage and planter receipt indices compared, 1949–58

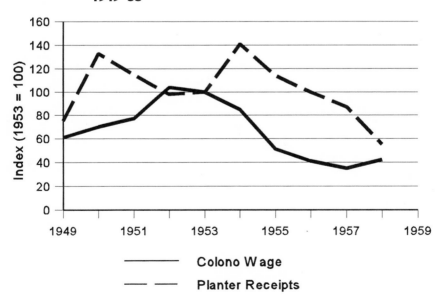

———— Colono Wage

— — Planter Receipts

FIGURE 3. São Paulo rural strikes reported in the Communist press, 1949–64

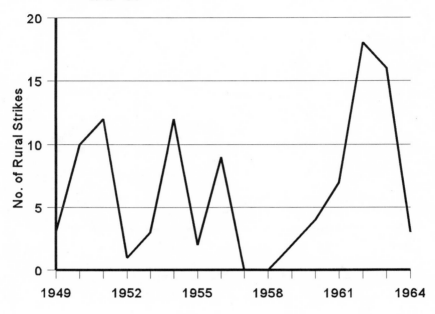

TABLE 1. Gubernatorial Election Results in São Paulo, 19 January 1947

Candidate	A	B	C	D
Adhemar de Barros	48%	23%	393,637	35%
Hugo Borghi	32%	29%	340,502	31%
Mario Tavares	13%	38%	289,575	26%
A. de Almeida Prado	6%	10%	93,169	8%
Total vote	535,096	581,787	1,116,883	

SOURCES: TRE/SP; French, "Adhemarista Populism in São Paulo," 22.

KEY: Column A is the percentage of votes won by the candidate in urban industrial regions, including the electoral zones of greater São Paulo, Campinas, Jundiai, Santos, and Sorocaba. Column B is the candidate's percentage of the vote in the remaining rural areas of the state. Column C is each candidate's statewide tally. Column D gives the total statewide percentages.

TABLE 2. Gubernatorial Election Results in the Alta Mogiana,
19 January 1947

Candidate	108	109	133	135
Adhemar de Barros (PSP)	4,509	505	321	340
Hugo Borghi (PTB)	3,824	729	1,550	1,380
Mario Tavares (PSD)	2,907	952	775	1,026
A. de Almeida Prado (UDN)	680	134	897	186
Total vote	12,001	2,320	3,543	2,932
Center/left (PTB/PSP) as percentage of total vote	70%	53%	52%	58%

SOURCE: TRE/SP.

NOTE: The 1947 electoral zones above were chosen at random from those located within the Alta Mogiana region. The selected zones were composed of the following cities and towns: Zone 108—Ribeirão Preto, Guarapiranga, Dourado, Boa Esperança, Trabiju, and Dumont; Zone 109—Cravinhos, Serrana, Guaturano, and Guatapará; Zone 133—São Simão, Icaturana, Luiz Antônio, and Serra Azul; Zone 135—Sertãozinho, Cruz dos Posses, Barrinhos, and Pontal. According to the 1950 census, the economically active populations (EAP) of all but Zone 108 were predominantly engaged in agriculture. In Zone 108, greater Ribeirão Preto, only one quarter of the 1950 EAP was engaged in agriculture.

TABLE 3. Municipal Election Results in the Alta Mogiana,
9 November 1947

Candidate categories	Ribeirão Preto	Miguelópolis	São Simão	Sertãozinho
Mayor				
Winning party	PTB	PSD	UDN	PTN
% of vote	37%	53%	69%	54%
City Council				
Center/left votes	7,768	897	698	1,629
Conservative Party votes	5,388	963[a]	1,336[b]	395[c]
Center/left % of vote	59%	48%	34%	80%

SOURCE: TRE/SP.

NOTE: The role of the UDN and its ideological nature in the interior of São Paulo needs further study. In the case of Miguelópolis, although the PSD won the mayoralty, Moraes says that the victor, José Santana, was so compromised with the PCB that he promised to deliver his post to the popular leader of the peasant league who had run as his vice mayor. Welch and Geraldo, *Lutas camponesas no interior paulista,* 92–94.

[a] PSP-UDN/PSD-PR
[b] PSP/UDN
[c] PSP-PTB-PTN/UDN

TABLE 4. **Quantity and Value of Coffee Exported Annually from the Port of Santos, São Paulo, 1942–53**

Harvest	60-kilogram sacks	Value (Cr$)	Cr$/sack
1942/43	4,704,335	1,373,412,222	291.95
1943/44	9,641,967	2,828,555,686	293.36
1944/45	9,492,210	2,813,794,515	296.43
1945/46	11,809,854	4,107,630,554	347.81
1946/47	10,334,788	5,501,425,662	532.32
1947/48	10,810,054	6,240,052,067	577.25
1948/49	11,283,649	6,400,539,018	567.24
1949/50	9,635,842	8,092,789,683	839.86
1950/51	8,505,149	10,406,745,032	1,223.58
1951/52	7,714,026	9,557,684,408	1,239.00
1952/53	7,781,498	9,840,517,231	1,265.00

SOURCE: Constantino C. Fraga, "Resenha histórica do café no Brasil," *ASP* 10:1 (January 1963), 21.

TABLE 5. Comparison of Coffee Export Prices from the Port of Santos, São Paulo, and the Prices Received by Planters, 1948–58

Year	Median export price[a] (U.S.$)*	Median planter price[b] (U.S.$)*	Index of export price	Index of planter price	Planter price as % of exports
1948	30.83	23.77	45	33	77%
1949	30.30	30.77	44	44	102%
1950	44.86	58.23	66	83	130%
1951	65.36	54.49	97	77	83%
1952	66.19	56.62	98	80	86%
1953	67.57	70.51	100	100	104%
1954	71.46	85.21	106	120	119%
1955	100.23	82.49	148	116	82%
1956	69.75	67.42	103	96	97%
1957	33.37	32.51	49	46	97%
1958	29.27	22.73	43	32	78%

*Price is per sixty-kilogram sack, deflated in current U.S. dollars. Current U.S. dollar/cruzeiro exchange rates derived from tables in Armin K. Ludwig, *Brazil: A Handbook of Historical Statistics* (Boston: G. K. Hall, 1985), 431–32.

[a] SOURCE: Fraga, "Resenha histórica do café," 21
[b] SOURCE: Rubens Araujo Dias, "Levantamento dos preços medios recebidos pelos lavradores," *ASP* 7:2 (February 1960), 47.

TABLE 6. Comparison of Coffee Planter and *Colono* Purchasing Power in São Paulo, 1949–58

Year	Cost of living index[a]	*Colono* wages[b]	Planter receipts[c]	*Colono* wage index[d]	Planter receipt index[e]
1949	58	1,250	576	61	75
1950	62	— [f]	1,090	— [f]	133
1951	67	1,800	1,020	77	115
1952	82	3,000[g]	1,060	104	98
1953	100	3,500	1,320	100	100
1954	118	3,500	2,200	85	141
1955	141	2,500	2,130	51	114
1956	173	2,500	2,280	41	100
1957	206	2,500	2,360	35	87
1958	237	3,500	1,720	42	55

[a] Cost of living index in the capital city of São Paulo, from Ludwig, *Brazil: A Handbook of Historical Statistics*, 448.

[b] Wages paid to *colonos* annually in cruzeiros for the care (*trata*) of every one thousand coffee trees. Figures for 1949 and 1951 are from *ASP* 2:4 (April 1952), 25; and those for 1953 are from *ASP* 3:9 (September 1953), 19. All others were extracted from *processos* stored in the archive of the Justiça do Trabalho, JT/RP, including *processos* numbered 238/62, 1694/64, 354/57, 589/60, 845/61, 467/61, and 332/64.

[c] Annual prices received in Cr$ by São Paulo planters for a sixty-kilogram sack of clean (*beneficiado*) coffee beans, averaged month-to-month by region. Dias, "Levantamento dos preços medios recebidos pelos lavradores," 47.

[d] *Colono* wages deflated by cost of living index.

[e] Planter income deflated by cost of living index.

[f] No data available.

[g] This amount, paid on Sitio Santo Antônio de Grotão (Ribeirão Preto), was considerably higher than the minimum standard rate of Cr$2,000 set by FARESP in July 1952. This difference may be explained by the proximity of the *sitio* to the competition of the urban labor market. The lower rate gives an index of 70, quite below the number used to draw the graph in Figure 2. "Imigrantes agrícolas italianos," *Brasil Rural* 120 (July 1952), 10.

TABLE 7. Immigration to the State of São Paulo, 1920–70

Years	Brazilians	Immigrants	Total	Percentage of immigrants in total
1920–29	230,790	503,568	734,358	68.6
1930–39	435,864	198,104	633,968	31.2
1940–49	528,000	66,000	594,000	11.1
1950–59	1,280,000	370,000	1,650,000	22.4
1960–69	758,000	78,800	836,800	9.3

SOURCES: Vicente Unzer de Almeida and Octavio Teixeira Mendes Sobrinho, *Migração rural-urbana: Aspectos da convergência de população do interior e outras localidades para o capital do estado de São Paulo (Com um estudo sobre zonas de colonização do estado de São Paulo)* (São Paulo: Secretária da Agricultura, Directória de Publicidade Agrícola, 1951), 79; and Rosa Ester Rossini, "Estado de São Paulo: A intensidade das migrações e do exodo rural/urbano," *Ciência e Cultura* 29:7 (July 1977), 783.

TABLE 8. Persons Occupied on Large and Medium-Sized Plantations in the State of São Paulo, 1950–70

Category	1950	1960	1970
Employers	32,696 (4.5%)	36,367 (4.8%)	32,640 (6.5%)
Permanent employees	519,629 (71.9%)	419,729 (56.0%)	288,308 (57.3%)
Temporary employees	170,429 (23.6%)	292,816 (39.2%)	181,962 (36.2%)
Total	722,754 (100%)	748,812 (100%)	502,910 (100%)
% Change in total	0	+3.6%	−30.5%

SOURCE: Adapted from table 44, São Paulo, in Secretaria da Economia e Planejamento (SEPLAN), *Trabalho volante na agricultura paulista* (Estudos e pesquisas no. 25) (n.d.), 170.

TABLE 9. São Paulo Gubernatorial Election Results and Municipal Breakdown, 3 October 1954

Governor	Total	77	108	109	133	135	146
Quadros	660,264	5,145	1,996	540	2,269	2,568	1,259
Barros	641,960	4,633	5,899	738	1,037	1,216	988
Prestes Maia	492,518	3,667	5,353	1,598	1,183	1,445	786
Toledo Piza	79,783	83	6,500	184	120	243	39
Blank	38,239						
Annulled	16,967						
Total	1,929,731	13,528	19,748	3,060	4,609	6,352	3,072
Vice Governor							
Porfirio da Paz	658,132	3,646	8,227	701	2,318	2,553	1,204
Salzano	625,455	4,613	5,492	712	1,017	1,144	965
Cunha Buena	532,641	5,089	5,359	1,624	1,250	1,721	829
Blank	95,994						
Annulled	17,509						
Total	1,929,731	13,348	19,078	3,037	4,585	5,418	2,998

SOURCE: TRE/SP.

NOTE: Table 2 lists the towns included in electoral zones 108, 109, 133, and 135. Zone 77 contains Monte Aprazivel, and Zone 146 includes Valparaiso; in both of these rural zones, the PCB was active organizing rural laborers.

TABLE 10. Presidential Election Results in Alta Mogiana,
3 October 1955

Presidential candidates	São Paulo total[a]	Interior total[b]	Zone 108[c]	Zone 109[d]	Zone 133[e]	Zone 135[f]
Barros	867,320	520,307	7,345	1,185	1,566	2,248
Tavora	626,627	395,000	5,502	1,513	2,301	2,369
Kubitschek	240,940	152,833	3,607	423	450	751
Salgado	159,051	128,141	2,534	420	146	954
Blank	21,497	13,541	161	66	63	97
Annulled	46,850	33,439	621	189	119	221
Total	1,962,285	1,243,260	19,770	3,778	4,645	6,640
Vice Presidential candidates						
Campos	726,069	463,318	7,766	1,660	2,271	2,900
Coelho	608,337	371,955	3,579	822	975	1,445
Goulart	384,083	254,921	6,212	684	837	1,383
Blank	205,401	127,382	1,714	474	490	785
Annulled	38,395	25,684	499	128	72	127
Total	1,962,285	1,243,260	19,770	3,778	4,645	6,640

SOURCE: TRE/SP.

[a] Total votes for the city of São Paulo and rural electoral zones in the state of São Paulo.
[b] Total votes for São Paulo state electoral zones outside the city of São Paulo.
[c] Ribeirão Preto.
[d] Cravinhos, Serrana, Dumont, and Guatapará.
[e] São Simão, Icaturama, Luiz Antônio, Serra Azul, and Santa Rosa de Viterbo.
[f] Sertãozinho, Pontal, Barrinha, and Cruz dos Posses.

TABLE 11. Ribeirão Preto Regional Labor Court: Rural Labor Claims and Claimants, May 1957–December 1964

Year	Claims Filed			Claimants		
	Rural claims	Total claims	Rural claims as % of total claims	Rural claimants	Total claimants	Rural claimants as % of total claimants
1957	205	756	27.1%	345	1,557	22.2%
1958	223	802	27.8%	351	1,085	32.4%
1959	147	866	17.0%	216	1,174	18.4%
1960	184	670	27.5%	225	843	26.7%
1961	401	1,050	38.2%	588	1,959	30.1%
1962	573	1,669	34.3%	1,032	3,001	34.4%
1963	798	2,144	37.2%	1,312	3,103	42.3%
1964	621	2,122	29.3%	1,454	3,622	40.1%
Totals	3,179	10,079	31.5%	5,523	16,344	33.8%

SOURCE: *Protocolos dos Processos (1957–1964)* (hereafter *Protocolos*), JT/RP.

NOTE TO TABLES 11 AND 12: Claims listed in the court ledger were considered rural if the accused firm (*reclamada*) was listed by one of the following distinct agricultural titles: *fazenda, sitio, chacara,* or *agro-industria.* This method of identification was chosen as the most efficient, since the most accurate method would have required consulting every one of the ten thousand claim files housed in the court archive. As I later learned, some workers entered claims against the owners of agricultural establishments. Not knowing the names of all owners, I was unable to quantify these claims, making the numbers above conservative estimates.

The total number of claimants for each claim was listed in the *protocolos.* As the difference between rural claims and rural claimants in Table 11 shows, some claims were filed by more than one worker. It is possible to argue that some of these claimants were not rural workers. Randomly selecting fifty case files from the archive, I found several claimants who listed their vocations as machine operators, mechanics, and other occupations that could be defined as industrial in nature. More than a few of these workers had to defend their position as industrial workers on farms in order to claim certain legal rights, demonstrating the transitional nature of the period.

TABLE 12. Ribeirão Preto Regional Labor Court: Claimants and Rural Claims Filed, May 1957–December 1964, Categorized by Agricultural Establishment

Year	Fazenda		Sitio/Chacara		Agro-Indústria		Total	
	Claims	Claimants	Claims	Claimants	Claims	Claimants	Claims	Claimants
1957	182	311	4	4	19	30	205	345
1958	202	324	5	7	16	30	223	351
1959	156	198	7	7	11	11	174	216
1960	160	197	11	12	13	16	184	225
1961	356	502	20	31	25	55	401	588
1962	473	851	62	84	38	97	573	1032
1963	699	1166	57	71	42	75	798	1312
1964	436	781	41	58	144	615	621	1454
Totals	2664	4330	207	274	308	919	3179	5523
Total as % of overall total (1957–64)	83.8%	78.4%	6.5%	5.0%	9.7%	16.6%	100%	100%

SOURCE: *Protocolos*, JT/RP.

BIBLIOGRAPHY

Archives and Libraries

Arquivo do Arquidiocese de Ribeirão Preto, Ribeirão Preto
Arquivo da Confederação Nacional dos Trabalhadores na Agricultura, Brasília
Arquivo da Primeira Junta de Conciliação e Julgamento, Ribeirão Preto
Arquivo da Tribunal Regional Eleitoral do Estado de São Paulo, São Paulo
Arquivo de História Contemporânea, Universidade Federal de São Carlos, São Carlos, São Paulo
Arquivo Nacional do Brasil, Rio de Janeiro
    Fundo da Secretária da Presidência da República
    Ministério da Agricultura
    Ministério do Trabalho, Indústria, e Comércio
    Secretaria da Justiça e Negócios do Interior do Estado de São Paulo
Arguiro Público e Histórico de Ribeirão Preto
Biblioteca da Sociedade Rural Brasileira, São Paulo
Biblioteca de Direito Social, Faculdade de Direito de São Paulo, São Paulo
Biblioteca do Instituto de Economia Agrícola, Secretaria da Agricultura do Estado de São Paulo, São Paulo
Biblioteca Municipal "Mario Andrade," São Paulo
Biblioteca Nacional do Brasil, Rio de Janeiro
Casa de Cultura, Ribeirão Preto
Casa de Rui Barbosa, Rio de Janeiro
Centro de Pesquisa e Documentação de História Contemporânea do Brasil, Fundação Getúlio Vargas, Rio de Janeiro
    Arquivo Gustavo Capanema
    Arquivo Lindolfo Collor
    Arquivo Osvaldo Aranha
    Coleção da História Oral
Library of Congress, Washington, D.C.
National Agricultural Library, Beltsville, Maryland
Pontifical Universidade Católica, São Paulo
    Biblioteca da Pôs-Graduação
    Centro de Documentação do Instituto Católico
United States National Archives, Washington, D.C.
    Brazilian Post and Decimal Files, Department of State (1920–65)
Universidade Estadual de Campinas
    Arquivo Edgard Leuenroth
    Centro de Memórias

Periodicals (including place of publication and years consulted)

Agricultura em São Paulo (São Paulo, 1951–76)
Boletim da FARESP (São Paulo, 1950–52)
Boletim de Agricultura (Rio de Janeiro, various)
Boletim do Ministério da Agricultura, Indústria e Comércio (Rio de Janeiro, 1912–44)
Boletim do Ministério do Trabalho, Indústria e Comécio (Rio de Janeiro, 1934–64)
Boletim Eleitoral da Tribunal Regional Eleitoral do Estado de São Paulo (São Paulo, 1947–61)

Brasil Rural (São Paulo, 1952–62)
Cidade, A (Ribeirão Preto, 1984)
Diário da Manhã (Ribeirão Preto, 1945–64)
Diário de Notícias (Ribeirão Preto, 1945–64)
Dirigente Rural, O (Rio de Janeiro, 1961–64)
Estado de São Paulo, O (São Paulo, various)
Folha de Londrina (Londrina, 1985)
Folha de São Paulo (São Paulo, various)
Lavoura, A (Rio de Janeiro, 1930–62)
Notícias de Hoje (São Paulo, 1953–59)
Novos Rumos (Rio de Janeiro, 1959–64)
Revista Brasileira de Geografia (Rio de Janeiro, various)
Revista Brasiliense (São Paulo, 1958–64)
Revista da Sociedade Rural Brasileira (São Paulo, 1930–55)
Revista de Direito Social (São Paulo, 1941–45)
Revista Legislação do Trabalho (São Paulo, 1941–64)
Rural, A (São Paulo, 1956–65)
Terra Livre (São Paulo, 1954–64)
Última Hora (São Paulo and Rio de Janeiro, 1954–65)

Government Documents and Reports

Brazil

Comissão de Desenvolvimento Industrial, *O problema da alimentação no Brasil* (Rio de Janeiro, 1954).
Comissão Nacional de Política Agrária, *Reforma agrária no Brasil: Estudos e projetos* (Rio de Janeiro: Serviço de Informação Agrícola, 1956).
————, *Reforma agrária no Brasil: Premeiros estudos e projetos* (Rio de Janeiro: Serviço de Informação Agrícola, 1953).
Consolidação das leis do trabalho (Rio de Janeiro: Imprensa Nacional, 1943).
Instituto Brasileiro de Geografia e Estatística, *Censo agrícola do estado de São Paulo: Recensamento do 1960* (Rio de Janeiro, 1963).
Instituto Brasileiro de Geografia e Estatística, *Censo demográfico: Estado de São Paulo,* Tomo I, vol. 25 (Rio de Janeiro, 1954).
Joint Brazil/United States Economic Development Commission, *The Development of Brazil* (Washington, D.C.: U.S. Government Printing Office, 1954).
Ministério da Agricultura, *A reforma agrária na VI Conferência Rural* (Rio de Janeiro: Serviço de Informação Agrícola, 1962).

São Paulo

Amaral, Roberto Ferreira do, ed., *Diagnóstico: Sexta região administrativa: Ribeirão Preto* (São Paulo: SEPLAN, August 1972).
Bosco, Santa Helena, and Antônio Jordão Netto, *Migrações: Estudo especial sôbre as migrações internas para o estado de São Paulo e seus efeitos* (São Paulo: Setor de Estudos e Pesquisas Sociológicas, Departamento de Imigração e Colonização, Secretaria da Agricultura do Estado de São Paulo, 1967).
Mendes Sobrinho, Octávio Teixeira, *Planejamento da fazenda de café: Separata of the Boletim de Agricultura* (São Paulo: Diretoria de Publicidade Agrícola, 1962).
São Paulo, Secretaria da Economia e Planejamento, *Trabalho volante na agricultura paulista* (São Paulo: Estudos e pesquisas, no. 25, 1978).

United Nations Documents

Department of Economic and Social Affairs, Joint Working Group of the Banco Nacional do Desenvolvimento Econômico (Brazil) and the United Nations Economic Commission for Latin America (ECLA), *The Economic Development of Brazil*, pt. 1 of *Analyses and Projections of Economic Development* (New York, 1956).

ECLA, *Coffee in Latin America: Productivity, Problems, and Future Prospects* (New York: United Nations, 1958).

ECLA, *Theoretical and Practical Problems of Economic Growth* (Santiago, Chile: ECLA, 1951).

FAO, ECLA, Instituto Brasileiro do Café, and Secretaria da Agricultura do Estado de São Paulo, Divisão da Economia Rural, *A indústria do café em São Paulo* (São Paulo: Diretoria de Publicidade Agrícola, 1961).

Personal Interviews

All interviews were conducted in Brazil, unless otherwise noted. Those interviews for which audio tapes and transcripts can be found in the Arquivo Edgard Leuenroth, Universidade Estadual de Campinas, São Paulo, are marked with an asterisk(*).

Interviews Conducted by Cliff Welch

Caixe, Vanderlei, Ribeirão Preto, 11 June 1997.
Ciavatta, Nazareno, Ribeirão Preto, 20 October 1988.*
Correa Neto, Jofre, Ribeirão Preto, 24 August 1988.
Cruz, Antônio Crispim da, Ribeirão Preto, 31 March 1989.*
Desterro, Zildete Ribeiro do, Ribeirão Preto, 5 July 1989.
Faleiro, Airton, Brasília, 18 July 1997.
Fishburn, John, Woodstock, Virginia, 27 April 1985.
Ganzer, Avelino, Taguatinga, 20 July 1997.
Gasparini, Welson, Ribeirão Preto, 25 July 1991.
Geraldo, João, Ribeirão Preto, 7 July 1989.
Girotto, Antônio, Ribeirão Preto, 19 October 1988.*
Gomes, Guilherme Simões, Ribeirão Preto, 22 May 1991.
Guindalini, Nelson Luis, Dumont, 13 May 1995.
Lepera, Luciano, Ribeirão Preto, 18 October 1988.
Marino, Divo, Ribeirão Preto, 20 June 1997.
Marques, Lilian Arruda, Brasília, 17 July 1997.
Moraes, Irineu Luís de, Ribeirão Preto, 22 August 1988.*
Moretti Pires, Aurea, Ribeirão Preto, 11 June 1997.
Neves, Elio, Araraquara, 22 July 1997.
Portela, José Alves, São Paulo, 23 August 1988.*
Rampazzo, Tulio Marco, Pradópolis, 23 July 1991.
Salla, Pedro, Dumont, 14 May 1995.
Silva, Lindolfo, São Paulo, 16 August 1988* and 18 July 1989.
Siviero, Natal, Ribeirão Preto, 20 October 1988.*
Syllos, Celso Ibson de, São Paulo, 19 and 26 January 1989.*
Teixeira, Arlindo, Ribeirão Preto, 18 October 1988.*

Interviews Conducted by Sebastião Geraldo

Ciavatta, Nazareno, Ribeirão Preto, n.d., 1988.
Girotto, Antônio, Ribeirão Preto, 28 November 1988.

Lepera, Luciano, Ribeirão Preto, n.d., 1988.
Moraes, Irineu Luís de, Ribeirão Preto, 20 February 1989.
Siviero, Natal, Ribeirão Preto, 1988.

Interviews Conducted by Cliff Welch and Sebastião Geraldo

Guerreiro Filho, João, São Paulo, 11 July 1989.
Moraes, Irineu Luís de, Ribeirão Preto, 27 May 1989.
Santos, Sérgio Luís dos, Serrana, 11 July 1997.

Interviews Conducted by Centro de Pesquisa e Documentação, Fundação Getúlio Vargas

Julião, Francisco, interviewed by Aspásia Camargo, Yxcatepec, Morelos, Mexico, December 1977.
Lemos, Francisco de Assis, interviewed by Eduardo Raposo, João Pessoa, January 1978.

Contemporary Sources

Barreto, Lêda, *Julião, nordeste, revolução* (Rio de Janeiro: Civilização Brasileira, 1963).
Barriguelli, José Cláudio, ed., *Subsídios à história das lutas no campo em São Paulo (1870–1956)*, 2 vols. (São Carlos: Universidade Federal de São Carlos, Arquivo de História Contemporânea, 1981).
Beraldo, João Marcos, et al., *O colono paulista e o Instituto de Açucar e Álcool* (São Paulo: Revista dos Tribunais, 1945).
Bernardes, Lysia Maria Cavalcanti, "O problema da 'frente pioneiras' no estado do Paraná," *Revista Brasileira de Geografia* 15:3 (July–September 1953), 335–81.
Bernardes, Nilo, "Expansão do povoamento no estado de São Paulo," *Revista Brasileira de Geografia* 14:4 (October–December 1952), 426–54.
Blair, Thomas Lucien, "Social Structure and Information Exposure in Rural Brazil," *Rural Sociology* 25:1 (March 1960), 65–75.
British Chamber of Commerce of São Paulo and Southern Brazil, *Personalidades no Brasil* (São Paulo: n.p., 1933).
Calazans, Julieta, "Cartilha sindical do trabalhador rural," publication of the Serviço de Assistência Rural, Natal, Rio Grande do Norte (1961). Mimeographed.
Callado, Antônio, *Tempo de Arraes: A revolução sem violência*, 3d ed. (Rio de Janeiro: Paz e Terra, 1980). Originally published as articles in Rio de Janeiro's *Jornal do Brasil* between 7 December 1963 and 19 January 1964.
Camargo, José Francisco de, *A cidade e o campo: O êxodo rural no Brasil* (Rio de Janeiro: Livro Técnico, 1968).
Carmen, Cagno, et al., *Ribeirão Preto: Memória fotográfica* (Ribeirão Preto: Colêgio, 1985).
Carone, Edgard, ed., *O P.C.B. (1922–1943)*, vol. 1 (São Paulo: Difel, 1982).
Carvalho, Hernani de, *Sociologia da vida rural brasileira (Subsídios para o seu estudo)* (Rio de Janeiro: Civilização Brasileira, 1951).
Catharino, José Martins, *O trabalhador rural brasileiro (proteção jurídica)* (Rio de Janeiro: Livraria Freita Bastos, 1958).
Cavalcanti, Coutinho, *Um projeto de reforma agrária* (Rio de Janeiro: Instituto Nacional do Livro, 1959).
Cavino, Romulo, "Proteção social ao trabalhador agrícola," *Revista do Serviço Público* (April 1950), 25–28.

César, Afonso, *Política cifrão e sangue: Documentário do 24 de agôsto* (Rio de Janeiro: Editorial Andes, 1955).

Chasin, José, "Contribuição para a análise da vanguarda política do campo," *Revista Brasiliense* 44 (November–December 1962), 102–29.

Confederação Nacional dos Trabalhadores na Agricultura, *Anais: IV Congresso Nacional dos Trabalhadores Rurais* (Brasília: Gráfica e Papelaria Tipogresso, 1985).

————, *Anais do VI Congresso Nacional dos Trabalhadores Rurais* (Brasília: Nossagráfica, 1995).

Confederação Rural Brasileira, *A reforma agrária no VI Conferência Rural* (Rio de Janeiro: Serviço de Informação Agrícola, 1962).

Costa, Luiz Flávio Carvalho, ed., *O Congresso Nacional Camponês: Trabalhador rural no processo político brasileiro* (Rio de Janeiro: Editora Universidade Rural, 1993).

Cruz, Adelina Alves Novaes e, et al., eds., *Impasse na democracia brasileira, 1951/ 1955: Coletânea de documentos* (Rio de Janeiro: Centro de Pesquisa e Documentação, Editora da Fundação Getúlio Vargas, 1983).

Davidson, Theresa Sherrer, "The Brazilian Inheritance of Roman Law," in *Brazil: Papers Presented in the Institute for Brazilian Studies*, edited by James B. Watson, Theresa Sherrer Davidson, and Earl W. Thomas (Nashville: Vanderbilt University Press, 1953), 56–90.

Dorin, Lannoy, "Notas sôbre o ensino rural no estado de São Paulo," *Revista Brasiliense* 44 (November–December 1962), 92–101.

Dozier, Craig L., "Northern Paraná, Brazil: An Example of Organized Regional Development," *Geographical Review* 46 (1956), 319–21.

Duarte, Gonçalo, "Ligas camponesas," *O Observador: Econômico e Financeiro* (Rio de Janeiro) 24:286 (December 1959), 29–32.

Duarte, Nestor, ed., *Reforma agrária* (Rio de Janeiro: Ministério de Educação e Saude, Serviço de Documentação, n.d.).

Faria e Silva, Mario Penteado de, ed., *Legislação agropecuária (relativa ao período de 1937–1947)* (São Paulo: Secretaria da Agricultura, 1952).

Ferrari, Fernando, *Escravos da terra* (Rio de Janeiro: Globo, 1963).

Ferreira, Waldemar Martins, *Princípios de legislação social e direito judiciário do trabalho*, vol. l (São Paulo: Editorial Limitada, 1938).

Frei Celso [Maria], *Os Cristãos e o sindicato na cidade e o campo* (São Paulo: Saraiva, 1963).

Galjart, Benno, "Class and 'Following' in Rural Brazil," *América Latina* 7:3 (July/ September 1964), 3–23.

Heller, Frederico, "O êxodo do campo como fator de desenvolvimento," *Sociologia* 5:1 (1943), 57–67.

Homen de Mello, Fernando B., "A política econômica e a setor agrícola no período pôs-guerra," *Revista Brasileira de Economia* 33:1 (January/March 1959), 33–35.

Instituto de Direito Social, *Anais do Primeiro Congresso Brasileiro de Direito Social*, 4 vols. (Rio de Janeiro: Serviço de Estatistico da Previdência e Trabalho, 1943–45).

James, Preston E., "The Coffee Lands of Southeastern Brazil," *Geographical Review* 22 (1932), 225–44.

Jesus, Carolina Maria de, *A Child in the Dark* (New York: E. P. Dutton, 1962).

Leal, Victor Nunes, *Coronelismo: The Municipality and Representative Government in Brazil* (New York: Cambridge University Press, 1977).

Lecocq-Muller, Nice, "Contribuição ao estudo do norte do Paraná," *Boletim Paulista de Geografia* 22 (1956), 55–97.

Leitão, Evaristo, Romulo Cavina, and João Soares Palmeira, *O trabalhador rural brasileiro* (Rio de Janeiro: Departamento de Estatística e Publicidade, Ministério do Trabalho, Indústria e Comércio, 1937).

Lima, Lorenço Moreira, *A coluna Prestes: Marchas e combates,* 3d ed. (São Paulo: Alfa Omega, 1979).

Lopes, Waldemar, "O projeto do código rural," *Boletim do Ministério da Agricultura, Indústria e Comércio* 10:109 (September 1943), 145–69.

Marcondes, J. V. Freitas, "O Estatuto do Trabalhador Rural e o problema da terra," *Cadernos Brasileiros* 5:4 (1963), 55–59.

Marques, Acrisio, *Relatório do Departamento de Terras e Colonização do Estado do Paraná em 1947* (Curitiba: DTC, 1947).

Martins, Araguaya Feitosa, "Alguns aspectos da inquietação trabalhista no campo," *Revista Brasiliense* 40 (March/April 1962), 132–41.

———, *Revolução branca no campo* (São Paulo: Brasiliense, 1962).

Martins, Ibiapaba, "Proletariado e inquietação rural," *Revista Brasiliense* 42 (July–August 1962), 62–81.

Meinberg, Iris, "Discurso," in *A Reforma agrária na VI Conferência Rural* (Rio de Janeiro: Ministério da Agricultura, Serviço de Informação Agrícola, 1962).

Melo Franco, Virgílio de, *A campanha da UDN* (Rio de Janeiro: Zelio Valverde, 1946).

Monteiro Lobato, José Bento, *Zé Brasil* (Rio de Janeiro: n.p. 1951).

Moraes Filho, Evaristo de, *O problema do sindicato único no Brasil* (São Paulo: Alfa Omega, 1952).

Mota, Lourenço Dantas, ed., *A história vivida: Documetos abertos,* vol. 1 (São Paulo: O Estado de São Paulo, 1981).

Muller, Nice L., *Sítios e sitiantes no estado de São Paulo* (São Paulo: VSP Boletim, 1951).

Pimpão, Hirosé, "Proteção jurídica ao trabalhador rural," *Boletim do Ministério do Trabalho, Indústria e Comércio* (1944), 131–40.

Pinheiro, Paulo Sérgio, and Michael M. Hall, eds., *A classe operária no Brasil (1889–1930),* 2 vols. (São Paulo: Alfa Omega, 1979).

Pinho, Pericles Madureira de, *O problema da sindicalização rural* (Rio de Janeiro: n.p., 1939).

Prado Junior, Caio, *A questão agrária,* 4th ed. (São Paulo: Brasiliense, 1987). Originally published as articles in *Revista Brasiliense* between 7 December 1963 and 19 January 1964.

———, *A Revolução brasileira,* 2d ed. (São Paulo: Brasiliense, 1966).

Prebisch, Raul, *The Economic Development of Latin America and Its Principal Problems* (Lake Success, N.Y.: United Nations, 1950).

Prestes, Luis Carlos, "Como enfrentar os problemas da revolução agrária e anti-imperialista," *Problemas* 9 (April 1948).

Price, Robert E., "Rural Unionization in Brazil," Land Tenure Center, University of Wisconsin, Madison, 1964. Mimeographed.

Rabello, Ophelina, *A rede sindical paulista: Tentativa de caracterização* (São Paulo: Instituto Cultural do Trabalho, 1965).

Ramos, Augusto, *O café no Brasil e no estrangeiro* (Rio de Janeiro: Papelaria Santa Helena, 1923).

Rezende Puech, Luiz Roberto de, *Direito individual e coletivo do trabalho (estudos e comentários)* (São Paulo: Revista dos Tribunais, 1960).

Rolim, Frei Antônio, "Levantamento sócio-religioso da arquidiocese de Ribeirão Preto, estado de São Paulo," Arquidiocese Católica de Ribeirão Preto (24 June 1963). Mimeographed.

Rostow, W. W., *The Stages of Economic Growth: A Non-Communist Manifesto* (New York: Cambridge University Press, 1960).

Rowe, J. W. F., *The World's Coffee: A Study of the Economics and Politics of the Coffee Industries of Certain Countries and of the International Problem* (London: n.p., 1963).

Russomano, Mozart Victor, *Comentários ao Estatuto do Trabalhador Rural,* 2 vols., 2d ed. (São Paulo: Revista dos Tribunais, 1969).

Sales, Apolônio, *O Ministério da Agricultura no govêrno Getúlio Vargas (1930-1944)* (Rio de Janeiro: Serviço de Documentação, 1945).

Sampaio, Aluysio, *O que é reforma agrária* (São Paulo: Fulgor, 1962).

Santos, Oto, "O programa do partido, a questão agrária, a organização e a luta dos camponeses," *Problemas* 64 (January 1955), 244-54.

Segadas Vianna, José de, *O Estatuto do Trabalhador Rural e sua aplicação (comentários à lei no. 4.214 de 2 de março de 1963),* 2d ed. (Rio de Janeiro: Livraria Freitas Bastos, 1965).

Silva, José Gomes da, *Noções sôbre associativismo rural (organização da classe rural brasileira)* (Campinas: Secretaria da Agricultura, Centro de Treinamento, 1962).

Simão, Assis, "O voto operário em São Paulo," *Revista Brasileira de Estudos Políticos* 1:1 (December 1956), 130-41.

Souza Duarte, Carlos de, *O trabalho agrícola no Brasil* (Rio de Janeiro: Imprensa Nacional, 1925).

Taylor, Carl C., "A contribuição da sociologia à agricultura," *Sociologia* 5:1 (1943), 1-55.

Torres, Vasconcelos, *Ensaio de sociologia rural brasileira* (Rio de Janeiro: A. Coelho Branco Filho, 1943).

Watson, James B., "Way Station of Westernization: The Brazilian Caboclo," in *Brazil: Papers Presented in the Institute for Brazilian Studies,* edited by James B. Watson, Theresa Sherrer Davidson, and Earl W. Thomas (Nashville: Vanderbilt University Press, 1953), 9-55.

Watson, Virginia Drew, "An Example of Rural Brazilian Acculturation," *Acta Americana* 3:3 (July-September 1945), 152-62.

Willems, Emilio, "Some Aspects of Cultural Conflict and Acculturation in Southern Rural Brasil," *Rural Sociology* 7:4 (1942), 375-84.

Vargas, Getúlio, *A campanha presidencial* (Rio de Janeiro: José Olympio, 1951).

———, *O governo trabalhista no Brasil,* 4 vols. (Rio de Janeiro: José Olympio, 1952-69).

———, *A nova política do Brasil,* 11 vols. (Rio de Janeiro: José Olympio, 1938-47).

———, *A política trabalhista no Brasil* (Rio de Janeiro: José Olympio, 1950).

Vera, Nestor, "O congresso camponês em Belo Horizonte," *Revista Brasiliense* 39 (January-February 1962), 43-50.

Vinhas, Moisés, *O partidão: A luta por um partido de massas, 1922-1974* (São Paulo: Hucitec, 1982).

Other Sources

Adelman, Jeremy, "Against Essentialism: Latin American Labour History in Comparative Perspective. A Critique of Bergquist," *Labour/Le Travail* 27 (Spring 1991), 175-84.

Alexander, Robert J., *Juscelino Kubitschek and the Development of Brazil* (Athens: Ohio University Center for International Studies, 1991).

Andrade, Manuel Correia de, *The Land and the People of Northeast Brazil* (Albuquerque: University of New Mexico Press, 1980).

Araújo, Rosa Maria, *O batismo do trabalho: Experiência de Lindolfo Collor* (Rio de Janeiro: Civilização Brasileira, 1981).

Aued, Bernardete Wrublevski, *A vitória dos vencidos (Partido Comunista Brasileiro—PCB—e Ligas Camponesas, 1955–64)* (Florianópolis: Editora da UFSC, 1986).

Azevêdo, Fernando Antônio, *As ligas camponesas* (Rio de Janeiro: Paz e Terra, 1982).

Baer, Werner, *Industrialization and Economic Development in Brazil* (Homewood, Ill.: Richard D. Irwin, 1965).

Bak, Joan, "Cartels, Cooperatives, and Corporations: Getúlio Vargas in Rio Grande do Sul on the Eve of Brazil's 1930 Revolution," *Hispanic American Historical Review* 63:2 (May 1983), 255–75.

Bandeira, Moniz, *O govêrno João Goulart: As lutas sociais no Brasil, 1961–1964*, 6th ed. (Rio de Janeiro: Civilização Brasileira, 1983).

Barros, Fatima Regina de, "A organização sindical dos trabalhadores rurais: Contribuição ao estudo do caso do estado de São Paulo, entre 1954–1964" (master's thesis, Universidade de Campinas, 1986).

Bastos, Elide Rugai, *As ligas camponesas* (Petrópolis: Vôzes, 1984).

Beatie, Peter, "Was Távora There?" *New York Review of Books,* 7 November 1991, 61.

Beloch, Israel, and Alzira Alves de Abreu, eds., *Dicionário histórico-biográfico brasileiro, 1930–1983,* 4 vols. (Rio de Janeiro: Forense-Universitária, 1984).

Benevides, Maria Victoria de Mesquita, *O govêrno Kubitschek: Desenvolvimento econômico e estabilidade política (1956–1961)* (Rio de Janeiro: Paz e Terra, 1976).

———, *O PTB e o trabalhismo: Partido e sindicato em São Paulo (1945–1964)* (São Paulo: Brasiliense, 1989).

———, *O PTB e o trabalhismo* (São Paulo: Brasiliense, 1988).

———, *A UDN e o udenismo: Ambiguidades do liberalismo brasileiro (1945–1965)* (Rio de Janeiro: Paz e Terra, 1981).

Bergquist, Charles, "Latin American Labour History in Comparative Perspective: Notes on the Insidiousness of Cultural Imperialism," *Labour/Le Travail* 25 (Spring 1990), 189–98.

Bergson, Joel, and Arthur Candal, "Industrialization: Past Success and Future Problems," in *The Economy of Brazil,* edited by Howard S. Ellis (Berkeley and Los Angeles: University of California Press, 1969), 29–73.

Berardo, João Batista, *O político Cândido Torquato Portinari* (São Paulo: Populares, 1983).

Berlin, Ira, "Time, Space, and the Evolution of Afro-American Society on British Mainland North America," *American Historical Review* 85:1 (February 1980), 44–78.

Besse, Susan K., *Restructuring Patriarchy: The Modernization of Gender Inequality in Brazil, 1914–1940* (Chapel Hill: University of North Carolina Press, 1996).

Bezerra, Gregório, *Memórias: Segunda parte, 1946–1969,* 2d ed. (Rio de Janeiro: Civilização Brasileira, 1980).

Boito, Armando, *O golpe de 1954: A burguesia contra o populismo* (São Paulo: Brasiliense, 1982).

Brandão, Octavio, *Combates e batalhas: Memórias,* vol. 1 (São Paulo: Alfa Omega, 1978).

Brant, Vinicius Caldeira, "Do colono ao bóia-fria: Transformações na agricultura e constituição do mercado de trabalho na Alta Sorocabana de Assis," *Estudos CEBRAP* 19 (January/March 1977), 37–91.

Bruneau, Thomas C., *Católicismo brasileiro em época de transição* (São Paulo: Loyola, 1974).

Cabellero, Manuel, *Latin America and the Comintern, 1919–43* (New York: Cambridge University Press, 1986).

Camargo, Aspásia de Alcântara, "Autoritarismo e populismo: Bipolaridade do sistema político brasileiro," *Dados* 12 (1976).

————, "A questão agrária: Crise de poder e reformas de base (1930–1964)," in *História geral de civilização brasileira,* Tomo III, *O Brasil republicano,* vol. 3, *Sociedade e política (1930–1964),* edited by Boris Fausto, 3d ed. (São Paulo: Difel, 1986), 121–224.

Carneiro, Maria Esperança Fernandes, *A revolta camponesa de Formoso e Tombas* (Goiânia: Editora da Universidade Federal de Goiás, 1986).

Castelo Branco, Carlos, *Introdução á revolução de 1964,* vol. 2 (Rio de Janeiro: Artenova, 1975).

Castro Gomes, Angela Maria de, "Confronto e compromisso no processo de constitucionalização," in *História geral da civilização brasileira,* Tomo III, *O Brasil republicaño,* vol. 3, *Sociedade e política (1930–1964),* edited by Boris Fausto, 3d ed. (São Paulo: Difel, 1986), 7–74.

————, *A invenção do trabalhismo* (Rio de Janeiro: Vertice/IUPERJ, 1988).

Castro Gomes, Angela Maria de, Lúcia Lahmeyer Lobo, and Rodrigo Bellingrodt Marques Coelho, *Burguesia e trabalho: Política e legislação social* (Rio de Janeiro: Campus, 1979).

————, "Revolução e restauração: A experiência paulista no período da constitucionalização," in *Regionalismo e centralização política: Partidos e constituinte nos anos 30,* edited by Angela Maria de Castro Gomes (Rio de Janeiro: Nova Fronteira, 1980), 237–337.

Cegalla, Domingos Paschoal, *Novíssima gramática da lingua portuguesa,* 29th ed. (São Paulo: Companhia Editora Nacional, 1985).

Cehelsky, Marta, *Land Reform in Brazil: The Management of Social Change* (Boulder, Colo.: Westview Press, 1979).

Chaui, Marilena, *Seminários,* 2d ed. (São Paulo: Brasiliense, 1982).

Chaves Neto, Elias, *Minha vida e as lutas de meu tempo* (São Paulo: Alfa Omega, 1978).

Cohen, Yousef, *The Manipulation of Consent* (Pittsburgh: University of Pittsburgh Press, 1990).

Colnaghi, Maria Cristina, "Colonos e poder: A luta pela terra no sudoeste do Paraná" (master's thesis, Universidade Federal do Paraná, 1984).

Conceição, Manuel da, *Essa terra é nossa: Depoimento sôbre a vida e as lutas de camponeses no estado do Maranhão* (Petrópolis: Vôzes, 1980).

Conniff, Michael L., "The Tenentes in Power: A New Perspective on the Brazilian Revolution of 1930," *Journal of Latin American Studies* 10:1 (1977), 61–82.

Corrêa, Anna Maria Martinez, *A rebelião de 1924 em São Paulo* (São Paulo: Hucitec, 1976).

Costa, Emilia Viotta da, *The Brazilian Empire* (Chicago: University of Chicago, 1985).

Costa Alves, Francisco José da, "Modernização da agricultura e sindicalismo: Lutas dos trabalhadores assalariados rurais da região canavieira de Ribeirão Preto" (master's thesis, UNICAMP, 1991).

Cross, Gary, "Time, Money, and Labor History's Encounter with Consumer Culture," and responses by Michael Rustin and Victoria de Grazia, *International Labor and Working Class History* 43 (Spring 1993), 2–30.

D'Aguiar, Hernani, *A revolução pro dentro* (Rio de Janeiro, 1976).

Daniel, Cletus E., "César Chávez and the Unionization of California Farmworkers," in *Working People in California,* edited by Daniel Cornford (Berkeley and Los Angeles: University of California Press, 1995), 371–404.

D'Araújo, Maria Celina, Glaúcio Ary Dillon Soares, and Celso Castro, *Visões do golpe: A memória militar sôbre 1964* (Rio de Janeiro: Relume Dumará, 1994).

D'Araújo, Maria Celina Soares, *O segundo govêrno Vargas, 1951–1954* (Rio de Janeiro: Zahar, 1982).

Dean, Warren, *Rio Claro: A Brazilian Plantation System, 1820–1920* (Stanford: Stanford University Press, 1976).

———, *The Industrialization of São Paulo, 1880–1945* (Austin: University of Texas Press, 1969).

———, "The Planter as Entrepreneur: The Case of São Paulo," *Hispanic American Historical Review* 46:2 (May 1966), 138–52.

Decca, Edgar de, *1930: O silêncio dos vencidos: Memória, história, e revolução,* 6th ed. (São Paulo: Brasiliense, 1994).

Delfim Netto, Antônio, and Carlos Alberto de Andrade Pinto, "The Brazilian Coffee: Twenty Years of Set-Backs in the Competition on the World Market, 1945/ 1965," in *Essays on Coffee and Economic Development* (Rio de Janeiro: Instituto Brasileiro do Café, 1973), 279–315.

Delgado, Lucilia de Almeida Neves, *PTB: Do getulismo ao reformismo (1945–1964)* (São Paulo: Marco Zero, 1989).

Dias, Eduardo, *Um imigrante e a revolução: Memórias de um militante operário, 1934– 1951* (São Paulo: Brasiliense, 1983).

D'Incao, Maria Conceição, *O "bóia-fria": Acumulação e miséria,* 8th ed. (Petrópolis: Vôzes, 1975).

———, "O movimento de Guariba: O papel acelerador da crise econômica," *Política e Administração* 1:2 (July–September 1985), 201–22.

D'Incao, Maria Conceição, and Moacyr Rodrigues Botelho, "Movimento social e movimento sindical entre os assalariados temporários da agroindústria canavieira no estado de São Paulo," in *Movimentos sociais na transição democrática,* edited by Emir Sader (São Paulo: Cortez, 1987), 53–81.

Dreifuss, René Armand, *1964: A conquista do estado: Ação política, poder e golpe de classe* (Petrópolis: Vôzes, 1981).

Dulles, John W. F., *Unrest in Brazil: Political-Military Crises, 1953–1964* (Austin: University of Texas Press, 1970).

———, *Vargas of Brazil: A Political Biography* (Austin: University of Texas Press, 1967).

Eckert, Cordula, "Movimento dos Agricultores Sem Terra no Rio Grande do Sul, 1960–1964" (master's thesis, Universidade Federal Rural do Rio de Janeiro, 1984).

Fabris, Annateresa, *Portinari, pintor social* (São Paulo: Perspectiva, 1990).

Fausto, Boris, *A revolução de 1930: Historiografia e história* (São Paulo: Brasiliense, 1970).

Felismino, Pedro Paulo, "A guerra de Porecatú," *Folha de Londrina,* 14–28 July 1985. Ten-part series.

Font, Mauricio, *Coffee, Contention, and Change in the Making of Modern Brazil* (New York: Basil Blackwell, 1990).

———, "Coffee Planters, Politics, and Development in Brazil," *Latin American Research Review* 22:3 (1987): 69–90.

Forman, Shepherd, *The Brazilian Peasantry* (New York: Columbia University Press, 1975).

Foweraker, Joe, *The Struggle for Land: A Political Economy of the Pioneer Frontier in Brazil from 1930 to the Present Day* (New York: Cambridge University Press, 1980).

French, John D., *The Brazilian Workers' ABC: Class Conflict and Alliance in Modern São Paulo* (Chapel Hill: University of North Carolina Press, 1992).

———, "Industrial Workers and the Birth of the Populist Republic in Brazil, 1945– 1946," *Latin American Perspectives* 16:4 (Fall 1989), 6–28.

———, "Workers and the Rise of Adhemarista Populism in Sao Paulo, Brazil, 1945–1947," *Hispanic American Historical Review* 68:1 (February 1988), 1–43.

Garcia, Maria Angélica Momenso, "As greves de 1912 e 1913 nas fazendas de café de Ribeirão Preto," *Estudos de História* (Franca) 2:2 (1995), 167–79.

Gebara, José Jorge, "A estrutura agrária do município de Sertãozinho: Evolução, caracterização e efeitos" (master's thesis, Escola de Administração de Empresas de São Paulo, Fundação Getúlio Vargas, 1976).

Geraldo, Sebastião, "Comunicação oral: O resgate da memória proletária em Ribeirão Preto" (master's thesis, Universidade de São Paulo, 1990).

———, "Relatório para o exame geral de qualificação para obtenção do grau de mestre em ciências da comunicação" (Universidade de São Paulo, 1988). Mimeographed.

Gifun, Frederick Vincent, "Ribeirão Preto, 1880–1914: The Rise of a Coffee County or the Transition to Coffee in São Paulo as Seen Through the Development of Its Leading Producer" (Ph.D. diss., University of Florida, 1972).

Giovanetti Netto, Evaristo, *O PCB na Assembléia Constituinte de 1946* (São Paulo: Novos Rumos, 1986).

Gnaccarini, José Cesar, *Estado, ideológia e ação empresarial na agroindústria açucareira do estado de São Paulo* (São Paulo: n.p., 1972). Mimeographed.

Gomes, Iria Zanani, *1957: A revolta dos posseiros* (Curitiba: Crias Edições, 1986).

Gorender, Jacob, *Combate nas trevas: A esquerda brasileira das ilusões perdidas à luta armada,* 2d ed. (São Paulo: Atica, 1987).

Gramsci, Antonio, "Notes on Italian History: The City-Countryside Relationship During the Risorgimento and the National Structure," *Selections from the Prison Notebooks* (New York: International Publishers, 1971).

Graziano da Silva, José, *Progresso técnico e relações de trabalho na agricultura* (São Paulo: Hucitec, 1981).

Grynszpan, Mario, "O campesinato fluminense: Mobilização e controle político, 1950–1964," *Revista Rio de Janeiro* 1 (April 1986), 19–27.

Grzybowski, Cândido, "Rural Workers' Movements and Democratisation in Brazil," in *The Challenge of Rural Democratisation: Perspectives from Latin America and the Philippines,* edited by Jonathan Fox (London: Frank Cass, 1990), 19–43.

Guilherme Velho, Otavio, *Capitalismo autoritário e campesinato* (São Paulo: Difel, 1979).

Hall, Michael M., "The Origins of Mass Immigration in Brazil, 1871–1914" (Ph.D. diss., Columbia University, 1969).

Hall, Michael, and Verena Martinez Alier, "Greves de colonos na Primeira República," paper presented at the II Seminário de Relações de Trabalho e Movimentos Sociais, Campinas, São Paulo, May 1979. Mimeographed.

Hammond, Jack, "The Landless Workers' Movement of Brazil," paper presented at the Latin American Studies Association Congress, Guadalajara, Mexico, April 1997. Mimeographed.

Harding, Timothy Fox, "The Political History of Organized Labor in Brazil" (Ph.D. diss., Stanford University, 1973).

Hewitt, Cynthia, "Brazil: The Peasant Movement in Pernambuco, 1961–1964," in *Latin American Peasant Movements,* edited by Henry A. Landsberger (Ithaca: Cornell University Press, 1969), 374–98.

Hippolito, Lucia, *PSD: De raposas e reformistas* (Rio de Janeiro: Paz e Terra, 1985).

Holloway, Thomas H., *Immigrants on the Land: Coffee and Society in São Paulo, 1886–1934* (Chapel Hill: University of North Carolina Press, 1980).

Huber, Evelyne, and John D. Stephens, "Conclusion: Agrarian Structure and Political

Power in Comparative Perspective," in *Agrarian Structure and Political Power: Landlord and Peasant in the Making of Latin America,* edited by Evelyne Huber and John D. Safford (Pittsburgh: University of Pittsburgh Press, 1995), 183–232.

Ianni, Octavio, *A luta pela terra,* 3d ed. (Petrópolis: Vôzes, 1981).

———, *Origens agrárias do estado brasileiro* (São Paulo: Brasiliense, 1984).

Ioki, Zilda Grícoli, *Igreja e camponeses: Teologia da libertaçâo e movimentos sociais no campo (Brazil e Peru, 1964–1986)* (São Paulo: Hucitec/FAPESP, 1996).

James, Daniel, "Something Old, Something New? The Emerging Parameters of Latin American Labor History," paper presented at Princeton University, 9 April 1993.

Katzman, Martin T., "Social Relations of Production on the Brazilian Frontier," in *The Frontier: Comparative Studies,* vol. 1, edited by David H. Miller and Jerome Steffen (Norman: University of Oklahoma Press, 1974), 275–96.

Keck, Margaret, *The Workers Party and Democratization in Brazil* (New Haven: Yale University Press, 1992).

Labaki, Amir, *1961: A crise da renuncia e a soluçâo parlamentarista* (São Paulo: Brasiliense, 1986).

La Cava, Gloria, "As origens da emigraçâo italiana para a América Latina após a segunda guerra mundial," *Novos Cadernos* 2 (1988), 49–77.

Lamounier, Maria Lúcia, *Da escravidão ao trabalho livre* (Campinas: Papírus, 1988).

Leff, Nathaniel, *Economic Policy-Making and Development in Brazil, 1947–1964* (New York: John Wiley & Sons, 1968).

Lenharo, Alcir, *Sacralização da política* (Campinas: Papírus, 1986).

———, "A terra para quem nela não trabalha," *Revista Brasileira de História* 6:12 (March/August 1986), 47–64.

Levi, Darrell E., *The Prados of São Paulo: An Elite Family and Social Change, 1840–1930* (Athens: University of Georgia Press, 1987).

Lewin, Linda, "The Oligarchical Limitations of Social Banditry in Brazil: The Case of the 'Good' Thief Antônio Silvino," *Past and Present* 82 (February 1979): 116–46.

———, *Politics and Parentela in Paraibá: A Case Study of Family-Based Oligarchy in Brazil* (Princeton: Princeton University Press, 1987).

Lichtenstein, Nelson, *The Most Dangerous Man in Detroit: Walter Reuther and the Fate of American Labor* (New York: Basic Books, 1995).

Loner, Beatriz Ana, "O PCB e a linha do manifesto de agosto: Um estudo" (master's thesis, Universidade Estadual de Campinas, 1985).

Lopes, Juarez Rubens Brandão, *Do latifúndio á empresa: Unidade e diversidade do capitalismo no campo,* 2d ed. (Petrópolis: Vôzes, 1976).

Love, Joseph L., *São Paulo in the Brazilian Federation, 1889–1937* (Stanford: Stanford University Press, 1980).

Love Joseph L., Verena Stolcke, and Mauricio Font, "Commentary and Debate," *Latin American Research Review* 24:3 (1989), 127–58.

Ludwig, Armin K., *Brazil: A Handbook of Historical Statistics* (Boston: G. K. Hall, 1985).

Macaulay, Neill, *The Prestes Column: Revolution in Brazil* (New York: New Viewpoints, 1974).

Machado, Maria Helena, *O plano e o pânico: Os movimentos sociais na década da abolição* (Rio de Janeiro: UFRJ, EDUSP, 1994).

Mainwaring, Scott, *The Catholic Church and Politics in Brazil, 1916–1985* (Stanford: Stanford University Press, 1986).

Mallon, Florencia E., *Peasant and Nation: The Making of Postcolonial Mexico and Peru* (Berkeley and Los Angeles: University of California, 1995).

———, "Peasants and Rural Laborers in Pernambuco, 1955–1964," *Latin American Perspectives* 5:4 (Fall 1978), 49–70.

Maranhão, Ricardo, *Sindicatos e democratização (Brasil 1945/1950)* (São Paulo: Brasiliense, 1979).

Margolis, Maxine L., *The Moving Frontier: Social and Economic Change in a Southern Brazilian Community* (Gainesville: University of Florida Press, 1973).

Martinez-Alier, Verena, and Armando Boito Junior, "The Hoe and the Vote: Rural Labourers and the National Election in Brazil in 1974," *Journal of Peasant Studies* 4:3 (April 1977), 147–70.

Martins, Ibiapaba, "Proletariado e inquietação rural," *Revista Brasiliense* 42 (July–August 1962), 62–81.

Martins, José de Souza, *Os camponesas e a política no Brasil* (Petrópolis: Vôzes, 1981).

Marx, Karl, "The Eighteenth Brumaire of Louis Bonaparte," in *Surveys from Exile: Political Writings,* vol. 2, edited and introduced by David Fernbach (New York: Vintage Books, 1974), 143–249.

Maxwell, Kenneth, "The Mystery of Chico Mendes," *New York Review of Books,* 28 March 1991, 39–48.

Maybury-Lewis, Biorn, *The Politics of the Possible: The Brazilian Rural Workers' Trade Union Movement, 1964–1985* (Philadelphia: Temple University Press, 1994).

Medeiros, Leonilde Sérvolo de, *História dos movimentos sociais no campo* (Rio de Janeiro: FASE, 1989).

Mendes, Chico, *Fight for the Forest: Chico Mendes in His Own Words* (London: Latin American Bureau, 1989).

Moisés, José Alvaro, *A greve de massa e crise política (Estudo da greve dos 300 mil em São Paulo, 1953–1954)* (São Paulo: Polis, 1978).

Moraes, Clodomir Santos de, "Peasant Leagues in Brazil," in *Agrarian Problems and Peasant Movements in Latin America,* edited by Rodolfo Stavenhagen (New York: Doubleday, 1970), 453–501.

Moraes, Dênis de, *A esquerda e o golpe de 64* (Rio de Janeiro: Espaço e Tempo 1989).

Moraes, Dênis de, and Fernando Viana, *Prestes: Lutas e autocríticas* (Petrópolis: Vôzes, 1982).

Morais, Fernando de, *Chatô: O rei do Brasil* (São Paulo: Companhia das Letras, 1994).

———, *Olga,* 13th ed. (Rio de Janeiro: Globo, 1986).

Mourão Filho, General Olympio, *Memórias: A verdade de um revolucionário,* 4th ed. (Porto Alegre: L + PM, 1978).

Nicholls, William H., "The Agricultural Frontier in Modern Brazilian History: The State of Paraná, 1920–1960," in *Cultural Change in Brazil: Papers from the Midwest Association for Latin American Studies, October 30–31, 1969* (Muncie: Ball State University Press, 1969), 36–64.

Page, Joseph A., *The Revolution That Never Was: Northern Brazil, 1955–1964* (New York: Grossman Publisher, 1972).

Paiva, Ruy Miller, Salomão Schattan, and Claus F. Trench de Freitas, *Setor agrícola do Brasil: Comportamento econômico, problemas e possibilidades* (São Paulo: Secretaria da Agricultura, 1973).

Paiva, Vanilda, ed., *Igreja e questão agrária* (São Paulo: Loyola, 1985).

Palmeira, Moacir, "The Aftermath of Peasant Mobilization: Rural Conflict in the Brazilian Northeast Since 1964," in *The Structure of Brazilian Development,* edited by Neuma Aguiar (New Brunswick: Transaction Books, 1979), 71–97.

Parker, Phyllis R., *Brazil and the Quiet Intervention, 1964* (Austin: University of Texas Press, 1979).

Pearson, Neale J., "Small Farmer and Rural Worker Pressure Groups in Brazil" (Ph.D. diss., University of Florida, 1967).

Pereira, Anthony W., *The End of the Peasantry: The Rural Labor Movement in Northeast Brazil (1961-1984)* (Pittsburgh: University of Pittsburgh Press, 1996).

Pinheiro Neto, João, *Jango: Um depoimento pessoal* (Rio de Janeiro: Record, 1993).

Portelli, Alessandro, *The Death of Luigi Trastulli and Other Stories* (New York: State University of New York Press, 1991).

————, "Uchronic Dreams: Working Class Memory and Possible Worlds," in *The Myths We Live By*, edited by Raphael Samuel and Paul Thompson (New York: Routledge, 1990), 143-60.

Porto, Mayla Yara, "De bóias-frias a cortadores de cana: O direto ao progresso com desordem na região de Ribeirão Preto" (master's thesis, Faculdade de Direito, USP, 1993).

Pureza, José, *Memória camponesa* (Rio de Janeiro: Marco Zero, 1982).

Revkin, Andrew, *The Burning Season: The Murder of Chico Mendes and the Fight for the Amazon Rain Forest* (Boston: Houghton Mifflin, 1990).

Rocha, Frances, "Conflito social e dominação: Um estudo sôbre as leis de regulação das relações de trabalho na empresa agrícola, 1897-1930" (master's thesis, Pontifical Universidade Católica, São Paulo, 1982).

Rodrigues, Leôncio Martins, "O PCB: Os dirigentes e a organização," in *História geral da civilização brasileira*, Tomo III, *O Brasil republicano*, vol. 3, *Sociedade e política (1930-1964)*, edited by Boris Fausto, 3d ed. (São Paulo: Difel, 1986).

Sampaio, Regina, *Adhemar de Barros e o PSP* (São Paulo: Global, 1982).

Samuel, Raphael, and Paul Thompson, eds., *The Myths We Live By* (New York: Routledge, 1990).

Santos, Raimundo, *A primeira renovação pecebista: Reflexos do XX Congresso do PCUS no PCB (1956-1957)* (Belo Horizonte: Oficina de Livros, 1988).

Saunders, V. D., "A Revolution of Agreement Among Friends: The End of the Vargas Era," *Hispanic American Historical Review* 44:2 (May 1964), 197-213.

Shirley, Robert W., *The End of Tradition: Cultural Change and Development in the Município of Cunha, São Paulo* (New York: Columbia University Press, 1971).

————, "Law in Rural Brazil," in *Brazil: Anthropological Perspectives*, edited by Maxine Margolis (New York: Columbia University Press, 1979), 343-62.

————, "Patronage and Cooperation: An Analysis from São Paulo State," in *Structure and Process in Latin America*, edited by Arnold Stricken and Sidney M. Greenfield (Albuquerque: University of New Mexico, 1972), 139-58.

Sigaud, Lygia, "Congressos camponeses (1953-1964)," *Reforma Agrária* 11:6 (November/December 1981), 3-8.

————, *Greve nos engenhos* (Rio de Janeiro: Paz e Terra, 1980).

————, *Os clandestinos e os direitos: Estudo sôbre trabalhadores da cana-de-açucar de Pernambuco* (São Paulo: Duas Cidades, 1979).

Silva, Francisco Ribeiro da, "A lei americana sôbre o açucar—'Sugar Act'—seus propositos e como funciona," *Brasil Açucareiro* (Rio de Janeiro) 4 (April 1971), 10.

Skidmore, Thomas E., *Politics in Brazil (1930-1964): An Experiment in Democracy* (New York: Oxford University Press, 1967).

————, *The Politics of Military Rule in Brazil, 1964-1985* (New York: Oxford University Press, 1988).

Soares, Glaúcio Ary Dillon, *Sociedade e política no Brasil* (São Paulo: Difel, 1973).

Sodero, Fernando Pereira, *Direito agrário e reforma agrária* (São Paulo: Livraria Legislação Brasileira, 1968).

Souza, Amaury de, "The Cangação and the Politics of Violence in Northeast Brazil," in *Protest and Resistance in Brazil and Angola*, edited by Ronald Chilcote (Berkeley and Los Angeles: University of California Press, 1972).

Souza, Márcio, *A expressão Amazonense* (São Paulo: Alfa Omega, 1977).

Souza, Maria de Carmo Campello de, *Estado e partidos políticos no Brasil (1930 a 1964)* (São Paulo: Alfa Omega, 1983).

Souza Carneiro, Honório de, "A CAIC: Companhia de Agricultura, Imigração e Colonização, 1928-1961" (master's thesis, Universidade do Estado de São Paulo, Araraquara, 1985).

Spruit, Troy, "Ribeirão Preto Labor Court Analysis," Grand Valley State University, 14 April 1993. Mimeograph in author's possession.

Stolcke, Verena, *Cafeicultura: Homens, mulheres e capital (1850-1980)* (São Paulo: Ed Brasiliense, 1986).

————, *Coffee Planters, Workers, and Wives* (New York: St. Martin's Press, 1988).

Stolcke, Verena, and Michael M. Hall, "The Introduction of Free Labour on São Paulo Coffee Plantations," *Journal of Peasant Studies* 10:2/3 (January/April 1983), 184-205.

Szmrecsanyi, Tomas, "O desenvolvimento da produção agropecuária (1930-1970)," in *História geral da civilização brasileira*, Tomo III, *O Brasil republicano*, vol. 4, *Economia e cultura (1930-1964)*, edited by Boris Fausto, 2d ed. (São Paulo: Difel, 1986), 107-207.

Toplin, Robert Brent, "Upheaval, Violence, and the Abolition of Slavery in Brazil: The Case of São Paulo," *Hispanic American Historical Review* 49:4 (1969), 639-55.

Vangelista, Chiara, *Os braços da lavoura: Imigrantes e "caipiras" na formação do mercado de trabalho paulista (1850-1930)* (São Paulo: Hucitec, 1991).

Vasconcellos, Maria Theresinha de, "Transcurso do primeiro decenio da Junta de Conciliação e Julgamento de Ribeirão Preto" (Ribeirão Preto, [1967?]). Mimeographed.

Vilaca, Marcos, and Roberto Albuquerque, *Coronel, coroneis* (Rio de Janeiro: Tempo Brasileiro, 1965).

Vinhas, Moisés, *Operários e camponeses na revolução brasileira* (São Paulo: Fulgor, 1963).

Walker, Thomas, "From Coronelismo to Populism: The Evolution of Politics in a Brazilian Municipality, Ribeirão Preto, São Paulo, 1910-1960" (Ph.D. diss., University of New Mexico, 1974).

Weffort, Francisco, "As origens do sindicalismo populista no Brasil (a conjuntura do após-guerra)," *Estudos CEBRAP* 4 (April/June 1974), 65-104.

————, *O populismo na política brasileira* (Rio de Janeiro: Paz e Terra, 1978).

Weinstein, Barbara, *For Social Peace in Brazil: Industrialists and the Remaking of the Working Class in São Paulo, 1920-1964* (Chapel Hill: University of North Carolina Press, 1996).

Welch, Cliff, "Jofre and the Brazilian Revolution: Peasant Mobilization, Land Reform, and History in São Paulo, Brazil," paper presented at the thirteenth annual Latin American Labor History Conference, Duke University, 19-20 April 1996. Mimeograph.

————, "Labor Internationalism: U.S. Involvement in Brazilian Unions, 1945-1965," *Latin American Research Review* 30:2 (1995), 61-89.

————, "'Rivalry and Unification': Mobilising Rural Workers in São Paulo on the Eve of the Brazilian Golpe of 1964," *Journal of Latin American Studies* 27 (1995), 161-87.

————, "Rural Workers and the Law in São Paulo, Brazil, 1930-1970," in *Identity,*

Consciousness, and Class Action: New Approaches to the Study of Latin American Workers, edited by John D. French and Daniel James (Durham: Duke University Press, forthcoming).

Welch, Cliff, and Sebastião Geraldo, *Lutas camponesas no interior paulista: Memórias de Irineu Luís de Moraes* (São Paulo: Paz e Terra, 1992).

Wirth, John, *The Politics of Brazilian Development* (Stanford: Stanford University Press, 1970).

Wolfe, Joel, *Working Women, Working Men: São Paulo and the Rise of Brasil's Industrial Working Class, 1900–1955* (Durham: Duke University Press, 1993).

Young, Jordan M., *The Brazilian Revolution of 1930 and the Aftermath* (New Brunswick: Rutgers University Press, 1967).

Zaidan Filho, Michel, *PCB (1922–1929): Na busca das origens de um marxismo nacional* (São Paulo: Global, 1985).

INDEX

ABOUT THE AUTHOR

Cliff Welch, a former Wyoming ranchhand and co-founder of the National Writers Union, is now Coordinator of Latin American Studies and Associate Professor of History at Grand Valley State University in Allendale, Michigan.

RCL

TEXAS A&M UNIVERSITY-TEXARKANA